MW00579485

The Shenandoah Valley
Campaign of 1864

MILITARY CAMPAIGNS OF THE CIVIL WAR

The Shenandoah Valley Campaign of 1864

EDITED BY GARY W. GALLAGHER

The University of North Carolina Press | Chapel Hill

© 2006 The University of North Carolina Press
All rights reserved

Designed by April Leidig-Higgins
Set in Monotype Bulmer by Copperline Book Services, Inc.
Manufactured in the United States of America

This book was published with the assistance of the Fred W.
Morrison Fund for Southern Studies of the University of
North Carolina Press.

The paper in this book meets the guidelines for perma-
nence and durability of the Committee on Production
Guidelines for Book Longevity of the Council on Library
Resources.

Library of Congress Cataloging-in-Publication Data
The Shenandoah Valley Campaign of 1864 / edited by
Gary W. Gallagher.
p.   cm. — (Military campaigns of the Civil War)
ISBN 978-0-8078-3005-5 (cloth: alk. paper)
ISBN 978-0-8078-5956-8 (pbk: alk. paper)
1. Shenandoah Valley Campaign, 1864 (August –
November)   I. Gallagher, Gary W.   II. Series.
E477.33.G35   2006
973.7'37 — dc22   2005031386

cloth   10 09 08 07 06   5 4 3 2 1
paper   12 11 10 09   5 4 3 2 1

For Shigeru Gallagher,

with whom I look forward to
exploring the Shenandoah Valley

CONTENTS

INTRODUCTION

ON JUNE 12, 1864, Gen. Robert E. Lee summoned Lt. Gen. Jubal A. Early to discuss an important assignment. The principal armies in the Eastern Theater had been battering one another for five weeks from the Rappahannock–Rapidan river line to the outskirts of Richmond, but Lee had another part of Virginia on his mind. He wanted Early to take his Second Corps on an independent operation far removed from the rest of the Army of Northern Virginia. Since early May, Union general in chief Ulysses S. Grant had sent two forces into the Shenandoah Valley to disrupt Confederate logistical production and play havoc with crucial rail lines. The first of those expeditions, under Maj. Gen. Franz Sigel, had ended in defeat at the battle of New Market on May 15. The second, commanded by Maj. Gen. David Hunter, had penetrated the upper Valley to Lexington, burned the Virginia Military Institute, and then turned southeastward to strike Lynchburg, a center for communications, transportation, and hospitals. Lee's oral instructions to Early on June 12, confirmed by written orders that evening, laid out several objectives. "I was directed to move . . . for the Valley," Early wrote shortly after the war, ". . . to strike Hunter's force in the rear, and, if possible, destroy it; then to move down the valley, cross the Potomac . . . and threaten Washington City." On June 15, Lee reported to Confederate president Jefferson Davis, who harbored deep concerns about Federal operations in the Valley, that Early had departed. Although worried about the danger of detaching one of his three infantry corps in the face of Grant's powerful army, Lee stated that "success in the Valley would relieve our difficulties that at present weigh heavily upon us."[1]

Early's movement to Lynchburg signaled the opening of what would become the longest, largest, and most important military campaign waged in the Shenandoah Valley. Its two distinct phases extended over four months. During the first phase, Early conjured memories of "Stonewall" Jackson's celebrated successes in the 1862 Valley campaign. He defeated Hunter outside Lynchburg on June 17–18, pursuing the Federals toward West Virginia before marching rapidly down the Valley and crossing the Potomac River into Maryland on July 5–6. Then Early's Army of the Valley, which numbered approximately 14,000 men of all arms, traversed the South Mountain and Catoctin ranges, descended

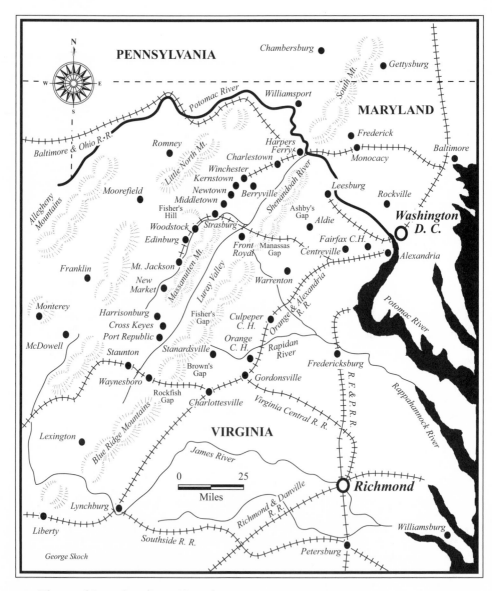

Theater of Operations, June–November 1864.

on Frederick, Maryland, and defeated a ragtag Union force under Maj. Gen. Lew Wallace in the battle of the Monocacy on July 9. Two days' march through stifling heat took the Confederates to the outer fortifications of Washington, where they probed the Union lines. Early soon realized that he could not over-power the defenders, who had been reinforced by veterans of the Union Sixth

Corps from the Army of the Potomac, and on July 13–15 he withdrew to the south side of the Potomac via White's Ford.

By any measure, Early had completed a masterful month's campaigning. He touched on one element of his success in a humorous comment to Henry Kyd Douglas on the evening of June 12: "Major, we haven't taken Washington, but we've scared Abe Lincoln like h[ell]!" Indeed, the presence of a Confederate army at Washington greatly vexed Lincoln. On the afternoon of July 10, as Early's soldiers moved toward Washington from the Monocacy, Lincoln wrote to Grant that Chief of Staff Henry W. Halleck "says we have absolutely no force here fit to go to the field." "Now what I think," continued Lincoln, "is that you should provide to retain your hold where you are certainly, and bring the rest with you personally, and make a vigorous effort to destroy the enemie's force in this vicinity." Grant answered that night from City Point, assuring the president that "I have sent from here a whole corps commanded by an excellent officer [Maj. Gen. Horatio G. Wright and the Sixth Corps], besides over three thousand other troops. One division of the Nineteenth Corps, six thousand strong is now on its way to Washington." Mindful that a more substantial diversion of strength from Petersburg to deal with Early could undermine northern civilian morale, Grant added, "I think on reflection it would have a bad effect for me to leave here. . . . I have great faith that the enemy will never be able to get back with much of his force." Lincoln soon calmed down, though he still hoped to smash the rebel invaders. His private secretary, John Hay, recorded on July 11 that the president's "only concern seems to be whether we can bag or destroy this force in our front."[2]

Robert E. Lee rendered a positive verdict about Early's operations a few days after the Army of the Valley returned to Virginia. He began a letter to Confederate secretary of war James A. Seddon with a statement about why Early was sent to the Valley: "Finding that it would be necessary to detach some troops to repel the force under Genl Hunter, which was threatening Lynchburg, I resolved to send one that would be adequate to accomplish that purpose effectually, and if possible strike a decisive blow. At the same time Genl Early was instructed, if his success justified it, and the enemy retreated down the Valley, to pursue him, and, if opportunity offered, to follow him into Maryland. It was believed that the Valley could then be effectually freed from the presence of the enemy, and it was hoped that by threatening Washington and Baltimore Genl Grant would be compelled either to weaken himself so much for their protection as to afford us an opportunity to attack him, or that he might be induced to attack us." Early had accomplished everything Lee hoped and now stood guard in the lower Valley. "[T]he value of the results obtained need not be further stated at present," Lee concluded, "as there are yet some to be expected in the future. I may, however, say that so far as the movement was intended to relieve our territory in that section of the enemy, it has up to the present time been successful."[3]

The Army of the Valley continued to operate along the Potomac frontier through the rest of July and into August. Elements of Early's force struck at the vital Baltimore and Ohio Railroad and skirmished with Federals in various parts of Virginia, West Virginia, and Maryland, inspiring hope in the Confederacy and frustration among northerners who had expected a quick end to the war when Grant took the field against Lee in the spring of 1864. Confederate bureaucrat John Beauchamp Jones, whose diary assiduously charted the ebb and flow of morale in Richmond, noted in mid-July that the "excitement on the news of our successes in Maryland is intense, and a belief prevails that great results will grow out of this invasion of the country held by the enemy." On July 27, David H. Strother, an officer serving with General Hunter, glumly recorded that "[a]bout this date in 1861 the remnant of [General Robert] Patterson's army abandoned the Valley. Annually since that date we have been driven out. Here we are in 1864 in the same position." Strother thought it "essential that our Government take the upper hand in this Valley," predicting that "[t]o remain on the defensive on the line of the Potomac is suggestive of continual excitement and disaster without cessation."[4]

Two events during the final days of July helped persuade Lincoln and Grant that greater resources should be deployed to gut the Valley's logistical capacity and remove Confederate forces from the area. At the battle of Second Kernstown, fought a short distance south of Winchester on July 24, Early defeated Brig. Gen. George H. Crook and subsequently followed the retreating Federals all the way to the Potomac. More ominously, on July 30 some of Early's cavalry under Brig. Gen. John McCausland burned Chambersburg, Pennsylvania, after the city's political leaders refused to pay $100,000 in gold or $500,000 in greenbacks as compensation for private property destroyed by some of Hunter's units. "For this act, I, alone, am responsible," wrote a defiant Early in his 1866 memoir, "as the officers engaged in it were simply executing my orders. . . . I am perfectly satisfied with my conduct on this occasion, and see no reason to regret it." Hunter's actions against civilians and Early's retaliation revealed that the war in the Valley had taken a more brutal turn—a trend that would accelerate over the next three months.[5]

The second and decisive phase of the 1864 Shenandoah campaign began on

August 7 with Maj. Gen. Philip H. Sheridan's appointment to head all Union forces in the theater. A week earlier, Grant had explained to General Halleck that he wanted Sheridan to pursue Early relentlessly and sever the rail connections between the Valley and Lee's army: "Wherever the enemy goes let [our] troops go also. Once started up the valley they ought to be followed until we get possession of the Va. Central rail-road." A few days later, Grant minced no words in explaining what lay in store for the economy of the Valley. "In pushing up the Shenandoah Valley . . . ," the general in chief told Sheridan, "it is desirable that nothing should be left to invite the enemy to return. Take all provisions, forage and Stock wanted for the use of your Command. Such as cannot, be consumed destroy. . . . Bear in mind, the object, is to drive the enemy South." Grant harbored few doubts about the outcome of the impending campaign, confiding to his friend William Tecumseh Sherman on August 7 that he had "put Sheridan in command who I know will push the enemy to the very death." Sherman answered the same day, predicting that Sheridan "will worry Early to death[.]" "Let us give these southern fellows all the fighting they want," added Sherman, "and when they are tired we can tell them we are just warming to the work[.]"[6]

A relatively uneventful five weeks ensued after Sheridan took charge. Early maintained an aggressive presence in the lower Valley, continuing to interfere with the B&O Railroad's operation, protecting the upcoming harvest, and serving as a galling irritant that contributed to deepening pessimism across the North about prospects for United States victory. At the same time, Sheridan methodically gathered a force, christened the Army of the Shenandoah, that would number more than 40,000 by mid-September.

The opposing armies in the Valley contended for immense stakes in September and October. Sheridan succinctly described the situation in his memoirs: "[T]he possession of the Valley of the Shenandoah at this time was of vast importance to Lee's army, and on every hand there were indications that the Confederate Government wished to hold it at least until after the crops could be gathered in to their dépôts at Lynchburg and Richmond. Its retention, besides being of great advantage in the matter of supplies, would also be a menace to the North difficult for General Grant to explain, and thereby add an element of considerable benefit to the Confederate cause."[7] Beyond logistics and morale, events in the Valley would affect Lincoln's chances for reelection in the November canvass. An absence of success against Early, coupled with the grinding stalemate between Grant and Lee at Petersburg, could diminish the long-term impact of Sherman's triumph at Atlanta, which Federals occupied on September 2. Should Democrats benefit from a perception that the conflict could drag on interminably, Republican failure at the polls would inspirit the Confederate people, compromise the northern war effort, and place at risk all progress toward emancipation.

The protracted drama in the Valley came to a rousing and bloody climax between September 19 and October 19. During those four weeks, the Shenandoah represented a true second front in Virginia, providing the landscape across which 60,000 soldiers marched and fought. Characterized by rapid movements, important battles, and systematic destruction of agricultural resources, the duel between Sheridan's and Early's armies contrasted sharply with the siege of Petersburg, which to observers behind the lines offered scant evidence that one side or the other had seized the upper hand. In the Valley, Sheridan's striking victories at Third Winchester (September 19), Fisher's Hill (September 22), Tom's Brook (October 9), and Cedar Creek (October 19) broke Confederate military resistance, and "The Burning," carried out in late September and early October, left much of the area an economic ruin. Well before Sherman's march to the sea laid a heavy hand on the interior of Georgia, Sheridan's army applied Grant's strategy of exhaustion—as some scholars have labeled the effort to wreck the economic infrastructure that fed, clothed, and armed Confederate soldiers—to the Shenandoah Valley. Unequivocal in its military and economic outcome, the 1864 Valley campaign also boosted Lincoln's candidacy for reelection, a fact that rendered it all the more decisive.[8]

A few comparative observations regarding the 1862 and 1864 Valley campaigns are instructive. In terms of scale and casualties, the 1864 campaign dwarfed that waged between Jackson and his Federal opponents in April and May of 1862. The meticulous Jedediah Hotchkiss, who served as mapmaker for both Jackson and Early, estimated that the Confederates marched 1,670 miles between June and early November of 1864, a distance roughly two and one-half times that logged by Jackson's command in the Valley. As for casualties, Jackson lost approximately 3,200 men and his opponents 5,450 (prisoners accounted for half of the Federal total), very modest numbers compared to those in 1864. Sheridan's losses in a single day at Third Winchester and again at Cedar Creek roughly equaled the toll among all Union forces during the entire 1862 campaign, and the butcher's bill for combined Union and Confederate forces in 1864 exceeded 25,000.[9] Strategically and politically, as already suggested, the impact of operations in 1864 far surpassed that in 1862. Although Jackson's Valley campaign almost surely will continue to inspire more popular attention, anyone seeking the moment when the Shenandoah loomed largest in the history of the Civil War should look to the summer and autumn of 1864.[10]

This volume, the ninth and largest in the Military Campaigns of the Civil War series, engages its subject from a number of perspectives. The eleven essays do not compose a seamless military narrative. Readers unfamiliar with the series should be advised that they must look elsewhere for comprehensive descriptions of all the major commanders, maneuvers, and battles. Such descriptions of the first phase of the campaign are available in Frank E. Vandiver's *Jubal's Raid: General Early's Famous Attack on Washington in 1864* (New York: McGraw-Hill, 1960) and B. F. Cooling's *Jubal Early's Raid on Washington, 1864* (Baltimore, Md.: Nautical & Aviation, 1989). For the campaign's more famous second phase, the best treatment is Jeffry D. Wert's *From Winchester to Cedar Creek: The Shenandoah Campaign of 1864* (Carlisle, Pa.: South Mountain, 1987). As with all titles in the series, this one seeks to highlight the important connections between the home front and the battlefield, examining some of the ways in which military affairs, civilian experiences, and politics played off one another. The contributors, also as in earlier volumes, do not always agree with one another.

The opening essay focuses on the campaign's two most important commanders. Philip H. Sheridan and Jubal A. Early entered the Valley with solid reputations, though Early's resume boasted more accomplishment at a higher level of responsibility. Events in the Valley sent their reputations hurtling in opposite directions. In the wake of Cedar Creek, Sheridan stood behind only Grant and Sherman as a Union hero, while Early endured savage criticism in the Confederacy as the man who "lost the Valley." This essay looks at each man's performance with an eye toward their respective resources, the degree to which they achieved the goals laid out by their superiors, and the soundness of their strategic and tactical decisions.

Sheridan took his orders from General in Chief Grant, who saw the Valley as part of a much larger military chessboard but understood how important it loomed in the thinking of politicians in Washington. Joseph T. Glatthaar traces the process by which Grant reached key decisions regarding commanders and strategy in the Valley. Juggling military and political considerations at a time when his own reputation had suffered some erosion in the North, Grant labored diligently to satisfy Abraham Lincoln while also putting in place the components for long-term success in the Valley. Bureaucratic resistance, an impending presidential election, and the transcendent importance of protecting

Washington all played roles in shaping Grant's actions, which, as Glatthaar's essay demonstrates, revealed his growth as the nation's senior commander.

The Confederate defeat at Cedar Creek spawned a long-running debate about whether Jubal Early ordered a "fatal halt" that squandered the morning's offensive gains and set up the ensuing disaster. Maj. Gen. John B. Gordon, Early's top subordinate, led those who blamed "Old Jube"; others blamed Gordon, whose soldiers were among the first to give way in the face of Sheridan's mid-afternoon counterattack. In the third essay, Keith S. Bohannon sifts through a mass of conflicting evidence to render a mixed verdict. He finds that Gordon sometimes dissembled and always sought to protect his own reputation in fastening blame on Early. For his part, Early was too quick to blame his soldiers, ill-informed about the state of affairs on Gordon's end of the line when Sheridan struck, and unwilling to concede that he had issued crucial orders to halt the tactical offensive. Neither man could stake a clear claim to the high ground, but Bohannon holds Early most responsible for the collapse of the Army of the Valley on the afternoon of October 19.

Maj. Gen. Horatio G. Wright temporarily headed the Army of the Shenandoah at the time of Early's surprise attack at Cedar Creek. He relied on his Sixth Corps to slow Confederate progress and constructed a solid defensive line well before noon. With Sheridan's arrival on the battlefield, Wright reverted to corps command and watched his chief orchestrate one of the war's most devastating counterattacks. A quiet engineer by training, Wright never received much credit for his role at Cedar Creek. William W. Bergen's essay, the first detailed exploration of Wright's career, brings out of the shadows an important officer whose soldiers formed the veteran core of Sheridan's army. Bergen assesses Wright's mixed record in the Valley, which included a fumbling effort at the outset of the battle of Third Winchester but rebounded at Fisher's Hill and closed with a stalwart effort at Cedar Creek. Perhaps the most surprising feature of Bergen's essay is how it shows the degree to which a senior officer in the most studied theater of the Civil War has remained almost invisible.

The next pair of essays shift attention directly to battlefields. The most one-sided clash between elements of Sheridan's and Early's commands occurred on October 9 at Tom's Brook, a few miles above Strasburg near the western slope of Massanutten Mountain, and highlighted the overwhelming superiority of Federal cavalry over their Confederate counterparts. In the fifth essay, William J. Miller evaluates leadership on both sides, narrates the tactical story of the fight, and gauges the importance of Union advantages of equipment and horseflesh. He believes that Tom's Brook, the aftermath of which featured the spectacle of Confederates fleeing for many miles up the Valley, confirmed total Federal dominance over a Confederate mounted arm that played no further notable role in the Valley.

Confederate infantry logged their worst performance of the campaign at Fisher's Hill on September 22, sprinting away from the field in confusion after being flanked. Robert E. L. Krick's essay mines a lode of evidence to reconstruct the southern debacle. Krick holds Jubal Early responsible for drawing a weak defensive line, though the numerical odds against the Confederates severely limited any chance of success. He argues that the battle permanently damaged morale in the Army of the Valley by planting seeds of doubt among the soldiers about themselves, their comrades, and the competency of their leaders. Although Early's army would recover to fight again at Cedar Creek, it was a far different force than the one that on September 20 had occupied the defensive lines at Fisher's Hill.

Most readers probably assume that news of Union victories in the Valley prompted universal applause in the North. After all, the slaughter of the Overland campaign and the steady attrition at Petersburg had fed growing frustration with the absence of good news from Virginia battlefields. But as Andre M. Fleche's essay demonstrates, many northern Democrats, hoping to unseat Lincoln in 1864, directed harsh criticism toward the president for the manner in which Sheridan conducted operations in the Valley. Democrats claimed that Federal depredations against civilians, including the seizure of slaves and destruction of private property, unmasked Republican willingness to threaten individual rights, white racial control, and widely held gender conventions. Moreover, Lincoln's critics averred, the Valley campaign would harden anti-Union sentiment among white southerners, thereby thwarting Democratic efforts to craft an easy peace and lasting reconciliation. They held up George B. McClellan's gentle handling of Confederate civilians as the best model to entice the South back into the Union. Sheridan's stunning triumphs, asserts Fleche, symbolized Republican tyranny and mismanagement of the war for Democrats who called for victory through more "civilized" means.

William G. Thomas's essay picks up this theme from the perspective of southern civilians caught in the track of military campaigning. Thomas portrays a population whipsawed by changing military fortunes and subjected to constant uncertainty regarding the safety of their families and property. Using literary sources as well as economic statistics, he finds that social and economic dislocation, while significant, fell short of the catastrophic level often described by Confederate wartime and postwar accounts. Still, their experience caused many residents of the Valley to wonder why God had chosen them for such trials, though most retained a strong allegiance to the Confederacy and a determination not to capitulate to what they saw as a barbarous enemy.

Many of the soldiers who fought under Early hailed from Virginia, and like comrades from other Confederate states they participated in a series of bitter defeats in September and October. Much of the literature on the Valley campaign has depicted Confederate soldiers as being well aware of an unfolding crisis that pointed directly toward ultimate national defeat. In the ninth essay, Aaron Sheehan-Dean counters this view. He describes men buffeted by a series of setbacks but, unlike historians, unaware that Appomattox lay just a few months in the future. They recalled that Sigel's and Hunter's invasions had been turned back before Sheridan arrived in the Valley and, though certainly depressed by Third Winchester and Cedar Creek, faced 1865 chastened but far from resigned to defeat. Echoing Thomas's conclusions, Sheehan-Dean suggests that Sheridan's victories and the burning of crops, barns, and mills both shook the confidence and hardened the resolve of Confederate soldiers and civilians.

Two biographical pieces, one with a Union and one with a Confederate emphasis, close the volume. Few United States officers in the Valley rivaled twenty-nine-year-old Col. Charles Russell Lowell in terms of his ability to inspire extravagant praise from his superiors. Of distinguished New England lineage, Lowell led a brigade in Brig. Gen. Wesley Merritt's cavalry division. Joan Waugh's essay takes Lowell from his promising youth as a scholar at Harvard to his heroic death at Cedar Creek, explaining how he envisioned his duty to the nation and why he symbolized the ideal citizen-soldier for many in New England and the North. Lowell's example reminds modern readers that Civil War armies reflected the societies for which they fought, with well-connected sons of elite families fighting alongside men of far more modest means. The death of the gifted Lowell also serves as a reminder of the conflict's immense toll in terms of lost potential in the postwar decades.

Although not as eminent as the Lowells of Boston, the Pattons of Virginia counted among their clan Revolutionary War hero John Mercer as well as national and state political figures. Three Patton brothers—John Mercer Jr., Waller Tazewell, and George S.—became Confederate colonels, and George S., whose flamboyant grandson and namesake led the American Third Army during World War II, fought in the Shenandoah Valley in 1864 until mortally wounded at Third Winchester. Robert K. Krick's essay follows the lives and careers of the

Patton colonels from their time at the Virginia Military Institute to the points at which they met their various fates. Their story, as with those of untold families on both sides, underscores both the war's voracious appetite for men and its demand for great sacrifice.

This volume in Military Campaigns of the Civil War pairs nicely with *The Shenandoah Campaign of 1862*, published in 2003. Collectively, the nine volumes in the series have dealt with every important operation in the Eastern Theater from the spring of 1862 through Spotsylvania, except Second Bull Run. The pace of publication in the series has slowed, as loyal readers will know, and there is little prospect for resuming the former one-volume-per-year pace. Future titles on the Richmond campaign of 1864, the siege of Petersburg, and the Appomattox campaign should appear over the next several years. After that, it may be time to head west to Shiloh or Chickamauga.

SINCE 1994, thirty-one scholars have contributed essays to Military Campaigns of the Civil War. Keith Bohannon, Bill Miller, Bob Krick, and R. E. L. Krick worked on previous volumes, and I am delighted to tender them continuing thanks. George Skoch, our series cartographer, also once again deserves grateful acknowledgment. Bill Bergen, Andre Fleche, Joe Glatthaar, Aaron Sheehan-Dean, Will Thomas, and Joan Waugh are first-time contributors to whom I offer my warmest gratitude. All of these friends and colleagues exhibited great patience as the process of publishing this volume stretched on and on. Full responsibility for the delays rests with me, and I can only hope that the authors are pleased with the result. As with the 1862 Valley collection, I finished much of the editorial work for this book while a fellow at the Henry E. Huntington Library in San Marino, California. I renew my thanks to Robert C. Ritchie and the Huntington staff. The dedication is to my grandson, whose first visit to the Shenandoah Valley lies in the future.

Notes

1. Jubal A. Early, *A Memoir of the Last Year of the War for Independence, in the Confederate States of America* (Toronto: Lovell & Gibson, 1866), 42; Robert E. Lee, *The Wartime Papers of R. E. Lee*, ed. Clifford Dowdey and Louis H. Manarin (Boston: Little Brown, 1961), 782–83. Lee initially resisted the idea of weakening his army to protect the Valley. On June 11, he wrote Jefferson Davis: "I acknowledge the advantage of expelling [the] enemy from the Valley. The only difficulty with me is the means. It would [take] one corps of this army. If it is deemed prudent to hazard the defense of

Richmond, the interests involved by thus diminishing the force here, I will do so. I think this is what the enemy would desire. A victory over General Grant would also relieve our difficulties" (Lee, *Wartime Papers*, 774–75).

2. Henry Kyd Douglas, *I Rode with Stonewall* (Chapel Hill: University of North Carolina Press, 1940), 295–96; Abraham Lincoln, *The Collected Works of Abraham Lincoln*, ed. Roy P. Basler, 9 vols. (New Brunswick, N.J.: Rutgers University Press, 1953), 7:437–38; John Hay, *Inside Lincoln's White House: The Complete Civil War Diary of John Hay*, ed. Michael Burlingame and John R. Turner Ettlinger (Carbondale: Southern Illinois University Press, 1997), 221. On July 8, Secretary of the Navy Gideon Welles painted a troubling picture of the Union high command: "The President has been a good deal incredulous about a very large army on the upper Potomac, yet he begins to manifest anxiety. But is under constraint I perceive, such as I know is sometimes imposed by the dunderheads at the War Office, when they are in a fog or scare and know not what to say or do" (Gideon Welles, *Diary of Gideon Wells, Secretary of the Navy under Lincoln and Johnson*, ed. Howard K. Beale, 3 vols. [New York: W. W. Norton, 1960], 2:69–70).

3. Lee to Seddon, July 19, 1864, in Lee, *Wartime Papers*, 823.

4. J. B. Jones, *A Rebel War Clerk's Diary at the Confederate States Capital*, 2 vols. (1866; reprint, Alexandria, Va.: Time-Life Books, 1982), 2:248; David Hunter Strother, *A Virginia Yankee in the Civil War: The Diaries of David Hunter Strother*, ed. Cecil D. Eby Jr. (Chapel Hill: University of North Carolina Press, 1961), 282–83.

5. Early, *Memoir of the Last Year of the War*, 74.

6. Grant to Sheridan, August 7, Grant to Halleck, August 1, Grant to David Hunter, August 5 (Grant subsequently gave these same instructions to Sheridan), Grant to Sherman, August 7, 1864, in Ulysses S. Grant, *The Papers of Ulysses S. Grant*, ed. John Y. Simon, 28 vols. to date (Carbondale: Southern Illinois University Press, 1967–), 11:379–80, 358–59, 381; Sherman to Grant, August 7, 1864, in William Tecumseh Sherman, *Sherman's Civil War: Selected Civil War Correspondence of William T. Sherman, 1860–1865*, ed. Brooks D. Simpson and Jean V. Berlin (Chapel Hill: University of North Carolina Press, 1999), 684.

7. Phillip H. Sheridan, *Personal Memoirs of P. H. Sheridan*, 2 vols. (1888; reprint, Wilmington, N.C.: Broadfoot, 1992), 1:460–61.

8. For a discussion of the strategy of exhaustion, see Herman Hattaway and Archer Jones, *How the North Won: A Military History of the Civil War* (Urbana: University of Illinois Press, 1982), 489–96.

9. Jedediah Hotchkiss, *Make Me a Map of the Valley: The Civil War Journal of Stonewall Jackson's Topographer*, ed. Archie P. McDonald (Dallas, Tex.: Southern Methodist University Press, 1973), 244. For a convenient reckoning of casualties during both campaigns, see the dates for the principal battles in E. B. Long and Barbara Long, *The Civil War Day by Day: An Almanac, 1861–1865* (Garden City, N.Y.: Doubleday, 1971). As with all estimates of casualties during the Civil War, the Longs' numbers should not be considered definitive. Losses for battles in the 1862 Valley campaign break down as follows: Kernstown (March 23), 590 U.S. and 720 C.S.; McDowell (May 8), 250 U.S. and 500 C.S.; Front Royal (May 23), 900 U.S. and 50 C.S.; First Winchester (May 25),

2,019 U.S. and 400 C.S.; Cross Keys (June 8), 685 U.S. and 690 C.S.; Port Republic (June 9), 1,000 U.S. and 800 C.S.—total, just fewer than 5,450 U.S. (more than half of whom were captured) and 3,200 C.S. Casualties for the 1864 Valley campaign were: Lynchburg (June 16–18), 950 U.S. and 500 C.S.; Monocacy (July 9), 2,000 U.S. and 700 C.S.; Second Kernstown (July 24), 1,200 U.S. and 500 C.S.; Third Winchester or Opequon (September 19), 5,000 U.S. and 4,000 C.S.; Fisher's Hill (September 22), 525 U.S. and 1,200 C.S.; Cedar Creek (October 19), 5,600 U.S. and 2,900 C.S.—total, just more than 15,000 U.S. and just fewer than 10,000 C.S. (about half of whom were prisoners at the last three battles). These figures are approximate, especially on the Confederate side, and do not include all of the smaller engagements and skirmishes in each campaign.

10. For a specific comparison of Early and Jackson in the Valley, see Gary W. Gallagher, "Revisiting the 1862 and 1864 Valley Campaigns: Stonewall Jackson and Jubal Early in the Shenandoah," in *Lee and His Generals in War and Memory* (Baton Rouge: Louisiana State University Press, 1998), 182–98.

The Shenandoah Valley
Campaign of 1864

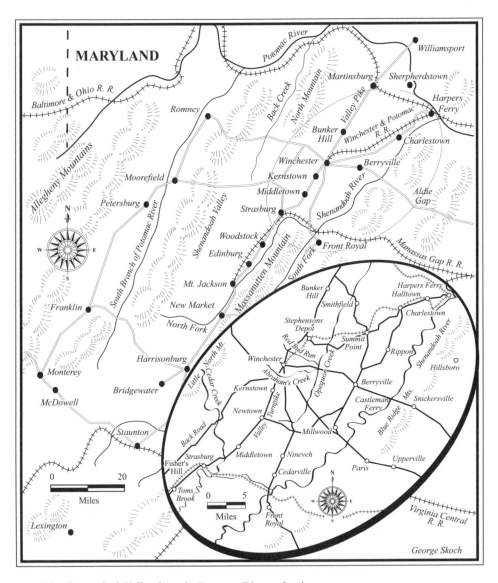

The Shenandoah Valley from the Potomac River to Lexington.

GARY W. GALLAGHER

Two Generals and a Valley

Philip H. Sheridan and Jubal A. Early in the Shenandoah

Abraham Lincoln and his son Tad listened to a torch-carrying crowd of serenaders outside the Executive Mansion on October 21, 1864. Recent events in the Shenandoah Valley prompted the president to "propose that you give three hearty cheers for Sheridan" as well as "three cheers for General Grant, who knew to what use to put Sheridan." The next day, Maj. Gen. Philip Henry Sheridan, who three days earlier had completed an extraordinary month-long campaign with a victory at Cedar Creek, received a warm message from Lincoln: "With great pleasure I tender to you and your brave army, the thanks of the Nation, and my own personal admiration and gratitude, for the month's operations in the Shenandoah Valley; and especially for the splendid work of October 19, 1864." A few days later, William Tecumseh Sherman acknowledged how success in the Valley had boosted Sheridan's reputation, affirming that among northern generals "Grant Sheridan & I are now the popular favorites." In sharp contrast to Sheridan's ascending star, Lt. Gen. Jubal Anderson Early's reputation dropped precipitately in the wake of repeated defeats in the Valley. In mid-September, before the battle of Third Winchester inaugurated a disastrous run of Confederate failure, a Georgia newspaper had observed that "Old Jubal Early, or, as Gen. Lee calls him, his 'bad old man,' has won a name during his sojourn in the Valley of Virginia, of which he is well worthy." Several defeats later, a woman in Albemarle County, Virginia, spoke for many Confederates in acidly noting in her diary, "Oh! How are the mighty fallen! Gen. Early came in town this evening with six men having been hid somewhere in the mountains. He used to be a very great man."[1]

Did the two men's performances in the Valley justify such dissimilar fates? Using the campaign's ultimate result as the sole criterion for judgment, the answer must be yes. Sheridan vanquished Early in utterly convincing style. But with other questions as part of the analytical equation, the contrast becomes less stark. How well did each man meet the strategic goals laid out by his superiors? How did their tactical efforts compare? Did one or the other exhibit greater initiative and imagination? Did either possess an edge in terms of personal leadership on the battlefield? Finally, within the realm of counterfactual conjecture, how would they have fared if their positions had been reversed?

Before moving on to explore these questions, attention to the two men's earlier Civil War careers and a reckoning of their respective human and material resources in the Valley will furnish helpful context. Sheridan's emerging from the Valley as a great national hero likely would have surprised anyone thoroughly conversant with his career prior to August 1864. A West Pointer who graduated in the bottom third of his class in 1853, Sheridan had a well-earned reputation for personal pugnacity, aggressiveness on the battlefield, and profane outbursts. Well below average height, he struck many who saw him as oddly put together. A staff officer penned a memorable portrait of his chief: "The general was short in stature . . . square-shouldered, muscular, wiry to the last degree, and as nearly insensible to hardship and fatigue as was consistent with humanity. He had a strangely-shaped head, with a large bump of something or other—combativeness, probably—behind the ears. . . . His face was very much tanned by exposure, but was lighted up by uncommonly keen eyes, which stamped him anywhere as a man of quickness and force, while its whole character betrayed him to be a soldier, with its firm chin, high cheekbones, and crisp mustache."[2]

Sheridan had seen a great deal of action by the late summer of 1864. He fought well in the Western Theater as a cavalry colonel before crafting a more mixed record as an infantry division commander at the battles of Stones River, Chickamauga, and Chattanooga. He impressed U. S. Grant at Chattanooga with what one historian of the battle called "an enthusiastic pursuit of the enemy . . . when everyone else seemed content to bivouac," thereby gaining invaluable entry into the future general in chief's circle of favorites.[3] Summoned east with Grant in the spring of 1864, Sheridan took charge of the Army of the Potomac's Cavalry Corps, joining Maj. Gens. Winfield Scott Hancock, Gouverneur K. Warren, and John Sedgwick—who led the Second, Fifth, and Sixth Corps respectively—as the only new face in the second tier of the army's command.

Sheridan's record during the Overland campaign featured high and low points. More than once during the battles of the Wilderness and Spotsylvania, his cavalry failed to carry out its essential missions of screening the ar-

Maj. Gen. Philip Henry Sheridan in the field. A woodcut of this photograph appeared on the front page of *Harper's Weekly* on October 8, 1864. Francis Trevelyan Miller, ed., *The Photographic History of the Civil War*, 10 vols. (New York: Review of Reviews, 1911), 4:263.

my's movements and gathering intelligence about the enemy. Sheridan seemed intent on using the troopers more like infantry and clashed openly with the Army of the Potomac's commander, Maj. Gen. George G. Meade, who stood by helplessly when Grant supported "Little Phil's" wish to cut loose from the army for a raid on Richmond in the midst of fighting at Spotsylvania. Grant had prized Sheridan's eagerness to pummel the rebels since getting to know him in the Western Theater, and that trait looked all the better amid a culture of caution bequeathed to the eastern army by George B. McClellan. Sheridan's raid on Richmond resulted in the mortal wounding of Maj. Gen. James E. B. "Jeb" Stuart at the battle of Yellow Tavern on May 11, a heavy blow to the Confederacy, but it also left Meade without sufficient cavalry strength. The most careful student of the Overland campaign persuasively argues that "Sheridan, in his avidity to win a point against Meade, had severely handicapped Grant in fighting Lee at Spotsylvania."[4]

Although Sheridan undeniably enjoyed Grant's respect when he took command in the Valley,[5] others entertained doubts about his qualifications. President Lincoln and Secretary of War Edwin M. Stanton headed the list of those with misgivings, initially opposing the thirty-three-year-old's appointment because of his youth. Sheridan's largest command had been the 12,500 troopers of the Cavalry Corps, a fact that invited questions about his capacity to control a vital theater containing scores of thousands of United States soldiers. Lt. Col. Theodore Lyman of Meade's staff offered a sound assessment on August 11, describing Sheridan as "an energetic and very brave officer" with greater capacity for field service than any of the generals who had opposed Jubal Early to that point. "This command, however, is a very large one," added Lyman in reference to Sheridan's previous service, "larger than he ever had before." Sheridan recalled in his memoirs that at a meeting with the president and secretary of war on August 5, "Mr. Lincoln candidly told me that Mr. Stanton had objected to my assignment to General Hunter's command, because he thought me too young, and that he himself had concurred with the Secretary." Grant had converted Lincoln, who pronounced himself satisfied and "hoped for the best." As for Stanton, he "remained silent during these remarks, never once indicating whether he, too, had become reconciled to my selection or not."[6] Most northerners probably would have seconded Lyman's belief that Sheridan should do better than his predecessors in the Valley—scarcely a high standard to meet—but might ultimately find himself out of his depth at the head of an important army.

Jubal Early went into the climactic phase of the Valley campaign with a more substantial record and reputation than Sheridan. A West Pointer who graduated eighteenth out of fifty in the class of 1837, Early had won the trust and affection of his commander. Robert E. Lee, who doubtless knew that "Old Jube" virtually idolized him, displayed rare public affection for the notoriously profane and sarcastic Early by calling him "my bad old man." Between 1862 and 1864, Early often exercised responsibility at a level beyond his rank, at times temporarily directing a division while a brigadier and a corps while a major general. In late May 1864, Lee secured his promotion to lieutenant general and assigned him to replace Richard S. Ewell at the head of Jackson's old Second Corps, the body of troops that would constitute the heart of the Confederate force in the Valley.

Early cut a remarkable physical figure. Nearly six feet tall but badly stooped by arthritis, he nevertheless conveyed an impression of ceaseless activity. Col. David Gregg McIntosh, an artillerist in the Second Corps who pronounced

Early "without a superior in the Army of Northern Virginia" as a brigade and division leader and "equal to the command of a corps," commented to members of Early's staff that the general seemed to be constantly in motion, "prowling around at all hours to see if everything was in shape." "[H]e spends all night in the saddle," a staff officer replied with at least a touch of hyperbole, "for he has the rheumatism so badly, that if he once gets out of his saddle, he can't get into it again." Early affected a hat with a large black plume but otherwise would not have evoked images of gallant cavaliers. He reminded one soldier of "a plain farmer-looking man . . . but with all, every inch a soldier." At the time of the Valley campaign, another witness left a vivid description of him as "one of the great curiosities of the war. He is a man of considerable corporosity, with a full face, which has the appearance of a full moon, when at its height. . . . His voice sounds like a cracked Chinese fiddle, and comes from his mouth . . . with a long drawl, accompanied by an interpolation of oaths." To ward off the cold, continued this man, Early wore a "striped woolen skull cap down over his ears," a "cloth overcoat striking his heels," and "leggings . . . wrapped from the feet upwards as high as the knee with white tape. He is as brave as he is homely, and as homely a man as any man you ever saw."[7]

Early had fought in all the Army of Northern Virginia's campaigns prior to his deployment to the Valley. He received praise from Lee and Stonewall Jackson for his actions at Second Bull Run, Antietam, Fredericksburg, and Chancellorsville. At Chancellorsville, Lee left him to hold the Rappahannock River line at Fredericksburg against long odds while the rest of the army marched west to confront Joseph Hooker's flanking force. This semi-independent assignment underscored a firm belief in Early, and Lee's report on the campaign stated that "Major-General Early performed the important and responsible duty intrusted to him in a manner which reflected credit upon himself and his command." FitzGerald Ross, a foreign officer who traveled with the Army of Northern Virginia during the Gettysburg campaign, commented about Early's professional stature at the mid-point of the war: "We . . . met General Early, a gruff-looking man, but with a high reputation as a soldier." By the summer of 1864, with Jackson long dead and Lt. Gen. James Longstreet absent because of a serious wound, Early was the best corps commander in the Army of Northern Virginia. Confederate artillery officer Robert Stiles, whose *Four Years Under Marse Robert* rates high among southern military memoirs, accurately observed that Lee showed "the utmost confidence" in Early "by selecting him so frequently for independent command, and to fill the most critical, difficult, and I had almost said hopeless, positions." Stiles also spoke of Early's "resource, his

Lt. Gen. Jubal Anderson Early
in a wartime portrait that be-
trays a casual approach to both
the style of his uniform and
the need to present a formal
appearance to the photogra-
pher. Francis Trevelyan Miller,
ed., *The Photographic History
of the Civil War*, 10 vols. (New
York: Review of Reviews,
1911), 10:245.

self-reliant, self-directing strength" — qualities Lee sought in any officer who
would operate beyond his immediate control.[8]

In mid-June 1864, only Jubal Early among all of Lee's lieutenants possessed
those qualities. As noted in the introduction, the first phase of the Valley campaign added luster to his already considerable reputation. Jedediah Hotchkiss
had been at Stonewall Jackson's side in the Valley in 1862 and participated in
both the Antietam and Gettysburg campaigns. Well equipped to offer a comparative evaluation, he wrote a revealing letter to his wife soon after Early's
army returned to Virginia in mid-July. "We have been over 3/4 of the State of
Maryland, scared 'Old Abe' so that he has ordered a good portion of his force
away from Richmond," stated Hotchkiss, "[c]aptured thousands of horses
and cattle, whipped the enemy in a regular battle and with small loss, returned
safely to a position that threatens Washington and Pa. at the same time, and are
ready to move in any direction." Rating Early's campaign compared to previous operations, the perceptive cartographer labeled it "by all odds the most
successful expedition we have ever made into the enemy's country." The *Times*
of London took a similar view in suggesting that Early's Maryland venture
proved the "Confederacy is more formidable as an enemy than ever." Closer
to the Valley, the editor of Charlottesville's *Daily Chronicle*, who manifested
both enthusiasm and an uncertain grasp of biographical details, deployed more

colorful language in rendering a positive verdict. "Early is in the ascendant," he observed: "He has unilaterally helped matters at Petersburg. Jubal is an outlandish designation, but it . . . [bids] fair to achieve an entrance into the history of the times. Long live Jubal Adam Early—if his name is Adam!"[9]

Sheridan and Early not only brought contrasting military experiences to the Valley, but once on the ground they also operated with vastly different bases of manpower and materiel. Indeed, numbers played a crucial role in the events of September and October. They also figured prominently in postwar writings of participants, nearly all of whom sought to address the question of odds in a manner favorable to their side. Although numbers for the final phase of the Valley campaign cannot be pinned down with great precision, it is possible to offer good estimates. At the outset of the campaign, the Army of the Shenandoah comprised approximately 35,000 infantry and artillery and 8,000 cavalry, for a total of 43,000. Sheridan's Middle Military Division also included 5,000 Federals at Harpers Ferry, 29,000 near Washington, and 8,600 elsewhere. Early's Army of the Valley consisted of fewer than 9,000 infantrymen and artillerists and between 3,500 and 4,000 cavalrymen, for a total of not more than 13,000. "As Sheridan prepared to move against his opponent," concluded Jeffry D. Wert in the best overall treatment of the campaign, "the Federal army enjoyed a superiority of at least three-to-one."[10]

The odds had not changed much by the time of Cedar Creek. Theodore C. Mahr addressed the question in a meticulous appendix to his study of the battle. He concluded that Sheridan's army fielded 22,254 infantrymen, 7,500 cavalry troopers, and 1,856 artillerymen who served 90 guns on October 19, with another 4,000 infantry within easy marching range. Early's attacking Confederate infantry numbered between 9,200 and 9,800, with support from 3,000 cavalrymen and 1,091 artillerists serving 34 guns. Totaling at most 14,000 men on October 19, the Army of the Valley confronted a foe two and one-half times its size.[11]

Debates about numbers raged after Appomattox between Federals and former Confederates, with Lost Cause writers often attributing southern defeat to the Union's advantage in men and resources. Jubal Early, who stood second to none in shaping the Lost Cause interpretation, larded his writings and speeches with allusions to powerful Federal battalions. Scholars have dismissed much of the Confederate fascination with numbers as special pleading. In light of the fact that former rebels sought to rewrite history in many ways, most notably in playing down the importance of slavery in the sectional breakup, skepticism about Confederate assessments of relative military strengths makes sense. In the case of the 1864 Valley campaign, however, Early's memoirs hewed much closer to the actual numbers than either Sheridan's or Grant's. He gave his strength just prior to Third Winchester as between 12,500 and 13,000 and Sheridan's as "at least 35,000 infantry" — estimates almost identical to those in the best modern scholarship. For Cedar Creek, Early thought his army fought with about 11,000 men on the field and another 1,700 cavalry nearby, a total some 1,300, or about 10 percent, lower than Theodore Mahr's figure.[12]

Sheridan's memoirs, in contrast, greatly underestimated his own force and overestimated Early's at the outset of the campaign. "The Confederate army at this date was about twenty thousand strong . . . ," he wrote, and the "force that I could take with me into the field at this time numbered about 26,000 men." The remaining tens of thousands of soldiers under his control, claimed Sheridan, had to be deployed to protect cities, guard the Baltimore & Ohio Railroad, and cover supply lines. Because he made no further estimates of strengths before he narrated the battle of Third Winchester, Sheridan left readers with a sense that he outnumbered Early by just 6,000 men, giving him an advantage of one and one-third to one rather than the true ratio of three to one.[13]

Although clearly disingenuous in dealing with numbers in the Valley, Sheridan came closer to the truth than did Grant. The commanding general's memoirs advanced the utterly unsupportable claim that each side initially fielded about 38,000 troops. "But the superior ability of the National commander over the Confederate commander was so great," remarked Grant in a well-executed jab at Early, "that all the latter's advantage of being on the defensive was more than counterbalanced by this circumstance." Grant went on to make the amazing statement that Early "lost more men in killed, wounded and captured in the valley than Sheridan had commanded from first to last." Confederate casualties from the beginning of August to the end of October — the vast majority of which came at Third Winchester, Fisher's Hill, Tom's Brook, and Cedar Creek — probably fell between 9,000 and 10,000. At its weakest, Sheridan's force in the field during the same period numbered more than 30,000. Grant thus tripled Confederate casualties or undercounted Federal strength by two-thirds. He did so, most likely, by way of getting even with Early for pieces published in the 1860s and 1870s suggesting that Grant lacked military talent and had triumphed over Lee only because an unforgiving preponderance of manpower and matériel worked decisively in his favor. In correspondence with Horatio Wright five years after Grant's death, Early alluded to the comment in *Personal Memoirs* about his casualties and Sheridan's strength as "curious."[14]

Unlike some of the leading commanders during the postwar years, participants and observers in the Valley and elsewhere seemed to have a good grasp of the relative numbers. On the Confederate side, Brig. Gen. Bryan Grimes of Maj. Gen. Stephen Dodson Ramseur's division informed his wife in mid-August that the Confederates had been demonstrating against Sheridan in the direction of Harpers Ferry. "I have no idea that we are going to fight him," said Grimes, "for the enemy out numbers us three to one, and Early knows too well the importance of preserving his army and will not risk too much in a fight of this character." At about the same time, the *Richmond Dispatch* informed readers that "Sheridan's entire force in the Valley amounts to 41,000 men." A month later, the *Charlottesville Daily Chronicle* professed to approve of Early's withdrawal southward from Winchester, where he had been "exposed to the flanking movements of the enemy, who watched him, with double his force of infantry, and harassed him continually with a superior force of cavalry." Jedediah Hotchkiss avoided guessing at specific numbers while impressing upon his wife that Early and his army faced very long odds. "[O]ur ranks are depleted by the many bloody battles of this mighty campaign," he wrote on October 11, "and we must have our lines strengthened to oppose those of the insolent foe that has added thousand upon thousands to his from every household in the North. The enemy is determined to do all that numbers can do this year."[15]

Many on the Federal side also realized Sheridan faced a much smaller foe. Secretary of the Navy Gideon Welles believed from the first that the Confederates entering Maryland in July lacked the power to mount a serious threat if Union resources were marshaled effectively. "It strikes me that the whole demonstration is weak[,]" he wrote in his diary on July 11, "that the Rebels have but a small force." Four days later, as Early withdrew unmolested to Virginia, Welles disparaged generals and War Department officials who "insisted there was a large force. We have done nothing, and it is more gratifying to our self pride to believe there were many of them, especially as we are likely to let them off scot-free." In early August, Welles held to the "opinion that the [Confederate] force is small and the scare great." Surgeon Daniel M. Holt of the 121st New York Infantry, a Sixth Corps unit, shared Welles's exasperation. Amid constant marching and countermarching in the lower Valley during August, Holt felt ashamed that Sheridan's army seemed unwilling to engage the less numerous rebels. From Halltown, he wrote on August 24, "Shall I say that we *retreated* before an inferior force? It looks like it, surely, for all the way down here, they were poking their jokes at us in the shape of shot and shell in a very provoking way." An artillery officer with the Army of the Potomac followed the action from a distance, marveling at "the audacity of Early attacking an entrenched force three times his own numbers" at Cedar Creek.[16]

Unlike so many others, Robert E. Lee unaccountably failed to grasp the odds against Early. Douglas Southall Freeman, the most influential historian of the Army of Northern Virginia, stated bluntly that no other "mathematical calculation made by Lee during the war was so much in error." Perhaps Lee's own disadvantage vis-à-vis Grant colored his attitude. After all, he had first sent to the Valley Early's Second Corps, with the fine divisions commanded by Maj. Gens. Robert E. Rodes, Dodson Ramseur, and John B. Gordon, and later reinforced it with the First Corps division of Maj. Gen. Joseph B. Kershaw and several brigades of cavalry. All of these deployments weakened his position at Petersburg, and Lee surely resented having to deplete his army to bolster another theater. But that should not have blinded him to Early's situation, and some of his correspondence suggests he must have known roughly how many soldiers served under Sheridan. On August 12, for example, he reported to Jefferson Davis that the "forces opposed to Genl Early consist of the 6th, 8th, two divisions of the 19th & the 13th Corps," as well as Brig. Gen. Alfred T. A. Torbert's cavalry division. Leaving aside the fact that there was no "13th Corps" in the Valley (or anywhere else), these units composed a formidable army. Yet on October 12, Lee insisted that with Kershaw's division at hand Early possessed the means to defeat the enemy. "I do not think Sheridan's infantry or cavalry numerically as large as you suppose," stated Lee to Old Jube, "but either is sufficiently so not to be despised and great circumspection must be used in your operations." Aware that Early's cavalry had been humiliated at Tom's Brook on October 9, Lee offered a stunningly wrong-headed analysis: "Although the enemy's cavalry may exceed ours in numbers, and I know it does in equipment, still we have always been able to cope with them to advantage, and can do so again by proper management. You have the greater proportion of the cavalry in Virginia and it must be made effective."[17]

Within the larger arithmetical reality in the Valley, the Federal mounted arm constituted the most critical factor favoring Sheridan. In his exhaustive study of Union horsemen, Stephen Z. Starr remarked that "Sheridan's cavalry enjoyed an overwhelming numerical superiority over Early's mounted troops . . . [and] its superiority in firepower was nothing short of awesome." The Army of the Shenandoah boasted the highest ratio of cavalry to infantry of any major United States force during the entire war, and Sheridan's troopers often outnumbered Early's by as much as three or four to one. Armed to a significant extent with

Spencer carbines and other repeating weapons, much better mounted, and generally well led, Federal horsemen repeatedly made the difference. Conceding Early's personal bias against cavalry and his occasional misuse of mounted units, the fact remains that Sheridan possessed the means for total dominance. "Time and again the events of the campaign resulted in a requirement that the [Confederate] cavalry do near impossibilities at moments of decision," Robert K. Krick noted in the best analysis of Early's cavalry, with the result that "the poor caliber of the men and units was exposed under an unblinking spotlight, and the shortcomings of their leadership were magnified manifold."[18]

Abundant testimony from both Confederates and Federals leaves no doubt about the northern cavalry's supremacy. In the wake of Third Winchester, Dodson Ramseur commented that "we whipped their infantry but their cavalry 7000 or 8000 strong broke our cavalry on the left [and] got in behind us followed by a strong column of infantry." Jedediah Hotchkiss echoed Ramseur, praising the Confederate infantry's effort on September 19 until "the enemy massed his cavalry on our left and they made a splendid charge; our cavalry broke and ran away, creating a stampede." A private in the 1st Virginia Cavalry agreed, lambasting "the cavalry on our left . . . as usual part of it gave way without making a stand. . . . There was no cause or excuse for all this, but was disgraceful in the highest degree." The Confederate cavalry also collapsed at Fisher's Hill and Cedar Creek, prompting many southern infantrymen to excoriate them for precipitating routs. Jubal Early, who often sneered at some of his mounted regiments as "buttermilk rangers," wrote Lee with substantial justification after Third Winchester and Fisher's Hill that the "enemy's immense superiority in cavalry and the inefficiency of the greater part of mine has been the cause of all my disasters."[19]

Men in the Army of the Shenandoah combined admiration for their own cavalry with sometimes open scorn for Early's. A member of the 65th New York Infantry observed after Cedar Creek that the "cavalry of this department have earned fame and reputation they may well feel proud of, and they could not well be other than successful when led by such gallant spirits as Torbert, [Brig. Gen. George A.] Custer, and [Brig. Gen. Wesley] Merritt. The fruits of the victory just gained the country owes to them." Col. James H. Kidd of the 6th Michigan Cavalry proudly averred that the "Cavalry gained the day at 'Winchester' the 19th September, and the Cavalry saved the day at Cedar Creek the 19th October." Evincing an almost total lack of respect for his southern opponents, Kidd added, "The Rebel Cavalry is of little account. Fighting them is only a *side-show*." Sheridan's success in the Valley depended on more than his advantage in cavalry, but Colonel Kidd's comments remind students of the campaign to be aware of that factor.[20]

With the prior careers of the opposing commanders and the strengths of the two armies in mind, we can return to the questions regarding their generalship posed at the beginning of this essay. We will turn first to how successfully each man met his strategic goals. U. S. Grant wanted Sheridan to accomplish three major tasks: first, to drive the Confederates from the Potomac River line and the lower Valley, pursuing them southward up the Shenandoah; second, to destroy the Valley's capacity to send food and other logistical goods to Lee's army; and third, to disrupt the Virginia Central Railroad, which crossed the Blue Ridge between Staunton and Charlottesville and connected with the Orange and Alexandria line in the Piedmont.

The first task was most important because its success would both facilitate completion of the other two and yield enormous dividends in the realms of politics and public morale in the United States. Grant initially circumscribed his naturally aggressive young lieutenant's options. On August 12, the general in chief directed Chief of Staff Henry W. Halleck to inform Sheridan "that it is now certain two Divisions of Infantry have gone to Early and some Cavalry and twenty pieces of Artillery. . . . He must be cautious and act now on the defensive until movement here force them to detach and send this way. Early's force with this increase can not exceed 40,000 men but this is too much for Sheridan to attack." Sheridan's priority throughout August lay in marshaling his forces, and he avoided battle on several occasions while marching to and fro in the lower reaches of the Valley. As we have seen, that behavior frustrated Federals such as Surgeon Holt of the 121st New York, who wondered why Sheridan did not strike a smaller foe; it also convinced Jubal Early that his opponent lacked audacity. Sheridan described his operations for the first five weeks as "almost wholly of offensive and defensive manœuvring for certain advantages, the enemy confining himself meanwhile to measures to counteract my designs." By mid-September, the Army of the Shenandoah, more than 40,000 strong, included Maj. Gen. Horatio G. Wright's Sixth Corps (3 divisions); Brig. Gen. William H. Emory's Nineteenth Corps (2 divisions); Brig. Gen. George Crook's Eighth Corps, also known as the Army of West Virginia (2 divisions); Brig. Gen. Alfred T. A. Torbert's cavalry (3 divisions); and the attendant artillery for all the infantry and cavalry commands.[21]

Sheridan assumed the offensive on September 19 and within a month had extinguished any significant Confederate military threat in the lower Valley. The Federal victories at Third Winchester, Fisher's Hill, and Cedar Creek, each of which ended with flanked Confederates abandoning the field in considerable disorder, demonstrated that Sheridan could thrash the rebels seemingly at will. Although Early's little army remained intact after Cedar Creek and ventured north of Strasburg and Front Royal as late as the second week of November, no one in touch with reality could have believed that the Confederacy might regain firm control of the lower Valley. No one but Abraham Lincoln, perhaps, who on February 25, 1865, having misunderstood a message from Sheridan, sent a telegraphic note to Grant expressing his and Secretary of War Stanton's concern: "Have you well considered whether you do not again leave open the Shenandoah-valley entrance to Maryland and Pennsylvania? — or, at least, to the B&O Railroad?"[22] Grant quieted down the president, who should have known that Cedar Creek had broken Confederate power in the Valley. After that battle, Washington experienced no more scares, the B&O Railroad functioned free of interruption, and Early could represent nothing more than a nuisance — all evidence that Philip Sheridan had carried out the first of his three tasks.

He did equally well with the second task, laying waste to large stretches of the Valley between Staunton and the Potomac River as well as to much of the Luray Valley east of the Massanutten Range. Contrary to local legend in the Valley and Lost Cause propaganda, Sheridan's troopers and soldiers did not put all barns, mills, and stocks of grain and hay to the torch. Neither did they slaughter or carry off all livestock and burn private dwellings indiscriminately. But during The Burning in late September and early October, as well as more generally during the entire campaign, they did severely damage the Valley's logistical output. One Union officer rendered a judicious verdict in stating, "It fell to General Sheridan to desolate this fertile valley, and the orders were carried out literally but not riotously, and so far as his authority could be exercised there was no unnecessary destruction." From Woodstock on October 7, Sheridan reported to Grant that his men had "destroyed over two thousand barns filled with wheat, hay, and farming implements; over seventy mills filled with flour and wheat; have driven in front of the army over 4,[000] head of stock, and have killed and issued to the troops not less than 3,000 sheep." He planned to continue the work on down toward Fisher's Hill, predicting that "[w]hen this is completed the Valley, from Winchester up to Staunton, ninety-two miles, will have but little in it for man or beast." The production of the lower Valley, emphasized Sheridan, had been reserved to supply Early's army in the winter, while that above Staunton had been shipped to Lee's army.[23]

The third of Grant's goals for Sheridan, disruption of the Virginia Central Railroad, went unmet. Grant had sought to disable the line since the beginning of the 1864 campaigning, but Maj. Gens. Franz Sigel and David Hunter, in May and June respectively, had failed to do so. After driving Early well up the Valley after Third Winchester and Fisher's Hill, Sheridan seemed perfectly positioned to hit the Virginia Central and move across the Blue Ridge toward Charlottesville and Gordonsville. But he told Grant on October 12 that he objected "to the opening of the R.R. and an advance on the old Rapidan line, on account of The waste of fighting force to protect R. Rds, and the additional waste of force, as some would have to be left in this valley." Two days later, Grant responded, "What I want is for you to threate[n] the Va. Central railroad & canal in the manner your judgement tells you is best holding yourself ready to advance if the enemy draw off their forces. If you make the enemy hold a force equal to your own for the protection of those thoroughfares it will accomplish nearly as much as their destruction." Sheridan met with Grant, Halleck, and Stanton in Washington on October 17, where he pressed his case on this issue. "The upshot," he wrote in his memoirs, "was that my views against such a plan were practically agreed to." Grant clearly did not hold Sheridan's obstinacy against him, for just three days after the meeting, with news of Cedar Creek in hand, he told Stanton that he considered Little Phil "one of the ablest of Generals."[24]

Jubal Early also met his strategic goals for more than four months. During the first phase of the Valley campaign, he saved Lynchburg, cleared the Valley of Federals, invaded the United States, menaced Washington, and compelled Grant to send thousands of soldiers from the Army of the Potomac to Washington and the Shenandoah. Lee then instructed Early to remain in the Valley, hoping that his presence would protect logistical production and open a true second front in Virginia that would siphon more troops from Grant's army.

From early August through October, Early maneuvered in the lower Valley and along the Potomac River in such a way as to supply his own army and allow part of the fall harvest to reach Lee's soldiers at Petersburg. "I have never known a more active campaign," Jedediah Hotchkiss wrote on August 28, "but it is the only kind to protect us from the movements of the Yankees. We must keep them busy all the time or their roving disposition will cause them to annoy us." In addition to protecting Confederate farmers, Early's army also gathered material from Maryland. Hotchkiss wrote that on one foray across the Potomac the Confederates seized "150 horses, 2,000 bush. of corn, a large lot of leather, etc." Soldiers in Lee's army appreciated the efforts of their comrades in the Valley. The *Petersburg Express* reported in late August that "Not a few of the well-fed, fat cattle of Maryland, captured by Gen. Early's forces, have reached Petersburg, and our troops are now enjoying the luxury of real good beef. . . . This army sends its compliments to Gen. Early, and hopes he will find it convenient to 'gobble up' a sufficiency of beeves, sheep, hogs, &c., to last them through the coming winter." Even after Cedar Creek, Early's army remained in position to block Federal access to rich agricultural areas in the upper reaches of the Valley.[25]

Early also occupied a great many United States soldiers in the Valley and along the Potomac River line throughout the late summer and autumn. With a force that never numbered as many as 15,000, he compelled Grant to detach for lengthy service away from Richmond and Petersburg one of his most trusted lieutenants, the veteran Sixth Corps, and two-thirds of the Cavalry Corps. These men joined many thousands of others brought together under Sheridan in the Middle Military Division. In all, between 85,000 and 90,000 Federals stood watch one way or another against the Army of the Valley. Thousands of them spent at least some time guarding the B&O Railroad, yet Early, in the words of the B&O's leading historian, "struck a heavy blow," shutting down the line for virtually the entire period between the first week of July and the end of September.[26]

Lee consistently pressed Early to use the soldiers sent from the Army of Northern Virginia aggressively or to return as many as possible to Petersburg. Early did his best, managing to hold Sheridan in the Valley and inflict significant losses on the Army of the Shenandoah. One reckoning of Sheridan's casualties placed the total at 16,952—including 1,939 killed, 11,893 wounded, and 3,121 captured or missing; another indicated 1,290 killed and 10,006 wounded, with no estimate of captured and missing. It seems likely that Sheridan's loss at least approached, and perhaps exceeded, the size of Early's army at its largest—an interesting reversal of Grant's statement about strengths and casualties in the Valley. At least 5,000 additional Federals had been killed, wounded, or captured during the first phase of the Valley campaign, pushing the total in the four-month operation above 20,000. Early lost approximately 10,000 killed, wounded, and captured against Sheridan and perhaps another 2,500 prior to August.[27]

Although Early's campaign represented a sound trade-off for the Confederacy that, over a period of four months, met Lee's logistical goals and created a sizeable second front, his efforts ultimately took on the aspect of an unmitigated disaster. Events on the battlefield triggered a rapid change in attitude toward him. Shortly before he was mortally wounded at Third Winchester, General Robert Rodes, one of Early's gifted division commanders, termed the

Valley operations "the grandest campaign of the war, considering the forces engaged." Rodes had fought under Lee in many famous engagements but "prided
himself on being with Early more than any part of his career." A lieutenant in
the 44th Georgia, writing in early August, thought that if "any man can give
the yankees 'tit for tat,' Gen. Early can. He is very popular with his command."
Just a few weeks later, in the aftermath of Third Winchester, Fisher's Hill, and
The Burning, Virginia's Governor William Smith urged Lee to sack Early: "I
am in frequent correspondence with the Valley, and speak confidently when
I say that it is of the greatest consequence to the country that General Early
should be relieved." One resident of the Valley went over the governor's head
to make her case to Jefferson Davis. "There will never be anything but defeat &
disaster," she stated, "until Genl Early is relieved of the command . . . if things
continue to go on as they have done for the last month we will have no army
to command in the valley." A Georgian in the Chatham Artillery—stationed
in the Department of South Carolina, Georgia, and Florida—voiced a similar
sentiment shortly after Cedar Creek: "We are all very much depressed just now,
resulting from a recent thrashing administered to Gen. Early, in the Valley, this
last defeat is the severest from our accounts, that has yet befallen him, and some
change must be made in the Valley District."[28]

Rumors that alcohol had affected Early's conduct in the Valley spread rapidly
after Cedar Creek. "As usually the newspapers are lying about things which
happened here and accuse our Old Man and several officers of having been
drunk," wrote a supportive staff officer in his diary on October 23. Resorting
to strained humor, he added, "I wish I had had something to drink myself at the
time." No creditable evidence supports the charge against Early, but perceptions mattered more than reality. A resident of Fishersville, in Augusta County,
raised the issue in a letter to Jefferson Davis. He claimed to have spoken with
many soldiers from Early's army as they passed by his place. "They do not
hesitate to say that they are going home," reported this civilian, "the men &
officers have become discouraged that there will never be any thing but defeat
& disaster until Genl Early is relieved. . . . I am sorry to say it is the general
opinion of the country & attributed to two free use of ardent spirits both by
officers of high & low & the request I have to make is this that you remove Genl
Early." A woman in eastern North Carolina, whose diary traced the campaigns
in Virginia via newspaper reporting, lamented "the serious disgrace" at Cedar
Creek, noting that the *Richmond Examiner* "says Apple Brandy did it all!"[29]

Early lingered in the Shenandoah for another four and one-half months after
Cedar Creek, though Lee recalled most of his troops to the Army of North-

ern Virginia. By March 1865, following a final humiliating defeat at Waynesboro, public opinion solidified against Old Jube. "While my own confidence in your ability, zeal, and devotion to the cause is unimpaired," Lee wrote Early on March 30, "I have nevertheless felt that I could not oppose what seems to be the current of opinion, without injustice to your reputation and injury to the service. I therefore felt constrained to endeavor to find a commander who would be more likely to develop the strength and resources of the country, and inspire the soldiers with confidence." Lee closed by thanking Early for "the fidelity and energy with which you have always supported my efforts, and for the courage and devotion you have ever manifested in the service of the country." With that compassionate message in hand, Jubal Early went home, his part in the conflict having closed on a bitterly disappointing note.[30]

Turning from the level of strategic goals, the next question concerns how well Early and Sheridan performed tactically. The short answer is that each man had good days and bad, but only Early achieved moments of imagination and risk-taking distinction. Early's negatives may be summed up quickly. He badly underestimated Sheridan prior to Third Winchester, dividing his infantry in a manner that invited disaster on September 19. This behavior grew out of his reaction to Sheridan's apparent unwillingness to fight a decisive battle. As he phrased it in his memoirs, "Events of the last month had satisfied me that the commander opposed to me was without enterprise, and possessed an excessive caution which amounted to timidity. If it was his policy . . . to convince me that he was not an able or energetic commander, his strategy was a complete success."[31] Early had no way of knowing that Grant, through Halleck, had instructed Sheridan to be cautious in August and early September.

At Fisher's Hill, Early may have erred by placing veteran infantry atop strong ground on the right and entrusting his left flank to dismounted cavalry. A soldier in the 60th Georgia, stationed near the Confederate right, pronounced that part of the position so strong "a single line of resolute men might have held back a dozen colums of the advancing foe," while on the left "the advantage in ground was not so much in our favor, and the main strength of the enemy was massed against that point."[32] But two caveats must be entered in Early's favor: first, he lacked enough manpower to defend in any depth the four-mile line that ran from Little North Mountain to the North Fork of the Shenandoah at Fisher's Hill (the only defensible position in the lower Valley); and second, the one part of the line he absolutely could not relinquish was his right, which protected the vital Valley Turnpike. Had he buttressed his left at the expense of his right, he could have lost access to the pike and found himself even more vulnerable in the wake of Sheridan's assaults. Still, the placement of dismounted horsemen on his vulnerable left flank must be adjudged a poor tactical choice.

That placement seems all the more odd because, from first to last in the campaign, Early so distrusted his cavalry that he relied almost solely on his veteran infantry and artillery. Anyone tempted to render too negative a verdict regarding this element of his generalship, however, should keep in mind that Confederate cavalry units from the Shenandoah Valley were so undisciplined and poorly led (a legacy of Turner Ashby's influence from 1862) that it made scant sense to depend on them for serious work.

Perhaps the most persistent criticism of Early's tactics relates to Cedar Creek, where he has been chided for calling a "fatal halt" after Confederates had won enormous success early in the morning. Although the myth of a fatal halt grew largely out of John B. Gordon's self-serving statements during and after the war, some evidence — most notably Jedediah Hotchkiss's journal entry for October 23 — suggests that Early second-guessed himself soon after the battle. "General Early told me not to tell General Lee that we ought to have advanced on the morning at Middletown," wrote Hotchkiss, "for, he said, we ought to have done so." But could Early's soldiers have accomplished more, even if pushed harder? They had been campaigning on short rations for some time and spent the night of October 18 moving into position to attack. Tired and hungry when they commenced their assault just after dawn on the nineteenth, they probably had reached their physical limits by the time they drove back the Nineteenth and Eighth corps at mid-morning. Although Gordon denied it, unimpeachable testimony describes thousands of men who fell out of the ranks to plunder the Union camps. Hotchkiss, for example, writing two days before he made the journal entry about Early, did not mention a fatal pause. "We halted near Middletown and reformed our lines, preparatory to another advance," he stated with no hint of disapprobation regarding Early's conduct, "but so many of our troops had left the ranks to plunder the Yankee camps that it was a long time before it could be done—in the meantime, . . . the enemy rallied . . . and attacked our left, which was seized with a sudden, unexpected, and unnecessary panic." An engineer officer on Early's staff used fewer words to say the same thing: "Everything seems to go to the dogs. We really were beaten by our own men, who, instead of being on the front, were busy plundering."[33]

Apart from the debate over the fatal halt, Early can be criticized for three other decisions at Cedar Creek. He deployed his cavalry poorly, sending Maj. Gen. Lunsford L. Lomax's division toward Front Royal, allocated too few men to control the Valley Pike north of Middletown, and left his infantry in an exposed position in the mid-afternoon. A good part of the problem in the last two instances, yet again, arose from his having so few infantry with which to cover a huge battlefield.

Against these negatives must be reckoned Early's deft use of a much inferior force to keep the Federals off balance through much of the campaign. His marching, skirmishing, and feinting compared favorably to Stonewall Jackson's storied maneuvering in May and June 1862. Early also handled his infantry divisions very effectively at Third Winchester, utilizing the talents of John B. Gordon, Robert E. Rodes, and Dodson Ramseur to neutralize Sheridan's infantry assaults for most of a long day's action. Old Jube's high point came in planning a tactical masterpiece at Cedar Creek. The war produced nothing to rival this audacious flanking maneuver, which called for a nighttime march that required two crossings of the North Fork of the Shenandoah River and the coordination of three columns in an assault at daybreak—all in the face of an enemy nearly three times Early's strength. Carried out magnificently in the beginning, the plan faltered when the Confederate assaults lost impetus against a solid defense from the Union Sixth Corps. Before the day was out, Early's army had suffered another reverse. Both Third Winchester and Cedar Creek might have been victories if Early had been permitted even a slight margin for error. But the Federal numerical advantage was such that only tactical perfection would have yielded Confederate triumph, and Early fell short of that impossible standard.

Sheridan, in contrast, survived tactical lapses at least as serious as his opponent's precisely because he could call on ample reserves of infantry and powerful cavalry. Before moving on to specific tactical decisions, it is important to credit Sheridan with coordinating cavalry operations with those of his infantry and artillery as well as any army commander during the war. Not content to have troopers screen his movements and seek out the enemy, he effectively employed their repeating firepower to demoralize and break Confederate infantry. This splendid coordination of infantry and cavalry on the battlefields at Third Winchester and Cedar Creek represented a unique feature of the 1864 Valley campaign.

Less impressively, Sheridan sent Wright's Sixth Corps and Emory's Nineteenth Corps through the Berryville Canyon at Third Winchester on a single road, where they predictably became bogged down. He also left Crook's Eighth Corps far behind without orders for a time before sending it in to bolster Emory's position. Crook eventually used Col. Isaac H. Duval's division to get around Early's left, a movement that, in conjunction with Federal cavalry surging up the turnpike to their right, broke the Confederate line. Much to Crook's displeasure, Sheridan later took credit for Duval's decisive tactical maneuver. Sheridan did not "write his report until after the war was over," a disgruntled Crook observed in his memoir, "and then instead of giving me the credit I deserved, he treated the subject something in this wise: that I was placed in a fortunate position where I could turn the enemy's flank, giving the impression that my turning the enemy's flank was part of his plan, whereas so far as I know the idea of turning the enemy's flank never occurred to him, but I took the responsibility on my own shoulders." Capt. Henry A. Du Pont, an artillerist in the Eighth Corps who was present on the scene, concurred that Crook "turned the Confederate left, when, entirely upon his own responsibility, he instantly made the movement which decided the Union victory." Once Early's army had left the field in confusion, Sheridan neglected to mount a rapid pursuit.[34]

At Fisher's Hill, Sheridan exhibited a spectacular lack of appreciation for the ground by suggesting an assault against Early's well-protected right flank astride the Valley Pike. Crook countered with a proposal for a movement around the Confederate left, where a thin line of dismounted troopers posed the weakest of obstacles. Sheridan embraced Crook's idea and implemented it on September 22. Once again, he claimed credit for the tactical success — and again Crook took exception. "Gen. Sheridan's first idea was for me to turn the enemy's right flank," remembered Crook after the war, "but after discussion saw the folly of such an undertaking, and finally let me go to the right, their left." Sheridan's official report implied that he devised the flank attack: "I resolved to use a turning column again, and that I would move Crook unperceived, if possible, over onto the face of Little North Mountain and let him strike the left and rear of the enemy's line." Col. Rutherford B. Hayes, who served under Crook as a brigade and later a division commander, wrote four days after the battle that at "Fisher's Hill the turning of the Rebel left was planned and executed by Crook against the opinions of the other corps generals," a statement with which Henry Du Pont agreed. "[S]o far as it relates to Crook's conception of the project," affirmed Du Pont, Hayes's statement "was fully corroborated by my personal recollections."[35]

Absent when Early struck at Cedar Creek, Sheridan arrived on the scene to find that Horatio Wright, who temporarily led the Army of the Shenandoah, had set up a strong defensive line north of Middletown. Early's army had shot its offensive bolt, and only sporadic firing erupted across the landscape. Yet the notion that Sheridan saved his fleeing army from imminent defeat with a desperate ride from Winchester quickly gained wide currency. It achieved its most popular expression in Thomas Buchanan Read's poem titled "Sheridan's

Brig. Gen. George Crook as he appeared in *Harper's Weekly* following the battles of Third Winchester and Fisher's Hill. *Harper's Weekly*, October 15, 1864.

Ride" (which inflated the distance Sheridan covered from about twelve miles to twenty), but it also became, along with the battle of Gettysburg and the naval duel between the ironclads *Monitor* and *Virginia*, one of the three most painted scenes of the Civil War. *Harper's Weekly* featured Sheridan, in the saddle on his horse Rienzi, galloping toward Cedar Creek from Winchester. Much of the popular conception of Sheridan's role at Cedar Creek amounted to romantic nonsense, and poor General Wright never received credit for his role in stabilizing the Union army. George Crook offered an unflattering anecdote about Sheridan on the evening of October 19: "Sitting around the campfires that night, Gen. Sheridan was feeling very good. He said, 'Crook, I am going to get much more credit for this than I deserve, for, had I been here in the morning the same thing would have taken place, and had I not returned today, the same thing would have taken place.' This saying was full of meat, but it made little impression on me at the time."[36]

Sheridan showed at his tactical best in preparing to counterattack at Cedar Creek. The last phase of fighting on October 19 highlighted his edge over Early in our fourth category of analysis—personal leadership during battle. Sheridan's fiery presence had helped rally Federals at Third Winchester, and his ride along the lines before the climactic assault at Cedar Creek greatly inspired the men. Capt. George B. Sanford of the First United States Cavalry, who witnessed Sheridan in action in the Valley, emphasized that he exercised up-close leadership, often moving around in combat with few or no aides and encouraging the men. "He was a wonderful man on the battle field, and never in as good humor as when under fire," stated Sanford, adding that "[t]his pre-supposes, however, that everyone about was doing his duty as he deemed it should be done. If he judged the contrary one might as well be in the path of a Kansas cyclone. Explanations were not in order, and the scathing torrent of invective that poured out, his shrill voice rising ever higher as his anger grew, while his piercing eye seemed absolutely to blaze, was a sight once seen not likely to be forgotten." An example of that invective issued from Sheridan when, en route to the battlefield at Cedar Creek, he berated Federal stragglers along the Valley Pike: "God *damn* you, don't cheer me! There's lots of fight in you men yet! God damn you! Come up!"[37]

Sheridan's soldiers at Cedar Creek almost unanimously lavished praise on him for reinspiriting the army after the morning's travails. Four witnesses will convey a sense of their reaction. When Sheridan appeared on the field at about ten thirty in the morning, wrote a surgeon with the 12th West Virginia on October 21, "his arrival infused new courage into our soldiers. 'Twas said to be like a reinforcement of twenty thousand men, . . . he remarked that 'Early should that day get the *damndest thrashing* he ever got,' and the battle turned to our favor; and such a victory as we had *that day* I never saw." Abiel Edwards of the 29th Maine matched the surgeon's enthusiasm, if not his spelling skills: "[A]t first it seemed as though it would be a defat to us But our Brave Sheridan wrung a *great victory* from the very jaws of defeat. . . . He rode right on the feild told the boys they wasn't half whipped Turned on the Rebels drove them from our works way beyond fishers Hill Capturing hard up to 70 peices of Artillary." A New Yorker also gauged Sheridan's value as equal to twenty thousand reinforcements, declaring that "General Sheridan has got the full confidence of all his men, and when he came down the line the air rang with cheers. . . . A new spirit entered us, and we were determined to drive the Rebels back, or die in the attempt."[38]

Captain Sanford narrated Sheridan's galvanizing impact on the army's high command. Present when the general rode west from the Valley Pike to meet with Wright, Sanford said the latter "had dismounted, and was sitting on the grass on the hillside. He looked tired and a little disspirited." Greeting Sheridan, Wright said, "Well, we've done the best we could." Sheridan responded with

"Sheridan at Cedar Creek." Unlike most artistic representations of Sheridan at Cedar Creek, which evoke a sense of stirring action, this late nineteenth-century treatment has a static, staged quality. Lew Wallace and others, *The Story of American Heroism* (Chicago: Werner, 1896), 553.

a reassuring, "That's all right; that's all right." General Emory, whose Nineteenth Corps had not acquitted itself as well as Wright's Sixth Corps to that point, rode up and reported that he had deployed one of his divisions to cover a retreat to Winchester. Sheridan snapped at Emory, "Retreat—Hell—we'll be back in our camps tonight." "When I listened to this conversation I did not exactly appreciate the fact that it was going to be an historical occasion," explained Sanford, "but I did understand that it was an interesting one, and the more so from the fact that until that moment it had never occurred to me that it was possible to even hope for anything more than an orderly retreat to Winchester, and an opportunity there to recuperate and recruit, preliminary to a new effort for the control of the Valley."[39]

This episode revealed the essence of Sheridan's appeal to U. S. Grant. Undismayed by the morning's misfortune and impatient with a subordinate's talk of retreat, he trained his eye on the enemy with no thought but how best to contrive an offensive victory. And with his superb ability to inspire his soldiers, he soon had them in motion against the rebels. Superior Union numbers, as always in the Valley, clearly helped Sheridan mount his counterattack. No one can know whether he would have been able to rally heavily outnumbered troops.

Whatever the answer to that question, it is clear that Early lacked his opponent's magnetic presence in battle. Courageous almost to a fault, Early placed himself at risk in vain attempts to slow fleeing troops at Third Winchester, Fisher's Hill, and Cedar Creek. Simon Baruch, a surgeon with a South Carolina unit, recalled that at Cedar Creek he "saw Gen. Early with waving flag imploring the men to stop the rout." The fleeing troops paid little heed, an embarrassment Early readily acknowledged in his memoirs. "Every effort was made to stop and rally Kershaw's and Ramseur's men," he wrote, "but the mass of them resisted all appeals, and continued to go to the rear without waiting for any effort to retrieve the partial disorder." During the retreat southward on the Valley Pike, Early sought to organize a stand. "I tried to rally the men immediately after crossing Cedar Creek, and at Hupp's Hill, but without success," he confessed. "Could 500 men have been rallied, at either of these places, who would have stood by me, I am satisfied that all my artillery and waggons and the greater part of the captured artillery could have been saved, as the enemy's pursuit was very feeble."[40]

Irascible and caustic, Early never forged the type of bond with his soldiers that paid dividends in a crisis. A few Confederates tempered criticism with praise after Cedar Creek, like a North Carolinian who called for the "most rigid discipline" to make the army fight again. A new commander would be necessary, he believed, because "Genl Early is no disciplinarian." Yet he called Early "one of the best military men of the present time. Take Genl Lee out and I don't think he has his equal." Many others offered far more negative comments. A soldier in the 5th Virginia assumed a common tone in contrasting how the troops responded to Stonewall Jackson and Early: "Oh what a difference between Jackson's Army & the *fire* he put into us & the *will* to fight & how it all *dried up* under Early!" Not surprisingly, cavalrymen produced some of the harshest invective. John M. Opie, whose reminiscence is quite good-natured in many ways, retained a fierce dislike of Early despite the passage of many years. "[A]s a commander, he was utterly inefficient and incapable," sputtered Opie. "His whole career, as an independent fighter, was a failure and a farce. . . . When Sheridan got through with him, he was seen sitting on top of the Blue Ridge Mountains. . . . I suppose he was looking at this beautiful and fruitful valley—the granary of Virginia—which was lost to the Confederacy by his own imbecility."[41]

Early's lack of judgment when it came to building morale surfaced in spectacular fashion in a statement addressed to "Soldiers of the Army of the Valley" on October 22. This remarkable document excoriated the men, directly questioning their courage and attributing to them all blame for the debacle at Cedar Creek. "Had you remained steadfast to your duty and your colours," read a typical passage, "the victory would have been one of the most brilliant and decisive of the war. . . . But many of you, including some commissioned officers, yielded to a disgraceful propensity for plunder, & deserted your colours to appropriate to yourselves the abandoned property of the enemy. . . . Had any respectable number of you listened to the appeals made to you and made a stand even at the last moment, the disaster would have been averted and the substantial fruits of victory secured." The text quickly became known far beyond the army, provoking widespread, and mostly censorious, reaction. The tone of Early's language, which would have been more appropriate during his career as a commonwealth's attorney in Rocky Mount, Virginia, caused offense even if much of what he said had merit. One Georgia soldier expressed a combination of insulted pride and anger that surely would have resonated among many of his comrades. "I suppose that Gen. Early's address to his army will be published in most of the papers, and I am not satisfied for the impression it is likely to create, to remain uncorrected," wrote John Y. Bedingfield. Early had "made a sweeping accusation of cowardice, and bad conduct, and thus endeavors to shift the responsibility, which rightly rests upon him alone." [42]

Jubal Early and Philip Sheridan labored under vastly different circumstances in the Shenandoah Valley. Early fought from a position of relative weakness, coaxing the maximum from his small army. In the last three months of this campaign, during which he opposed the able and confident Sheridan, he managed to meet most of Lee's strategic expectations despite making a number of tactical mistakes. At Cedar Creek, he formulated and almost carried to fruition a plan of battle as complex as any other in the war. His actions in the Valley marked him as an energetic, resourceful officer entitled to a position just below Stonewall Jackson and James Longstreet on the roster of Confederate corps commanders. In terms of ability in semi-independent operations, only Jackson excelled him among Lee's lieutenants. Yet he suffered ignominious defeat in the end, sent home from the army to watch the final scenes of the conflict in disgrace. "I think Gen. Early did everything a commander could do in the valley with the number of men he had in his command," wrote John H. Worsham in tribute to his old chief, "and as an humble member of that army, I would like to ask those who have criticized Gen. Early if they ever thought of the great disparity in numbers in the two armies?"[43] Whether yes or no, the answer to that question almost always counted for less than the ultimate result for those evaluating Early in the Valley.

Sheridan proved himself a dependable army commander who implemented most of Grant's strategic design and thereby significantly furthered the Union cause. He relied on his preponderant strength, and especially his marvelous cavalry, to overcome tactical mistakes as well as to deliver powerful blows. Although he lacked Early's intellectual capacity and never devised a tactical plan equal to his opponent's at Cedar Creek, he nonetheless used personal charisma to motivate his soldiers in ways Early could not duplicate. Men in the ranks generally gave Little Phil full credit for their triumphs, often overlooking entirely or slighting the work of his subordinates. A coveted major general's commission in the regular army gave tangible expression to the gratitude of his military and civilian superiors. More than that, Sheridan's success in the Valley propelled him to a position in the Union pantheon behind only Grant and Sherman. For the rest of his life, he enjoyed substantial fame as a member of the triumvirate credited with orchestrating final United States victory, and he would follow Grant and Sherman as just the third officer to wear four stars as general in chief of the United States Army.

One question about the two generals cannot be answered. Early proved he could accomplish a great deal with minimal resources in the 1864 Valley campaign. Sheridan proved he could do the same with ample resources. If given Sheridan's advantages, it seems likely that Early would have achieved even more. Whether Little Phil could have done as well in Early's place is more uncertain.

Acknowledgments

I wish like to thank William W. Bergen, Keith S. Bohannon, R. E. L. Krick, Robert K. Krick, William J. Miller, and Joan Waugh for sharing some of their research materials pertinent to this essay's topic.

Notes

1. Abraham Lincoln, *The Collected Works of Abraham Lincoln*, ed. Roy P. Basler, 9 vols. (New Brunswick, N.J.: Rutgers University Press, 1953), 8:58, 73–74; Sherman to Ellen Ewing Sherman, October 27, 1864, in William T. Sherman, *Sherman's Civil War: Selected Civil War Correspondence of William T. Sherman, 1860–1865*, ed. Brooks D. Simpson and Jean V. Berlin (Chapel Hill: University of North Carolina Press, 1999), 743; "Phax" in the *Mobile Advertiser*, September 15, 1864; Sarah Strickler Fife diary, entry for March 7, 1865, Special Collections, Alderman Library, University of Virginia, Charlottesville [repository hereafter cited as UVA]. Fife recorded her thoughts after Early's defeat at the battle of Waynesboro, which marked the very end of operations in the Valley.

2. Frederick C. Newhall, *With Sheridan in the Final Campaign against Lee*, ed. Eric J. Wittenberg (Baton Rouge: Louisiana State University Press, 2002), 3.

3. Peter Cozzens, *The Shipwreck of Their Hopes: The Battles for Chattanooga* (Urbana: University of Illinois Press, 1994), 392.

4. Gordon C. Rhea, *The Battles for Spotsylvania Court House and the Road to Yellow Tavern, May 7–12, 1864* (Baton Rouge: Louisiana State University Press, 1997), 120–21. See also pp. 9–10, 36–37, 40–42, 67–69 for Rhea's overall analysis of Sheridan's actions at Spotsylvania. On Sheridan in the Wilderness, see Rhea, *The Battle of the Wilderness, May 5–6, 1864* (Baton Rouge: Louisiana State University Press, 1994), 433–34, which concluded that Sheridan "failed miserably . . . permitting Lee's entire army to approach undetected."

5. See Joseph T. Glatthaar's essay in this volume for a full discussion of the process that led to Sheridan's selection.

6. Theodore Lyman, *Meade's Headquarters, 1863–1865: Letters of Colonel Theodore Lyman from the Wilderness to Appomattox* (Boston: Atlantic Monthly, 1922), 210; Phillip H. Sheridan, *Personal Memoirs of P. H. Sheridan*, 2 vols. (1888; reprint, Wilmington, N.C.: Broadfoot, 1992), 1:460–61. On Sheridan's youth, see also Wesley Merritt, "Sheridan in the Shenandoah Valley," in Robert Underwood Johnson and Clarence Clough Buel, eds., *Battles and Leaders of the Civil War*, 4 vols. (New York: Century, 1887–88), 4:501.

7. David Gregg McIntosh Manuscript, 80–82, Southern Historical Collection, University of North Carolina, Chapel Hill [repository hereafter cited as SHC]; C. C. Blacknall diary, August 7, 1861, North Carolina Department of Archives, Raleigh [repository hereafter cited as NCDA]; "Phax" in the *Mobile Advertiser*, September 15, 1864.

8. U.S. War Department, *The War of the Rebellion: A Compilation of the Official Records of the Union and Confederate Armies*, 127 vols., index, and atlas (Washington: Government Printing Office, 1880–1901), ser. 1, 25(1):803 (hereafter cited as *OR*, with all references to ser. 1); FitzGerald Ross, *Cities and Camps of the Confederate States*, ed. Richard B. Harwell (Urbana: University of Illinois Press, 1958), 50; Robert Stiles, *Four Years Under Marse Robert* (1903; reprint, Dayton, Ohio: Morningside, 1977), 188–89.

9. Jedediah Hotchkiss to his wife, July 15, 1864, frame 786, microfilm roll 4, Jedediah Hotchkiss Papers, Manuscripts Division, Library of Congress [repository hereafter cited as LC]; *Times*, July 25, 1864, as quoted in Frank E. Vandiver, *Jubal's Raid: General Early's Famous Attack on Washington in 1864* (New York: McGraw-Hill, 1960), 174; *Charlottesville Daily Chronicle*, July 29, 1864.

10. Jeffry D. Wert, *From Winchester to Cedar Creek: The Shenandoah Campaign of 1864* (Carlisle, Pa.: South Mountain Press, 1987), 26. The official Federal field returns for August 1864 place Sheridan's overall "present for duty" strength in the Middle Military Division at 3,883 officers and 90,143 men: General Headquarters, 144; Department of Washington, 28,790; Department of the Susquehanna, 2,668; Middle Department, 5,870; Department of West Virginia, 21,868; Sixth Corps, 12,615; Nineteenth Corps, 13,176; cavalry, 8,895 (*OR*, 43[1]:974). The field return for September 10, 1864, places the strength of the Sixth, Eighth, and Nineteenth corps and the cavalry at 40,672, with another 4,815 at Harper's Ferry (*OR*, 43[1]:61).

11. Theodore C. Mahr, *The Battle of Cedar Creek: Showdown in the Shenandoah, October 1–30, 1864* (Lynchburg, Va.: H. E. Howard, 1992), 367–72.

12. Jubal A. Early, *A Memoir of the Last Year of the War for Independence, in the Confederate States of America* (Toronto: Lovell & Gibson, 1866), 88, 119–20. In his figures for Cedar Creek, Early counted "about 8,500 muskets," artillery "about the same strength as at Winchester" (just more than 1,000), and "about 1,200 cavalry." The rest of the cavalry, "which numbered less than 1,700, did not get up" (p. 120). For a partial estimate of Confederate strength in the Valley district on August 31, 1864, see *OR*, 43(1):1011, which records 8,963 men in the divisions of Robert E. Rodes, John B. Gordon, and Stephen Dodson Ramseur and their supporting artillery units.

13. Sheridan, *Personal Memoirs*, 1:470–71, 474–75.

14. Ulysses S. Grant, *Personal Memoirs of U. S. Grant* (1885; reprint of 2-vol. original in one vol., Lincoln: University of Nebraska Press, 1996), 531, 541; Jubal A. Early to Horatio G. Wright, December 3, 1890, Jubal A. Early Papers, LC. On literary jousting between Grant and Early prior to publication of Grant's *Personal Memoirs*, see William A. Blair, "Grant's Second Civil War: The Battle for Historical Memory," in Gary W. Gallagher, ed., *The Spotsylvania Campaign* (Chapel Hill: University of North Carolina Press, 1998), 223–54.

15. Bryan Grimes to his wife, August 21, 1864, Bryan Grimes Papers, SHC; *Richmond Dispatch*, August 22, 1864; *Charlottesville Daily Chronicle*, September 22, 1864; Jedediah Hotchkiss to his wife, August 11, 1864, frame 794, microfilm reel 4, Hotchkiss Papers.

16. Gideon Welles, *Diary of Gideon Wells, Secretary of the Navy under Lincoln and Johnson*, ed. Howard K. Beale, 3 vols. (New York: W. W. Norton, 1960), 2:72–73, 77, 89; Daniel M. Holt, *A Surgeon's Civil War: The Letters and Diary of Daniel M. Holt, M.D.*, ed. James M. Greiner, Janet L. Coryell, and James R. Smither (Kent, Ohio: Kent State University Press, 1994), 241–42; Charles S. Wainwright, *A Diary of Battle: The Personal Journals of Colonel Charles S. Wainwright, 1861–1865*, ed. Allan Nevins (New York: Harcourt, Brace, 1962), 473–74.

17. Douglas Southall Freeman, *Lee's Lieutenants: A Study in Command*, 3 vols. (New

York: Scribner's, 1942–44), 3:611; Robert E. Lee, *The Wartime Papers of R. E. Lee*, ed. Clifford Dowdey and Louis H. Manarin (Boston: Little, Brown, 1961), 833–34; *OR*, 43(2):891–92.

18. Stephen Z. Starr, *The Union Cavalry in the Civil War*, 3 vols. (Baton Rouge: Louisiana State University Press, 1979–85), 2:256; Robert K. Krick, "'The Cause of All My Disasters': Jubal A. Early and the Undisciplined Valley Cavalry," in *The Smoothbore Volley That Doomed the Confederacy: The Death of Stonewall Jackson and Other Chapters on the Army of Northern Virginia* (Baton Rouge: Louisiana State University Press, 2002), 213.

19. Stephen Dodson Ramseur to David Schenck, October 10, 1864, folder 17, Stephen Dodson Ramseur Papers, SHC; Jedediah Hotchkiss to "My Dear Sara," September 21, 1864, frames 791–92, microfilm reel 4, Hotchkiss Papers; Charles Figgatt to his wife, September 20, 1864, item 61, *Catalogue 61 — Christmas 1991* (Gettysburg, Pa.: Sword and Saber, 1991), 30; Jubal A. Early to R. E. Lee, September 25, 1864, in *OR*, 43(1):558.

20. "Franconi" of 65th New York Infantry to *New York Sunday Mercury*, October 28, 1864, in William B. Styple, ed., *Writing and Fighting the Civil War: Soldier Correspondence to the New York Sunday Mercury* (Kearny, N.J.: Belle Grove, 2000), 304; James H. Kidd to "Dear Father," October 21, 1864, in James H. Kidd, *One of Custer's Wolverines: The Civil War Letters of Brevet Brigadier General James H. Kidd, 6th Michigan Cavalry*, ed. Eric J. Wittenberg (Kent, Ohio: Kent State University Press, 2000), 115–16.

21. Ulysses S. Grant, *The Papers of Ulysses S. Grant*, ed. John Y. Simon, 28 vols. to date (Carbondale: Southern Illinois University Press, 1967–), 11:403; Sheridan, *Personal Memoirs*, 1:475. The Army of the Shenandoah's order of battle in mid-September is in Sheridan, *Personal Memoirs*, 2:11–21.

22. Lincoln, *Collected Works*, 8:316. Lincoln had thought Sheridan meant to leave just 2,000 soldiers to protect the Potomac line when in fact he allocated 12,000–14,000 along the B&O and thousands more at Harpers Ferry and elsewhere in the lower Valley (ibid., 317). For Early's movements after Cedar Creek, see Early, *Memoir of the Last Year*, 121–24.

23. Frederick C. Newhall, *With Sheridan in the Final Campaign against Lee*, ed. Eric J. Wittenberg (Baton Rouge: Louisiana State University Press, 2002), 9; *OR*, 43(1):30–31.

24. Grant, *Papers*, 12:313, 312, 327; Sheridan, *Personal Memoirs*, 2:66.

25. Hotchkiss to "My Dear Wife," August 28, Hotchkiss to "My Dear Sara," August 10, 1864, frames 789, 787, microfilm roll 4, Hotchkiss Papers; article from the *Petersburg Express*, reprinted in the *Countryman* (Turnwold, Georgia), August 23, 1864.

26. *OR*, 43(1):61; Festus P. Summers, *The Baltimore and Ohio in the Civil War* (1939; reprint, Gettysburg, Pa.: Stan Clark Military Books, 1993), 123–24.

27. *OR*, 43(1):59–60, 144. Losses prior to Sheridan's arrival included, but were not limited to, the following: Lynchburg (June 16–18), 950 U.S. and 500 C.S.; Monocacy (July 9), 2,000 U.S. and 700 C.S.; Cool Spring (July 18), 425 U.S. and 400 C.S.; Stephenson's Depot (July 20), 200 U.S. and 250 C.S.; Second Kernstown (July 24),

1,200 U.S. and 500 C.S. Some of these figures are approximate, and all the smaller engagements are omitted.

28. [Alexander M. Garber Jr.], . . . *A Sketch of the Life and Services of Maj. John A. Harman* (Staunton, Va.: "Spectator Job Print," 1876), 32; J. B. R. [Lt. J. B. Reese] to Mr. Countryman, August 5, 1864, printed in the *Countryman*, August 23, 1864; *OR*, 43(2):894; Sarah L. McComb to Jefferson Davis, October 24, 1864, in Jefferson Davis, *The Papers of Jefferson Davis*, ed. Lynda L. Crist and others, 11 vols. to date (Baton Rouge: Louisiana State University Press, 1971–), 11:117; Robert Saussy to Joachin R. Saussy, October 23, 1864, Joachin R. Saussy Jr. Papers, Perkins Library, Duke University, Durham, North Carolina.

29. Oscar Hinrichs diary, October 23, 1864, copy in possession of Robert K. Krick; T. L. McComb to Jefferson Davis, October 24, 1864, C.S.A. Secretary of War, Letters Received, item #544, roll 136, National Archives, Washington; Catherine Ann Devereux Edmondston, *"Journal of a Secesh Lady": The Diary of Catherine Ann Devereux Edmondston, 1860–1866*, ed. Beth Gilbert Crabtree and James W. Patton (Raleigh: North Carolina Division of Archives and History, 1979), 627–28 (entry for October 29, 1864).

30. Lee to Early, March 30, 1865, George H. and Katherine M. Davis Collection, Manuscripts Section, Howard-Tilton Memorial Library, Tulane University, New Orleans, Louisiana. Early printed this letter, with some small errors of transcription, as appendix A in *Memoir of the Last Year*.

31. Early, *Memoir of the Last Year*, 85.

32. John Y. Bedingfield to "Dear Ma," September 26, 1864, Bedingfield Family Civil War Letters, acc. #13119, UVA.

33. Jedediah Hotchkiss, *Make Me a Map of the Valley: The Civil War Journal of Stonewall Jackson's Cartographer*, ed. Archie P. McDonald (Dallas, Tex.: Southern Methodist University Press, 1973), 241; Hotchkiss to "My Dear Wife," October 21, 1864, frame 794, microfilm reel 4, Hotchkiss Papers; Oscar Hinrichs diary, October 19, 1864, copy in possession of Robert K. Krick. For a full discussion of the "fatal halt," see Keith S. Bohannon's essay in this volume, which assigns more blame to Early than does my treatment.

34. George Crook, *General George Crook: His Autobiography*, ed. Martin F. Schmitt (Norman: University of Oklahoma Press, 1960), 126–27; Henry A. Du Pont, *The Campaign of 1864 in the Valley of Virginia and the Expedition to Lynchburg* (New York: National Americana Society, 1925), 125. For Sheridan's taking credit for Duval's attack, see *OR*, 43(1):47 and Sheridan, *Personal Memoirs*, 2:24. In his official report, dated February 3, 1866, Sheridan stated that Crook "was directed to act as a turning column, to find the left of the enemy's line, strike it in flank or rear, break it up, and that I would order a left half-wheel of the line of battle to support him."

35. Crook, *General George Crook*, 129; *OR*, 43(1):48; Du Pont, *Campaign of 1864*, 134–35.

36. For a detailed discussion of Sheridan's Ride in art, see Harold Holzer and Mark E. Neely Jr., *Mine Eyes Have Seen the Glory: The Civil War in Art* (New York: Orion, 1993), 152–65; Crook, *General George Crook*, 134. Crook went back to Cedar Creek

and Fisher's Hill on December 26, 1889. His diary for that day betrayed his lingering bitterness. "After examining the grounds and the position of the troops after twenty five years which have elapsed and in light of subsequent events, it renders Gen. Sheridan's claims and his subsequent actions in allowing the general public to remain under the impressions regarding his part in these battles, when he knew they were fiction, all the more contemptible. The adulations heaped on him by a grateful nation for his supposed genius turned his head, which, added to his natural disposition, caused him to bloat his little carcass with debauchery and dissipation, which carried him off prematurely" (Crook, *General George Crook*, 134).

37. George B. Sanford, *Fighting Rebels and Redskins: Experiences in Army Life of Colonel George B. Sanford, 1861–1892*, ed. E. R. Hagemann (Norman: University of Oklahoma Press, 1969), 269; A. Wilson Greene, "Union Generalship in the 1864 Valley Campaign," in Gary W. Gallagher, ed., *Struggle for the Shenandoah: Essays on the 1864 Valley Campaign* (Kent, Ohio: Kent State University Press, 1991), 72.

38. Alexander Neil, *Alexander Neil and the Last Shenandoah Valley Campaign: Letters of an Army Surgeon to His Family, 1864*, ed. Richard R. Duncan (Shippensburg, Pa.: White Mane, 1996), 74; Abial Edwards to "My Dear Sister," October 21, 1864, in Beverly Hayes Kallgren and James L. Crowthamel, eds., *"Dear Friend Anna": The Civil War Letters of a Common Soldier from Maine* (Orono: University of Maine Press, 1992), 106–7; "Excelsior" to editor of *New York Sunday Mercury*, October 31, 1864, in Styple, *Writing and Fighting the Civil War*, 304–5.

39. Sanford, *Fighting Rebels and Redskins*, 291.

40. Simon Baruch, *Reminiscences of a Confederate Surgeon* (New York: n.p., 1915), unnumbered pp. 1–2; Early, *Memoir of the Last Year*, 116–17.

41. Samuel P. Collier to his parents, October 22, 1864, #416, Samuel P. Collier Papers, NCDA; quotation from George McClellan Mooney (5th Virginia) courtesy of Robert K. Krick; John M. Opie, *A Rebel Cavalryman with Lee, Stuart and Jackson* (1899; reprint, Dayton, Ohio: Morningside, 1972), 252–53.

42. Copy of Early's address to his soldiers, frame 47, microfilm 36, Hotchkiss Papers; John Y. Bedingfield to "Dear Ma," October 30, 1864, Bedingfield Family Civil War Letters.

43. John H. Worsham, *One of Jackson's Foot Cavalry: His Experience and What He Saw during the War 1861–1865* (1912; reprint, Alexandria, Va.: Time-Life, 1982), 279.

JOSEPH T. GLATTHAAR

U. S. Grant and the Union High Command during the 1864 Valley Campaign

A mid the literally hundreds and hundreds of important decisions that an army commander makes, there are often a handful that prove decisive in the outcome of a war. Sometimes they are orders that commanders must dispense in an instant, without much reflection, almost instinctively; at other times, army leaders agonize over these situations, drawing on all their intelligence, training, and character to help them see the way. Frequently, it is not just the decisions themselves, but how they meld with other events that dictates their critical success or failure. Nor do commanders always know the magnitude of their problems and the full consequences of their decisions. Snap judgments on seemingly minor matters can sometimes blossom into major events with dramatic repercussions. It is only in the fullness of time that we, the armchair quarterbacks of the past, gain that glimpse of clarity.

In the Civil War career of Ulysses S. Grant, historians have posited numerous critical moments that shaped the outcome of both his career and the war. His decision to counterattack at Fort Donelson after a rebel assault had broken his line won him the first great Union victory of the war. After the disastrous losses at Shiloh, Maj. Gen. Henry W. Halleck superseded him in command, relegating Grant to a position stripped of responsibility. For a month, he stewed, until finally he resolved to seek his own removal. William T. Sherman urged Grant to stay, explaining that his friend could never restore his reputation and contribute to the war effort from the sidelines. Grant remained. When President Abraham Lincoln called Halleck to Washington in July 1862, Grant resumed command. Nine months afterward, having failed at sundry attempts to get at the Confederates at Vicksburg, Grant's plan to march down the western bank and shuttle across the Mississippi River would rank as one of the most decisive in his military life. From there, he could maneuver, fight his opponent on ground of his choosing, and ultimately crack the Confederate grip on Vicksburg.[1]

Another of those pivotal events for Grant was his handling of Jubal Early's raid on Washington and into Maryland and Pennsylvania in the summer of 1864. Unlike most of those other defining moments and decisions, Grant had assumed the position of lieutenant general, with responsibility for overall command of the entire Union Army. Early's raid exploited the weakness of an odd command structure that Grant himself had devised. The crisis, moreover, extended beyond Grant's ability to formulate fresh plans or dig deep within himself to find the resolve to see matters through to their conclusion, as it had in other pivotal moments.

Early's raid was one of the most critical events in Grant's tenure as commanding general. It took place at a time when his hard-earned reputation had begun to tarnish, and just months before the presidential election of 1864. The threat compelled Grant to stretch beyond his military talents and judgment of personnel to test both his political savvy and the strength of his relationship with Lincoln.

After Grant's selection as lieutenant general in March 1864, he considered for a time remaining out west. Having served, fought, and won there, Grant understood war in the Western Theater, with its vast distances, river operations, and emphasis on marching as well as fighting. A western man himself, Grant felt a bond with the soldiers he commanded there. They had evolved together, and, justifiably, he felt great confidence in them, as they did in him.

But after coming east to meet with the president, his cabinet, and other politicians, it became clear that the government and the public had their own set of expectations of the new commanding general. They demanded that Grant confront Lee's army directly — he had previously proposed a massive raid from southern Virginia, slashing deep into North Carolina and wrecking all the railways leading to Virginia, making the state untenable for Lee's force — and insisted that he maintain his headquarters in the East.[2]

Grant designed an unusual solution. To avoid the continual barrage of visitors and to oversee the operations of the Union forces against Lee's troops, he elected to travel alongside the Army of the Potomac. There, he could observe and, if necessary, supervise the army and its generals directly, while leaving Maj. Gen. George G. Meade in command. At the same time, he could remain relatively close to the political epicenter, Washington, D.C.

To handle everyday military affairs, Grant would retain former commanding general Halleck under a new title, chief of staff. Halleck would serve as

Lt. Gen. Ulysses S. Grant in the autumn of 1864. Francis Trevelyan Miller, ed., *The Photographic History of the Civil War*, 10 vols. (New York: Review of Reviews, 1911), 10:39.

Grant's link to various field commanders. Usually, he would summarize their messages and relay them to Grant for decisions and instructions. Occasionally, he issued orders or offered military advice on his own.

Grant's novel command structure offered several advantages. It freed him from personnel burdens and huge amounts of paperwork, allowing him to concentrate on fighting the war. The new system, moreover, exploited the talents of several key subordinates. Halleck, a man beaten down by the military and political pressures of the commanding general's job, no longer had to shoulder the responsibility for important decisions and could perform the staff work at which he excelled. Because Meade was a strong administrator and knew the key personnel in the Army of the Potomac, Grant retained him as well. Once again, this decision enabled Grant to focus on the strategic and operational levels of war, and it stifled much of the hostility that a westerner coming in to take over the primary eastern army could engender.[3]

But this new command structure was not without serious flaws. Despite all Grant's efforts to act with tact and discretion, his mere presence undercut Meade's authority. It quickly proved awkward for both men and first embarrassing, then insulting, to Meade. More important, by positioning Grant with the army in the field and away from the seat of government, the structure created a power vacuum. The Prussian military theorist Carl von Clausewitz emphasized that the military establishment is part of the political sphere and that war is policy by other means. Without Grant's presence in Washington, without daily interaction between the commanding general and the political leadership, a problem of communication inevitably developed. And it was precisely this failure that Early's raid exploited.[4]

Over the initial five weeks of the spring 1864 campaign in the East, Grant had sustained almost 60,000 casualties in some of the heaviest fighting in the war. Although Lee parried each successive blow, Grant inched his way around Lee's right flank. Then, in a deft maneuver, Grant swung his army across the James River and struck at Petersburg from the south. Weak Federal assaults failed to carry the lightly manned Confederate works, and Grant and Lee settled into a siege.

While Grant would continue to seek opportunities to break through the rebel line or outflank it, he decided on a plan to war against Lee's logistics, severing the railroads that hauled essential food and materiel to Richmond and the enemy army. During that time, Maj. Gen. David Hunter had taken over command of Union troops in the Shenandoah Valley from Maj. Gen. Franz Sigel and had advanced south toward Lynchburg, a major Confederate rail nexus. In an effort to protect this vital railroad connection, Lee detached Early's Second Corps to drive back Hunter's columns. Combining with rebel soldiers in the Valley under Maj. Gen. John C. Breckinridge, Early routed Hunter's command, compelling it to flee all the way to West Virginia for sanctuary. With the door now wide open, Early's force of 10,000 infantry, 4,000 cavalry, and a sprinkling of artillerists stormed down the Valley to threaten Washington and Maryland.

The raid northward was a stroke of brilliance on the part of Lee and Early. In an effort to replace his massive losses, Grant had denuded Washington of effective defenders, leaving behind disabled veterans, organized into the Veterans' Reserve Corps, and a smattering of quartermaster troops to shield the nation's capital. As long as the Army of the Potomac remained between Washington and Lee's army, Grant effectively protected Washington. But once Grant swung his forces below Petersburg, he exposed the Union capital.

Early's advance shifted the Union focus away from Petersburg, the site of Grant's major effort, and toward protection of Washington and the defense of Maryland and Pennsylvania. If the Confederate general could capture Washington, even temporarily, it would be a monumental boost for the rebel war effort. Even if Early's men did not occupy Washington, though, a successful Confederate campaign might compel Grant to withdraw northward, and it would certainly ease pressure on Lee's entrenched soldiers when Grant detached substantial forces to protect the seat of government. Meanwhile, Early's men could gather foodstuffs and animals to replenish dwindling supplies.

And while Early's raid could have proven militarily disastrous for Grant and the Lincoln administration, it was undoubtedly a public relations nightmare. In a presidential election year, with all the fanfare of the final push to win the war, to have a Confederate force threaten or actually seize Washington and invade Maryland and Pennsylvania spelled disaster for the Federals. In 1862, Stonewall Jackson had threatened Washington, and Lee had invaded Maryland. The following year, Lee had once again returned to Maryland and penetrated to the outskirts of Harrisburg, Pennsylvania. If it happened again in mid-1864, how could anyone justly argue that the war was anywhere close to over?[5]

The raid also occurred at a crucial time for Grant and the Lincoln administration. The stunning Union losses in the campaign thus far — after the initial fights at Petersburg, they had climbed to 70,000 for Union troops fighting under Grant's direct supervision — shook the northern public, and the glacial progress toward the defeat of Lee's army convinced many northerners that the price for victory might be too high. This decline of public confidence in ultimate Union success was reflected in the rising price of gold as compared to Federal paper notes, which achieved its peak for the entire war during Early's raid. As northerners lost faith in the war effort, their confidence in Union paper notes plummeted.[6]

Meanwhile, many in both Congress and the Republican Party expressed a lack of confidence in Lincoln himself. Congress had recently passed its own version of Reconstruction, called the Wade-Davis Bill, which Lincoln pocket vetoed. In retaliation, Wade and Davis issued their famous manifesto, which excoriated the president as a tyrant. The Wade-Davis Manifesto went too far, and many Republicans pronounced it offensive, but such divisions within the party during a presidential election year could spell political disaster that fall.

They fed into a simmering opposition to Lincoln's candidacy, led by former secretary of the treasury Salmon P. Chase and Maj. Gen. John C. Frémont.[7]

Early's approach sparked quite a furor in Washington. Attorney General Edward Bates commented that "some of our townspeople are in ludicrous terror, lest Washington itself should be taken." With no active-duty units left, disabled troops in the Veterans' Reserve Corps manned the critical defenses. Soldiers in the Quartermaster Department rallied to aid their ailing comrades, and locals grabbed weapons and offered their services temporarily. War Department employees continued to work at their stations, but with weapons alongside their desks. A navy admiral even took it upon himself to prepare a fast steamer in case Lincoln had to abandon the city.[8]

Officials in Washington functioned as if they were in a fog. They had no good intelligence on the size of Early's columns and little understanding of what to do. Secretary of War Edwin M. Stanton exhibited "none of the alarm and fright I have seen in him on former occasions," thought Secretary of the Navy Gideon Welles. Stanton simply had no clue how to react. The various bureau chiefs were "alarmed and ignorant," noted Welles, and Chief of Staff Halleck, the man whom Grant supplanted as commanding general, "is a perfect maze, bewildered, without intelligent decision or self-reliance." At first, Halleck viewed Early's operation as a raid, with little promise of genuine success, so long as Federals held Washington, Baltimore, Harpers Ferry, and Cumberland. But the closer Early came to the nation's capital, the more unsure Halleck grew.[9]

Maj. Gen. Ethan Allen Hitchcock, who had been brought out of retirement in 1862 to advise the administration and help coordinate military activities before Halleck took over, also felt increasingly "apprehensive" of a movement on Washington once Grant shifted below Petersburg. On July 4, he visited Halleck, whom he found "quiet and passive." Halleck explained that he had protested Grant's removal of troops and artillery from Washington, warning him "if the enemy did not make a movement this way it would show an ignorance of the art of war, of which they could not be accused." Grant then rescinded his most recent order for more men. Yet Hitchcock emerged from the meeting convinced that "Grant knew nothing of the real state of things here, and that the authorities here had been content to send him advice but no orders, leaving him to judge, from a local and distant stand point, of what was required here."[10]

From Halleck's office, Hitchcock went to visit Stanton. He, too, projected a calm image, even though Hitchcock could tell he was distressed by Early's advance and the condition of the capital defenses. Yet Stanton refused to act. Stanton expressed a sense of resignation over the situation, claiming Grant had been "informed of everything." This kind of passivity only annoyed Hitchcock more, "as if the authorities here had nothing to do but report the capture of the capital when that fact should occur."[11]

Lincoln, meanwhile, kept his own counsel during those early days of the Confederate raid. When Hitchcock visited the president on July 4 after he obtained little satisfaction from Halleck and Stanton, he found Lincoln "exceedingly depressed; more so than I had ever seen him before." Hitchcock expressed his fears that "the Capital was in great danger." To this, Lincoln replied vaguely, "We are doing all we can." Dissatisfied with the response, Hitchcock sensed that Lincoln had yielded too much control to Grant. Critics had stung the president with accusations of interfering far too much with military affairs, especially in the case of McClellan, and now he was distancing himself too much from his duties as commander in chief. Hitchcock believed that Grant's proper place was in Washington, not with a local army. Had the commanding general been at his proper post, he could handle the threat on the nation's capital properly, but from the Petersburg area, he simply did not grasp the full extent of the peril. To jolt Lincoln, Hitchcock asserted that if Stonewall Jackson commanded the rebels, they "would be in Washington in three days." The old general told Lincoln that he understood the president's reticence to interfere with Grant's decision making, but the consequences of failure were too great. The campaign against Richmond paled in comparison to the importance of protecting Washington. It might be humiliating to Grant, but the occupation of Washington, even briefly, would be mortifying to Grant and the entire nation. He then asked if it would not be prudent to have troops on steamers at City Point, ready to reinforce Washington by telegraphic notice in case they needed them.[12]

The president did not commit himself to any course of action that day, but he did not have to do so. As he followed the message traffic between Grant and Halleck carefully, he realized that Grant had begun to perceive Early's raid as something more serious than a show of force. But by contrast with everyone else, Grant saw opportunity, not hazard, in Early's raid. Initially, he believed Hunter's force, combined with any troops in the Washington area, ought to be enough to put Early to flight. As the level of fear in Washington rose, Grant realized he must increase the troop strength to deal with the rebel invaders. On July 5, the day after Hitchcock's meetings, Grant sent back to Washington from Petersburg the Sixth Corps commanded by Maj. Gen. Horatio Wright. A division of the Nineteenth Corps en route from Louisiana and 3,000 dismounted cavalry joined them. That force, combined with Hunter's men, should cut off Early, crush his command, and then advance up the Shenandoah Valley to the

Staunton area, destroying rails and depots and gobbling up food and livestock as it went. Grant even offered to return to Washington and take charge personally, if Lincoln wanted him to do so.[13]

As Early's raid unfolded, Lincoln, like Grant, perceived this as an opportunity, and when he read Grant's offer to come north to direct the offensive operation in person, the president jumped at it. "Now, what I think is that you should provide to retain your hold where you are, certainly, and bring the rest with you personally, and make a vigorous effort to destroy the enemy's force in this vicinity," Lincoln counseled Grant. "I think there is really a fair chance to do this if the movement is prompt." He offered this, Lincoln emphasized, as a suggestion, and not an order. Above all else, the president wanted Grant to take charge.[14]

Within a day, however, Grant changed his mind on commanding in person. By coming to Washington, Grant worried that he would feed those in the northern public and the army who saw Early's campaign as a crisis. Instead, the lieutenant general elected to remain at his City Point headquarters. "I think, on reflection, it would have a bad effect for me to leave here," he explained to the president. All three Union field commanders there, Maj. Gens. David Hunter, E. O. C. Ord, and Horatio G. Wright, impressed Grant, and the commanding general possessed "great faith that the enemy will never be able to get back with much of his force." Also weighing on Grant's decision was seniority around Petersburg. If the lieutenant general left, command would devolve on Maj. Gen. Benjamin Butler, a political bigwig before the war. In Grant's opinion, Butler was prompt, always courteous, an excellent administrator, and utterly incapable of executing a military operation. Lincoln replied that Grant's plan was "very satisfactory."[15]

Unfortunately, Union execution failed to live up to the concept. Early pummeled Yankee troops under Maj. Gen. Lew Wallace at the Monocacy and then turned his command on the Federal capital. Fortunately for the Federals, Early did not know how light Union manpower around the capital was. Acting with prudence, Early probed, but before the Confederates could launch an effective attack, reinforcements from Wright's corps rushed to the defenses north of the city. Rebels postured and threatened and burned down the home of Postmaster General Montgomery Blair. Yet the Confederate commander refused to be goaded into an assault on a fortified position. After putting the scare in Washingtonians, Early gathered up all the food and animals his troops could manage and slipped back across the Potomac River virtually unscathed. Federals simply could not cut the rebels off. Hunter had fled so far to the northwest that it took his command two weeks to reenter the area of operations. And Horatio Wright took too long organizing and marched too slowly to block Early.

Although Early deserves credit for directing a skillful campaign, the lackluster performance of the Union field commanders accentuated his elusiveness. "Evidently disgusted" with Wright's pursuit, Lincoln sarcastically grumbled that the Union commander pursued slowly "for fear he might come across the rebels & catch some of them." But in fairness to Wright, he was no more blameworthy than numerous others. Wright, a prewar engineer who graduated second in his West Point class, had no one to direct him intelligently, and his troops arrived piecemeal, sometimes without equipment. Overall, his performance in the campaign typified the behavior of corps commanders in the Army of the Potomac, who fussed too much over details and moved their columns too slowly. Certainly Wright was no more culpable than Hunter, whose defeated command fled in the wrong direction, away from Washington, and literally took itself out of the campaign for a couple of weeks. Wallace also failed to shine, but at least in the rout he and his subordinates had the good sense to flee to Baltimore, the city he was assigned to protect.[16]

The real problem lay with the Union high command, both civilian and military. Lincoln, for his part, hesitated to interfere, trusting his commanding general to handle arrangements. Secretary of War Stanton did so, too, even though his faith in Grant had begun to show signs of cracking. And Grant's management in the first two weeks of Early's raid did little to bolster the secretary's confidence.[17]

Grant, preoccupied with defeating Lee and distracted by petty personality and professional disputes among the ranking officers around Petersburg, responded slowly to Early's threat. It took him more than three weeks to realize that Early and his command had left the Petersburg defenses. Once Grant did recognize its seriousness, he detached the Sixth Corps, forwarded several thousand dismounted cavalry, and redirected part of the Nineteenth Corps to Washington.[18]

Grant's principal problems were distance and a divided command structure, and both were his own doing. His headquarters at City Point were more than a hundred miles from Washington. Communications traveled slowly, and for a brief time, they were severed. From that distance, he could neither manage the Union response nor provide detailed instructions for his subordinates to the north.[19]

Even worse, the Union lacked an overall commander on the scene. Early's raid crossed over or affected troops in four separate military districts. No one coordinated their responses effectively, and no one combined their strength into a unified whole. Grant finally ordered Wright to act as overall commander, regardless of rank, and directed him to move against Early. But by the time he got underway, it was too late.[20]

The obvious person to pull these disparate strands together was Halleck, but he refused to act. Over the past two years, "Old Brains," as some fellow officers nicknamed the bookish Halleck, had gained a terrible reputation as someone who dodged important responsibility. Gossip claimed he had a drinking problem. In the crisis, Halleck failed to step forward and take control of the situation. He overestimated Early's strength by more than double, and according to Assistant Secretary of War Charles A. Dana, Halleck "strenuously opposed sending Wright out" after Early until Grant's order arrived. In fact, Dana elaborated for the secretary, throughout the raid Halleck issued no commands without receiving orders. Various cabinet members and powerful politicians had grown to loathe Halleck for what they perceived as a character weakness, and during Early's raid, Stanton actually contemplated removing him.[21]

Part of the problem lay in Halleck's aggravation with Grant. It most likely was not about the elevation of Grant, his junior, above him. The military and political burden of serving as general in chief had exacted quite a toll on Halleck. What annoyed Halleck was that Grant had not heeded his warning. When the lieutenant general swung the Army of the Potomac below the James River, Halleck predicted "Lee would play the same game of shuttle-cock between him & Washington that he did with McClellan." Worse yet, Grant had stripped many of Washington's defenders as replacement troops for his horrendous casualties. His decision not only had invited Early's raid but also made it all the more burdensome by forcing Federal leaders to protect the nation's capital with almost no effective troops.[22]

Individuals like Postmaster General Blair, who had his home torched by Early's men, placed the blame for the destruction and threat to the nation's capital squarely on "these men to whom the Capitol has been a peculiar charge," which listeners interpreted as including Halleck. In another version, Blair allegedly charged that "the officers in charge about Washington are poltroons." Once again, the accusation would have covered the chief of staff. When Halleck complained in a note through Stanton to Lincoln about the insults and then demanded that he either dismiss Blair from the cabinet or strike those officers from the commissioned rolls, Lincoln brushed the complaint aside. He did not endorse the remarks, nor did he know if Blair even said them. But he refused to dismiss a cabinet member for critical comments made in the passion of a great

Maj. Gen. Henry W. Halleck, whose conduct during the initial stage of Early's campaign prompted Attorney General Edward Bates to express "contempt" for Halleck and anger about "the ignorant imbecility of the late military operations." Courtesy of the Library of Congress.

loss. Then, in firm language that expressed his irritation, he concluded, "I propose continuing myself to be the judge as to when a member of the Cabinet shall be dismissed."[23]

The raid and the aggravation were Grant's fault, and Halleck wanted no part of them. Thus, when Grant's aide Col. Cyrus Comstock visited Halleck to explain the lieutenant general's views on the campaign, Halleck sneered at him and spoke sarcastically about when Grant was going to take Richmond.[24]

Once Early retreated to safety, Grant had to weigh his priorities. Because the Confederate general escaped with his command intact, Grant felt pressure to keep the Sixth Corps near the nation's capital. He could not risk the fall of Washington or even its partial occupation for a second time. With the presidential election just four months away, the political repercussions of another successful invasion or the capture of Washington could be disastrous. In an optimistic moment, Grant hoped the combined commands of Wright and Hunter could advance up the Shenandoah Valley, disrupting rebel logistics as they went. In that way, they could shield Washington and aid his army near Petersburg. But at the same time, Grant kept in mind the big picture—the defeat of Lee's army. He had almost completed preparations for an attack on the Weldon Railroad, one of Lee's primary supply lines. Its capture and destruction could inflict serious damage to the Confederate war effort in Virginia. Those units he had transferred north might provide the margin for success in the operation, and he was sorely tempted to recall them.[25]

Before he could resume offensive operations with the troops he wanted, Grant knew he had to resolve two problems: maintaining adequate forces to defend Washington and creating a command structure that would exploit rather than squander the combined strength of all the troops there. First, Grant tried to bolster defenses around the Potomac so that they could repel Early's advance without the Sixth Corps, which he would recall to Petersburg. He proposed the establishment of schools of instruction for all troops raised east of Ohio at Washington, Baltimore, and Harpers Ferry. "By doing this," Grant explained to Halleck, "we always have the benifit of our increased force and they in turn improve more rapidly by contact with veteran troops." He would also send to Washington all soldiers whose enlistment would expire by August 20, which "will give quite a force around which to rally new troops."[26]

Halleck, however, balked at the plan and opposed the transfer of Wright's corps. The schools of instruction would take months to develop, and "new organizations of fragments of regiments are almost worthless," deemed Old Brains. He predicted that if Wright's corps left, the Confederates would renew their raid, but he insisted that Grant would have to judge whether he left a large enough force behind to protect Washington and Maryland. Ultimately, Halleck's argument carried the day. After leaning in one direction and then the next, Grant told Halleck to retain Wright's corps. "I would prefer a complete smashup of the enemy's roads about Gordonsville & Charlottesville to having the same force here," Grant conceded.[27]

On the surface, the second issue, the creation of an effective command structure, was not nearly so difficult. The Union forces in the region lacked a unity of command. With delays in communications, Grant could not direct operations from such a distance. He needed someone in charge on the scene, someone who could draw on all military resources in the area to deal with any raids. Grant proposed that the administration create a military division that would encompass the Departments of Washington, Western Virginia, the Middle, and the Susquehanna.

The real struggle came over the choice of commander. Wright had demonstrated little initiative, and his slowness earned him Lincoln's ire. He could serve in the department but could not head it. Grant first proposed Maj. Gen. William B. Franklin. A classmate of Grant's at West Point who had ranked first in the class of 1843, Franklin had risen to corps command. His close friendship with Maj. Gen. George B. McClellan ran him afoul of the Radical Republican-dominated Joint Committee on the Conduct of the War, and its investigation blamed him for the Union disaster at Fredericksburg. He was resurrected as a corps commander on Nathaniel P. Banks's ill-fated Red River campaign, where Franklin suffered a wound. By mid-July, he had recovered enough for duty, and he needed a new job. Unfortunately for Franklin, the Lincoln administration found him unacceptable. Simply put, Franklin had too much political and military baggage.[28]

In lieu of Franklin, Halleck suggested another classmate of Grant's, Maj. Gen. Christopher C. Augur. Augur graduated five places ahead of Grant and had seen combat in the Shenandoah Valley campaign of 1862 and the Port Hudson campaign of 1863. In October 1863, Augur took over the Department of Washington. Frequent interaction earned him Halleck's esteem. The former commanding general described Augur as "capable & efficient" and insisted, "I see no good reason for removing or superseding" him. But Augur had lost the confidence of the secretary of war. Assistant Secretary of War Dana, an ally and close friend of both Grant and his headquarters personnel since the Vicksburg campaign the previous year, warned Grant's chief of staff John A. Rawlins that Stanton considered Augur incompetent. "Indeed the Secretary has very sharply reprimanded him for want of attention to his duties," Dana relayed.[29]

Some Republicans floated George B. McClellan as a commander of a newly created Middle Division. He had no assignment, and the Republicans thought active duty might keep McClellan from accepting the Democratic party's nomination for the presidency. Neither Lincoln nor Grant took it seriously. There was no way that Lincoln would give McClellan another chance to win acclaim on the battlefield. A McClellan military success, regardless of how unlikely that was, would enhance his presidential stature, not diminish it. The entire proposal was ludicrous.[30]

The lieutenant general had reached an impasse with Stanton and Halleck, and he immediately appealed to Lincoln. On July 26, Rawlins delivered a letter and spoke on Grant's behalf, explaining the entire situation and proposing the creation of a "Military Division" with George G. Meade, commander of the Army of the Potomac, as its head. Since the opening of the spring campaign, Meade had been embarrassed by Grant's presence, as though he were incompetent to run an army without supervision. Grant understood the awkwardness of the situation and tried to make it as tolerable as possible, but military and political concerns convinced the lieutenant general that he belonged with the Army of the Potomac. As the campaign extended and Grant became more familiar with the officer corps, Meade's value had declined. Although Grant liked him and respected his talents, virtually no one else among the high-ranking officers in the Army of the Potomac did. Meade had an irascible disposition. His explosive temper convinced others that he had a "kill the messenger" mentality. Few could work with him, and Grant thought this transfer was an ideal solution. Meade was an excellent administrator and a good army commander, especially on the defensive. And Grant had a ready replacement in mind for commander of the Army of the Potomac, Maj. Gen. Winfield Scott Hancock. "With Meade in command of such a division," Grant explained in writing to the president, "I would have every confidence that all the troops within the military division would be used to the very best advantage from a personal examination of the ground, and [he] would adopt means of getting the earliest information of any advance of the enemy, and would prepare to meet it."[31]

The president was not convinced. In Lincoln's mind, Meade was not the right man for the job. Nor was the president satisfied with the way Union officials handled the first raid. By the time Rawlins met with Lincoln, both the president and the commanding general had read reports that Early had launched another raid. He wanted to meet face to face, to get the right person and execute the right plan.[32]

Because of the demands around Petersburg, Grant could not rendezvous with Lincoln until the last day of July. In the meantime, he ordered Wright to merge with Hunter and to go after Early. In response to Halleck's insistence that Lee had reinforced Early, Grant forwarded the rest of the Nineteenth Corps and six cavalry regiments.[33]

On the same day, Grant also notified officials in Washington that someone on the scene had to be in charge. Slow communications made it imperative that "some one in Washington should give orders and make dispositions of all the forces within reach of the line of the Potomac." Lincoln concurred. He directed Stanton to place Halleck in charge of all troops in the four military departments and directed him to "take all military measures necessary for defense against attack of the enemy and for his capture and destruction."[34]

Despite a unified command under Halleck, the rebel raiders wreaked more havoc. Early seized a line near the Potomac River and hurled cavalry forces well into Maryland and Pennsylvania. They gathered more military supplies and burned Chambersburg, Pennsylvania. For the second time in a few weeks, Early made his escape as, once again, Union resistance was a fiasco. Attorney General Bates sized up the mood well when he recorded in his diary, "We are disgraced."[35]

By the time Lincoln and Grant met, it was evident that Halleck could not handle the job. Grant again argued for Meade, and Lincoln opposed it once again. Later, Grant explained to Meade that the Joint Committee on the Conduct of the War, the congressional body that monitored and criticized the Union war effort and military personnel, had attacked him, and Lincoln had to intervene to save the general. If they transferred Meade from command of the Army of the Potomac, it would look like a demotion and damage Meade's reputation further. That may have been true, but Lincoln most likely still harbored resentment over Meade's unwillingness to follow up after the Union victory at Gettysburg. Meade had sensible arguments why he could not attack then, but Lincoln believed a golden opportunity had slipped away as Lee's wounded army escaped back to Virginia. Meade was not the man for the job.[36]

Instead, Grant and Lincoln settled on Maj. Gen. Philip H. Sheridan. Sheridan was one of the two best division commanders Grant had ever seen, and he helped instill a new level of aggressiveness in the cavalry of the Army of the Potomac. Lincoln and Grant had concluded that the Union needed a hard-driving commander who would fight relentlessly and seek the destruction not only of Early's troops but also of the resources of the Valley. It was a perfect job for the feisty Sheridan.[37]

"I am sending General Sheridan for temporary duty whilst the enemy is being expelled from the border," Grant notified Halleck. "Unless General Hunter is in the field personally, I want Sheridan put in command of all the troops in the field, with instructions to put himself south of the enemy and follow him to the death." Along with Sheridan, Grant transported enough cavalry from the Army of the Potomac, armed with repeating carbines, to neutralize the strength of Early's horsemen.[38]

On the surface, Grant's appointment and instructions seemed specific, but somehow the execution lacked purpose. Both Stanton and Halleck had grown irritated with Grant's failures and inability to check Early's raids. The disastrous attack on the Crater at Petersburg just a few days before merely strengthened their disappointment in Grant. Neither man would lift a finger to help implement Grant's directive. Stanton openly doubted that the tough little cavalryman possessed the ability and experience to direct such a campaign. Halleck did not object to Sheridan but opposed the division of power. Because Hunter commanded in the field, he retained control of the operation, and the aggressive Sheridan lapsed to a position as head of the cavalry force. Halleck thought little of Hunter but refused to intervene on Sheridan's behalf, petulantly informing Grant, "Had you asked my opinion in regard to Genls Hunter & Sheridan it would have been freely & frankly given." This was Grant's decision to make, not his, the chief of staff contended.[39]

For two days, Lincoln observed from the sidelines as the War Department's gears ground. Yet nothing emerged. After three and a half years in the White House, Lincoln had learned how the bureaucracy, even at the highest levels, could stifle or circumvent carefully conceived plans and directives. Now, the sage president coached his commanding general, offering to share this hard-won knowledge. To Grant, he telegraphed that the orders placing Sheridan south of Early with instructions to pursue the Confederates until his columns destroyed them "is exactly right as to how our forces should move." He then warned Grant that directives and implementation were two distinct matters. "Please look over the dispatches you may have received from here even since you made that order, and discover, if you can, that there is any idea in the head of any one here of 'putting our army south of the enemy,' or of 'following him to the death' in any direction." With words of wisdom, earned through nearly four years of political battles in Washington, Lincoln counseled, "I repeat to you it will neither be done nor attempted, unless you watch it every day and hour and force it."[40]

Had Grant been on the scene, his plans would have been executed promptly, but from one hundred miles distant, nothing happened. Two hours after receiving Lincoln's advice, Grant boarded a steamer headed north. At Monocacy, Maryland, he consulted with Hunter, who requested that Grant replace him. Sheridan finally assumed command with specific instructions.

Grant awarded his subordinate extensive powers to remove incompetent or uncooperative officers, regardless of rank. This time, the lieutenant general demanded results. "What we want is prompt and active movements after the enemy," he explained. And Sheridan fulfilled Grant's expectations. By the time he assumed command, Early and his little Army of the Valley had slipped back across the Potomac River into Virginia. Grant kept Sheridan on a short leash for five weeks, assuming that Early and his reinforced corps outnumbered the Federals. When Lee recalled a portion of the command, Grant, in person at Sheridan's headquarters, endorsed a plan of aggressive action. At Winchester, in mid-September, Sheridan delivered a powerful blow, followed up three days later by the rout of Early's depleted ranks at Fisher's Hill. His mission accomplished, Sheridan began to withdraw his army, gobbling up food and livestock and torching barns and mills as he marched. Grant had asked that the Federals strip the countryside so bare that crows flying over the Valley would have to tote haversacks. Sheridan did, to some extent.

But belief in the demise of Early's force was premature. Reinforcements from Lee enabled the Confederate general to attack once more, in mid-October, at Cedar Creek. In the morning hours, Early whipped the Federals, but by afternoon the tide turned. Sheridan, absent from the command that morning, rallied his troops, and in the late afternoon struck with fury. The Confederate line crumbled. Not only had Sheridan reversed the day's fortunes, but he also had captured much of Early's artillery and wagon train. Yet Sheridan failed to fulfill Grant's goal of destroying Charlottesville, Gordonsville, and the Virginia Central Railroad. For month after month, Sheridan concocted lame excuses. Finally, in late February 1865, he executed Grant's orders. Had he done so promptly, Sheridan might have shortened the war by a couple of months.[41]

Yet Grant's confidence in Sheridan, and Lincoln's in Grant, had paid great dividends during the closing weeks of the presidential campaign. Coupled with the fall of Atlanta to Sherman in September, the triumph over Early in the Valley secured Lincoln's reelection.

A few months later, Grant tackled what seemed like another crisis when Confederate Gen. John Bell Hood's Army of Tennessee invaded Tennessee. With Hood's forces near Nashville, Union major general George H. Thomas carefully gathered his resources but put off an attack because of terrible weather. An impatient Grant did not understand the situation clearly and believed Thomas was acting indecisively. He sent a replacement for Thomas and then concluded that he had to oversee the situation personally. Just as the lieutenant general was boarding a train for Nashville, a message arrived announcing Thomas had attacked and won a resounding victory. Critics later accused Grant of acting against Thomas hastily, yet the experience during Early's raid, fresh in his mind, doubtless guided Grant's decisions.

For Grant, Early's operations in the summer and autumn of 1864 tested his ability to formulate overall plans, to select competent personnel, and to oversee their execution. The rebel invasion occurred at a time of failure in the Eastern Theater and limited success out west. Opposition to Lincoln seemed to be gaining strength in and out of his party. By exploiting a weak command system, one designed by Grant himself, Early nearly battled his way into Washington, which would have been a political catastrophe for the administration. Throughout the crisis, opposition mounted against Grant. Halleck had voiced dissatisfaction, and while Secretary of War Stanton was more circumspect in his criticism, his conduct — especially his lack of support — indicated his displeasure with Grant as well as with numerous other subordinates. Only Lincoln continued to endorse his lieutenant general, and this faith was born out by success.

Early's raid was one of the critical moments in Grant's tenure as commanding general. He learned the importance of an effective command structure and that he had to oversee his directives to ensure that the bureaucracy, both military and civilian, executed them fully and properly. For all the applause that scholars have offered for Grant's unique command system, most prominently, in T. Harry Williams's classic, *Lincoln and His Generals*, it failed him badly in the late summer and fall of 1864. Wanting no further part of Halleck, who undercut him badly, Grant attempted to transfer him to the Pacific Coast for the remainder of the war. Halleck's collaborator Stanton balked at the change, and Grant dropped the proposal.[42]

But most important, Grant came to grips with the political realities of the job of commanding general. During the course of the war, Grant had developed a healthy respect for the political aspects of military command. Yet even he underestimated just how much the position of commanding general straddled both the military and the political worlds.[43]

Away from Washington, Grant lost out on the regular interactions with policy makers and public-opinion shapers. Had he been there, they would have exposed him to their daily interests and concerns and would have reminded him just how tightly military and political events dovetailed, especially in a presidential election year. At that stage of the war, an ultimate Confederate victory had to begin with a defeat of Lincoln or the prowar politicians at the polls, and perhaps only the occupation of the Union capital could ensure that. The 1864 military campaigns against the Confederates, especially the one against Lee, absorbed Grant so wholly that he temporarily lost sight of the army's principal mission of protecting the seat of government.

Early's Valley campaign forced Grant to draw on more than just his military skills and judgment of personnel. In order to direct an effective campaign against Early's raiders, he had to ride herd over field commanders and the military and political bureaucrats and officials who had mastered the art of resistance to policies and directives they did not like, even if the ranking general officer and the president supported them. He also had to become a quick study on the political nature of the commanding general's position. Fortunately for Grant, he had Lincoln, a consummate politician, as his commander in chief.

Notes

1. Many scholars, beginning with Bruce Catton, have emphasized Grant's continuation of the Overland campaign after the fight in the Wilderness. There, Gen. Robert E. Lee and his forces rocked the Army of the Potomac with a surprise assault. Despite suffering huge losses, Grant did not hesitate to order the army to continue its advance to the southeast. By doing so, Grant certainly sent a message to both sides that this campaign would be a long and costly struggle, one that a single battle would not decide. But Grant could not have terminated the campaign after a single battle. From his standpoint, he had no choice except to continue the campaign.

2. For Grant's plan and Halleck's letter of rejection, see Grant to Halleck, January 19, Halleck to Grant, February 17, 1864, in U.S. War Department, *The War of the Rebellion: A Compilation of the Official Records of the Union and Confederate Armies*, 127 vols., index, and atlas (Washington, D.C.: Government Printing Office, 1880–1901), ser. 1, 33:394–95, 32(2):411–13 [hereafter cited as *OR*; all future references are to volumes in ser. 1]. See also U. S. Grant, *Personal Memoirs of U. S. Grant* (1885; reprint of 2-vol. original in one vol., Lincoln: University of Nebraska Press, 1996), 404–5.

3. See Joseph T. Glatthaar, *Partners in Command: The Relationships between Leaders in the Civil War* (New York: Free Press, 1994), 206–8.

4. See Carl von Clausewitz, *On War*, ed. and trans. by Michael Howard and Peter Paret (Princeton, N.J.: Princeton University Press, 1976), for the views of Clausewitz. The practice of establishing army headquarters outside the national capital had prece-

dents. After the War of 1812, the War Department divided the U.S. Army into a Northern and a Southern Department, with Maj. Gen. Jacob Brown and Maj. Gen. Andrew Jackson in charge. Although Brown technically outranked Jackson, they functioned as coequals. When Zachary Taylor served briefly as president, commanding general Winfield Scott maintained his headquarters in New York City. Scott returned to Washington for Millard Fillmore's presidency, but he went back to New York when Franklin Pierce defeated him for the presidency in the election of 1852. Even though tensions eased after James Buchanan became president, Scott stayed in New York. He returned to Washington, though, during the secession crisis. See Russell F. Weigley, *History of the United States Army*, enlarged ed. (Bloomington: Indiana University Press, 1984), 192–93, 199.

5. See Grant to Hon. E. B. Washburne, July 23, 1864, in U. S. Grant, *Papers of Ulysses S. Grant*, ed. John Y. Simon, 28 vols. to date (Carbondale: Southern Illinois University Press, 1967–), 11:300.

6. The ratio peaked on July 11, 1864, at $2.85 worth in paper for $1.00 in gold. See William Ernest Smith, *The Francis Preston Blair Family in Politics*, 2 vols. (1933; reprint, New York: Da Capo, 1969), 2:248.

7. For examples, see Gideon Welles, *Diary of Gideon Welles, Secretary of the Navy under Lincoln and Johnson*, ed. John T. Morse, 3 vols. (Boston: Houghton Mifflin, 1911), 2:102–3 (entry for August 13, 1864), and Marsena R. Patrick, *Inside Lincoln's Army: The Diary of Marsena Rudolph Patrick, Provost Marshal General, Army of the Potomac*, ed. David S. Sparks (New York: Yoseloff, 1969), 403 (entry for July 27, 1864).

8. Edward Bates, *The Diary of Edward Bates, 1859–1866*, ed. Howard K. Beale (1933; reprint, New York: Da Capo, 1971), 384 (entry for July 10, 1864). See also Welles, *Diary*, 2:72 (entry for July 11, 1864); Benjamin P. Thomas and Harold M. Hyman, *Edwin M. Stanton: The Life and Times of Lincoln's Secretary of War* (New York: Knopf, 1962), 318–20; Dana to Grant, July 11, 1864, in Grant, *Papers*, 11:229.

9. Welles, *Diary*, 2:72, 76, 78 (entries for July 8, 11, 13, 1864). See also Welles, *Diary*, 2:70, 72–73 (entries for July 9, 11, 1864); Halleck to Grant, July 5, 1864, in Grant, *Papers*, 11:171.

10. E. A. Hitchcock to Mrs. Mann, July 14, 1864, Ethan Allen Hitchcock Papers, Library of Congress. See also Herman Hattaway and Archer Jones, *How the North Won: A Military History of the Civil War* (Urbana: University of Illinois Press, 1983), 99–102.

11. E. A. Hitchcock to Mrs. Mann, July 14, 1864, Hitchcock Papers.

12. Ibid. See also Welles, *Diary*, 2:91–92 (entry for August 2, 1864); John Hay, *Lincoln in the Civil War in the Diaries and Letters of John Hay*, ed. Tyler Dennett (New York: Dodd, Mead, 1931), 209 (entry for July 11, 1864).

13. See Grant to Halleck, July 4, 5 (12:30 P.M. and midnight), Halleck to Grant, July 5 (12:30, 4:30, and 10:30 P.M.), Grant to Halleck, July 6, 9, Meade to Grant, July 6, 9, 1864, in Grant, *Papers*, 11:169, 170–71, 178–79, 198–99, 202; Meade to Grant, July 16, 1864 (with enclosure), H. J. Hunt to Humphreys, July 16, 1864, in *OR*, 40(2):276–77. The division from the Nineteenth Corps was coming from New Orleans to reinforce Grant's forces.

14. Grant to Halleck, July 9, Lincoln to Grant, July 10, 1864, in *OR*, 37(2):134, 155.

15. Grant to Lincoln, July 10, Lincoln to Grant, July 11, 1864, in ibid.,155–56, 191.

16. Hay, *Diaries and Letters*, 210 (entry for July 14, 1864).

17. See Dana to Grant, July 12, 1864, in Grant, *Papers*, 11:229–30.

18. See William B. Feis, "A Union Military Intelligence Failure: Jubal Early's Raid, June 12–July 14, 1864," *Civil War History* 36 (September 1990):209–25.

19. See E. A. Hitchcock to Mrs. Mann, July 14, 1864, Hitchcock Papers.

20. See Grant to Halleck, July 12, Dana to Rawlins, July 24, 1864, in Grant, *Papers*, 11:221, 301–2.

21. Dana to Rawlins, July 13, Dana to Grant, July 12, 1864, in Grant, *Papers*, 11:244, 229–30. See also Thomas and Hyman, *Stanton*, 318–21; Bates, *Diary*, 385–86 (entries for July 15, 16, 1864); Hay, *Diaries and Letters*, 209 (entry for July 13, 1864).

22. Halleck to Lieber, July 7, 1864, Francis Lieber Papers, Huntington Library, San Marino, Calif. Thanks to John Marszalek for helping me locate a copy of the Halleck letter.

23. Lizzie [Blair Lee] to Phil, August 1, 1864, in Elizabeth Blair Lee, *Wartime Washington: The Civil War Letters of Elizabeth Blair Lee*, ed. Virginia Jeans Haas (Urbana: University of Illinois Press, 1991), 416; Halleck through Stanton to Lincoln, July 14, Lincoln to Stanton, July 14, 1864, in Abraham Lincoln, *The Collected Works of Abraham Lincoln*, ed. Roy P. Basler, 9 vols. (New Brunswick, N.J.: Rutgers University Press, 1953), 7:439–40.

24. See Patrick, *Inside Lincoln's Army*, 409–10 (entry for August 5, 1864); Cyrus B. Comstock, *The Diary of Cyrus B. Comstock*, ed. Merlin E. Sumner (Dayton, Ohio: Morningside, 1987), 280 (entry for July 15, 1864); Brooks D. Simpson, *Ulysses S. Grant: Triumph Over Adversity, 1822–1865* (Boston: Houghton Mifflin, 2000), 357.

25. Grant to Halleck, July 22, 23, 1864, in Grant, *Papers*, 11:295, 299.

26. Grant to Halleck, July 15, 17, 1864, in ibid., 255, 268.

27. Halleck to Grant, July 28, 22, Grant to Halleck, July 23, 24, 1864, in ibid., 355, 295, 299, 303.

28. Grant to Halleck, July 18, Halleck to Grant, July 21, 1864, in ibid., 274, 286.

29. Halleck to Grant, July 21, Dana to Rawlins, July 12, 1864, in ibid., 286, 231.

30. See Patrick, *Inside Lincoln's Army*, 410 (entry for August 5, 1864); Smith, *Blair Family*, 2:279–81.

31. Grant to Lincoln, July 25, 1864, in *OR*, 37(2):433–34. See also Dana to Stanton, July 7, 1864, in ibid., 40(1):35–36; Dana to Rawlins, July 15, Stanton to Grant, July 26, 27, Grant to Stanton, July 26, 1864, in Grant, *Papers*, 11:252, 315–16; Patrick, *Inside Lincoln's Army*, 385, 403 (entries for June 18, 23, July 27, 1864). See also Meade letters to his wife in 1864, George G. Meade Papers, Historical Society of Pennsylvania, Philadelphia.

32. See Stanton to Grant, July 26, 27, Grant to Stanton, July 26, 1864, in Grant, *Papers*, 11:315–16.

33. Grant to Halleck, July 25, 26, Halleck to Grant, July 26, 1864, in ibid., 317.

34. Stanton to Halleck, July 27, 1864, in *OR*, 40(3):501–2. See also Grant to Halleck, July 26, Stanton to Grant, July 27, 1864, in Grant, *Papers*, 11:315–17.

35. Bates, *Diary*, 392 (entry for July 31, 1864). See also ibid., 391–92 (entries for July 29, August 1, 1864).

36. See Lincoln to Meade, July 14, 1863 [unsent], in Lincoln, *Collected Works*, 6:327–28; Meade to his wife, August 3, 1864, in George Gordon Meade, ed., *The Life and Letters of General Meade, Major-General United States Army*, 2 vols. (New York: Scribner's, 1913), 2:218.

37. See Grant to Halleck, June 24, 1864, in Grant, *Papers*, 11:124; *New York Times*, August 9, 1864.

38. Grant to Halleck, August 1, 1864, in *OR*, 37(2):558.

39. Halleck to Grant, August 5, 1864, in Grant, *Papers*, 11:360. See also Grant to Halleck, August 1, 3, 4, Halleck to Grant, August 2, 3, 4, 1864, in ibid., 359–61; Patrick, *Inside Lincoln's Army*, 403–4, 409–10 (entries for July 27, August 4, 5, 1864); Welles, *Diary*, 2:94 (entry for August 5, 1864).

40. Lincoln to Grant, August 3, 1864, in *OR*, 37(2):582.

41. Grant to Sheridan, August 7, 1864, in ibid., 43(1):719.

42. Grant to Stanton, August 15, Stanton to Grant, August 18, 1864, in ibid., 50(2):945, 949.

43. See Brooks D. Simpson, *Let Us Have Peace: Ulysses S. Grant and the Politics of War and Reconstruction, 1861–1868* (Chapel Hill: University of North Carolina Press, 1991), for Grant and politics during his military service.

KEITH S. BOHANNON

"The Fatal Halt" versus "Bad Conduct"

John B. Gordon, Jubal A. Early, and the Battle of Cedar Creek

I n the late nineteenth century, former Confederate general John Brown Gordon began compiling his memoir of service in the Army of Northern Virginia. At the time he started writing, Gordon was one of the most distinguished living Confederate veterans, having held public offices at the state and national level and having been a spokesman for the New South and Lost Cause movements. Gordon's *Reminiscences of the Civil War* describes numerous Civil War campaigns and battles but pays particular attention to the October 19, 1864, battle of Cedar Creek. Gordon concluded two lengthy chapters of reminiscences dealing with Cedar Creek by explaining that it was "one of the most imperative duties devolving upon me . . . to guide the future historian to a clear apprehension of the truth in regard to the chivalrous character and conduct" of the men who served under him in the final major engagement of the 1864 Shenandoah Valley campaign.[1]

"No battle of the entire war," claimed Gordon, "with the single exception of Gettysburg, has provoked such varied and conflicting comments and such prolonged controversy" as Cedar Creek. Gordon and the Valley army's commanding officer, Lt. Gen. Jubal A. Early, formed differing versions of what happened at Cedar Creek soon after the battle and defended them for many years until their deaths. Gordon had the final word on the matter when his *Reminiscences* appeared in 1903, a decade after Early's death. Many writers and historians have uncritically accepted the version of Cedar Creek in *Reminiscences*, failing to acknowledge Gordon's desire to protect his own reputation and those of his division and the rest of the Confederate Army of the Valley, even at the expense of the truth.[2]

Prior to the spring and summer of 1864, John B. Gordon was little known outside of the Army of Northern Virginia. Within that army, his performances commanding a brigade of Georgians during the Chancellorsville and Gettysburg campaigns had earned him a reputation as one of Robert E. Lee's best brigadier generals. Gordon's subsequent participation in the Overland campaign, particularly in the Wilderness and on May 12, 1864, at Spotsylvania Court House, won him attention throughout the Confederacy. On May 13, 1864, Robert E. Lee telegraphed Jefferson Davis recommending that Gordon receive an immediate promotion to major general to replace Maj. Gen. Edward "Allegheny" Johnson, who had been captured the day before. Davis responded that he would nominate Gordon for the position the next day.[3]

When Gen. Jubal Early assumed command of the Army of Northern Virginia's Second Corps in late May 1864, Gordon took over Early's old division. Relations between Gordon and Early became increasingly strained that spring and summer due to tactical disagreements on several battlefields, including the Wilderness and Lynchburg. The friction continued into the fall of 1864, as intimated in an October 16 letter to Gordon from his wife Fanny in which she asked if he had "seen anything of Gen. Early or heard any news of his ill natured remarks."[4]

Gordon's superior leadership abilities and bravery under fire earned him the undying respect of the men in his division, one of whom wrote in late July 1864 that the general had "won the name of the Bayard of our Army." Gordon's wife, Fanny, witnessed this devotion on the Wilderness battlefield, where wounded men from her husband's command were "extravagant in their expressions of admiration and love." They claimed that the general "knew how to lead men," she wrote, and "said if they loved anybody in this world it was Genl. Gordon."[5]

The laurels that Gordon earned at battles like the Wilderness, Spotsylvania, and the Monocacy came at a terrible price for the men in his command. By the fall of 1864, Gordon's division of three brigades had been decimated by hard fighting and desertions. One of these brigades consisted of his old command, six regiments and a battalion of Georgians. His other two brigades, which had been nearly destroyed in the Mule Shoe at Spotsylvania Court House, incorporated the remnants of fourteen Virginia regiments (including the famed Stonewall Brigade) and ten Louisiana regiments. The regimental consolidations within the Virginia and Louisiana commands resulted in widespread bitterness. "Strange officers command strange troops," wrote an army inspector in August 1864, "and the difficulties of fusing this incongruous mass are enhanced by constant marching and frequent engagements." Pvt. Richard Colbert of the

Maj. Gen. John Brown Gordon. National Archives.

9th Louisiana expressed his resentment of the changes in a July 1864 letter. "I am tired of our being pulled & hauled about as we are no officers no Brigade no Re[g]t taken all the flags out of our brig but one," he wrote, "all played out and the men are playing out too."[6]

Casualties in Colbert's 9th Louisiana and the rest of Gordon's division had been especially heavy among noncommissioned and commissioned officers. During the July 1864 expedition against Washington, for example, the division lost 55 officers and 624 men killed and wounded and 21 men missing, most of them in the July 9 battle of the Monocacy. On August 20, 1864, an inspecting officer recorded that a majority of the officers in Brig. Gen. William Terry's Virginia brigade were absent, "including nearly all the original regimental and company commanders." The same inspector observed deteriorating conditions among the Georgia regiments and lax discipline in the consolidated Louisiana command, attributing problems in the latter organization to "new officers, not thoroughly acquainted with their commands." The humiliating Confederate defeats at the battles of Winchester and Fisher's Hill in late September 1864, which resulted in the loss of hundreds of additional officers and men from the division, worsened the crisis.[7]

The constant marching of Early's men in the summer and fall of 1864 made it difficult to supply the Valley army. By late September, a Louisiana captain wrote that the roughly 1,800 men in Gordon's division were "shoeless, pantless, jacketless, sockless and miserable," resembling "Falstaff's Army more than any Corps in the Confederacy." Maj. Thomas H. Bomar of the 38th Georgia noted around the same time that his regiment had between twenty and twenty-five barefoot men, many more who had only pieces of shoes, and some who were "almost naked." The inadequate issuance of quartermaster and commissary supplies to Gordon's regiments, combined with the division's lax discipline and low morale, undoubtedly affected their performance at Cedar Creek.[8]

By the third week of October 1864, Early's Valley army lay encamped at Fisher's Hill. Facing a chronic shortage of supplies and under pressure from General Lee to mount an offensive, Early decided to attack the Federal Army of the Shenandoah encamped five miles to the north along the winding banks of Cedar Creek. In order to determine where best to attack, Early ordered Gordon and several other officers to reconnoiter the Federal position. On October 17, Gordon and a small party that included Jedediah Hotchkiss, Early's chief engineer, rode and then climbed on foot to a signal station atop Signal Knob, or Three Top Mountain, on the northern end of Massanutten Mountain. There they got a spectacular view of the Union army's position.

Using field glasses, the Confederates could observe Federal breastworks, camps, artillery, wagons, and even Sheridan's headquarters at Belle Grove mansion. Amazed at how lightly the Federals had guarded the eastern end of their line, Gordon and Hotchkiss agreed that an attack against that flank could succeed if a way was found to get southern troops around the northern end of the Massanutten and across Cedar Creek without being detected. As Gordon and Hotchkiss descended the steep slopes of Signal Knob, they discussed at length the plan they would suggest to Early. The two officers undoubtedly agreed with another member of the party, Brig. Gen. Clement A. Evans, who wrote his wife the next day that "we can utterly rout them, if we attack their left flank."[9]

Hotchkiss met with Early on the night of the seventeenth, describing the reconnaissance and giving the army commander a sketch of the Federal position and camps. The next morning Early met with Hotchkiss and Gordon. Gordon confirmed the cartographer's account of the previous day's reconnaissance and offered assurances that an attack on the Federal left would be successful. Early had previously contemplated attacking the other end of the Union line, but this new information caused him to change his mind. Later that morning, Gordon and Hotchkiss went to see if there was a way to move troops around the northern base of the Massanutten. After discovering a narrow foot path that would prove suitable, the two officers returned to army headquarters to attend a 2:00 P.M. conference between Early and his division commanders.

Early began the meeting by explaining the findings of the previous day's reconnaissance on the enemy's left flank. Using a sketch map drawn by Hotchkiss, Gordon described the Federal position in detail. After the war, Gordon claimed that he "was so positive of success" that he announced at the meeting that he would "bear all the blame" in case the flank attack failed. Following some general discussion, Early adopted Gordon's plan over one suggested by Brig. Gen. John Pegram to assault the Federal right flank.[10]

Early planned to launch a three-pronged attack against the Federals. Gordon was given command of a column consisting of his own division under General Evans, two other divisions under Brigadier General Pegram and Maj. Gen. Stephen Dodson Ramseur, and a cavalry brigade under Col. William H. Payne. Gordon's force was to move after dark on October 18 across the North Fork of the Shenandoah River on a makeshift bridge, then traverse the northern slope of Massanutten Mountain to a point on the Shenandoah River known as Bowman's Ford. There the men would wait until 5:00 A.M., when the various columns of the Army of the Valley would advance, with Gordon's men crossing the river and attacking the rear of the Union Eighth Corps.

Shortly after dusk on the extremely cold evening of the eighteenth, Gordon's men left Fisher's Hill with admonitions to keep quiet during the march. Canteens, swords, and anything else that might make noise were left behind. It took nearly the entire night for the troops to make the slow, exhausting march to the base of the Massanutten and then to move more than two miles in single file along the difficult trail around the base of the mountain and get into position on the bottomland at Bowman's Ford. Most of the men had about an hour's rest before getting into position along the fog-shrouded banks of Cedar Creek.

At the appointed hour, Colonel Payne's cavalrymen dashed across the creek, scattering Union pickets. The infantrymen then plunged into the frigid waters, crossing in three columns and "keeping their files dressed and well closed up." After clambering up the steep, muddy banks on the opposite side of the creek, the men pushed northward by the right flank at the double quick with skirmishers thrown out to guard the flanks of the columns.

Upon reaching the Cooley house, which Gordon had seen from the signal station, the Confederates halted and formed battle lines with sharpshooters deployed in front. Gordon's old division under Evans formed with the Georgia brigade under Col. John H. Lowe on the left, the Louisianans under Col. William R. Peck in the center, and General Terry's Virginians on the right. Ramseur's division formed on the right of Evans, with Pegram's brigades deployed in rear of Evans as a reserve. The gray battle lines faced toward the west and northwest into the left and rear of the Union Eighth Corps camps.[11]

After advancing across undulating and partially wooded ground, the charging southerners came within sight of the Federal camps. Before attacking, gray-clad officers ordered a brief halt to reform the men. The oblique direction of the subsequent Confederate assault resulted in Evans's division pushing ahead of Ramseur's and Pegram's divisions. Although the majority of the Federals were able to form lines of battle to the west of their camps, the yelling Confederates killed, wounded, and captured some of them in their tents.

The ensuing fight lasted half an hour at most before the outnumbered Federals began falling back toward the Valley Turnpike. Gordon's troops pursued them, moving through the enemy camps and wagon yards. The piles of winter clothing, blankets, and rations lying about proved too great a temptation for many of the ragged and famished southerners to resist, even though Early had issued orders prohibiting plundering.[12]

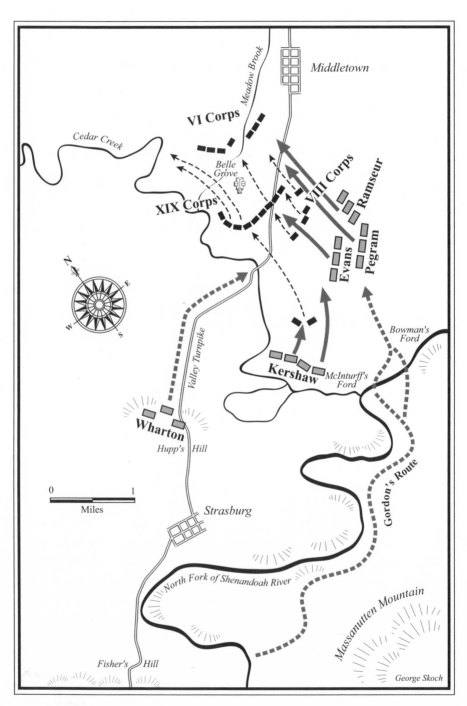

Confederate Attacks, 5:40 A.M. – 7:30 A.M., October 19, 1864.

Confederates under Gordon routing elements of the Union 19th Corps at Cedar Creek. Robert Underwood Johnson and Clarence Clough Buel, eds., *Battles and Leaders of the Civil War*, 4 vols. (New York: Century, 1887–88), 4:515.

Despite the "brief but somewhat stubborn resistance" put up by one Union brigade, Gordon's troops soon joined with Maj. Gen. Joseph B. Kershaw's division advancing from the south. The combined force surged through dense abatis and across the entrenchments of the Union Nineteenth Corps along the Valley Turnpike, capturing several cannon, which a detachment of the 12th Georgia Artillery Battalion of Evans's brigade turned on their former owners. The Confederates then charged across the open fields south and southeast of the Belle Grove mansion before hitting the center of a Federal line containing the remnants of the Eighth and Nineteenth Corps. For approximately thirty minutes, the Union line held, but then collapsed after being flanked, and the Federals retreated northward toward the ravine of Meadow Brook.[13]

As Gordon's and Kershaw's men continued northward, they encountered two divisions of the Federal Sixth Corps deployed on a series of ridges just north of Meadow Brook Valley. By this time, General Early had crossed Cedar Creek on the Valley Turnpike, accompanied by the Confederate artillery and an additional infantry division. As Early rode northward along the Valley Pike, he encountered Gordon sometime between 7:00 and 7:30 A.M. atop a rise just east of the pike and across from the lane leading to Belle Grove.[14]

Determining exactly what transpired in the ensuing meeting between Early and Gordon is impossible because the generals and their allies left irreconcilable accounts of the incident. In a letter written two days after the battle, Lt. Thomas G. Jones of Gordon's staff told his father, "Early in joyous extacy, gave no orders, did nothing, allowed precious moments to slip thru his grasp." Several decades after the war, Gordon claimed that Early rode up ecstatic over the morning's victory, declaring, "Just one month ago today General we were going the other way!" and proclaimed, "Well Gordon, this is glory enough for one day!"[15]

Gordon supposedly responded by pointing through the dense fog and smoke to the Union Sixth Corps forming to the north on Red Hill and said, "It is very well so far, general; but we have one more blow to strike and then there will not be left an organized company of infantry in Sheridan's army." Gordon then explained that he had planned to order a concerted infantry attack against the Sixth Corps after bombarding it with several dozen pieces of artillery massed along the Valley Turnpike. Early replied, "No use in that; they will all go directly." Thomas G. Jones claimed that Early said, "in substance," that the Sixth Corps would "go to the rear with the rest. They are all trying to get away now." At this point, wrote Gordon in his *Reminiscences*, "My heart went into my boots. Visions of the fatal halt on the first day of Gettysburg, and of the whole day's hesitation to permit an assault on Grant's exposed flank on the 6th of May [at the Wilderness] . . . rose before me." A furious Gordon returned to his division, and Early again took command of the Second Corps.[16]

Early and his staff officers vehemently denied Gordon's version of this meeting. Early's postwar version noted only that Gordon "briefly informed me of the condition of things and stated that Pegram's division, which had not been engaged, had been ordered in." Gordon then returned to his division, at which time Early claimed that he "rode forward on the Pike" amidst heavy fog and smoke "to ascertain the position of the enemy in order to continue the attack." Early and his chief of staff, Samuel J. C. Moore, then claimed that the army's commander posted a large concentration of artillery along a high point on the turnpike south of Middletown with orders to bombard the Federals. Old Jube was clearly ecstatic that morning, probably believing the Union troops would offer little further serious resistance. He was not, however, ready to give up pursuing the Federals at this point in the battle.[17]

After being temporarily checked along the banks of Meadow Brook, Gordon's

Northern artist James E. Taylor's sketch of Gordon asking Early for reinforcements to complete the rout of Union forces on the morning of October 19, 1864. Courtesy of the Western Reserve Historical Society, Cleveland, Ohio.

division reformed, advanced across the stream, and obliqued to the northwest, moving after the remnants of the Nineteenth Corps. Slowed by stiff enemy resistance, the Confederates took shelter behind a stone wall and fired into a Federal line near the Shipley house and orchard. By 9:00 A.M., the Confederate infantry attacks were losing momentum; their rapid pursuit of the enemy over a considerable distance had resulted in southern units becoming scattered.[18]

Hoping to coordinate attacks against a Union division on Cemetery Hill west of Middletown, Early sent staff officers to Gordon and Kershaw with orders to turn the right flank of the Federal position on the hill. According to Early's official report written three days after the battle, Gordon and Kershaw "stated in reply that a heavy force of cavalry had got[ten] in their front, and that their ranks were so depleted by the number of men who had stopped in the camps to plunder that they could not advance them." Early offered a different version of this exchange immediately after the war, writing that the staff officer sent to Gordon with orders to advance returned without delivering them, the aide claiming that he had seen Gordon's division reforming and that it was in no condition to attack. Gordon denied in his *Reminiscences* that either he or Kershaw told Early during the battle that their commands could not advance.

"The truth is we were not only urgently anxious to advance," wrote Gordon, "but were astounded at any halt whatever."[19]

By 11:30 A.M., Early's lines had reformed on the northern outskirts of Middletown, with Gordon's depleted division stretched thin to hold the army's left flank. At approximately 1:00 P.M., Gordon's, Kershaw's, and Ramseur's divisions advanced one half mile beyond the main Confederate line before halting in a country lane that ran northwest from the Valley Pike. Southern skirmishers continued northward for some distance before encountering the main Federal line and retiring.

Gordon's thinned division held the far left of this advanced Confederate infantry line. On the right of Gordon's division, General Terry's Virginians connected with Kershaw's command. The Louisianans held the center of Gordon's line with the 12th Georgia Artillery Battalion of Evans's brigade on the far left. Several Confederates described gaps between the weakened units holding Gordon's position, a man in the Stonewall Brigade calling it "a thin skirmish line." Clement Evans's brigade, minus the 12th Georgia Battalion and half of the 38th Georgia, deployed along a wooded ridge and in a large open field several hundred yards to the west of the rest of the division and the main infantry line.[20]

The army's "fatal halt," as Gordon later termed the afternoon lull, lasted from the time that Gordon's, Kershaw's, and Ramseur's divisions advanced northward at 1:00 P.M. until around 4:00 P.M. Early gave several reasons in his official report and memoirs for halting the southern advance. The immense Federal cavalry force, which threatened the flanks of the Confederate army, made an attack "extremely hazardous," claimed Early. He also noted that the exhausted and famished conditions of the southern soldiers that afternoon resulted in many of them going to the rear to plunder the captured camps.

Several other Confederates suggested that widespread plundering influenced Early's decision to stop the advance. Jedediah Hotchkiss told his wife that, following the halt near Middletown, "so many of our troops had left the ranks to plunder the Yankee camps that it was a long time" before another advance could be made. Early's chief of artillery, Col. Thomas H. Carter, recalled asking the army commander why he did not continue the advance. Early's responded that "he intended to pursue the enemy as soon as the line could be put in order."[21]

Many men in Gordon's division and throughout Early's army gathered battlefield spoils during the afternoon lull, their jaunts made easier by the scarcity of experienced commissioned and noncommissioned officers who could impose discipline. Richard Waldrop of the 21st Virginia wrote on October 21 that, during the Confederate advance, "a large proportion, probably a majority of the men—fell back and, notwithstanding that the most positive orders had been issued against it, commenced plundering the captured camps. . . . The plundering was indulged in by officers as well as men. . . . Our army is little better than a band of thieves and marauders." George B. Hamilton, a soldier in the 8th Louisiana Infantry, wrote a friend that "in the afternoon about five oclock more than one half our men and officers were plundering and straggling to the rear." "Do not be surprised when I tell you," he continued, "that officers of high rank and some of them well known to you had from three to ten men detailed to carry off plunder."[22]

Hamilton's comments regarding well-known officers engaging in plunder may have been a reference to his division commander. At least one wartime and several postwar accounts claim that General Gordon plundered by proxy. Surg. Robert T. Myers of the 16th Georgia Infantry wrote in his diary of encountering a wagon in the enemy's captured camps during the afternoon which he was told belonged to Gordon. Myers claimed that an aide of the general "was loading it with eatables—camp fixtures &c." At least three other Confederates, two of them officers, remembered encountering a captured wagon appropriated for Gordon's headquarters being escorted to the rear by men from his division.[23]

A number of Confederates noted the inability of Gordon, his depleted officers corps, and the army's provost marshal to halt the plundering. General Evans confessed to his wife two days after Cedar Creek that "the immense amount of plunder on the battlefield caused a great deal of straggling and proper steps were not taken to prevent it." Pvt. Isaac G. Bradwell of the 31st Georgia remembered straggling with a comrade and returning to their regiment in the afternoon with haversacks full of Yankee beef and hardtack. The two Georgians found "only a handful" of their comrades at the front, with no effort being made to bring up the stragglers or strengthen their position.[24]

Throughout the afternoon, Gordon and his subordinates grew concerned about reports they received from Brig. Gen. Thomas L. Rosser warning of Union cavalry and infantry forces massing in their front. Gordon sent several messages to Early requesting reinforcements to strengthen the army's left flank, eventually dispatching Lt. Thomas G. Jones to speak to the army commander. Jones remembered that Early "did not seem to attach much importance" to the opinion that a Federal attack might fall on the Confederate left. Early instructed

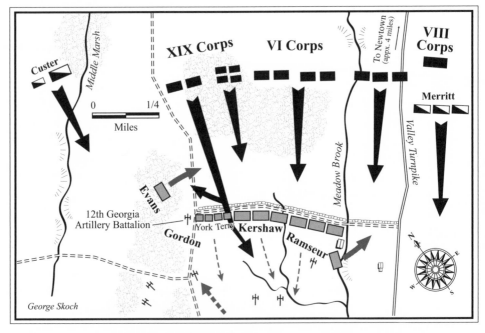

Sheridan's Counterattack West of the Valley Turnpike and the Collapse of Gordon's Division, October 19, 1864.

Jones to "tell General Gordon that it is probably a demonstration to cover the retreat . . . and that he must show a fierce front to the enemy and hold on," as the Federals would retreat before nightfall.[25]

Gordon eventually rode to see Early, but the army commander had no infantry reserves. Instead, Early could send only a few artillery batteries to bolster Gordon's line. As Gordon galloped back to his division, he reached it in time to see charging Federal infantrymen bearing down upon the attenuated southern line.[26]

The Federals soon penetrated the gap between Gordon's main line, which was "temporarily fortified with rails," and Evans's detached brigade. The Louisianans and Virginians in the main line found themselves nearly enveloped by advancing enemy troops, and the Confederates broke to the rear. Alexander S. Baird of the 2nd Virginia Infantry told his mother on October 22 that he "was obliged to run out between two Yankee lines of battle or be taken a prisoner." Baird escaped from what he termed "the hottest place I ever was in," but many of his comrades did not.[27]

Upon seeing the imminent collapse of the main southern line, General Evans wheeled his brigade to attack the flank and rear of the advancing Federals. The assault by Evans's troops drove one Union brigade back for a short distance, the Federal commander reporting that his men "encountered a most murderous fire from [a] hidden enemy on the right and rear." Soon, however, the Georgians found themselves cut off from the rest of Gordon's division, and they retreated southward in confusion.[28]

In an address delivered to his brigade shortly after Cedar Creek, General Evans blamed "much of the disaster" on those men in his command "who stopped to plunder during the glorious victory of the morning and those who threw away their arms in the evening." Some men in the ranks also attributed their command's poor performance in the late afternoon of the nineteenth to plundering. Sgt. John F. Charlton of the 5th Louisiana wrote in his diary on October 20 that when the enemy advanced the day before, the Confederates, "being scattered" and "pillaging the deserted Yankee camps," could not "withstand the charge and fled." George H. Lester of the 38th Georgia admitted years later that his comrades were "somewhat demoralized by the immense amount of the spoils" when the enemy made their final charge.[29]

Gordon and several of his subordinate officers performed heroic service throughout the evening of October 19, rallying troops and fighting rearguard actions as the Confederates retreated southward. The first of these engagements took place on the Old Forge Road, a half mile south of the site of the initial Confederate collapse. General Terry "rallied some two or three hundred men behind a stone fence" along the Old Forge Road and fought until the enemy again threatened his left. This time the menacing Federals consisted of Brig. Gen. George A. Custer's cavalry division, the advance of which Gordon described as a "dull heavy, swelling sound like the roar of a distant cyclone."[30]

Custer's cavalry charge forced the Confederates to retreat to the high ground overlooking Meadow Brook just north of Belle Grove. Although several artillery pieces bolstered the Confederate line, blue-clad horsemen again turned the southern left and sent Gordon's men retreating southward. "We finally got into a perfect run," remembered a member of the 61st Georgia, "with the cavalry getting nearer all the time, and some of our men surrendering." When the Confederates reached the abandoned earthworks of the Union Nineteenth Corps near Cedar Creek on the west side of the Valley Pike, they put up a brief stand before once again having their left flank enveloped by Union horsemen.

Finding it impossible for his command to wade across Cedar Creek by the flank without sustaining heavy casualties, Clement Evans ordered "a precipitate retreat" in which his brigade lost all semblance of organization. During

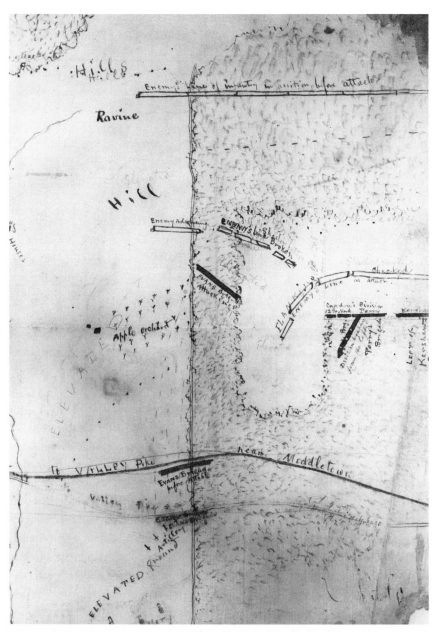

Portion of a map of the Cedar Creek battlefield, showing the brigades of Gordon's division (in dark lines) being outflanked and driven back by attacking Federals. The map was probably drawn to accompany the official report of Confederate general Clement A. Evans. Evans-Stephens Papers, Folder 13, Box 3, Ms. 2946, Hargrett Rare Book and Manuscript Library, University of Georgia.

this scramble, pursuing Union troops captured many Confederates who fell behind. Of the 737 casualties sustained by Gordon's division at Cedar Creek, 455 (62 percent) of them were taken prisoner while 282 (38 percent) were killed or wounded.[31]

In the days immediately following Cedar Creek, a frustrated and depressed Jubal Early sent telegrams and an official report to Lee blaming the Valley army's defeat on its "bad conduct" and "uncontrollable propensity" to plunder, claiming that the men ran "without sufficient cause." Early gave Gordon credit for his reconnaissance on Signal Knob and for commanding the Second Corps in its flank march and subsequent attack, but he unfairly stated that Gordon's division gave way north of Middletown, "not because there was any pressure on them, but from an insane idea of being flanked." Although portions of Gordon's division rallied "and with the help of the artillery" checked the enemy for some time, "a great number of the men could not be stopped."[32]

Three days after Cedar Creek, Early publicly lashed out against his army. "Many of you, including some commissioned officers, yielded to a disgraceful propensity for plunder," he announced, "subsequently those who had remained at their post, seeing their ranks thinned by the absence of the plunderers . . . yielded to a needless panic and fled the field in confusion." Early's address insinuated that Gordon had participated in the plundering, something the army commander believed based on rumors that Gordon had appropriated a captured wagon for his own use during the battle. "The officer who pauses in the career of victory to place guard over a sutler's wagon for his private use," stated Early, "is as bad as the soldier who halts to secure for himself the abandoned clothing or money of a flying foe."[33]

The address provoked resentment in Gordon and many others, and letters from soldiers excoriating Early appeared in southern newspapers for several weeks after Cedar Creek. Almost every letter mentioned wide-scale plundering by Confederates and admitted that it was one of the primary reasons for defeat. None of them, however, singled out Gordon's division as the primary culprit in the disaster.[34]

Many newspaper correspondents credited Gordon with the initial Confederate success at Cedar Creek. "Gordon's genius had won the most brilliant victory of the war," wrote a soldier to the *Richmond Daily Examiner*, "the plan was his entirely." A contributor to the *Selma Dispatch* said that Gordon's "masterly flank attack" at Cedar Creek "forcibly reminds us that the spirit of the glorious Jackson still lives and moves." Gordon "seems destined to fill the void occasioned by the fall of Jackson," the correspondent predicted. Peter W. Alexander, a popular war correspondent who had hinted in his columns that Jubal Early had problems with alcohol, wrote five days after Cedar Creek of rumors circulating about Early being relieved of command. Alexander claimed that Gordon was one of several candidates who might succeed Early, characterizing the Georgian as "the most promising young officer in the Army of Northern Virginia, and . . . a temperate man."[35]

A missive in the October 27, 1864, *Richmond Enquirer* signed "Argus" but clearly written by an officer who was with Gordon at Cedar Creek, particularly outraged Jubal Early. Argus was Lt. Frank Markoe, a twenty-four-year-old signal officer on Gordon's staff. Markoe claimed that Gordon planned the "brilliant and successful" Confederate attack at Cedar Creek and would have won a resounding victory had not Early interfered and made the "fatal mistake" of "resting and waiting three hours to reorganize." Early did not know the identity of Argus but believed that his letter had been inspired by Gordon.[36]

The Argus letter and others like it clearly incensed the quarrelsome Early, as revealed in a letter he wrote a few days after Cedar Creek to his friend, Confederate congressman Alexander A. Boteler. After claiming that Cedar Creek would have been a glorious Confederate victory "had my troops behaved as they ought to have done," Early groused that "as usual the want of final success has been followed by vituperation of me." The irascible general found it particularly galling that "for all that was done well, credit is given to others and for all the disaster I am blamed." Early stressed that "if there was any merit" in the attack plan it was his, since he "had to entrust its execution to others & my whole energies were given to its superintendence."[37]

On October 28, Early met with his division commanders to ascertain the Valley army's condition and its level of confidence in the commanding general. Lt. Oscar Hinrichs of Pegram's staff predicted a confrontation between the "Old Man," as he termed Early, and Gordon. "There seems to spring up an animosity between Early and Gordon," wrote Hinrichs in his diary that day, "and it won't need much to blow this up into a roaring flame." Clement Evans echoed these sentiments in a letter to his wife, claiming that "Early is desperately jealous and will do everything in his power to work the downfall of Gen. Gordon, for he fears that Gordon's genius will obscure him as a department commander in the same way that it did last year as a division commander."[38]

During the October 28 meeting, Early confronted Gordon about the Argus letter, intimating that the Georgian had inspired it and other accounts. Gordon denied these charges but admitted that "the facts had been truly stated as to our unfortunate halt and delay." The exchange between the two generals, Gordon later told one of his staff officers, was at first "polite and cold" but grew more heated with "much plain speaking on both sides." Little is known about the exact nature of the exchange, but Gordon claimed that it centered on whether the afternoon halt or the men's "bad conduct" had been the primary reason for the disaster at Cedar Creek.[39]

Early's charge that Gordon appropriated a sutler's wagon during the battle also greatly incensed Gordon. According to Lieutenant Jones of Gordon's staff, the story originated from an incident that took place on the morning of October 19 when Gordon encountered two wagons. One of the vehicles had a black cover on it similar to those on ordnance wagons, and Gordon told the driver that ammunition wagons should not go to the rear since they might be needed. The driver replied that the vehicle with the black cover was an officer's headquarters wagon, and Gordon told the man to drive on to the rear. Gordon undoubtedly explained these circumstances to Early on October 28, and according to Jones, Early "soon became satisfied that the sutler's wagon story was a great injustice to Gordon."[40]

Despite Early's concession that Gordon had not been personally involved in plundering, a "mutual strong dislike" existed between the two officers. Gordon considered requesting a court of inquiry against Early but desisted, confessing to an aide that "were it not for his attachment to his men, and the effect of dissension and bitterness between Generals, when the cause was in such a gloomy period, he would have asked to be sent elsewhere to duty." Clement Evans predicted that "the result of the quarrel between Gordon & Early will be their separation," but it was mid-December 1864 before Gordon and the Second Corps left Early and the Shenandoah Valley to rejoin Lee's besieged army in Petersburg.[41]

Jubal Early steadfastly maintained during and after the Civil War that wide-scale plundering and an unnecessary panic and retreat were the primary causes of the Confederate defeat at Cedar Creek. He did, however, concede on a few occasions that he had made mistakes. On October 23, 1864, as Jed Hotchkiss departed from the Valley for Richmond to meet with Robert E. Lee, Early instructed the mapmaker "not to tell Lee that we ought to have advanced in the morning [on October 19] at Middletown for . . . we ought to have done so." In a printed November 28 letter to the chairman of the Committee on Military Affairs in the Confederate Senate, Early admitted that he had "committed blunders" during the late campaign and saw where he "might have done things that were not done" but unfortunately did not elaborate on his mistakes.[42]

Although John B. Gordon might not have known about the Argus letter, it resembled in all but one aspect the general's postwar statements about Cedar Creek. The difference concerned plundering. Argus claimed that one-third of the Confederates went to the rear to plunder, while Gordon steadfastly refused to admit that such was the case. In 1870, the general wrote in a private letter, "I state with emphasis and most positively that I never saw less straggling on any battlefield during the war." Gordon claimed that this was "the testimony of the Inspectors after the battle" and that he had also been on the ground and remarked upon the absence of plundering. "It is a great injustice to the private soldiers," declared Gordon, who believed that he could not let mistaken assertions of plundering "go down to the future as history if I can prevent it."[43]

Gordon apparently spoke publicly about Cedar Creek for the first time on the evening of July 2, 1888, while in Gettysburg to honor the 25th anniversary of that battle. While talking to a *Boston Herald* reporter, Gordon claimed that he had suggested, planned, and executed the Confederate attack at Cedar Creek. Gordon had victory in his grasp, he explained, when Early arrived on the field, stopped the advance, and refused to order up artillery to bombard the Federals. Early justified the halt by claiming that "we've won a great victory, we've done enough for one day; we will stop here." When Gordon insisted that they could destroy the Federals "in an hour," Early again said no, that "the men had seen fighting enough, and we have won glory enough for one day."[44]

Jubal Early read the *Boston Herald* interview with Gordon when it appeared in the *New Orleans Sunday States* in September 1888. Early claimed that he did not believe that Gordon had made the statements attributed to him by the reporter but immediately wrote the Georgian asking about the interview. Gordon did not reply, "preserving a profound silence on the subject," according to Early's former chief of staff, Samuel J. C. Moore.[45]

Gordon's comments caused a stir among ex-Confederate officers who had served under Early in the Valley. A former member of Thomas Rosser's staff told Early that the *Boston Herald* interview was "almost a literal publication of the account of the matter given to me by Gen. Gordon in the winter of 1887 on the way to New York." Several other ex-Confederates, including Gens. William H. F. Payne and Lunsford L. Lomax, privately repudiated Gordon's version of the affair. Lomax claimed that if Gordon made the statements attributed to him in the *Herald*, one could "only account for it by his vanity — of which he possesses a large amount."[46]

The most detailed public refutation of Gordon's comments appeared in an article written by Samuel J. C. Moore. Moore wrote that Early "was always willing to listen to advice and suggestions properly given by his subordinates" but "was not inclined to yield to any one in executing his plans in his own way." The Confederate plan to attack at Cedar Creek belonged to Early, who formulated the complex operation, arranged its details, and gave orders to the various division commanders. Moore concluded that Gordon's "imagination, heightened by personal vanity and desire for self-exultation," and perhaps inflamed by "the adulation of sycophantic flatterers, has led him . . . to believe that he alone achieved the great victory." Moore concluded that the Army of the Valley had been defeated at Cedar Creek because many men had "abandoned duty for plunder," the Confederate cavalry under Rosser had not adequately protected the army's left flank, and Gordon's division had abandoned its position in the last line.[47]

By the time Gordon began writing his memoirs in the late 1890s, the question of whether Confederate soldiers had plundered at Cedar Creek had grown in significance in the mind of the old soldier and politician. Because one of the main themes of Gordon's *Reminiscences* was the promotion of sectional reconciliation by praising the bravery and honor of both Union and Confederate soldiers, he could not allow charges of southern misconduct to go unchallenged. Such accusations also reflected poorly on Gordon and his division. "I insisted then, and still insist," Gordon wrote, "that our men deserved only unstinted praise" for what they did at Cedar Creek.[48]

Early's grave charge of plundering so directly concerned "the reputation, the honor, the character of Southern soldiers . . . as to demand the most exhaustive examination," explained Gordon. Gordon emphatically and repeatedly denied that his troops plundered at Cedar Creek, his main supporting evidence being heavily edited excerpts from postwar letters written to him by prominent ex-Confederate officers. The Confederate defeat at Cedar Creek, Gordon insisted, had been "due solely to the unfortunate halting and delay after the morning victory."[49]

The publication of Gordon's *Reminiscences* in 1903 met with universal public praise and glowing reviews. Most southern veterans undoubtedly felt as Gordon did, that the book's patriotic message justified the use of literary license and the denial of unpleasant aspects of their service. Ex-staff officer Thomas G. Jones proofread the Cedar Creek chapters of *Reminiscences* and told his former chief that the book "was a great work." Jones, who loved Gordon "as a father" during the war, thought that "one of the grandest things" in the general's memoir was his assertion that "the great conflict should not be presented to our children from passionate sectional standpoints."[50]

Gen. Clement Evans also assisted with *Reminiscences*, loaning his official re-

John Brown Gordon at
Gettysburg, September
1894 (albumen by William
H. Tipton). Courtesy of
Jeff Kowalis.

port of Cedar Creek to Gordon and reviewing the chapters of the book that dealt
with the controversial battle. Evans had always believed that Early's "want of
Generalship" was the primary cause for the Confederate defeat at Cedar Creek,
but immediately after the battle, Evans had admitted in letters home and in a
speech to his brigade that plundering had been a serious problem in his command. He also conceded that "proper steps" had not been taken to prevent this
from happening, and that "much of the disaster" had been due to both looting
and fleeing before the enemy in the evening.[51]

Extracts from postwar correspondence between Evans and Gordon that appear in *Reminiscences* contain no admission of wide-scale plundering. Evans
instead claimed that after passing through the enemy's camps on the morning
of October 19, 1864, he "had small details sent over the ground . . . to bring up

every man who had fallen out for any cause except wounds." At the time of the decisive Federal attack in the late afternoon, Evans stated that "his command was not straggling and plundering." "The Cedar Creek disaster was caused by the halt," wrote Evans to Gordon, "which you did not order and which I know you opposed."[52]

At least a few southern veterans privately resented Gordon's biased treatment of Cedar Creek in *Reminiscences*. John Warwick Daniel, who served as Early's chief of staff for a time during the war, admitted that Gordon was "as fine a figure in battle as I ever saw" but believed the general "befogged and confused" every battle he wrote about in his memoirs. When Daniel confronted his friend Thomas G. Jones about Gordon's assertions, Jones defended his former chief by claiming that "Gordon did not intentionally misstate anything, though, after the lapse of nearly forty years, it is easy for one to make the mistake."[53]

Gordon claimed in *Reminiscences* that whatever his men had been in the great battles of 1863 and early 1864, "they were the same at Cedar Creek." "They had not changed," he asserted, "except perhaps to grow . . . into a more self-sacrificing manhood as the demands upon them became more exacting." He believed that if his official report of Cedar Creek and Confederate army inspection reports of Early's Valley army had appeared in the U.S. War Department's *Official Records*, they would have vindicated his beliefs. While Gordon's Cedar Creek report has never surfaced, inspection reports and wartime testimony from southern soldiers contradict Gordon's claims about conditions in the Valley army in October 1864. These sources instead reveal the problems that undoubtedly contributed to the plundering and collapse of Gordon's division at Cedar Creek: exhaustion, extreme hunger and raggedness, and deteriorating discipline due to a shortage of officers. John B. Gordon's wish to protect the reputation of his command and the Lost Cause image of the southern soldier, combined with his intense pride and vanity, prevented him from being completely honest about the Confederate disaster at Cedar Creek.[54]

Yet Gordon and his division do not deserve all the blame for what happened at Cedar Creek. Jubal Early gave the crucial orders to halt during the early afternoon of October 19 that ultimately cost his army a victory. Early defended his decision two days later by arguing that fatigue and excessive plundering had depleted the southern ranks and that a heavy Federal cavalry force opposite his right flank north of Middletown made a further Confederate advance hazardous. Unfortunately for the Confederates, Early failed to acknowledge warnings of a Federal concentration against his left until it was too late. Old

Jube's contention that Gordon's division gave way solely from the "insane idea of being flanked" reveals the army commander's ignorance of the situation on his left flank at the decisive moment of the day.[55]

Several sources indicate that Early thought the enemy was in retreat toward Winchester by the afternoon of October 19. If he believed this, why did he relinquish the offensive momentum his troops had sustained in their successful morning assaults? Maintaining such a momentum was Early's best chance of inflicting a decisive defeat against a larger enemy army. A comment Early made to Jedediah Hotchkiss, probably in the late evening of October 19, may help explain the halt. "The Yankees got whipped and we got scared," Early told Hotchkiss in reference to the day's incredible turn in affairs. The "we" in Early's statement undoubtedly referred to the routed Confederate soldiers, but Old Jube might also have meant it to apply to himself.[56]

Acknowledgments

The author thanks the following individuals for their assistance with this essay: Marshall Burnett, John M. Coski, Ralph L. Eckert, Gary W. Gallagher, Jeff Kowalis, Robert E. L. Krick, Robert K. Krick, Eric J. Mink, Donald C. Pfanz, and Gregory C. White.

Notes

1. John B. Gordon, *Reminiscences of the Civil War* (New York: Scribner's, 1903), 371. The best biography of Gordon is Ralph L. Eckert, *John Brown Gordon: Soldier, Southerner, American* (Baton Rouge: Louisiana State University Press, 1989).

2. Gordon, *Reminiscences*, 332. Those historians who have been critical of Gordon's version of Cedar Creek in *Reminiscences* include Eckert, *Gordon*, 93–104; Theodore C. Mahr, *The Battle of Cedar Creek: Showdown in the Shenandoah, October 1–30, 1864* (Lynchburg, Va.: H. E. Howard, 1992), 91, 248–52, 345–56; Jeffry D. Wert, "Jubal A. Early and Confederate Defeat," in Gary W. Gallagher, ed., *Struggle for the Shenandoah: Essays on the 1864 Valley Campaign* (Kent, Ohio: Kent State University Press, 1991), 38.

3. Edward A. Pollard, *Lee and His Lieutenants* (New York: E. B. Treat, 1867), 540–45; "General John B. Gordon," *Montgomery Advertiser*, July 3, 1864; Robert E. Lee to Jefferson Davis, telegram dated May 13, 1864, Compiled Service Record of John B. Gordon, M 331, National Archives, Washington [repository hereafter cited as NA]; Jefferson Davis, *The Papers of Jefferson Davis*, ed. Lynda L. Crist and others, 11 vols. to date (Baton Rouge: Louisiana State University Press, 1971–), 10:207, 417.

4. Campbell Brown, "Early's Expedition to Lynchburg after Hunter," folder 6, box

2, Brown-Ewell Papers, Tennessee State Library and Archives, Nashville; Eckert, *Gordon*, 64–70; Fanny Gordon to John B. Gordon, October 16, 1864, box 3, series 3, Bell Wiley Papers, Special Collections, Emory University, Atlanta, Ga. [repository hereafter cited as EU].

5. George P. Ring to wife, July 27, 1864, George P. Ring Letters, Louisiana Historical Association Collection, Special Collections, Tulane University, New Orleans; Fanny Gordon to John B. Gordon, May 15, 1864, box 3, series 3, Wiley Papers.

6. U.S. War Department, *The War of the Rebellion: A Compilation of the Official Records of the Union and Confederate Armies*, 127 vols., index, and atlas (Washington: Government Printing Office, 1880–1901), ser. 1, 43(1):609 [hereafter cited as *OR*; all references are to ser. 1); Richard Colbert to Mrs. E. M. Potts, July 27, 1864, folder 57, North Louisiana Historical Association, Centenary College, Shreveport.

7. Field Return of Gordon's division, July 15, 1864, folder 318, Frederick Dearborn Collection, Houghton Library, Harvard University, Cambridge, Mass.; Inspection Reports dated August 20, 1864, for Terry's, Evans's, and Stafford's/York's brigades, 7-P-17, 8-P-17, 9-P-17, M 935, Inspection Reports . . . Received by the Inspection Branch in the Confederate Adjutant and Inspector General's Office, NA. For an article that plays down the negative effects of consolidation in Terry's brigade, see A. T., "From General Early's Army," *Richmond Dispatch*, November 2, 1864. Gordon's division lost a total of 445 men killed or wounded at Winchester and Fisher's Hill. The published returns do not estimate the prisoners lost in these battles, but they numbered in the hundreds.

8. Field return of Gordon's division, September 10, 1864, Chicago Historical Society; Jubal A. Early, *A Memoir of the Last Year of the War for Independence in the Confederate States of America* (Lynchburg, Va.: C. W. Button, 1867), 92; Mahr, *Cedar Creek*, 367; George P. Ring to wife, September 21, 1864, Ring Letters; Thomas H. Bomar to sister, September 17, 1864, Bomar Family Papers, Ms. 86, EU; *OR*, 43(1):557.

9. Robert Grier Stephens Jr., *Intrepid Warrior: Clement Anselm Evans, Confederate General from Georgia, Life, Letters, and Diaries of the War Years* (Dayton, Ohio: Morningside, 1992), 479–80; Jedediah Hotchkiss, *Make Me a Map of the Valley: The Civil War Journal of Stonewall Jackson's Topographer*, ed. Archie P. McDonald (Dallas, Tex.: Southern Methodist University Press, 1973), 237; "Flanking 'Little Phil,' the Man Who Almost Spoiled Sheridan's Ride," *Boston Herald*, August 19, 1888; Mahr, *Cedar Creek*, 81. In 1888, Gordon claimed that members of Early's staff were present on Signal Knob and were "utterly incredulous" when he proposed to march around the mountain and strike the Federal left flank.

10. Hotchkiss, *Make Me a Map*, 238; Early, *Memoir of the Last Year*, 83–84; Stephens, *Intrepid Warrior*, 481, 486; Thomas G. Jones to father, October 21, 1864, Thomas G. Jones Papers, Alabama Department of Archives and History, Montgomery; Gordon, *Reminiscences*, 335. General Evans claimed in an October 18, 1864, letter that Early "favors the attack on their right flank."

11. Stephens, *Intrepid Warrior*, 487; Janet B. Hewett and others, eds., *Supplement to the Official Records of the Union and Confederate Armies*, 100 vols. (Wilmington, N.C.: Broadfoot, 1994–2000), pt. 1, 7:607 [hereafter cited as *ORS*; all references are to

pt. 1]; Mahr, *Cedar Creek*, 122; George W. Nichols, *A Soldier's Story of His Regiment* (1898; reprint, Kennesaw, Ga.: Continental Book Company, 1961), 193–94; Argus, *Richmond Daily Enquirer*, October 27, 1864; Oscar Hinrichs diary, October 19, 1864, copy in possession of Robert K. Krick; Gordon, *Reminiscences*, 339.

12. *ORS*, 7:607; *OR*, 43(1):563. For a discussion of Jubal Early's unfair postwar contention that Gordon was late in launching his attack on the morning of the 19th, see Mahr, *Cedar Creek*, 123.

13. *ORS*, 7:607; Stephens, *Intrepid Warrior*, 489; Isaac G. Bradwell, "Battle of Cedar Creek," *Confederate Veteran* 27 (November 1919):411.

14. Samuel J. C. Moore, "In Defence of General Early," *Clarke County (Va.) Courier*, October 17, 1889 (a handwritten draft of this article is in folder 7, Samuel J. C. Moore Papers, Mss 1M7864a18, Virginia Historical Society, Richmond [repository hereafter cited as VHS]); Early, *Memoir of the Last Year*, 86; Thomas G. Jones to John W. Daniel, December 24, 1905, Lewis Leigh-Peters Collection, U.S. Army Military History Institute, Carlisle Barracks, Pa.

15. Thomas G. Jones to father, October 21, 1864, Jones Papers; Gordon, *Reminiscences*, 341, 357; *ORS*, 7:612; "Flanking 'Little Phil.'" Gordon's account of this meeting in his *Reminiscences* is nearly identical to the version given by Thomas G. Jones to John W. Daniel in a July 3, 1904, letter.

16. Gordon, *Reminiscences*, 341; "Flanking 'Little Phil,'" *Boston Herald*, August 19, 1888; Pollard, *Lee and His Lieutenants*, 546; Thomas G. Jones to father, October 21, 1864, Jones Papers; Stephens, *Intrepid Warrior*, 488; *ORS*, 7:612; George P. Hawes, "The Battle of Cedar Creek," *Confederate Veteran* 31 (May 1923):169; C. R. Hatton, "The Valley Campaign of 1864," *Confederate Veteran* 27 (May 1919):171.

17. Moore, "In Defence of General Early"; Early, *Memoir of the Last Year*, 86.

18. Mahr, *Cedar Creek*, 195, 199–200.

19. *OR*, 43(1):561; Early, *Memoir of the Last Year*, 88; Gordon, *Reminiscences*, 365.

20. Lt. Col. Phillip E. Davant, "Casualties in the 38th Georgia Regiment, Evans' Brigade," *Macon Daily Telegraph*, November 1, 1864; undated map of Cedar Creek drawn to accompany the official report of General Clement Evans, folder 13, box 3, Clement Evans–Robert G. Stephens Papers, Ms. 2946, University of Georgia Special Collections, Athens [repository hereafter cited as UGA]; Calvin D. Bowles, comp., *Atlas to Accompany the Official Records of the Union and Confederate Armies* (Washington: Government Printing Office, 1891–95), plate 82, no. 9; *ORS*, 7:610; Mahr, *Cedar Creek*, 250, 261. Only half of the 38th Georgia Infantry saw action on October 19, the other half "being on picket the night before, were deployed as skirmishers on the right to protect the flank of the army."

21. *OR*, 43(1):561; Early, *Memoir of the Last Year*, 89–90; Jedediah Hotchkiss to wife, October 21, 1864, frame 794, reel 4, Jedediah Hotchkiss Papers, Library of Congress, Washington [repository hereafter cited as LC]; Thomas H. Carter to Samuel J. C. Moore, October 15, 1889, folder 6, Samuel J. C. Moore Papers. For postwar criticism of Early's "inexcusable delay," see Jedediah Hotchkiss, *Virginia*, vol. 4 of *Confederate Military History*, ed. Clement A. Evans (Atlanta: Confederate Publishing Com-

pany, 1899), 508. In *Reminiscences*, Gordon unfairly claimed that Early's concern for the right flank of his final line was unwarranted (*Reminiscences*, 344).

22. Richard Waldrop to father, October 21, 1864, Richard Waldrop Papers, Southern Historical Collection, Wilson Library, University of North Carolina, Chapel Hill [repository hereafter cited as SHC]; George B. Hamilton to W. T. Sutherlin, January 4, 1865, Sutherlin Papers, SHC.

23. Robert T. Myers diary, October 22, 1864, Museum of the Confederacy, Richmond, Va. [repository hereafter cited as MOC]; Mahr, *Cedar Creek*, 426–27. The other eyewitnesses included Robert B. Winston of Kirkpatrick's battery, commissary sergeant James R. Sheldon of Bryan's brigade, and Capt. George T. McGhee, quartermaster of Humphreys's brigade.

24. Stephens, *Intrepid Warrior*, 483; Bradwell, "Battle of Cedar Creek," 411. For other accounts from Gordon's division that mention plundering, see Nichols, *Soldier's Story*, 195; John H. Worsham, *One of Jackson's Foot Cavalry* (1912; reprint, Jackson, Tenn.: McCowat-Mercer Press, 1964), 177; William E. Trahern, *William Eustace Trahern: An Autobiography, September 21, 1926* (privately printed, 1993), 48. Despite the frank admission of plundering at Cedar Creek by George W. Nichols, John B. Gordon endorsed *Soldier's Story* as "a simple recital of facts connected with our great civil war" (Nichols, *Soldier's Story*, vi).

25. *ORS*, 7:607–8, 610; Thomas G. Jones to John W. Daniel, December 25, 1904, Jones Papers; *OR*, 43(1):563; Early, *Memoir of the Last Year*, 93; Gordon, *Reminiscences*, 346. Early told Lee on October 21 that the final, decisive Federal attack at Cedar Creek had been a "demonstration, hoping to protect his stores, &c. at Winchester."

26. Gordon, *Reminiscences*, 347–48; *ORS*, 7:608; Moore, "In Defense of General Early." For a critical account of the supposedly feeble resistance put up by Terry's brigade, see Henry Robinson Berkeley, *Four Years in the Confederate Horse Artillery: The Diary of Private Henry Robinson Berkeley*, ed. William H. Runge (Chapel Hill: University of North Carolina Press for the Virginia Historical Society, 1961), 106. For Early's ignorance of events unfolding at this time on his left flank, see Daniel A. Wilson Jr. to "My Dear Col," October 21, 1864, Beverly R. Welford Papers, VHS.

27. Alexander S. Baird to mother, October 22, 1864, bound volume no. 334, Fredericksburg and Spotsylvania National Military Park, Fredericksburg, Va. Thomas G. Jones claimed after the war that the Federals penetrated a gap left when Gordon ordered "two regiments out of his left brigade" to support several artillery pieces posted "in a little hollow near and a little in rear of our [left] flank" (*ORS*, 7:611).

28. *ORS*, 7:608; *OR*, 43(1):310; Stephens, *Intrepid Warrior*, 488. Evans believed that the Federal attack could have been repulsed if the main Confederate battle line had extended an additional four hundred yards westward (*ORS*, 7:608).

29. Handwritten speech by Clement A. Evans on the back of Jubal A. Early, *Soldiers of the Army of the Valley . . .* (n.p., 1864), MOC; John F. Charlton diary, October 19, 1864, copy in possession of Robert E. L. Krick; Gussie Reese, ed., *This They Remembered, 1861–1865* (Washington, Ga.: Washington Publishing Company, 1965), 108; Thomas G. Jones to John W. Daniel, December 26, 1905, Leigh-Peters Collection.

Weariness and exhaustion probably contributed to the collapse of Gordon's division; the men "had been marching from sundown the evening before, been up all night, and . . . been ordered to leave their canteens behind" (Jones to Daniel, December 26, 1905).

30. "Another Statement of the Battle of Strasburg," *Richmond Dispatch*, October 29, 1864; Gordon, *Reminiscences*, 348; Thomas G. Jones to Daniel, December 25, 1904, Jones Papers; Mahr, *Cedar Creek*, 298.

31. *ORS*, 7: 608–9, 611; Nichols, *Soldier's Story*, 196; Mahr, *Cedar Creek*, 310; "Report of casualties in Gordon's Division in engagement at Cedar Creek . . . October 19, 1864," box 3, Evans-Stephens Papers. For a sarcastic statement by Early regarding the relatively light casualties in Gordon's division compared to other Confederate units at Cedar Creek, see Early, *Memoir of the Last Year*, 93.

32. *OR*, 43(1):560–63.

33. Early, *"Soldiers of the Army of the Valley"*; Stephens, *Intrepid Warrior*, 490, 493. Early's address appeared in broadside form and in newspapers across the Confederacy.

34. For newspaper references to plundering, see "The Valley," *Richmond Daily Examiner*, October 24, 1864; "The Late Fight in the Valley," *Richmond Whig*, October 25, 1864; "The Battle of Strasburg," *Richmond Dispatch*, October 27, 1864; "The War News," *Richmond Daily Examiner*, October 27, 1864; Asa Tennet, "Another Statement of the Battle of Strasburg," *Richmond Dispatch*, October 29, 1864; "A Great Defect," *Charleston Mercury*, November 2, 1864.

35. "The War News," *Richmond Daily Examiner*, October 27, 1864; P., "Maj. Gen. John B. Gordon," *Macon Daily Telegraph and Confederate*, December 21, 1864. See also Gamma, "Our Richmond Correspondence," *Mobile Advertiser and Register*, November 6, 1864; P. W. A., "Army Correspondence of the Savannah Republican," *Charleston Daily Courier*, November 2, 1864.

36. Argus, October 21, 1864, *Richmond Daily Enquirer*, October 27, 1864; Thomas G. Jones to John W. Daniel, December 25, 1904, Jones Papers; Stephens, *Intrepid Warrior*, 493. Thomas G. Jones, who identified Argus as Frank Markoe, stated that Early believed Argus was Maj. Robert W. Hunter of Gordon's staff.

37. Jubal Early to Alexander R. Boteler, October 31, 1864, Chicago Historical Society.

38. Oscar Hinrichs diary, October 28, 1864; Stephens, *Intrepid Warrior*, 491.

39. Thomas G. Jones to John W. Daniel, December 25, 1904, Jones Papers; Hotchkiss, *Make Me a Map*, 241. Gordon admitted in his *Reminiscences* that "there were a number of strongly controverted points" between him and Early on October 28, but he did not go into detail about them (*Reminiscences*, 357, 360–61).

40. Thomas G. Jones to John W. Daniel, December 25, 1904, Jones Papers. For accounts that mention the wagon appropriated by Gordon, see Robert T. Myers diary, October 22, 1864; Mahr, *Cedar Creek*, 426–27. If true, these circumstances would explain the accounts of soldiers who saw the captured wagon supposedly appropriated by Gordon for his headquarters.

41. Thomas G. Jones to John W. Daniel, December 25, 1904, Jones Papers; Stephens, *Intrepid Warrior*, 492, 497.

42. Jubal Early to Alexander R. Boteler, October 31, 1864, Chicago Historical Society; *OR*, 43(1):560–61; Early, *Memoir of the Last Year*, 93; Hotchkiss, *Make Me a Map*, 241; Jubal A. Early, *Letter from Lieutenant-General J. A. Early Asking Further Enquiry into the Causes of the Recent Reverses in the Valley of Virginia. Headquarters Valley District, November 28, 1864* (Richmond, Va.: n.p., 1865).

43. John B. Gordon to George F. Holmes, December 29, 1870, George F. Holmes Papers, vol. 1, LC; Stephens, ed., *Intrepid Warrior*, 497; Robert E. Lee to John B. Gordon, January 8, 1867, folder 4, box 5, John B. Gordon Papers, UGA; John B. Gordon to Robert E. Lee, February 6, 1868, Lee Headquarters Papers, Mss 3L515a603, VHS; Gordon, *Reminiscences*, 332–33, 368. Gordon's official report of Cedar Creek, which he had completed by November 5, 1864, has never appeared in print and is not in the collection of his personal papers at the University of Georgia. In response to a January 1867 request from Robert E. Lee for copies of official reports from the final year of the war, Gordon answered that he had "not been able to recover" his reports covering the 1864 Valley campaign. In *Reminiscences*, Gordon intimated that his Cedar Creek report might not have been forwarded by Early to Lee or that it might have been lost when Lee's "official papers were captured" (*Reminiscences*, 333).

44. Moore, "In Defence of General Early"; "Flanking 'Little Phil,'" *Boston Herald*, August 19, 1888. Even though Gordon may have spoken publicly about Cedar Creek for the first time in 1888, his version of events had been in print for some time, as may be seen in an 1870 biographical sketch in Pollard, *Lee and His Lieutenants*, 546. For Gordon's influence on Pollard, see John B. Gordon to Rev. J. W. Jones, February 10, 1867, item #132, *Remember When Auctions Catalog No. 48*, May 21, 2000.

45. Jubal Early to John B. Gordon, September 12, 1888, Jubal A. Early Papers, LC; Moore, "In Defense of General Early."

46. Holmes Conrad to Jubal Early, June 27, Lunsford Lomax to Jubal Early, September 19, 1888, Jubal A. Early Papers.

47. Moore, "In Defence of General Early." Gordon's silence when questioned about Early's sobriety at Cedar Creek particularly incensed Moore.

48. Gordon, *Reminiscences*, 355. For an excellent analysis of Gordon's *Reminiscences*, see Eckert, *Gordon*, 331–35.

49. Gordon, *Reminiscences*, 355, 360–68, 370.

50. John B. Gordon to Thomas G. Jones, June 11, 1902, Thomas G. Jones to John W. Daniel, February 29, 1904, Jones Papers; Thomas G. Jones to John B. Gordon, November 10, 1903, folder 3, box 4, Gordon Papers; "Eloquent Orators Tell of Gordon's Brave Deeds on Fields of Battle and of His Private Life," undated newspaper clipping in box 10, ibid. For numerous glowing newspaper reviews of *Reminiscences*, see clippings in folder 3, box 12, ibid.

51. John B. Gordon to Clement Evans, August 7 [no year given, but prior to 1899], folder 10, Evans-Stephens Papers; Stephens, *Intrepid Warrior*, 482–83, 491; handwritten speech by Evans on the back of Early, *Soldiers of the Army of the Valley*, MOC.

52. Gordon, *Reminiscences*, 361, 365; Clement Evans to J. S. McNeilly, November 23, 1904, box 21, John W. Daniel Papers Acc. 158, Special Collections, Alderman Library, University of Virginia, Charlottesville. Evans wrote in 1904 that he had resented

Early's official charge that defeat at Cedar Creek "was due to straggling, plundering, and misconduct" and that Early had been "misinformed" in this matter.

53. John W. Daniel to Robert D. Johnston, July 22, 1905, copy of original in possession of Gary W. Gallagher. For other criticisms of Gordon's *Reminiscences*, see Y. J. Pope to John W. Daniel, March 14, 1905, and J. S. McNeilly to Y. J. Pope, box 21, Daniel Papers Acc. 158; M. R. Tunno to Samuel J. C. Moore, January 1904, folder 6, Moore Papers.

54. Gordon, *Reminiscences*, 370–71.

55. *OR*, 43(1):561–63.

56. *OR*, 43(1):563; Thomas G. Jones to John W. Daniel, December 25, 1904, Jones Papers; Hotchkiss, *Make Me a Map*, 240.

WILLIAM W. BERGEN

The Other Hero of Cedar Creek

The "Not Specially Ambitious" Horatio G. Wright

Our truest, bravest heart is gone,
And we remember well
The bitter anguish of that day
When noble Sedgwick fell.
But there is still another left,
To lead us to the fight,
And with a hearty three time three
We'll cheer our gallant Wright.
— *God Bless the Old Sixth Corps*

ew know that Washington, D.C.'s Memorial Bridge spanning the Potomac River symbolizes reconciliation between North and South. Completed in 1932, the elegantly arched span links the Confederate states with the Federal capital. Those crossing from Virginia approach the Lincoln Memorial head on. Those leaving Washington glimpse Arlington House, once Gen. Robert E. Lee's home. Linked forever, then, are Lincoln and Lee, the two towering figures on their respective sides.[1]

This intentional juxtaposition reflects the emerging national consensus first seen in the 1890s. As the war's passions cooled, as veterans aged and their numbers dwindled, as new issues demanded attention, the nation put aside, and papered over, the past. By the time the bridge was completed, even Arlington cemetery, the graveyard founded in 1864 by Union authorities on Lee's lands to ensure that he would never again live there, had spawned symbols of reconciliation. The most prominent of these, a thirty-two-foot-high ornate Confederate monument surrounded by more than 400 graves of those who wore the gray, would have astounded the hardened U.S. officers who established the cemetery.[2]

Still, reminders of the war's intensity crowd the view. Challenging the spirit of consensus are two massive monuments visible on the hillside just below Arlington House's portico. Both mark graves of Union generals who did much to defeat Lee and his army. On one monument, one can easily read the word "SHERIDAN" in metal letters embedded in the stone. A bronze, flag-draped medallion displays Gen. Philip H. Sheridan's likeness, familiar to students of the Civil War. The monument opposite it, equal in size but of a different shape, is adorned only by a bas-relief portrait depicting a general even Civil War scholars would be hard-pressed to identify. To find whose grave the monument marks, visitors must brush aside overgrown shrubbery to read the plaque on its back. Only then does one learn that there lies Maj. Gen. Horatio Gouverneur Wright and that veterans of the Sixth Corps erected the monument to honor their former commander.[3]

Wright's remains resting near Sheridan's suggests his close association with the hero of Cedar Creek. While heading the Department of the Ohio, Wright, recognizing Sheridan's worth, cosigned a September 12, 1862, telegram to the War Department that prompted Sheridan's promotion to brigadier general. "We have no good generals here and are badly in want of them," he wired. "Sheridan is worth his weight in gold. Will you not try and have him made a brigadier at once? It will put us in good shape." Wright later served loyally under his former subordinate during the 1864 Shenandoah Valley campaign, at the battle of Sailor's Creek, and in postwar Texas. Both men would reach the top of their army branches, Wright retiring as chief of engineers the same year that Sheridan became commanding general of the army.[4]

Although his monument ranks with Sheridan's, Wright's renown does not. A book about the Civil War has been published for every day since the end of the conflict, yet not a single biography, monograph, or article has focused on Wright.[5] The breadth of his war experience invites attention. Wright fought the Civil War as an engineer, as a War Department insider, as a recruiting officer, as a general in amphibious operations in the Deep South, as a major department head in the Midwest, and as a senior infantry commander through the bloody final two years of the Army of the Potomac's existence. He watched the war come from his top staff position in the War Department, guided troops in the first battle of Bull Run, played a major role in turning back Gen. Braxton Bragg's 1862 invasion of Kentucky, fought at Gettysburg, and saw the war end at Appomattox Court House. He was captured once early in the war and

Horatio G. Wright's monu-
ment at Arlington National
Cemetery in 2002, with the
portico of the Custis house
in the background. Collection of William W. Bergen.

twice wounded while serving as a major general. At the July 12, 1864, battle of
Fort Stevens, Wright's thoughtless invitation for Abraham Lincoln to join him
on the parapet nearly resulted in a disaster for the Union cause. Twice, at Rappahannock Station in 1863 and at Petersburg in 1865, he directly commanded
troops that broke formidable Army of Northern Virginia fortifications and completely routed the defenders, a claim few generals could make. Most striking,
Wright's personal heroism and sound decisions under the most confusing of
circumstances enabled Sheridan to win his signal victory at the battle of Cedar
Creek.

Wright's obscurity becomes more curious given that his contemporaries described him with superlatives. Within a month of starting his 1864 campaign
against the Army of Northern Virginia, Lt. Gen. Ulysses S. Grant wrote that
Wright was "one of the most meritorious officers in the service and with opportunity will demonstrate his fitness for any position." To Maj. Gen. George G.
Meade, Wright was an "excellent officer." A Sixth Corps surgeon, George Stevens, dedicated the second edition of his book, *Three Years in the Sixth Corps*,
to Wright, describing him as a "Brave, Honored, and Able Leader." Wright was
"distinguished both for gallantry and ability" according to Col. Elisha Hunt
Rhodes of the 2nd Rhode Island Volunteer Infantry.[6]

When Wright is mentioned in the literature, writers often muddle his career and identity. In *The Generalship of Ulysses S. Grant* (1929), the distinguished British military historian J. F. C. Fuller confuses H. G. Wright with George Wright, a general who spent the Civil War in command of the Department of the Pacific. The index of Clifford Dowdey's widely read *Lee's Last Campaign, The Story of Lee and His Men Against Grant—1864* (1960) confuses Horatio Wright with Ambrose R. Wright, a Confederate general. In James E. Taylor's invaluable sketchbook chronicling the 1864 Valley campaign, the author mistakes Wright's middle name as "Gates," an error repeated in John Henry Cramer's *Lincoln Under Enemy Fire* (1948), a study of events at Fort Stevens. Curious errors occurred even in Wright's lifetime. The authors of *The Life of Gen. Philip H. Sheridan, Its Romance and Reality* (1888), published shortly after Sheridan's death, identify Wright variously as "Horatio J." and "Marcus D."[7] Wright remains invisible even among leading Civil War figures born in Connecticut. An 1869 book that celebrated Connecticut's contributions to victory published sixty portraits of prominent civilian and military leaders, yet Wright's visage was omitted in favor of those who achieved far less. The authors praised Wright as a "brave, skillful, and effective fighter" but jumbled the details of his career. Time would not correct the omission; a centennial-era book on Connecticut's favorite sons dwells on lesser generals.[8]

Wright would always claim Connecticut as home, writing late in life that he was "more attached to Clinton [Connecticut] than any other place in our extended country." He descended from Benjamin Wright, a Roman Catholic and a soldier who settled in Clinton as early as 1660. There Horatio Wright was born March 6, 1820, to a family that had gained prominence in exporting lumber to the West Indies in exchange for sugar, salt, molasses, and rum. In his fourteenth year, he enrolled at the Norwich Academy (now Norwich University), a military school founded by Alden Partridge, a graduate and former superintendent of West Point.[9]

Wright entered the U.S. Military Academy on July 1, 1837. One of his references praised him as "a young man of talents, of an amiable disposition & first rate character, he is esteemed & beloved by all who know him." In his application papers, Wright described himself as five feet nine, free from any infirmity, able to read and write, and to "perform with facility all that is required in arithmetic." In the September 1838 roll of cadets, Wright ranked eighth, but he rose to second by graduation. He finished first in his class in artillery and second in engineering but won his most outstanding marks in conduct, leading the class in the annual ratings in 1839, 1840, and 1841. Although less celebrated than other classes in the same decade, Wright's peers provided competition for honors. Of the thirty-seven members of the West Point Class of 1841 still living in 1861, twenty-one became general officers in either the Union or Confederate armies, including Don Carlos Buell, Robert S. Garnett, Josiah Gorgas, Nathaniel Lyon, and John F. Reynolds.[10]

Commissioned a second lieutenant of engineers, Wright became an assistant to the Board of Engineers, followed by two years as an instructor at West Point, first of French and then of engineering. On August 11, 1842, he married Louisa Marcella Bradford of Culpeper, Virginia. Louisa's mother was a member of the Slaughter family, a clan that included several civic and military leaders in Virginia's Piedmont. Her father's family traced its lines to early settlers, including the Bradfords of Plymouth Colony, and Louisa grew up in a household whose wealth included several dozen slaves. In his years at the academy as a leading student and a professor, Wright became acquainted with dozens of those who would lead forces on both sides in the Civil War, yet no firsthand recollection of him during those years has been found. This pattern of achieving prominence and yet escaping notice would persist throughout his life.[11]

Early in his career, Wright attracted the attention of chief of engineers colonel Joseph S. Totten. Pursuant to Totten's exacting instructions, he performed detailed experiments with various mortars to be used in constructing fortifications. The results pleased the chief, who in 1845 praised Wright's study as "by far the best book yet written on mortars; and the publication of it would confer a very great service on the act of building." That same year, Wright accompanied the secretary of war on an inspection trip, another high-visibility assignment for the twenty-five-year-old second lieutenant.[12]

Unlike most of his West Point classmates, Wright saw no action in the Mexican War. When hostilities broke out in 1846, he was serving as superintending engineer on the first construction phases of Fort Jefferson, on Dry Tortugas, Florida, an island located sixty miles west of the Florida Keys. Although an important assignment, the task was lonely and daunting — the site on which the fort was built rises barely three feet above sea level. Fort Jefferson would become the largest and most remote of the masonry coastal fortifications built during the antebellum years. Slaves performed most of the labor. Wright's many problems included mysterious fevers, escaped slaves, hurricanes, scarcity of fresh water, lack of supplies of any kind, and periodic shortfalls in congressional appropriations. Although Fort Jefferson's foundations barely showed above water by 1856, the fact that foundations existed at all showed considerable progress given the difficulties of obtaining materials and labor as well as the state of engineering knowledge and technology. The effort was wasted: Wright spent ten years overseeing construction of a citadel rendered obsolete before its completion by the development of rifled cannon.[13]

Following the extraordinarily long tour of duty in Florida, Wright spent the six years before the Civil War as an assistant to Totten in Washington. He worked closely with top military officials, including Bvt. Lt. Gen. Winfield Scott and, during 1856–57, Secretary of War Jefferson Davis. Wright's duties included replying to congressional inquiries, researching the requirements and limitations of law, compiling estimates requested by members of Congress, corresponding about appointments to West Point, and making recommendations on congressional appropriations.[14]

On the eve of the Civil War, as Washington officials temporized about resupplying or reinforcing Fort Sumter, Wright read dispatches that passed between President James Buchanan's administration and army officers based in Charleston. He tried to focus attention on the urgent request for instructions from Capt. John G. Foster, a fellow engineer stationed at Fort Sumter. Wright watched carefully the actions of Adj. Gen. Samuel Cooper and Secretary of War John B. Floyd, both of whom would soon become Confederate generals. On a December 2, 1860, letter from Foster asking for arms and ammunition for his civilian employees, Wright wrote a meticulous record of what had transpired: "Handed to adjutant-general and by him laid before the Secretary of War on the sixth of December. Returned by adjutant-general on the seventh. Action deferred for the present. See Captain Foster's letter of December 4." Although Wright failed to obtain a decision from his superiors, he corresponded separately with Foster. In a February 25, 1861, dispatch, Foster thanked Wright for the "interesting private information."[15]

Winfield Scott's regard for Wright, together with his experience in coastal installations, probably led to his playing a key role in one of the United States government's first moves against the Confederacy. Six days after the surrender of Fort Sumter, Scott ordered Wright to assume command of the army forces in a seaborne expedition to the Gosport navy yard at Norfolk. Federal authorities hoped to save this key base for the Union or, barring that, to destroy the yard to prevent anything useful falling into the enemy's hands. The expedition arrived to find all the ships except the USS *Cumberland* already scuttled and a yard superintendent unwilling or unable to defend the installation.[16]

Orders to destroy the yard brought Wright under fire for the first time in his military career. He and naval commander John Rodgers were assigned to blow up the yard's dry dock. After lighting the fuses to a ton of gunpowder, Wright

Maj. Gen. Horatio Gouverneur Wright. This photograph, taken in May 1865, shows the scar on Wright's left cheek from his wound at the battle of Cedar Creek as well as a Sixth Corps commemorative ribbon on his uniform. Library of Congress.

and Rogers began rowing a small boat to the safety of the *U.S.S. Pawnee*. Confederate militia fired on them, however, and forced their surrender. The two officers were handed over to Virginia authorities who arranged for a prisoner exchange, and Wright soon returned to Washington.[17]

In May 1861, Wright served as an aide in an excursion by Federal forces to seize Arlington Heights and Alexandria, Virginia. On a hill just west of Alexandria, he selected the site for Fort Ellsworth and supervised the start of its construction. Other assignments in erecting Washington's defenses continued into July. On July 21, Wright joined the march to Manassas as chief engineer for Brig.

Gen. Samuel P. Heintzelman's Third Division of Brig. Gen. Irvin McDowell's army in northern Virginia. Wright and two fellow engineers directed the march of a flanking column to cross Blackburn's Ford over Bull Run. Heintzelman cited Wright in his report as one of several officers who performed in an "able and fearless manner."[18]

On September 14, Wright was appointed brigadier general of volunteers and assigned the next day to command a brigade then forming in Washington. His promotion was prompted by Brig. Gen. Joseph F. K. Mansfield, a fellow engineer then in charge of the Washington defenses. In a September 11 memo to Secretary of War Simon Cameron, Lincoln wrote, "This day Gen. Mansfield personally appears, and urges that Horatio G. Wright, of Topographical Engineers, be a Brigadier General of Volunteers, as a Connecticut appointment. Gen. Totten concurs, as Gen. Mansfield says." Totten did concur. "Wright has been constantly employed in a way to develop a bright intelligence, sound judgment, and an ever-ready earnestness and zeal," Totten had written in an unaddressed May 5, 1861, letter apparently designed to help Wright win a promotion. "No one is better qualified for regimental command," Totten continued, and Wright was "distinguished for energy, efficiency & every other soldiery quality."[19]

Wright performed a variety of duties between the autumn of 1861 and the summer of 1862. In late October 1861, his command sailed with an amphibious force that seized Port Royal, South Carolina. His soldiers participated in a number of actions along the coast over the next several months, including the series of nearly bloodless captures of Fernandina, Jacksonville, and St. Augustine, each a Florida rail center or harbor. The June 16, 1862, battle of Secessionville — a Union defeat suffered in the first attempt to seize Charleston — marked the only heavy fighting for Wright and his troops. His superior cited him for "gallantry and good conduct" at Secessionville, and Charles Francis Adams Jr., a cavalry officer at the battle, wrote to his father that during the fight Wright appeared "a little excited at times but growing genial and kindly as the fire got hot." His regiments were soon merged with a force operating in southeastern Virginia, and Wright journeyed north in July to assist New England governors in speeding new regiments to Washington. He had completed a similar assignment a year earlier, making him a natural choice for this duty. Less than two weeks before the battle of Second Bull Run, John Pope requested Wright's services as a division commander, but Wright was by then reporting from Boston on Massachusetts's regiments and their progress in mustering into Federal service.[20]

The first year of the war had brought Wright a general's commission and favorable notice. Naval captain Samuel F. Du Pont, soon to command the expedition to Port Royal, met Wright in July 1861 and wrote that he "should be made a colonel and have the first military authority." In October 1861, the 2nd Connecticut Infantry's correspondent told the readership of the *Hartford Evening Press* that the new commander of their brigade "has sustained a high reputation in the regular army." Overall, however, Wright remained unknown. As would be seen throughout his career, he had performed competently but always in a manner that garnered little notice. Nor would he attract much attention to himself; Wright detested the "notoriety" that came with a "love for newspaper fame."[21]

On August 16, 1862, General in Chief Henry W. Halleck summoned Wright to Washington, and within the week he traveled west to head a reorganized and expanded Department of the Ohio with the acting rank of major general. His new command included Ohio, Michigan, Indiana, Illinois, Wisconsin, and the part of Kentucky east of the Tennessee River. Upon becoming general in chief in July, Halleck had found that the administration and the Congress were dissatisfied with Maj. Gen. Don Carlos Buell, commander of the Army of the Ohio. Kentucky's unreliable Unionist government, trying to assert itself in a state with divided loyalties, also concerned the administration. The strategic stakes were high. As Lincoln was said to have remarked, "I hope to have God on my side, but I must have Kentucky."[22]

Wright made an unlikely choice for such a key command. He had compiled a solid but unremarkable war record, lacked high-level political connections, and remained largely unknown. Though they had never served together, Halleck knew Wright as an underclassman at West Point, as a fellow engineer, and as a top West Point graduate. Winfield Scott, who had named Halleck as best suited to succeed him as general in chief, in turn thought highly of Wright, once calling him an "engineering officer of high science and judgment."[23]

Wiring Washington from Cincinnati on August 31, Wright told Halleck that he had found "matters here in a very bad condition." Two Confederate armies had invaded Kentucky and by early September threatened Cincinnati and Louisville, creating an atmosphere bordering on hysteria. Alarmed municipal and state officials — and Wright's subordinates — pleaded for troops to defend their localities and did not hesitate to contact the War Department or Lincoln when they did not receive satisfaction from the department commander. Friction with elected officials began soon after Wright's arrival in Cincinnati. Ohio governor David Tod wired the secretary of war on September 10 that he possessed the "fullest confidence" in Wright but expressed concern that the general had "some difficulty with our Indiana friends." Two days later, Tod reaffirmed his "entire confidence in Major-General Wright's ability for the duty of the position he fills. His forces, both officers and men, are extremely raw, but if not interfered with I have no doubt he will efficiently perform his whole duty." Struggling to make do with underequipped, undisciplined militia and untrained green regiments rushed to the front, Wright also endured unrealistic expectations of what he could accomplish with his limited resources.[24]

Wright assigned field control to Maj. Gen. Lewis (Lew) Wallace, who had been without a command since his failure to march to the front on the first day of the battle of Shiloh. Wright worked to check the two-pronged rebel advance by fortifying Cincinnati and moving troops to the most threatened points. He also cooperated with his classmate, General Buell, forwarding troops to his Army of the Ohio. Having successfully petitioned for Philip Sheridan to be promoted, Wright wired Buell to ask if he "could spare me General Sheridan for the cavalry force I hope to raise? I need him much." There is no record of a reply, but Sheridan was soon named commander of an infantry division in Buell's army.[25]

Confederate armies began withdrawing from Kentucky after the battle of Perryville on October 8, 1862. Wallace and other officers took credit for a successful defense of Cincinnati, and Phil Sheridan won renown at the battle of Perryville. Wright, whose efforts had helped make both successes possible, received little notice. The departmental commander wrote to Halleck on October 25 that the Confederate army had left Kentucky and that a large concentration of Union forces remained. As the crisis faded, Wright turned to more routine administrative duties.[26]

Wright began his third month as departmental commander under attack from a new direction. "I ought . . . to inform you that a committee of gentlemen from the West visited the War Department some days ago to ask your removal," wired Halleck on November 18. The committee contended that Wright pursued "too milk and water a policy toward the rebels in Kentucky." One specification noted that Wright had revoked "Buell's Orders, No. 49," the key provision of which required that "all persons who have actively aided or abetted in the invasion of Kentucky by rebel troops within the last three months will be sent to Vicksburg and forbidden to return to Kentucky." Wright replied on November 21, explaining at great length the obvious difficulty in carrying out Buell's directive. Asking that he be relieved if his actions did not meet with Washington's approval, Wright vowed to continue to do his best and not be influenced by those who demanded his removal "without even asking what my policy was or seeking to ascertain whether their impressions were true or not." Halleck replied that Wright's explanations were "perfectly satisfactory." He had simply passed on the complaints about Wright, said Halleck, who closed with a warning about listening too much to Kentucky's "Union men." On his part, Wright showed little skill in cultivating political support. When former senator and cabinet member Thomas Ewing (William Tecumseh Sherman's stepfather) wrote describing the havoc Confederate guerrillas who crossed the Ohio River caused, Wright replied that such small bands were thieves and that the civil authorities ought to deal with them. "The citizens living upon the border must aid in their own protection," he curtly wrote Ewing.[27]

Wright suffered criticism from more than local delegations. Soon after Wright reached Cincinnati, Ohio senator John Sherman (General Sherman's influential brother), wrote to Secretary of the Treasury Salmon P. Chase that Wright impressed him as "a good soldier — but a very careful — prudent one. It is manifest he looks only to defensive warfare." Chase agreed and began maneuvering for Wright's replacement, as evidenced by a letter from Brig. Gen. James A. Garfield to his wife on December 26, 1862: "Mr. Chase told me a day or two ago that the Secretary of War said he was going to make me a Major General and give me General Wright's department with authority to go into East Tennessee and hold that count[r]y." Such an assignment probably would not occur, Garfield continued, because the "War Department will not hold one mind for a week."[28]

The effort to remove Wright bore fruit on March 12, 1863, when the Senate rejected his promotion to major general of volunteers by a vote of twenty to fifteen. Such a defeat was unusual, especially for a general of good character who had suffered no military defeats. A coalition of Radical Republicans from the Midwest and Northeast formed the majority; senators supporting the nomination included moderates and Democrats from Kentucky, Maryland, Connecticut, and Rhode Island, as well as New Jersey's newly elected senator, William Wright, a cousin of the nominee. No record of the debate exists, and it is unknown what factors figured into the Senate's action, but it nonetheless appears that the Senate majority believed Wright did not share their hard-line stance toward the prosecution of the war. To the Radicals, Wright may have resembled the recently dismissed Buell and Maj. Gen. George B. McClellan, conservative West Pointers noted for their lack of aggressiveness and Democratic political views at odds with the Republican agenda.[29]

Wright knew his nomination was in trouble because rumors of his replacement had reached the newspapers. He wired the War Department on March 15: "The recent action of the Senate, in refusing my confirmation as major-general . . . can be looked upon only as a condemnation of my administration of the affairs of this department, and will naturally occasion in the public mind a want of confidence which will seriously impair my usefulness in my present position. In this view of the case, I feel bound to suggest to the military authorities at Washington my removal from this command." The next day, Maj. Gen. Ambrose E. Burnside — an Indiana native removed from command of the Army of the Potomac in January — was ordered to the Department of the Ohio.[30]

After briefly commanding the Louisville District, Wright returned east. The Senate action received little notice in Ohio and Kentucky newspapers, a reflection of Wright's low profile. The *Louisville Journal* editorialized briefly that "Kentucky will not refuse to be comforted" by the defeat. Assessments of Wright's tenure as department commander are few. An officer in one of the untrained Ohio regiments hurried to meet the threat posed by Bragg's invasion echoed common themes regarding Wright's wartime service. Describing Wright as a "cool, level-headed, faithful organizer," the soldier opined, "His administration of the short-lived Department of the Ohio will always remain a testimony of the highest soldierly steadfastness and remarkable executive ability" of one who lacked the "power to inspire men to supreme exertion." Wright left a lasting, albeit minor, mark on the region. Fort Wright, today a Kentucky suburb of Cincinnati, takes its name from a stronghold named for Wright in the defense line built in 1862.[31]

Following a vacation to the South Carolina coast in the company of his wife and John Hay, President Lincoln's secretary, Wright received orders in May 1863 to take command of the First Division in the Sixth Corps of the Army of the Potomac. He reported to Maj. Gen. John Sedgwick, the Sixth Corps chief, less than two weeks after the Chancellorsville campaign. The force Wright joined ranked among the Union army's largest and best fighting units — well trained, well led, and well provisioned. The men of the Sixth Corps took pride in wearing the Greek cross identification badge on their caps.[32]

Horatio Wright's two-year association with the Sixth Corps produced most of what is known about him today. The artist and journalist James E. Taylor, who observed him during the 1864 Shenandoah Valley campaign, described Wright as having "a rounded face of florid hue with puffy cheeks and bulging forehead," brown curly hair, and a mustache and goatee of a lighter shade. Slightly above middle height and stout, he was characterized as courtly, formal, and kind. The most cited description came from a subordinate, Brig. Gen. Joseph Warren Keifer. Wright's "characteristics as a soldier were of the unassuming, sturdy, solid kind — never pyrotechnic," Keifer recalled more than thirty-five years after they served together. "He was modest, and not specially ambitious."[33]

Yet descriptions remain scarce, and few comrades seem to have known Wright well. Sixth Corps rank and file had much to say about their superiors — especially Sedgwick and Sheridan — but seldom mentioned Wright in letters and diaries. When accounts do refer to him, they rarely include much detail. Typical of such chronicles are letters written by Lewis Bissell, a private in the 2nd Connecticut Heavy Artillery. He left a vivid initial impression of Sheridan as "a small man with black beard and hair and two of the blackest and sharpest eyes you ever saw in anyone's head." Yet Bissell's first mention of Wright — "I have seen Maj. Gen. Wright who is in command of our corps" — lacks any details whatsoever, and his other references to the general provide no further illumination.[34]

Though Keifer thought him "ideally suited to command infantry," Wright appears to have seen himself as an engineer doing his duty as a soldier before returning to quieter work. Wright's high standing in the Engineering Corps finds confirmation in his being ordered to West Point as superintendent in November 1863 — a posting rescinded three days later. Why the reversal occurred is unknown, but Wright may have protested the order, not wishing to return to a staff command while armies remained in the field. Moreover, while the superintendent's post invariably went to an engineer of promise, most officers considered it more trouble than the honor was worth. Wright's engineering skills remained in demand in Washington, and he spent the early months of 1864 there serving on a board studying the nation's seacoast fortifications, a curious assignment in the middle of the war.[35]

The Sixth Corps saw limited action during the Gettysburg campaign, though its march of more than thirty miles all through the night on July 1 and into the following day brought reinforcements to the Army of the Potomac at a critical time. Just after Lee's army escaped across the Potomac, Wright wrote the first of only two known surviving wartime letter to his wife. The lengthy July 18 missive, addressed to "My darling Wife," shows that Wright shared much with his Virginia-born spouse. "Our corps is now here waiting our turn for crossing the ever memorable Potomac," Wright wrote. "We shall probably be again on the sacred soil of Va before your good people in Washington have your breakfast tomorrow." The detailed letter reflects the caution that Wright and the army's high command showed in looking for a way to bring Lee to bay. "In an equal fight I have no doubt we could whip him [Lee] not withstanding his superior numbers," he wrote, overestimating the size of the Confederate army, "but give him the advantage of position, in addition, and the chances are largely against us."[36]

As acting commander of the Sixth Corps, Wright earned a brevet promotion for seizing the Confederate fortified bridgehead at Rappahannock Station on November 7, 1863. After the inconclusive Mine Run campaign, the Army of the Potomac went into winter camp in the fields near Culpeper, an area Wright certainly knew well from visits to his wife's family. Residing there as a senior commander in the invading army, Wright must have found it awkward, especially as several in-laws fought for the South, including a cousin of his wife, James E. Slaughter, who became a brigadier general. Afton, the home of his brother-in-law, Slaughter S. Bradford, and formerly the residence of his wife's father, became a Federal headquarters whenever the army occupied the Culpeper vicinity. Mrs. Wright's relatives and their property thus received some protection, and Wright twice intervened when Slaughter Bradford was arrested as a possible spy. Perhaps he welcomed the respite provided by the temporary engineering duties in Washington.[37]

Wright's first extended engagement as division commander occurred during the May 5–6 battle of the Wilderness, where he accomplished little more than other generals who attempted to maneuver troops through the heavily wooded terrain. During the May 6 Confederate flank attack, Wright kept his division from panicking and helped contain damage done to the Union line. In the early evening of May 7, Sedgwick led the Sixth Corps out of the lines at the Wilderness as the armies moved toward the strategic crossroads at Spotsylvania Court House. Late on the next afternoon, Wright's jaded division joined the Fifth Corps in attacking lead elements of the Confederate army that blocked their way to the crossroads. The disjointed attacks failed and both sides began entrenching. The following day, May 9, a rebel sharpshooter killed Sedgwick near the front lines. One officer remembered it as "the saddest day the Sixth Corps ever knew." Wright had just left Sedgwick when word came of the latter's death, and he took command in his friend's place.[38]

Wright's permanent promotion to succeed Sedgwick was not at all certain. He was not the army's senior brigadier; even Brig. Gen. James B. Ricketts, a fellow Sixth Corps division head, outranked him. Moreover, promoting a general from another corps had been recently considered. In early April, Meade had contemplated transferring Sedgwick to head forces in the Shenandoah Valley and replacing him with Brig. Gen. John Gibbon of the Second Corps, perhaps the army's best division commander. That idea did not come to fruition, and

Gibbon remained a division commander for several months more. Sedgwick had made clear his preference for Wright to be his successor, and that probably sealed his promotion. On May 12, Meade recommended to Grant that Wright be promoted to major general, and Grant forwarded the recommendation to Washington. The Senate quickly approved Wright's nomination, and on May 16 he received permanent command of the Sixth Corps. Years later, a messenger from Grant recalled giving the news to Lincoln that Sedgwick had been killed. "General Wright must have that promotion," the courier recalled Lincoln saying: "We have not treated him fairly." Lincoln's statement may have referred to the administration's ineffective support for Wright as head of the Department of the Ohio.[39]

Wright earned a second brevet promotion for his actions at Spotsylvania, and he ably handled the Sixth Corps in a May 21 rear-guard action. He had been wounded on May 12 during the gruesome struggle at the "Bloody Angle." A shell exploded near him and his staff, the blast throwing Wright several feet and a shell fragment badly bruising his thigh. Wright remained in command, drawing the comment of a staff officer who found him "smiling away despite his bruises."[40]

The bloody Overland campaign cost the Sixth Corps dearly. The Wilderness and Spotsylvania together deprived it of more than a third of its strength, 43 percent of its officers, and Sedgwick. Like his fellow corps commanders, Wright compiled a mixed record at Spotsylvania, at Cold Harbor, in the movement across the James River, and during the opening weeks of the stalemate in the trenches of Petersburg. Days of solid achievement, such as the Sixth Corps' rapid march to Cold Harbor, were balanced by instances of failure, such as Wright's uncertain handling of the corps at the June 21–23 battle of Jerusalem Plank Road.[41]

Grant's coordinated spring offensive included an advance by a small Federal army up the Shenandoah Valley to threaten Confederate communications and deprive Lee of supplies from that fertile region. That force, ineptly commanded by Maj. Gen. Franz Sigel, marched south on the same day Grant crossed the Rapidan River en route to the Wilderness. Defeated by a Confederate army commanded by Maj. Gen. John C. Breckinridge at the May 15 battle of New Market, Sigel retreated back down the Valley. While Sigel's force regrouped, Breckinridge crossed most of his force over the Blue Ridge to reinforce Lee. Grant remained determined to seize the Valley, and by early June a new Union advance had brushed aside a small Confederate force at the battle of Piedmont and reached Staunton. Commanded by Maj. Gen. David Hunter, the Federals marched on to Lexington, then turned southeast toward Lynchburg, a strate-gic rail center.[42]

Lee countered this threat by dispatching Lt. Gen. Jubal A. Early and his Second Corps to Lynchburg. Early's timely arrival not only blocked Hunter, but also sent him retreating west into the mountains. With the Shenandoah Valley now clear of Yankees, Early's veterans marched north down the familiar hard surface of the Valley Turnpike, past the fields of their triumphs during Stonewall Jackson's 1862 Valley campaign. Grant did not know Early's corps had left the Petersburg front until the Confederates crossed the Potomac River in early July. With Early's little army threatening Washington and Baltimore, Grant sent the Sixth Corps north. The corps' location closest to the embarka-tion point made it the natural choice for the job. On July 6, the corps' Third Division, under Ricketts, steamed by water to Baltimore. Ricketts's men then sped westward by rail to form the bulk of General Lew Wallace's scratch force that, in the battle of the Monocacy on July 9, delayed Early's progress toward Washington for a day.[43]

Two days later, Wright and two divisions landed in Washington just in time to stop Early at Fort Stevens. Wright quickly sized up the Confederate threat as no more than a probing movement. Much of official Washington turned out to cheer the Union troops as they marched to the front lines north and west of the city. Lincoln, cabinet members, Mrs. Lincoln, Wright's wife, and members of Congress followed them, hoping to see a little of the war. On July 12, Wright ordered up a brigade to push the Confederate lines back.[44]

Other than his official reports and messages, Wright left only a few accounts of his wartime actions. The most complete of these outlined his role in nearly getting President Lincoln killed during the fighting at Fort Stevens. In an 1870 letter, Wright recalled that he had "thoughtlessly invited" Lincoln to watch his troops advance. "A moment after," Wright wrote, "I would have given much to have recalled my words." Lincoln took his place on the parapet, where he parried Wright's initial entreaties to get down, even after an officer standing near the president was wounded. The general opined that Lincoln retired after several anxious minutes only "in deference to my earnestly expressed wishes." Well into the twentieth century, Oliver Wendell Holmes, who in 1864 was a captain on Wright's staff and later would become a justice on the U.S. Supreme Court, said that he did not recognize the president and shouted, "Get down you damn fool!" Though that incident cannot be discounted entirely, the weight of evidence from other recollections suggests that Wright's account remains the more accurate description, and that Holmes's great story was just that.[45]

Grant named Wright to command a force to pursue Early as the Confederates withdrew from the capital's outskirts, crossed the Potomac, and falling back through Leesburg, Virginia, reconnected with their supply line from the Valley. The pursuing army at first included Wright's two Sixth Corps divisions and two divisions of the Nineteenth Corps sent from Louisiana, where they had fought in Maj. Gen. Nathaniel P. Banks's ill-fated Red River campaign. They would be joined later by some of David Hunter's troops, now returning from their roundabout retreat from Lynchburg. Grant's orders reflected conflicting aims, a confusion not helped by Henry Halleck, now Grant's Washington chief of staff, who conveyed and sometimes interpreted the commander in chief's intent. On July 12, Grant ordered that Wright "should push Early to the last moment, supplying himself from the country." Halleck told Wright on July 15 that Grant intended him to live off the land—an unlikely prospect for a cobbled-together army lacking sufficient cavalry and operating in the war-ravaged northern Virginia Piedmont—and that he was probably expected to exercise his own judgment. On July 16, Grant ordered Wright to return to Petersburg with his troops as soon as it became apparent that Early's Confederates were retreating. On July 22, Grant urged more aggressive action, wiring Halleck that Wright should venture south and destroy the railroads between Charlottesville and Gordonsville.[46]

Inadequate transport and insufficient—and to one infantryman, "unreliable"—cavalry hobbled the makeshift Union army's pursuit of Early, frustrating Grant's hopes of cutting off the Confederate army or destroying the railroads near Charlottesville. Poor intelligence prompted caution, as Halleck estimated the Confederate force at 40,000, a force considerably greater than that commanded by Wright and triple the enemy's actual strength. After a minor clash with Early at the battle of Cool Spring on July 18, Wright's force followed Early into the lower Valley. The Confederates appeared to be retreating south, apparently on their way back to Lee. Considering his mission accomplished, Wright marched his Sixth Corps back to Washington to sail again for Petersburg. His pursuit had lasted barely a week but proved hard on his men. Sixth Corps veterans recalled these hot and dusty July marches as among their most arduous and began to call themselves "Wright's Walkers" and "Wright's Cavalry." By the time the Sixth Corps reached Washington on July 23, Wright told Halleck that his men needed two days to refit themselves with, among other items, shoes. Discovering that Wright's Sixth Corps had departed from Virginia, Early turned around and on July 24 successfully attacked part of Hunter's force under Brig. Gen. George Crook at the second battle of Kernstown. The resulting Union rout opened the lower Valley again to invasion, and Early used the opportunity to recross the Potomac and send cavalry into Pennsylvania, where they burned the town of Chambersburg on July 30. The Sixth Corps, which was poised to embark for Petersburg, marched instead into Maryland.[47]

One by one, Federal commanders in the Valley had come to grief: Sigel at New Market in May, Hunter near Lynchburg in June, and Crook at Kernstown in July. During his brief time in the Valley, Wright had fared little better. One veteran nonetheless thought criticism of Wright unjust, writing that he "had an army, but a large part of it was unwieldy, and could not be formed into an offensive weapon in the few days of hasty marching. Great allowance must be made for the heterogeneous and extemporized mass which had thus been brought together." Thus hampered, Wright had acted with characteristic quiet competence but demonstrated little instinct for aggressive warfare or for independent command. Like so many Army of the Potomac generals before him, he proved unable to overcome logistical and intelligence challenges so that he could bring his greater numbers to bear. This continued failure prompted Grant to assign Philip Sheridan to command the newly created Middle Department.[48]

Wright's Sixth Corps, along with two of the Army of the Potomac's cavalry divisions, formed the backbone of Sheridan's new Army of the Shenandoah. Other infantry units included Crook's force, now designated the Eighth Corps, and the two divisions of the Nineteenth Corps commanded by Maj. Gen. William H. Emory. Throughout August, the opposing armies maneuvered in the lower Valley, each trying to catch the other at a disadvantage. Not until September 19 did Sheridan finally commit to engage the enemy on the field that would become known as the Opequon or Third Winchester.[49]

Sheridan planned for a rapid advance against a segment of Early's army, hoping to defeat it before "Old Jube" could concentrate his scattered divisions. He predicated this plan on the Sixth and Nineteenth corps marching quickly through the long, narrow, and steep Berryville Canyon, located just east of Winchester, to support a cavalry division that would lead the advance. Recognizing that moving more than 24,000 infantry on a single road would cause problems, Sheridan ordered that "all regimental and other wagons that will inconvenience the quick movement of troops" be kept out of the line of march. The army commander, apparently intending to lead from the front, further directed that the Sixth Corps would spearhead the advance and Emory would follow Wright's orders during the march. Despite measures taken to expedite the advance through the canyon, the Federal infantry experienced delays getting to the battlefield — to the point that Sheridan's plan to attack before the Confederates could consolidate their forces failed. The delay had several causes, but Wright bore some responsibility for failing to act promptly in clearing the bottleneck.[50]

Despite being driven back in the early part of the action, the Sixth Corps participated in the final counterattack that swept Confederates from the field. Early reformed his army just south of Strasburg at a formidable series of bluffs known collectively as Fisher's Hill. On September 20, following a reconnaissance with Sheridan, Wright directed his forces in seizing high ground about 700 yards from the center and right of rebel lines. The following day, Sixth Corps skirmishing helped occupy the Confederates' attention as Crook's Eighth Corps marched to attack the Confederate flank. Wright followed up with an assault that contributed to flushing the rebels out of their lines. He led from the front and took an active role in encouraging the men and directing movements and artillery. The result was a second complete rout of the rebels in three days. "Nothing but night," Wright wrote in his report, saved Early's army "from utter annihilation."[51]

Pursuing Early up the Valley, the Sixth Corps participated in "The Burning," the systematic destruction of crops, barns, and mills and the confiscation of livestock in the region between Staunton and Strasburg. On their return, the Army of the Shenandoah stopped along the quiet banks of Cedar Creek just north of Strasburg. While camped there, Sheridan decided to travel to Washington to resolve questions raised by headquarters about future operations. As next ranking officer, Wright assumed temporary command of the Army of the Shenandoah.[52]

Sheridan expected to be absent only briefly, and no one anticipated that the Federals would establish a base at Cedar Creek. The army had paused there in August, but Sheridan, considering the position indefensible, had withdrawn to the north. Believing the twice-defeated Confederates incapable of offensive action, Sheridan posted his army with an eye more for the troops' comfort than for defense. Farthest south and east, Crook's Eighth Corps camped on high ground overlooking the creek valley, positioned mostly to contest a movement along the Valley Turnpike to their right. Emory's divisions pitched their tents on the west side of the pike and slightly to the north of Crook's position. Farther west and north, Wright's Sixth Corps camped in the open fields. The rolling ground did not lend itself to defense, and Sheridan weakened his army further by scattering it over five miles along six separate ridges.[53]

On October 16, Federal signalmen intercepted a bogus message composed by Early to prevent reinforcements being sent to Grant. The message, purportedly from Lt. Gen. James Longstreet, ordered Early to remain in place until he arrived and the pair could "crush Sheridan." Wright forwarded the message to Sheridan, who had reached Front Royal. Wright added that if "the enemy should be strongly reinforced in cavalry, he might by turning our right, give us a great deal of trouble. I shall hold on here until the enemy's movements are developed and shall only fear an attack on my right, which I shall make every preparation for guarding against and resisting."[54]

Sheridan thought the message a ruse but returned Brig. Gen. Wesley Merritt's cavalry division, which had accompanied him, to Cedar Creek as a precaution. In his reply to Wright, Sheridan said, "Make your position strong. . . . If the enemy should make an advance, I know you will defeat him. Look well to your ground and be well prepared." Sheridan also told Wright to "close in" the cavalry division posted at Front Royal so the horsemen could help protect the army's left flank along Cedar Creek. This small division, commanded by the recently promoted Col. William H. Powell, had been posted at Front Royal, about ten miles to the west, to watch for advances from that direction.[55]

The Federal army, expecting to stay put for a few days, began to entrench. In a predawn raid on October 17, a mixed Confederate force of infantry and cavalry surprised a Union cavalry outpost near the western fringe of the Federal encampment. While casualties were slight, the incident strengthened Wright's belief that any attack would come on the seemingly more vulnerable western end of the Union line. For that reason, he posted two of the army's cavalry divisions — Merritt's and Brig. Gen. George A. Custer's — on that flank. Wright followed Sheridan's instructions by bringing Powell's division closer to his eastern flank. Wright, Crook, and cavalry commander Brig. Gen. Alfred T. A. Tolbert believed that these orders had been carried out. However, Powell had moved his pickets only as far west as Buckton Ford, apparently believing that Crook had covered Bowman's Ford, which afforded a crossing of the North Fork of the Shenandoah River a mile southeast of the Eighth Corps lines. On October 17, Wright, accompanied by other general officers, inspected the army's entire front but apparently never checked the ground between the Eighth Corps lines and fields adjoining fords across Cedar Creek and the North Fork. Various reconnaissances, including that of one of Crook's brigades on October 18, found no indication of enemy activity. Wright, not fully trusting the reports, ordered Emory to reconnoiter with one of his divisions on the morning of October 19.[56]

On the day before the climactic clash of the Valley campaign, Wright attended to administrative chores, including finishing his report on Third Winchester and Fisher's Hill. He closed his account by praising soldiers of the Sixth Corps, saying "their crowning achievements in the battles of the Valley will be looked upon with pride by each and every one of them, whose greatest glory will be the claim to have belonged to the Army of the Shenandoah." The words reflect a view, widely shared in the army's peaceful camps, that Early's depleted army could not long sustain itself in a region stripped of supplies and had retreated, or would soon retreat, without giving battle. Wright acted according to that belief. On both October 17 and 18, the temporary commander ordered the army to be roused at 4:00 A.M. and ready for action by sunrise. But for October 19, he decided against waking his entire force in the predawn hours. On the morning of the battle, most of the Army of the Shenandoah slept in.[57]

Jubal Early's surprise attack ranks among the greatest feats of the war. From a vantage on Three Top Mountain, Early's lieutenants had devised a complex attack plan involving several columns and intricate timing. That the twice-routed, outnumbered, underfed, and undersupplied Army of the Valley achieved all its initial objectives remains a signal accomplishment. On the United States side, Early's successful surprise assault constitutes the blackest mark on Wright's Civil War record. Soon after Early's troops attacked Crook's position, a staff officer from Emory carrying word of the fighting to headquarters found Wright preparing to mount. "He knew what I had to tell him," the officer recalled, "but he listened to my brief message patiently and replied with the formal courtesy of the regular army." Wright soon galloped toward the sound of guns to begin five hours of commanding an army staggered by one flanking move after another. The nature of the Confederate offensive was both literally and figuratively shrouded in fog. Wright did not know whether Early had been substantially reinforced, and in the early hours of the battle mist obscured the direction and strength of the southern attack.[58]

Wright seemed ubiquitous that chilly October morning. Several accounts mention his presence on the front lines, directing forces down to the regimental level, dispatching aides to gather intelligence, and conferring repeatedly in person with Crook, Emory, and other officers. In contrast to the few, unspecific mentions on other fields, those who saw Wright at Cedar Creek recorded details. Besides remembering the general's presence and his orders, several accounts highlight his unfailing courtesy in the most desperate situations. Capt. John K. Bucklyn remembered one such incident, which also illustrates the confusing nature of the battle's early stages. Dispatched by Wright to see if troops on a nearby bluff were friend or foe, Bucklyn was fired upon by the entire Confederate line occupying the hill. He survived his close call and eventually circled

General Sheridan and his corps commanders on the Valley Pike near Belle Grove, sketch by James E. Taylor. Wright is the figure in the middle, with Sheridan and George Crook to his right and William H. Emory and Alfred T. A. Torbert to his left. Courtesy of the Western Reserve Historical Society, Cleveland, Ohio.

back to headquarters. "My dear fellow," Wright exclaimed upon seeing him, "I thought you were killed." Years later Bucklyn wrote that the "memory of his kindly words and manner have always been cherished by me."[59]

About thirty minutes after the Confederate assault began, Wright and Emory met Col. Thomas F. Wildes at the head of an Eighth Corps brigade near the Valley Turnpike. Although Wildes's brigade had just fought a determined delaying action in the face of overwhelming numbers, Wright ordered it to return to the fray to buy time so Emory's Nineteenth Corps could form a line perpendicular to their entrenchments and parallel to the pike. By forming such a line and connecting it to Col. Rutherford B. Hayes's Eighth Corps division, Wright hoped to stem the Confederate tide by holding the high ground along the pike.[60]

Rallying two of his regiments, Wildes turned around and returned to the fight. "We formed at once for the charge for which the most we could hope would be time for the 19th corps to turn its line to meet the enemy," Wildes wrote:

Every officer and man in our little band knew he was going to meet over-whelming numbers in those woods, but they never hesitated. Fixing bayo-nets, we started on the way back down the hill from the pike, and as we started to ascend to the woods, raised the old yell and dashed forward. Just after we started, General Wright rode out in our front and most gallantly led the charge. We advanced close to the edge of the woods, where we met with a terrible fire and a counter charge from ten times our number, which swept us back again to the pike. General Wright was wounded in the face, and came back bleeding freely. He displayed great personal courage, but gallant as he and the men who followed him were, they were obliged to give way before the awful fire they met at the edge of the woods.[61]

Wildes's accounts merit emphasis: Wright invited death by leading a forlorn hope of an attack. He had never led an assault in his many other times under fire, though he had earned a reputation for always being close to the action. He would have been captured had not General Crook and an aide bravely inter-vened to help the dazed Wright off the field. Most accounts mention Wright's being shot in the chin, but he described the wound as being on his "face," and subsequent photographs show a distinct scar on his left cheek even with his mouth.[62]

After the rout of Wildes's force, Wright rode west to confer for at least the second time with Emory. The Nineteenth Corps commander wished to pull his remaining brigades out of their southward-facing entrenchments and make a stand west of the pike. Wright apparently approved that decision, then de-parted to form the Sixth Corps' First and Third divisions he had ordered for-ward. One officer remembered him "bare-headed, with the blood trickling down his beard" as the corps' First Division formed. Keifer, in command of the Third Division, recorded that Wright rode up around 8:00 A.M., display-ing confidence that the battle could be won. "He was tranquil, buoyant, and self-possessed," Keifer recalled. "General Wright and Sheridan's staff worked bravely and vigorously, endeavoring to stop the rout and reform the stragglers," recalled another veteran, "the gallant General riding wounded over the field, his bleeding face bound with a handkerchief." Wright personally ordered the 15th New Jersey to fall back to a new position, one member of the regiment re-membering his "chin bleeding from a bullet-wound." At another point, as the 9th New York began to abandon a hill under heavy fire, Wright rode among them and ordered them back to the crest to buy time for their brigade to reform.

As they traded volleys with the oncoming Confederates, a brigade staff officer arrived with orders to withdraw. The 9th's commander, Maj. James W. Snyder, refused, pointing out that Wright was nearby, and that the "general has ordered me to hold this crest, and I shall obey his orders."[63]

The Confederate attack was designed both to surprise the Army of the Shenandoah and to defeat it piecemeal. In this, Sheridan's faulty dispositions, not Wright's failure to picket the fords along Cedar Creek, hurt the Union force badly. While the Eighth Corps had been surprised, both the Nineteenth and Sixth corps had adequate time to form before coming under attack. But they were hindered by the nature of the ground, the fog, and later in the morning, the sun that blinded Union troops as they fought facing east. In addition to the fog and the sun, rebel attackers enjoyed the further advantage of knowing the uneven terrain over which the fighting raged. By repeated flanking movements, Early's army forced the Nineteenth Corps and then the Sixth Corps' First and Third divisions to quit the field. Wright faced a crucial choice: he could fully commit his remaining unbloodied division, or he could begin to disengage and draw off to the north and west to buy time to rally. Wright chose to order a general withdrawal, with a view toward circling back toward the vital Valley Turnpike. He later explained that a "change of front was necessary, and this must be made to a position which would place our force between the enemy and our base." With this goal in mind, he summoned Merritt's and Custer's cavalry divisions from their positions on the army's far right. These two decisions — to disengage the infantry and to reinforce his left by shifting cavalry to hold the pike — proved critical to the ultimate Union victory.[64]

The single unbloodied division, the Sixth Corps' Second, helped secure time for the withdrawal. Camped farthest from the fight when the battle began, the division, led by the dependable Brig. Gen. George Washington Getty, advanced more directly south than the rest of the Sixth Corps. Seeing the other divisions disengaging, Getty pulled back to a cemetery located on a hill northwest of Middletown. There the Second Division drove back repeated Confederate attacks, as Early sought to rout the one Union force that refused to quit the field. Eventually Getty's command, like every other Federal infantry division at Cedar Creek, would be flanked out of its position. It retired to a new, south-facing line about a mile farther north. Wright began to form the rest of the Sixth Corps on Getty's right, while Custer's and Merritt's cavalry kept their position on the left astride the pike.[65]

Once Wright had reformed the army north of Middletown, he ordered preparations for a counterattack to begin in early afternoon. "General Wright was active in his effort to retrieve the day," remembered one officer who witnessed him personally bringing up the Nineteenth Corps to extend the Sixth Corps line. "He has never admitted that he had given up the battle or had lost hope of renewing the offensive." Another officer recalled carrying orders to various commands, telling their officers to ready their troops for an advance at 3:00 P.M. Writing soon after the war, a veteran of Getty's division recalled that Wright "frequently said that he could yet defeat the enemy, and his staff have claimed that he issued orders looking to a counter-attack, but it is doubtful if such a movement would have been successful, as the army was much disheartened." He characterized the army as being in "sort of a dogged gloom." General Keifer concurred, writing that though "the army loved Wright, and believed in him, his temperament was not such as to cause him to work an army up to high state of enthusiasm." A member of the Nineteenth Corps similarly remembered doubting that a counterattack led by Wright would be successful, though he had the "entire confidence of the corps."[66]

Whatever preparations Wright had made for a counterattack, Sheridan's arrival around 10:30 A.M. made all believe that it could, and would, happen. His return from Washington had taken longer than planned, and Sheridan had spent the night in Winchester. Discomforted by the sound of battle early on October 19, Sheridan elected to ride to Cedar Creek and, once there, to rally the army. One veteran's reaction typified that of the entire army: "The magnetism of his fiery energy electrified the army with a kindred spirit, and they fought with just that desperate valor that was needed to turn the tide of affairs in our favor." Sheridan conferred briefly with Wright, who had been meeting with Crook and others near the pike. After taking time to interrogate prisoners to assure himself that Longstreet's First Corps had not reinforced Early, Sheridan ordered a counterattack that swept the rebel army from the field in the late afternoon. Wright, still bleeding from his painful wound, resumed command of the Sixth Corps. He took an active part in coordinating the afternoon attack, twice intervening in person with his Third Division to ensure it kept up with the advance. One of Sheridan's staff officers remembered carrying orders to the corps commander for the counterattack. "I found General Wright just in rear of his corps, lying on the ground," he wrote. "He sat up as I reported, and I saw that his beard was clotted with blood and his neck and chin swollen, and he spoke with something of an effort." After listening to the message, Wright replied simply, "Very well." As Sheridan's staffer rode away, he heard Wright giving orders in a clear, calm voice. A while later, during the counterattack, the same Nineteenth Corps staff officer who had brought news to Wright of the predawn assault found the corps commander standing with his staff in an exposed position, still "composed and kindly in manner and gentle in voice," when he delivered a message from Emory.[67]

Sheridan's counterattack achieved decisive results. The seemingly miraculous rally, together with final defeat of the Confederate army in the Valley where it had often embarrassed Federal forces, prompted an unusual outpouring of prose and poetry. The beauty of a valley framed by mountains clad in autumnal colors, the eerie sight of butternut-clad Confederates emerging from the morning fog, and the drama of the Confederate surprise assault and of Sheridan's arrival combined to produce, in the words of one major's official report, a "memorable morning." As a veteran observed more than a century ago, "It seems impossible, for writers of histories even, to avoid the romantic and write soberly about this battle." No event in that battle, and perhaps none in the entire war, thrilled northerners as much as Sheridan's dramatic return to his army and the rally that ensued. "Little Phil's" feat became the subject of an enormously popular poem titled "Sheridan's Ride," composed by a prominent poet, Thomas Buchanan Read. From its first reading on October 31, 1864, "Sheridan's Ride" quickly caught the public's imagination and would be featured for generations at veteran reunions, patriotic exercises of all kinds, and in classrooms across the northern states.[68]

Many in the Sixth Corps who believed that they, and their commander, had not received credit for their accomplishments at Cedar Creek blamed the poem. A New York soldier voiced a typical opinion: "Buchanan Read's poetical description of Sheridan's ride from Winchester to the army on that day seems to have hidden the deeds of our grand corps commander, and deprived him of his just mede of praise. His own corps knew what he did and what they did, and gave him his just reward by their admiration for the heroic part he performed at the battle." An early historian of the Army of the Potomac, war correspondent William Swinton, agreed. Writing in 1866, Swinton contended that the "dramatic incidents attending the arrival of Sheridan have perhaps caused General Wright to receive less credit than he really deserves. The disaster was over by the time Sheridan arrived; a compact line of battle was formed, and Wright was on the point of opening the offensive. Wright certainly had not the style of doing things possessed by Sheridan, but no one who knows the steady qualities of that officer's mind can doubt that he would have himself retrieved whatever his troops had lost of honor." Hazard Stevens, a veteran of the fight who wrote one of the first scholarly accounts of the battle, offered a balanced assessment. "If I had been with you this morning," Stevens remembered Sheridan shouting as he arrived, "this disaster would not have happened." Though Stevens believed Sheridan might have prevented the surprise, he thought the remark "unjust to Wright and his army." Emphasizing the soundness of the Confederate plans and the skill with which they were executed, Stevens opined that "Achilles himself could not have withstood the terrific force" of the assault once it began.[69]

How did Wright assess what happened on that remarkable day? In his most immediate account, a letter written to his wife a week after the battle, he said he would have led the army in a successful counterattack had not Sheridan arrived. Still, Wright added, Sheridan's arrival "was a relief to me, and had, naturally enough, more influence over the entire army than I have." He gave the most complete description of his part in the battle, with detail that could not have comforted his spouse, but omitted any specific description of his leading troops into battle. He told of working to stabilize Union units in the line just east of the Valley Turnpike, using "words of encouragement, command, and I fear profanity." After that line broke, he was left "alone with a single orderly (the staff officers with me having been sent on various duties) and for a mile I rode without other attendance, getting a bullet thro' my chin, another thro' the brim of my hat, and two at least through my horse, and another thro' the horse of my orderly—Both of us were dismounted and rode the horse of another orderly thro' the rest of the day, my own spare ones having gone to the rear." Apparently responding to his wife's concern that Sheridan would get too much credit while her husband received censure, Wright observed, with remarkable detachment, that "the final result was more signal than a repulse in the beginning would have been; so that in spite of the mortification I feel, I still believe that 'what is, is right'."[70]

In his November 1865 official report on the battle, Wright sought to add "something in the way of explanation of the causes of the comparatively easy success of the enemy in early part of the action." That explanation, he continued, would interest "the professional soldier . . . even if it is lost on others." Unfortunately, Wright offered few insights. Part of the problem lay in a lack of information. In Galveston, his headquarters as commander of the Department of Texas when he wrote, Wright lacked copies of his subordinates' reports that had long since been turned in to the War Department. He gave a few reasons why the army had been surprised, including the impression left by Crook's October 18 reconnaissance that the enemy "had doubtless retreated up the Valley." He noted that the scarcity of supplies in the Valley had fostered the belief that Early must either fight or quit their position, and that Crook's report helped foster that belief. Nonetheless, Wright noted that he had ordered another reconnaissance by the Nineteenth Corps for the morning of October 19. He speculated about one cause of the surprise not found elsewhere in the literature — that the Confederates dressed in blue uniforms to fool Union pickets — and did not address his failure to ensure that all fords were picketed.[71]

Wright assigned the most blame to the inability of the Eighth and Nineteenth corps to withstand attack. In his view, the line he helped form just east of the Valley Turnpike should have held until the Sixth Corps reinforced it. "Here the battle should have been fought and won, and long before midday the discomfited enemy should have been driven across Cedar Creek stripped of all the captures of his first attack," he argued in a long and crucial sentence, "but from some unexplainable cause the troops forming this part of the line would not stand but broke under a scattering fire, which should not have occasioned the slightest apprehension in raw recruits much less in old soldiers like themselves." Here Wright ignored the effect of surprise, the uncertainty caused by the fog, and most of all, the well-planned and executed Confederate attack that repeatedly flanked the Union divisions out of their positions.[72]

Other than his official report, Wright never gave another public account of his actions at Cedar Creek. The only other surviving comment suggests that he believed Sheridan received too much credit. "I had the troops in good shape when Sheridan came up," Wright wrote to a friend a few months before he died in 1899, adding, "In fact he made no changes in the dispositions I had made, and naturally carried out the plans for the movement I had formed. I think the command proudly understood this."[73]

Unhappily for Wright, the newspaper accounts, history's first draft, followed the outlines of Read's poem. In the poet's eyes, the army was retreating before the arrival of Sheridan, whose force of character turned things around:

> And the wave of retreated checked its course there, because
> The sight of the master compelled it to pause.
> With foam and with dust the black charger was gray;
> By the flash of his eye, and his red nostril's play,
> He seemed to the whole great army to say:
> "I have brought you Sheridan all the way
> From Winchester down to save the day."

If early newspaper stories cited Wright at all, they mentioned his being wounded. A long account by the *New York Herald* reporter on the scene referred to Wright's wound and his being near the front lines "during the whole day" but offered few other details. While no newspaper blamed Wright for the morning's reverses, none gave him credit for steadying the army before Sheridan arrived. Most surprisingly, no major newspaper recounted how Wright led Wildes's brigade into battle. Back in Petersburg, artillerist colonel Charles S. Wainwright read the accounts and formed an opinion about Sheridan's victory and who was responsible. "Sheridan made no change in Wright's dispositions until after the repulse; yet in neither of his dispatches to General Grant does he give Wright any credit whatever, but leads one to suppose that it was he alone who saved the day," he wrote in his diary. "The best informed here," concluded Wainwright, "believe that Wright would have done quite as much had Sheridan not come up." Soon after the battle, Sheridan himself attributed the morning's rout to Wright's posting Merritt's and Custer's cavalry divisions on the right. In his memoirs, Sheridan admitted that "the surprise of the morning might have befallen me as well as the general on whom it did descend." Still, he assumed no responsibility for posting his army haphazardly on terrain he had earlier believed indefensible.[74]

With the 1864 Valley campaign finally finished, Wright and the Sixth Corps returned to the Petersburg trenches in December. Wright may have felt chagrin as he greeted his Army of the Potomac colleagues, as Read's poetry had started to crowd out the facts. Col. Theodore Lyman, a member of Meade's staff, recorded this impression of Wright's return. "General Wright, though always pleasant is, I think rather in low spirits," Lyman wrote. "He has had poor luck, on numerous occasions, and it culminated at Cedar Creek, where he chanced to have command of the army when it was surprised. He had rallied it, when Sheridan arrived on the field; but of course Sheridan had the credit of the victory, and indeed he deserved it. All the officers say that Wright made prodigious exertions and rode along all parts of the line in the hottest fire."[75]

By early 1865, as the Army of the Potomac prepared for its final campaign, Wright adopted much of Ulysses S. Grant's steely determination to end the war quickly. On February 25 — well before any anticipated advance — Wright issued stern orders to the corps: "As any movement on the enemy's part is at once to be followed up, the entire corps, without striking tents, will be held ready to move in pursuit at a moment's warning." He described "the utmost vigilance on the part of the pickets, and readiness on the part of the whole command to move promptly, as of first importance," expressing "trust that the corps will not be behind the others in the army in this particulars." One of Grant's aides, Adam Badeau, recalled that Wright had been "full of confidence ever since the beginning of the movement. He was ready to assault at any time, and inspired not only his subordinates but his superiors with his own belief in victory."[76]

Grant noticed. On March 31, as Sheridan prepared to attack Confederate forces holding the strategic intersection at Five Forks, he asked Grant to reinforce him with the Sixth Corps. The general in chief demurred, explaining that Wright's troops were too far away. But he added a significant sentence: "Wright thinks he can go through the line where he is and it is advisable to have troops and a commander there who feels so." Late the next day, as Wright's troops crept into position for their assault on the enemy's lines, Meade's chief of staff, new to his job, sent a message to the Sixth Corps commander to "assault as you please." Wright did not care for the newcomer's casual tone and sent a curt reply: "Everything will be ready. The corps will go in solid, and I am sure will make the fur fly. . . . If the corps does half as well as I expect we will have broken through the rebel lines fifteen minutes from the word 'go.'" This message prompted Grant to say, "I like the way Wright talks."[77]

In a well-planned and executed attack early on the morning of April 2, the Sixth Corps fulfilled Wright's promise. Led by Getty's division arrayed in an unconventional wedge formation, the corps smashed through the formidable, albeit undermanned, rebel fortifications. Wright's success broke the stalemate and hastened Lee's abandonment of Petersburg. The victory did not come without considerable cost, however, as the Sixth Corps lost more than a thousand men.[78]

During the pursuit to Appomattox, Sheridan and Wright cooperated for a final time on April 6 at the battle of Sailor's Creek, where their commands trapped nearly a third of Lee's army. Sheridan's cavalry delayed forces commanded by Lt. Gens. Richard H. Anderson and Richard S. Ewell long enough for the Sixth Corps to catch up. Though Wright remained under Meade's direct command, he cooperated with Sheridan to work out a plan of attack. The cavalry would seek to block Anderson's march by working south and then circling back east. Wright's corps would assault the force's rear, where Ewell's infantry had formed along the banks of Sailor's Creek. After some spirited combat, including a Confederate counterattack led by G. W. Custis Lee, Robert E. Lee's oldest son, Wright's veterans overwhelmed Ewell's force. More than 5,000 Confederates surrendered, among them Ewell, Custis Lee, and four other generals. The southern counterattack astounded Wright, who had ordered his artillery to stop firing because, from his vantage point, he could see the Confederate forces almost surrounded and looked "upon them already as our prisoners." The futile counterattack probably prompted the single recorded instance of Wright's being less than courteous. Custis Lee, a student of Wright's at West Point, encountered the Sixth Corps commander after his capture and tried to shake hands. Wright refused and ordered his chief of staff to escort Lee to the rear.[79]

After the war, Custis Lee and Ewell, seeking to explain their force's collapse, exaggerated the number of Union soldiers they confronted at Sailor's Creek. Wright, replying to an inquiry from Keifer, who was writing his own account, penned a rare letter on his war experiences that he intended for others to publish. Writing in 1888, Wright denied claims that Union forces numbered 30,000 but, not having a copy of his reports, declined to give an estimate of his own (Wright probably had 7,000 men in his attacking force, and Sheridan may have had as many as 8,000, for a total of about 15,000). He had "never seen or before heard" of Lee's and Ewell's accounts, Wright assured Keifer, indicating disinterest in historical controversy if not in his own war record.[80]

Wright's innate cordiality may have contributed to hastening the war's end. In the evening after the battle, a dejected Ewell was taken to Wright's headquarters. "I am glad to see you Ewell," Wright remarked to his old friend, who had graduated a year ahead of him at West Point. "I'll be blank-blanked if I'm glad to see you," Ewell snapped in reply. They were soon talking easily, however, with other officers, including Sheridan. Ewell's remarks suggesting that Sheridan ask for Lee's surrender impressed a Dr. Smith, a Union army surgeon. Encountering Grant the next day, Smith recounted Ewell's recommendation, one of several factors encouraging the Federal commander to initiate the correspondence with Lee that would lead to the latter's capitulation.[81]

Wright's aggressiveness continued on April 7. At one point, he became so anxious to aid the cavalry in an engagement that Grant had to reassure him that the horsemen were holding their own. Wright was not present during the surrender discussions between Grant and Lee on April 9, but the Sixth Corps was close enough to witness the Confederate commander leaving the McLean House. Wright called his soldiers to attention as Lee rode past en route to inform Confederates that they were surrendered. In the celebrations that followed the surrender, Wright and Meade were "almost dragged from their horses in the mad rejoicing."[82]

Soon after Appomattox, the Sixth Corps and most of the cavalry were ordered south to join William Tecumseh Sherman as he advanced against Gen. Joseph E. Johnston's Confederate army. Wright continued to show determination, marching his men to Danville, Virginia, a distance of nearly 120 miles, over poor roads in hot weather in just four days. There Wright learned that Johnston had surrendered. A week later, the Sixth Corps was ordered north to Washington, D.C. Having missed the Grand Review, it marched before a smaller crowd on June 8, 1865, parading past a reviewing stand adorned with a large Greek cross of evergreens. The final march of "Wright's Walkers" was, appropriately, a strenuous one. One participant wrote that "hundreds of our men fell down by sunstroke and exhaustion, fainting and reeling before the stand of reviewers." Wright led the Sixth Corps march into history, riding, as one reporter wrote, "a dark bay horse, decorated with flowers." The correspondent's account remains the single known description of Wright's horse, which attracted notice only when leading a Washington parade.[83]

After the Sixth Corps disbanded, Wright became commander of the Provisional Corps, which constituted the remnant of the Army of the Potomac. In July 1865, he was appointed commander of the Department of Texas, reporting once again to Phil Sheridan, now the district commander. Sheridan was pleased, telling Grant that Wright "would be very acceptable" for the post. After about a year, when Wright showed himself to be too reasonable for Sheridan's taste in his dealings with the state's elected governor, Sheridan arranged to have his associate mustered out of the volunteer army. Wright may have wanted out because he felt isolated. In January 1866, he remarked to a friend that he was "about as much separated from the officers of the Corps [of Engineers] out here as tho' I did not belong to it."[84]

Now a lieutenant colonel of engineers, Wright returned to his peacetime duties. He spent the next eighteen years working on dozens of public works projects, the Brooklyn Bridge and the Washington Monument most famous among them. At a time when many of his fellow officers were publishing their accounts of the war, Wright's only publication was to coauthor *Report on the Fabrication of Iron for Defensive Purposes and Its Uses in Modern Fortification, Especially in Works of Coast Defense*, a treatise on his core specialty in military engineering. Wright retired in 1884 after five years as a brigadier general and chief of engineers. Counting his time as a Norwich Military Academy cadet, he had spent nearly fifty years in uniform.[85]

Wright lived quietly in retirement in Washington, spending his summers in Clinton, Connecticut. When asked to take an active role in organizing the Society for the Army of the Potomac, he demurred. Wright told his correspondent that "he was but a poor hand at getting up such things, and moreover think that the initial steps at any rate would come with more propriety from others than from myself." He presided over the May 1887 dedication of the monument marking where Sedgwick was killed at Spotsylvania, but he left the speeches to others. The ceremony's commemorative booklet described Wright as "a tall, well preserved man, with the carriage and bearing of a solder, one would scarce conceive that with his quiet, easy, gracious manners that he once commanded the fighting Sixth Corps; but he did, and he did it well." Wright took pride in his corps, telling one author that "as marchers they were unsurpassed, and as fighters they were as good as the best, if not a little better." Wright received some recognition outside of army circles for his service. On June 14, 1865, he was voted the thanks of the Connecticut legislature, which cited him for "his eminent services in the late war." He received an honorary doctorate from Norwich University in 1897.[86]

Wright died at the age of seventy-nine in Washington on July 2, 1899. The then chief of engineers, Brig. Gen. John M. Wilson, selected Wright's burial site and, in a florid general order, paid tribute to his predecessor as a "peerless, accomplished, knightly soldier. For the nobility of his character, for gentleness of disposition, for all the grand attributes of the beau-ideal soldier, General Wright stood pre-eminent. Of commanding presence, brave and strong to act, equally at home on the field or in the council chamber, the memory of our hero will ever be held in reverence by his fellow countrymen."[87]

Wilson's prediction did not come true, as Wright's renown never matched the prominence of his Arlington Cemetery monument. By neither writing memoirs or articles nor leaving papers to any institution, he contributed to his own obscurity. His distaste for the "disease" of "love of newspaper fame" assured that he would not receive prominent mention in contemporary journalistic accounts. Wright failed to write several of his official reports—odd for such a meticulous officer—and those he did write are seldom quoted. Few with whom he served wrote anything substantive about Wright, and the most complete description, that penned by Warren Keifer, did not appear until the year after his death.

Wright's most lasting contribution to Civil War literature consisted of a few passages in the second edition of Dr. George Stevens's *Three Years with the Sixth Corps*. In the preface to the revised edition, dated April 10, 1867, Stevens wrote that he was "especially indebted" to Wright for "the great assistance he has rendered me in correcting the narrative and furnishing new material for this edition." Comparing the two texts reveals what he probably thought important about his war record. Few now remember the complete if minor victory at Rappahannock Station, but Wright took pride in it. In small type below the second edition's text, he credited himself for the success. As temporary commander of the Sixth Corps, he placed the artillery and devised an assault that commenced when the sun was at an angle that blinded Confederate defenders. "The plan," wrote Wright with uncharacteristic informality and immodesty, "worked liked a charm." The complete description of the action at Fort Stevens, and Wright's forthright account of his endangering Lincoln, also became part of the second edition. Breaking the Confederate line at Petersburg on April 2 and the battle of Sailor's Creek received more attention in a later version, which quoted Wright's official report. The descriptions of the Overland and Valley campaigns, however, remained almost identical in both books.[88]

Wright's combat career has not undergone scholarly examination, though a few historians have commented briefly on his performances in individual battles and campaigns. One authority on Spotsylvania evaluated his performance as that of "a general promoted beyond his ability." In the opening stage of the siege of Petersburg, Wright stumbled badly on June 21–23 in fighting at the Jerusalem Plank Road. Angry at what he saw as Wright's lack of nerve and poor handling of troops on that occasion, General Meade contemplated removing him, a fact noted by a least one historian. Among Wright's contemporaries, Lt. Col. Horace Porter of Grant's staff assessed Wright's performance during the Overland campaign in flattering terms, stating that Wright had "assumed command of the Sixth Corps at a critical period of the campaign, and under very trying circumstances; but he had conducted it with such heroic gallantry and marked ability that he had commended himself highly to both Grant and Meade." Taking a different view, Maj. Gen. Gouverneur K. Warren's first biographer rated several senior commanders of the Army of the Potomac, including Wright, as no better than "honest mediocrities."[89]

Wright compiled a mixed record during the 1864 Valley campaign. Circumstances — poor transport, the enemy's head start, conflicting orders, inadequate cavalry, and coordination with unfamiliar units — probably precluded success in his brief tenure in independent command during his pursuit of Early after the action at Fort Stevens. One authority on the campaign thought Wright's effort "sluggish," and the fact remains that he marched his troops many hot and dusty miles for very little result. Serving under Sheridan, his poor handling of the march through Berryville Canyon probably contributed to the Army of the Shenandoah's poor showing in the first phases at Third Winchester, and several chroniclers have justly criticized him for it. His Sixth Corps seized the key ground that made possible the victory at Fisher's Hill, but most of the attention in that battle has gone to Crook for the turning movement and to Sheridan for urging on the attack from the front lines. At Cedar Creek, the routing of two-thirds of the army he commanded so embarrassed Wright that he could not write coherently about it a year later. Nonetheless, the numerous battle accounts of Wright's frontline visibility, courtesy, and calm demeanor attest to his effect on steadying men rocked by arguably the war's best-executed surprise attack. Most important, the decisions he made in withdrawing from contact with the assaulting Confederates and transferring the cavalry to the army's left set up Sheridan's counterattack. "After the war, Sheridan would receive all the accolades for the surprising and electrifying comeback later in the day and Wright would be cast as the inept leader who had invited disaster," wrote Theodore Mahr, the foremost modern historian of the battle. "This simply was not true," insisted Mahr. "Without Wright's tactical judgment in the morning's fight, the potential for Sheridan's great victory in the afternoon would not have been there."[90]

In contrast to his earlier mixed record, Wright performed laudably during the Appomattox campaign. He clearly appreciated the need for speed and determination and exercised both. In breaking the Confederate lines on April 2 and seizing the opportunities presented at Sailor's Creek, Wright seemed almost a different general than the sometimes tentative officer seen earlier in the war. Growth and experience may explain the difference. Unlike many of his Army of Potomac peers, Wright never commanded troops before the war and had risen quickly to corps command. While he had led a brigade and two different divisions for nearly two years before promotion to head of a corps, Wright had directed infantry in combat only a few times before the Wilderness. He learned about handling large numbers of troops on the job, and that during the war's final year. Perhaps Wright, always a thoughtful officer, used the winter of 1864–65 to reflect on his own performance and decided to emulate the aggressive tactics Sheridan employed with success in the Valley campaign. He may have concluded that a careful but determined use of superior numbers and materiel would bring victory.

Sixth Corps staff officer major Charles A. Whittier suggested that drunkenness might have explained Wright's inconsistent battlefield performance. In an unpublished memoir written nearly twenty-five years after the war, Whittier stated that "Wright had the appearance and the reputation of being a well mannered, temperate man — not all deficient in physical courage, but when responsibilities came on him he took to drink." Specifically, Whittier accused Wright of drinking too much at Third Winchester and Cedar Creek. In both instances, his account lacks specifics, and in the case of Cedar Creek contradicts the testimony of many other witnesses. His allegations cannot be refuted, but they remain unsupported. The lack of confirmation in other accounts renders Whittier's assertions particularly problematical, as it is unlikely that a senior commander's drinking problem would be overlooked in the competitive and often gossipy Army of Potomac.[91]

Sixth Corps veterans presented the most balanced views of Wright. One recalled that Wright was unpopular, and that he angered many by "some ill-judged sentences which the General Order announcing the death of Sedgwick contained. I cannot now recall the offensive passage, but I remember its effect upon our men." He was probably referring to a bracing order that Wright issued two weeks after he assumed corps command, one that undoubtedly angered many who had just bled through the Wilderness and Spotsylvania: "The general commanding the corps has noticed with regret indications of a failure upon the part of some to appreciate the full importance of the struggle in which we are engaged, and the absolute exertion and vigilance far beyond what is required by the mere letter of duty." Citing the death of so many, including "the noble and beloved leader who fell in your front rank," Wright told his men that "indifference at this time to anything that may advance the general good is criminal." Others remembered with bitterness some of the most severe and, in their view, needless marches. These included the pursuit of Early in July 1864, the trek to Danville in April 1865, and the march to Washington after the war ended. "Thirty miles a day when the war was over was more than the men of the 6th Corps hoped for, and Gen. Wright lost much respect due him, as he was in command, and such marching was needless," grumbled one veteran about the march to Danville.[92]

Most members of the Sixth Corps, however, remembered Wright with respect and some affection, albeit with some distance. Some viewed Wright favorably from the start. Writing in his diary the day after Sedgwick was killed, Sgt. Cyrenus Stevens thought "the loss was severe but we have nearly or quite his equal (H. S. Waight)." A Sixth Corps officer wrote two weeks later that Wright "is an able commander and was much relied on by Gen. Sedgwick." Postwar accounts echo the same themes. An 1869 chronicle of the Vermont brigade's experiences nicely summarized a common view. Maj. Aldace F. Walker noted that "some quiet grumbling was, of course, occasionally heard; but General Wright . . . was an exceedingly careful and pains-taking officer, prompt and energetic almost to excess," whose strict professionalism sometimes caused "his men to think him unnecessarily severe." Behind all the comments, positive and negative, is a larger truth: Wright's diligence ensured that the Sixth Corps remained an effective outfit, compiling arguably the Army of the Potomac's best combat record in the final year of the war. Grant recognized this, telling Sheridan on the morning of the battle of Sailor's Creek, "The Sixth Corps will go in with a vim any place you may dictate."[93]

Besides Sixth Corps veterans and his fellow engineers, few noted the passing of Horatio Wright. His obscurity stems from several factors beyond his own reticence. Arriving in mid-1863, he was a latecomer to the Army of the Potomac who accomplished nothing memorable during the Gettysburg campaign, the campaign that boosted the memory of so many of his peers. For example, Joshua Chamberlain's role in that battle and his eloquent memoirs led to several books and countless articles, while Wright, a more consequential Army of the Potomac figure, remains invisible. The nature of his victories also figures in Wright's obscurity. His successes were either minor, such as Rappahannock Station, or overshadowed by larger events. In this latter category, news of breaking through the Confederate lines on April 2, 1865, was obscured by the spectacular victory at Five Forks on April 1 and the fall of Petersburg and Richmond on April 3. Similarly, the victory at Sailor's Creek was eclipsed by the surrender two days later at Appomattox. At Cedar Creek, there seems to be room in the public imagination for only one hero, and Phil Sheridan's ride to victory trumped Wright's considerable feats on that day. Sheridan deserves the accolades—as one scholar put it, the ride remains "by far the best example of how a charismatic officer could infuse spirit into soldiers on the battlefield." But Sheridan never conceded that Wright's efforts to retrieve the day had made his victory possible. Wright's accomplishments at Cedar Creek appear all the more remarkable because he made crucial decisions with a confidence and certainty that belied his temporary status as army commander and did so despite not knowing the size or position of the enemy he faced and while coping with a painful wound. There is much truth in Colonel Lyman's observation that Wright was unlucky.[94]

Yet it remains remarkable that Wright could be so thoroughly forgotten. A final cause of that obscurity lies in the character of the man. "My beau ideal of a soldier," wrote George G. Meade, hardly overgenerous with praise, of the cadet who had finished first in conduct in his West Point class. Recollections of Wright most often remark on his courtesy, calm, and good character under all circumstances. Buchanan Read, the author of "Sheridan's Ride," in a January 1863 newspaper account, summed up this view, calling Wright "a General whose gentlemanly bearing in all capacities makes him an ornament to the American army." As a gentleman and as a soldier, Wright would not call attention to himself during or after the war. Wright's leading Colonel Wildes's brigade back into the fog and the fray at Cedar Creek underscores the phenomenon of his obscurity. Many who were there wrote about seeing Wright bleeding; only Colonel Wildes recorded how it happened, and he did so in an obscure book published many years later. By 1864, army commanders did not lead troops into battle, but Wright's supreme sense of duty that day moved him to the most courageous, even foolhardy, of acts. Then, characteristically, he seems never to have mentioned it. As a result, Wright's heroism attracted no notice.[95]

And so Wright remains forgotten, his solitary reminder a monument on Arlington Heights erected by the Sixth Corps veterans who knew what they and their commander had achieved. Horatio Wright's grave lies on the ridge he helped seize, facing the Washington Monument he helped build, seen by millions but noticed by only a few.

Acknowledgments

Without the assistance of many, this essay would not have been possible, and the author expresses his thanks to his colleagues and friends. Those pointing out sources and providing material included Stephen Wright, Michael P. Musick, Richard J. Sommers, John J. Hennessy, Ed Banning, Kristol Prohl, Roger Sherry, and David Ward. Librarians at the Historical Society of Pennsylvania and at the Alderman and law school libraries at the University of Virginia were unfailingly helpful. The only other person in the world who approaches my level of interest in Horatio Wright is Jan Jones, and she helped with support and a startling amount of varied information. Abbot Kominers and Gil Hahn provided encouragement and editorial suggestions. Special thanks go to my colleagues Robert K. Krick, William Miller, and Robert E. L. Krick for their help with sources and ideas. Will Thomas assisted with every step of the project, from conception, to research, to composition. To Gary Gallagher go my deepest thanks for providing the opportunity to delve into unanswered questions and for the inspiration to carry the project through.

Notes

1. James M. Goode, *The Outdoor Sculpture of Washington, D.C., A Comprehensive Historical Guide* (Washington: Smithsonian Institution Press, 1974), 193.

2. James W. Loewen, *Lies Across America: What Our Historic Sites Get Wrong* (New York: New Press, 1999), 333; James Edward Peters, *Arlington National Cemetery, Shrine to America's Heroes* (Washington: Woodbine House, 1986), 23–26, 251, 262; Goode, *Outdoor Sculpture of Washington*, 197.

3. Peters, *Arlington National Cemetery*, 209–11, 244–45. The author paid a personal visit to the site in September 1999.

4. U.S. War Department, *The War of the Rebellion: A Compilation of the Official Records of the Union and Confederate Armies*, 127 vols., index, and atlas (Washington: Government Printing Office, 1880–1901), ser. 1, 16(2):510 [hereafter cited as *OR*; all references are to series 1 unless otherwise noted].

5. David J. Eicher, *The Civil War in Books: An Analytical Biography* (Urbana: University of Illinois Press, 1997), xxi.

6. Ulysses S. Grant, *The Papers of Ulysses S. Grant*, ed. John Y. Simon, 28 vols. to date (Carbondale: Southern Illinois University Press, 1967–), 10:469; George Meade, *The Life and Letters of George Gordon Meade; Major General, United States Army*, 2 vols. (New York: Scribner's, 1913), 2:213; George T. Stevens, *Three Years in the Sixth Corps*, 2nd ed. (New York: D. Van. Nostrand, 1870), frontispiece; Elisha Hunt Rhodes, "The Second Rhode Island Volunteers at the Siege of Petersburg, Virginia," in Rhode Island Soldiers and Sailors Historical Society, *Personal Narratives of Events in the War of the Rebellion, Being Papers Read Before the Rhode Island Soldiers and Sailors Historical Society*, 10 vols. (1878–1915; reprinted as part of the *Military Order of the Loyal Legion of the United States*, 66 vols. [Wilmington, N.C.: Broadfoot, 1993]), 41:434 [set cited hereafter as *MOLLUS*].

7. J. F. C. Fuller, *The Generalship of Ulysses S. Grant* (1929; reprint, New York: Da Capo, 1991), 222; Clifford Dowdey, *Lee's Last Campaign: The Story of Lee and His Men Against Grant—1864* (Boston: Little, Brown, 1960), 415; James E. Taylor, *With Sheridan Up the Shenandoah Valley in 1864: Leaves from a Special Artist's Sketch Book and Diary*, ed. Dennis E. Frye, Martin F. Graham, and George F. Skoch (Dayton, Ohio: Morningside, 1989), 123; John Henry Cramer, *Lincoln Under Enemy Fire: The Complete Account of His Experiences During Early's Attack on Washington* (Baton Rouge: Louisiana State University Press, 1948), 138; Frank A. Burr and Richard J. Hinton, *The Life of Gen. Philip H. Sheridan, Its Romance and Reality: How an Humble Lad Reached the Head of an Army* (Providence, R.I.: Reid, 1888), 67, 445.

8. Letter to Dr. A. H. Stevens, February 2, 1899, Clinton Historical Society, Clinton, Conn. [repository hereafter cited as CHS]; W. A. Croffut and John M. Morris, *The Military and Civil History of Connecticut during the War of 1861–1865*, 3rd ed., (New York: Ledyard Bill, 1869), frontispiece, 535; Ezra J. Warner, *Generals in Blue: Lives of the Union Commanders* (Baton Rouge: Louisiana State University Press, 1992), 208, 219–20, 514–15, 33–34; John Niven, *Connecticut for the Union: The Role of the State in the Civil War* (New Haven, Conn.: Yale University Press, 1965), ix; Mark Mayo Boatner III, *The Civil War Dictionary*, rev. ed. (New York: David McKay, 1987), 730, 204. These examples represent only a few of many that underscore the degree to which Wright has been slighted or misidentified in the literature.

9. Croffut and Morris, *Military and Civil History*, 535; *Tercentenary Homenoscitt Plantation, 1663 Clinton, Conn. 1963* (Hartford, Conn.: Connecticut Historical Society, 1963), 27, 88; William A. Ellis, *Norwich University 1819–1911: Her History, Her Graduates, Her Roll of Honor*, 2 vols. (Montpelier, Vt.: Capital City Press, 1911),

2:260–61; Robert G. Poirier, *"By the Blood of Our Alumni": Norwich University Citizen Soldiers in the Army of the Potomac* (Mason City, Iowa: Savas, 1999), 2–6; "Records Relating to U.S. Military Academy, Application Papers of Cadets, 1805–1866," RG 94, M688, Roll 106, National Archives, Washington [repository hereafter cited as NA]. The written record contains some conflicting information about Wright's early years. For example, Crofutt and Morris put Wright's birthplace at Orange, Connecticut, with his family moving to nearby Clinton during his childhood.

10. "Records Relating to U.S. Military Academy, Application Papers of Cadets, 1805–1866," RG 94, M688, roll 106, NA; "Semi Annual Rolls of Cadets, 1818–1869," RG 94, box 2, NA; Warner, *Generals in Blue*, 510, 575.

11. Though how Wright met his future wife is unknown, at least two Slaughter family members married army officers, and Louisa's aunt was married to a West Point professor. George W. Cullum, *Biographical Register of the Officers and Graduates of the U.S. Military Academy at West Point, N.Y., from Its Establishment in 1802, to 1890, with the Early History of the United States Military Academy*, 3rd ed., 3 vols. (Boston: Houghton Mifflin, 1891), 2:61–62; "Slaughter S. Bradford," *Culpeper Star-Exponent*, August 9, 1912; "Country Landmarks," *Culpeper Star-Exponent*, May 14, 1953; William Whitman Bailey, "My Boyhood at West Point," in *MOLLUS*, 38:84.

12. "Letters and Reports of Col. Joseph G. Totten, Chief of Engineers (1838–1864)," RG 77.2.8, entry 145, 6:317, 7:146, NA; Cullum, *Biographical Register*, 2:61.

13. Cullum, *Biographical Register*, 2:61; Robert B. Roberts, *Encyclopedia of Historic Forts: The Military, Pioneer, and Trading Posts of the United States* (New York: Macmillan, 1988), 178; Albert Manucy, "The Gibraltar of the Gulf of Mexico," *Florida Historical Quarterly* 21 (April 1943):303–10; Albert Manucy, "A Construction History of Fort Jefferson, 1846–1874" (paper written for National Park Service, Dry Tortugas National Park, Fla., 1961), 23, 33.

14. Patricia L. Faust, ed., *Historical Times Illustrated Encyclopedia of the Civil War* (New York: Harper & Row, 1986), 759; Jefferson Davis, *The Papers of Jefferson Davis*, ed. Lynda L. Crist and others, 11 vols. to date (Baton Rouge: Louisiana State University Press, 1971–), 6:390, 464, 483, 591, 621, 630.

15. Stewart L. Woodford, "The Story of Fort Sumter," *Personal Recollections of the War of the Rebellion, Addresses Delivered before the Commandery of the State of New York, Military Order of the Loyal Legion of the United States*, ed. James M. Wilson and Titus Coan (New York: Commandery, 1891), 260–61; W. A. Swanberg, *First Blood: The Story of Fort Sumter* (New York: Scriber's, 1957), 91–92; *OR*, 1:186.

16. *OR*, 2:19–23; Bern Anderson, *By Sea and By River: The Naval History of the Civil War* (1962; reprint, New York: Da Capo, 1977), 29.

17. *OR*, 2:19–23; F. N. Boney, "Turn About and Fair Play," *Connecticut Historical Society Bulletin* 31 (April 1966):34–35.

18. Benjamin Franklin Cooling III and Walton H. Owen II, *Mr. Lincoln's Forts: A Guide to the Civil War Defenses of Washington* (Shippensburg, Pa.: White Mane, 1988), 38, 41; *OR*, 5:684; Cullum, *Biographical Register*, 2:62; Joseph Mills Hanson, *Bull Run Remembers: The History, Traditions, and Landmarks of the Manassas (Bull Run) Campaigns Before Washington, 1861–1862* (Manassas, Va.: National Capitol Pub-

lisher, 1961), 20; *OR*, 2:404. Traces of Fort Ellsworth remain visible on the grounds of the George Washington Masonic National Memorial.

19. Abraham Lincoln, *The Collected Works of Abraham Lincoln*, ed. Roy P. Basler, 9 vols. (New Brunswick, N.J.: Rutgers University Press, 1953), 6:517; "Letters and Reports of Col. Joseph G. Totten, Chief of Engineers (1838–1864)," RG 77.2.8, entry 145, 10:48, NA; Connecticut Adjutant-General's Office, *Record of Service of Connecticut Men in the Army and Navy of the United Sates during the War of the Rebellion* (Hartford, Conn.: Case, Lockwood & Brainard, 1889), 257, 290. Lincoln, who probably was acquainted with Wright, erred in describing him as a member of the Topographical Engineers. Lincoln's reference to Wright's native state may reflect an attempt by him to distribute equitably the appointments of generals among the several states.

20. Herbert M. Schiller, *"Sumter Is Avenged": The Siege and Reduction of Fort Pulaski* (Shippensburg, Pa.: White Mane, 1995), 65; *OR*, 6:96–97, 124–125, 127, 220, 255; Patrick Brennan, *Secessionville: Assault on Charleston* (Campbell, Calif.: Savas, 1996), 62–63, 141–42, 239–40, 280–81, 290–93; *OR*, 14:53; Worthington Chauncey Ford, ed., *A Cycle of Adams Letters, 1861–1865*, 2 vols. (Boston and New York: Houghton Mifflin, 1920), 1:157; *OR*, ser. 3, 1:466, 12:576, ser. 2, 2:384.

21. Samuel Francis Du Pont, *Samuel Francis Du Pont: A Selection from His Civil War Letters*, ed. John D. Hayes, 3 vols. (Ithaca, N.Y.: Cornell University Press, 1969), 1:116. See also Gideon Welles's comments in Gideon Welles, *Diary of Gideon Welles, Secretary of the Navy under Lincoln and Johnson*, ed. John T. Morse, 3 vols. (Boston: Houghton Mifflin, 1911), 1:46.

22. *OR*, ser. 3, 2:398, 16(2):375; Stephen D. Engle, *Don Carlos Buell: Most Promising of All* (Chapel Hill: University of North Carolina Press, 1999), 278–83; James Lee McDonough, *War in Kentucky: From Shiloh to Perryville* (Knoxville: University of Tennessee Press, 1994), 61–63.

23. John S. D. Eisenhower, *Agent of Destiny: The Life and Times of General Winfield Scott* (New York: Free Press, 1997), 393, 397, 403; *OR*, 2:33.

24. *OR*, 16(1):907, 16(2):385, 404, 447–48, 447–78, 483–85, 495, 503–5, 507–8, 550.

25. *OR*, 16(2):491–92, 550, 595; Lew Wallace, *Smoke, Sound and Fury: The Civil War Memoirs of Major-General Lew Wallace, U.S. Volunteers*, ed. Jim Leek (Portland, Ore.: Strawberry Hill Press, 1998), 156–72; Engle, *Don Carlos Buell*, 282–83.

26. *OR*, 16(2):643. "In this connection," Wright wrote Halleck, "I will say what I have for some time desired saying, and that is that a commander of all the forces in the West should be at once appointed. Until this is done it is certain but that little can be accomplished. Leaving out of consideration any jealousies that may exist and arise, it is impossible that several independent commanders can act with the same effect as a single controlling head." Wright assured Halleck that he was not nominating himself; neither did he mention any possible candidates for the post.

27. Stewart Sifakis, *Who Was Who in the Union* (New York: Facts on File, 1988), 368, 414; *OR*, 20:68, 76, 80–82, 101–2; Faust, *Historical Times Illustrated Encyclopedia*, 681. A Kentucky delegation that included Joshua Speed, one of Lincoln's oldest friends, met with the president in September 1862 to complain of the handling of the war in their

state. See Robert L. Kincaid, *Joshua Fry Speed: Lincoln's Most Intimate Friend* (Harrogate, Tenn.: Department of Lincolniana, Lincoln Memorial University, 1943), 26–27.

28. *OR*, 16(2):504; Salmon P. Chase, *The Salmon P. Chase Papers*, ed. John Niven and others, 5 vols. (Kent, Ohio: Kent State University Press, 1993–98), 3:262–63; James A. Garfield, *The Wild Life of the Army: Civil War Letters of James A. Garfield*, ed. Frederick D. Williams ([East Lansing]: Michigan State University Press, 1964), 204.

29. *Journal of the Executive Proceedings of the Senate of the United States of America from December 1, 1862, to July 4, 1864, Inclusive* (Washington: Government Printing Office, 1887) 23:297; Sifakis, *Who Was Who in the Union*, 8, 82, 90, 107, 114, 116, 139–40, 141–42, 167, 177, 179–80, 195, 202, 213, 229–30, 254, 278, 279, 314–15, 320, 326, 367, 383–84, 399, 417, 431, 454, 458–59, 466; *Homenoscitt Plantation*, 88; James L. Morrison Jr., *"The Best School in the World": West Point, the Pre–Civil War Years, 1833–1866* (Kent, Ohio: Kent State University Press, 1986), 132–33. See also Meade, *Life and Letters*, 1:360; Elizabeth Blair Lee, *Wartime Washington: The Civil War Letters of Elizabeth Blair Lee*, ed. Virginia Jeans Laas (Urbana: University of Illinois Press, 1991), 252. The apparently unwarranted rejection has baffled historians, most notably Kenneth P. Williams and Ezra J. Warner. See Kenneth P. Williams, *Lincoln Finds A General; A Military Study of the Civil War*, 5 vols. (New York: Macmillan, 1949–59), 3:194–95; Warner, *Generals in Blue*, 672.

30. *OR*, 20:68, 80–88; *Louisville Journal*, March 11, 1863; *New York Times*, March 8, 1863; *OR*, 23(2):144–45; William Marvel, *Burnside* (Chapel Hill: University of North Carolina Press, 1991), 222.

31. *OR*, 23(2):193–94; *Louisville Journal*, March 14, 1863; Geoffrey R. Walden, "The Defenses of Cincinnati," *Blue & Gray Magazine* 3 (May 1986):26; Albion W. Tourgee, *The Story of a Thousand, Being a History of the Service of the 105th Ohio Volunteer Infantry, in the War for the Union from August 21, 1862 to June 6, 1865* (Buffalo: S. McGerald, 1896), 69–70.

32. John Hay, *Inside Lincoln's White House: The Complete Civil War Diary of John Hay*, ed. Michael Burlingame and John R. Turner Ettlinger (Carbondale: Southern Illinois University Press, 1997), 53; *OR*, 23(2):341, 25(2):520, 585. How Hay and Wright became acquainted is unknown. Hay makes several references to Wright and his wife in the diary. The most likely explanation is that Wright and Hay became friends while Wright was still stationed at the War Department in 1861.

33. Taylor, *With Sheridan Up the Shenandoah*, 122; Joseph Warren Keifer, *Slavery and Four Years of War: A Political History of Slavery in the United States* (New York: Knickerbocker Press, 1900), 105.

34. Lewis Bissell, *The Civil War Letters of Lewis Bissell*, ed. Mark Olcott and David Lear (Washington, D.C.: Field School Educational Foundation Press, 1981), 249, 298, 352, 371, 387–88, 390, 396. In an April 10, 1865, letter written the day after Lee's surrender at Appomattox Court House, Bissell records a charming rumor that Lee had surrendered his sword to Wright because his corps was the first to break the lines at Petersburg (372).

35. Letter to Dr. A. H. Stevens, February 2, 1899, CHS; Morrison, *"Best School,"*

37; *OR*, 24(1):111. For Wright's preference for field command, see *OR*, 6:242. It is also reasonable to assume that Wright, once the Senate had rejected his promotion to major general, had some leverage to be assigned where he wished. The West Point superintendent's job was eventually assigned to Zealous Bates Tower.

36. H. G. Wright to Louisa M. Wright, July 18, 1863, Charles Bedmar Collection, United State Army Military History Institute, Carlisle, Pa.

37. Slaughter Family Papers, box 2, no. 1006, Alderman Library, University of Virginia, Charlottesville; *Historic Culpeper* (Culpeper: Culpeper Historical Society, 1974), 36; Marsena Rudolph Patrick, *Inside Lincoln's Army: The Diary of Marsena Rudolph Patrick, Provost Marshal General, Army of the Potomac*, ed. David S. Sparks (New York: A. S. Barnes, 1964), 296–97; Lincoln, *Collected Works*, 6:536–37, 7:51, 8:175.

38. Richard Elliott Winslow III, *General John Sedgwick: The Story of a Union Corps Commander* (Novato, Calif.: Presidio, 1982), 161–62; Gordon C. Rhea, *The Battles for Spotsylvania Court House and the Road to Yellow Tavern: May 7–12, 1864* (Baton Rouge: Louisiana State University Press, 1997), 37–38, 72–74, 83–85; Martin T. McMahon, "The Death of General John Sedgwick," in Robert Underwood Johnson and Clarence Clough Buel, eds., *Battles and Leaders of the Civil War*, 4 vols. (1887–88; reprint, Edison, N.J.: Castle, n.d.), 4:175; Mason Whiting Tyler, *Recollection of the Civil War, with Many Original Diary Entries and Letters Written from the Seat of War, and with Annotated References*, ed. William S. Tyler (New York: Putnam, 1912), 166; Charles A. Whittier manuscript, February 13, 1888, Boston Public Library.

39. John Gibbon, *Personal Recollections of the Civil War* (New York: Putnam, 1928), 209–10; Meade, *Life and Letters*, 2:185; McMahon, "Death of General John Sedgwick," 175; *OR*, 26(1):577, 654, 698, 646, 763, 882; Charles S. Wainwright, *A Diary of Battle: The Personal Journals of Colonel Charles S. Wainwright, 1861–1865*, ed. Allan Nevins (1962; reprint, New York: Da Capo, 1998), 360; David B. Parker, *A Chautauqua Boy in '61 and Afterward, Reminiscences*, ed. Torrance Parker (Boston: Small, Maynard, 1912), 42.

40. Cullum, *Biographical Register*, 2:62; Jack D. Welsh, *Medical Histories of Union Generals* (Kent, Ohio: Kent State University Press, 1996), 380; Theodore Lyman, *Meade's Headquarters, 1863-1865: Letters of Colonel Theodore Lyman, from the Wilderness to Appomattox*, ed. George R. Agassiz (Boston: Atlantic Monthly, 1922), 112.

41. Gordon C. Rhea, *To the North Anna River: Grant and Lee, May 13–25, 1864* (Baton Rouge: Louisiana State University Press, 2000) 370; Rhea, *Battles for Spotsylvania Court House*, 316, 319; Lyman, *Meade's Headquarters*, 176; J. Michael Miller, *The North Anna Campaign: "Even to Hell Itself," May 21–26, 1864* (Lynchburg, Va.: H. E. Howard, 1989), 6–7.

42. Jeffry D. Wert, *From Winchester to Cedar Creek: The Shenandoah Campaign of 1864* (1987; reprint, Mechanicsburg, Pa.: Stackpole, 1997), 5–7.

43. Ibid., 7–8; A. Wilson Greene, *Breaking the Backbone of the Rebellion: The Final Battles of the Petersburg Campaign* (Mason City, Iowa: Savas, 2000), 9.

44. Wert, *From Winchester to Cedar Creek*, 8; Cramer, *Lincoln Under Enemy Fire*, 49.

45. Stevens, *Three Years in the Sixth Corps*, 382.

46. *OR*, 37(1):222, 261, 338, 350, 414, 419, 422, 426; Alanson A. Haines, *History of the Fifteenth Regiment New Jersey Volunteers* (New York: Jenkins and Thomas, 1883), 229.

47. *OR*, 37(1): 330–31, 338, 413–14, 422, 423; Haines, *History of the Fifteenth Regiment*, 229; *New York Herald*, July 25, 1864; Peter J. Meaney, *The Civil War Engagement at Cool Spring, July 18, 1864 (The Largest Battle Ever Fought in Clarke County, Virginia)* (Berryville, Va.: Clarke County Historical Association, 1979–80), 47–53; Benjamin Franklin Cooling, *Jubal Early's Raid on Washington: 1864* (Baltimore: Nautical & Aviation, 1989), 214–20; "A Private in Company E," *Winsted Herald*, August 26, 1864.

48. Haines, *History of the Fifteenth Regiment*, 233–34.

49. Wert, *From Winchester to Cedar Creek*, 18–22, 43–45.

50. The Sixth Corps started promptly at 2:00 A.M. on September 19 and found the Nineteenth Corps, which had a shorter distance to march, waiting at the eastern end of the canyon. Over the next several hours, infantry filed through the defile. The march was slowed first by fording the Opequon and then by the steep grade and wet surface of the road. Emory, described as "swearing mad," lost patience when he saw Sixth Corps wagons on the road and received permission from Wright for his lead division to "hurry forward regardless of the order of march and, so as far as the trains were concerned, to pass them." As a result of that delay, Sheridan failed to attack before Early's reinforcements arrived.

A week after the battle, responding to Emory's protest about a newspaper report faulting the Nineteenth Corps commander for delay in reaching the battlefield, Wright deplored the "misstatement" and summarized the events as he remembered them. The Sixth Corps head expressed confidence that the Nineteenth Corps had moved to the front as quickly as possible "after it had been decided to park the trains on the east side of the Opequon." Sheridan seconded Wright's account. Wright elaborated in his report filed shortly after the battle. He reported obtaining Sheridan's permission to halt all trains and to advance promptly with only one battery of artillery, the remainder of the cannon "being held back till it could be ascertained that it would not impede the advance of the infantry columns through the narrow gorge." None of the Sixth Corps reports mentions a significant delay, suggesting that Wright's trains or artillery did not slow the march. Moreover, Brig. Gen. Cuvier Grover, commanding the Nineteenth Corps' lead division, stated in his report that his men moved "in advance of" the Sixth Corps ordnance and ambulance train. Wright's statement that a decision had been made to halt trains on the east side of the Opequon implies that some congestion occurred there rather than in Berryville Canyon. A postwar account by a veteran of the 15th New Jersey, among the last Sixth Corps regiments to reach the field, appears to confirm that corps trains in the road east of the creek caused delay.

Other, subsequent accounts mention a bottleneck caused by Wright's "baggage train," "ammunition wagons," and "headquarters wagons, ammunition trains and ambulances." In these writings, the Nineteenth Corps moved ahead by leaving the road to walk along the steep slope on either side. Emory, in an 1872 account sent to the adjutant general, contended that the trains of the Sixth Corps obstructed his march to the battlefield and faulted Wright because he did not allow the Nineteenth Corps to precede the Sixth Corps trains. Emory may have believed that because his corps had reached the entrance to the canyon first, his men should have led the way, though that contradicted Sheridan's orders for the march.

Reports dated closest to the action suggest relatively little difficulty with delays caused by any wheeled vehicles, and a close reading of other writings refer to bottlenecks that probably occurred at the western end of the canyon. Such problems could have been caused, at least in part, by the opening phases of the battle itself and the natural flow of men and materiel to the rear. Besides wagons, some of which would have been necessary, accounts include references to such impediments as the now disengaged cavalry, hospitals, noncombatants, skulkers, and wounded. The differing versions cannot be fully reconciled, though there seems little basis for the charge that Wright disobeyed Sheridan's orders to leave the regimental baggage wagons behind. Emory's orders to push his men forward past all obstacles reflects a sense of urgency and a demonstration of initiative that Wright, in overall command of the two corps during the march, should have exercised. Ultimate Federal victory at the Opequon relieved the parties responsible from fully answering for the delay, yet Wright bears partial responsibility for the Union forces' tardy opening of the battle and the early reverses that they suffered. In his memoirs, Sheridan regretted the "unavoidable delays" caused by Wright's ammunition wagons but took no personal responsibility for his plan that required two army corps to ford a stream and march rapidly up a steep grade though a narrow canyon. See *OR*, 43(1): 61, 149, 162, 189, 242, 226, 253, 266, 279, 318, (2):153; Wesley Merritt, "Sheridan in the Shenandoah Valley," in Johnson and Buel, *Battles and Leaders*, 4:158–59; George E. Pond, *The Shenandoah Valley in 1864* (New York: Scribner's, 1883), 158–59; John William De Forest, *A Volunteer's Adventures: A Union Captain's Record of the Civil War* (New Haven, Conn.: Yale University Press, 1946), 173; Wert, *From Winchester to Cedar Creek*, 49–51; A. Wilson Greene, "Union Generalship in the 1864 Valley Campaign," in Gary W. Gallagher, ed., *Struggle for the Shenandoah: Essays on the 1864 Valley Campaign* (Kent, Ohio: Kent State University Press, 1991), 52; Phillip H. Sheridan, *Personal Memoirs of P. H. Sheridan* (1888; reprint, New York: Da Capo Press, 1992), 288, 295, 300–303; Wilbur Fisk, *Hard Marching Every Day: The Civil War Letters of Private Wilbur Fisk, 1861–1865*, ed. Emil and Ruth Rosenblatt (Lawrence: University Press of Kansas, 1992), 258–59; Frank M. Flinn, *Campaigning with Banks in Louisiana, '63 and '64 and with Sheridan in the Shenandoah Valley in '64 and '65* (Boston: W. B. Clarke, 1889), 176–77.

51. Sheridan, *Personal Memoirs*, 300–303; Fisk, *Hard Marching Every Day*, 258–59.

52. Theodore C. Mahr, *The Battle of Cedar Creek: Showdown in the Shenandoah, October 1–30, 1864* (Lynchburg, Va.: H. E. Howard, 1992), 74–77; Merritt, "Sheridan in the Shenandoah Valley," 512–14.

53. Raoul S. Naroll, "Sheridan and Cedar Creek—A Reappraisal," in *Military Analysis of the Civil War: An Anthology by the Editors of Military Affairs* (Millwood, N.Y.: KTO Press, 1977), 380; Merritt, "Sheridan in the Shenandoah Valley," 512–14.

54. *OR*, 43(1):423–33, (2):367; Sheridan, *Personal Memoirs*, 314–15.

55. Sheridan, *Personal Memoirs*, 314–15.

56. Mahr, *Battle of Cedar Creek*, 79, 82, 87, 94, 96–97; De Forest, *Volunteer's Adventures*, 202.

57. *OR*, 43(1):154.

58. De Forest, *Volunteer's Adventures*, 209.

59. *OR*, 43(1):154, 226–28, 233, 256; De Forest, *Volunteer's Adventures*, 210; Mahr, *Battle of Cedar Creek*, 123–25, 127, 132–34, 140, 163, 204, 207; John K. Bucklyn, "Battle of Cedar Creek, October 19, 1864," in *MOLLUS*, 34:405, 409.

60. Mahr, *Battle of Cedar Creek*, 127.

61. Thomas F. Wildes, *Record of the One Hundred and Sixteenth Regiment, Ohio Infantry Volunteers, in the War of the Rebellion* (Sandusky, Ohio: F. Mack, 1884), 205.

62. Taylor, *With Sheridan Up the Shenandoah*, 489; Wildes, *Record of the One Hundred and Sixteenth*, 205. For examples of Wright leading from the front ranks, see Lyman, *Meade's Headquarters*, 112–14, 145, 175–77; Oliver Wendell Holmes Jr., *Touched with Fire: Civil War Letters and Diary of Oliver Wendell Holmes, Jr., 1861–1864*, ed. Mark de Wolfe Howe (Cambridge, Mass.: Harvard University Press, 1946), 104–7; Fisk, *Hard Marching Every Day*, 258–59. For Wright's personal statements as to where he was wounded, see Horatio Wright to George Cullum, January 10, 1866, Special Collections and Archives Division, United States Military Academy Library, West Point, N.Y.; "U.S. Army Generals Reports of Civil War Service, 1864–1887," VI, 473–477, R22, NA.

63. Haines, *History of the Fifteenth Regiment*, 227; Wert, *From Winchester to Cedar Creek*, 191; Hazard Stevens, "The Battle of Cedar Creek," in *Papers of the Military Historical Society of Massachusetts*, 14 vols. (1895–1918; reprint in 15 vols. with a general index, Wilmington, N.C.: Broadfoot, 1989–90), 6:108; Aldace F. Walker, *The Vermont Brigade in the Shenandoah Valley 1864* (Burlington, Vt.: Free Press Association, 1869), 138; *OR*, 43(1):256.

64. Naroll, "Sheridan and Cedar Creek—A Reappraisal," 380; Mahr, *Battle of Cedar Creek*, 171–73.

65. Mahr, *Battle of Cedar Creek*, 171–73.

66. Stevens, *Three Years in the Sixth Corps*, 427; John K. Bucklyn, "Battle of Cedar Creek," 407–8; Mahr, *Battle of Cedar Creek*, 239; Walker, *Vermont Brigade*, 146; H. M. Pollard, "War Papers and Personal Reminisces, 1861–1865: Read Before the Commandery of the State of Missouri Military Order of the Loyal Legion of the United States," in *MOLLUS*, 14:286.

67. Mahr, *Battle of Cedar Creek*, 239–45, 264–69; Fisk, *Hard Marching Every Day*, 269; George A. Forsyth, *Thrilling Days in Army Life* (New York: Harper, 1900), 159; De Forest, *Volunteer's Adventures*, 224.

68. *OR*, ser. 2, 5:500; E. D. Hadley, "The Battle of Cedar Creek, Popular History Refuted," in *MOLLUS*, 56:469; Harold Holzer and Mark E. Neely Jr., *Mine Eyes Have Seen The Glory: The Civil War in Art* (New York: Orion, 1993), 152–65.

69. Isaac O. Best, *History of the 121st New York State Infantry* (1921; reprint, Bal-

timore: Butternut and Blue, 1996), 200. See also Isaac Oliver Best, "Sheridan in the Shenandoah," Schoff Civil War Collection, William L. Clements Library, University of Michigan, Ann Arbor; Haines, *History of the Fifteenth Regiment*, 280–81; William Swinton, *Campaigns of the Army of the Potomac* (1882; reprint, Secaucus, N.J.: Blue and Grey, 1988), 563; Hazard Stevens, "The Battle of Cedar Creek," 223.

70. H. G. Wright to Louisa M. Wright, October 26, 1864, Gilder Lehrman Collection, Morgan Library, New York.

71. *OR*, 43(1):159.

72. Ibid., 158–61.

73. Letter to Dr. A. H. Stevens, February 2, 1899, CHS.

74. *New York Times*, October 21, 22, 1864; *New York Herald*, October 22, 1864; Wainwright, *Diary of Battle*, 474–75; Cyrus Comstock, *The Diary of Cyrus B. Comstock*, ed. Merlin E. Sumner (Dayton, Ohio: Morningside, 1987), 295; Sheridan, *Personal Memoirs*, 336.

75. Lyman, *Meade's Headquarters*, 300.

76. Adam Badeau, *Military History of Ulysses S. Grant, From April, 1861, to April, 1865*, 3 vols. (New York: Appleton, 1885), 3:504.

77. *OR*, 46(3):423; Bruce Catton, *Grant Takes Command* (Boston: Little, Brown, 1968), 443; Badeau, *Military History of Ulysses S. Grant*, 3:504.

78. Haines, *History of the Fifteenth Regiment*, 302.

79. Chris M. Calkins, *The Appomattox Campaign, March 29–April 9, 1865* (Conshohocken, Pa.: Combined Books, 1997), 105–11; *OR*, 46(1):905–8; M. L. Butterfield, "Personal Reminiscences with the Sixth Corps, 1864–65," in *MOLLUS*, 49:91.

80. Isaac R. Pennypacker, *General Meade* (New York: Appleton, 1901), 379–80; *OR*, 46(1):683, 980; Keifer, *Slavery and Four Years of War*, 305. A modern source puts Wright's attacking force at 7,000 men. (Calkins, *Appomattox Campaign*, 108.) Sheridan estimated his own numbers at 9,000 enlisted men on March 31, 1865. How many of those men were available a week later after the battle of Five Forks and the pursuit of Lee through Southside Virginia is a matter of conjecture. (Sheridan, *Personal Memoirs*, 267.)

81. Donald C. Pfanz, *Richard S. Ewell: A Soldier's Life* (Chapel Hill: University of North Carolina Press, 1998), 440–42; Horace Porter, *Campaigning with Grant* (1897; reprint, Secaucus, N.J.: Blue and Grey, 1987), 459.

82. Keifer, *Slavery and Four Years of War*, 217–18, 228; Paul Stephen Beaudry, *The Forgotten Regiment: History of the 151st New York Volunteer Infantry Regiment* (Cleveland, Ohio: InChem, 1995), 197. Beaudry consistently refers to "Horace" Wright as commander of the Sixth Corps.

83. David G. Martin, ed., *The Monocacy Regiment: A Commemorative History of the Fourteenth New Jersey Infantry in the Civil War, 1862–1865* (Hightstown, N.J.: Longstreet House, 1987), 129; Augustus Woodbury, *The Second Rhode Island Regiment: A Narrative of Military Operations* (Providence, R.I.: Valprey, Angell, 1875), 359–60; Stevens, *Three Years in the Sixth Corps*, 445.

84. Cullum, *Biographical Register*, 2:63; *OR*, 48(2):1086; Roy Morris Jr., *Sheridan:*

The Life and Wars of General Phil Sheridan (New York: Crown, 1992), 276–77; Horatio Wright to George Cullum, January 10, 1866, Special Collections and Archives Division, United States Military Academy Library.

85. J. G. Barnard, H. G. Wright, and Peter S. Michie, *Report on the Fabrication of Iron for Defensive Purposes and Its Uses in Modern Fortification, Especially in Works of Coast Defense* (Washington: Government Printing Office, 1871).

86. Horatio Wright to Norton Galloway, July 24, 1887, Historical Society of Pennsylvania, Philadelphia [repository hereafter cited as HSP]; *Society of the Army of the Potomac: Record of Proceedings, at the Third Annual Re-Union Held in the City of Boston, May 12th, 1871* (New York: Crocker, 1872), 4; Horatio Wright to Major Edmund K. Russell, June 24, 1869, HSP; *Sedgwick Memorial Association, 6th Army Corps, Spotsylvania Court House, Va., May 11, 12, and 13, 1887* (Philadelphia: Dunlap & Clarke, 1887), 104; Cullum, *Biographical Register*, 2:64; William Arba Ellis, *Norwich University 1819–1911*, 260.

87. *Army and Navy Register* 26 (July 1899):45.

88. Letter to Dr. A. H. Stevens, February 2, 1899, CHS; Stevens, *Three Years in the Sixth Corps*, 289–90, 382, 401, 411, 440, 443–44. Stevens's first edition (Albany, N.Y.: S. R. Gray, 1866) is 436 pages long. The second edition includes 445 pages and a two-page appendix. The second edition's version of the Valley campaign adds a few words of detail to the battle of Fisher's Hill account. In both versions, the delay on moving the Nineteenth Corps through Berryville Canyon is blamed vaguely on "some misconception of orders." For some reason, Time-Life Books reprinted the first edition in its Collector's Library of the Civil War series (Alexandria, Va.: Time-Life Books, 1982). Because the second edition contains significant additional material, Time-Life Books would have perhaps been best advised to reprint the 1870 version.

89. Rhea, *Battles for Spotsylvania Court House*, 316; Noah Andre Trudeau, *The Last Citadel: Petersburg, Virginia, June 1864–April 1865* (Boston: Little, Brown, 1991), 81; Porter, *Campaigning with Grant*, 166; Emerson Gifford Taylor, *Gouverneur Kemble Warren: The Life and Letters of An American Solder, 1830–1882* (Boston and New York: Houghton Mifflin, 1932), 194.

90. Cooling, *Jubal Early's Raid*, 236, 250; Merritt, "Sheridan in the Shenandoah Valley," 507; Pond, *Shenandoah Valley in 1864*, 158–62; De Forest, *Volunteer's Adventures*, 173–75; Wert, *From Winchester to Cedar Creek*, 49–51; A. Wilson Greene, "Union Generalship in the 1864 Valley Campaign," in Gallagher, *Struggle for the Shenandoah*, 52; Mahr, *Battle of Cedar Creek*, 173.

91. *OR*, 36(3):579; Charles A. Whittier manuscript, Boston Public Library. The Whittier allegations are referenced in Rhea, *Battles for Spotsylvania Court House*, 316 and Rhea, *To the North Anna River*, 15. A. Wilson Greene discounts Whittier's allegations, writing that there "is no other hint in the literature that Wright abused alcohol under stress." (Greene, *Breaking the Backbone of the Rebellion*, 52.) Whittier was not the only member of Sedgwick's staff to be cool toward Wright. After Sedgwick's death, Thomas W. Hyde continued to serve on Wright's staff before eventually commanding a brigade in the Sixth Corps. In *Following the Greek Cross*, Hyde hardly mentioned Wright. His only attempt at a description is in a single phrase noting that Wright had

recently retired as chief of engineers. (Hyde, *Following the Greek Cross: Memories of the Sixth Army Corps* [Boston: Houghton, Mifflin, 1894], 196.)

92. E. R. Jones, *Four Years in the Army of the Potomac* (London: Tyne, 1914), 132–33; *OR*, 36(2):79; David G. Martin, ed., *The Monocacy Regiment* (Hightstown, N.J.: Longstreet House, 1987), 126.

93. Cyrenus Stevens, May 10, 1864, typescript in bound vol. 36, Fredericksburg and Spotsylvania National Military Park Library, Fredericksburg, Va. [repository hereafter cited as FSNMP]; Charles Harvey Brewster, *When This Cruel War Is Over*, ed. David W. Blight (Amherst: University of Massachusetts Press, 1992), 307; Walker, *Vermont Brigade*, 17; Grayson M. Eckberger, typescript memoir in bound vol. 327, FSNMP; James M. Tescler, typescript in bound vol. 41, FSNMP; Bruce Catton, *Bruce Catton's Civil War* (New York: Fairfax, 1984), 555, 669–70; Sheridan, *Personal Memoirs*, 384.

94. Greene, *Breaking the Backbone of the Rebellion*, 32; Earl J. Hess, *The Union Soldier in Battle: Enduring the Ordeal of Combat* (Lawrence: University Press of Kansas, 1997), 121.

95. Meade, *Life and Letters*, 1:360; Frank Moore, *The Civil War in Song and Story, 1860–1865* (New York: P. F. Collier, 1889), 537.

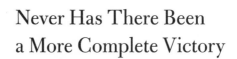

WILLIAM J. MILLER

Never Has There Been
a More Complete Victory

The Cavalry Engagement at
Tom's Brook, October 9, 1864

B rig. Gen. George Armstrong Custer, United States Volunteers, was in high spirits on October 10, 1864. He
wore the uniform coat of a Confederate general of cavalry, a fact he found immensely amusing. The gleeful
Custer shared the joke with the men of his Third Cav-
alry Division by cantering ostentatiously through their camps clad in the gray
coat, and the men, too, saw high comedy in the charade. Custer purposely cut
an absurd figure—sleeves drooping and lapels tucked under his armpits—but
the veteran troopers understood the more subtle humor of the performance as
well. They had themselves captured Custer's costume the day before, and they
knew that the original owner was no mere Confederate officer. Custer wore the
purloined coat of Brig. Gen. Thomas Lafayette Rosser, an old friend of Custer's from West Point. The classmates had each risen within the past week to
division command, and each bore both an excellent war record and the high
expectations of their men. When they had met on the banks of Tom's Brook,
in Shenandoah County, Virginia, however, Custer had erased old memories
and old comparisons and inflicted upon his friend Tom Rosser the greatest drubbing any Federal cavalry force had ever visited upon a Confederate
counterpart.

Beyond its clownish braggadocio, Custer's farce held a symbolism that any
of those Federal cavalrymen might well have enjoyed contemplating. For much
of the war, the Confederacy's horse soldiers in the Eastern Theater had been
routinely superior to the North's mounted arm. Having learned well from their
early defeats and embarrassments, however, the Federals had gained ground
and produced a mounted arm superior in equipment, logistics, organization,

tactics, and leadership. The northerners had attained parity on some cavalry battlefields in 1863, but the southerners had remained formidable opponents. Not until October 9, 1864, did the Union horsemen at last decisively step to the fore and complete the reversal of roles. At Tom's Brook, the Federal cavalry assumed figuratively what Custer donned literally — the mantle of mounted supremacy previously owned by the Confederates.

After Maj. Gen. Philip H. Sheridan defeated Lt. Gen. Jubal A. Early's small but active Confederate army at the battles of Third Winchester and Fisher's Hill in September 1864, the southerners withdrew in disarray to near Staunton in the upper Shenandoah Valley. No portion of Early's army suffered more from the chaos of defeat than did the cavalry. Two tiny divisions comprised Early's entire mounted arm. Maj. Gen. Lunsford Lindsay Lomax, a former staff officer with little experience in the cavalry, led one of these "divisions," which consisted of just six regiments, four partial regiments (battalions), and the attendant light artillery batteries, all organized into two brigades. Despite the elaborate order of battle, Lomax commanded just 800 men in the field — about what a colonel of cavalry might have hoped to command two years earlier. Early's other cavalry division was larger but still troubled. It had been commanded by Maj. Gen. Fitzhugh Lee, a competent and experienced officer, until he had fallen wounded at Third Winchester. Lee's replacement was Rosser, whose command experience extended only to control of a brigade of no more than four regiments. Blunt, burly, and brave, the twenty-eight-year-old Rosser had served since the war's outset. West Point trained, he had obeyed his conscience and resigned on the cusp of graduation to go south. He had sustained no fewer than four wounds in serving the Confederacy and had established an unquestioned reputation as one of the most aggressive and successful cavalry commanders in the Army of Northern Virginia. Rosser was also among the more brash and flamboyant. He had christened his command the "Laurel Brigade" and prescribed that his men should trim their uniforms and regimental colors with leaves of laurel. When "the Laurels" joined Early in the first week of October 1864, Rosser had declared them "the saviors of the valley." Had Rosser wished to alienate his new commander he could have scarcely done so more effectively. The curmudgeonly Early later wrote that he thought Rosser's "ridiculous vaporing" absurd and resented the implication that the Laurel Brigade would "show the rest of my command how to fight."[1]

Sheridan wore laurels only figuratively in early October 1864, but he would not rest even on those. In mid-August, Lt. Gen. U. S. Grant had stressed the importance of controlling the Shenandoah as a theater of operations and elimi-

Maj. Gen. Lunsford
Lindsay Lomax. Francis
Trevelyan Miller, ed., *The
Photographic History of the
Civil War*, 10 vols. (New
York: Review of Reviews,
1911), 4:111.

nating it as a granary for Lee's army. "Give the enemy no rest," the commanding general had written to Sheridan. "Do all the damage to railroads and crops
you can. Carry off stock of all descriptions, and negroes, so as to prevent further planting. If the war is to last another year, we want the Shenandoah Valley
to remain a barren waste."[2] Sheridan had begun the destruction immediately
in portions of the lower Valley. After gaining control of the upper Valley in late
September, he put torches in the hands of his cavalrymen and turned them
loose on a broader scale.[3]

Sheridan's cavalry chief, Delawarean brigadier general Alfred Thomas Archimedes Torbert, was a thirty-one-year-old West Pointer with a long record of
capable service as an infantry commander. At the beginning of the tenth month
of 1864, Torbert commanded in the field about 9,000 men organized into three
divisions. The Second Division, smallest of the three, under Col. William H.
Powell, had been detached for duty east of the Blue Ridge. Custer had ascended
to command of the Third Division only on the last day of September, but the
veteran First Division, previously Torbert's, had been in the capable hands of

Maj. Gen. Thomas Lafayette Rosser. Francis Trevelyan Miller, ed., *The Photographic History of the Civil War*, 10 vols. (New York: Review of Reviews, 1911), 4:73.

Brig. Gen. Wesley Merritt since early August. Though thirty years old, Merritt was but four years out of West Point. In that time, he had proved himself intelligent and able, both as a staff officer and as a cavalry commander. Like Custer, he was one of the "boy generals" given their stars in June 1863 and charged with, in Sheridan's words, "giving life to the Cavalry Corps." Sheridan later declared that both had fulfilled every expectation.[4]

The people of the Shenandoah Valley came to call Sheridan's campaign of destruction "The Burning." Beginning on October 5 in Augusta County, Sheridan's infantry divisions moved northward on the Valley Turnpike, while the cavalry brought up the rear, ranging across the Valley, torches in hand. "The cavalry as it retired," wrote Sheridan in his memoirs, "was stretched across the country from the Blue Ridge to the eastern slope of the Alleghenies, with orders to drive off all stock and destroy all supplies as it moved northward." Early responded swiftly. Keeping his infantry and artillery behind, he ordered Rosser and Lomax to "pursue the enemy, to harass him and ascertain his purposes." Lomax set off after Merritt on the Valley Turnpike, and Rosser chased

Brig. Gen. Alfred Thomas Archimedes Torbert. Francis Trevelyan Miller, ed., *The Photographic History of the Civil War*, 10 vols. (New York: Review of Reviews, 1911), 4:251.

his old friend and classmate Custer on the Back Road, west of and roughly parallel to the Pike.[5]

The emotional impact of The Burning on Rosser and his men cannot be overestimated. Rosser well understood that many of the defiled homesteads belonged to men in his command, and it was clear to him that they were moved to hatred. Years later, after time had dulled passions, an officer of the Laurel Brigade recalled with horror the spectacle of hundreds of fields, mills, barns, and even dwellings ablaze. The Federals, he wrote, left "a smoky trail of desolation to mark the footsteps of the devil's inspector-general, and show in a fiery record, that will last as long as the war is remembered, that the United States, under the government of Satan and Lincoln, sent Phil. Sheridan to campaign in the Valley of Virginia."[6]

A Confederate colonel confessed that many "who might have been spared as a prisoner atoned with his life, for the valley men, in many cases, took no prisoners." Another officer declared that his men were "blinded with rage at the sight of their ruined homes" and drove onward, "impelled by a sense of personal injury." Custer's rear guard was hard pressed to fend off vigorous attacks on October 6 and again on the seventh, but the Federals were not interrupted in their destruction.[7]

Snow squalls and a ragged gray sky set a dreary tone on the morning of October 8. Merritt's men, specifically the 9th New York Cavalry and the 1st New York Dragoons of Col. Thomas C. Devin's brigade, continued the work of destruction along the Valley Pike, burning mills, barns, and at Woodstock, a locomotive and the railroad depot. Col. James H. Kidd's Michigan brigade brought up the rear, finishing off what Devin had missed and parrying the occasional thrust by Lomax's pursuers. Kidd's men arrived at Woodstock to find the village burning. Flames from the barns and the depot torched by Devin's men had spread to dwellings, and troopers of the 1st and the 6th Michigan regiments dismounted to help citizens fight the fires. Watching from afar, Lomax's men saw the flames and were enraged. They charged into the town and drove the Michiganders out, including the bucket brigades. The Wolverines reformed north of the village where, according to Kidd, they invited an attack that did not come.[8]

On the Back Road, Rosser's no less angry men dogged the Federals closely. A New Yorker on the Back Road recalled that the rear of Custer's column was "menaced considerably" throughout the day. Maj. John W. Phillips, who commanded the 18th Pennsylvania, Custer's rear guard, declared, "In all the hard service which the regiment did, it had no harder day's work than that of the 8th

Sheridan and several subordinates who played important roles at Tom's Brook, in a photograph taken after Appomattox. In order from left: Sheridan, Brig. Gen. James William Forsyth (Sheridan's chief of staff, who was a lieutenant colonel in the 1864 Valley campaign), Maj. Gen. Wesley Merritt (a brigadier general in the Valley), Brig. Gen. Thomas Casimer Devin, and Maj. Gen. George Armstrong Custer (a brigadier general in the Valley). Francis Trevelyan Miller, ed., *The Photographic History of the Civil War*, 10 vols. (New York: Review of Reviews, 1911), 4:260.

of October, 1864. It was one continued running fight." The Pennsylvanians lost eight killed and five captured that day, and given the enflamed passions of Rosser's men, it can be assumed that the prisoners soon numbered among the dead.[9]

Sheridan was displeased. The impertinence of the Confederate cavalry galled him. Ten minutes before noon he wrote to Torbert that he wished this harassment stopped. "I want General Merritt to turn on them," he ordered, "and follow them with either the whole or such portion of his force as he may deem necessary. This will be done to-day."[10]

Sheridan was doubtless annoyed by the mere necessity of having to order what Torbert should have had done on his own. The cavalry chief had fallen into Sheridan's bad graces two weeks earlier during the Fisher's Hill operations. Sheridan had sent Torbert on a long flanking march up the Luray Valley in an attempt to get in Early's rear at New Market, the result of which, Sheridan had hoped, would be the destruction of Early's already badly whipped army. Torbert's movement was, in Sheridan's words, "an entire failure."[11] That same week, Sheridan had found one of the more experienced cavalrymen in the Union army, Brig. Gen. William Woods Averell, irresolute and sluggish and promptly fired him. Torbert could have had no doubts that he might be next.

Torbert, who had his headquarters at Strasburg on October 8, was aware of the southern cavalry's extreme aggressiveness and had responded. Knowing that Custer had his hands full on the Back Road, Torbert ordered Merritt to send help. Late on the dark, gray afternoon, Merritt dispatched Col. Charles Russell Lowell's reserve brigade (composed mostly of U.S. Regular cavalry) and portions of Devin's brigade. From the hamlet of Tom's Brook, Lowell's and Devin's men passed westward through the bottoms of the watercourse of the same name. On the Back Road, they found Custer had withdrawn to the north bank and that Rosser had not hesitated in following. Whether Custer realized it or not, he had drawn Rosser into a trap. Merritt's brigades closing in from the east were in position to cut Rosser off from his retreat route. Merritt saw the opportunity and pressed his men forward, expecting a counterthrust from Custer along the Back Road. Rosser only escaped when a citizen alerted him to Merritt's approach, and even then the Virginians had to brush aside Lowell's men with a saber charge.[12]

Merritt's troopers returned to the Valley Pike and went into camp, all except for Kidd's Michiganders. In compliance with Sheridan's earlier directive, Torbert ordered Merritt to send a force southward on the pike to determine the enemy's strength, so Kidd's tired men retraced their steps to Woodstock. Late in the evening, they rejoined the rest of the division at the northeastern foot of Round Hill, a prominent mound of wooded sandstone rising conspicuously 300 feet above the Valley floor southwest of Strasburg.[13]

Sheridan found rest elusive. After his noon dispatch to Torbert, the Confederate activity in his rear had somehow increased, and his own cavalry seemed unable or unwilling to stop it. "Tired of these annoyances," he wrote in his memoirs, "I concluded to open the enemy's eyes in earnest, so that night I told Torbert I expected him either to give Rosser a drubbing the next morning or get whipped himself."[14]

Having returned from his meeting with the army commander before midnight, Torbert dashed off orders to Merritt and Custer. The former was to have his men in the saddle ready to move at 6:00 A.M. Custer would by that time be advancing southward toward Tom's Brook, where the skirmish with Rosser had ended indecisively that evening. Custer was to communicate with Merritt so the two could coordinate their advance. Torbert explained that though they did not know where to find the main body of the Confederate cavalry, they knew it had been on the Back Road the night before. Merritt was thus to move toward the scene of the skirmish, near where the Back Road crossed Tom's Brook. He would establish a link with Custer while having scoured the intervening country for Confederates. At the same time, Merritt was to send "a strong reconnaissance" southward on the Valley Pike to find the enemy and learn his strength. Torbert closed by making clear to Merritt that half measures would not suffice: "You must put every available man in the fight."[15]

Custer had his men in the saddle early, and at sunrise Col. Alexander C. M. Pennington had his brigade, accompanied by Capt. Charles H. Peirce's battery of the Second U.S. Artillery, moving southward on the Back Road. Col. William Wells's brigade soon broke camp and followed.[16]

During the night, Rosser had taken part of his command well south of Tom's Brook but had left at least a portion of the Laurel Brigade and all four regiments of Brig. Gen. Williams Carter Wickham's brigade, commanded in Wickham's absence by Col. Thomas T. Munford, on Spiker's Hill, the high ground just south of where the Back Road crossed the brook. Munford commanded just 800 men in those four regiments, and he knew well that many more Federals than he could handle lay opposite him. Custer had been retiring for four days, so when Pennington's pickets moved southward, filling the predawn darkness with gunfire, Munford knew he would have to react briskly.[17] He reinforced his picket line, deployed the 1st Virginia and 2nd Virginia on the west of the Back Road, placed the 3rd Virginia just to the east of the road, and sent for help.[18]

Rosser hastened forward at Munford's call, taking with him a section of artillery under Lt. John W. "Tuck" Carter. These two guns belonged to the horse artillery of Capt. Roger Preston Chew, renowned for its long and superior service, especially in the Shenandoah Valley, where it had fought under Stonewall Jackson and Turner Ashby in the 1862 Valley campaign. The current commander was twenty-year-old Capt. James Walton Thomson, and Rosser directed that the rest of the battery should follow as soon as it could move.

Rosser arrived with Carter's two guns, the rest of the Laurel Brigade, and Col. William H. F. Payne's small brigade. The sun was up, and the same raw, gloomy weather — wind and threatening snow — chilled the men gathering on the hills above Tom's Brook. More chilling for the Confederates, perhaps, was the view of the meadows north of the creek. Pvt. George M. Neese, one of Carter's artillerymen, "saw the fields blued all over with hosts of Yankee horsemen in full battle array in line and column." A cavalryman peering through the tree cover found that "every opening disclosed moving masses of bluecoats . . . covering the hill slopes and blocking the roads with apparently countless squadrons."[19]

As Rosser sat upon his mount on Spiker's Hill that morning, the weight of command must have pressed upon him heavily. He was far from the nearest infantry support, new to his command, and did not enjoy the confidence of his superior, Jubal Early. In years to come, Munford and Rosser would feud bitterly, and it is unclear whether the animosity began at Tom's Brook or had already existed—the colonel had begun the war senior in rank to Rosser, but the latter had been promoted over Munford's head. On this day, the two would have to work together. Finally, Rosser was in pain. He had been shot in the leg at the battle of Trevilian Station in June—the fourth of six wounds he would suffer in the war—and the lesion, still open and draining, pained him so much he confided to his wife that he wished to be at home. What effect these burdens had on Rosser's decisions we cannot know. According to witnesses, he gazed across the valley at the blue hordes and calmly listened to Munford brief him on the situation. Munford later wrote that he said frankly that they could not hope to fight Custer's entire division, that he could not hold his position long without strong support, and that his left flank, though on a high hill, was "in the air." According to Munford, Rosser replied in "a vaunting manner" and declared, "I'll drive them into Strasburg by 10 o'clock."[20]

Rosser deployed his troopers in a shallow arc across the northern face of Spiker's Hill. Munford held the left of the line. Keeping the 3rd Virginia in reserve, he sent his 2nd Virginia with the 1st Virginia down to where the Back Road crossed the creek to oppose the Federal advance. Colonel Payne's tiny brigade of about 300 men fell in to the right of Munford's 3rd Virginia. Col. Richard H. Dulany of the 7th Virginia Cavalry commanded the Laurel Brigade, about 600 strong, and he put his men into position on Payne's right. The 35th Battalion, Virginia Cavalry, also known as White's Battalion, formed a portion of Dulany's Laurels. Composed of six companies of Virginians and Marylanders—some of them born and reared not far from the hills on which they would fight that day—the men of White's Battalion coveted the nickname "the Comanches," earned in a ferocious charge at the battle of Parker's Store in November 1863. On the morning of October 9, they numbered almost 200 and made up about a third of Dulany's brigade.[21]

The Laurels carried a variety of arms, including Sharps carbines, Henry repeaters, Burnside carbines, Colt revolvers, and sabers.[22] Lt. Nicholas W. Dorsey sent about forty of the better-armed Comanches into the creek bottom on

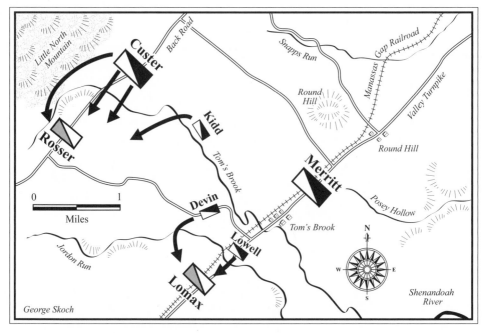

Battle of Tom's Brook, October 9, 1864.

foot as skirmishers.[23] Behind them stood the rest of the brigade: 11th Virginia dismounted with Henrys and beside them, mounted and atop the hill from west to east, the rest of Dorsey's men in the 7th Virginia and the 12th Virginia. Tuck Carter's two rifled guns went into battery on the face of Spiker's Hill behind Munford's position.[24]

The 5th New York Cavalry led Pennington's advance, and after driving in Munford's pickets at an easy trot, the New Yorkers felt the Confederate defense stiffen.[25] Custer deployed Pennington's brigade in long lines extending away on both sides of the Back Road. Custer rode ahead, the brigade immediately behind, colors and guidons jumping in the raw breeze. As the line crested a ridge and took into view the brook and its bottom, the division commander called for a halt. He studied the field before him and what he could make out of the Confederate positions. He saw a cluster of horsemen on Spiker's Hill and at length gleefully recognized his old friend from West Point days. Custer, ever flamboyant, gratified his taste for the theatrical by cantering forward alone, removing his hat, and making a sweeping bow in Rosser's direction.

Peirce's battery deployed on a hill to the east of the road and opened fire at long range. High winds hindered the gunners' accuracy, so when the Confed-

James E. Taylor sketched Custer's theatrical action on the morning of October 9, describing the incident in his postwar memoir: "Out rode Custer from his staff on his handsome black mare, far in advance of his line, his glittering figure in plain view of both armies. Sweeping off his broad sombrero, he threw it down to his knee in a profound salute to his honorable foe. It was like the action of a Knight in the Lists!" Courtesy of the Western Reserve Historical Society, Cleveland, Ohio.

erate artillery made no reply Peirce moved to a second hill, west of the Back Road and only about 800 yards from Carter's guns. There Peirce enjoyed more success.

Custer sent three regiments forward. The 3rd New Jersey held the center, and the 2nd Ohio spread out to the left. The 5th New York, deployed as skirmishers, stood on the right of Custer's line. The 18th Pennsylvania stood in the hollow, behind the 5th New York, just west of the Back Road, and the 1st Connecticut stood in reserve. Custer had an abundance of men at his disposal, and through the increasing smoke he considered how they might be used to best advantage.[26]

At last stung into action, the Confederate gunners opened an accurate, plunging fire that impressed both Custer and Peirce. The Federals replied in kind. George Neese, serving one of the Confederate guns, thought he and his comrades were "fully exposed to a raking fire of their guns all the time and all over. . . . Their shell and shrapnel and solid shot raked and plowed up the sod all around our guns."[27]

Beneath the umbrella of shot and shell, the cavalrymen, mounted and on foot, went to work. The opponents searched and probed, looking for an opening, content to let skirmishers and sharpshooters in the wooded bottom set the pace.[28] Attempting to exploit an opening on the Confederate left, the 18th Pennsylvania charged at the road crossing, but Munford's men, aided by Thomson's guns, stymied the advance. On the Federal left, Pennington led a mounted charge that dispersed the skirmishers of the 35th Battalion and pushed back the dismounted troopers of the 11th Virginia. From high on the hill, the balance of the Comanches charged down the slope, rallying the wavering skirmishers of the 35th and the 11th Virginia and repelling Pennington's foray.[29]

Custer grew more active in seeking an advantage, and the fighting waxed furious at times as charge and countercharge kept the contest in balance. In the ebb and flow, Payne's brigade made three countercharges against the Federals. Colonel Dulany went down wounded, and Col. Oliver R. Funsten succeeded to command of the Laurel Brigade. Custer had suffered few casualties but came to realize he would make no headway with frontal attacks. He began to look for other avenues of approach.[30]

A mile and a half beyond Rosser's right flank, Lunsford Lomax presided over a bad situation that held every promise of worsening. Arrayed on a high ridge just south of Jordon Run, Lomax's eight-hundred-man command was, in truth, nothing like a division and very little like cavalry. Before him, in the streets of the hamlet of Tom's Brook, advanced Merritt's division. If well armed, Lomax's men might have been able to make up some of the disparity in numbers between them and their enemies, but they were not. An officer from the Confederate inspector general's office examined Lomax's men two weeks after the action at Tom's Brook and described them as "very poorly armed." "Very few of the men have any arms, except long Rifles, which cannot be handled on horseback. [It is] owing entirely to this fact, that this division is generally overpowered by the enemy, when engaged in an open country. The troops of the enemy having from seven to twenty two shots to each man whilst our men have but one long Rifle, and that very unwieldy on horseback." The officer concluded that Lomax's division "cannot properly be termed Cavalry." Lomax's command was clearly in no condition to oppose Wesley Merritt's division. By Lomax's own admission, he could not hope to resist a mounted charge because his men had no arms with which to fight on horseback, "not a saber or pistol being in the command."[31]

Lomax's subordinate commanders were battle tested. Marylander Bradley T. Johnson, a brigadier general of long experience, commanded about a third of Lomax's men, while William P. Thompson, lieutenant colonel of the 19th Virginia Cavalry, led Lomax's other, larger brigade.[32] Nominally, the wounded Col. William Lowther Jackson, 19th Virginia, was commander of the brigade, but Thompson led in his absence. Lomax placed the Valley Pike in the middle of his line, with Johnson's men to the east and Thompson's on the west. The six guns — captured 3-inch ordnance rifles — of Lt. John R. McNulty's Baltimore light artillery, also known as the Baltimore Battery and the 2nd Maryland Battery, stood in the middle of the line in the road.[33]

Perhaps a half hour after Custer's division had advanced at 6:00 A.M., the Reserve Brigade, composed of three U.S. Regular regiments and the superb 2nd Massachusetts Cavalry, led Merritt's division southward. Torbert's plan was to advance on both the Back Road and the Valley Pike and gradually concentrate on the Back Road, where the enemy had been most aggressive the night before. Merritt divided his command. Colonel Lowell, forming the division's left, moved southward on the Pike. Kidd, the division's right, moved westward by a side road through the bottoms by the brook with orders to attack the enemy's flank near the Back Road. Devin, in the center, moved across country to seize the high ground south of Tom's Brook. As Merritt explained in his report, Lowell was to move his men southward through the village and on to the high ridge just south of the brook. Then, having secured the high ground, Lowell was to turn westward to the Back Road. The entire division could then concentrate on the flank of whatever enemy force was there and, with Custer, rout it.[34]

Lowell learned almost immediately that the day's program was not to go as expected. When his brigade cleared the southern edge of the village and hit the brook, Lowell sent out an advance guard. Less than a quarter of a mile on, where the ground began to rise south of Jordon Run, the Federal scouts met Lomax's pickets. The greater portion of Lowell's command had remained in column on the Valley Pike — in traveling, not fighting, formation. With the first shots, Lowell ordered out a skirmish line to explore more fully what lay ahead. Lomax, however, did not await such investigation. McNulty's Baltimorean gunners opened fire from the pike, and Thompson's brigade, deployed west of the pike, charged with a yell.[35]

Most of the Federal column was too far back in the road to be affected by surprise, especially because the Confederates did not press their advantage. After the briefest of thrusts, the Confederates fell back and regrouped. Lomax dismounted a portion of his force and concealed them in some woods. In the lull, Lt. Frank E. Taylor's guns, First U.S. Artillery, attached to Devin's brigade, went into battery on high hills west of the pike. Lowell deployed his brigade to force a passage of Jordon Run and the ridge beyond. The 2nd Massachusetts took the lead, and Lowell himself advanced to the dismounted picket line.[36]

Meanwhile, on Lowell's right, Devin's brigade gained Lomax's ridge west of the pike. Because he was well beyond the Confederate left, Devin met no opposition. Hearing the firing on Lowell's front, he turned eastward toward the Confederate flank and prepared to assist Lowell. As he came upon southerners, presumably some of Thompson's men, on the edge of a patch of woods, Devin dismounted two squadrons of the 1st New York Dragoons and advanced them as skirmishers, supported by the Fifth U.S. Cavalry, which belonged to Lowell's brigade but had been on duty at Merritt's headquarters. Having ridden to the sound of the guns, the regulars had arrived at the right place and time, and Devin sent them forward.[37]

Despite the advantage of the high, steep ridge, Lomax's position had become untenable. Neither flank was anchored on anything like a formidable feature of the terrain, and with but 800 men the Confederates were probably just strong enough to contest the 600 men of Lowell's Brigade. As soon as Devin turned eastward on the Confederate flank, Lomax had little hope of standing.[38]

Meanwhile, with firing audible ahead of and behind them, Colonel Kidd's Michigan brigade of Merritt's division moved westward along the bottomland between the high ridges that bordered Tom's Brook.[39] Just ten days earlier, this had been Custer's brigade. He and the Michiganders had risen to fame together, and the troopers adored their old commander as much as they loathed his transfer to another division. They had gone out of their way to mimic his affectations of dress, and each man sported a red neckerchief like that Custer habitually wore. One account states that it was these bandannas that Custer noticed when he looked to his left and saw reinforcements arriving and that he happily seized upon the arrival of his beloved brigade to launch a charge and break the stalemate below Spiker's Hill. In truth, Custer had begun planning for the decisive charge before Kidd's men came into view.[40]

Knowing that he outnumbered Rosser, Custer extended his line westward. If Rosser discovered this extension, he would be forced to abandon his position or to extend his own line to prevent the Federals from moving around his western flank. By attempting to protect more ground with his small force, Rosser would necessarily weaken his line elsewhere. If Rosser did not discover the extension to the west, his left flank would be caught by surprise, turned, and the entire Confederate position rendered untenable. Custer would have been pleased with either eventuality.

Custer began by strengthening his skirmish line. The 18th Pennsylvania advanced on the 5th New York's right to the creek and tore down fences to let mounted carbineers through. The Pennsylvanians extended westward along the creek and the base of the hill. At the same time, the 8th and 22nd New York, from Wells's brigade, moved behind the Pennsylvanians through woods and ravines to extend the flank even more. The two regiments together totaled about 350 men, all under the command of Lt. Col. William H. Benjamin of the 8th New York. Benjamin deployed his force in three parallel columns, aimed eastward at Spiker's Hill and Munford's flank. Leaving nothing to chance, Custer arranged a diversion on the Back Road by bringing forward the 1st New Hampshire and the 1st Vermont, both of Wells's brigade. In column of fours, the 1st Vermont charged across the ford and directly up the road, which was lined on both sides by fences. As the head of the column topped the crest, it sustained a heavy shock from canister. The rest of the column threw down fences on the right of the road and shifted to the west, where it reformed and charged again, firing its Spencers as it went in.[41]

All the while, rounds from Peirce's Battery had had a telling effect on the Confederate batteries in their exposed position. Overmatched by counterbattery fire and the approach of the New Englanders, the southern gunners limbered up and withdrew to a new position to the rear, farther up Spiker's Hill, a position very near where Colonel Benjamin's flanking attack would soon appear quite suddenly.[42]

Seeing the arrival of Kidd on the left and knowing that his flanking column would soon attack on his right, Custer launched the final push upon Spiker's Hill from his center. He rode in among the men of the 5th New York, still skirmishing along in the bottom by the brook, and, gathering a few companies from the left of the 18th Pennsylvania with the New Yorkers, personally led a charge up the hill.[43]

Kidd's Michiganders arrived to find some of Pennington's men making progress. A battalion of the 2nd Ohio had worked its way around the Confederate right flank and rear and had poured in fire from their Spencers. Kidd saw that "the enemy's line . . . was rather thin," for the reason that the heaviest part of Rosser's force had been massed in front of Custer. Without communicating with Custer, Kidd put his men in line and immediately attacked. The mounted portion of Lt. Col. George A. Purington's 2nd Ohio, along with Kidd's 6th and 7th Michigan regiments, charged with sabers upon the Laurel Brigade's right. Capt. Joseph W. Martin's 6th New York battery supported the charge with an accurate enfilading fire.[44]

The slashing attack upon Rosser's right stove in the flank of the 12th Virginia, which at once fell back. The dismounted skirmishers of White's Battalion and the 11th Virginia, who had stood in the bottom since dawn, now saw themselves flanked on both sides — by Kidd and the Ohioans on their right and Custer's thrust with the New Yorkers and Pennsylvanians on the left. Capt. Mottrom D. Ball of the 11th Virginia turned to see "the whole country to my left rear covered with the flying regiments of other brigades, the enemy pressing them close." With their supports crumbling, the foot-bound Laurel skirmishers ran for the rear, but the Federals were already among them. The 7th Virginia, in the center of the Laurel Brigade's line, held firm to give the dismounted men in front an opportunity to get to their horses.[45]

The troops Custer had sent around to the far right were not behind time in throwing their weight onto the scale. Colonel Benjamin and his 8th New York charged up the western face of Spiker's Hill, angling left toward Custer's main line. The Federals crested the hill with Thomson's battery on the road to their right rear. The New Yorkers quickly wheeled and took the guns.[46]

Thomson and his gunners stood firm as Payne's brigade, which had been detailed as the gunners' support, charged across the hill to save the guns. But it was too late. Artilleryman George Neese later claimed that the fire from Peirce's battery "was too hot for us, and a large body of cavalry was advancing on our position on both flanks with but a few scattering cavalrymen on our side to oppose them. . . . And we left our position not a moment too soon, for it was not long after we retired until I saw the blue horsemen swarm all over the hill we had just left."[47]

With the appearance of New Yorkers of the 8th and 22nd on the Confederate left and rear, Rosser's men were gripped by a fatal panic. As one southerner later wrote, "Every soldier knows that it only requires a shout in the rear to keep a stampeded force on the run, and it was so now, for the author saw fully six hundred veteran Confederate troops flying madly along the 'back road.'" Munford's brigade dissolved and headed for the rear in chaos, followed closely by Payne's brigade and, bringing up the rear, the Laurels. The engagement at Tom's Brook was over, and what would become known as "the Woodstock Races" had begun. Years later, Munford wrote succinctly, "It became more a contest of speed than valor."[48]

Rosser's officers, from brigadier to lieutenant, joined in the flight, but many of them endeavored to rally their men and several succeeded in doing so. Munford regrouped some distance to the rear,[49] and Rosser ordered him to charge to save some of the division train, parked by the Back Road. Munford deployed the 1st Virginia in the road, the 3rd and 4th to the west and the 2nd Virginia to the east, but the Federals appeared in such numbers that Munford and Rosser agreed that resistance was futile and the southerners withdrew.[50]

Most of Rosser's men fled southwestward on the Back Road, while some took a side road just in the rear of Spiker's Hill and headed almost due southward through the village of Saumsville and toward Woodstock. The Federals pressed both groups. On the Back Road, Custer's men followed Rosser all the way to Columbia Furnace, perhaps nineteen miles from Spiker's Hill, where Payne's men and Funsten's Laurels rallied.[51]

On the Valley Pike, matters were little different. After the short engagement on Jordon Run, an action more of maneuver than combat, Lomax had begun his retreat. Lieutenant McNulty and his Marylanders got their guns away from the advancing Federals and, with urging from Lomax and assistance from Colonel Thompson and his men, helped establish rear-guard stands on advantageous hills and ridges along the Valley Pike. "General Lomax was everywhere on the field," recalled one man of Thompson's brigade, "animating and cheering his men in the hour of defeat as well as in victory." Less than three miles from their initial position, however, the Confederates struck the open country just north of Woodstock. With no place to hide or to make a stand, there was nothing to do but run.[52]

The four guns of Capt. John J. Shoemaker's veteran battery of horse artillery had remained near New Market to receive fresh horses when Rosser's and Lomax's men had followed the Federals northward the day before. About noon, the battery halted north of Woodstock to feed and water the teams. All morning, the men had heard the boom of artillery, but now they noticed the firing had stopped. A courier sent ahead for instructions from Lomax suddenly reappeared at the gallop, bearing news of the collapse above Jordon Run. Shoemaker at once put his guns in position on the pike, hoping to serve as a rallying point for Lomax's fugitives. In a very few minutes, he recalled, "we saw them coming at a gallop. They didn't pay the slightest attention to us, but kept on going faster than ever, if it were possible." Among Shoemaker's men, shock quickly gave way to indignation. "Neither Munford's, Rosser's or Wickham's brigades, who were on the backroad, would have deserted us that way," Shoemaker wrote. One of the artillerymen began shouting, "Run, damn you, run: the Yankees are right behind you!" and the rest of the gunners jeered and laughed at the cowards.[53]

Expecting a Federal charge at any moment, the Virginians attempted to forestall the inevitable with a slow, methodical fire that sent one round down the pike at intervals of half a minute "as regular as clockwork." When the Federals did not immediately advance, Shoemaker and his officers decided to sacrifice one gun and its crew to ensure the escape of the rest of the battery. After a few minutes, when the Federals still did not come on, Shoemaker, who had remained behind with the sacrificial piece, withdrew under the protection of a second gun planted some distance to the rear. The second gun soon did the same under the flying shells of a third. The undulating country offered plenty of knolls from which Shoemaker's successive guns could fire, and the battery successfully withdrew one piece at a time at high speed for sixteen miles to south of Mount Jackson. Shoemaker lost not a gun, but his horses, fresh that morning, were completely broken down.[54]

Shoemaker's account, written long after the war, suggests a lull between the passage of Lomax's refugees and the appearance of the Federals. Merritt's report, penned just days after the event, declared that "not a moment's delay now occurred; the enemy was pressed at every step." With Lowell pressing southward on the pike and Devin moving on the Confederate flank, Merritt took no official notice of Shoemaker's heroes. He had met Devin on the pike shortly after the collapse of Lomax's line and ordered him to press the enemy. Lowell's First and Fifth U.S. Cavalry regiments came on as well, and the 2nd Massachusetts moved across country on both sides of the pike to gain the flanks of any Confederate rear guard. Moving at a trot, Devin reached Woodstock with little opposition and then bore off to the west on a byroad, driving a gaggle of Lomax's fugitives through woods and across Narrow Passage Creek. In the meantime, Lowell's men had come upon Lieutenant McNulty's battery just south of Woodstock. There, after a run of perhaps four miles, the battery horses, which Lomax declared were in "miserable condition" to begin with, gave out. The Marylanders unlimbered their guns and tried to hold off the pursuers, but the fresher Federal mounts bore their riders forward, and the northerners took two of the six guns. A few miles later, north of Edinburg, Lowell's men took two more guns.[55] Lomax did not fare much better. In the swirling fights along the pike, the Federals captured the division commander — but could not hold him. Lomax escaped by knocking one of his captors to the ground and joining in a Federal charge upon his own men. He later joked that he was the bravest among the Yankees, "for he charged right into the rebels."[56]

Lomax's deliverance was perhaps all that went right for the southerners that day, for the Federals were utterly relentless in their chase. When Lowell's brigade slowed at Edinburg, Devin, leading the 9th and 6th New York Cavalry, plucked up the baton and surged forward on a four-mile gallop to near

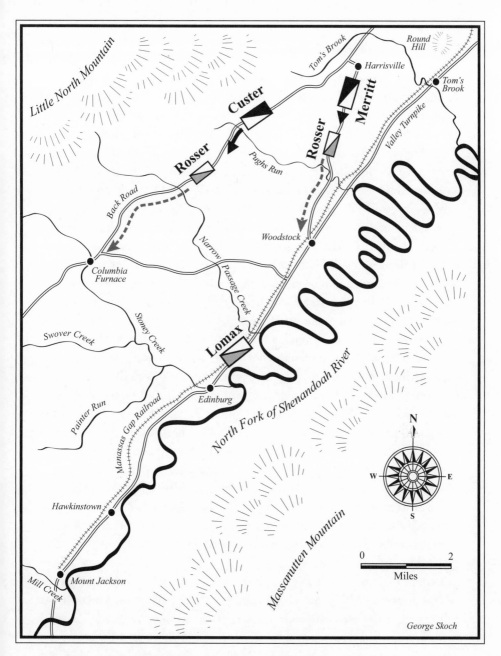

Federal Pursuit after Battle of Tom's Brook, October 9, 1864.

Little North Mountain

Tom's Brook

Round Hill

Harrisville

Custer

Merritt

Rosser

Rosser

Pughs Run

Valley Turnpike

Tom's Brook

Back Road

Woodstock

Narrow Passage Creek

Columbia Furnace

Swover Creek

Stoney Creek

Lomax

North Fork of Shenandoah River

Painter Run

Manassas Gap Railroad

Edinburg

Hawkinstown

Massanutten Mountain

N

W   E

S

0   2

Miles

Mill Creek   Mount Jackson

George Skoch

Hawkinstown. Lieutenant McNulty, struggling along with his last two weary teams, could not outrun the New Yorkers. McNulty abandoned one gun in the hope of saving the other. Determined to have the last cannon, Devin split his command to pursue on two roads. The men of the 6th New York thundered through Mount Jackson but found they were too late to snap up the last field piece. With all of Shoemaker's battery and the more fortunate of Lomax's fugitives, McNulty and his gun had crossed to the south side of the Shenandoah River. Merritt declared that when last seen, the enemy was "flying" southward across Meem's Bottom in disorder; "where they stopped the terror-stricken wretches could scarcely tell themselves, I cannot." The Federals ever afterward laughingly recalled the pursuit as "the Woodstock Races."[57]

A paucity of records makes it difficult to determine the casualties and captures on October 9, 1864. The marching and skirmishing of the days previous to the engagement made enumeration of the men present for duty difficult for the officers present, and the long-running fight made it impossible for Confederate leaders to distinguish among their killed, wounded, and captured. Understandably reluctant to chronicle the extent of the disaster, Rosser made no report and called for none from his subordinates. The more forthright Lomax admitted his material losses but did not enumerate them or suggest a figure for his losses in men or animals. The meticulous Merritt reported the capture of forty-three wagons full of ordnance, arms, and stores; five pieces of artillery with limbers (all but one of McNulty's guns); three ambulances; more than four dozen prisoners; and caissons, forges, mules, horses, and sets of harness without number. Custer had taken six pieces of artillery; the headquarters wagons of Rosser and Munford; the division's ordnance, ambulance, and wagon trains; "a large number of prisoners"; and General Rosser's coat.[58] Sheridan informally estimated the number of prisoners at about 330, and Torbert simply stated that "my losses in this engagement will not exceed sixty killed and wounded, which is astonishing when compared with the results."[59]

In addition to his many other trophies gained that day, Custer was able to capture in his report both the near helplessness of the Confederate fugitives and the arrogance of their powerful pursuers. "Vainly," he wrote, "did the most gallant of this affrighted herd endeavor to rally a few supports around their standards and stay the advance of their eager and exulting pursuers, who, in one overwhelming current, were bearing down everything before them." Torbert trumpeted that "there could hardly have been a more complete victory and rout. The cavalry totally covered themselves with glory, and added to their long list of victories the most brilliant one of them all and the most decisive the country has ever witnessed." Merritt merely concluded succinctly that "never has there been, in the history of this war, a more complete victory than this of Tom's Creek."[60]

If Torbert and his commanders expended no energy in affectations of modesty, it was likely due in part to reflection on the long road they had traveled to the evening of October 9, 1864. Confederates had argued, and would continue arguing for decades, that northern advantages in manpower and materiel accounted for their victories. Captain French Harding, who fought at Tom's Brook with the 20th Virginia Cavalry of Lomax's division, declared in his memoirs that the battle "was wholly a cavalry fight between General Early's half-starved and equipped few and General Sheridan's over-fed and well equipped many."[61]

Given the Federal ascendancy in all arms in 1864, it is tempting to accept Harding's argument that he and his comrades had had no hope at Tom's Brook. Yet granting all of the Confederates' arguments as to the advantages enjoyed by the Federal cavalry, physical superiorities alone cannot explain the northern victory. After all, Federal generals had for much of the war been proving that advantages in numbers, weaponry, and supply did not translate into victory if leadership was wanting. Whatever their level of relative disadvantage in numbers and equipment, the southern cavalry had managed a vigorous harassment of the withdrawing Federals on October 6, 7, and 8. And their commanders had chosen to stand and fight on October 9 against an enemy they knew to be more numerous and better armed. Given an opening by virtue of their effective maneuvering and fighting as well as by their material and numerical edge, Sheridan's horsemen had driven Lomax and Rosser and their men for two dozen miles, reaping every advantage along the way.

Tom's Brook had been a clear victory with real consequences. Jubal Early's cavalry never again played an important role in the Shenandoah Valley, leaving Torbert's brigades largely free to roam unchecked. The engagement also held symbolic importance for Federal cavalrymen who had labored so long in the shadow of their opponents. Indeed, there had never been an affair quite like Tom's Brook. Victories and routs there had been on both sides, but nothing had approached the one-sidedness of the thumping that the Federals had visited upon Rosser and Lomax. In this respect, what was accomplished tactically at Tom's Brook paled in comparison to what had been demonstrated in a larger sense. Custer and Merritt had not only shown beyond dispute their troopers' superiority to the southern cavalry on October 9 but also their parity, or more, with any cavalry in any theater of the conflict.

"For four centuries, or since the invention of gunpowder," wrote an officer of the First U.S. Cavalry, who had fought at Tom's Brook, "the great masters of the art of war had sought in vain to produce a soldier that could do effective fighting both on horseback and on foot." Thanks to the happy coincidence of technology, enlightened leadership, and suitable terrain, the American Civil War produced such soldiers, and Merritt's and Custer's men at Tom's Brook represented the highest state of development of this "hybrid cavalryman." Not only had the men of the First and Third Cavalry Divisions fought well in the saddle and on foot (Lomax was convinced he had faced Federal infantry on October 7, 8, and 9 when in fact he had only brushed with Merritt's dismounted troopers), they also had executed a prodigious pursuit unlike anything seen in the war.[62] "The fact is," Jubal Early wrote to Robert E. Lee on October 9, 1864, "that the enemy's cavalry is so much superior to ours, both in numbers and equipment, and the country is so favorable to the operations of cavalry, that it is impossible for ours to compete with his." From the date of Tom's Brook, it was the Union horsemen who would bear the standard of the finest American cavalry, and twenty years later when the armies of Europe revamped their mounted arms, they did so upon the model of the Federal cavalry of 1864–65.[63]

Acknowledgments

The author gratefully acknowledges the generous assistance of Garland Hudgins, Richard Kleese, Horace Mewborn, Robert K. Krick, Keith Bohannon, and Richard Griffin.

Notes

1. U.S. War Department, *The War of the Rebellion: A Compilation of the Official Records of the Union and Confederate Armies*, 127 vols., index, and atlas (Washington: Government Printing Office, 1880–1901), ser. 1, 43(1):613 [hereafter cited as *OR*; all references are to series 1]; Jubal Early in "Generals Early and Rosser," *Philadelphia Weekly Times*, May 17, 1884. An officer of the 35th Battalion of Virginia Cavalry of Rosser's command recalled that Rosser said "he is going to 'run over everything in the Valley'" (Frank M. Myers, *The Comanches: A History of White's Battalion, Virginia Cavalry* [1871; reprint, Marietta, Ga.: Continental, 1956], 335, 341).

2. *OR*, 43(1):917.

3. A quarter of a century after the war, an officer of the First U.S. Cavalry wrote with displeasure of having to discharge "this disagreeable and demoralizing duty" (Moses Harris, "With the Reserve Brigade," *Journal of the United States Cavalry Association* 3 [1892]:15).

4. *OR*, 43(2):248, 158, 177, 218, (1):421; Philip Henry Sheridan, *Personal Memoirs of Philip Henry Sheridan*, enlarged ed., ed. Michael V. Sheridan, 2 vols. (New York: Appleton, 1902), 1:474.

5. Sheridan, *Personal Memoirs*, 2:55–56; *OR*, 43(1):559.

6. Thomas L. Rosser, "Annals of the War: Rosser and His Men," *Philadelphia Weekly Times*, March 22, 1884; Myers, *Comanches*, 335–36.

7. Thomas T. Munford, "Annals of the War: Munford on Rosser," *Philadelphia Weekly Times*, May 17, 1884; William N. McDonald, *A History of the Laurel Brigade, Originally the Ashby Cavalry of the Army of Northern Virginia and Chew's Battery* (1907; reprint, Gaithersburg, Md.: Olde Soldier Books, 1987), 303; Louis N. Beaudry, *War Journal of Louis N. Beaudry, Fifth New York Cavalry*, ed. Richard E. Beaudry (Jefferson, N.C.: McFarland, 1996), 176. See also Henry Norton, *Deeds of Daring, or History of the Eighth New York Volunteer Cavalry* (Norwich, N.Y.: Chenango Telegraph Printing House, 1889), 94.

8. Beaudry, *War Journal*, 176; *OR*, 43(1):477; J. H. Kidd, *Personal Recollections of a Cavalryman* (Ionia, Mich.: Sentinel Printing, 1908), 400; "The Cavalry—Letter From 'A Soldier,'" in *Richmond Sentinel*, November 10, 1864.

9. Beaudry, *War Journal*, 176; *OR*, 43(1):540; *History of the Eighteenth Regiment of Cavalry Pennsylvania Volunteers (163rd Regiment of the Line)* (New York: Wynkoop Crawford, 1909), 28. See also A. B. Nettleton, "How the Day Was Saved at the Battle of Cedar Creek," in *Glimpses of the Nation's Struggle: A Series of Papers Read Before the Minnesota Commandery of the Military Order of the Loyal Legion of the United States*, 6 vols. (St. Paul, Minn.: St. Paul Book and Stationery, 1887–1909), 1:260. Nettleton served in the 2nd Ohio Cavalry.

10. *OR*, 43(2):320.

11. Ibid., 43(1):28–29.

12. Kidd, *Personal Recollections*, 400; *OR*, 43(1):446–47, 477, 491; Rosser to wife, October 12, 1864, Thomas L. Rosser Papers, MSS 1171-g, box 1, University of Virginia, Charlottesville [repository hereafter cited as UVA]; McDonald, *History of the Laurel Brigade*, 303.

13. *OR*, 43(2):320, (1):446–47. One regiment each from Devin and Lowell accompanied the reconnaissance. See also Hillman Hall, *History of the Sixth New York Cavalry (Second Ira Harris Guard), Second Brigade, First Division, Cavalry Corps, Army of the Potomac, 1861–1865* (Worcester, Mass.: Blanchard Press, 1908), 231.

14. Sheridan, *Personal Memoirs*, 2:56.

15. *OR*, 43(2):320–21. Torbert's orders suggest that Custer encamped northwest of Round Top.

16. *OR*, 43(1):550, 520, 549, 543, 545. Peirce's command consisted of the remnants of Batteries B and L of the Second U.S. and contained two light 12-pounders under Lt. Samuel B. McIntire and two rifles under Lt. Edward Heaton. Peirce reported leaving camp at between 8:00 and 9:00 A.M.

17. The 5th New York Cavalry, Pennington's vanguard, struck pickets of the 4th Virginia near Mt. Olive. (Ibid., 520.)

18. Munford, "Annals of the War."

19. McDonald, *History of the Laurel Brigade,* 305–6; Munford, "Annals of the War"; George M. Neese, *Three Years in the Confederate Horse Artillery* (New York: Neale, 1911), 322.

20. Jack D. Welsh, *Medical Histories of Confederate Generals* (Kent, Ohio: Kent State University Press, 1995), 189; Rosser to wife, October 12, 1864, Rosser Papers.

21. Munford, "Annals of the War"; John E. Divine, *35th Battalion Virginia Cavalry* (Lynchburg, Va.: H. E. Howard, 1985), 16, 42, 76; Myers, *Comanches,* 337, 338.

22. Inspection Reports and Related Records Received by the Inspection Branch in the Confederate Adjutant and Inspector General's Office, M935, 8-J-39, National Archives, Washington [repository hereafter cited as NA].

23. Lt. E. J. Chiswell of Company B commanded these dismounted skirmishers. They deployed in a line a quarter mile long. (Myers, *Comanches,* 338–39.)

24. McDonald, *History of the Laurel Brigade,* 305; Myers, *Comanches,* 338–39; Neese, *Three Years,* 323.

25. *OR,* 43(1):520.

26. Ibid., 541, 520.

27. Ibid., 549, 521; Neese, *Three Years,* 323. Custer claimed Peirce's fire dismounted one of the Confederate guns, but neither Neese nor any other Confederate account confirms this (*OR,* 43[1]: 521).

28. McDonald, *History of the Laurel Brigade,* 306.

29. George Baylor, *Bull Run to Bull Run or Four Years in the Army of Northern Virginia* (n.d.; reprint, Washington: Zenger, 1983), 252. Company B (led by Capt. George Baylor) of the 12th Virginia disobeyed Dulany's orders and joined the Comanches in the charge.

30. "The Cavalry Fights in the Valley—The Fight of Sunday Last," letter signed by "A Soldier" in *Richmond Sentinel,* October 15, 1864; McDonald, *History of the Laurel Brigade,* 307.

31. Inspection Reports and Related Records Received by the Inspection Branch in the Confederate Adjutant and Inspector General's Office, M935, 9/3-J-39, NA; *OR,* 43(1):612–13.

32. "The Cavalry," *Richmond Sentinel,* November 10, 1864. For a discussion of the elusive Thompson, see Robert K. Krick, *Lee's Colonels: A Biographical Register of the Field Officers of the Army of Northern Virginia* (Dayton, Ohio: Morningside, 1991), 371; for a synopsis of his service record, see Richard L. Armstrong, *The 19th and 20th Virginia Cavalry* (Lynchburg, Va.: H. E. Howard, 1994), 175–76. The comparison of the relative sizes of the brigades is based upon Lomax's statement that he commanded about 800 men and Armstrong's revelation, based on brigade returns, that Thompson's (Jackson's) brigade numbered 528 men, aggregate present, on October 25, 1864, two weeks after the battle (Armstrong, *19th and 20th Virginia,* 80).

33. Armstrong, *19th and 20th Virginia,* 134; George Perkins, "Yankee Hoplite: George Perkins's Three Years with the Sixth New York Independent Battery" (unpublished and unpaginated manuscript, private collection of Richard N. Griffin, Kaneohe, Hawaii).

34. *OR,* 43(1):460, 447, 483.

35. Ibid., 491; W. W. Goldsborough, *The Maryland Line in the Confederate Army, 1861–1865* (Baltimore: Guggenheim, Weil, 1900), 292. In the absence of abundant evidence, historians have speculated about Lomax's initial deployment. Though Lomax's report states that Johnson's brigade stood west of the pike later in the afternoon, the source relied upon here, a firsthand account by a participant, who, regrettably, did not identify himself, makes clear that at the beginning of the fight Lomax had deployed Jackson's brigade, commanded by Thompson, west of the Valley Pike and Johnson's brigade east of the road ("Cavalry," *Richmond Sentinel*).

36. "Cavalry," *Richmond Sentinel*; *OR*, 43(1):491.

37. *OR*, 43(1):483, 447, 492. The Fifth U.S. Cavalry was part of Lowell's Reserve Brigade (James R. Bowen, *Regimental History of the First New York Dragoons during Three Years of Active Service in the Great Civil War* [Battle Creek, Mich.: published by the author, 1900], 247).

38. *OR*, 43(1):445.

39. Kidd moved minus the 1st Michigan Cavalry, which served on the Valley Pike in the early morning and later operated with Lowell's Reserve Brigade (ibid., 448).

40. *Grand Rapids Daily Eagle*, July 8, 1876.

41. *OR*, 43(1):543–44, 521; *History of the Eighteenth Regiment*, 60; W. G. Cummings, "Six Months in the Third Cavalry Division under Custer," in *War Sketches and Incidents as Related by Companions of the Iowa Commandery, Military Order of the Loyal Legion of the United States* (Des Moines, Iowa: P. C. Kenyon, 1893), 299.

42. *OR*, 43(1):521.

43. Beaudry, *War Journal*, 176; *OR*, 43(1):541.

44. *OR*, 43(1):539, 465, 447; Kidd, *Personal Recollections*, 401.

45. M. D. Ball, "Annals of the War: Rosser and his Critics," *Philadelphia Weekly Times*, July 12, 1884; Myers, *Comanches*, 339; "The Cavalry Fights in the Valley," *Richmond Sentinel*, October 15, 1864.

46. *OR*, 43(1):544.

47. McDonald, *History of the Laurel Brigade*, 306–7; Neese, *Three Years*, 323.

48. Myers, *Comanches*, 340; Munford, "Annals of the War."

49. The site of Munford's rally cannot be determined with any certainty. Participants estimated it at between one and two miles south of the Spiker's Hill position. Maj. Walter C. Hull, 2nd New York Cavalry, reported skirmishing with an organized body of troops about two miles north of Columbia Furnace (*OR*, 43(1):537–38).

50. Munford, "Annals of the War."

51. Kidd, *Personal Recollections*, 402.

52. "Cavalry," *Richmond Sentinel*.

53. John J. Shoemaker, *Shoemaker's Battery, Stuart Horse Artillery, Pelham's Battalion, Afterwards Commanded by Col. R. P. Chew, Army of Northern Virginia* (1908; reprint, Gaithersburg, Md.: Butternut, 1980), 84–85.

54. Ibid., 87–88.

55. *OR*, 43(1):447, 492, 613; Goldsborough, *Maryland Line*, 292. A Federal artilleryman who saw McNulty's teams immediately after their capture was shocked by their condition. The guns, he wrote, "were dragged by the poorest and scraggiest speci-

mens of horses I had ever seen. The harness was all assorted, odds and ends, anything to get along. Some of them had four horses, and some only 2. One had two mules." This account is all the more remarkable because Lomax testified that the Baltimore Battery had just been newly equipped for the field (George Perkins, "Yankee Hoplite"; *OR*, 43(1):612–13).

56. "Cavalry," *Richmond Sentinel*; Jedediah Hotchkiss, *Virginia*, vol. 3 of *Confederate Military History*, ed. Clement A. Evans (Atlanta: Confederate Publishing Company, 1899), 628–30. The first source states that Lomax was captured twice, but no other account verifies that statement.

57. *OR*, 43(1):483, 448.

58. Ibid., 448, 521. The Rev. Frederic Denison, regimental historian of the 1st Rhode Island Cavalry, declared that the six guns taken from Rosser by Custer's men at Tom's Brook were, ironically, the very same pieces that had been captured from the Third Cavalry Division during a raid at Ream's Station, south of Petersburg, in the summer of 1864 (Frederic Denison, *Sabres and Spurs: The First Regiment Rhode Island Cavalry in the Civil War, 1861–1865* [Central Falls, R.I.: Regimental Association, 1876], 410).

59. *OR*, 43(2):327, (1):43.

60. Ibid., 43(1)521, 431, 448.

61. Joseph French Harding, *French Harding: Civil War Memoirs* (Elkins, W.Va.: McClain, 2000), 175.

62. Moses Harris, "The Union Cavalry," *Journal of the United States Cavalry Association* 5 (1892):3–4; *OR*, 43(1):612. Merritt remarked that the extent of the victory was due in no small part to the training and discipline through which his men had kept their animals in such good condition. Despite the active service of the first week of October, the Federals were able to chase a beaten enemy fifteen to twenty miles or more at rapid gait (*OR*, 43[1]:447).

63. *OR*, 43(1):559; Theodore F. Rodenbough, "Cavalry War Lessons," *Journal of the United States Cavalry Association* 2 (1889):106, 119, 121–22.

ROBERT E. L. KRICK

A Stampeede of Stampeeds

The Confederate Disaster at
Fisher's Hill

W hen the weary remnants of Lt. Gen. Jubal A. Early's Confederate army pulled into their entrenchments at Fisher's Hill on the morning of September 20, 1864, they stood on the brink of a crisis. The day before, the Army of the Valley had experienced a painful defeat at Winchester. With ranks that seemed to dwindle in direct proportion to the swelling numbers of the Union army, Early's little band now faced the double-edged task of repairing its morale while defending itself against pursuing Federals. There was some cause for optimism. Everyone recognized that only an overwhelming inferiority in numbers had produced defeat at the battle of Third Winchester on the nineteenth, and the new position at Fisher's Hill certainly balanced some of that inequality. The soldiers also knew it was the most defensible spot in the lower Shenandoah Valley, a valley that had been exclusively their preserve in three memorable campaigns. But advantages of terrain and tradition were not enough to renew the army's spirit. Two days later a small, well-executed flank attack drove Early's army in chaos from Fisher's Hill. Although those same Confederates regrouped to fight another day, it now seems apparent that the drubbing they received on September 22 proved to be an essential ingredient in the ultimate dissolution of Early's Valley army later that autumn.

Other famous Civil War hills — Henry Hill at Manassas, Malvern Hill below Richmond, and Snodgrass Hill at Chickamauga, for example — have well-defined boundaries that are easily discerned on the spot. Fisher's Hill is unlike those sites because it is not an obvious, free-standing geographic feature. The ground Jubal Early chose to defend on September 20 was a series of low knobs more than a hill. A gentle country stream, aptly named Tumbling Run, flowed at the base of the ridge and protected approaches from the north. To the west, the imposing bulk of Little North Mountain represented the left end of Early's line of defense. His eastern flank rested in great security on the North Fork of the Shenandoah River, which there abuts an arm of Massanutten Mountain sometimes called Three Top Mountain. This entire position was denominated Fisher's Hill and spanned 3.9 miles from the base of the mountain to the edge of the river.[1]

General Early indisputably understood the dimensions of this line. His army had spent several days there in mid-August building the very entrenchments it now manned on September 20. Even with the larger force he had then, the same strengths and flaws of the position must have been apparent. The collection of hills and plateaus that formed the heart of his stronghold abruptly ended less than a mile east of Little North Mountain. The final thousand yards to the base of the mountain was mostly flat. That ground's featureless appearance stood in direct contrast to the wrinkly set of hills that shielded the bulk of Early's force. He hardly could view a front of four miles, with the last stretch virtually barren of naturally defensible ground, as a secure spot. Early elected to stop and perhaps fight at Fisher's Hill because, as he subsequently explained, "it was the only place where a stand could be made." Early's claim was correct, as farther south the Valley grows progressively wider, with no natural stopping point available until Brown's Gap, southeast of Harrisonburg and sixty-five miles distant. If the army retreated to that mountain refuge, it would throw open the bulk of the Shenandoah Valley to the enemy, thus undoing all the good work achieved by Early's men during the course of their summer campaign. That move also would endanger the important railroad town of Staunton, one of the local lifelines for the Army of Northern Virginia. Seen in that light, Jubal Early's decision to stop at Fisher's Hill seems sound.[2]

Sluggish pursuit from Winchester by Maj. Gen. Philip H. Sheridan's Federal army gave the Confederates a welcome window of opportunity. As stragglers from the ranks wandered into the lines on the twentieth and twenty-first, Early reorganized the officer corps that commanded them. The death of Maj. Gen. Robert E. Rodes at Winchester not only deprived Early of his ablest subordinate, but it also eroded the morale of Rodes's division, which had greatly admired its old commander. To repair that sizable gap, Maj. Gen. S. Dodson Ramseur shifted over from a different division. It was a wise move, as Ramseur's old brigade belonged to Rodes's division, and he was known and liked there. Brig. Gen. John Pegram from Virginia then ascended to command Ramseur's former division. Pegram was another competent officer, well suited to lead a division in Early's army. For several months, Maj. Gen. John C. Breckinridge had commanded the two small divisions of Maj. Gen. John B. Gordon and

Brig. Gen. Gabriel C. Wharton. On September 21 he received orders directing him to another department in southwest Virginia, leaving Gordon and
Wharton independent of any higher authority than Early himself. The loss of
Breckinridge delivered a further blow to Early's organization, as the departing
Kentuckian had stood second only to Rodes in popularity. In only forty-eight
hours, Jubal Early's top two subordinates disappeared, and three of his top five
command slots changed hands. Very good officers remained in place at each
of those posts, but the juggling surely must have further unsettled the skittish
army.[3]

The alignment Early selected for his hastily retooled army is perhaps the
most controversial Confederate subject associated with the battle. Veterans
and historians alike have pointed out, with varying degrees of asperity, that
the configuration of the Confederate army at Fisher's Hill was the root of the
ensuing disaster. Early arranged his divisions, from right to left, in the following order: Wharton, Gordon, Pegram, Ramseur, and the cavalry. Gabriel C.
Wharton's two small brigades showed shocking evidence of hard use from
Third Winchester. One diarist in the division estimated that Wharton lost two-
thirds of his strength in the fight on the nineteenth. Inspectors visiting the two
brigades at the end of September, after the fight at Fisher's Hill, found that
the entire division numbered fewer than 700 muskets. Many companies were
without even noncommissioned officers. One can easily imagine the consequence that arrangement would have on discipline and in turn on battlefield
performance. Wharton's portion of the defenses took advantage of the steepest
hills on the battlefield. The river anchored his right, and the Valley Turnpike
climbed the hill on his left at a particularly steep grade.[4]

The line continued west of the turnpike with John B. Gordon's division.
The bed of the Manassas Gap Railroad bisected Gordon's position on its way
south to Mount Jackson. Two of Gordon's three brigades were tiny and probably ineffective. They represented the remnants of the once proud brigades
overrun at Spotsylvania's Bloody Angle back in May. Army of Northern Virginia headquarters had consolidated the various regiments into new brigades
that looked, on paper, unlike anything the army ever had seen. At Fisher's Hill,
Brig. Gen. William Terry's brigade of Gordon's division numbered fourteen
separate regiments, while the Louisiana brigade had ten. The loss of their well-
established identities sat poorly with the men of those reconstituted brigades,
sapping their spirit and reducing their usefulness. As a counterweight to those
two suspect brigades, Gordon had his old Georgia brigade, one of the largest
and best in the army. Its normal commander, Brig. Gen. Clement A. Evans,

was absent during this part of the campaign, but Col. Edmund N. Atkinson brought veteran leadership to a good collection of units.[5]

Farther west, separated from Gordon's division by the Middle Road, John Pegram's division also had only three brigades. Brig. Gen. Robert D. Johnston commanded five North Carolina units. The other two brigades had new commanders: Lt. Col. William S. Davis of the 12th North Carolina was brought in from a different brigade to lead the remnants of Godwin's four regiments, and Col. John S. Hoffman of the 31st Virginia replaced Pegram in command of five Virginia regiments. Some of these units resembled sickly companies more than seasoned regiments. The 13th Virginia, for example, only had forty men present at the battle. On Pegram's left, four very fine brigades composed Ramseur's division and represented the left of the infantry line. Each of the four brigades (Brig. Gen. Philip Cook's Georgians, Brig. Gen. William R. Cox's North Carolinians, Brig. Gen. Cullen A. Battle's Alabamians, and Brig. Gen. Bryan Grimes's North Carolinians) possessed distinguished reputations, and at Fisher's Hill each enjoyed reliable leadership. The ground Ramseur defended was the heart of Jubal Early's position, for there the craggy hills softened somewhat, making a Federal attack a more realistic option.[6]

Last, and in the army's mind least, came the collected cavalry brigades led by Maj. Gen. Lunsford L. Lomax. Some of the best cavalry in the state, commanded by Col. Thomas T. Munford, was absent in the Page Valley to the east, performing valuable duty in blocking the path of Federal cavalry toward Early's right and rear. Munford's loss left only Lomax's command to assist the infantry of the Valley army. Excoriated by nearly everyone, Lomax's five brigades were indeed an undistinguished lot. Brig. Gen. John McCausland's old brigade had been sent off to the right, near the base of Three Top Mountain, and played no part in the fight at Fisher's Hill. That left Brig. Gen. John C. Vaughn's mixed brigade and three mostly Virginian brigades to hold down Early's flank: Smith's, Johnson's, and Jackson's. Col. George H. Smith of the 62nd Virginia commanded what generally was known as Imboden's Brigade, after its longtime leader, and it certainly was the least bad of the trio. Brig. Gen. Bradley T. Johnson brought a winning attitude with him from the Army of Northern Virginia, but the material composing his cavalry brigade was not the best. Brig. Gen. William L. Jackson's regiments may have been worse than Johnson's. The bulk of the units in those latter two brigades had spent the war fighting in the irregular fashion of western and southwestern Virginia. Traditional battles, in the eastern-Virginia style, were unfamiliar and unwelcome, and nothing in their past service had prepared them for combat with the powerful legions of frontline Federal cavalry.

Vaughn's brigade is an organization little known to students of the battles in Virginia. Indeed, its precise composition at Fisher's Hill remains uncertain. Some of the units present with Early's army below Strasburg included less than half the 16th Battalion Georgia Cavalry together with the 1st Tennessee Cavalry, the 16th Battalion Tennessee Cavalry, the 43rd Tennessee Mounted Infantry, and the 59th Tennessee Mounted Infantry. There may have been fragments of other organizations lumped into this peculiar mass as well. General Vaughn had been knocked out with a wound earlier in the campaign, and Lt. Col. Onslow Bean assumed Vaughn's responsibilities. The brigade's role in the battle is poorly documented, and the organization does not even appear in the order of battle in the standard modern history of the 1864 Valley campaign.[7]

These four cavalry brigades, all far below effective strength, held responsibility for the last stretch of nearly flat ground from Ramseur's position to the foot of Little North Mountain. At least one of every four men had duty in the rear as horse holders, further diminishing the efficiency of an already weak force.

Morale in Early's army seems not to have followed any predictable pattern. Some soldiers, confronted with unaccustomed defeat at Third Winchester, were gloomy about their prospects. Capt. James M. Garnett, a staff officer long associated with the Second Corps, wrote on the twenty-first of being "fatigued in body and spirit, especially the latter." Although Buckner M. Randolph of the 49th Virginia was not present at Fisher's Hill, he rejoined the army on the twenty-fourth and reported to his family that when his comrades had pulled into their position on Fisher's Hill four days earlier, they had felt "ashamed of the Winchester affair & were resolved to fight to the last should the enemy attack their breastworks." In Cook's Georgia brigade, Joseph Ansley sounded cautiously optimistic on the twenty-first when he wrote, "I think there is but little prospect of a fight here, and if it does come, I cant see why the yankees wont get badly whipped, as we have a strong position." "We wait, with patience, the coming of the enemy," echoed Joseph B. Reese of the same brigade. In Cullen Battle's Alabama brigade, two men wrote letters on September 20, perhaps in sight of each other, and offered divergent views. Surgeon Abner McGarity of the 61st Alabama boldly predicted, "We can't be driven from here." Nearby, an unidentified soldier of the same brigade penned a hasty note saying he expected an attack that morning, adding, "I don't like the aspect of affairs much." A civilian correspondent in Richmond, in a very revealing passage that addresses the public's perception of the Valley army's status, reported that "it is generally understood that Early's men would not fight after their repulse near Winchester . . . and much is said about 'want of confidence' and a 'cowardly fear of being flanked.'"[8]

Those men in the Confederate ranks anxious to expunge the memory of Third Winchester probably were alone in welcoming the approach of the Federal army on the twenty-first. General Sheridan moved his troops leisurely as he struggled to adapt his plans to the sudden changes wrought by the battle on the nineteenth. An overwhelming numerical advantage helped ease Sheridan's transition. One modern historian has estimated that army's strength at "approximately 35,000" men on September 21. Facing Sheridan from atop the string of knobs at Fisher's Hill, Jubal Early could muster far fewer fighting men. Maj. Samuel J. C. Moore, later Early's chief of staff, suggested after the war that the army took only about 11,000 men into the fight at Third Winchester, which would mean that Early's strength at Fisher's Hill was perilously close to 8,000. Clarence R. Hatton, an officer attached to the staff of a North Carolina brigade, later claimed to have seen a morning report after the battle at Fisher's Hill that showed Early's army with 7,248 soldiers, meaning it would have numbered between 8,000 and 8,500 effectives on September 22. By any calculation or combination of sources, it is clear that Sheridan's army outnumbered the Confederates almost four to one. Standing strictly on the defensive at Fisher's Hill could not be enough to balance those slanted figures. Each man in Early's army must have been responsible, on average, for nearly three feet of the line, a terrible ratio.[9]

From their lofty position, southern infantrymen observed with interest as Sheridan's army approached on the twenty-first. Great clouds of dust hanging over the Valley floor marked the Federals' progress and visually reminded the Confederates of the great strength of the Union army. A Confederate officer on one of the highest hills enjoyed watching the maneuver, cheerfully terming it "an animating spectacle." Jubal Early chose not to defend the town of Strasburg, just northeast of the Fisher's Hill position, but he did contest the ground just north of Tumbling Run. Another chain of hills, mostly unwooded, lay across the stream from the primary Confederate line. Where the Middle Road crossed Tumbling Run, the ground on the northern bank had a separate identity, called "Flint Hill," and reached an elevation equal to that of the terrain defended by Gordon's and Pegram's divisions on the other side. For any direct assault to stand a chance of success, Sheridan's army needed possession of not only Flint Hill but also the smaller knobs flanking it. The scuffle for that terrain on September 21 was part of the preliminary groundwork necessary for the next day's Union offensive. Many brigades in Early's army had organized sharpshooter battalions by the autumn of 1864, and those units occupied rifle pits and imperfect barricades on the northern bank of Tumbling Run. Late in the day, vigorous assaults by men of the Federal Sixth Corps succeeded in securing the coveted heights, forcing the Confederate skirmishers to melt back into the primary line of defense.[10]

As every eye followed those obvious preliminaries, the most important pre-battle maneuver went unseen. The Federal division of Brig. Gen. George Crook did not accompany the rest of Sheridan's army in its noisy march through Stras-burg. Instead it took shelter in the wooded vales north of the town. Its presence there seems to have escaped the notice of the men manning the Confederate signal stations, and apparently Early was unaware of Crook's position before the battle. The Shenandoah Valley is an unlikely venue for secret movements, particularly at its narrowest point. The Federals' success in shielding Crook's detour emphasizes the inefficiency of the Confederate cavalry and stands as an indictment of Early's signalmen.

While blue-coated infantry wrested Flint Hill away from its thin line of Con-federate defenders, General Sheridan conspired with his top subordinates to use Crook's hidden division as a strike force that would pry the Confederates loose from their bastion at Fisher's Hill. Officers of the Nineteenth Corps could testify to the impracticability of storming the eastern end of the position, which had the steepest ascent. Maj. Gen. Horatio G. Wright's Sixth Corps occupied the center of the line, where offensive prospects looked mixed. On the west-ern end of his front, Sheridan had his cavalry, mostly dismounted, facing the unhorsed Confederate cavalry. It was clear to everyone on both sides that the most vulnerable section of the Fisher's Hill line was the portion near the base of Little North Mountain. Not only was the ground friendlier for an attack, but the feeble Confederate cavalry also offered a likelier target than the reliable infantrymen farther east along the line. After pondering those facts, Sheridan chose to launch Crook's men on a flanking march up the eastern face of Little North Mountain. This would be the decisive movement of the ensuing battle and the key to the Confederate collapse in the Valley.[11]

Crook's march to the scene of action on the twenty-second took him toward the Back Road, a dirt thoroughfare that paralleled the western edge of the Val-ley all through its northern section. While Crook's column snaked southwest-ward through crevices and along wooded paths, the Confederates at Fisher's

Hill seem to have been paralyzed. They had been in the entrenchments there for two days by the morning of the twenty-second, yet nobody claimed then or afterward to have a clear conception of what lay ahead. The men had been strengthening their old entrenchments on the twentieth and twenty-first. Because the western end of the line seemed like an obvious weak point, Lomax's cavalry even commenced new fortifications a few yards into the woods up the slope of Little North Mountain. Despite those precautions, generals Lomax and Ramseur expressed doubts about their ability to resist a Federal onslaught at that point.[12]

Having determined that he would stand and fight, Jubal Early seems at first to have been content to await developments. At the same time, it began to dawn on many in the army that the position could not be held against Sheridan's massive force. By September 22, the army commander and his men had drifted toward an unsettling void between confidence and doubt. Early wrote a few weeks later that on the twenty-second he "discovered that the position could be flanked," causing him to decide to retreat in the darkness that night. It is not apparent why it took General Early three days — on his second occupation of the position — to understand the weakness of Fisher's Hill. Early deserves more criticism for the uncertainty and malaise that infected the Army of the Valley at Fisher's Hill than he does for his army's physical alignment at that position.[13]

As bad as that indecision was, worse events developed on the twenty-second that are even harder to explain. Once Sheridan and Crook agreed on their flanking maneuver, Crook's column spent the afternoon executing the plan. His four brigades, probably numbering a few more than 5,500 men, dodged among the woodlots north of Fisher's Hill, slowly angling toward the Back Road and the foot of Little North Mountain. As with any tactical end around, secrecy was vital. Not only did the flankers hope to remain unseen by the Confederates atop the hills south of Tumbling Run, they also knew that a careless step would alert the signal station on Three Top Mountain. If spotted too early in the march, Crook's men would lose their advantage and perhaps fail in their mission when faced by Confederate countermeasures. George Crook led the march himself, weaving among hillocks and through ravines, always, as he later wrote, "keeping my eyes on the signal station."[14]

If Crook could keep his eyes on the signal position, it seems likely that the men manning that post could see him. In this instance, diligent observers on the mountain did see Crook's column and reported it to Early's headquarters. Pvt. B. L. Wynn, assigned to the Valley army on signal duty, wrote in his diary on the twenty-second that his colleague William B. Kleinpeter "reports the enemy preparing for a general advance. Sends several messages about enemy appearing in front and on the flank of Gen. Ramseur's forces." Maryland cavalryman Joseph R. Stonebraker chose the twenty-second to ride up Three Top Mountain, and a signal officer there "said to me that he thought that Sheridan was massing troops on our left, under cover of the timber." More than a few of the soldiers in the trenches at Fisher's Hill wrote then and later in the same vein. George Q. Peyton of the 13th Virginia remembered seeing the Federals "marching across a naked field on the side of North Mountain for hours before we heard the firing from there." Gen. Bryan Grimes, commanding a brigade near the left of Early's line, maintained that he saw Crook's brigades climbing the face of the mountain and urged division commander Dodson Ramseur to react quickly. Grimes complained that Ramseur refused to do anything until General Early had been notified — a process that apparently took more than a few minutes. The remaining hour between the discovery and the attack seemed excruciating for Grimes, who waited for the axe to fall. "My anxiety for the fate of the army was intolerable," he later wrote. Artillerist Henry Berkeley explicitly chronicled the same event in his diary: "We can see them plainly climbing up the side of North Mountain. I suppose Gen. Early knows this and has troops there to meet them, and unless he has, we will have to get from this position, and very quickly too."[15]

Another artillerist, writing twenty-five years later, told how some of his battery mates found General Ramseur and pointed out Crook's regiments struggling up the mountain, prompting Ramseur to scoff that it probably was a fence line. Nonetheless, he looked through his field glasses and said loudly, "My God! Two lines of the enemy's infantry!" Enough evidence of this sort survives to make it reasonably certain that Ramseur and many of the men in his division, at least, saw the disaster in its infancy and were powerless to arrest its progress.[16]

In later years, Jubal Early remained entirely silent on the subject of the early warning. It never has been explained when if ever the intelligence of Crook's movement reached him. The efforts of the signalmen and General Ramseur to reach Early may have failed, and no source gives his personal location when the attack finally struck. Even his warmest enemies could not accuse Old Jube of neglecting his duty. He had no agenda to prosecute, no point to prove, and could not possibly earn anything other than misery and embarrassment by ignoring that flanking column. We must conclude that Early somehow remained unaware of Crook's movement until too late to muster a response.[17]

Only the dismounted Confederate cavalry division stood between Ramseur's

Maj. Gen. Stephen Dodson Ramseur, who described himself as "much mortified" after Fisher's Hill because the soldiers of his division were "very much stampeded & did not keep cool or fight as well as they have heretofore done." Robert Underwood Johnson and Clarence Clough Buel, eds., *Battles and Leaders of the Civil War*, 4 vols. (New York: Century, 1887–88), 4:242.

infantry and Crook's mountain-climbing bluecoats. Lunsford Lomax could count open terrain to his front and the presence of a few batteries of horse artillery among his assets, but he had ample cause for pessimism otherwise. The army blamed the cavalry for every setback these days, usually with cause, and confidence within the mounted arm waned. Outnumbered and outgunned soldiers, riding emaciated horses, left Lomax with a sadly ineffective and unreliable force. To their credit, his regiments had been laboring hard since the twentieth to improve their vulnerable position. Fresh breastworks of logs and stacked rails stood four feet high and were chinked with dirt and rocks. These had sprung up in the low ground near the base of the mountain in the previous forty-eight hours. Some artillery crews constructed their own redoubts, while other cavalrymen continued to work on the thin line of rifle pits in the woods part way up the side of Little North Mountain. These were wise moves and showed that the army's cavalry retained some energy. General Lomax estimated his entire strength at about 1,000 men, but that seems like an incredibly low sum for four brigades. Charles T. O'Ferrall, who commanded the collection of horseless cavalrymen that operated with Lomax's division, thought there were 300 men in his own force alone at Fisher's Hill.[18]

Well-planned flank attacks often employ diversions to fix the attention of the victims in the wrong direction. This seemed especially important as Crook's line wriggled along the base and side of the mountain less than a mile from Lomax's cavalry. Brig. Gen. William W. Averell's Federal cavalry division earnestly skirmished with the Confederates along the Back Road all day on the twenty-second. When Crook disappeared up the side of the mountain, Averell launched an attack on Lomax's western flank. E. P. Goggin of General Lomax's staff remembered the "dense black columns" that appeared directly in front. Although Bradley Johnson's brigade was there to snub the Union advance, the probe achieved its loftier purpose of distracting the southern horsemen. Hard on the heels of this small victory, Lomax's men turned to find fresh bluecoats coming down the mountain squarely on their flank. Averell had remained in contact after his preliminary repulse, and now the Confederates found themselves "vigorously pressed" in front while being flanked by Crook from the west.[19]

By late afternoon, with the autumn sun just above the rim of the mountain, Crook had maneuvered his force high enough up the slope of Little North Mountain to achieve his desired alignment. He halted his columns and faced them left ninety degrees. The view they saw must have been a memorable one. "The slope of the mountain was one mass of rocks . . . covered with a small growth of timber," wrote Crook. Peering through the trees into the low ground ahead, the Federals could see directly down the line of Confederate cavalry. Like a skillful admiral leading a line of ships, Crook had achieved the ideal "tee" formation, directly on the flank of Lomax's cavalry. A country lane that crawled part way up the slope probably divided the Federal position, with two brigades on its left and two on its right. There was little time to admire this alignment. With belated vigilance, Lomax's pickets in the trees near the foot of the mountain's slope spied Crook's men and opened the action. Although the advantage of surprise was not entirely lost, the Federals in this instance did not inflict the complete, jaw-dropping sort of shock usually associated with Stonewall Jackson's famous flank attack at Chancellorsville from the year before.[20]

There is little doubt that despite the preliminary picket firing, the bulk of Lomax's men were unprepared for the onslaught coming off the mountain. Bradley Johnson had seen it and sent a staff officer to alert Lomax, but before any precautionary steps could be taken the Federals were upon them. The arrangement of Lomax's brigades when the flank attack struck is not entirely cer-

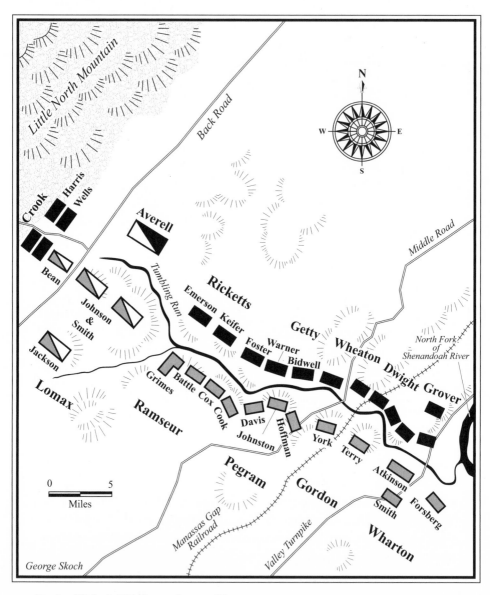

Battle of Fisher's Hill, September 22, 1864.

tain. General Johnson reported that the brigades stood, from left to right, in the following order: Bean, Smith, Johnson, Jackson. The 8th Virginia Cavalry, of Johnson's own brigade, was for some reason "up in the woods on the North Mountain dismounted, fighting as infantry." That regiment, separated from its parent brigade, anchored the left of the entire line, on Bean's left. Reactions to the attack varied by command. "Had the heavens opened, and we been seen descending therefrom, the surprise of the Confederates could not have been greater," wrote an officer in the 34th Massachusetts. In some instances that was true. Norval Baker of the 18th Virginia Cavalry in Smith's brigade had drawn duty as a horse holder that morning, and was to the rear of the main line when Col. Rutherford B. Hayes's division struck among the vulnerable led horses. "The horse I had next to me was wounded and tore from me with such force that the bridle strap tore some flesh from my hand," Baker wrote in his diary. "I pulled my gun and commenced fighting. The other boys let the horses go and did the same." Where the 8th Virginia Cavalry stood, the Federals' charge passed somewhat to the rear, leaving the 8th with an opportunity to turn the tables and smite Crook's flank. Col. Alphonso F. Cook ordered the 8th to turn around and attack southward, "which we did, and struck the rear of Crooks corps who about-faced and poured a hot fire into us," wrote James D. Sedinger. General Johnson claimed great success for the 8th, writing that its counterattack succeeded in "driving the enemy back into the mountain." Union sources make no mention of this episode, and it cannot have been more than a brief bump in Crook's path.[21]

Elsewhere along Lomax's front, the reaction to Crook's advance was in keeping with the formula for a flank attack. Bean's cavalry brigade was taken entirely by surprise. Capt. Reuben Clark of the 59th Tennessee Mounted Infantry recalled, somewhat ludicrously, that the first he knew of the Unionists' approach was when one of his men yelled out, "Look here, Captain, behind us!" Clark spun around to see Crook's men "within a few steps behind us." Bean's brigade, predictably and understandably, dissolved. Bradley Johnson's brigade, next in line, apparently gave way in short order, though the general was under fire long enough to have a bullet clip his pants leg and another smash through his saddle bag. The men of Smith's regiments also broke and ran, which Colonel Smith admitted, though he sharply countered subsequent criticism by pointing out that his brigade "made a stand when it got up with the infantry and stood until the infantry ran away." An artillerist in Ramseur's division left little room for misunderstanding when he wrote that the Confederate cavalry "rushed down like the swine with an overdose of devils."[22]

When the fight started Jackson's brigade stood either on the far right of Lomax's division or in reserve. "Our regiment did not start to retreat until we were enclosed in . . . an acute angle," wrote French Harding of the 20th Virginia Cavalry. In response to the increasing scorn directed toward the Valley cavalry by southern newspapers, a soldier in that same brigade wrote to the *Richmond Sentinel* after the battle to defend his unit's reputation. At Fisher's Hill, he complained, the standard reports mistakenly placed blame for the disaster on Jackson's men, "whilst in truth they were not in line, but were ordered up . . . and actually charged through the Yankee lines and temporarily re-took the fortifications, and were compelled to fall back because of the infantry giving way on their right." The 2nd Maryland Cavalry fought in Jackson's brigade at Fisher's Hill, and accounts from its ranks hardly confirm that bold claim. Col. Gustavus W. Dorsey led a counterattack into Crook's flank, "but the charge only availed to release some prisoners and to get the horses of the dismounted men out of the way." Those horses were essential military booty. Without them the Valley cavalry would have ended the war as infantry. While Dorsey parried and thrust, George W. Booth of General Bradley Johnson's staff organized the escape of the horses. All went well until the last of the cavalry gave way. This created a "semi-panic," with "the men leading the horses into a gallop, and soon the whole outfit was in a helpless state of rout; saddles were slipping and turning, horses were breaking away from their holders, baggage and bundles were being spilled all along the road in the utter confusion. It was not within the limit of human ability to stop or stem the mad flying column."[23]

General Lomax was one of the earliest and loudest defenders of the Confederate cavalry's performance at Fisher's Hill. Writing just six weeks after the battle, he offered no apologies and actually assumed the offensive, noting that his men blocked Crook's regiments "and drove them back some distance. . . . The infantry failed to come to my support." He closed his argument by claiming that if his men "had been supported . . . the enemy would have been forced back." Such implausible and unnecessary statements diminish Lomax's credibility and make it harder to believe anything he wrote. Clearly the cavalry did what it could in isolated episodes. Not every man ran, and some units with able leaders probably counterattacked. Outnumbered at least five to one, fighting dismounted, with pressure from two directions, it is unremarkable that the cavalry broke and scattered. Pretending otherwise, and assuming the air of an abandoned hero, was a graceless and ill-considered ploy by Lomax.[24]

A few batteries of horse artillery occupied knobs and rises along Lomax's line. They were damned by implication, being lumped into the general outcry against the cavalry. Micajah Woods commanded a section of guns in Jackson's battery of Virginia Horse Artillery and left a descriptive account of his role in the fight. Once Crook's position became apparent, Woods's guns delivered a steady barrage of canister and shell that had no apparent influence on the Federals. Woods wrote in disgust that his fire had little chance of becoming effective because the cavalry stationed in the entrenchments closer to the mountain "rushed from the works in confusion, neither officers nor men seeming to know what to do." Firing until the last possible second, the horse artillerists dragged their guns by hand a few yards to the rear and limbered up, making good their escape by a narrow margin. They left behind two guns in the hands of the bluecoats.[25]

The decisive moment of the battle of Fisher's Hill occurred when Crook's men passed along Lomax's line of entrenchments to confront the left of the Confederate infantry position. The excitement of the chase and the distance covered must have made it difficult for Crook's subordinates to keep their commands in hand. If those four brigades succeeded in retaining their formation, would they have sufficient energy to drive off the Confederate infantry? Dodson Ramseur's division was the equal of any other in the Army of Northern Virginia. The next stage of the fight at Fisher's Hill, then, would bring two fundamental battlefield attributes — momentum and skill — into direct conflict. If anyone present that afternoon had a chance to anticipate the contest, they must have been disappointed by the reality. On September 22, at least, Ramseur's division was not up to the challenge.

General Ramseur apparently had tried to send word of the blossoming crisis to Jubal Early but took no other immediate steps to prepare for the advent of battle. His first move occurred only after the sound of small-arms fire erupted along Lomax's sector of the line. Alive to the danger of stripping his own front too severely, Ramseur chose to send nothing more than the trusty North Carolina brigade of General William R. Cox. Pulling Cox's men from the right-center position in his four brigade front, Ramseur ordered them off to the west without any specific objective other than to move toward the sound of the guns. Wandering through the pastures behind the main line of battle at a double quick pace, Cox's regiments clipped a corner of Crook's force and bounced away, eventually ending up on a "high ridge" directly behind the fleeing Confederate cavalry and not far from the Back Road. There Cox met Lomax, and the latter, Cox reported, "kindly conducted me by the nearest route to the turnpike." Edmund P. Goggin of Lomax's staff held a different view of the encounter, recalling instead that Lomax asked Cox for assistance in launching a counterattack into Crook's flank. "A half dozen bullets" scared Cox's men away, claimed Goggin, and the Carolinians "disgracefully wheeled & ran." Soldiers in the 14th North Carolina partially corroborated both stories, writing that the brigade was prepared to battle with Crook but instead was maneuvered out of its position by the collapse of the primary Confederate line to the north. The Carolinians marched parallel to the Valley for a time before turning back toward the turnpike and the rest of the army.[26]

While Cox's brigade disappeared toward the Back Road, Gen. Bryan Grimes's brigade braced to receive the shock of Crook's attack. Grimes's men were Tar Heels, too, and their general had done all in his power to prepare for the contest. As the westernmost unit in the army's line of infantry, this brigade bore responsibility for flank protection, although the screen of dismounted cavalry in the ground below represented the literal flank. Grimes's men already had constructed a small line of entrenchments facing west as a contingency—a visual example of their derision for the cavalry. Everyone in the ranks at this part of the line had seen the Union column in its flank march and had heard or witnessed the collapse of the cavalry line. The 32nd North Carolina, 45th North Carolina, and 2nd North Carolina Battalion all shifted into the perpendicular line of fortifications to confront Crook's men face to face, leaving only two of Grimes's regiments facing north toward the Federal Sixth Corps. This was the spot where Early's army had its best chance to stall the momentum of the Union advance. Success and adrenaline undoubtedly drove the Federals onward, but a steep hill defended by tough veterans and supported by artillery should have been adequate to blunt the approaching blue-clad infantry. Nonetheless that combination proved insufficient, and the failure of Grimes's brigade even to dent Crook's front is typical of the degree of the Confederate collapse at Fisher's Hill.[27]

The 45th North Carolina anchored the left of Grimes's new alignment and "acted very gallantly on this occasion." In twisting to face Crook, those three units exposed themselves to a perfect enfilading fire from Wright's Union infantry blasting away in front of the main Confederate line. The steepness of the hill directly west of Grimes's left may have limited the effectiveness of the supporting Confederate artillery, and the oncoming Federal line extended far enough south to overlap the 45th North Carolina. Rounding out the bleak picture, some bluecoats brought captured artillery—probably some of the horse artillery run over in the initial onslaught—to bear on Grimes's position. The combination of all these factors proved too great an obstacle for the five North Carolina units to overcome. Bryan Grimes fought among them for a time, but even his on-the-spot leadership could not subdue the dark shadow of despondency that infected nearly every Confederate heart that day.

Grimes stayed as long as he could, leaving only when General Ramseur "came up and told me to save my brigade if possible." By General Crook's own admission, the Tar Heels briefly had dulled his momentum. Wright's Sixth Corps line was less than 100 yards away when Grimes left, but men from Crook's command already had infiltrated behind the 45th North Carolina, leaving the brigade in a dangerous predicament. Col. David G. Cowand of the 32nd reported that his regiment "did not retire until nearly surrounded," and Thomas P. Devereux at brigade headquarters estimated that some of the Federals were a full half mile to the south when Grimes's line dissolved. The Tar Heels abandoned their ground because they were maneuvered out of it. This was far from the sort of head-on collision that normally was needed to drive this proud organization from a battlefield. The inability of General Ramseur to squelch every crisis simultaneously had ensured Grimes's defeat. Without other units to extend the flank and buttress the front facing Wright's corps, there was no hope for a successful defense.[28]

Phil Cook's Georgia brigade stood on the far right of Ramseur's division. It, too, suffered from reduced numbers and an inadequate number of officers, leaving it ill-prepared to confront the surging Crook-Wright collaboration. A member of the brigade, writing on the morning of the twenty-second, placed Cook's strength at roughly 340 men — the equivalent of an ordinary Confederate regiment as recently as five months earlier. Although there is no explicit account of the fight at Fisher's Hill from the pen of any member of Cook's brigade, the sources that do survive all admit to being pried out of the breastworks by the flanking maneuver of George Crook's division. "In neither of the late fights was our Infantry whipped," wrote John L. Johnson of the 4th Georgia, "but forced to fall back because the cavalry let the Yankees flank our position and get behind us." Capt. Asbury H. Jackson of the brigade staff echoed that diagnosis, blaming the cavalry for leaving "an open field for the enemy to continue his flanking without opposition, which they did until they had 2 Brigades of our Div. all most surrounded & firing on their backs before they knew it, while fighting in front." Cook's brigade seems not to have been one of the pair fighting for its life. On his map of the battlefield, army cartographer Jedediah Hotchkiss showed Cook's brigade pulling out of the line and moving to the southwest. In his journal, Hotchkiss wrote of an unnamed brigade of Ramseur's division that "instead of marching by the line of works, was marched across an angle by its commander. The enemy seeing this movement rushed over the works and the brigade fled in confusion." Because Cox's brigade moved out of the fortifications in that direction, Hotchkiss may have drawn Cook but meant Cox; or, perhaps Cook's brigade really did move in the same direction as Cox's but without operating under General Ramseur's orders. Either way, Cook's brigade made no mark on Crook or on the course of the battle.[29]

Cullen Battle's Alabama brigade was the last command in the division with a chance to block the Federals. More accounts of the battle survive from this brigade than from any other Confederate outfit on the battlefield. "We were all ready for them on our portion of the line, and thought every thing was going on right," reported a surviving Alabamian four days later. The men were surprised, then, when other brigades nearby began to pull back or march away. Battle's men were all alone when Jubal Early rode up and personally ordered General Battle to take the brigade out of its entrenchments and march it southward, parallel to the Valley Pike. The army commander finally had reached a spot far enough ahead of the toppling Confederate line where he could rearrange his intact brigades and take steps to salvage what remained. Clearly the Sixth Corps had not yet attacked this far east, and Grimes's brigade must have left the field only moments earlier. The left of the Alabama brigade pulled out first, while Early rode along the front repeating the order. After delivering it in person to the 3rd Alabama on the eastern end of Battle's brigade, the general continued along the ridge into the left of Pegram's line.[30]

By the time the 3rd Alabama received its marching orders, the rest of the brigade had filed off to the south. Col. Charles Forsyth of Mobile commanded what was left of the 3rd and found himself in "a critical and trying moment. I did not know the back country and was only guided by the direction in which I thought the pike road was." Striking off on its own, the 3rd Alabama soon came upon the remnants of Grimes's brigade making a stand in some woods about 800 yards south of the original hilltop position, and now probably facing northwest. The 3rd affixed itself to the left flank of the 45th North Carolina, and with an anxious eye on the setting sun it engaged in a fierce duel with pursuing Federals. The western half of Early's army now had dissolved into separate clusters, the larger chunks resembling islands among the frothing mass of fugitives. Cox's brigade and the cavalry were on a separate route near the western end of the Valley floor, while Cook's brigade and most of Battle's brigade moved independently farther east. Some of Grimes's men and the 3rd Alabama fought their own action. All of them were beyond the reach of any coordinating hand, though General Ramseur did help to arrange the stand of the latter group and ordered it out of its second position at the last moment. Broadly speaking, command and control had reached an unimaginable low.[31]

While Ramseur's division moved southward in many unconnected parts, the chaos on top of the Fisher's Hill line continued. The extent to which Sheridan's various divisions achieved tactical coordination is an impressive sidelight to the story of the battle. Unchecked momentum continues to build, at least while energy lasts, but the distance covered by Crook's men from where they struck the cavalry line to the left of Pegram's division should have destroyed any chance of close cooperation with Wright's Sixth Corps. Instead, the North Carolinians and Virginians of Pegram's division found themselves in a fix similar to that encountered by Ramseur a few minutes earlier—and with the same results. The wooded terrain on their part of the line prevented close observation of events off to the west, but the officers and men of the brigade surely knew that their flank was growing less secure by the minute. The aggressiveness of the Sixth Corps troops opposite Pegram also demanded attention and ultimately provided the primary difference on this section of the line. It was Wright's men, not Crook's, who initiated the collapse of John Pegram's three brigades.[32]

The details of Pegram's disintegration almost mirror those of Ramseur's from a few minutes earlier. Learning that his left was threatened and perhaps uncovered, General Pegram pulled out his own old brigade, now under the myopic Col. John S. Hoffman, from the division's right and sent it to the left. There it was supposed to form facing west toward the greatest danger. Under the circumstances, this was the competent move to make. Just to the east of Hoffman's new position, Davis's (formerly Godwin's) North Carolina regiments remained in the primary entrenchments, with R. D. Johnston's brigade to their right. There is no evidence that the gap caused by Hoffman's realignment ever was filled, but it is of little importance because Pegram's line began to crumble almost at once.[33]

In the absence of detailed accounts from the Tar Heels, the testimony of men from the Virginia brigade must suffice. Capt. Samuel D. Buck of the 13th Virginia put the blame for the first gap in the division's front on Johnston's brigade, which he accused of fleeing. The North Carolinians erroneously thought, wrote Buck, that General Pegram was unfairly protecting his own beloved Virginians by giving them a head start toward the rear. Unwilling to stand for favoritism, Johnston's men "stampeded" and "ran over" Hoffman's brigade. This opened the way for Getty's Sixth Corps division to climb the hill unopposed. Jubal Early was on the ground at that time, spreading the alarm like a Paul Revere in gray. Old Jube saw Johnston's men break and told the Virginians to fire at them if they failed to stop. Apparently nobody took this command seriously, and in fact Hoffman's brigade could not recover from being trampled and left the battlefield "without any organization."[34]

Archibald "Baldy" Henderson of the 12th North Carolina in Johnston's brigade, unaware that the Virginians were defaming his command, wrote a week later that his regiment "staid in the works until ordered twice to leave" and lost about thirty men that afternoon. J. F. Coghill in the same brigade left no details, writing only that "the entire line gave way leaving a good meny peaces of artillery behind. . . . After this our men would not rally and every man was for himselfe so you may believe that was a stampeede of stampeeds." Contrasting recollections aside, the three brigades under General Pegram's leadership shared a common result. They all left the field without offering anything more than a token resistance and with very light casualties.[35]

Jubal Early did more than sound the alarm among the brigades of Pegram's division. Once the dimensions of the Union attack became apparent, he reacted by calling for his easternmost division, that of Gabriel Wharton, to abandon its position beyond the turnpike and shift westward to face Crook's onslaught. If there had been sufficient time to execute this maneuver, it would have required the right of Gordon's division to sidle to its right, filling the gap left by Wharton. On the fronts of Ramseur and Pegram, the removal of certain brigades within those divisions to face west also required shuffling and rearranging. The effect of these intricate movements, if they all had been carried out successfully, would have caused troops to move simultaneously to the right, left, and rear. The speed and success of Crook's attack prevented most of those adjustments from occurring.

The panic, now irreversible, communicated itself to Gordon's brigades astride the railroad. General Gordon had witnessed the collapse of Pegram's troops and in fact had meddled with the Virginian's dispositions toward the end. Now his own division stood between the converging arms of Sheridan's army. Gordon's division occupied an especially important position very close to the Valley Pike, the ultimate destination of every Confederate on the battlefield. General Gordon's soldiers fired a volley or two toward Brig. Gen. Frank Wheaton's and Brig. Gen. William Dwight's blue-clad divisions and then scampered in every direction. Some were caught up in the throng of traffic along the road. Others chose to make for the wooded slopes of Massanutten Mountain, hoping to scuttle far enough east to avoid the descent of the Nineteenth Corps. The few casualty figures available suggest that this division did not stand firm for very long. Certainly there was little left to be gained by stubbornness. William J. Seymour of the Louisiana brigade confirmed that the division "stood not upon the order of going; it was altogether too late to retire in order, for it required the greatest fleetness of foot to enable us to keep from being captured." An unidentified man in that brigade tearfully implored his comrades to stand and fight, calling out, "I say, men, for God's sake let us stop and fight them right here! We are ruined forever." Prudence overcame sentiment, and the Louisianans moved away with everyone else, hoping to avoid prison and survive to fight another day.[36]

The Georgia brigade in Gordon's division, formerly commanded by General Gordon himself, rested its right flank on the Valley Pike. A steep hill there overlooked a rustic stone bridge quite similar in design to Burnside's Bridge at Sharpsburg. The approach to that position from across Tumbling Run was so precipitous that the Nineteenth Corps made no real effort to storm the defenses. The Georgians could see enough to know that they were in danger anyway, and when the brigade found Federals in its rear, it fell apart. "We did not know what it meant at first, for we saw our men leaving our works on our left and begin to fall back in a run," recalled G. W. Nichols. Col. Edmund N. Atkinson, who commanded the brigade, was captured late in the battle after vainly attempting to salvage a lone Confederate cannon in the Valley Turnpike. General Clement Evans resumed command of the brigade a few days after the disaster and learned from his men of "the most lamentable confusion" that had reigned. He estimated that 400 of his soldiers had fled to the mountains, the other half of the brigade escaping under the leadership of Col. John H. Lowe of the 31st Georgia. H. P. Fortson of the 31st, one of the mountain climbers, described how the Federals "cut a portion of us off from the pike, [and] marched down our breastworks." Fortson skirted the base of Massanutten Mountain until opposite the village of Edinburg, where he climbed over the heights and into the Page Valley. Although "the yankees were all around me," he succeeded in rejoining the army near Port Republic several days later, having displayed remarkable initiative and perseverance. Stragglers from the mountain route continued to trickle into the brigade as late as October 6, but many were without weapons and were not of much use for many days to come.[37]

Gabriel Wharton's fought-out division stood last in line and defended the strongest, steepest section of the entire position. Once Early appreciated the extent of the crisis, he sent Jedediah Hotchkiss of the army staff to pull Wharton's men out of the line and hustle them to the west, where everyone hoped they could stall the Union success. Borrowing troops from Wharton's front was not all that dangerous. Even a skirmish line of infantry left behind could make a bold showing from that formidable position for a few minutes. By the time Hotchkiss fetched Wharton, however, it was too late to matter. The Virginians marching west across the turnpike collided with Georgians from Gordon's division fleeing east toward the mountain. Looking south, Wharton could see scattered bluecoats on the turnpike more than a thousand yards to his rear. The best Wharton could do was to use his division — about the only unbroken unit of any size left in Early's army — to force open a passage and assume a belligerent stance along the turnpike to keep that road available as long as possible. The army's artillery, its wagon train, and the growing mass of fugitives all needed that reliable surface to speed their escape. Writing in retrospect, W. F. Claughton of Wharton's division refused to differentiate between the twin disasters at Third Winchester and Fisher's Hill, noting only that both battles fully tested his athleticism as he made his way to safety. "I was never accused of being a very clumsy boy," Claughton remarked drolly to explain his successful escapes.[38]

The performance of the army's artillery stood in direct contrast to that of the infantry and cavalry. Even the usually skeptical General Early agreed that "the artillery behaved splendidly." Several dozen guns from the battalions of Lt. Cols. Carter M. Braxton, William Nelson, and J. Floyd King occupied knobs along the Confederate ridge. They naturally became islands of resistance in the rearward path of the infantry. Nelson had posted his pieces among the infantry brigades of Ramseur's division. Those cannon did well in firing toward the Sixth Corps and apparently also directed some rounds at Crook's four brigades. Milledge's Georgia Battery probably anchored the division left, with the Fluvanna (Va.) Artillery in the middle and the Amherst (Va.) Artillery on the right, amidst Battle's regiments. These batteries all had seen grueling duty at Third Winchester and felt the loss of horses and equipment quite severely. The Fluvanna battery had 12-pounder Napoleons. Early in the action it split in half, with two guns staying in the breastworks and the others probably going to reenforce Battle and the Amherst battery. The two guns left in the original position divided their efforts, one piece firing north toward the Sixth Corps, the other swiveling left and firing down the line of entrenchments just abandoned by Grimes. As the guns ran out of canister rounds, they attempted to leave the field, but at least one was overtaken and captured. Not far from there, the Amherst unit faced similar problems. It too lost at least one gun to the surging Union infantry.[39]

The batteries of Braxton's battalion strengthened Pegram's and Gordon's defenses. When disaster overtook the foot soldiers, the artillery there stood firm, in some instances for longer than was wise. The Alleghany (Va.) Artillery, known

A somewhat romantic rendering of the stone bridge that carried the Valley Pike across Tumbling Run at Fisher's Hill. Benson J. Lossing, *Pictorial Field Book of the Civil War*, 3 vols. (Hartford, Conn.: T. Belknap, 1870–76), 3:373.

as Carpenter's Battery from the earliest days of the war, had trod the Valley Pike two years before with Stonewall Jackson. Devastating casualties at Third Winchester impaired its efficiency somewhat, and the battery's position on a wooded hill near the left of Pegram's division ensured its destruction on September 22. One Union source commended Carpenter's guns for their "splendid service" at Fisher's Hill. Late in the day the battery was "almost surrounded, and about to be pounced upon," recorded its earliest historian, when the four guns fell silent and the cannon crews "had to fly to the rear." Excited soldiers from Brig. Gen. George W. Getty's Sixth Corps division snatched the trophies and pressed on toward the turnpike in search of more. Farther to the east, along the same ridge, similar scenes produced other losses in Braxton's command. The Stafford (Va.) Artillery lost two of its pieces, the first time any of its guns had been captured during the war. The Lee Lynchburg (Va.) Battery, also of that battalion, lost two of its guns as well, bringing the day's loss to eight guns for Braxton—certainly more than half of his ordnance. Two years later, Jubal Early still remembered that Braxton came up that evening and "told me with tears in his eyes about the loss of his guns."[40]

Sam Moore, soon to become General Early's chief of staff, watched the army "leave the field almost without a fight." It was "the first time in my life" he had seen such a spectacle, and it was painful. By the time Early and his staff joined the mob on the turnpike, the evacuation was complete. The entire original Confederate position on the chain of hills looking down upon Tumbling Run now lay empty. The Nineteenth Corps crossed the picturesque stone turnpike bridge virtually unchallenged, and the full weight of that fresh corps bore down the road in pursuit. Federal cavalry, a few brigades of the Sixth Corps, and perhaps some of Crook's men all swung toward the Valley Pike, bent on inflicting the maximum damage possible before sunset ended their day's work. But Jubal Early's army slipped away without much further loss. There were several reasons for the escape, including total darkness and the scattered condition of the pursuers. Good work by Early's subordinate officers is a third reason for the success of his army's retreat. All over the edges of the battlefield, regimental commanders and staff officers worked hard to establish pockets of resistance. The defense of a hillock near Mount Prospect was particularly effective. Mount Prospect was a cluster of a half-dozen buildings on a midsized ridge that bisected the turnpike just more than one mile south of Fisher's Hill and a few hundred yards northeast of the oddly shaped Valley landmark called Round Hill. In the gathering twilight, several prominent officers built a hasty line of defense hoping to block Federal pursuit and hold open the turnpike to allow the last few Confederates to escape.[41]

Early's chief of staff, Lieut. Col. Alexander S. "Sandie" Pendleton, was the animating spirit in this resistance. Using his authority and popularity, he snared everyone he could to build up a firing line. Two pieces of artillery, under orders from Captain Carpenter, wheeled into position. Some of Cullen Battle's Alabama brigade, which had left the battlefield nearly intact, also came up, as did part of Cox's wayward North Carolina brigade, fresh from its circuitous march to the west and south. Captain Buck of the 13th Virginia was present with a few men from that regiment, together with an unknowable number of others from miscellaneous units. Little organization was evident, and "most of our men went on," grumbled Jedediah Hotchkiss, "officers and all, at breakneck speed." Union troops feeling their way along the turnpike just at twilight met canister delivered from the cannon, which served to slow down the pursuit long enough for total darkness to cover the retreat.[42]

Lt. Col. Alexander Swift
"Sandie" Pendleton. Courtesy
of Tony Marion.

This successful roadblock cost the army the services of Sandie Pendleton. Riding along the line on a prominent white horse, the famous staff officer made an obvious target. Maj. Henry Kyd Douglas, engaged in supervising a section of the line, unsuccessfully urged Pendleton to dismount. Soon thereafter a rifle bullet hit Pendleton in the body with an audible thud, toppling him from the horse. Young Sandie correctly diagnosed his injury as a mortal wound and began composing farewell messages for his family. His friend Douglas rescued Pendleton's watch, Bible, and other effects, while Thomas T. Greene, an Alabamian from Battle's brigade, secured the bright horse and the colonel's field glasses. Friends saw Pendleton into an ambulance and had him carried along the turnpike as far as Woodstock, where he was placed in the house of Dr. Murphy. The army's chief of staff survived only into the next day, dying on the twenty-third. Because the town was in the hands of Sheridan's army by then, Pendleton received a temporary burial in the Lutheran Cemetery. His body was retrieved a few weeks later when Early moved back down the valley, and Pendleton's family gave him a permanent burial in the Stonewall Jackson Cemetery in his native Lexington.[43]

Elsewhere other competent officers were laboring mightily to save the army's logistical base. Jedediah Hotchkiss focused his efforts on the wagon train. Riding full tilt to the south, he overtook the train, "which was fairly flying." Fleet-footed stragglers fled with the wagons and stoked the panic by spreading grim rumors about the proximity of Federal cavalry. "I saw one poor fellow, who had both legs broken, and another dead, both caused by being run over," recollected Joseph Stonebraker. Hotchkiss fought his way through the mob and reached its head at the little village of Hawkinstown. He then took measures to protect the various bridges along the supply train's route, especially the one over a stream that fed the North Fork of the Shenandoah River near Mount Jackson. His actions stand as an example of model staff work. Off to the west, on the Back Road, Booth and Dorsey continued to labor on behalf of the cavalry's led horses. The success of these endeavors helped limit Fisher's Hill to a serious defeat instead of a catastrophic disaster. The experience of General Bryan Grimes probably was more typical than those of Hotchkiss, Booth, and Dorsey. The brigadier did his best to restore order along the turnpike, but "it was fall back all the time, and I was carried along in the current." When the men assessed the battle in the next few days, many admitted that darkness was all that saved their small army from destruction.[44]

The Valley army finally pulled up at Mount Jackson the next day, spooked beyond precedent. Stragglers wandered in for the next several weeks. The loss of at least a dozen guns required reorganization in that arm. Those who felt inclined to write about their experiences at Third Winchester and Fisher's Hill generally directed their blame at two culprits: the army's cavalry and General Early. The majority of correspondents clearly labeled the horsemen as the cause of the army's woes. Some went further and criticized Early, too, for having demonstrated "inexcusable improvidence" in placing the cavalry in a situation where its worthlessness could be so harmful. Lomax's men seem not to have had any supporters at all outside their own ranks. Fisher's Hill was only another in a long series of actions in which the Confederate cavalry proved to be a weak link, and that cumulative effect added virulence to the ire of its critics. Colonel Forsyth of the 3rd Alabama assured his readers that the army was in good shape, "and but for the conduct of the cavalry, and that they cannot be depended upon, all would be well. One or two brigades of these are noble fellows, as for the rest, if the Yankees had the whole concern it would be better for this army." "All of our misfortunes were caused by depending on our cavalry to protect our flanks," agreed John L. Johnson of the 4th Georgia. "In neither of the late fights was our Infantry whipped but forced to fall back because the cavalry let the Yankees flank our position and get behind us." A correspondent in Cox's brigade blamed virtually everyone involved but did complain that after "a few shots" on the left, "our miserable cavalry broke and fled."[45]

Many others in the army attacked Early for what they perceived to be an injudicious arrangement of his command at Fisher's Hill and for allowing his command's morale to sink. When Gen. Clement A. Evans rejoined his brigade shortly afterward, he canvassed his infantrymen for their opinions and concluded "that if the forces had been properly distributed along the line that [there would have been] no disaster." "It is apparent to every man in this army . . . that there is something radically wrong in the management of this command," complained one survivor of the battle. "The men do not believe they were whipped but out-generalled badly," argued a North Carolinian in Johnston's brigade. Gen. John B. Gordon, who developed into the chief postwar critic of Jubal Early, showed unusual restraint in his memoirs. He remarked upon Early's poor disposition of troops and then made a point of reminding his readers that the soldiers were not to blame for Fisher's Hill. "There are conditions in war when courage, firmness, steadiness of nerve, and self-reliance are of small avail," the Georgian sapiently explained. The record clearly disputes Gordon's implication. Few men of any rank displayed unshakable nerves atop Fisher's Hill on September 22.[46]

J. Floyd King, who commanded the battalion of artillery attached to Wharton's division, maintained that he reflected the views of the enlisted men in the army when he wrote that General Breckinridge would be a suitable replacement for Early: "Genl. Early, they say, drinks!" King claimed to have the best interests of the soldiers in mind but confessed that if Early "succeeds in leading them to victory again it will be a happy and grateful surprise to us all." George Peyton in the 13th Virginia wrote that as Crook's men swept along the lines, he had seen Early behind the lines taking a swig from a bottle of whiskey. "Perhaps that was the reason he did not know Sheridan had turned his flank," suggested Peyton. Although most sources abstain from making direct accusations of drunkenness against Old Jube, the reputation plagued him. Samuel J. C. Moore, of Early's staff, felt compelled to defend his chief in a letter dated November 1, 1864. "Much has been said, and has found its way into the newspapers, about Genl Early being a man of intemperate habits, and in this way accounting for his defeats, but . . . I have been on his staff since Aug. 1st, now 3 months, and I have never, at anytime, seen him under the effects of liquor. I have seen him drink, and believe that he takes a little every day, but I have never seen him intoxicated." The accuracy of the army's beliefs regarding Early and liquor are of little importance. The perception held by some of his men that he was subject to alcohol's crippling effects was enough to erode further the army's confidence in its leader.[47]

Fisher's Hill certainly was a low point in Jubal Early's career. He gave it scant attention in subsequent writings, and at times attempted to play down its significance and the degree of his defeat. He devoted only two paragraphs to Fisher's Hill in his initial report on the army's September operations in the lower Valley. His *Autobiographical Sketch and Narrative* is scarcely more complete, offering only five paragraphs on the subject and no commentary at all. An anecdote from later in the campaign gives vivid evidence that the memory of Fisher's Hill was a sore point with Old Jube. After the disastrous fight at Cedar Creek, a column of disenchanted infantrymen marched past Early and hooted at him, someone calling out, "Give that dog a bone and let him go." Early responded by yelling, "Fisher's hill, G.D. you," as though invoking the battle's name was a sufficient epithet. On a later occasion he bristled at the suggestion that his army was routed at Fisher's Hill, retorting that "routed" was not a term "applicable to the affair at Fisher's Hill, where my force again made front the next day, and drove back a pursuing force. My retreat was not only orderly, but it exhibited a spectacle rarely seen in war, an inferior force retreating in line of battle for miles, in perfect order." Early referred in that passage to his retreat up the Valley from Mount Jackson toward New Market and ultimately Port Republic. This is a mild case of dissembling, as no Confederate on the field at Fisher's Hill claimed anything short of a rout for the bulk of the army that day. Early never assigned himself any blame for the disaster.[48]

Many others in the army merited criticism as well. Lunsford Lomax may have done all in his power to prepare his cavalry command for a Federal attack, but even so his horsemen proved no obstacle to Crook's flank attack. If Lomax was indeed as ill-equipped to defend that flank as he subsequently claimed, it surely was his responsibility to hammer that point home to the army commander. If Lomax did so, there is no record of it. On the hill to the east, Dodson Ramseur displayed little generalship until it was too late. He may have shrugged off the news of a flanking column, and clearly he was not prepared to deal with Crook's men when the crisis arose. His ardor and energy during the subsequent fighting helped to rehabilitate his reputation. Beyond individual criticism, some soldiers blamed the army as a whole. Artillerist Micajah Woods pointed fingers in all directions and confronted the facts in an assessment written only twenty-four hours after the battle: "The victory was more easily won & less dearly bought by the enemy than any ever achieved on this continent."[49]

George Crook's flank attack had been wildly successful. It drove most of Early's army across the Valley, onto the turnpike, and then up the Valley toward Tom's Brook. Crook's division paid an incredibly low price in human blood for that achievement. Published casualty returns for General Crook's four brigades show that he lost a total of eight men killed and 142 wounded. If that sum is literally true, it means that the Confederate defenders managed to kill one of their attackers about every half mile—a ridiculous statistic. Judged by traditional standards, Fisher's Hill must be termed a skirmish rather than a battle. Truly the Second Corps had seen better days and done much better work.[50]

Even at this late date it is hard to see the proper path among the tangle of Early's options before the battle of Fisher's Hill. He arranged his line in a position that had been adequate one month earlier, in the same formation he had used before. If he had exchanged his alignment, sending his reliable infantry to occupy the susceptible left flank, his weak cavalry would have been responsible for at least 3,000 yards, supposedly with only about 1,000 men. Lomax's dismounted cavalry clearly could not have defended that stretch against the infantry of the Sixth and Nineteenth Corps. With a tiny army, new commanders in key positions, and a terrible shortage of company and regimental officers, it is difficult to devise any formula with which Early could have succeeded at Fisher's Hill. This makes his defeat at Third Winchester that much more important, because it forced Early to confront a series of problems that had no solution.

There are several ways to view the results of Fisher's Hill. Early's little army hardly could afford to lose any significant portion of its dwindling strength, especially without inflicting any defeat on Sheridan. The Confederate army incurred between 600 and 1,000 casualties, and the loss of at least a dozen cannon proved damaging to its artillery branch as well. Worst of all, the army's retreat from Fisher's Hill exposed the majority of the Shenandoah Valley to the rapacious Federal cavalry. The ensuing "Burning" injured the Confederate war effort, discouraged and harmed the civilian population in the Valley, and reduced the conduct of the war to a lower, more unseemly level.[51]

Most important of all, the wretched afternoon at Fisher's Hill mortally wounded the Army of the Valley. For the first time, the men of the famous Second Corps felt twinges of self-doubt. Morale dipped to an alarmingly low level. Although some talked bravely, enough men in the ranks felt dubious about their army's chances that it must have made a difference. "Of the prospects & condition of the army I forbear to speak," wrote Micajah Woods on the twenty-third, but "I can confidentially say to you that I regard its future career in the Valley with by no means hopeful anticipation." Henry R. Berkeley, another artillerist, despondently concluded his September 22 diary entry with a dark passage: "Surely the future looks gloomy and hopeless for the South just at present. May God help us." In what little remained of the 13th Virginia, diarist George Peyton described his comrades as "nervous and restless" on the twenty-third, judging "it would not take much to stampede them." Buckner Randolph of the same brigade returned from furlough on the twenty-fourth and found his friends "considerably demoralized." "They are not so much dispirited themselves," he wrote revealingly, "as that they have lost confidence in each other." W. F. Claughton eloquently assessed the army's condition, admitting "it has lost that buoyancy of spirit and cheerfulness of soul that it possessed before the Winchester fight." In the 21st Virginia, Richard Waldrop predicted that of the men in his regiment "a large number of them if attacked would run without firing a gun." Not every soldier felt that way, and some of them insisted that all they wanted was better cavalry or a new commanding general to restore their spirits entirely. But the tremendous majority of surviving testimony displays an unprecedented dejection.[52]

The very principles that bind an army together can work against it in the proper setting. Teamwork and unity of purpose, once compromised, are not easily restored and can nurture dissatisfaction and unrest. The orderly retreat of Jubal Early's army up the Valley toward Staunton, and its reorganization and return to the lower Valley in October, may have deceived some into thinking that the army was healed. Subsequent events clearly showed that far from being rejuvenated, the army—as then configured—was irreparably injured. The men in the ranks no longer entirely trusted each other, lacking the confidence to stand firm without casting doubtful glances at those around them. Most soldiers probably were willing to do their individual part, but the fresh memory of the wild stampede at Fisher's Hill undoubtedly diminished their faith in the army and their comrades. The moral effect of the defeat proved greater than the physical. Seeds of doubt and demoralization, sown on September 22, sprouted an ugly fruit four weeks later in the even greater disaster at Cedar Creek. Faced with adversity there, the army collapsed at the smallest excuse. Fisher's Hill had confirmed the unhappy results of Third Winchester and set the tone for Cedar Creek. It proved to be a crucial bridge between the two great battles of the 1864 Valley Campaign.

Notes

1. U.S. Department of the Interior Geological Survey, Mountain Falls, Va., 1997 Quadrangle.

2. Jedediah Hotchkiss, *Make Me a Map of the Valley: The Civil War Journal of Stonewall Jackson's Topographer*, ed. Archie P. McDonald (Dallas, Tex.: Southern Methodist University Press, 1973), 222; U.S. War Department, *The War of the Rebellion: A Compilation of the Official Records of the Union and Confederate Armies*, 127 vols., index, and atlas (Washington: Government Printing Office, 1880–1901), ser. 1, 43(1):555 [hereafter cited as *OR*; all references are to ser.1]. Hotchkiss's journal for this period was printed in *OR* 43(1):574–75. Subsequent citations will be to the 1973 version, which is preferable because of its annotations. Many Confederate accounts talk of occupying the earthworks left over from their time there in August, but a significant number also describe the construction of new or improved fortifications in September. In 1862, Stonewall Jackson had expressed doubts about the feasibility of Fisher's Hill as a defensive position during his operations in the Valley, according to Edward A. Pollard, *The Lost Cause: A New Southern History of the War of the Confederates* (New York: E. B. Treat, 1866), 596.

3. *OR*, 43(2):876.

4. Jeffry D. Wert, *From Winchester to Cedar Creek* (1987; rev. ed., Mechanicsburg, Pa.: Stackpole Books, 1997), 110, 128; Douglas Southall Freeman, *Lee's Lieutenants: A Study in Command*, 3 vols. (New York: Scribner's, 1942–44), 3:583–84; Vernon H. Crow, ed., "The Justness of Our Cause: The Civil War Diaries of William W. Stringfield," *East Tennessee Historical Society's Publications* 56 and 57 (1984–1985), 97; *OR*, 43(1):596–97. Although the inspection reports for Wharton's brigades are dated September 29, their observations can be considered germane to Fisher's Hill because the division saw virtually no action on the twenty-second. Examples of the soldiers' dissatisfaction with the details of their alignment will appear in the body of this essay. When Breckinridge arrived at Staunton he told acquaintances there that the army's position at Fisher's Hill was entirely secure (Robert G. Stephens Jr., comp., *Intrepid Warrior: Clement Anselm Evans, Confederate General from Georgia* [Dayton, Ohio: Morningside, 1992], 445).

5. William J. Seymour, *The Civil War Memoirs of William J. Seymour*, ed. Terry L. Jones (Baton Rouge: Louisiana State University Press, 1991), 142. Terry's brigade included what little remained of the old Stonewall Brigade. The Louisiana brigade had lost its commander, Zebulon York, to a war-ending wound at Third Winchester. At Fisher's Hill, it probably was under the shared leadership of Col. William R. Peck of the 9th Louisiana and Col. Eugene Waggaman of the 10th Louisiana.

6. George Q. Peyton diary, September 20, 1864, transcript provided by Peyton's grandson to Robert K. Krick, Fredericksburg, Virginia. Peyton served in the 13th Virginia.

7. John B. Lindsley, *Military Annals of Tennessee* (Nashville: J. M. Lindsley, 1886), 525, 758; *OR*, 43(2):869–70; Willene B. Clark, ed., *Valleys of the Shadow: The Memoir of Confederate Captain Reuben G. Clark* (Knoxville: University of Tennessee Press, 1994), 105–6.

8. "Diary of Captain James M. Garnett," in *Southern Historical Society Papers*, ed. J. William Jones and others, 52 vols. (Richmond, Va.: Southern Historical Society, 1876–1959), 27:7 [hereafter cited as *SHSP*]; Buckner M. Randolph to his mother, September 29, 1864, Randolph Family Papers, Virginia Historical Society, Richmond [repository hereafter cited as VHS]; Joseph A. Ansley letter, *Macon Daily Telegraph*, September 30, 1864; J. B. Reese letter, *Countryman* [Eatonton, Georgia], October 18, 1864; Abner E. McGarity letter, September 20, 1864, in Edmund C. Burnett, ed., "Letters of a Confederate Surgeon," *Georgia Historical Quarterly* 30 (1946):43; Gamma, "Our Richmond Correspondence," *Mobile Advertiser and Register*, October 4, 1864.

9. Wert, *From Winchester to Cedar Creek*, 110; Samuel J. C. Moore, "Early's Strength at Winchester," *Confederate Veteran* 11 (September 1903):396; C. R. Hatton, "The Valley Campaign of 1864," *Confederate Veteran* 27 (May 1919):170; "The Shenandoah Campaign, Generals Sheridan and Early," *New Orleans Daily Picayune*, January 14, 1868. The author of this 1868 letter almost certainly was Maj. John P. H. New, an officer on General Pegram's staff. For a further discussion of this subject, including an excerpt from the New letter, see John Esten Cooke, *Wearing of the Gray* (New York: E. B. Treat, 1867), 101–4.

10. Seymour, *Civil War Memoirs*, 143; Peyton diary, September 21, 1864.

11. George Crook, *General George Crook: His Autobiography*, ed. Martin F. Schmitt (Norman: University of Oklahoma Press, 1946), 129–30. Sheridan and Crook later disputed the particulars of the plan, Crook reporting that it was his idea to turn the Confederate left after Sheridan had proposed flanking the Confederate right, near the river. Although the precise truth remains uncertain, the weight of the evidence is on Crook's side, as is Sheridan's long record of sophistry. For a more complete discussion, see Wert, *Winchester to Cedar Creek*, 111–12.

12. Garnett Diary, *SHSP*, 27:8. General William N. Pendleton, chief of artillery for the entire Army of Northern Virginia, reported later that Early's senior artillerist, William Nelson, suggested "certain precautions" before the battle to protect the delicate western flank, but that advice was ignored "owing to some misapprehension or oversight." Pendleton's source for that statement must have been some communication from Nelson, his kinsman, now long lost (*OR*, 42[1]:863). Subsequently, Ramseur blamed the defeat at Fisher's Hill on the army's poor alignment (Gary W. Gallagher, *Stephen Dodson Ramseur: Lee's Gallant General* [Chapel Hill: University of North Carolina Press, 1985], 151).

13. *OR*, 43(1):556.

14. Ibid., 390; Crook, *Autobiography*, 130. The residents around Fisher's Hill believed that General Crook had the assistance of an unnamed local guide (John W. Wayland, *A History of Shenandoah County* [Strasburg, Va.: Shenandoah Publishing House, 1927], 345).

15. B. L. Wynn diary, September 22, 1864, Mississippi Department of Archives and History, Jackson; Joseph R. Stonebraker, *A Rebel of '61* (New York and Albany: Wynkoop, Hallenbeck, Crawford, 1899), 65; Peyton diary, September 22, 1864; Bryan Grimes, *Extracts of Letters of Major-General Bryan Grimes to His Wife, Written While in Active Service in the Army of Northern Virginia*, comp. Pulaski Cowper (Raleigh,

N.C.: Alfred Williams, 1884), 69; Henry R. Berkeley, *Four Years in the Confederate Artillery*, ed. William H. Runge (Chapel Hill: University of North Carolina Press, 1961), 99–100. Private Wynn's diary is not specific as to where either Kleinpeter or Wynn was when these reports were sent. The language used implies that Kleinpeter was on the mountain and Wynn at or near army headquarters. Kleinpeter was a veteran of the 7th Louisiana Infantry.

16. John H. Lane, "The Battle of Fisher's Hill," *Richmond Dispatch*, June 14, 1891. Lane served in the Fluvanna (Virginia) Artillery. His account was published under the same title in *SHSP*, 19:289–95.

17. In his report of the ensuing disaster (*OR*, 43[1]:556), Early took the position that he was unaware of the movement, saying only that Crook's force "moved under cover of the woods on the left."

18. James E. Taylor, *With Sheridan Up the Shenandoah Valley in 1864: Leaves from a Special Artist's Sketch Book and Diary*, ed. Dennis E. Frye, Martin F. Graham, and George F. Skoch (Dayton, Ohio: Morningside, 1989), 409; Micajah Woods letter, September 23, 1864, Woods Papers, box 1, Albert and Shirley Small Special Collections Library, University of Virginia, Charlottesville [repository hereafter cited as UVA]; Charles T. O'Ferrall, *Forty Years of Active Service* (New York and Washington: Neale, 1904), 118. Thanks to the gracious Mary Edwards of Albemarle County for providing me with a typescript of the fine letter by Woods.

19. Bradley T. Johnson letter, September 29, 1864, Johnson Papers, box 3, William R. Perkins Library, Duke University, Durham, North Carolina [repository hereafter cited as DU]; E. P. Goggin to L. L. Lomax, September 27, 1867, Chicago Historical Society [repository hereafter cited as CHS]. The Johnson letters are typescripts, prepared by General Johnson himself around 1900 from the original documents. Although the typescripts retain the form of letters, there clearly is some postwar material mixed into the original language. In his Fisher's Hill letter, for example, Johnson includes information on troop positions and movements he could not have known in September 1864. He also uses information from Lomax's official report without attributing it to that source. The result is a disconcerting letter-memoir hybrid.

20. Crook, *Autobiography*, 130; M. S. Watts, "General Battle and the Stolen Colt," *Confederate Veteran* 30 (May 1922):169. Watts is the source for the sun's position atop the mountain. The road that ran up the eastern slope of Little North Mountain is there today, a narrow dirt track that leads to a few isolated houses.

21. George W. Booth, *Personal Reminiscences of a Maryland Soldier in the War between the States* (Baltimore: Fleet, McGinley, 1898), 147; Bradley T. Johnson letter, September 29, 1864, Johnson Papers; James D. Sedinger, "Diary of a Border Ranger," West Virginia Division of Culture and History, Charleston, West Virginia; *OR*, 43(1):611; Alfred Dibble, "With Sigel in the Shenandoah Valley," *National Tribune*, June 9, 1927; Garland R. Quarles and others, eds., *Diaries, Letters and Recollections of the War between the States* (Winchester, Va.: Frederick County Historical Society, 1955), 112; Micajah Woods letter, September 23, 1864, Woods Papers. Woods confirmed that from where he stood Crook's flanking movement was unseen and "not discovered till it had been actually accomplished." General Lomax contended that he

was not surprised, that he swung his left around in time to blunt Crook's onslaught, and that he was forced to give way from lack of support. Lomax's version is discarded because it conflicts with most other Confederate accounts and because his report is riddled with exaggerations and claims of questionable accuracy.

22. Clark, *Valleys of the Shadow*, 41; Bradley T. Johnson letter, September 29, 1864, Johnson Papers; George H. Smith, "Imboden's Brigade," *Richmond Daily Whig*, October 12, 1864; Watts, "General Battle and the Stolen Colt," 169. Clark's recently published memoir is the only narrative source found thus far from Bean's brigade at Fisher's Hill. The *Athens Southern Watchman*, November 30, 1864, published a casualty list for the 16th Battalion Georgia Cavalry without comment. The list shows four men wounded and nine captured in that unit at Fisher's Hill.

23. [Joseph] French Harding, *Civil War Memoirs* (Parsons, W.Va.: McClain, 2000), 171–72; A Soldier, "The Cavalry," *Richmond Sentinel*, November 10, 1864; W. W. Goldsborough, *The Maryland Line in the Confederate Army, 1861–1865* (Baltimore: Guggenheimer, Wiel, 1900), 213; Booth, *Personal Reminiscences*, 147–48. French Harding remembered after the war that Jackson's brigade occupied the left center of Lomax's front, but he is overruled by the contemporaneous evidence from Bradley Johnson and Soldier, though the latter pair do not agree with each other. One of the landmarks just in front of Lomax's line was the Barbe House (pronounced without the second vowel), which still stands. A highly overwrought version of the family's September 1864 experiences, including romance and ghosts, appears in Emma Howard Wright, "The Old Farm-House at North Mountain," *Blue and Gray* 1 (March 1893):223–25.

24. *OR*, 43(1):611. "The Cavalry at Fisher's Hill," *Confederate Veteran* 3 (February 1895):51–52, gives another vigorous defense of the cavalry's performance. The writer was a member of Munford's brigade who was present on the twenty-second delivering a dispatch to Lomax. He argues that the cavalry did all it could and conducted a fighting withdrawal. Several factual errors cast suspicion on the quality of the reminiscence.

25. Micajah Woods letter, September 23, 1864, Woods Papers. Woods reported the loss of a gun from his own section, together with another from McClanahan's battery of Virginia horse artillery.

26. *OR*, 43(1):1027; Julius L. Schaub memoir, Troup County Archives, La Grange, Georgia; William R. Cox, *Address on the Life and Character of Maj. Gen. Stephen D. Ramseur* (Raleigh, N.C.: E. M. Uzzell, 1891), 43; E. P. Goggin to L. L. Lomax, September 27, 1867, CHS; T. B. Beall, "That Stampede at Fisher's Hill," *Confederate Veteran* 5 (January 1897):26; Walter Clark, comp., *Histories of the Several Regiments and Battalions From North Carolina in the Great War, 1861–'65*, 5 vols. (Goldsboro, N.C.: Nash Brothers, 1901), 1:173; Letter of "Nat," September 21, 1864, printed in *Our Living and Our Dead*, November 12, 1873; *Raleigh North Carolina Standard*, October 14, 1864; Hotchkiss, *Make Me a Map*, 230. Jedediah Hotchkiss wrote several months later that "an attempt was made to throw the whole line back and more to the left to meet the movement of the enemy," but the maneuver failed. There is no other evidence of an armywide realignment, and if Early truly did ponder such an effort, he made no progress in implementing it. Even if one adopts an uncompromising interpretation of

the actions of Cox's brigade at Fisher's Hill, there remains some need for tolerance. It was an emaciated organization. The 2nd North Carolina Infantry was commanded by a lieutenant, and the 4th by a captain. The latter regiment numbered only about 50 men on September 22. The strengths of the other units in the brigade are not known, but there is no reason to suspect that they were much different. The 14th North Carolina incurred twenty-seven casualties at Fisher's Hill — two-thirds of them captured.

27. *OR*, 43(1):605. Despite high hopes and a reasonable number of sources, I have not been able to reconcile the conflicting accounts regarding the alignment of Ramseur's brigades at the beginning of the battle. The one certainty is that Grimes's brigade anchored the division's left. The positions shown on the map accompanying this essay and mentioned in the text above are, unhappily, only one of several defensible interpretations.

28. Grimes, *Extracts of Letters*, 69–70; Crook, *Autobiography*, 131; Thomas P. Devereux letters, September 23 and 25, 1864, Devereux Letterbook, North Carolina State Archives, Raleigh; "Correction," "Grimes' Brigade," *Richmond Daily Whig*, November 25, 1864; *OR*, 43(1):605. When Grimes's brigade regrouped the next day, its five units could muster a total of only 300 men.

29. T[homas] B[anks] C[abaniss], "Battle Near Winchester," *Macon Telegraph and Confederate*, October 6, 1864; John L. Johnson to cousin, October 4, 1864, J. C. Bonner Collection, Georgia College, Milledgeville [repository hereafter cited as GC]; Asbury H. Jackson letter, October 2, 1864, Harden Family Papers, DU; Hotchkiss, *Make Me A Map*, 230; "Cook's Brigade," *Milledgeville Southern Recorder*, October 18, 1864. The Milledgeville newspaper account confirms the strength of Cook's brigade, reporting that it numbered about 350 men on September 29.

30. M, "Extract from a Private Letter from a Member of the Third Alabama," *Mobile Advertiser and Register*, October 6, 1864; Justice, "Brigadier General Battle of Alabama," *Richmond Whig*, November 10, 1864; Charles Forsyth, "The Third Alabama Regiment, How it Escaped Capture," *Mobile Advertiser and Register*, October 13, 1864.

31. Forsyth, "Third Alabama Regiment"; "Correction," "Grimes's Brigade"; P. J. Rast, "Fisher's Hill," *Confederate Veteran* 22 (March 1915):123; M, "Extract From a Private Letter." Rast located the stand of the 3rd Alabama/Grimes combination as "hardly more than three hundred yards from the road [Valley Pike]."

32. Hatton, "Valley Campaign," 170.

33. Samuel D. Buck, *With the Old Confeds: Actual Experiences of a Captain in the Line* (Baltimore: H. E. Houck, 1925), 114–15; Robert K. Krick, *Lee's Colonels: A Biographical Register of the Field Officers of the Army of Northern Virginia*, rev. 4th ed. (Dayton, Ohio: Morningside, 1992), 194–95.

34. Buck, *With the Old Confeds*, 115; S. D. Buck, "Battle of Fisher's Hill," *Confederate Veteran* 2 (November 1894):338; S. D. Buck to J. A. Early, September 9, 1888, J. A. Early Papers, Library of Congress, Washington, D.C. [repository hereafter cited as LC]. Because Buck's memoir was published in 1925, some may be skeptical about the veracity of his tale regarding Early's orders to fire on the Tar Heel brigade. However, the 1888 Buck letter to Early cited above says essentially the same thing: ". . . at Fisher's

Hill . . . [I] remember you calling upon us to *shoot* some of the N.C. Brigade who had stampeded and were running over us — and you were certainly perfectly collected."

35. Archibald E. Henderson letter, September 29, 1864, Henderson Papers, DU; J. F. Coghill letter, October 6, 1864, James O. Coghill Papers, DU.

36. Peyton diary, September 22, 1864; Seymour, *Civil War Memoirs*, 144; Lane, "Battle of Fisher's Hill." Lt. Col. Henry D. Monier of the 10th Louisiana reported in his diary that "our boys remain[ed] bravely in the works until all others had left" (Napier Bartlett, *Military Record of Louisiana* [New Orleans: L. Graham, 1875], 53). Casualties in the 21st Virginia, for example, were only one killed, five wounded, and eleven missing or captured (*Richmond Examiner*, October 31, 1864). Peyton claimed that most of the 31st Virginia was captured because of General Gordon's interference, which forced the regiment to stay in the entrenchments longer than was necessary.

37. I. G. Bradwell, "Troops Demoralized at Fisher's Hill," *Confederate Veteran* 25 (March 1917):109; George W. Nichols, *A Soldier's Story of His Regiment* ([Jessup, Ga.]: privately printed, 1898), 189; Stephens, *Intrepid Warrior*, 450, 455; H. P. Fortson letter, October 11, 1864, Barnes Family Papers, UVA; Thomas A. Mann letter, October 6, 1864, Mann Collection, Georgia State Archives, Atlanta [repository hereafter cited as GSA]. There may have been local counterattacks by the Georgia brigade. Stephen C. Murray of the 26th Georgia told his grandson that his unit pressed the Federals back across the Manassas Gap Railroad only to be driven into the cut themselves and captured. (Alton J. Murray, *South Georgia Rebels: The True Wartime Experiences of the 26th Georgia Volunteer Infantry* [Jacksonville, Fla.: Allied Printing, 1976], 186.) The gun Colonel Atkinson labored to save probably was from King's battalion, attached to Wharton's nearby division.

38. Hotchkiss, *Make Me A Map*, 231; Gabriel C. Wharton to John C. Breckinridge, October 5, 1864, quoted in Michael West, *30th Battalion Virginia Sharpshooters* (Lynchburg, Va.: H. E. Howard, 1995), 167; Steven A. Birchfield, comp., *Civil War Letters*, 2 vols. (Melber, Ky.: Simmons Historical Publications, 1996), 2:122–23. The Wharton letter quoted from West actually is at the Chicago Historical Society. Efforts to secure a legible photocopy failed because of faded ink on the original document. Claughton, whose letters are published in Birchfield, was a member of the 45th Virginia Infantry. For a really splendid account of the Nineteenth Corps' reluctance to attack, see William B. Jordan, ed., *The Civil War Journals of John Mead Gould* (Baltimore: Butternut & Blue, 1997), 405–8. Gould noted that as late as 5:55 P.M., most of that corps lingered north of Tumbling Run and was subjected to sternly worded orders from Sheridan to push forward and ignore the frightening terrain. It is to be regretted that there is no Confederate account equivalent to Gould's in content.

39. *OR*, 43(1):556; Berkeley, *Four Years*, 99–100; Lane, "Battle of Fisher's Hill"; Watts, "General Battle and the Stolen Colt," 169; David G. Martin, *The Fluvanna Artillery* (Lynchburg, Va.: H. E. Howard, 1992), 115; W. Cullen Sherwood and Richard L. Nicholas, *Amherst Artillery, Albemarle Artillery and Sturdivant's Battery* (Lynchburg, Va.: H. E. Howard, 1996), 60–62; *OR*, 42(1):863. Nelson was acting as the army's chief of artillery at Fisher's Hill in the place of Col. Thomas H. Carter, who had been lightly wounded three days earlier. Nelson probably retained command of his

own battalion on the twenty-second. Lane wrote years later that the men of Ramseur's division "occupied the breastworks to the right and left of our battery." The *Richmond Whig*, October 3, 1864, citing the *Lynchburg Republican* of uncertain date, reported that the Fluvanna Artillery lost one gun and the Amherst Battery lost two. Berkeley's diary says his unit lost only one gun, not two.

40. Keith S. Bohannon, *The Giles, Alleghany and Jackson Artillery* (Lynchburg, Va.: H. E. Howard, 1990), 49; Taylor, *With Sheridan Up the Shenandoah*, 413; C. A. Fonerden, *A Brief History of the Military Career of Carpenter's Battery* (New Market, Va.: Henkel, 1911), 53–54; *OR*, 43(1):192, 203; Homer D. Musselman, *The Caroline Light, Parker and Stafford Light Virginia Artillery* (Lynchburg, Va.: H. E. Howard, 1992), 121; Robert H. Moore, *The Charlottesville, Lee, Lynchburg and Johnson's Bedford Artillery* (Lynchburg, Va.: H. E. Howard, 1990), 103; Jubal Early to Thomas H. Carter, December 13, 1866, Lee Family Papers, VHS. A nominal list of the casualties in the Alleghany Artillery was published in the *Richmond Whig*, October 6, 1864. For evidence on the postbattle plight of Carpenter's Alleghany artillery, see Nemo [Mary Catherine McVicar], "When We Were Changing Hands," *Winchester Evening Star*, February 14, 1912, which quotes a September 1864 letter from a central Valley resident who met Carpenter after Fisher's Hill. Most reliable summaries of the battle place the number of Confederate cannon captured at twelve or thirteen. Based on the available evidence, it appears that those guns included two from the Stafford Artillery, two from the Lee Lynchburg Battery, four from the Alleghany Artillery (three ordnance rifles and one Napoleon), one from the Fluvanna Artillery, one from the Amherst Artillery, and two from the horse artillery.

41. Samuel J. C. Moore letter, October 3, 1864, Moore Papers, Southern Historical Collection, University of North Carolina, Chapel Hill [repository hereafter cited as SHC]; Wayland, *History of Shenandoah County*, 31, 187. Hotchkiss (*OR*, 43[1]:1028) places this defense "on the hill in front of Mount Prospect." Maj. Marcellus N. Moorman, executive officer of Braxton's artillery battalion, suggested that one purpose of the stand was to allow the remnants of that battalion to get away (M. N. Moorman, "Recollections of Cedar Creek and Fisher's Hill, October 19th, 1864," *SHSP*, 30:372). Anyone exploring the battlefield today must remember that the course of the turnpike was changed in 1923 to eliminate the switchback descent from Wharton's position to the stone bridge over Tumbling Run. The ruins of the bridge survive among the weeds, making for an atmospheric stop on a battlefield tour.

42. Cox, *Address on Ramseur*, 43–44; W. H. May, "Reminiscences of the War between the States," 288, typescript, GSA; Garnett, "Diary," 9; Hotchkiss, *Make Me a Map*, 231. In addition to Pendleton, other officers present at different times during this stand included Generals Gordon, Pegram, Cox, and perhaps Battle. Henry Kyd Douglas and Jedediah Hotchkiss of the army staff also were there. Carpenter's role in this affair is confusing. Most sources indicate that he lost all his guns on the main battlefield. If he was present among the men Pendleton rallied, then perhaps he was directing the fire of some other guns collared from among the retreating masses (see note 40 above). The guns could have been from the Amherst Artillery, as two guns from that battery apparently participated in some twilight engagement (Lane, "Battle

of Fisher's Hill"). Major Moorman recalled that Pendleton "collected about one hundred men." (Moorman, "Recollections of Cedar Creek," 372.) Captain Buck of the 13th Virginia left four accounts of the battle, and while they are all very similar, they vary in some specifics. Regarding the fight at Mount Prospect, Buck wrote in 1894 that he helped to gather "about fifty men" and two cannon (Buck, "Battle of Fisher's Hill," 338), while in the later draft of his memoirs he says he rallied twenty men and two cannon (Samuel Buck typescript memoir, DU.). When his full memoirs reached print in 1925, the numbers had changed to "about twenty men" and only one cannon (Buck, *With the Old Confeds*, 115). At least Buck consistently identified Captain Carpenter as the artillerist in every account. Captain May of the 3rd Alabama remembered firing a volley here and insisted later that Colonel Pendleton had said the volley "saved the army." Douglas claimed to have been officially in charge of the army's rear guard. If the stand at Mount Prospect was as unharmonious as its survivors' reminiscences, no part of the army would have escaped.

43. Marginalia of Henry Kyd Douglas in his personal copy of Mary Anna Jackson, *Life and Letters of General Thomas J. Jackson* (New York: Harper & Brothers, 1892), 306, at the library of Antietam National Battlefield Park, Sharpsburg, Maryland; Henry Kyd Douglas, *I Rode With Stonewall* (Chapel Hill: University of North Carolina Press, 1940), 312–13; Thomas T. Greene letter, October 4, 1864, Greene Family Papers, VHS; M, "Extract from a Private Letter"; W. G. Bean, *Stonewall's Man: Sandie Pendleton* (Chapel Hill: University of North Carolina Press, 1959), 210–11, 216. Douglas described Pendleton's wound as being "in the groin and through the body," while Bean said Pendleton was shot in the abdomen, the ball passing entirely through. A sketch in John Lipscomb Johnson, *Biographical Sketches of Alumni of the University of Virginia* (Baltimore: Turnbull Brothers, 1871), 656–57, states that the wound was in the groin. Another very eloquent and emotional obituary of Pendleton is in the *Richmond Daily Enquirer*, October 18, 1864. The correspondent M (cited above) wrote that Dan Wheeler of the 3rd Alabama was beside Pendleton when the latter was hit.

44. Hotchkiss, *Make Me a Map*, 231; Stonebraker, *Rebel of '61*, 65; Grimes, *Extracts of Letters*, 71; Buckner Randolph letter, September 29, 1864, Randolph Family Papers. The Randolph letter provides a good example of the army's views on the degree of its defeat, suggesting that with "even two hours more of day light they would have completely destroyed our army." Unlike the reality of the war's larger battles, the destruction of an army—in this case Early's—was a possibility at Fisher's Hill. Encircling or permanently smashing an army of fewer than 10,000 men is a reasonable goal. This seems especially evident when compared to some of the battles traditionally viewed as lost opportunities for overwhelming victories, such as the Confederate retreats from Maryland in 1862 and 1863, or McClellan's narrow escape from Lee's combinations in the latter half of the Seven Days battles below Richmond.

45. Seaton Gales diary, September 22, 1864, printed in *Our Living and Our Dead*, March 11, 1874; Forsyth, "Third Alabama Regiment"; John L. Johnson letter, October 4, 1864, GC; UUD, "Army Correspondence of the Journal," *Wilmington Daily Journal*, October 26, 1864. UUD recently has been identified as Dr. Thomas F. Wood of the 3rd North Carolina Infantry. See Thomas Fanning Wood, *Doctor to the Front: The*

Recollections of Confederate Surgeon Thomas Fanning Wood, 1861–1865, ed. Donald B. Koonce (Knoxville: University of Tennessee Press, 2000).

46. Stephens, *Intrepid Warrior*, 455; Micajah Woods letter, September 23, 1864, Woods Papers; Archibald E. Henderson letter, September 29, 1864, Henderson Papers; John B. Gordon, *Reminiscences of the Civil War* (New York: Scribner's, 1903), 326. Asbury H. Jackson, a staff officer in Cook's brigade, admitted to being "badly demoralized and stampeded twice . . . not because we were whip'd, but for the want of generalship, Genl. Early being completely out-*generaled* & out numbered." (Asbury H. Jackson letter, October 2, 1864, DU.)

47. J. Floyd King letter, October 11, 1864, in King's Compiled Service Record, M331, roll 149, National Archives, Washington, D.C.; Peyton diary, September 22, 1864; Samuel J. C. Moore letter, November 1, 1864, Moore Papers. After the war, community gossips spread the word that Early had been drinking on the day of the battle (Wayland, *History of Shenandoah County*, 328).

48. *OR*, 43(1):556; Jubal A. Early, *Lieutenant General Jubal Anderson Early, C.S.A.: Autobiographical Sketch and Narrative of the War between the States* (Philadelphia: Lippincott, 1912), 429–31; James A. Milling, "Jim Milling and the War, 1862–1865," photocopy of typescript memoir in author's possession; Jubal A. Early to George F. Holmes, May 6, 1871, vol. 1, Holmes Papers, LC.

49. Micajah Woods letter, September 23, 1864, Woods Papers.

50. *OR*, 43(1):123.

51. The published returns for Fisher's Hill (*OR*, 43[1]:556–57) show fewer than 600 Confederate casualties, although Early's report on an adjacent page admits to almost 1,000 men missing. Presumably many hundreds of those absentees came back to camp before the official tabulation was posted. Even a thorough scouring of the service records for each unit engaged at Fisher's Hill probably would not yield a firm figure because of the loss of so many army muster rolls from the war's last six months.

52. Micajah Woods letter, September 23, 1864, Woods Papers; Berkeley, *Four Years*, 101; Peyton diary, September 23, 1864; Buckner Randolph letter, September 29, 1864, Randolph Family Papers; Birchfield, *Civil War Letters*, 2:123; Richard Waldrop letter, September 24, 1864, Waldrop Papers, SHC. One rustic Georgian rejoined his unit after the battle and "was sorey to see thee bouys so bad whipt—i dont think that they will ever dough well a gin" (Thomas A. Mann letter, October 6, 1864, Micro Drawer 171, 27, Mann Collection). For an example of soldiers who professed no demoralization, see especially the Thomas P. Devereux letter, September 25, 1864, Devereux Letterbook. Devereux wryly headed his letter from "Camp Stampede." Despite its gloomy memories, Fisher's Hill became one of the most popular spots for Confederate reunions in the Shenandoah Valley. The first to occur on the battlefield was in 1891, but they became frequent events for many years afterward (Wayland, *History of Shenandoah County*, 28).

ANDRE M. FLECHE

Uncivilized War

The Shenandoah Valley Campaign, the Northern Democratic Press, and the Election of 1864

On October 13, 1864, Abraham Lincoln pessimistically predicted the outcome of the impending presidential election. Although state contests in Pennsylvania, Ohio, and Indiana went well for the Republicans in October, Lincoln "was still gloomy over the prospects." He believed he would defeat Democratic candidate George B. McClellan by the narrow margin of 120 to 114 in the Electoral College. The president prepared to concede Pennsylvania, New Jersey, New York, Kentucky, Maryland, and Delaware to his rival. The capture of Atlanta and Union victories in Virginia's Shenandoah Valley had lifted Lincoln from the despair he faced in late August, when he saw no hope for his own reelection, but the outcome of the presidential contest remained unclear. The Democrats made campaign issues of conscription, confiscation, emancipation, restrictions on the freedom of the press, arbitrary arrests, and other controversial policies the Lincoln government passed in pursuit of victory. The harsh war measures that paid dividends during the autumn of 1864 still faced ratification by voters at the polls.[1]

The military events of 1864 marked the culmination of a shift in Lincoln's strategic thinking. Early in the war, the president embraced a conciliatory strategy that rested on the belief that most white southerners remained loyal Unionists who would quickly return to the national fold after a restrained but decisive show of force by the Federal government. In Lincoln's first annual message to Congress, delivered in December 1861, he announced that he would specifically avoid measures that might alienate southern civilians. "In considering the policy to be adopted for suppressing the insurrection, I have been anxious and careful that the inevitable conflict for this purpose shall not degenerate into a violent and remorseless revolutionary struggle," he stated. "We should not be in haste to determine that radical and extreme measures, which may reach the loyal as well as the disloyal, are indispensable." Three long years of war had proved the ineffectiveness of such an approach. Gradually but surely, Lincoln abandoned the idea of widespread southern loyalism and accepted as necessary the confiscation of Confederate property, the abolition of slavery, the arming of African American soldiers, and the destruction of the economic infrastructure of the Confederacy.[2]

In early 1864, he took the final step in moving to what historian Mark Grimsley has termed "hard war" when he brought Ulysses S. Grant, newly promoted to the rank of lieutenant general, east to serve as general in chief of all Union forces in the field. During the Vicksburg and Meridian, Mississippi, campaigns, Grant and Maj. Gen. William Tecumseh Sherman, his principal subordinate, had experimented with a new raiding strategy that encompassed the destruction of private property, civilian food supplies, crops, railroads, and warehouses. Lincoln seized on these tactics as the surest means to victory and promoted Grant accordingly. Once he arrived in Virginia, Grant applied his ideas with energy and determination. While the Army of the Potomac grappled with Robert E. Lee's Army of Northern Virginia from the Wilderness to Petersburg in a grueling battle of attrition, Grant dispatched Maj. Gen. David Hunter and subsequently Maj. Gen. Philip H. Sheridan with orders to devastate the Shenandoah Valley. Under Sheridan, the new way of making war on the South, devised in part by Grant and approved by Lincoln, reached its apogee. Union forces burned barns, destroyed crops, liberated slaves, confiscated private property, and did all in their power to make the Valley a barren waste.[3]

Historians have long treated Sheridan's campaign, along with the fall of Atlanta, as the final blows shattering any prospect of Democratic victory at the polls in 1864. The Democratic Party had adopted a "war failure" plank at their convention that summer, which declared that Lincoln's policy of continued fighting, emancipation, and harsh treatment of southern civilians had no reasonable prospect of success. Although presidential candidate George B. McClellan demanded reunion as the basis of any peace, he and the Democrats advocated immediate discussion of terms. Union victories in September and October, however, proved "that the Democrats' war failure plank was a palpable lie." Historian Christopher Dell asserted that the conservative tradition that resisted emancipation, confiscation, and the destruction of southern

Harper's Weekly ran this full-page portrait of Democratic candidate George B. McClellan a few weeks before the election. *Harper's Weekly*, September 17, 1864.

civilian property met defeat on the field. William Zornow agreed that "the far-reaching military achievements of Sherman, Sheridan, and Farragut broke the back of the opposition, both southern and northern Democratic."[4]

In the long run, Sheridan's dramatic successes in the Shenandoah Valley may have contributed to the defeat of the Democrats; in the short term, however, the opposition party used the harsh military campaign to attack the Lincoln administration's ways of making war. Sheridan's Valley campaign epitomized all that Democrats perceived as wrong in the Republican-led war effort. The wanton destruction of cropland, confiscation of private property, and emancipation of slaves, Democrats argued, would only alienate southern civilians, making reunion harder to achieve. Unlike Lincoln, northern Democrats and their supporters proved unwilling to give up the notion of widespread southern unionism. Their perception of southern civilians as oppressed by both secessionist tyrants and ruthless Federal armies governed Democratic criticisms of military strategy and fueled political debate during the autumn of 1864. Democratic editors presented an image of white southerners that could be used both to criticize administration war policy and urge support for Democratic politicians. Electoral politics, military strategy, and representations of the South came together in closely related fashion. In short, the policies that brought the Lincoln administration its biggest successes provided the issues on which Democrats hoped to deal the Republicans their biggest defeat.

Historians who seek to minimize the seriousness of this threat ignore the strength and longevity of the Democratic Party. Mark Grimsley observes that "the shift to hard war occasioned little public debate among northern policy and opinion-makers," in part because "the Democratic Party proved unable or unwilling to capitalize on the issue." While acknowledging that Democrats objected to a "war of subjugation" and nominated George B. McClellan, who "had been one of the most fervent defenders of the old conciliatory policy," Grimsley does not explore how the Democrats used the issue of hard war during the campaign of 1864. The Democrats remained a powerful opposition party throughout the war and forced Lincoln to make tough choices about what kind of war he would fight. As Joel Silbey points out, "Democrats were acceptable enough to enough voters to offer competitive opposition to the dominant Republicans and posed, therefore, significant strategic problems for the majority party." Michael Holt concurs that "the Democratic party remained a potent challenger to Republicans in the North." Democrats managed to offer coherent opposition to the Republicans despite the defection of War Democrats and policy differences between advocates of peace at any price and the majority who remained committed to union first. In the words of Michael Holt, "the menace of a Democratic comeback . . . was no chimera."[5]

The prewar relationship between the Democratic Party and southerners provided one of the biggest obstacles to a Democratic comeback. The secession of the South during the winter and spring of 1861 posed a peculiar problem for northern Democrats. Much of the party's traditional support had come from the South, and antebellum Democrats pointed to that fact as a source of strength in their contests with the newly formed Republicans. "In the years before the Civil War one way to express nationalism was to be a Democrat," suggests Jean Baker. As a result, "their party's relationship to the South became a means of exhibiting patriotism." Unlike their Republican opponents, Democrats enjoyed a base of support that transcended section and allowed them to stake a claim as the true defenders of national unity. Constitution and union became key tenets of the Democratic faith even before the war, and the party's identity and patriotic credentials came to rest on its close relationship with the South.[6]

The secession of the South and ensuing Civil War destroyed the validity of such claims. When war broke out, Republicans rather than Democrats did the most to uphold the Union. If anything, Democratic loyalty came into question because of prewar association with southerners. Democrats scrambled to retain their image as a national, patriotic party in the midst of a conflict fought under the direction of the self-consciously sectional Republicans. The editors of Democratic newspapers recognized the precarious nature of their party's position. The *Indianapolis Daily Sentinel* reprinted an article from the *Times* of London pointing out that the Democratic Party occupied "at this moment a position as strange and as exceptional as ever fell to the lot of any political combination in any country. They are fighting for a cause to which they profess, and doubtless feel, the most boundless devotion; but they are fighting . . . in support of a party which they hate with all the bitterness of a defeated faction."[7]

The biggest problem that the war posed for Democrats lay in reconciling military service and loyalty to the Union with political opposition to Republican policymakers. While, in the words of Jean Baker, "Democrats established their nationalism as Union soldiers," their relationship with their former southern allies remained ambivalent. Most Democrats retained a positive view of the majority of southerners. A small minority led the South to secession, they argued, and most southerners remained loyal unionists, ready to return to the national fold once the misguided few met defeat on the battlefield. Such a view held important implications for both military strategy and the election of

1864. Sheridan's harsh methods in the Shenandoah Valley, insisted Democrats, would only alienate the loyal southern masses and hinder reunion. Democrats claimed that their party, with its more conciliatory approach to war-making, represented the best political alternative and the surest means of ending the war with the South on the basis of Union.[8]

Gen. George B. McClellan, nominated in the summer of 1864 as the Democratic presidential candidate at the party's convention in Chicago, positioned himself perfectly to take advantage of such a strategy. His nomination represented a defeat for New York governor Horatio Seymour and the wing of the party that favored immediate peace, and McClellan acted immediately to remind voters that he had once led the effort to achieve reunion through military force. Acknowledging that he "could not look in the face of my gallant comrades of the Army & Navy who have survived so many bloody battles" and maintain that the war "had been in vain," McClellan declared that "the restoration of the Union in all its integrity is and must continue to be the indispensable condition in any settlement."[9]

A McClellan administration, however, would conduct military policy much differently should "the dread arbitrament of war" continue. McClellan vowed in his letter accepting the Democratic nomination that he would fight "a war conducted strictly in accordance with those principles which I had so often had occasion to communicate when in the command of Armies." Although he deliberately omitted reference to his notorious address to President Abraham Lincoln penned in July 1862, McClellan's meaning remained clear. The war, he had written from Harrison's Landing, "should not be, at all, a War upon population; but against armed forces and political organizations. Neither confiscation of property, political executions of persons, territorial organization of states or forcible abolition of slavery should be contemplated for a moment. Pillage and waste should be treated as high crimes."[10]

Even if McClellan would have preferred not to dredge up his attempt to lecture Lincoln on war policy, Democrats eager to begin the campaign seized upon the theme. The *New York World* celebrated McClellan's nomination as the surest way to achieve peace. "After his inauguration, the character of the war will have so changed that the southern people will no longer have a sufficient motive to stand out. They will then see that submission to the Union does not involve the overthrow of their institutions, the destruction of their property, industrial disorganization, social chaos, negro equality, and the nameless horrors of a servile war." The *Philadelphia Age* declared that Democratic policy "will be guided by justice and humanity." Even Horatio Seymour, McClellan's main rival for the Democratic nomination who had attempted to make an issue out of the general's alleged mistreatment of Maryland civilians in 1861, now defended the actions of his ex-rival in campaigning for the Democratic ticket. Any apparent cooperation with Lincoln early in the war "must not be viewed in the light which events have since thrown upon the policy of the administration. Then, the President denounced measures which he has since adopted." The nature of the war had changed, Democrats argued, and their nominee stood prepared to turn back the clock.[11]

Republican politicians hoped to attract voters in a very different way. Lincoln, Grant, and congressional Republicans had come to realize that victories in the field held the key to political success on the home front. Increasingly, a vigorous war effort that targeted soldiers and civilians alike became the surest way to secure dramatic northern victories that would win over moderates and ensure Confederate defeat. In the Republicans' calculation, the Democrats —with their cries for conciliation, protection of civil liberties, and lenient treatment of southern civilians—would go down to defeat along with the Confederacy. As historian Michael Holt observed, "Congressional Republicans . . . approached the military conflict with the Confederacy and the political conflict with the Democracy in exactly the same way. In neither would they make concessions to induce cooperation, in neither did they seek compromise or accommodation. In both they demanded war to the hilt."[12]

In the midsummer and fall of 1864, northerners got just that from their commanders in the Shenandoah Valley. In June, David Hunter burned the Virginia Military Institute before being driven off by Jubal Early. When Philip H. Sheridan took command of Union forces in the area, the destruction began in earnest. After defeating Early at the battles of Third Winchester on September 19 and Fisher's Hill three days later, Sheridan's soldiers fanned out to burn barns, destroy and confiscate crops, and drive off livestock. After less than one month of this work, Sheridan could report having "destroyed over 2000 barns filled with wheat, hay and farming implements, and over 70 mills, filled with flour. The people here are getting sick of the war; hitherto they have had no reason to complain because they have been living in great abundance."[13]

Early signs suggested that many northerners agreed. The independent *New York Herald* joined Republicans in applauding the newly ferocious turn military strategy had taken. "Shenandoah. The Country Laid Waste. Affairs in the Valley Prospering," proclaimed one headline. The paper had no qualms about treating Confederate civilians harshly. Sheridan's destruction of barns, houses, and cropland brought tacit approval. The nonpartisan *Herald*, and its thousands of moderate readers, agreed with the Republican view that only punishing Confederate civilians could end the war speedily and achieve reunion. The *Herald* professed to want an end to the fighting but insisted that "the subjugation of the rebel armies" provided "the first essential" to peace. "Our only peacemakers are Lieutenant-General Grant and his subordinate major generals and the armies of the Union," the paper argued. As a result, Lincoln seemed the more prudent choice for president because he supported vigorous war measures. "We know the position of Mr. Lincoln," reasoned the *Herald*. "He is prosecuting the war and is pledged to fight it out." It appeared that stern war measures and Confederate defeat would bring Republican victory at the polls in 1864.[14]

Northern Democrats, however, used those very same issues to attack Lincoln, the Republicans, and the entire northern war effort during the fall's political battles. On September 29, as Sheridan's army stood poised to lay waste to the Valley and the election campaign heated up, a poem titled "My Southern Home" appeared in the *Cincinnati Enquirer*. The author identified himself only as "Johnson's Island," one of the most notorious Federal prisoner-of-war camps:

> Shall I not weep Virginia's hills, her slopes and grassy plains,
> Her cities and her villages; her cottages and lanes?
>
> Her sons so gallant, chivalrous; her bracing mountain air,
> Her daughters pure and beautiful, and true as they are fair?
>
> Shall not my harp remain unstrung, the captive sing no more?
> How can I wake the minstrelsy of "Old Virginia shore?"
>
> A curse, then, on my good right arm, a curse upon my tongue
> If I forget my Southern home — the loins of which I sprung.
>
> There let me go! My heart is there! There I may calmly die;
> Virginia's turf must wrap my clay, her win is my requiem sigh.[15]

This poem, "written for the *Cincinnati Enquirer*," appeared with a companion piece pleading for an end to the war:

> Oh give us back the joys of Peace!
> That filled the land in other years,
> And let this war of brothers cease
>
> That drenches it with blood and tears.
> Oh give us back the Government

Our fathers in their wisdom made
Its basis on the free consent
Of all the states they justly laid.

Now look upon the ruin wrought
By bigots in their power and pride —
The Constitution set at naught,
The laws ignored or else denied,
While frenzy reigns supreme,
And kindred meet as deadly foes,
And deal each other mortal blows,
Nor falter at the blood that flows
In many a ghastly stream.

Oh when will gentle peace return
And bless the blighted land again?
When will our haughty rulers learn
The lesson in a million slain?
When will the bigots see
That force of arms will not restore
The Union as it was before,
Though they should give a million more
To set the Negroes free?[16]

Although the two poems may be unusual for their romanticism and hyperbole, they call attention to the three important themes that converged in the northern Democratic press during the war. Democratic editors used the image of a loyal white South to criticize the harsh turn in administration war policy and to campaign for the election of Democratic politicians. Representations of the South and military strategy became linked during the autumn's political campaigns. The poems depicted the South as a verdant land characterized by abundance, peace, and harmonious social relations. White southerners should not be viewed as enemies but as wayward "brothers" unjustly smitten by a tyrannical government that threatened liberties in the North and South alike. Gentle persuasion would suffice to bring the southern people back into the Union and secure the "joys of peace" for all Americans.

Events in the Shenandoah Valley underscored how remote peace remained and offered clear evidence to Democrats of Republican intentions to destroy the South, subjugate its people, and frustrate efforts at reconciliation. In June 1864, Sheridan's predecessor David Hunter set fire to the Virginia Military Institute in Lexington before retreating from the Valley of Virginia. Confederate cavalry acting under orders from Gen. Jubal Early retaliated in July by burning the town of Chambersburg, Pennsylvania.

Democratic editors blamed the escalating violence on Republican willingness to prosecute a harsh war. Chambersburg's *Valley Spirit* concurred with the *Philadelphia Age* in attributing the tragedy in Pennsylvania to the ruthless actions of Hunter. Both papers printed comments from General Early excusing his behavior during his brief invasion of the North. "General Hunter in his recent raid to Lynchburg, caused wide-spread ruin wherever he passed. I followed him about sixty miles, and language would fail me to describe the terrible desolation which marked his path. Dwelling-houses and other buildings were almost universally burned; fences, implements of husbandry, and everything available for the sustenance of human life . . . were everywhere destroyed. We found many, very many, families of helpless women and children who had been suddenly turned out of doors, and their houses and contents condemned to the flames," recounted Early. "Such things of course, cannot be long endured, and must provoke retaliation whenever it is possible." The unrepentant Early even commented on the willingness of Democratic journals to exonerate him and asked directly a question editors in Chambersburg and Philadelphia implicitly seconded: "I saw with much pleasure . . . an able article in the National Intelligencer, which called upon the north to consider gravely whether such a mode of warfare as they had inaugurated is likely to yield a success commensurate to its cost."[17]

Democratic editors had not so far abandoned the Union cause that they could not applaud conventional victories as they occurred. The *Chambersburg Valley Spirit* celebrated Sheridan's "brilliant victory" over Early at Winchester on September 19. "The President and Secretary Stanton have at length — doubtless by mistake — placed at the head of the Army of the Valley of the Shenandoah a man of talents and military skill," the paper marvelled.[18]

When the Democratic press received reports of Sheridan's less conventional operations, however, a different tone emerged. "Our dispatches furnish details of the devastations of war," wrote the *Detroit Free Press*. "Mills, barns and dwellings of defenseless people are destroyed, their cattle and sheep taken from them, and, homeless and destitute, the old and infirm, and helpless women and children are left in their desolation to face the rigors of approaching winter." A correspondent of a New York paper reacted in horror to efforts to render the Valley a "barren waste." "What do the readers of the *World* think of the wanton burning of twenty-seven hundred barns, filled with wheat, and more than eighty mills for grinding wheat and corn? This was done by soldiers of 'The Union,' with the Union flag waving over them."[19]

Destruction of private homes prompted fiercer criticism: "The flames from the burning barns communicated, in many instances, to dwelling-houses contiguous, and houses and barns alike, in a few hours, with all their contents, were reduced to a mass of smouldering ruins." The worst was yet to come, according to the *Philadelphia Age*: "Sheridan intends to continue the destruction all the way north to Martinsburg. The damage has been immense. Not only barns but private dwellings have been destroyed. Half the village of New Market is in ashes. The people, deprived of food and homes, will have to wander off. Few, not accustomed to the desolations of war, can realize the extent of the destruction made, under orders from Grant, by Sheridan in the Shenandoah Valley."[20]

Grant's orders to Sheridan to make the Valley a "barren waste" received particular condemnation. The *Valley Spirit* asserted that, if Sheridan had not described the devastation in official reports to Grant, "we would be inclined to disbelieve the whole story. That an order so desperately wicked, so contrary to the spirit of Christianity, and so revolting to the civilization of this age, should have been issued and executed by officers commanding the armies of a free, civilized and religious nation, is, indeed, almost too incredible for human belief." Elsewhere the Chambersburg paper charged that Sheridan admitted the war now targeted civilians and private property, and summed up the developments in one succinct heading: "Vandalism."[21]

Democratic newspapers lamented the human and natural costs of a campaign that attacked civilians and the South's social and economic infrastructure. The *Cincinnati Inquirer* condemned Sheridan for burning the Valley, claiming that the Shenandoah before the war was "as fair a country as the sun ever shone on. It was old and settled and had many beautiful mansions and pleasant homes. It is now a waste and desolation . . . its old men murdered or starving to death; its women and children the victims of murder, lust and want of food and shelter." The *Philadelphia Age* held that it could not "tell the story any better" than a correspondent of the *New York Tribune*: "The Valley of the beautiful Shenandoah, from near the Natural Bridge to the gallows tree of John Brown, is a desolation." The *Valley Spirit* condemned the policies that produced such devastation: "No ordinary circumstances will justify a civilized people in resorting to a wholesale and indiscriminate destruction of private property. No common exigency will excuse a barbarous war upon non-combatants. Nothing but the most pressing necessity, will warrant a military commander in depopulating whole sections of country, wasting and burning up the property of the people, and making a rich, populous and fertile valley a howling wilderness, incapable of supporting any living thing."[22]

War in the Valley seemed to blur the lines between civilian and combatant in ways unimaginable in 1861. Besides targeting the crops, stores, and industries that provided sustenance for southern civilians and soldiers, Union generals had to deal with a civilian population overtly hostile to Federal troops. In the Shenandoah Valley, as in other areas of Union occupation, Confederate guerrillas operated behind enemy lines, harassing supply trains, and attacking isolated garrisons or companies of Union soldiers. In a letter to General Grant, Sheridan complained that, since his arrival in the Valley, "every train, every small party, and every straggler has been bushwhacked by the people." Sheridan concluded that only harshly punitive measures would put an end to guerrilla warfare. Like the cattle and crops that fed Robert E. Lee's Army of Northern Virginia, he decided that the civilians who sustained guerrilla fighters should be rooted out with fire and sword. When Lt. John R. Meigs, Sheridan's engineer officer and the son of Union quartermaster general Montgomery C. Meigs, was found dead near Dayton, Virginia, the Federal commander retaliated by burning all the houses within five miles of the town. Grant, it was rumored, agreed, giving orders to "shoot every guerilla, burn every house, and drive out men, women, and children from the guerilla-infested region of the Shenandoah Valley."[23]

The northern Democratic press attacked the policies of Grant and Sheridan as a merciless abandonment of the rules of warfare. The *New York World* described the vengeance visited upon Dayton: "This work was done with deliberation, and without any other than the briefest warning to the inmates. All appeals for mercy were vain. Tottering age and feeble infancy, delicate ladies, and women in that state which would find pity even in the eyes of a savage, were compelled to rush out of their houses, and then to witness their homes consumed before their eyes by devouring flames. What pen can describe the horrors of these scenes?" The premeditation of the burning made it especially horrible. "With a refinement of malignity worthy of the evil one himself, not only the seed for next year's crops, but even the very farming implements themselves were burned up."[24]

Punishing civilians for the deeds of Confederate irregulars, argued Democrats, represented the horrifically logical outcome of the emerging Republican policy of targeting the economic, industrial, and social infrastructure that supported the southern war effort. The *Detroit Free Press* echoed Chambersburg's

Union soldiers discover Lt. John R. Meigs's body in this sketch by James E. Taylor, whose memoir described the young officer's death as "a deplorable tragedy." Courtesy of the Western Reserve Historical Society, Cleveland, Ohio.

own *Valley Spirit* in blaming administration policies for the late July burning of the town. "The laying waste of the Shenandoah Valley will undoubtedly call out acts in retaliation equally terrible," the *Free Press* somewhat smugly predicted, adding that "when war degenerates into a contest of mere brutality, in which women and children, non-combatants and prisoners, are made to suffer, we elevate even a degraded enemy to a level with ourselves." The *Philadelphia Age* held that harsh Union war measures alone should shoulder the blame for increasing violence. "Sheridan's barbarous devastation in the Shenandoah Valley has already borne its fruits. The guerrillas are so numerous, and so savage in their attacks upon his rear-guards and his supply trains, that he finds himself unable to hold a position so far advanced as Strasburg." Another editor agreed: "General Grant's order, if it be really issued, will make the killing more general, and very much promote the operations which General Sheridan has begun, the whole ending in one grand result, namely, killing the whole population of the country, men and women and children."[25]

Democrats made sure to remind readers that war on Confederate civilians meant war on women as well. In his study of guerrilla warfare in Missouri, Michael Fellman suggests that for American society such a development meant nothing less than a "gender crisis." To treat women as participants in war meant blurring "gender boundaries and gender decorum in often horrifying ways." The situation proved little different in the more "conventional" Shenandoah Valley campaign. Like Sherman's more famous "March to the Sea," Sheridan's campaign in the Valley produced its share of "bummers" (though that word came into use regarding Sherman's men), Union stragglers and foragers who took or destroyed food and other goods on southern farms and in southern homes. Democratic editors accused them of visiting "nameless indignities" upon the white women of the South, who had to resort to carrying firearms in self-defense. One Democratic correspondent in the Valley attempted to explain the despair and "strange and fascinating beauty" of the rebel women. "War is nearer their hearts than ours, it is a sterner thing by far. . . . Is it strange, then," he asked, "that we who seek for tenderness in the hearts of those women must seek deep?" According to this reporter, a war that touched women transformed traditional gender characteristics. Where one should find tenderness, only cold desperation could be found. "One who commences speech with these damsels finds himself wondering what sort of beings have arisen on this soil in the place of the children of Eve. These women have suffered," remarked the reporter.[26]

The abolition of slavery in the Shenandoah Valley and elsewhere proved the most controversial wartime policy in the eyes of Democrats. Federal troops began enforcing the Emancipation Proclamation as they entered and occupied Confederate territory. Democratic Party editors attacked this war measure and appealed to property rights, constitutional principles, and sheer racism in support of their preferred candidates in 1864. Referring to the white southern civilians left without food or shelter by Sheridan's forces, one Democratic editorial self-righteously proclaimed that "it may be perfectly just in Mr. Lincoln to doom defenseless women and children of the white race to agony and starvation, while he supports one hundred and fifty thousand negroes at government expense." The *Valley Spirit* declared that the "object of the war" had been "subverted from a high and holy purpose to a mere crusade against African slavery." Democrats attempted to use both white racial solidarity and material interests to turn readers against Lincoln's policy of emancipation. "It becomes men of property to look at this matter with calm and considerate minds," reasoned one paper. Abolition, according to this editorial, dangerously involved the enforcement of "new principles of social life," the compelling of "special religious dogmas," and "the arbitrary change of domestic and state laws." As a result, Lincoln and abolition presented the nation with a future that threatened "the destruction of the safeguards of property." Democrats argued that the Federal power on display in the Shenandoah Valley threatened to transform the Constitution, the nation's social structure, and the war itself.[27]

Whether viewed through the lens of race, gender, the environment, or society, Democrats detected something new in the way Sheridan and his superiors fought. The *Cincinnati Enquirer* reprinted a headline from the *Montreal Gazette* that summed up for all Democrats the nature of the changes represented by the 1864 Valley campaign: "Uncivilized War." "The practice of civilized warfare, as now well recognized," continued the editorial, "holds sacred the lives and property of the people who are so unfortunate as to live in countries in which war prevails. When the contrary practice prevails, it is rightly called uncivilized." Like Lincoln, the Democratic Party recognized that targeting southern civilians, their crops, homes, and property represented a new departure in wartime policy. Unlike Lincoln, they argued that continued devastation would drown any prospects for peace in the blood of the once-loyal southern masses.[28]

Alarmist theories of genocidal Republican plots appeared in the Democratic press as editors watched what they perceived as the systematic destruction of the Shenandoah and the entire South. The *Cincinnati Enquirer* ran a headline declaring "Southerners To Be Exterminated." The accompanying article purported to be a letter "written by a New England gentleman high in the confidence of the administration." "To prosecute this war as it should be prosecuted, nay as it inevitably will be, it must be waged for the complete extermination of the adult population of the States in rebellion," the mysterious Republican suggested. Only that would ensure freedom for the slaves and the loyalty of the young generations of white southerners, even if it took "thirty years of war." The letter also implied that Lincoln could retain office through nefarious means should the reconstruction of the South take longer than four years. In a similar vein, the *Detroit Free Press* claimed Lincoln had inflicted more "wrongs and miseries" during his "four year sway" than any leader besides "Tamerlane, Atilla, and Ghengis Khan."[29]

According to the Democrats, most of the civilians Sheridan treated as enemies and rebels were loyal Americans. "These people too are our countrymen —their history our history," proclaimed one newspaper. The *Valley Spirit* agreed, stating that "this war was commenced to restore the Union. It was to be a war, whose object should be to bring back the citizens of the seceded States to their allegiance to the Government." Lincoln's policies had ruined all hope for such an achievement: "Does any man of sane mind think that the Southern people can be conciliated and brought back into the Union, by such acts of cold blooded barbarity as Gen. Sheridan relates in his official report? Will men who have been ruined and their property wholly destroyed love the Government that inflicts the wrong?" The *Indianapolis Daily Sentinel* reprinted the orders Grant issued to Sheridan in late August regarding treatment of Confederate property in the Valley: "Do all the damage you can to the railroad and crops. Carry off stock of all descriptions, and negroes, so as to prevent further planting. If the war is to last another year let the Shenandoah Valley remain a barren waste." This "looks like another year of war, and another, and another," opined the Democratic editor with disgust. The *Valley Spirit* gave voice to similar sentiments during the summer of 1864. "Under the policy of the present Administration, this war *can never end!* Their *policy* precludes the possibility of such a result. It is against the law of reason, of human nature, and of God. From the very nature of the case the war must be interminable."[30]

Such a prospect proved especially problematic for the editors of Chambersburg's *Valley Spirit*. "As citizens of Franklin County we have a deeper interest in the war policy of this administration, than other portions of the country removed from the scene of hostilities. To us it is a vital question, that private property shall be protected by both armies." Sheridan's tactics endangered northern and southern civilian alike. "If this is the way the war is to be carried on in the future, God save the people along the border!" one editor pointedly declared. Both Democrats and Republicans in Pennsylvania faced "revenge for the atrocities practiced in the Shenandoah Valley. In what condition do you suppose *they* would leave *our* beautiful Valley with its fine farm-houses and magnificent barns and mills?" The editors of the *Spirit* asked their readers whether there existed "a single man in our community who does not regret what has been done by Sheridan."[31]

The Union general's dramatic victories at Third Winchester, Fisher's Hill, and Cedar Creek posed a problem for Democrats, however. Having suffered through more than three years of war with little sustained good news, most northerners greeted the string of successes in the Valley with hope and renewed enthusiasm. The newfound prospect of peace boosted Lincoln's chances for reelection. Democrats devised several strategies to overcome the rising popularity of Lincoln, Grant, and Sheridan. Some editors suggested that the good news from the Valley was at best premature bragging and at worst deliberate deception from the administration. Both the *Chicago Times* and the *Indianap-*

olis Daily Sentinel reported that Early retained an army of 15,000 even after Cedar Creek. Secretary of War Edwin M. Stanton "is engaged in a wholesome humbugging of the people in order to induce them to re-elect Lincoln under the impression that he is carrying on the war vigorously and successfully," argued one editor.[32]

Some Democratic editors hoped for impending peace while asserting that the Lincoln administration remained intransigent on crucial issues. They insisted that rational people, North and South, would end the war rather than continue fighting over emancipation and secession. The *Cincinnati Enquirer* offered typical Democratic analysis: "There is no doubt that the peace sentiment is growing stronger day by day; and the evidence of a decided change in the public mind is multiplying on every hand. People who have been warm supporters of war are asking themselves: Why shall we sacrifice our substance and ourselves to benefit the negroes?" Democrats asserted that "a majority of the Southern people would most gladly find themselves under the old flag and the old Constitution if they could be permitted to save their honor and their record" by returning to the Union with their slave property intact.[33]

According to Democrats, however, Lincoln's fanatical commitment to emancipation made him unwilling to consider the possibility of an early peace. "How Peace Could Have Been Procured. Lincoln's Refusal of the Overture," ran one headline. Some Democrats even claimed that Republicans were the true secessionists, willing to endure limitless war and disunion for the sake of antislavery. "There are tens of thousands of Republicans who prefer the separation of the free and slave states into two independent governments than to have them remain under one government, part free and part slave," asserted the *Cincinnati Enquirer*. The *Valley Spirit* opined that the people "are beginning to realize the fact that under the present relentless and vindictive policy the war must be interminable; or at least that it can never end except through sheer exhaustion of both sections, when nothing but poverty, desolation, ruin and anarchy will be left as the inheritance of a once proud, prosperous and happy people."[34]

Democrats offered George B. McClellan as the perfect alternative to Lincoln and the Republicans. While serving early in the war as a major general and commander of the Army of the Potomac, McClellan, in the words of historian Mark Grimsley, had "epitomized the conciliatory policy." Always a firm Democrat, McClellan opposed confiscation, emancipation, and rough treatment of southern civilians. In the context of the 1864 election campaign, Democrats made sure to publicize McClellan's commitment to fighting a gentlemanly, conciliatory war. "Both McClellan and Lee have always labored to keep war within civilized rules," claimed the *Detroit Free Press*. Even the Confederate general who did the most to keep the hopes of Confederate independence alive merited praise in the eyes of some northern Democrats. Unlike Lincoln and his subordinates, Grant and Sheridan, Robert E. Lee continued to view war as a contest between opposing armies that left civilians relatively undisturbed. A victory by McClellan would represent an opportunity to roll back the Republican military and political policies on display in the Shenandoah Valley. Democrats argued that southern civilians, no longer tyrannized by Lincoln and his generals, would then gladly return to the Union. As a result, McClellan, if elected, would rank behind George Washington as the "second savior of his country." The *Valley Spirit* made the case more bluntly: "If you believe that in the prosecution of this war, all private property and unarmed persons should be strictly protected, vote for McClellan."[35]

In this Democratic formulation, McClellan and his party, not a Lincoln who favored continued war with southerners and fellow Americans, became the true Unionists. Samuel J. Tilden, while campaigning for McClellan, argued that the general "makes the union of the States under the Constitution of our fathers the sole condition of future peace. He puts nothing before the Union." McClellan, according to one editor, stood for an "honorable peace," one that "Americans can feel proud of. It will not beget hate, that centuries cannot weaken, but kindly brotherhood of States." Democrats often charged that rebel leaders hoped for Lincoln's election to help them hold sway over the Union-leaning masses of the South. The *Detroit Free Press* declared, "Lincoln the Rebel Candidate." "A sincere secessionist . . . hailed the proclamations of emancipation and confiscation, and the policy of plunder and devastation as sure pledges of ultimate triumph; they were terrible ordeals, but they most effectively eradicated every sentiment of Union," explained the *Cincinnati Enquirer*.[36]

One editor asserted that the type of war exemplified by Sheridan's Valley campaign held negative implications for the rights of northerners and southerners alike. "It is inconceivable how a war like that which is now carried on against the South can, if successful, do anything else than establish a government of force," wrote the editor. Harsh methods of making war ultimately strengthened the power of the presidency and the army and threatened the liberties of those on the home front. "All history teaches the lesson that a government of force over a conquered people abroad must become a government of force over a subject and disfranchised people at home," learned readers of the

Cincinnati Enquirer. Horatio Seymour often remarked while on the campaign trail that northerners could not "trample upon the rights of the people of another State" without trampling on their "own as well." Democrats insisted that Lincoln would stop at nothing less than despotic military rule over North and South together.[37]

Throughout the autumn of 1864, Democrats relentlessly criticized Lincoln's military and political policies on display in the Shenandoah Valley. In the Democratic view, events in the Valley underscored the degree to which Republican programs and strategy posed threats to constitutional protections of individual rights and freedoms, to white racial control, to widely accepted norms of gender behavior, and to the possibility of an easy peace and comfortable reintegration of the white South into the national fabric. Democratic editors and politicians presented a rival plan for ending the war. For them, George B. McClellan's vision of victory on the battlefield combined with conciliatory treatment of southern civilians provided the best way of attracting Confederates back to the Union. As a result, Sheridan's Valley campaign became a symbol of Republican tyranny and mismanagement of the war. Democrats hoped to gain electoral victory by criticizing military tactics that sought victory through "uncivilized" means.

The Democrats' campaign strategy did not pay dividends at the polls in 1864. Lincoln won a decisive 212 to 21 victory in the Electoral College, while on the battlefield General Sherman went on to employ many of the tactics that Democrats decried during his March to the Sea. Yet the election of 1864 was closer than it appeared. Democrats won 45% of the vote nationwide. Furthermore, according to one historian of the election, the "party's candidates ran surprisingly close races in states generally accounted as Republican strongholds." The overwhelmingly Republican soldier vote may have pushed Lincoln over the edge in key states such as New York, Pennsylvania, Indiana, and Illinois.[38]

As historian David Potter pointed out, hindsight is both "the historian's chief asset and his main liability." While Potter was referring to the decade of the 1850s, his warning applies equally well to the election of 1864. For too long, the perception that Sheridan's victories in the Shenandoah Valley and Sherman's capture of Atlanta foreordained Lincoln's victory has overshadowed the controversy surrounding the military tactics that brought Union success in 1864 and 1865. Lincoln faced difficult choices in approving emancipation, the destruction of crops and property, and the harsh treatment of southern civilians. Neither he nor the Democrats knew how they would fare at the polls in September and October 1864. The Shenandoah Valley campaign, and the destructive warfare that it represented, offers a fascinating window on the partisan political conflict waged during the autumn of 1864.[39]

Notes

1. William Zornow, *Lincoln and the Party Divided* (Norman: University of Oklahoma Press, 1954), 171, 194–95.

2. Mark Grimsley, *The Hard Hand of War: Union Military Policy toward Southern Civilians, 1861–1865* (Cambridge: Cambridge University Press, 1995), 1–6; James M. McPherson, "Lincoln and the Strategy of Unconditional Surrender," in *Lincoln the War President*, ed. Gabor S. Boritt (New York: Oxford University Press, 1992), 29–62; Abraham Lincoln quoted in Roy P. Basler, ed., *Abraham Lincoln: His Speeches and Writings* (New York: World, 1946), 630.

3. Grimsley, *Hard Hand of War*, 1–6; Edward Hagerman, *The American Civil War and the Origins of Modern Warfare* (Indianapolis: Indiana University Press, 1988), 275; Herman Hattaway and Archer Jones, *How The North Won: A Military History of the Civil War* (Urbana: University of Illinois Press, 1983), 501–677.

4. Christopher Dell, *Lincoln and the War Democrats* (Madison, N.J.: Fairleigh Dickinson University Press, 1975), 267–86; Harold M. Hyman, "The Election of 1864," in vol. 2 (1848–1896) of *The History of American Presidential Elections, 1789–1968*, ed. Arthur M. Schlesinger Jr. (New York: Chelsea House, 1971), 1170, 1172, 1179; Zornow, *Lincoln and the Party Divided*, 8, 133, 141.

5. Grimsley, *Hard Hand of War*, 171; Joel Silbey, *A Respectable Minority: The Democratic Party in the Civil War Era* (New York: Norton, 1977), x, 110, 115; Michael F. Holt, "Abraham Lincoln and the Politics of Union," in *Abraham Lincoln and the American Political Tradition*, ed. John L. Thomas (Amherst: University of Massachusetts Press, 1986), 113. For further discussion of historians' tendency to study intraparty divisions rather than interparty conflict, see Michael F. Holt, "An Elusive Synthesis: Northern Politics during the Civil War," in *Writing the Civil War: The Quest to Understand*, eds. James M. McPherson and William J. Cooper Jr. (Columbia: University of South Carolina Press, 1998), 112–34.

6. Jean Baker, *Affairs of Party: The Political Culture of Northern Democrats in the Mid-Nineteenth Century* (New York: Fordham University Press, 1983), 317, 319.

7. *Indianapolis Daily Sentinel*, September 15, 1862.

8. Jean Baker, *Affairs of Party*, 319.

9. Stephen W. Sears, *The Civil War Papers of George B. McClellan: Selected Correspondence, 1860–1865* (New York: Ticknor and Fields, 1989), 591.

10. Ibid., 591, 595, 344.

11. *New York World* quoted in the *Chambersburg Valley Spirit*, September 7, 1864, *Valley of the Shadow: Two Communities in the American Civil War*, Virginia Center for Digital History, University of Virginia ‹http://www.valley.vcdh.virginia.edu›; *Phila-*

delphia Age quoted in *Valley Spirit*, September 21, 1864, *Valley of the Shadow*; Horatio Seymour quoted in Stewart Mitchell, *Horatio Seymour of New York* (Cambridge, Mass.: Harvard University Press, 1938), 369, 371.

12. Holt, "Abraham Lincoln and the Politics of Union," 117.

13. Quoted in *Cincinnati Enquirer*, October 26, 1864.

14. *New York Herald*, October 20, 1864; *New York Herald*, October 27, 1864. The *Herald*, edited by James Gordon Bennett, championed its self-consciously independent style. It reached a large audience as "the most successful and widely circulated newspaper in mid-nineteenth-century America." The "popular, cheap, mass circulation newspaper" provides a reasonable reflection of the political views crafted to appeal to the northeastern general public not specifically aligned with either party. Indeed, Bennett supported the victorious Democrats in 1862 and endorsed Lincoln's reelection in 1864. See James Crouthamel, *Bennett's New York Herald and the Rise of the Popular Press* (Syracuse, N.Y.: Syracuse University Press, 1989), ix. Much has been written about how Republicans and Union soldiers viewed the South, white southerners, and harsh war measures—though authors sometimes treat these groups as if they spoke for the North as a whole. See, for example, Earl J. Hess, *Liberty, Virtue, and Progress: Northerners and Their War for Union* (New York: New York University Press, 1988); James M. McPherson, *For Cause and Comrades: Why Men Fought in the Civil War* (New York: Oxford University Press, 1997); Reid Mitchell, *Civil War Soldiers* (New York: Viking, 1988); and Charles Royster, *The Destructive War: William Tecumseh Sherman, Stonewall Jackson, and the Americans* (New York: Knopf, 1991).

15. *Cincinnati Enquirer*, September 29, 1864.

16. Ibid.

17. *Philadelphia Age* quoted in *Valley Spirit*, August 31, 1864, *Valley of the Shadow*.

18. *Valley Spirit*, September 28, 1864, *Valley of the Shadow*.

19. *Detroit Free Press*, October 21, 1864; *New York World* quoted in *Valley Spirit*, October 19, 1864, *Valley of the Shadow*.

20. *Valley Spirit*, October 19, 1864, *Valley of the Shadow*; *Philadelphia Age* quoted in *Valley Spirit*, October 19, 1864, *Valley of the Shadow*.

21. *Valley Spirit*, October 26, 1864, *Valley of the Shadow*; *Valley Spirit*, October 19, 1864, *Valley of the Shadow*.

22. *Cincinnati Enquirer*, October 26, 1864; *Philadelphia Age* quoted in *Valley Spirit*, October 19, 1864, *Valley of the Shadow*; *Valley Spirit*, October 26, 1864, *Valley of the Shadow*.

23. *Cincinnati Enquirer*, October 26, 1864.

24. *New York World* quoted in *Valley Spirit*, October 19, 1864, *Valley of the Shadow*.

25. *Detroit Free Press*, October 21, 1864; *Philadelphia Age* quoted in *Valley Spirit*, October 19, 1864, *Valley of the Shadow*; *Cincinnati Enquirer*, October 26, 1864.

26. Michael Fellman, "Women and Guerrilla Warfare," in *Divided Houses: Gender and the Civil War*, eds. Catherine Clinton and Nina Silber (New York: Oxford University Press, 1992), 147; *Cincinnati Enquirer*, August 31, October 26, 1864.

27. *Detroit Free Press*, October 21, 1864; *Valley Spirit*, July 20, 1864, *Valley of the Shadow*; *Indianapolis Daily Sentinel*, October 18, 1864.

28. *Cincinnati Enquirer*, October 26, 1864.

29. Ibid., October 29, 1864; *Detroit Free Press*, October 7, 1864.

30. *Detroit Free Press*, October 21, 1864; *Valley Spirit*, October 26, 1864, *Valley of the Shadow*; *Indianapolis Daily Sentinel*, October 27, 1864; *Valley Spirit*, July 6, 1864, *Valley of the Shadow*.

31. *Valley Spirit*, October 26, 19, 1864, *Valley of the Shadow*.

32. *Indianapolis Daily Sentinel*, October 26, 1864 (reprinted from the *Chicago Times*).

33. *Cincinnati Enquirer*, August 5, 1864.

34. Ibid., November 7, August 15, 1864; *Valley Spirit*, July 20, 1864, *Valley of the Shadow*.

35. Mark Grimsley, *Hard Hand of War*, 23; *Detroit Free Press*, October 7, 21, 1864; *Valley Spirit*, October 26, 1864, *Valley of the Shadow*.

36. Tilden quoted in Samuel Augustus Pleasants, *Fernando Wood of New York* (New York: Columbia University Press, 1948), 160; *Cincinnati Enquirer*, September 23, 1864; *Detroit Free Press*, October 1, 1864.

37. *Detroit Free Press*, October 11, 1864; Seymour quoted in Stewart Mitchell, *Horatio Seymour of New York* (Cambridge, Mass.: Harvard University Press, 1938), 375.

38. Harold Hyman, "Election of 1864," 1175–76.

39. David M. Potter, *The Impending Crisis: 1848–1861* (New York: Harper, 1976), 145.

WILLIAM G. THOMAS

Nothing Ought to Astonish Us

Confederate Civilians in the 1864 Shenandoah Valley Campaign

Nancy Emerson lived in Staunton, Virginia, and kept a diary intermittently throughout the Civil War. Emerson was raised in Massachusetts and moved south with her brother, a Lutheran minister, in the late 1850s. They became Confederates, transplanting themselves and driving deep roots into the new soil around them. Emerson intended her diary to be read by her "northern friends, should any of them have the curiosity to read [it]." She felt increasingly sick with what she thought might be typhoid fever, so she directed that the journal "be forwarded to" her northern friends "at some future time." She wondered what her friends in the North thought about the war and the South, and what they thought about the destruction of civilian property in Staunton and farther up the Valley in Lexington in June 1864. She wondered whether any of her friends in the North had even heard of the pillaging in the Valley and whether they favored "this unjust & abominable war." She decided that she could not guess what they thought anymore — their distance of mind and spirit were too great. "Such strange things happen these days," she concluded, "that nothing ought to astonish us."[1]

Confederate civilians in the Shenandoah Valley might have thought they knew what to expect of the war by 1864, but they soon found themselves taken aback by Union successes and Union aggressiveness, determination, and competence. They admitted to themselves that while nothing ought to astonish them, nearly everything in the summer and fall of 1864 did. The war changed from something largely distant and contained to something unpredictable and invasive. Union armies in the Valley were better led, more determined, and more hardened than before. Confederate armies in the Valley were less well led, less determined, and at times less courageous than in the past. Confederate civilians found themselves less sure of their security, their army, and their prospects.[2]

Valley civilians had good reason to be surprised at the changes in 1864. In the preceding years, they witnessed a more limited war, one in which Confederate armies swept enemy forces out of the Shenandoah and Federal forces never sustained a hard policy against civilians. In 1862, Confederate major general Thomas J. Jackson maneuvered and fought to clear the Valley of Union forces in a few short weeks. Panic shook Staunton in April 1862 when Union forces appeared nearby. One Confederate officer from Staunton called the excitement "exceedingly ludicrous and amusing." He chuckled at "women and children and negroes and especially the men and more especially the office-holding men—Quartermaster and Commissioner" who "were seen running to and fro through rain."[3]

Jackson's decisive engagements and brilliant marches dazzled Confederate civilians and gave them unsurpassed confidence in the supremacy of their army, its commanders, and its cause. The leading citizens of Augusta County drafted a testimonial of appreciation to Jackson for "protecting their homesteads from desolation, and themselves and their families from insult and oppression." The editors of the *Staunton Spectator* praised Jackson's service. "Their advance guards were at our very borders," the paper reminded readers, "and a general feeling of insecurity pervaded the community. In the midst of our apprehension, and when some of our citizens had begun to remove their families and property, a significant message was received from Gen. Jackson, urging our people to remain quiet, that the enemy were not yet in Augusta!" After the Valley was secure and Lee's forces were winning battles around Richmond, Nancy Emerson reflected, "Public thanks were offered for their [the Confederate forces'] deliverance. Our help is in God & in him alone."[4]

God's role in the struggle seemed apparent to Confederate civilians in the Valley before the 1864 campaign. When Confederate forces drove Maj. Gen. George B. McClellan's Army of the Potomac from Richmond in 1862, Nancy Emerson considered it evidence of God's justice and plan for the Confederacy. "This judgment from God has fallen upon the North because of their declension from him," Emerson affirmed. She could not "for one moment believe that a righteous God" would allow the Confederacy to "be trodden down as the mud of the streets, whatever our cruel and insolent invaders might threaten." Emerson knew that her neighbors, fellow parishioners, and friends had prayed fervently for direction: "Too many prayers have been ascending to heavens night & day for such an event to come to pass." Later, in early 1863, Emerson reflected on the previous year's events and concluded, "Blessed be the Lord who has not given us as a prey to their [Yankee] teeth. As a nation, we have in a measure acknowledged God, & he has appeared for us most wonderfully."[5]

Confederate civilians in the Valley believed they had been delivered in 1862 from desperate danger by the brilliance of Jackson as an instrument of their Christian God. Nancy Emerson continually referred to the dangers to the Valley in 1862. "We have much to be grateful for," Emerson thought. "For months we were under frequent apprehensions that the Yankees would come in & get posession of the Valley, but the Lord mercifully preserved us from the danger, & has delivered us from the fear." The southern newspapers were clear as well about the stakes in the war, informing citizens of the consequences of a northern victory: southerners, the editors predicted, would be "left without rights, without legal remedies, an inferior race creeping on the face of our own land." Less dramatically, Jedediah Hotchkiss, the gifted cartographer who served with Stonewall Jackson and his successors, wrote his ten-year-old daughter, Nellie, that the Yankees "would come and destroy us and our country if they could." Emerson also saw the dangers of a Yankee invasion, lamenting, "How many churches have they polluted, how many graves desecrated. How have they soaked our soil with the blood of our noblest & best. . . . May the righteous Lord plead our cause against an ungodly nation."[6]

Victories in the first half of 1863 reassured Valley Confederates and seemed to confirm their understanding of their role in the war. Lt. Gen. Richard S. Ewell's triumph over Maj. Gen. Robert H. Milroy at Winchester on June 14–15, together with Robert E. Lee's success at Chancellorsville in early May, caused Valley civilians to place their faith in the superiority of southern arms. When Nancy Emerson learned about Milroy's defeat, she rejoiced, calling it "glorious news" and noting the capture of "several thousand prisoners & stores without number." She had also heard comforting stories from Winchester about "an old negro who was kept on nothing but water for three days because he refused to work & said he was 'secesh.'" The story described Federal officers putting the black man in hard labor breaking rocks and starving him into submission, yet he refused to give in and insisted he was secessionist to the core. "Noble fellow. It does one good to hear such instances," Emerson affirmed with thorough sincerity, as if in 1863 even black slaves were completely unshakable in their commitment to the Confederate cause. The battle at Gettysburg, which marked the bloody culmination of Lee's invasion of Pennsylvania in June and July, registered in the Shenandoah Valley as no more than a temporary setback. A Valley newspaper called Gettysburg "one of the severest of the war, . . . a hard fought battle . . . in which we were successful, though with heavy loss." Southern newspapers gleefully reported that during the Pennsylvania campaign northern "fugitives . . . keep pouring into Harrisburg, Lancaster and other cities, in a state of complete terror, bringing their cattle, merchandise and household goods with them."[7]

Because Valley civilians had not fully experienced the destructive nature of the war at the beginning of the 1864 campaign, they had yet to understand their vital role as witnesses and participants in a changing conflict. Confederates took the 1862 Valley campaign as a mark of God's deliverance and the victories in 1863 as further evidence of divine favor. When Federal troops returned to the Valley in 1864, Confederate civilians faced anew their fears and expectations of the war. Their capacity for vengeance and retribution surprised them. Both emotions unnerved them, drew comment, and forced self-examination — but did not alter their purpose. The war, however strange it had become, was to be fought out, and Confederate civilians in the Valley remained determined to see it through.[8]

Confederate civilians took their bearings along lines of connection in their inner lives with family, neighbors, and God. They combined allegiance, friendship, and faith to find a fixed position on the war, and in so doing to better comprehend their reactions. As 1864 inaugurated more destructive capacities in the war, they were particularly attentive to the conduct of Confederate troops. When Confederate forces plundered farms, took the war to northern women and children, and exhibited reckless lack of discipline during battles, civilians became concerned about the rightness of their cause. Many Valley civilians expected their men in the field to act like southern Christian soldiers, in effect to represent the best values of the new nation. They defined Federal troops as barbarians, willing to set aside codes of morality, honor, and Christian faith and to behave in a reprehensible, immoral, and unchristian manner. "God grant that the day may soon come when we shall be separated from such a race," one Confederate wrote his wife in the summer of 1864, as he detailed the depredations of Maj. Gen. Philip H. Sheridan's Union cavalry. Later that fall, he encouraged her: "Don't you all feel discouraged. . . . Providence never will smile upon a people so lost to the best feelings of our nature and who conduct warfare in such uncivilized ways."[9]

The Shenandoah Valley harbored strong Confederate allegiances that grew among civilians not only from their faith in the divine but also from their experience in worldly affairs. The Valley's counties stood among the richest in Virginia in 1860. Augusta, Rockbridge, Frederick, and Rockingham in particular stood in the top twenty counties in Virginia for improved acreage in farms, value of livestock, and cash value of farms. Valley civilians increasingly found their economy and social experience tied to the institution of slavery. The region boasted 17 percent of Virginia's slaveowning households and 10 percent of Virginia's slaveholders. Neighboring counties in the Piedmont, which led Virginia in slaveholding and value of real estate and personal property, exerted a strong influence on the Valley's growth. With its rich farms and successful commercial development, the Valley, like most of Virginia, remained Unionist in sentiment throughout the secession crisis, but in 1861 the region committed itself to the Confederate cause. The depth of that commitment, while not as complete as in some other areas of Virginia, especially the Piedmont, placed the region overwhelmingly in the Confederate column. Enlistment patterns, for example, demonstrate that 65 percent of the eligible white men in the Valley joined the Confederate forces—compared to 75 percent in the Tidewater and 85 percent in the Piedmont. The Shenandoah Valley's commitment to the Confederacy, like its increasing connections to the institution of slavery, were evident in the broadsides that encouraged civilians to become soldiers: "Your soil has been invaded by your Abolition foes, and we call upon you to rally at once, and drive them back."[10]

By 1864, after years of general success in the Valley for the Confederate army, civilians in the Shenandoah Valley experienced a sharp change in the conduct of U.S. forces in the region. Federal soldiers came in June to occupy previously private civilian space, letting residents of the Valley know that their enemy could control them and their homes and that no rebel army could free them. Often in the Valley campaign, this presence of Federal troops in and among civilians brought a new urgency to the war. For its part, the Federal army continually tried to calibrate its orders for destruction. For example, at various points in the Valley campaign Union officers ordered the destruction of Confederate supply installations but not civilians' homes, the burning of a three-mile radius around the site of a particular killing, and the torching of barns with hay but not those without. These limitations were meant to maintain discipline and order in the Federal army as the war widened to include the destruction of civilian property.[11]

The Federal army swept into the Valley in 1864 in three phases: the first under Maj. Gen. Franz Sigel in May, the second under Maj. Gen. David Hunter in June, and the third under General Sheridan in September and October. Each operation grew in scope and determination. Lt. Gen. Ulysses S. Grant's orders for each of these operations developed more fully as well. He cautioned Sigel that "indiscriminate marauding should be avoided. Nothing should be taken not absolutely necessary for the troops, except when captured from an armed enemy." Grant's approach changed for the fall campaign. He directed Sheridan to "eat out Virginia clear and clean as far as they [Early's army] go, so that crows flying over it for the balance of the season will have to carry their provender with them."[12]

After Sigel's effort to control the Valley came to grief at the battle of New Market in May, General Hunter moved his force up the Valley with more purpose, defeating a hastily assembled Confederate force at Piedmont in Augusta County on June 5. The battle gave Valley civilians a taste of what the summer and fall would bring. It was a disaster for the Confederates, as two infantry brigades and the 3rd Battalion Valley Reserves tried to stop the more powerful and experienced Federal forces. The Reserves were local civilians, mostly boys and older men called into duty to protect their fellow citizens in an emergency. At the battle's crucial moment, Confederate cavalry failed to support the infantry, and the men ran from the battlefield in confusion. The cavalry picked their way south and east over the Blue Ridge at Rockfish Gap, leaving the entire Shenandoah Valley in Federal control for the first time in the war. Jacob Hildebrand, a Confederate supporter with three sons in the army, admitted that "from every indication we were routed." Two days later, Hildebrand went to the battlefield to help bury the dead but found only five bodies. He concluded optimistically that "the Yankees had more killed than we had." Joseph Waddell thought "no citizen of Staunton above the age of infancy, then living, will ever forget Sunday, the 5th of June, 1864." Waddell, a Confederate clerk, loaded all of his "valuable paper," mostly bonds and vouchers, into a trunk and headed for Waynesboro. He described the mood as "cheerful" and fully expected the Confederate army to regain supremacy in the Valley.[13]

A decidedly less optimistic atmosphere prevailed in Staunton, which Hunter occupied on June 11–12. For citizens of Augusta, like many others in the upper Valley, Hunter's army imposed the first major occupation of the war. The Federals entered the homes of civilians and took food and property. When northern soldiers arrived at the home of Nancy Emerson's neighbor, "they took everything they had to eat, all the pillow cases & sheet & towels & some of the ladies stockings . . . & destroyed things generally." According to Emerson, the soldiers "took off all the Negro men & boys they could, as well as all the horses" and "told the women they would take them *next* time they came." Waddell noted that "nearly all of the houses had been searched for provisions and arms," that "a large number of Negroes went off with the Yankees," and that "some persons here suffered much from the Yankees in loss of property [while] others escaped entirely." "Almost everybody lost horses," he reported. Waddell characterized the Federal army as full of "treachery" and "without motive, although characteristic of the people."[14]

Federal officers, for their part, considered the Confederate civilians equally full of treachery. They were unsure of some Confederate women, particularly those not in the elite class. Wealthier Confederate women often received guards at their houses and were treated with respect, but more common women, either on the yeoman farms or in the small towns, encountered suspicion and at times hostility. One Union soldier found "pretty girls abundant" in Harrisonburg but called them "detestable secesh." David Hunter Strother, a Virginian who served as Hunter's chief of staff during the Valley campaign, found himself in several discussions with women and girls along the army's route. Early on in the campaign he decided "to have no more social intercourse with the people of the country" because it interfered with his "military duties" and brought him face to face with "outrage and distresses which awaken my sympathies but which I could not prevent."[15]

Wary Union soldiers found some evidence of cooperation from Valley civilians. Federal officers convened groups of prominent citizens to inform them of Hunter's "retaliatory" orders against bushwhackers and guerrillas, asking them to identify the culprits. In Newtown, as in other towns, these citizens complied and "promised to give all the information in their power." They pointed out a Mrs. Wilson's house as a refuge for guerrillas, whereupon Hunter's troops arrested her, charged her with "feeding and harboring guerrillas," burned all of her possessions, and marched her six miles to a guard tent. When Hunter's troops moved into Staunton, remarked one Federal, the women "greeted us pleasantly, waved their handkerchiefs, . . . and brought buckets of water or milk to quench our thirsts." Some dressed up for the occasion in their "Sunday dresses" and handed out bouquets of flowers to the invading soldiers. Federal officers wondered whether this demonstration was "sincere and loyal" or meant to insult them.[16]

Nancy Emerson called the Federals a "cloud of locusts from the bottomless pit." She heard them say they would come back "to reap [the wheat harvest]." In telling the story of the occupation, Emerson described what happened at her home. She began her entry for July 9 with the intention of telling "about some Yankee raiders" and noted that General Hunter's June occupation of Staunton "will not soon be forgotten in these parts." When Federal troops arrived, they

Maj. Gen. David Hunter.
Francis Trevelyan Miller, ed.,
*The Photographic History of
the Civil War*, 10 vols. (New
York: Review of Reviews,
1911), 10:175.

demanded whiskey, flour, and bacon, in that order. Emerson watched as the
soldiers ransacked the house. They took the shoes of her older male cousin because shoes were "nearly impossible to get." In a moment of commercial bravery, the cousin bought the shoes back on the spot with a ten-dollar Ohio note.
Emerson recorded her sister-in-law's outrage that the Federal army was injur-
ing "innocent persons who had taken no part in the war." When she hurled
this insult at the Federals, one responded, "You need not tell me that, I know
all the people along here have sons in the army." Emerson reported that her
sister-in-law was "afraid to undress" that night and slept but a few hours, as the
household took turns keeping watch.[17]

The presence of armed and rowdy Federal troops terrified some women.
When Hunter's forces pushed into Rockbridge County, Eva Honey Allen, a
young woman living near Fincastle who had two brothers in Maj. Gen. George
E. Pickett's division, grew anxious. As Hunter slowly proceeded up the Valley,
swirling rumors preceded his army like a drop in barometric pressure before a
summer thunderstorm. Allen had yet to see her first Yankee, but she had heard
that they were buying barrels of whiskey several farms away. "We shall be much
more afraid of them now than ever," she worried. Later that day, she finally saw

her "first Yankees!" and confessed to feeling "relieved." They were polite and considerate, asking directions and moving off quickly, "shutting the gate after them," a gesture that surprised her. By the next day, rumors of "their doings are 'as thick as blackberries,'" Allen recorded. Allen was most troubled by "very alarming" rumors that "the Negroes" were spreading, one of which claimed that Hunter was approaching with "a very large army, including 8,000 Negroes." Another story circulated that 200 or 300 Negro men from the Bedford area had joined the Federal force in the Valley. Still another report ran that the Federal army "can't take the women off now, but will come back for them."[18]

Confederate civilians of means retreated to mountain hideaways to keep clear of the grasping invaders, taking personal property, slaves, and livestock with them. When Hunter's army arrived in Lexington, David Hunter Strother observed "a great deal of smoke in the mountains." When he inquired about it among the locals, they replied that "it came from the camps of the refugees who were hiding" from the army "with their Negroes and cattle." Strother was surprised at the "satisfaction" that Confederate civilians expressed about their slaves' loyalty. From his perspective, black people only feigned loyalty to their masters. "The Negroes take the first opportunity they find of running into our lines and giving information as to where their masters are hidden," Strother noted.[19]

When Federal troops swept into an area, Confederate men had much to fear. They often attempted to hide, running into corn or wheat fields or into the mountains. At the approach of Federal troops, Joseph Waddell evacuated Staunton and moved out of their path. He paid close attention to rumors about their return throughout the summer and fall, always ready to move again if necessary. In Winchester, the brothers of Matthella Page Harrison hid in their cornfield up to three times a day as rumors circulated about the imminent arrival of Federal troops. Even the Episcopal minister fled to avoid arrest. "The men & boys always kept out of the way," Nancy Emerson recorded, "as they were sometimes taken off & did not know what treatment they might receive." Some were shot down as they ran away; others escaped undetected and watched as Federal troops stood in their homes and yards. "They always fire upon those who run from them," Nancy Emerson noted. The women, she added, "were left to shift for themselves as best they could." She and her sister-in-law defended the home against Union soldiers who arrived on June 11. "Those who left their houses fared worse than others, at least their houses did," Emerson concluded. Emerson's brother Luther, a Presbyterian minister, abandoned the house to avoid capture by the Federal troops. The family considered the move wise because, according to Emerson, the northern army has "such spite against preach-ers & especially as he has written & spoken so freely, that his [pro-Confederate] sentiments are generally known."[20]

Contemporaries and later historians focused on Hunter's attacks on promi-nent Confederate civilians who seemed to stand symbolically for the rebellion. In Staunton, Hunter ordered the destruction of the Walkers' mill, Crawford and Young's woolen factory, J. A. Trotter's stables, and W. F. Smith's mill. All of these men operated factories that directly aided the Confederate military effort, and their families supported the Confederacy. Joseph Waddell reported that the "people of Staunton have not suffered at the hands of the Yankees, except the owners of mills and factories." Forces under Hunter targeted institu-tions and businesses that they considered clearly recognized extensions of the Confederate war machine. Hunter proceeded to Lexington, where he burned part of the Virginia Military Institute and Gov. John Letcher's home, both of which were intimately connected to the southern cause. Confederate newspa-pers expressed outrage at the burnings and destruction of property. The *Re-publican Vindicator* condemned Hunter's behavior at Lexington as "one of the most wanton and barbaric acts of the war." The paper compared Hunter to Maj. Gen. Benjamin F. "Beast" Butler, whose occupation of New Orleans in 1862 stood in southern minds for graceless and mindless violence against civil-ians, especially women. When Confederate lieutenant general Jubal A. Early defeated Hunter at Lynchburg on June 18 and pushed him out of the Valley, the Staunton newspaper hailed the Confederates and jeered Hunter. "He has accomplished nothing," the paper sneered, "as regards the overthrow of the Confederacy, having run away from the only point he could have materially damaged it."[21] The Shenandoah Valley remained largely free of a major Federal military presence from June 18 until early September.

In addition to its careful targeting of symbolic institutions and people, Hun-ter's army directed considerable anger toward Confederate women — behaviors that Valley civilians, such as Eva Honey Allen, sometimes linked in excoriat-ing their enemy. When Hunter issued a stirring statement from his headquar-ters in Wheeling, West Virginia, that his troops had accomplished $10 million worth of damage to Confederate property, Allen hoped Early "and his men will remember this, when they reach Pennsylvania." Hearsay in Rockbridge County confirmed Hunter's perfidy in her eyes. She learned from a reliable source "that one of his [Hunter's] objects in this expedition was to degrade the Va. women, 'that he was determined to break their proud spirit.'" Hunter, according to this source, thought "southern women had done more to bring

Ruins of the Virginia Military Institute. Francis Trevelyan Miller, ed., *The Photographic History of the Civil War*, 10 vols. (New York: Review of Reviews, 1911), 3:140.

on this rebellion than the men and they ought to be made to suffer for it." One older Rockbridge citizen told Allen that the Federal army's "mode of warfare was something new in history." He told her "a war between civilized nations was carried on by battles between opposing armies." But the Federal army, he said, "fought by burning homes or robbing women & children."[22]

Hunter's burning of V.M.I. and Governor Letcher's home attracted the attention of the Confederate press, but his army's actions against women and families struck more directly at the core of the southern household. Hunter's troops executed a Confederate civilian in Rockbridge County for defending his home and family. "The execution will take place in a few minutes," David S. Creigh wrote on June 10, in a last letter to his wife Emily. He explained that he was to be hanged and the house in which he was imprisoned burned around him. Creigh had shot a Federal soldier who ransacked his home and threatened his daughters. The soldier recovered from the wound, and Federal officers captured Creigh, imprisoned him, tried, and executed him. Micajah Woods, Creigh's nephew and a Confederate artilleryman whose unit served in the area with Jubal Early, reported to his father, Creigh's brother-in-law, that "Uncle David was certainly executed at Mr. Morrison's near Brownsburg." Federal troops buried Creigh in a shallow grave near the execution site. Family members, hearing of the execution, went to the place and "had him interred properly." According to Micajah Woods, another man who tried to protect his home "was treated terribly," and "his mind is said to be affected by the scenes he and his daughter have passed."

Creigh's case became a cause célèbre of the *Central Presbyterian*, a southern denominational newspaper and printing company, but it was not the only execution in Rockbridge. Fannie Wilson recorded the execution of Matthew White Jr.: "He was seen on Sunday afternoon marching out of town with a squad of soldiers, who shot him for bush-whacking." She noted that Federal troops carried out the execution "all the time deceiving his parents." When the parents asked about their son, they were told he was "at home." Wilson seemed to consider the deception particularly noteworthy. After the Federals left the area, "his body was found unburied in the woods near Mrs. Cameron's house."[23]

Many women drew clear distinctions between the honorable behavior of Confederate soldiers and the depredations of Federal troops. In Fauquier County in July, Lucy Johnson Ambler matter-of-factly recorded the destruction of her plantation. Federal soldiers "destroyed the mills. They burnt down our stacks of wheat. . . . They took the negroes' clothes and any little thing belonging to them they wanted. The officers heard the firing of the guns as they were killing the sheep, but let it go on." Ambler believed that the officers led and encouraged the destruction and turned a blind eye toward the inhumanity and cruelty of it. "All sense of shame and decency seems to have deserted them," she observed. They acted "in the most Godless manner."[24]

Confederate civilians cheered when Early's forces cleared the Valley of Federal troops and crossed the Potomac to threaten Washington. Mary Catharine Powell Cochran in Loudoun County followed the northern newspaper coverage of Early's raid. "We have all enjoyed intensely the panic in Yankeedom," she wrote in her diary on July 13. Cochran had heard some suggest that Early's troops "should pillage and burn as the Yankees have done," but she thought otherwise. "In our heart of hearts," she confessed, "we can't help feeling proud and pleased that they didn't [burn and pillage]." Cochran believed that "such dirty work" would "defile" the "hands" of the Confederacy's "sons and brothers and husbands." She considered Early's raid a "test" that would prove "Southern men cannot turn thieves and house burners at a moment's notice."[25]

When Federal troops terrorized southern women, their male relatives often swore vengeance within the boundaries of honor. Virginia Military Institute cadet Lawrence Royster, for example, stated the matter plainly. "Mother lost absolutely everything," he told his friend, John E. Roller. She was forced to become a refugee, became sick, and lost all means of survival. "If I am ever spared to get into yankee land," Royster swore, "I will respect nothing but a woman's person, I'll break, pillage and plunder."[26]

Given an opportunity to take such action in July, Early's army respected little in their path. Early's forces demanded levies from Frederick, Maryland, and Chambersburg, Pennsylvania, after they threatened Washington in late July. The burning of Chambersburg by Brig. Gen. John McCausland's cavalry struck some Confederate civilians as neither wise nor honorable. Joseph Waddell thought the reprisal burnings sure to further enrage the northern people and revive their "war spirit." "The Yankees," Waddell predicted, "will come back and burn a hundred for one." Waddell considered the Confederate raid bad policy because the Confederacy's only hope lay with northern public opinion, which could demand an end to the war. He thought "it would be far better to let their [the Federals'] outrages stand out before the world . . . to the disgust of even some of their own people." Waddell's opinion on this matter hardened, and he later called the destruction of Chambersburg "a miserable affair, . . . horribly stupid . . . a blunder." Yet Waddell admitted feeling a certain degree of pleasure that "the miserable Yankee nation, who have been burning and pillaging throughout our own country for so long, have now been made to suffer in their own homes."[27]

Other Confederates joined Waddell in experiencing a tangle of emotions regarding Early's actions north of the Potomac River—vindication mixed with chagrin, joy with fear, and spite with abhorrence. Waddell reported in his diary that the retaliation provoked much discussion in Staunton among its citizens. Jedediah Hotchkiss explained the burning of Chambersburg to his wife as directly connected and proportional to Hunter's burnings in Lexington. Hotchkiss observed that citizens of Chambersburg "laughed at General McCausland" and refused to pay the $100,000 demanded.[28] Although Waddell filled several pages in his diary with the reasons he considered the raids misguided, some newspapers in Staunton and Richmond called the actions "just retaliation" and argued that a reciprocal policy would continue until the Federal army returned "to that mode of warfare practiced by all civilized nations." Not all editors took this position. Some criticized the raid as "stupid" and feared its repercussions on the northern draft at a critical time when public morale in the United States seemed to be lagging. "As if to stimulate the tardy Pennsylvanians to rush to arms against us," one disgusted southern editor lamented, "Chambersburg is burned down."[29]

Eva Honey Allen learned of the raid from northern newspapers and rumor.

"The Yankees do not find burning such a pleasant pastime," she commented with relish, "when their own homes are in question." She vowed not to "waste" any "sympathy or pity" on the northern people. The burning at Chambersburg led Allen to make a private confession in her diary. She had "never recorded the fate of 'the star spangled banner' " that her brother brought her from Chambersburg after the Gettysburg campaign. She took the flag to her room, grabbed a pack of matches, locked the door, and burned it. "I took a 'savage pleasure' in burning that flag," she confessed.[30]

Despite a growing hatred among Confederates for what the United States flag represented, even some southern officers expressed dismay at the behavior of Early's troops in Pennsylvania and Maryland. Brig. Gen. Bradley T. Johnson, a cavalry commander under McCausland, filed a report with the office of the adjutant general on August 10, 1864, accusing Confederate forces of "outrageous conduct." Johnson's brigade had been routed in a small battle at Moorefield, and he was trying desperately to save his career. Jedediah Hotchkiss considered Johnson "culpably negligent" for the "extremely disgraceful" defeat at Moorefield. According to Hotchkiss, who served at Early's headquarters, Johnson had been asleep when his brigade came under attack and "barely escaped, in his stocking feet & on the bare back of a horse." Hotchkiss considered Johnson a "bold dashing fellow" who as an officer had "no discipline." For his part, Johnson considered the undisciplined behavior of his men at Chambersburg offensive both to himself and "the cause." "Every crime in the catalogue of infamy has been committed," he wrote, "except murder and rape." Johnson gave examples of outright robbery — even a Catholic priest was robbed of his watch on his way to service. "Thus, the grand spectacle of a national retaliation was reduced to a miserable huckstering for greenbacks," Johnson concluded. Worse than this, Johnson reported drunken Confederate soldiers back in Virginia who "knocked down and kicked an aged woman who has two sons in the Confederate army." After choking the woman's sister, they locked her in a barn and set fire to it — all because the woman would not give them fresh horses.[31]

While civilians such as Waddell considered the Confederate raid bad policy, others had the sinking feeling that it symbolized something more — a turning point in the conduct of Confederate arms, and in the course of the war, that would lead to even more severe consequences for civilians. For these individuals, the raid too much resembled Hunter's dishonorable, blatantly criminal campaign in June. The monetary levies appeared to be little more than highway robbery, and the burning of homes scarcely differed from what Hunter and his forces had done. Many civilians and soldiers had difficulty reconciling the behavior of Early's cavalry with Lee's order issued from Chambersburg in 1863. Lee held that the Confederate army would "only make war on armed men" and could not "take vengeance for the wrongs our people have suffered without lowering ourselves in the eyes of all." Lee presented his men with a clear statement that vengeance was for God not man, and he forbade "unnecessary or wanton injury to private property." Newspaper editors at the time admitted that not all southerners agreed with Lee's views. The Democratic paper in Staunton, for example, held that the only way to make "the mass of the Northern people see the outrageous impropriety of conducting the war on their uncivilized plan was to make them feel some of the burdens of that plan, and let them realize that plunder and destruction was not and could not be confined to one side alone." The paper considered Lee's orders the proper course of action but counseled that "the remembrance of wrongs so lately inflicted will cause many to feel disappointed."[32]

After Early burned Chambersburg, he telegraphed Lee, "I alone am responsible for this act." Early's actions in Pennsylvania and Lee's clear position in 1863 set up a running dispute after the war regarding Confederate conduct. The *Confederate Veteran* noted that the burning of Chambersburg initiated "much controversy" and that "many believed it was accidental." Southern civilians and soldiers who lived far from the Valley thought it an accident that seemed inconsistent with the conduct of Confederate armies. In 1884, a Baltimore lawyer who had served in McCausland's cavalry tried to explain his conduct in the burning. He maintained that the cavalry consisted of the "very first young men of our State, . . . guided by the strongest instincts of principle." He implied that such upstanding citizen soldiers would not behave in an immoral fashion; after all, they were now doctors and lawyers, prosperous, Christian, and dutiful. As for the fate of "your petty little town," he wrote a Chambersburg resident, it was burned because it happened to be "the nearest and most accessible place of importance for us to get to." This cavalryman had been captured at Moorefield and imprisoned: "For eight long, miserable, weary months we bewailed the day that Chambersburg was founded, builded, and burned."[33]

Southern civilians wanted to see their young men as gallant and good Christian soldiers. Nancy Emerson considered the South more civilized than the North, and she pointed to its Christian faith as one of the main reasons. She railed against some Boston newspapers' advertisements about the capture of 10,000 Bibles by blockading U.S. naval vessels. She thought it "outrageous for people calling themselves Christians to be chuckling over the infamous robberies of their countrymen." As if to convince herself of the truth of her statement,

Emerson addressed the subject of northern perfidy. "If you ask me how I know that their soldiers are more profane than ours," she wrote, "I answer the same way that I know most things, by testimony, abundant testimony."[34] Yet in the aftermath of the Chambersburg burning, some southern civilians questioned how God could favor such action on the part of their army and worried what the answer would mean for their future.[35]

The Maryland campaign in the summer of 1864 gave Confederate civilians in the Valley some confidence that the war might end soon and favorably for their cause. Early's army cleared the Valley of Federal troops, threatened Washington, and delivered retribution on northern civilians. The crops were safe and abundant, money worth more after currency reform. Civilians read northern newspapers and their "talk about starving the South." Southern newspapers scoffed lightheartedly that there was plenty to eat: "The young rook is eaten in England, and as we know of no difference between the rook, and the crow, we do not see why young crows may not be eaten, or, indeed, in war times, old crows."[36]

By the second week of September, Confederate hopes faded and civilians grew despondent. The fall of Atlanta on September 2 altered expectations about the war's course. "I have so much bad news to record," Eva Allen wrote, "that I scarcely know where to begin. . . . The general opinion is that the war is to be interminable now." Allen confessed a secret desire to "shut the book and sit me down and die." Other diarists recorded similar signs of collective depression. Waddell gave his first indication of anxiety on September 14, when he noted "a rather somber feeling in the community today — nothing to be hoped for from any peace party in the North." Waddell considered the Confederacy "about used up."[37]

The state of depression among Confederate civilians deepened in September when General Sheridan's army came into a region still rich in logistical production. General in Chief U. S. Grant famously instructed Sheridan to make the Shenandoah Valley a "barren waste" by carrying off or destroying anything of value to the Confederate military effort. The Valley in 1864 held large quantities of crops and supplies, despite the summer's long drought and the invasions of Union armies early in the summer. The Staunton newspaper reported in mid-July that the wheat crop was "of excellent quality and well filled." The paper predicted that the corn crop also would be successful. Hotchkiss wrote that Clarke and Jefferson counties had "abundance in them" of flour and noted that Early's commissary had "100,000 bushels of wheat at his command." Waddell reported Augusta County to be "rich in all that is needed to sustain an army. . . . The mills are full of wheat." Waddell worried that if the Federal troops came "the loss to our army will be irreparable." Even in late September, Sheridan reported from Harrisonburg that "the country from here to Staunton was abundantly supplied with forage and grain."[38]

Sheridan's troopers set crops and barns on fire throughout the lower Valley in August and September. These Federals, noted Sheridan in his official report, operated under "the most positive orders . . . not to burn dwellings."[39] According to Waddell, northern troops in Staunton "entered very few private houses and committed no depredations," but he heard of "great destruction in Rockbridge and all the Lower Valley." "Women were wringing their hands and crying while the men were carried off as prisoners and the barns and hay stacks were burning," Waddell wrote. Matthella Harrison witnessed the destruction at her family's plantation. "Every head of stock driven off," she dryly recorded: "Those young animals that refused to go were shot down." When the enemy's officers and soldiers came to her family's plantation, she heard the sound of an uncontrolled mob — "the shouts, ribald jokes, awful oaths, demonical laughter of the fiends." These soldiers also sought revenge. According to Harrison, their watchword was "Remember Chambersburg."[40]

From the top of Brown's Gap in the Blue Ridge Mountains in late September, Early's army, defeated recently in the battles of Third Winchester and Fisher's Hill, defended its last toehold in the Valley while Federal cavalry carried out Sheridan's orders to destroy Confederate supplies. The gap offered a particularly high vantage from which to see the destruction. Deployed in a close defensive perimeter along the ridge lines, soldiers could watch the fires on the Valley floor below. "Immediately in my view were burnt not less than one hundred hay stacks and barns," one artilleryman wrote his father; "nearly every farm large or small has been visited by the torch." This man admitted that the "whereabouts of the enemy" were "unknown precisely" and guessed that Federal cavalry bore responsibility for the burning. The Valley, he thought, was no longer "tenable" for any army, and he feared the same measures would be extended to the Confederate country as a whole.[41]

While Confederates speculated on the enemy's activities, Union soldiers and officers engaged in widespread destruction fueled not only by orders from Grant and Sheridan but also by determination to avenge Confederate guerrilla activity. When Lt. John Rogers Meigs, son of the Union quartermaster general and a favorite of Sheridan's, was killed near Harrisonburg on October 3 by Confederate cavalrymen, Little Phil ordered a complete burning of all property within a three-mile radius of the site. "Since I came into the Valley from

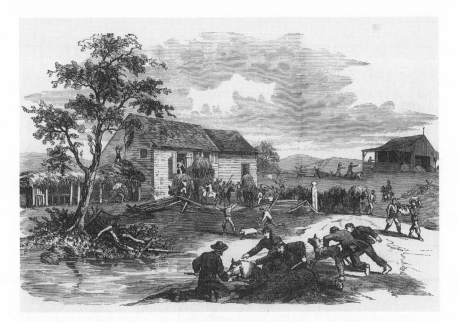

"Wilson's Cavalry Foraging in the Shenandoah Valley." This woodcut of a sketch by James E. Taylor gave readers of *Frank Leslie's Illustrated Newspaper* an idea of how Sheridan's campaign affected many civilians in the Valley. Paul F. Mottelay and T. Campbell-Copeland, eds., *The Soldier in Our Civil War*, 2 vols. (New York and Atlanta: Stanley Bradley Publishing Company, 1893), 2:345.

Harper's Ferry," Sheridan concluded, "every train, every small party, and every straggler, has been bushwhacked by the people." Rumors swirled that Confederate civilians, not uniformed cavalry, were responsible for Meigs's death, and Federal troops, especially Sheridan, viewed the killing as a "murder." The day after Meigs's death, Col. William H. Powell informed the citizens of Page County that two Confederate prisoners of war would be shot or hanged for every Union soldier killed by a southern bushwhacker. Indeed, that very day Powell reported that he "had two bushwackers shot to death" in retaliation for the killing of one of his soldiers.[42]

Despite the intensity of various accounts of The Burning and the escalation of reprisal violence in the region, some observers mentioned the destruction only in passing—as just another strange happening in a long war. Jedediah Hotchkiss, an astute observer, only mentioned the burning of civilian property once in his journal. On August 17, he stated matter-of-factly, "We found the enemy gone this morning and the smoke rising from all parts of the Lower

Valley from the burning of barns and hay and wheat stacks by the retreating Yankees." Hotchkiss's emphasis at end of his statement was on the retreating Yankees. The smoke of the burning appeared more as evidence of their retreat than of their pillage. A month later, Hotchkiss returned home to Staunton to find "the people are busy sowing grain." Shortly thereafter, he reported "some difficulty" gathering supplies "for the year" from his neighbors and friends. Even so, Hotchkiss thought that he "got along well."[43]

Hotchkiss's optimism about the limited scope of the damage somewhat obscured the fact that the Federals had burned great quantities of hay and barns, driven off large numbers of livestock, and enlisted or emancipated hundreds of slaves. Only Rockingham County undertook a complete survey of the damage and losses to the civilian population. The county acted in response to a memo from the Office Recorder of Virginia Forces, appointed by Governor William Smith. The governor charged the office "to carefully ascertain what wrongs and injuries, contrary to the rules of war, have been committed upon the people of Virginia." The offense considered "worse than all" was "offering insult, outrage, and violence to defenceless women."[44] Rockingham followed through on the request, one of the only counties in the Valley to do so. It reported in November that a committee of seventy-two citizens from every section of the county canvassed their neighbors and compiled a complete survey of the damage in the campaign. Their findings were part of the record of the county court and subject to the court's scrutiny (see table 1).

Rockingham County's estimate was, according to the newspaper, the conservative, lower total of the returns gathered by the committee. The newspaper put the estimate at more than $25 million in Confederate prices, or $5 million in real value. Rockingham County's losses likely ranked among the most significant in the Valley.

Heavy as these losses were, Sheridan's forces had inflicted limited and targeted damage that neither destroyed the entire Valley nor subjugated its population. The summer's drought and the war's loss of laborers lowered production levels from the 1860 highs, but perhaps by no more than 15 percent. Sheridan extravagantly claimed that his cavalry units struck so hard at civilian property that the Valley "will have little in it for man or beast." His final report claimed that Federals destroyed or captured 3,772 horses, 10,918 cattle, 12,000 sheep, 15,000 hogs, 20,397 tons of hay, 435,802 bushels of wheat, 77,176 bushels of corn, 71 flour mills, and 1,200 barns.[45] Rockingham apparently lost 450 of the 1,200 barns, 31 of 71 flourmills, and 6,000 of 20,000 tons of hay destroyed in the Valley.[46] In Rockingham, where Sheridan's cavalry admittedly visited

Table 1. Estimate of Rockingham County Losses in 1864 Valley Campaign
Compared with U.S. Census Agricultural Schedule Data for Rockingham
County

Property Damage or Loss	Amount or Number	1860 U.S. Census Agricultural Production
Dwelling houses burned	30	
Barns burned	45	
Mills burned	31	
Fencing destroyed (miles)	100	
Bushels of wheat destroyed	100,000	358,653
Bushels of corn destroyed	50,000	684,239
Tons of hay destroyed	6,233	19,174
Cattle carried off	1,750	13,299
Horses carried off	1,750	7,874
Sheep carried off	4,200	13,364
Hogs carried off	3,350	37,307
Factories burned	3	
Furnaces burned	1	

Sources: *Staunton Republican Vindicator*, November 18, 1864; 1860 U.S. Census
Agricultural Schedule, Rockingham County.

widespread destruction, the county's conservative estimate of total losses represented less than a quarter of production levels in 1860. Federal troops in Rockingham burned and destroyed more barns, hay, and wheat than any other agricultural products. Hogs, cattle, and corn remained in significant numbers. Citizens in Rockingham dutifully reported these losses, fully expecting that the process would eventually result in compensation from the state or Confederate government. They had reason to believe that the state government would come to their aid; in 1862 and 1863 it had proved attentive to the demands of a citizenry at war.[47]

Through this destruction, Federal officers openly challenged the Confederate civilians' sense of security and faith in their government. They destroyed Confederate supplies and buildings and threatened Confederate men. They also visibly demonstrated the weakness of Confederate institutions. When Federal troops occupied Staunton in September, an officer "offered for sale a Confederate $1,000 bond," as if to dare Confederates to invest in their government's shaky future. Waddell noted that after some time the seller "could find no purchaser." In an elaborate display of magnanimity, the officer gave the bond to Andrew Hunter, cousin of the Federal general, "as partial compensation for the burning of his house."[48]

Not surprisingly, many black residents of the Valley did not see U. S. forces as menacing invaders. In Augusta County, for example, Nancy Jenkins Jefferson had lived before the war as a free black woman who made her living as a housekeeper. She had two children in her household and owned real estate and some property. Some time after the war she married a freedman named Thomas Jefferson. She claimed her sympathies "were all the time with the Union." Nancy's brother, presumably a slave, was "in the Confederate Army" and "was forced to wait on an officer." "Our Loyalty is indisputable," Nancy and Thomas claimed in 1877, "because we are colored persons." In September 1864, Nancy harbored a Federal officer wounded in a nearby skirmish. "He was wounded at our door, and the Confederates would have stripped and murdered him after he was shot down, had he not been cared for by us," they claimed. The claim investigator looked into the matter and concluded that Nancy acted "at considerable risk to herself and property [and] kept him [the officer] concealed from the rebel troops until he could be removed to a place of safety." Nancy's claim was for compensation and services rendered during the 1864 Valley campaign — including the care and hospitalization of a Federal officer and the loss of one 180-pound hog and eight barrels of flour.[49]

Unionists in the Shenandoah Valley — whether free blacks, Dunkers, Mennonites, or independent-minded yeomen—could experience sharp treatment in 1864 from Confederate civilians, officers, and soldiers as well as from the invading Federals. In Winchester, Mordecai Purcell faced potential violence when a Confederate enlisted man promised to "shoot him if he did not give him a horse that he had and prove his loyalty to the Confederacy." Purcell watched helplessly as the soldier took the animal. Confederate soldiers camped at the farm of Christian Landis, a Dunker in Augusta County, for four days in the fall of 1864. Landis's son had been conscripted into the Confederate army in 1862, as Landis put it matter-of-factly, "against my will" and "by armed men from my house and was killed in the Wilderness." When Federal troops came into Augusta at "the time of the burning," they took his corn, and when Landis objected "threatened to burn my barn down." The beleaguered Dunker gave them "hay, oats, bacon, and provisions," and his wife "cooked for them all day." Although the Federal troops spared Landis's barn, they took his horses.

Unionists who objected to such seizures were told, according to one postwar claimant, "the less I said, the better for me."[50]

Like many Unionists, Landis shepherded his sons and daughters north or west out of the reach of Confederate conscription agents. Confederates imprisoned these resisters when possible and enforced conscription, even shooting at Unionists who ran from them. Confederate civilians viewed these resisters as potential enemies, and indeed some of them were. When Unionists fled north or west to reach Federal lines, some of them joined the U. S. Army. John D. Stover, a farmer in New Hope near Staunton, received aid from Unionist David Myers, who "advised and encouraged me to go" through the lines to the Federal army. Stover left the Valley in 1864, joined the 6th Ohio, and returned to the Shenandoah in Sheridan's command. John Yates, another Unionist in Augusta, was imprisoned in Castle Thunder for "aiding refugees across the lines." Moved to Staunton in September 1864 to stand trial for treason, he was liberated by Sheridan's army.[51]

When Federal troops moved through Rockingham and Augusta Counties, they did not just burn Confederate barns and liberate Unionists from prisons — they also freed many slaves. Although slaves had run away throughout the war, the pace picked up in the Shenandoah Valley in 1864. Civilians took notice, but newspapers only reluctantly admitted the hemorrhaging loss of black labor. The *Staunton Vindicator* offered no more than a veiled comment that "only white labor is available locally." Confederate civilians also took notice when the Union army began to use black troops in Virginia. Amanda Edmonds chastised Grant in June for bringing "the abominable wretches and negroes to the field." When black soldiers in the Ninth Corps suffered heavy casualties in late July during the battle of the Crater at Petersburg, some civilians in the Valley expressed paternalist pity. Mary Cochran described the black troops as "poor wretches stimulated with whisky and induced to think they would meet with no resistance." She considered the grisly result at Petersburg, which she attributed to poor conduct by the Federal officers, a sad betrayal of simple black men.[52]

Many African Americans took the opportunity to join the Federal army when it appeared in the Valley. In late September, Sheridan's force impressed both free and enslaved African Americans in Staunton to tear up the railroad. According to Waddell, the impressed crew were "very indignant and did much less damage . . . than they could have done." In the next sentence, however, Waddell conceded that "a considerable number of Negroes" went off with the

Union army. Federal officers apparently promised to take any willing African Americans to Washington, where "they could work for a living." Waddell, like Cochran, sneered at such a possibility and considered black men too deluded or infantile to know what was good for them. Confederate civilians simply could not admit to themselves that slaves felt no loyalty to either the southern cause or their masters.[53]

Although they typically failed to come to terms with black disloyalty, Confederate civilians turned a more realistic eye toward their soldiers. Civilians felt connected to the army and watched its every move. Earlier in the war, they had taken pride in the fortitude and resilience demonstrated by Confederate troops at Fredericksburg and Gettysburg and in the boldness and power of southern soldiers who fought at Second Manassas and Chancellorsville. In 1864 as earlier, they expected their soldiers to punish the Federal transgressors and to sting the northern will.[54]

Confederates in uniform were similarly connected to the home front, assessing reactions behind the lines in light of their own conduct. A soldier named John T. Cooley considered the South to be "in a war which we must fight out." In September 1864, he cited the old maxim, "The harder the storm the sooner it will be over," to give himself and his civilian relatives some comfort. In a letter to his cousin, Cooley listed three things he needed to stay in the field and keep up morale: "I can stand the storm very well if I get plenty to eat, and can enjoy good health, and be permitted to peruse the thoughts of my highly esteemed and affected cousin Julia!" In fact, this was not all Cooley needed. He went to prayer meetings, daydreamed about the "blue mountains" of southwest Virginia, and confessed to dreading another winter in the field. He feared "that we will suffer worse than we ever have." "War is all that can be heard," he admitted, "and everybody is tired of that."[55]

The battle of Fisher's Hill caused Confederate civilians in the Valley to examine closely themselves and their army. On September 22, Early's army fled the field at Fisher's Hill in disastrous order. Soldiers referred to it as a "stampede," "a panic" carried out "at breakneck speed" and in "the greatest confusion." Elements of the army scattered over Massanutten Mountain into the Page Valley, not to return to the main body for weeks. Officers and soldiers alike understood how embarrassing the loss at Fisher's Hill was for the Confederacy. They wrote home to offer explanations full of determination. One soldier, who shared his "darkest forebodings," considered the rout "woeful to our young country and its cause." Another blamed the "management of the command" and considered the army's future in the Valley over. A third called the battle a disgraceful stampede and pronounced the "cavalry so utterly worthless" that it could not stop a flank attack on the infantry under any circumstances. Yet this last witness sought to assure his mother that the soldiers had "quite recovered their morale."[56]

Civilians had their doubts. "To all appearance there is no help for us but in God," Joseph Waddell lamented. Fisher's Hill sent him into a spiral of depression. "A dull feeling of gloom seems to pervade the community," he recorded; ". . . there is little to hope for in the future. It is like walking through the Valley of the Shadow of Death." Incredulous at the depth of depression he witnessed, Waddell wondered whether any of his neighbors had not grown tired of the war. He claimed that "[a]nxiety and gloom were depicted on every countenance." "For myself," he confessed, "I feel staggered and overcome. Our cause seems to be desperate." When Waddell's sister heard that Sheridan's forces had crushed the Confederates at Fisher's Hill, she suffered "intensely from nervous apprehensions" and dreaded that "she and her children, would be slaughtered, or at least starved to death." Waddell regarded the Christianity of the northern people as hypocritical because they seemed to take pleasure in the "alarm and suffering" of Confederate women and children. Evidence of that suffering lay all too readily at hand, whether in Staunton, where Federal troops "destroyed publick property," or in the thirteen-mile stretch between Waynesboro and Staunton, along which one trooper in the 20th U.S. Cavalry traveled one night "guided along the way by blazing haystacks and large granneries."[57]

When Sheridan's army seemed poised to move out of the Valley in mid-October, Confederate civilians and soldiers could hardly believe what had happened to them. "I dislike very much to hear of our arms meeting so many reverses," one young man wrote his brother, a cavalryman in McCausland's brigade. The army previously had always won "victories." Also incensed at the conduct of Federal troops in the Valley, the man remarked, "It is almost enough to make the blood boil in one's veins to hear of the atrocities and vandalism Sheridan has committed." He admitted that the "country" was in a "terrible crisis" but tried not to believe that the northern army's cause would prevail. "Surely," he thought, "the South can never be subdued by men who commit such outrages! The vengeance of a just God will most certainly overtake them sooner or later." Joseph Waddell, an admitted pessimist, worried that "officials in Richmond" were in a "state of panic, . . . making no provision for the future." Apparently, he had heard the government was "staking everything on a single throw [of the dice]." That strategy seemed desperate to Waddell, who prayed to God that the Confederates "may be humble, submissive, and trustful" even in

Federal soldiers cheer Sheridan as he rides past, with plumes of smoke from burning crops and buildings rising in the background. James E. Taylor's sketch conveys strong images of Union triumph and destruction that would linger for years among the Valley's residents. Courtesy of the Western Reserve Historical Society, Cleveland, Ohio.

the face of slaughter and loss. Waddell, though, came around to seeing cheerful news on the horizon. He took comfort in reports of successes west of the Mississippi, where he thought "the Confederates appear to have things their own way." He thought things looked "a little brighter" on October 19.[58]

The battle of Cedar Creek, fought that October 19 near Middletown, proved Waddell wrong and shocked the Valley's civilians. The Confederate army plundered the enemy's camps after initial success and then ran pell-mell in the face of a counterattack. General Early criticized his men openly in the newspapers for their "misconduct" and "disgraceful propensity for plunder." He released his postbattle address for publication in the press at the same time it was read to his soldiers, an example of how closely Early linked the home front and battlefield. His address sought to shame the men, daring those who plundered to show their spoils. For each man who dropped out of the ranks at Cedar Creek to ransack Federals camps, insisted Early, the plunder would represent "badges of his dishonor, the insignia of his disgrace." Old Jube blamed officers as well as enlisted men for the turnaround loss. Success, he cautioned, came from discipline and from fighting with honor. In his last paragraph, Early appealed to the cause and to patriotism, calling on soldiers in the Army of the Valley "to do battle like men."[59]

With Early's public pronouncement circulating through newspapers in the state, his soldiers wrote home to describe the battle and their role in it. Most characterized Cedar Creek as a "painful" and "disgraceful affair." One young Virginia cavalryman admitted that "disaster after disaster attends this army." He considered it "very galling" to have to "acknowledge all this" but thought it "folly to attempt to smooth things over." After Cedar Creek, the trooper marched without a horse and tried to keep up with his unit on foot. He thought the army "demoralized" and suggested that Early should "sell out to another firm." Some soldiers tried to play down the loss at Cedar Creek, telling their families that the battle should be considered a draw. The quartermaster in Thomas L. Rosser's cavalry command mentioned "our Troops stopping to plunder their camps," but in his tabulation—which did not square with reality—Early's army came away from the field with the advantage in captured pieces and men.[60]

Word of Early's losses spread quickly across Virginia and beyond. It reached troopers in the 1st Battalion Kentucky Mounted Rifles just days after Cedar Creek as they traveled through southwestern Virginia to join Confederate forces in the Valley. "Our men generally go on this expedition," remarked Edward O. Guerrant, an officer in the unit, "with a heavy heart." At the same time, Guerrant recorded in his diary signs of economic and social collapse during the two-week journey. On one twenty-mile march through several small towns and past many farms, he "saw nobody" except "the wondering little negroes and children and the girls at 'Hollins Institute.'" He considered it "peculiar" to travel through so much of Virginia and see "not a face hardly." The journey brought unsettling moments, as when the Kentuckians heard that their horses "will surely starve, so all say." They marched through Augusta County, where Guerrant saw "not one in a dozen barns were left standing." Later, above Harrisonburg, he witnessed "utter desolation." "You might travel all day and night," Guerrant marveled, "and not see a dozen [people]. They were closed in their houses if they had [any]." When Guerrant and his unit arrived at Early's camp, they were directed to the lower Luray Valley to join Maj. Gen. Lunsford L. Lomax's cavalry division. En route the Kentuckians encountered part of the Laurel Brigade, "most of them drunk." Two days later, Guerrant noted, "Everybody joined in a Philippic against the war."[61]

Civilians also observed the deterioration in Confederate capacity to continue the war. Joseph Waddell recorded in October that "a considerable number of men from the town and county have run off to avoid military duty." When farmers were drafted into military service, some filed for a writ of habeas corpus in a local court "on the ground that the Government had entered into a contract to release them from military service" in return for their selling their produce to the government at the approved prices. According to Waddell, many of these men were "probably hiding in the mountains."[62]

Soldiers who found the Valley's destruction and the loss at Cedar Creek "humiliating" understandably feared that civilians would lose faith in the army's ability to defend them. One deemed it embarrassing "to come back up the Valley after another thrashing." As the fall campaign unfolded, Jedediah Hotchkiss urged his wife to spread word at home that the army would continue to fight. "Our men in the field have lost none of their accustomed courage," he emphasized, "their leaders none of their accustomed skills, but our ranks are depleted." He viewed the northern advantage as purely one of "numbers" of men, and exhorted those at home to "cheerfully come now, and in two months all will be well." Especially before the disaster at Cedar Creek, Hotchkiss insisted that time might still be on the side of the Confederates. "If we are able to keep the enemy at bay," he wrote home, ". . . we shall not be troubled by them another year." Hotchkiss heard rumors from the North that public opinion would not support another year of war. He was "confident" in "a conclusion of hostilities with the ending of 'Old Abe's' reign." "Everything indicates a strong peace movement in the North," Hotchkiss reported hopefully.[63]

Lincoln's reelection led many Valley civilians to question their prospects for victory. Most recognized that the Republican triumph meant "at least four more years of war." Joseph Waddell thought the election would be "discouraging" for the Confederate soldiers "after all they have endured." He also saw the election as evidence of a more determined foe in the North, where the people "have declared in favor of prosecuting the war, even to our extermination."[64]

Lincoln's immediate call for one million men further discouraged Confederate civilians, leading some to consider the cause "hopeless" and others to encourage more drastic measures to win the war. "Many of our people are ready to give up," Waddell observed, "especially the original secessionists." He heard rumors that many secessionists wanted to strike a deal with Lincoln, ending the war for southern independence with a bargain that preserved some aspects of slavery in the South. Waddell found this sentiment reprehensible. "I would rather lose slavery and everything and become a serf to Russia," he affirmed, than give up the cause. For Waddell, surrendering to save slavery was the ultimate admission of failure because it plainly revealed the emptiness of Confederate nationalism. An ambivalent supporter of slavery at best, Waddell preferred "independence without slavery" to capitulation with it. While Waddell considered the prospect of arming slaves to fight for the Confederacy, women from neighboring Rockingham County petitioned the secretary of war to allow them to raise a regiment of female soldiers "armed and equipped to perform regular service." The women affirmed their determination "to leave our hearthstones — to endure any sacrifice — any privation for the ultimate success of our Holy Cause."[65]

The war had yielded reversals of fortune, bitter harvests, and deep anxieties for its Confederate participants. Widespread destruction in the Valley and defeats on the battlefield left soldiers and civilians bewildered. A cavalry quartermaster named D. C. Snyder appealed to a "just God" and could not believe "that He will permit such a race of men to subjugate and destroy a people fighting for all that is dear to enlightened freemen." He was convinced that "retribution will surely overtake" an opponent "so lost to the best feelings of our nature and who conduct a warfare in such uncivilized ways." As the army moved to put detailed men into the ranks, Snyder voiced mixed emotions about leaving the security of his job and "fighting a foe that makes such warfare upon defenseless women and children." He preferred to defend his family at home where it counted the most. Instructing his wife in November to take rations from the Federal army rather than become a refugee, he urged her "to provide for yourself and [the] children" and to stay at home. Snyder described the region around the Valley as a world apart from the year before when supplies were plentiful. "You can form no idea of how scarce everything is," he warned, "and how much suffering must result the coming winter from the scarcity." While stationed in Rockingham County in December, Snyder was "surprised" that civilians who had lost so much "got along so well." He was less sure of the army. "Qualification for office [in the army] now seems to be that of whiskey drinking, swearing, deceitfulness and anything else calculated to deceive and take advantage," he lamented. "If this war is to continue until the morals of the army improve it will be of long duration."[66]

The Valley campaign of 1864 impressed upon Confederate civilians that the war and their perceptions of it were subject to constant negotiation. Many planters and yeomen saw their farms wrecked, barns burned, cattle driven off, and crops seized. The Confederate army conscripted nearly every available man, while it lost battles, cohesion, and moral direction. Eva Allen's brother Henry wrote home from the trenches at Petersburg to tell of a strange story of a "Negro man belonging to old Capt. Breckinridge." The former slave fled the plantation and "went off with Hunter" in June 1864. According to Henry, the man deserted from the Federal army and came over to the Confederate lines. He told them "he was 'sick of soldiering,' and said there were some other Botetourt Negroes in his Regt. all anxious to get back home." Henry was amazed at the strangeness of the report, not because a former slave in the Federal army had deserted to the Confederacy, but because slaves were actually fighting in the Federal army. "Who would have thought four years ago," he wondered, "that the time would come when we would be fighting our neighbor's Negroes?"[67]

Confederate civilians found that they did not quite know themselves, that their astonishment knew few boundaries. As noted earlier, Amanda Edmonds criticized Grant when black Federal soldiers were first deployed in Virginia. She wondered whether the Confederates would "ever blot out such a foe?" Later in September her question changed: "Will kind Providence forsake us in this day of adversity? Will he permit one of the most beautiful countries in the world to become enslaved and subjugated?"[68] The shift in her emphasis was subtle but startling. Confederate civilians, tired of the war but determined to fight it out, asked themselves in June 1864 whether they would eventually destroy the enemy, but by September they wondered whether they were forsaken. The answers to these questions eluded them, but the questions themselves hung in the autumn air. The Confederacy's enemy demonstrated such determination and capacity for war in the Valley that civilians knew the war had altered course. At the same time, the Confederate army showed such failure of command and lack of discipline that civilians knew they could not rely on it for protection. Despite this reversal and their astonishment at it, Confederate civilians in the Shenandoah Valley held fast to their desperate, losing cause, hoping, praying, and believing that they would not be forsaken.

Acknowledgments

The author would like to thank Anne S. Rubin, Aaron Sheehan-Dean, Doug Smith, Bill Bergen, and Edward L. Ayers for their helpful comments and careful reading of this essay.

Notes

1. Diary of Nancy Emerson, July 9, 1864, *Valley of the Shadow: Two Communities in the American Civil War*, Virginia Center for Digital History, University of Virginia ‹http://valley.vcdh.virginia.edu› [item hereafter cited as Emerson diary, with date].

2. Stephen V. Ash's *When the Yankees Came: Conflict and Chaos in the Occupied South, 1861–1865* (Chapel Hill: University of North Carolina Press, 1995) traces the changing experiences of what he calls "three worlds" of the occupied South: garri-

soned towns, the no man's land, and the Confederate frontier. Ash's description of no man's land in 1864 as engendering alienation—"in a strange land"—was clearly at work in the Shenandoah Valley. This essay, though, locates the processes at work on Confederate civilians in a specific time and place, seeing how Confederate views were shaped by their perceptions of their role in the war, the enemy's actions, and the conduct of the Confederate troops.

3. William H. S. Baylor to Mrs. Baylor, April 22, 1862, Special Collections Department, University Libraries, Virginia Tech, Blacksburg, Va.

4. *Staunton Spectator,* January 6, 1863; Emerson diary, June 30, 1862.

5. Emerson diary, July 4, 1862, January 1, 1863.

6. Jedediah Hotchkiss to Nellie Hotchkiss, December 17, 1862, Hotchkiss Family Papers, Albert and Shirley Small Special Collections Library, University of Virginia, Charlottesville [repository hereafter cited as UVA]; Emerson diary, March 6, 1863.

7. Emerson diary, June 26, 1863; *Staunton Spectator,* July 7, August 11, 1863.

8. Two recent studies of the experiences of Virginia civilians during the Civil War are William A. Blair, *Virginia's Private War: Feeding Body and Soul in the Confederacy, 1861–1865* (New York: Oxford University Press, 1998) and Daniel E. Sutherland, *Seasons of War: The Ordeal of a Confederate Community* (Baton Rouge: Louisiana State University Press, 1995). For two less scholarly accounts devoted to the 1864 Valley campaign specifically, see Michael G. Mahon, *The Shenandoah Valley, 1861–1865: The Destruction of the Granary of the Confederacy* (Mechanicsburg, Pa.: Stackpole Books, 1999) and John L. Heatwole, *The Burning: Sheridan in the Shenandoah Valley* (Charlottesville, Va.: Rockbridge, 1998).

9. D. C. Snyder to his wife, June 22, October 26, 1864, D. C. Snyder Letters, James Madison University, Harrisonburg, Va. See Ash, *When the Yankees Came,* 40–41, on southern citizens' views of occupation as degrading, polluting, and violating. For an excellent overview of Confederate views on Christian soldiers, see Reid Mitchell, "Christian Soldiers? Perfecting the Confederacy," in *Religion and the American Civil War,* eds. Randall M. Miller, Harry S. Stout, and Charles Reagan Wilson (New York: Oxford University Press, 1998), 297–309.

10. Aaron Sheehan-Dean, "'Give the Yankees Hell': Enlistment and Service in the Virginia Infantry" (paper, Annual Meeting of the Southern Historical Association, Louisville, Kentucky, November 9, 2000); Edward L. Ayers and Anne Sarah Rubin, *Valley of the Shadow: The Eve of War* (New York: W. W. Norton, 2000), 95. Some historians, such as John L. Heatwole, have played down the role of slavery in the Valley and the region's commitment to Confederate nationalism, emphasizing instead the strong Mennonite and Dunker presence in the area and the Unionist support in the secession crisis.

11. Mark Grimsley, *The Hard Hand of War: Union Military Policy toward Southern Civilians, 1861–1865* (New York: Cambridge University Press, 1995), 225. Grimsley argued that Union forces pursued a conciliatory policy toward civilians in the first two years of the war, hoping to lure Unionists back to the government and not to further alienate recalcitrant southerners. He viewed the "hard war" phase after 1863 as

proportional because soldiers were "thinking bayonets" who understood the calibration needed to defeat the South; they did not erase the line between combatant and noncombatant.

12. U.S. War Department, *The War of the Rebellion: A Compilation of the Official Records of the Union and Confederate Armies*, 127 vols., index, and atlas (Washington: Government Printing Office, 1880–1901), ser. 1, 40(3):223, 37(2):202 [hereafter cited as *OR*; all references are to ser. 1].

13. John R. Hildebrand, ed., *A Mennonite Journal, 1862–1865: A Father's Account of the Civil War in the Shenandoah Valley* (Shippensburg, Pa.: Burd Street Press, 1996), 49; Joseph A. Waddell diary, June 11, 1864, UVA.

14. Emerson diary, July 13, 1864; Waddell diary, June 13, 14, 18, 19, 1864. In the lower Valley, Federal forces as well took horses and liberated slaves. See Mathella Page Harrison diary, August 10, 11, 1864, Mathella Page Harrison Papers, UVA: "We are again relieved from the hated presence but their visit has been very disastrous to us for they have carried off George who has hitherto been a faithful servant."

15. John Price Kepner diary, July 26, 1864, Virginia Historical Society, Richmond [repository hereafter cited as VHS]; David Hunter Strother, *A Virginia Yankee in the Civil War: The Diaries of David Hunter Strother*, ed. Cecil D. Eby Jr. (Chapel Hill: University of North Carolina Press, 1961), 237–38.

16. Strother, *Virginia Yankee*, 235–36, 246.

17. Emerson diary, July 21, 1864. On the rarity of Union forces raping southern women, see Ash, *When the Yankees Came*, 200–201, who points out that twenty-two Union soldiers were executed for attempted rape, half of them black. Ash also points out that the far more common violation, or symbolic rape, of southern women was the complete invasion of private space in women's homes.

18. Civil War diary of Eva Honey Allen, June 14, 15, 1864, folder 4, Gilmer Speed Adam Collection, UVA.

19. Strother, *Virginia Yankee*, 254.

20. Harrison diary, July 28, 1864; Emerson diary, July 13, 1864.

21. Waddell diary, June 11, 1864; *Staunton Republican Vindicator*, July 22, 8, 1864.

22. Allen diary, July 8, 16, 28, 1864. See also Charles Royster, *The Destructive War: William Tecumseh Sherman, Stonewall Jackson and the Americans* (New York: Knopf, 1991), 340–41, who pointed out that Sherman's marches and destruction "were an exercise in reshaping people's perception of the United States by demonstrating what those who believed in the country's permanence could do to confirm their belief." According to Royster, Sherman hoped to use war to show civilians the emptiness of their quest for independence (Royster, *Destructive War*, 341). On the concept of total war, see Stig Forster and Jorg Nagler, eds., *On the Road to Total War: The American Civil War and the German Wars of Unification, 1860–1871* (New York: Cambridge University Press, 1997); Mark E. Neely Jr., "Was the Civil War a Total War?" *Civil War History* 37 (March 1991):5–28; and Lance Janda, "Shutting the Gates of Mercy: The American Origins of Total War, 1860–1880," *Journal of Military History* 59 (January 1995):7–26.

23. Micajah Woods to John Woods, June 28, 1864, Micajah Woods Papers, UVA; "A

Brief Sketch of the Life and Character of David S. Creigh, Esq.," in *Lewisburg Weekly Times Print*, 1865, Micajah Woods Papers; Fannie M. Lyle Wilson to father, June 17, 1864, Virginia Military Institute Archives, Lexington [repository hereafter cited as VMI]. For a mention of the Creigh killing, see also Cornelia McDonald, *A Diary with Reminiscences of War and Refugee Life in the Shenandoah Valley, 1860–1865* (Nashville, Tenn.: Cullom and Ghertner, 1934), 220.

24. Lucy Johnson Ambler diary, July 27, 1864, UVA.

25. Mary Catharine Powell Cochran diary, July 13, 1864, VHS.

26. Lawrence Royster to John E. Roller, July 28, 1864, John E. Roller Papers, VMI.

27. Waddell diary, July 22, August 4, 1864.

28. Ibid., August 6, 1864; Jedediah Hotchkiss to Sara Hotchkiss, August 10, 1864, Hotchkiss Family Papers. See also Fielder C. Slingluff to Ephriam Hiteshew, August 1, 1884, *Confederate Veteran* 17 (November 1909):560: "I saw this confidence, almost amounting to contempt, on our march to your town. . . . Knots of men on the corners poked fun at our appearance and jeered us."

29. *Staunton Republican Vindicator*, August 12, 1864; *Charleston Mercury*, August 16, 1864. See also the *Mercury* on September 28, 1864.

30. Allen diary, August 9, 1864.

31. Jedediah Hotchkiss to Sara Hotchkiss, August 10, 1864, Hotchkiss Family Papers; *OR*, 43(1):7–8. The *Charleston Mercury*, September 30, 1864, considered the raid a key factor in later losses in the Valley because it undermined discipline and morale in the army: "This excursion into the rich country of the enemy, the license allowed to officers and men, and the plunder that was secured, together with the free use of liquor since their return, have borne their natural fruit. Some of this fruit was gathered by the enemy at Winchester and Fisher's Hill."

32. *Staunton Republican Vindicator*, July 3, 1863.

33. *Confederate Veteran* 21 (July 1913):356; Fielder C. Slingluff to Ephriam Hiteshew, August 1, 1884, *Confederate Veteran* 17 (November 1909):560. I disagree with Beringer and others' treatment of Confederate faith and religion in *Why the South Lost the Civil War*. They contend that civilian will was "undermined by doubts of religion" and "could no longer supplement the force of arms." They suggest that Confederates considered fostering God's grace by reforming or eliminating slavery. Letters and diaries from the Valley reveal no evidence to support this argument. Confederate civilians instead used the suffering inherent in their Christian faith to give them will and to sustain their spirit rather than to open doubts about their actions (Richard E. Beringer, Herman Hattaway, Archer Jones, and William N. Still Jr., *Why the South Lost the Civil War* [Athens: University of Georgia Press, 1986]: 293). See also the especially thoughtful essay by Harry S. Stout and Christopher Grasso, "Civil War, Religion, and Communications: The Case of Richmond," in Miller, Stout, and Wilson, *Religion and the American Civil War*, 313–59.

34. Emerson diary, August 9, 1864.

35. For an analysis of Confederate behavior in the burning of Chambersburg, see Everard H. Smith, "Chambersburg: Anatomy of a Confederate Reprisal," *American Historical Review* 96 (April 1991):432–55. Smith focuses on the Confederate views of

northern women, particularly ethnic German civilians, to explain the making of the Chambersburg burning. Smith considers the 1863 Gettysburg campaign, when Lee's army was encamped in Chambersburg, as the crucial experience that led to the burning in 1864. Smith also focuses on the southern concept of honor and its implications for how Confederates expected to be treated in 1863. See also Blair, *Virginia's Private War*, 143, for an analysis of Virginians' views on Federal treatment of southern women and civilians, and John B. Gordon, *Reminiscences of the Civil War* (New York: Scribner's, 1903), 305, for a postwar view of the Chambersburg burning as having been against the orders of Robert E. Lee.

36. On Valley crops, see Allen diary, September 7, 1864, and Waddell diary, September 24, 1864. On the money supply and Confederate measures to reign in inflation, see John Monroe Godfrey, "Monetary Expansion in the Confederacy" (Ph.D. diss., University of Georgia, 1976). See also *Staunton Republican Vindicator*, September 9, 1864.

37. Allen diary, September 7, 1, 1864, Waddell diary, September 14, 1864. For further evidence of collective depression and the endlessness of the war, see Ash, *When the Yankees Came*, 211–15.

38. *OR*, 43(1):695, 719, 917; Jedediah Hotchkiss to Sara Hotchkiss, June 19, 1864, reel 4, Jedediah Hotchkiss Collection, Manuscripts Division, Library of Congress, Washington, D.C.; Waddell diary, September 24, 1864; *Staunton Republican Vindicator*, July 15, 1864; *OR*, 43(1):30. See also Blair, *Virginia's Private War*.

39. *OR*, 43(1):50. Many homes were burned, especially in Loudoun and Fauquier where Lt. Col. John S. Mosby's raiders irritated Sheridan's forces. On August 13, 1864, for example, Mosby's force captured a wagon train near Berryville and a few days later attacked the 5th Michigan. The 5th was sent back to Berryville to burn houses and devastate the farms there. See *OR*, 43(1):822.

40. Harrison diary, August 17, 1864. See also Lucy Rebecca Buck, *Shadows on My Heart: The Civil War Diary of Lucy Rebecca Buck of Virginia*, ed. by Elizabeth R. Baer (Athens: University of Georgia Press, 1997), 301.

41. Micajah Woods to John Woods, September 30, 1864, Micajah Woods to Sabina Woods, September 30, 1864, Woods Papers.

42. *OR*, 43(1):508; Heatwole, *Burning*, 89–115. See also Kepner diary, October 4, 1864, which notes: "To retaliate for the death of Lt. Meigs the buildings near Harrisonburg were burned for miles around."

43. Jedediah Hotchkiss, *Make Me a Map of the Valley: The Civil War Journal of Stonewall Jackson's Topographer*, ed. Archie P. McDonald (Dallas, Tex.: Southern Methodist University Press, 1973), 222, 228–29. Jacob Hildebrand focused most of his diary notes on the concerns of his farm and family, but he did report on the burning in the Valley. He traveled to Winchester in late August to visit his sons in camp. On the way, he observed, "Yankees are burning Every barn they come across that has either hay or grain in it. I seen a good many that were smoking yet as I passed up the Valey Pike." Later in September, when he was home in Augusta, Hildebrand reported that "the Yankee cavalry took possession of Staunton about 3,000 — this afternoon the Yankees burned all the hay near the C.R. Road. I saw them set fire to Mr. J. H. Coiners

hay stacks." And a few days later, he wrote "the Yankees made a General burning of barns in the lower end of this county and the uper end of Rockingham county and also some houses" (Hildebrand, *Mennonite Journal*, 228).

44. *Staunton Republican Vindicator*, July 29, 1864.

45. *OR*, 43(1):30–31, 37–38.

46. Michael G. Mahon's recent account of the Valley campaign suggests that Sheridan inflated his numbers to impress the public and Grant and that the destruction in the Valley had little impact on the overall capability of the Confederacy to wage war. He argues that the Valley was already depleted and no longer supporting the Confederate war effort. Mahon compiles little evidence to support his argument (Mahon, *Shenandoah Valley*).

47. On the responsiveness of Virginia and the Confederacy to citizen concerns, see especially Blair, *Virginia's Private War*, 4–5.

48. Waddell diary, September 26, 1864.

49. Claim of Nancy and Thomas Jefferson, Southern Claims Commission, Augusta County, National Archives and Records Administration, Washington, D.C. The claim for the care of the officer was not allowed, but the claims for the hog and flour were. Nancy and Thomas Jefferson received $42.00 in compensation.

50. Claim of Mordecai Purcell, Southern Claims Commission, Augusta County, quoted in Patrick Maiberger, "Civilian and Military Interactions in Winchester Virginia" (undergraduate thesis, University of Virginia, 2000); claim of Christian Landis, Southern Claims Commission, Augusta County.

51. Claims of David Myers, John Yates, and David W. Landes, Southern Claims Commission, Augusta County (Landes's claim addresses the shooting incident).

52. *Staunton Republican Vindicator*, September 15, 1864; Cochran diary, August, 1864; Amanda Virginia Edmonds diary, June 10, 1864, VHS. See Ash, *When the Yankees Came*, 156–57, for further evidence of Confederate views that the Federal army deluded slaves.

53. Waddell diary, October 10, 1864. See also, Allen diary for Eva Allen's commentary on the loyalty of her servants. On the number of runaways in Virginia during the Civil War, see Ervin L. Jordan Jr., *Black Confederates and Afro-Yankees in Civil War Virginia* (Charlottesville: University Press of Virginia, 1995): 72–90. Jordan, citing a Virginia governmental report, stated that as of 1863, 37,706 slaves out of a total population of 346,848 had absconded successfully. The number only increased in 1864. M. G. Harman, one of the largest slave owners in Augusta County, lost about half of his slaves by early 1865 (Blair, *Virginia's Private War*, 124).

54. Gary W. Gallagher, *The Confederate War* (Cambridge, Mass.: Harvard University Press, 1997): 8–9. Gallagher asserts that the stunning successes of Lee's army in the spring of 1863 created a feeling of invincibility that carried civilian morale to the end of 1864 and perhaps to the end of the war. Gallagher aimed his argument at historians who suggested that class tension, guilt about slavery, and women's growing unease about the war created a loss of will that destroyed the Confederacy. No evidence from the Valley points to loss of civilian "popular will" for these reasons.

55. John T. Cooley to Julia, September 17, 16, 1864, John T. Cooley Letters, VHS.

56. Micajah Woods to John Woods, September 23, 1864, Woods Papers; John Anthony Craig letter, October 15, 1864, VHS; William Francis Brand to Kate Armentrout, September 22, 1864, William Francis Brand Papers, UVA; diary of Capt. James M. Garnett, September 9, 1864, UVA.

57. Waddell diary, September 14, 20, 22, 23, 1864; Henry Chester Parry to his father, September 30, 1864, Henry Chester Parry Papers, VHS.

58. William Wilson to J. Francis Wilson, October 15, 1864, Elizabeth Ann Wilson Papers, UVA; Waddell diary, October 15, 19, 1864.

59. *Staunton Republican Vindicator*, October 28, 1864.

60. William Clark Carson to Jennie, October 23, 1864, William Clark Carson Letters, VHS; William J. Black diary, October 19, 1864, VMI; D. C. Snyder to wife, October 22, 1864, D. C. Snyder Letters. See also Robert Ryland Horne to Mollie Horne, October 29, 1864, Horne Family Papers, VHS, which mentions Early's newspaper address on the conduct of his men.

61. Edward O. Guerrant, *Bluegrass Confederate: The Headquarters Diary of Edward O. Guerrant*, ed. William C. Davis and Meredith L. Swentor (Baton Rouge: Louisiana State University Press, 1999), 559 (October 22), 561 (October 24), 563 (October 27), 564–65 (October 29), 566–67 (October 31, 1864).

62. Waddell diary, November 5, 1864.

63. Jedediah Hotchkiss to Sara Hotchkiss, October 11, November 5, August 20, September 3, 1864, Hotchkiss Collection; Garnett diary, October 26, 1864.

64. Waddell diary, November 12, 15, 1864.

65. Ibid., December 25, 26, 1864, January 16, 18, 26, 1865; Irene Bell, Annie Samuels, and others to Secretary of War Seddon, December 2, 1864, quoted in Gallagher, *Confederate War*, 77.

66. D. C. Snyder to wife, October 26, 31, November 12, December 14, 1864, D. C. Snyder Letters.

67. Allen diary, December 5, 1865.

68. Edmonds Diary, September 25, 1864.

AARON SHEEHAN-DEAN

Success Is So Blended with Defeat

Virginia Soldiers in the Shenandoah Valley

Colonel Edward T. H. Warren of Harrisonburg, Virginia, wrote to his wife frequently during his long tenure as an officer in Virginia's 10th Infantry Regiment. While stationed in Orange County in March 1864, he sent Ginnie a wish that surely represented the thoughts of many Virginia soldiers. "I hope my dear darling it will not be so very long before I can go home and put off the garb of a soldier and put on that of a citizen and be to you a kind affectionate husband and to my dear children a good and indulgent father." Warren looked forward to the time when he could rejoin his family, but he decided that his service would end only when the war ended. His family's secure position in the middle of Virginia's Shenandoah Valley bolstered Warren's commitment to the Confederacy. Although Union forces invaded the Valley repeatedly in 1864, Warren's family and the families of thousands of other Virginia soldiers remained well-fed and protected until late in the year. This security offered crucial reassurance for those men under arms who served away from their homes.[1]

Most historians of the Civil War see the 1864 Shenandoah Valley campaign as an example either of how the North won the war or why the Confederacy lost it. Scholars interested in identifying the ultimately successful aspects of Union military strategy describe the Valley campaign as an integral part of the North's efforts to block Confederate access to the material resources necessary to carry on the war and to confine the Virginia theater to the eastern side of the state.[2] Union commander Ulysses S. Grant's instructions to his subordinates to leave the Valley so barren that "crows flying over it for the balance of this season will have to carry their provender with them" are applied as both the forecast of events to come and proof of the events themselves.[3] Union soldiers did destroy substantial amounts of public and private property in the Valley, but historians too often use the observations of those men to evaluate the reaction of Virginians to that destruction. Northern soldiers' status as hostile invaders seriously compromised their ability to accurately assess the temper of Valley Confederates at this crucial juncture in the war.

For historians interested in explaining how Confederate failures rather than northern successes produced the war's outcome, the 1864 Valley campaign serves as a microcosm for the military defeat and collapse of civilian morale that plagued the Confederacy through its final year. The authors of *Why the South Lost the Civil War* have encapsulated this argument most fully. They assert that "Sheridan's victories over Early in the Shenandoah Valley . . . signaled the beginning of a marked rise in desertion from the Confederate army" and "helped to depress already depleted Confederate morale."[4] Despite their contrasting explanations of the war's course, the interpretations of Union success and Confederate failure do share a common orientation. Both begin with the war's conclusion in early 1865 and look back to the Valley campaign as a place where both historians and historical actors can see the end looming.

Perceiving the events of 1864 through the eyes and ears of Valley soldiers and civilians forces us to abandon the perspective that reads the battles of New Market, Lynchburg, Third Winchester, Fisher's Hill, and Cedar Creek as an inevitable story of declension for Confederate forces paralleling the Confederacy's military losses elsewhere in 1864. This imposed narrative misrepresents the reality of the war and distorts how people at the time understood the fortunes of the Confederacy.[5] From the perspective of citizens and soldiers in and from the Shenandoah Valley, no single narrative existed. Not knowing which battles would receive "names," they judged their prospects for achieving independence against their own history. Virginians and other Confederates had driven off northern troops and held Union policies at bay for three years. For most of the year, 1864 was no different. Confederate forces twice repulsed Union invasions of the Valley, giving Confederate civilians and soldiers strong reasons to maintain their expectations of independence. The battles of late September and October 1864 reversed this trend and left Confederates stunned at their losses. Disorganized and much less certain of the future, Valley Confederates ended the year badly shaken but not resigned to defeat.

The struggle for the Valley began early in the year for both soldiers and civilians. In early January, George Washington Miley, from Shenandoah County in the lower Valley, eyed Union troops uneasily across the upper Rapidan River.

Wishing he had been with his love during the recent holidays, Miley observed that "a Regiment of Yankees emerged from the woods and directed to march directly toward us — Oh! that I could have had at least one shot at them for disturbing my reverie. I longed for them to come a little nearer, but they took good care to keep out of range." Miley's family lived in Mt. Olive, just south of Winchester in territory continually contested by Union and Confederate troops, and later in the same letter Miley gave open vent to his fears. "Oh Tirzah! You can not tell how much anxiety I feel when I'm aware of your being in the enemy's lines," he wrote. "I don't know how soon a beast Butler or some other implacable enemy will be sent among you, who will war against our Mothers, Sisters, and lovers when they once find no other prey. May this never be so. Yet how long our lovely homes will escape the tyranny that reigns at New Orleans, Norfolk and the extending portions of N. Carolina no one can tell."[6]

Miley might have received some solace from observing the complacency with which another Confederate woman handled herself in the presence of hostile troops. Mathella Page Harrison, living about fifteen miles southeast of Winchester in Millwood, blandly recorded in her diary on January 19 that "I reached home today after a pleasant visit. The Yankees frequently dashed in upon us. Once they searched the house for Rebels." As with many other Confederates living in the Valley, Harrison continued her daily routine of visiting family and friends regardless of the occasional presence of hostile troops in the area. Perhaps she drew sustenance from the memories of T. J. "Stonewall" Jackson two years previously and his exploits in eradicating the Federal threats in the area. Or maybe simply living within a short drive of enemy soil had numbed her to the presence of the hated northerners. In any case, Harrison's diary casually mentioned interactions with Union soldiers alongside her daily activities. Like many Virginians, Harrison despised the northern interlopers and at times feared them, but she adapted to their presence and continued to support the Confederacy.[7]

Eighty miles up the Valley from Millwood lay Staunton, home to nearly 4,000 people in 1860 and a thriving commercial center for the region, channeling agricultural goods west across the Allegheny Mountains and down the Valley to markets in southern Pennsylvania. Several vital railroad lines that directed the Valley's resources into the arms and stomachs of Virginia's soldiers intersected in Staunton and made the town strategically important as well.[8] While Mathella Harrison contended with Union troops regularly, those Virginians farther south in the Valley did not, and they continued many of their prewar routines. Jedediah Hotchkiss, who served as the chief cartographer for Confederate forces in the area, spent time early in the year at home near Staunton with his family. On New Year's Day, 1864, he noted in his diary, "Went to Staunton; the day was pleasant in the morning but it turned intensely cold and windy. There were a great many people in Staunton, buying and selling srv'ts."[9]

A year before Hotchkiss penned that entry, President Abraham Lincoln had signed the Emancipation Proclamation, adding a new dimension to the struggle between North and South. But the prospect of the abolition of slavery apparently did not deter southerners' interest in buying or selling slaves, even on New Year's Day. As Hotchkiss revealed, Virginians maintained slavery at the center of their commercial and social lives. This stubborn refusal to recognize the goals of Union policy must have infuriated Lincoln, but for those Virginians who maintained their autonomy from Union soldiers, continuing their antebellum practices demonstrated their confidence that Confederate armies would secure their nation's independence.

For Jasper Hawse, the commissary sergeant for the 11th Virginia Cavalry, the first month of the new year ended auspiciously. On January 30, he wrote in his diary, "Attack & capture a train of 100 Yankee wagons all heavily laden with commissary stores; more than 50 of which were brought to the valley the other were destroyed by the Yankees." Capturing supplies from Union forces meant a slight reprieve from the rigors of foraging and provided Hawse's troops with delicacies like real coffee for which Confederate units had to invent substitutes. The long and usually boring winter interval between campaign seasons made absence from home even harder to bear for many soldiers. After an arduous thirty days of hard marching in the Virginia mountains, Richard Henry Watkins, a captain with the 3rd Virginia Cavalry, found winter comfort in the form of a fresh bath and a warm meal, provided, he playfully informed his wife, by an "old sweetheart of mine" in Harrisonburg.[10]

Like many Virginia Confederates, Warren, Miley, Robinson, and Watkins had volunteered their services almost immediately after Lincoln's call for Union troops in mid-April 1861. While some Virginia men avoided or refused military service, others who were too young at the start of the war waited and served in different capacities before joining the Confederate army. After working in the quartermaster and commissary departments at Hanover Junction, George Quintis Peyton enlisted in the 13th Virginia Infantry Regiment on February 9, 1864. Peyton served the Confederacy until he was captured at the battle of Cedar Creek in late 1864 and sent to the Union prisoner-of-war camp at Point Lookout, Maryland.[11] Other Virginians joined him, some publicly and others privately, in avowing their support for their nation at the start of 1864. "You are a most sensible woman in agreeing to adopt my opinion of the Tax Bills," Colonel Warren wrote to his wife in February. "I consider the tax enormously high but not one cent more than is absolutely necessary. Then the tax is levied on all alike. . . . The tax on bonds operates very hard on some people. For instance, on Mother and Grandma, but if such bonds were not taxed the richest men in the country would escape taxation—I am satisfied that the Bill is a good one because so universal in its application."[12]

George Washington Miley, serving under Warren in the 10th Infantry, gave his impressions of the unit's confidence in a letter to his future wife in late March. Although Miley desperately wanted to transfer to a cavalry regiment, he had reenlisted in October 1863. Many of his comrades seem to have done likewise: "The regiment was [re]formed a few days ago, and, after a brief address by Col. Warren, they were invited to rally 'round our flag, and the response was almost universal. A resolution was adopted by which all who stepped to the front avowed their determination never to lay down their arms while our soil is polluted with Lincoln's hireling crews. Those who did not come forward were old men and entitled to discharges." Miley noted that the reorganization was having the desired effect and that their weakened ranks were now growing again. "Officers and men are constantly returning," he observed. "Besides to see a recruit is no uncommon thing."[13]

Randolph Harrison McKim, a young soldier with the 2nd Virginia Cavalry, chose this interval to resign from the army, not because of a lack of faith in his purpose as a soldier, but rather to retrain himself so he could more effectively serve the men with whom he fought. Years later, he recalled, "In tendering my resignation . . . I stated that I had been 'looking forward to the Christian ministry for the last five years, and for several months had been a candidate for orders in the Protestant Episcopal Church.' I added that it was 'my desire to commence my studies at once at the seminary in order to be prepared for ordination the ensuing spring, at which time it is my purpose to reënter the service in the capacity of chaplain.'" After completing his studies with a minister in Staunton, McKim rejoined his old unit as the chaplain and served with them until the end of the war.[14]

Virginians in and out of military service found reason to look forward to an independent Confederacy and even seemed to relax a little in anticipation of the welcome peace they hoped lay just ahead. William Wirt Gilmer, a farmer from Albemarle County who served with the quartermaster's department and traveled with the 2nd Virginia Cavalry for a good portion of the war, reflected in March 1864, "I have no fear of Rich's falling into the hands of the enemy & if it should! we are then conquered! This country is hard to overrun, harder to beat & hardest of all to hold: we can never surrender while an army is left. [I]t would be nonsence to look for any favours from our guard [?] and brothers; for of all people on earth, brothers are hardest to reconcile, when once aroused & inflamed by collision of arms." Colonel Warren, in a letter home to his wife in Harrisonburg that same month, wrote that "everybody in the army seems to think that this is the last year of the war. Every one is in the finest spirits and confidently expecting an early peace. This is my feeling[.] I have strong reasons for believing this."[15]

Enlisted men shared this outlook as well. John William Carpenter, a private with the 18th Virginia Cavalry, concurred in Warren's assessment of the Confederacy's military prospects. Writing to his wife, Mary, from Rockingham County in mid-March, he stated, "The Yankees are reenforcing at Petersburg is the report but I don't know how true it is and if they are I suppose they will make a move on us in a few days. But I am in the hopes that peace will be made before we have any more fighting to do. The Yankees are fighting amongst themselves and the forin nations and I think that is a true report. The most of the boys thinks that there will be better times before long."[16] Although Carpenter's perception of the state of diplomacy may have been overly optimistic, his beliefs no doubt strengthened his confidence at the start of the new campaigning season.

Confederate civilians also held these hopes, and it gave some of them license to engage in activities usually reserved for the parlor during peacetime. Lt. John H. Jones of the 4th Virginia Infantry received a letter from his "cousin Marcey" in Lynchburg on March 21, 1864, in which she updated him on local gossip and begged him to come home for a visit. Although Marcey also anticipated peace within the year, she exaggerated the psychological status of her countrymen to tease her cousin. "It seems to be that the whole world is so much demoralized that they are not capable of making each other happy, pardon me, of course there are some exceptions, your fair *North Carolinian* for instance would you think me very inquisitive, were I to enquire her name? hope you'll bring her to Va. And let us behold the light of her countenance and judge for ourselves whether she is worthy the disposal of my Cousin's heart."[17]

John Jones, when he received his cousin's double-edged missive, was not the only soldier who found a way to enjoy both his personal and professional commitments. As Union and Confederate armies began preparing for the major spring campaigns in the East, Jedediah Hotchkiss met with Gen. Robert E.

Lee. After the meeting, Hotchkiss noted in his journal, "He said he wanted every man to his post, that we had hard work to do this year, but by the blessing of Providence he hoped it would turn out well. . . . Said he was glad to see me back was pleased that I had been able to attend to duty and yet be often at home." Although Hotchkiss had a more flexible schedule than most soldiers, he was not unique among Virginia Confederates in having successfully reconciled his loyalties to family and nation.[18]

Richard Watkins, who had reassured his wife early in the year that he was being well looked after by an old girlfriend, gave eloquent voice to the conflicting emotions he felt after his third year in the service:

My Precious Mary—I would give anything in the world to see you this evening. I am almost crazy to see you. I think of you and think of you; and I dream of you and dream of you, and wish to see you and long to see you; but the same old long miles still stretch themselves between us, and the days pass by, and pass by, and the cruel heartless war 'drags its slow length along,' and the rigid discipline of the army winds itself around me and contracts and still contracts as if it would wring the last drop of blood out of my heart. . . . When this history of the war is written many brilliant names will adorn its pages, but one whose name will never be mentioned therein, feels that he this day is exercising as much self-denial, in making as great a sacrifice for his country as any living man be he officer or private. And the greatest, the only sacrifice which I realize at all is absence from my Mary and those whom I love.

Like most Virginia Confederates, Watkins understood his duties to family and country as intertwined, for personal and national honor were closely linked. "God grant that I may so bear myself in the battle & in the camp & under all circumstances," he wrote, "as not to bring a reproach upon them [his children] for 'a good name is rather to be chosen than great riches.' "[19]

Colonel Warren, stationed in eastern Virginia and separated from his wife and family like Watkins, experienced similar doubts about how best to manage his competing obligations. In an April 5 letter to his wife Ginnie, he concluded, much as Watkins had, that continued military service would jointly satisfy God, country, and his family:

I must not write so much about you and home—of course it makes me happy, but the remembrance which always follows, that I am in the army and you at home overcomes me with sadness. I think you had better have me elected commonwealth's attorney this spring in May, over Woodson and thus keep me at home. Don't you think Ben and Nate could manage it. It is the only chance of my getting out of the war and to tell the truth I don't believe I ought to want to get out of it so long as the present necessity exists for my staying in it. I dont think you would have half as much respect for me as a civil officer as you have for me as a colonel. And I could not have that you know do you see the only chance is for me to do my duty here and trust in God for success and a speedy termination of the war which everybody seems to anticipate.

Warren decided that staying in the army would fulfill the expectations his wife held for him. From mid-February to early May he wrote her thirty letters, more than one every three days, and all contained long, plaintive memories of their meeting and early romance and his love for her and their children. In late April, Ginnie wrote to let him know that she had planted flowers at home with their daughter's help, and Warren replied that he had sent home a bedstead he had made for a daughter.[20]

For soldiers who could not reach the balance that Warren and Watkins found and who deserted, the consequences could be dire. Henry Robinson Berkeley, serving in an Amherst County artillery battery, wrote this diary entry early in 1864, from winter quarters in Orange County, just east of the Valley: "Slight snow. Saw a man shot to-day for desertion. Poor fellow: His crime was only going home to see after his wife & children. It was his third or fourth offense. His name was Martin. He was buried where he was executed. Did he not die for his country?" Just ten days after Edward Warren affirmed his love for his wife by recommitting himself to the army, another soldier was executed for deserting. Rufus Woolwine, a captain with the 51st Virginia Infantry, noted in his diary, "Lt Col. Wolfe had me to act as Adjt the Regt being formed in Two Battalions to march out to the execution of John Jones — of 30th Batt. (of Grayson) for desertion he was executed at 2 oclock P.M." The event drew the attention of soldiers and served as a clear warning about the results of abandoning one's post. John T. Cooley, a private from Wythe County serving in the 51st, was one of those men whom Capt. Woolwine marched out to witness the execution. Cooley noted, in a letter to his cousin, "A man from Grayson Co by the name of John Jones was shot here last Friday. Another from the Co named Widner will be executed at the same stake tomorrow." While new recruits might have blanched at these incidents, Cooley, by this time a two-year veteran, saw no need to elaborate. Following the two sentences he allotted to the execution, Cooley reported his regiment's position and announced, "Our rations are short, but I will be content while we stay in S.W.Va." For those still in the unit who were not content, the day's lesson may have encouraged them to lie low.[21]

The Confederate army exhibited similar efficiency and control in its efforts to secure food for soldiers. In mid-May, the Confederate quartermaster for central Virginia received a note from General Lee: "'Borrow all the corn you can from citizens and send me at once. If persons holding corn will not let you have it, impress it, I presume an impressment will not be necessary when the magnitude of the stake is thought of. Answer me at once what you can do.'" Lee requested "an answer from Lynchburg, Staunton, and Charlottesville." He also wanted "every artillery horse that can be had. Send by passenger train anything you can get." Lee, hard-pressed by Grant in eastern Virginia, turned to the Valley and the rich lands alongside it for supplies, as he had done since the war's beginning. The response, sent by Maj. H. M. Bell to Maj. Gen. John C. Breckinridge, came quickly and revealed the effectiveness of Confederate impressment and foraging efforts and the relative abundance of goods in the Valley:

I am arranging to send to every part of the country to get corn from the citizens, but as the emergency is great and pressing, I will ship from the corn here belonging to your command all that I can get off by mail train in the morning — say from 600 to 1,000 bushels. As you are in a good grass country, I hope you will be able to subsist without much grain, but I will, if you cannot spare this corn, replace what I take from the corn I hope to borrow from citizens. If you can spare it, I will send all I can get from citizens besides.[22]

Some of those Confederate civilians from whom Major Bell "borrowed" corn might have looked forward to encounters with Union troops which, while more capricious than those with Confederate forces, were sometimes less costly. Mathella Page Harrison, in Millwood, noted on May 10 that Federal troops "met Dr. H. [her husband] several times during the day and at last took his saddle from him. I hear they have taken my horse from Mr. Mitchell's." Harrison inserted this note in her diary alongside references to visiting friends and her concern for her brothers, who served as Confederate soldiers. Levi Pitman, a mechanic living in Shenandoah County just south of Winchester, treated his encounters with Union troops in the same offhand manner. On May 4, in his journal amongst recordings about the work he was doing and visits from family members, he noted that "the Federal troops are again among us."[23]

Indeed, by this time, Union soldiers had pushed up the Valley well past Winchester. Commanded by Maj. Gen. Franz Sigel, a northern force had made its way south into the Valley as far as New Market, where a motley collection of soldiers and youthful volunteers from the Virginia Military Institute, led by General Breckinridge, defeated Sigel and sent him fleeing from the region. Echoing scenes of Stonewall Jackson's outnumbered troops defeating Union forces in the Valley in 1862, this type of humiliation pleased Confederates in the area and reinforced their vision of southern military superiority.

Six days after Sigel's loss, the northern command replaced him with Maj. Gen. David Hunter. In 1862 and 1863, while stationed along the Sea Islands of South Carolina, General Hunter had raised the first black Union regiment but earned little real military experience in a region remote and relatively unimportant for both nations. His appointment to head the Department of West Virginia undoubtedly did little to trouble Confederates in the Valley. The casual references made by civilians to the presence of an invading army revealed a confidence among the Confederate population that bolstered their soldier relatives absent from their homes. Lt. Benjamin Lewis Blackford, who served with the 11th Virginia Infantry but was stationed temporarily in Wilmington, North Carolina, wrote home to his mother in early June 1864. After relating his anxiety over the girl he was courting and expressing relief that his soldier-brothers were still well, he remarked, "By the way I wish you would tell me all about what happened at Edgewood & Dewberry during the Yankee possession." The Blackford matriarch, who had five sons in Confederate military service, lived directly in the path of Hunter's troops, but all her son could muster was a "by the way" reference and a kind of morbid curiosity about the fate of his neighbors.[24]

Hunter initially met with more success than Sigel, defeating (and killing) Brig. Gen. William E. Jones at Piedmont, just east of Staunton, on June 5 and capturing 1,500 Confederate prisoners. Col. E. G. Lee, commanding the 33rd Virginia Infantry, wrote to General Lee with a frank assessment: "We have been pretty badly whipped." Hunter continued up the Valley, occupying Staunton, where he destroyed railroads and manufacturing facilities, before marching to Lexington where his troops burned the Virginia Military Institute. Nearly continuous fighting in early June occupied both sides, and Confederate brigadier general John D. Imboden, a native of Staunton, wrote to Breckinridge on June 11 that he intended to catch Hunter before he took Lynchburg. "My men are in fine spirits, and move with a will," Imboden bragged. They failed, however, to catch Hunter, who by mid-June had reached the outskirts of Lynchburg, where he hoped to destroy the East Tennessee and Virginia Railroad leading to Charlottesville and the fertile fields of the Piedmont.[25]

Lee detached Lt. Gen. Jubal A. Early and the Second Corps from the main force of the Army of Northern Virginia at Petersburg to join Breckinridge at Lynchburg. Eventually reorganized into the Army of the Valley, Early's corps mirrored the diverse makeup of Lee's army, with regiments from North Carolina, Georgia, Louisiana, and other Confederate states. Virginia supplied the main contingent of soldiers for the Army of the Valley, and of these, close to 30 percent were themselves natives of the Valley. For Confederate soldiers from the Valley assigned to defend it from the series of Union invasions, fighting in their own region helped fuse their need to protect their homes with loyalty to their country.[26]

Hunter's slow movement up the Valley gave Early and Breckinridge the opportunity to reinforce Lynchburg. After a brief fight on June 18, Hunter began to retreat west over the Allegheny Mountains into Union territory. Following his expulsion, Hunter occupied Liberty, just west of Lynchburg. Frederick Anspach, a resident of the town, wrote to his brother a week after the occupation and described the destruction Hunter's troops wrought on the town. After watching Union soldiers burn the hospital, two houses, and several bridges, Anspach "left town refugeeing Tuesday night and stayed at Uncle Caleb's." Anspach probably had little use for the verb "to refugee" in his prewar lexicon, but its incorporation into his wartime vocabulary revealed that the practice had become commonplace for residents of the Valley. The disturbance only increased his anger at the North. After celebrating Hunter's eventual defeat at Lynchburg, he wrote, "It is a pity we could not surround and kill, not capture or wound, every scoundrel of them, and if it shall ever be my lot to obtain revenge certainly I have more now to prompt and actuate me than ever before. I shall try to kill the last one of them."[27]

At least one of the Confederate soldiers engaged in the fight against Hunter at Liberty believed his troops had narrowly missed an opportunity to do just that. Buckner Magill Randolph reported that his unit "pushed on rapidly as advanced guard to Liberty where the enemy made a show of themselves. Attacked with Skirmishers, drove them, & started their rear guard moving, was reinforced & drove them through town. With fresh men or suitable Cavalry force could have captured numbers infantry. I don't think very well managed." But Randolph did not dwell on his regrets; following his account of the fight, he noted, "Liberty number of pretty girls & highly exhilerated at our entrance."[28]

In contrast, Anspach seems to have drawn his consolation in more economic terms. In his closing lines, he revealed how little lasting damage Hunter did to his area. "No mills were burnt down in this County that I know of, unless Ball's was. In some places along the road the crops were damaged but not sufficiently to materially injure the abundance, though it will bear hard on individuals. Wheat is ripening—some few are cutting, Ad. is for one. The crop I suppose will be a good yield—corn looks well but needs rain." In fact, the drought to which Anspach refers seems to have done more long-term harm than Hunter's troops.[29]

Robert Conrad, a lawyer from Winchester, traveled through the upper Valley in June, and he too believed Hunter's campaign did little lasting damage to civilian property and crops. News reports in the North and rampant rumors in the South spawned images of mass destruction, but Conrad offered a blunt assessment: "People in the Valley complaining of Yankee outrages . . . saw nothing to compare with our inflictions." Confederate officials concurred with Conrad's sarcastic evaluation. Col. E. G. Lee, reestablished in the Confederate headquarters in Staunton, wrote to the War Department on June 17, 1864, to summarize the effects of Hunter's campaign. He reported the burning of several public buildings and three miles of railroad. Advance warning of Hunter's approach enabled the Confederates "to get off 900 sacks of salt, a large lot of leather, &c. All the ammunition was saved, all the bacon, and most of the quartermaster's stores."[30] Although he predicted that several more weeks of work would be needed to repair the railroad, the telegraph was already back in order. Hunter's defeat at Lynchburg and subsequent expulsion from the Valley proved both an embarrassment for the North (following on the heels of Sigel's losses in the same region two months earlier) and a boon for the South. Repeating the pattern that Lee had established in the eastern Virginia theater, Confederate troops in the Valley drove back a series of Federal advances and protected the rich agricultural region as a main provisioner of both civilians and soldiers.

Hunter's commander, Ulysses Grant was probably more upset than Anspach. Grant had explicitly urged Hunter on several occasions to make the destruction of the Virginia Central Railroad "beyond the possibility of repair for several weeks" his primary goal; Hunter failed to do this before leaving the region. Worse yet, the destruction that Hunter's troops did commit, in Staunton and Lexington, including the burning of former governor John Letcher's home, renewed Confederate hatred for northern troops and added a new reason for soldiers to keep fighting. Thomas Cleveland, an artillerist with the Fluvanna battery, noted in a letter to his wife in late June, "It was truly mortifying to see the destruction at the beautiful Town of Lexington. . . . I believe a great many of our soldiers are determined to avenge themselves yet, but that cannot pay us back."[31]

Indeed, the damage Hunter's troops inflicted did not deter Confederate forces in the Valley, though Buckner Randolph, like most soldier-diarists during the summer of 1864, noted the destruction wrought by northern troops whenever he encountered it. Shortly after his unit left Liberty (no doubt reluctantly), Randolph noted: "Marched at 4 A.M. toward Salem, found Bonsacks large factory & flouring mills burnt[.] Miserable brutes they fear to straggle on account of their disgraceful conduct through our country." George Peyton participated with Randolph in the defeat of Hunter and continued down the Valley under Jubal Early's command. Marching north through Roanoke and Botetourt Counties, Peyton "heard that our officers are going to have a dance at the 'Springs' tonight [Peyton had washed his clothes the previous day at the springs]. If they all looked like me they might call it the dance of the rag man." The officers were hoping to draw partners from a local school, the Hollins Institute for the Education of Baptist Girls. Unlike Peyton, who could only describe the event, Randolph managed to attend. After finding dinner, he noted, "Came by Botetourt Springs found a sort of Soiree going on at femal sem. Went in was introduced by Gen R. Had a very pleasant evening, dancing & promenading."[32]

The next day, Peyton and his fellow soldiers found time to visit the Natural Bridge, a local geological wonder he had never before seen. As his regiment marched north, they received food from civilians along the way, either free or in exchange for services. "After breakfast went to house nearby and started to climb a cherry tree but the owner, a woman objected so I agreed to gather them on shares one half for the other," Peyton recorded. "According I went up the tree ate as many as I wanted. Put same in a basket and came down and divided with the woman."[33] Like Peyton, many Confederate soldiers found the Valley an inviting escape from the harsh siege life they had left behind in Petersburg. For those soldiers who lived in the Valley, the midsummer respite afforded an opportunity to visit friends and family. "Numbers of our Brig. have had an opportunity to get home," Randolph noted, "passing through their section of the country."[34]

Early's troops continued to push down the Valley as Hunter disappeared over the mountains to the west. Indeed, a corporal in the 45th Virginia Infantry wrote to his sister after the engagement at Salem, "I dont think old Hunter . . . will stop running." Robert Young Conrad, the Winchester lawyer who scoffed at Hunter's efforts at destruction, wrote an optimistic letter to his wife from

Staunton in late June that reflected the state of mind of many civilians and soldiers in the Valley at the time. He told his wife that he expected the army to reach Winchester in five days: "This movement seems to be important and promises great results. The force is over 15,000 — with a considerable number of our best general officers, and the pick of men. It will completely frustrate the Yankee plan of reaping our [illegible] harvest in the Valley." Isaac White, a surgeon assigned to the 62nd Virginia Mounted Infantry, concurred with Conrad's assessment in a letter to his wife written at about the same time. Having fought at Lynchburg and on down the Valley, he expressed his perceptions succinctly: "I think our prospects are fine more so than ever."[35]

Conrad's hope that the Confederate army would "frustrate the Yankee plan" testified to the diverse support that the young nation had drawn. A lawyer before the war, Conrad was elected by the citizens of Frederick County, in the lower Valley, to represent them in Virginia's secession convention in early 1861. A staunch Unionist at the time (like Jubal A. Early), Conrad had voted against secession at both opportunities during the convention but reluctantly affixed his signature to the ordinance of secession in May 1861. Having turned fifty-five in 1860, Conrad was entitled, by both age and position, to sit out the war in Winchester. Although he did not serve in the army, Conrad refused to take an oath of allegiance to the United States and was jailed repeatedly by Union officials as a result. This treatment, along with Union occupations of his home town, seems to have transformed Conrad's reluctance to support secession into hatred of the North. Conrad did not undergo that conversion alone; along with his five sons, more than 60 percent of the eligible men of Frederick County joined Confederate armies.[36]

By early July, the Confederates reached Frederick County, having "swept the Valley clean of Federals."[37] The townspeople of Winchester, and the "pretty women and girls" in particular, celebrated the return of Confederate soldiers. Those civilians north of Winchester, in Union territory, felt the hand of the Confederate confiscation machine just as their neighbors to the south had experienced Union raids earlier in the year. On July 3, Early wrote to Breckinridge, "General: Your note of 4 P.M. is just received. You will have secured for the use of the entire army such public stores as may have been left by the enemy. All shoes in the private stores will be secured in like manner. You will seize all other goods in the stores in Martinsburg, and place them in charge of a responsible and competent quartermaster, to be confiscated for the benefit of the Government; and take the most efficient measures to prevent all plundering or private appropriation of these goods or any other captures."[38]

Aside from the need to secure valuable goods, bringing a harder war to those new *West* Virginians, who had abandoned their prewar identity as part of the Old Dominion, helped define the physical borders of the Confederacy. At the same time, commanders in the Valley helped establish the cultural dimensions of Confederate identity in their effort to bolster soldiers' allegiance to their new nation. As Early's forces pushed Hunter's troops out of Lynchburg and proceeded down the Valley, most of the men passed through the town of Lexington and saw the grave of the late Confederate general Stonewall Jackson. Henry Robinson Berkeley was one of those soldiers who marched past what was becoming a Confederate shrine: "June 25 1864. Saturday. Passed through Lexington, all the Infantry filing by Stonewall Jackson's grave." Many of Berkeley's comrades made similar notes in their diaries and letters home, where the image of successful Confederate soldiers paying homage to their fallen leader could be repeated and absorbed into the emerging national culture.[39]

In July, Early's troops advanced north out of the Valley into Maryland, where they swung east, defeated a Federal force near Frederick in the battle of the Monocacy, and headed south toward Washington. Early's troops drew within sight of the Capitol but did not make a serious attempt on the heavily fortified city. Nevertheless, Lincoln was forced to call up local militia units before regular reinforcements arrived from Grant's army. Confederate papers chronicled the campaign closely, and civilians and soldiers gloated over the juxtaposition of Union troops stuck in the mud outside Petersburg and Early's forces nimbly cutting through northern territory to harass the Federal capital. Union commanders reluctantly recognized that Confederate troops had dominated northern forces in the Valley thus far in the year. Even as Grant vainly urged Hunter to "make all the Valley south of the Baltimore and Ohio Road a desert," he received a communication from Assistant Secretary of War Charles A. Dana that confirmed how ineffective Union forces had been against Early's men. On July 15, Dana noted that Early's units had reentered the Valley and assessed the Confederates' recent campaign: "The enemy will doubtless escape with all his plunder and recruits, leaving us nothing but the deepest shame that has yet befallen us."[40]

Following the raid on Washington, George Peyton and the 13th Virginia Infantry returned to the Winchester area, where they engaged in periodic skirmishes with Union troops and practiced a gentle form of food requisition on their Confederate neighbors. "Went foraging with John Moore," wrote Peyton. "After a long wait got a breakfast of Corn hoe cakes and fried meat at a Mr McCormicks near Berryville." This routine continued through July, with Pey-

This woodcut from *Frank Leslie's Illustrated Newspaper* shows skirmishing along
the works near Washington on July 12, 1864. For many civilians in the Valley, Early's
campaign across the Potomac seemed to continue a pattern of Confederate success in the
Shenandoah theater. Paul F. Mottelay and T. Campbell-Copeland, eds., *The Soldier in
Our Civil War*, 2 vols. (New York and Atlanta: Stanley Bradley Publishing Company,
1893), 2:297.

ton stopping once to sleep at a friend's house (though he confessed to sleeping
in the front yard rather than the feather bed his host offered). William Gilmer,
also traveling and fighting occasionally in the Valley, found an opportunity to
return to his home in Albemarle County for clean clothes. While at home he
noted that his wheat yield would be of smaller quantity but higher quality than
normal. Like many Virginia soldiers, Gilmer balanced his duties as a soldier
with his duties at home and helped ensure through either letters or periodic
visits that planting and harvesting continued on a regular schedule. Perhaps
because of the scarcer yield he anticipated or because of his evaluation of war
conditions, Gilmer wrote an article for the *Charlottesville Chronicle* toward the
end of July encouraging people to plant turnips, a good food for refugees.[41]

From a military perspective, the recent fighting in the Valley had worked as
Confederates hoped.[42] In late July, Robert E. Lee wrote to Confederate secretary of war James A. Seddon with a report on Early's operations for the preceding month. Early had accomplished the goals Lee had set for him: to drive

Hunter away from Lynchburg and march down the Valley as far as possible in the hope that Grant would withdraw troops from Petersburg to protect Washington. "General Early's report will explain his operations," Lee observed, "and the value of the results obtained need not be further stated at present, as there are yet some to be expected in the future. I may, however, say that so far as the movement was intended to relieve our territory in that section of the enemy, it has up to the present time been successful." Richard Watkins, under Early's command in the lower Valley, went beyond Lee's cautious optimism: "We are now between Charleston & Winchester all well & much cheered by the good news from Petersburg in the papers of the 27th. . . . Truly we must be approaching Peace, for Peace follows Justice, and a sense of justice seem to return, to the people both South and North."[43]

Virginians had successfully weathered two Union invasions in the first half of 1864, and they were preparing to meet the next challenge. "We find the people in the Valley still loyal," recorded Watkins. "I am greatly surprised at this for a large majority of them are without slaves very many never having owned them and their habits & mode of living is almost Yankee. They are the people for apple-butter in the world. They seem to live upon apples and milk and cold bread. . . . At the same time, they have the largest quantity of fat hogs." Not all Confederate soldiers had the time to stop and appreciate the sociology of Valley life. Henry C. Carpenter, with the 45th Virginia, wrote home to his sister in Bland County from camp near Berryville in mid-July. "I have had a very hard time of it lately," he reported. "We have not had one days rest for the last month and we have not been out of the sound of Artillery for the last 15 days and I know that Bro John and Ed sees much easier time in Prison than we do in the field some times I get so tiard marching that I am foolish anought to wish that I was with them."[44]

On August 9, William Gilmer complained in his diary about low prices the government was paying farmers, averring that "In our country, land & labor constitute the back-bone of the Gov. break down the farming interest, & you conquer us at once." Although Ulysses S. Grant and Maj. Gen. Philip H. Sheridan (just given full command in the Valley) were not privy to Gilmer's notes, they grasped this truth at the same time. They laid plans to eliminate the Valley as a source of food and fodder for the Confederacy, seeking to break the will of Confederate civilians and to starve out Confederate soldiers. For Valley residents facing their third Union general of the year, the situation closely resembled that of eastern Virginia in 1862 and 1863, when Robert E. Lee drove back a series of unsuccessful attacks as Lincoln searched for an effective military leader. On the same day Gilmer lodged his protests about government price fixing, Isaac White, the 62nd Regiment's chief surgeon, explained his perception of Confederate prospects and asserted his willingness to engage in the harder war that both Yankees and Confederates seemed to be waging: "The Lord I think is on our side & I hope he will soon put a stop to the diffusion of blood; for I & all of us are tired of it & desire peace (honorable)[.] I suppose you have seen an account of the burning of Chambersburg I am opposed to burning; but I supposed they deserved it & if they desire to retaliate we can play that game with them & play it well but I do hope such warfare may cease."[45]

Confederate soldiers in the Valley continued to live comfortably. George Peyton, whose unit contended with Union soldiers in the lower Valley, noted on August 30, "During this month we have been 'on the go' near all the time. Have hardly had time to bathe or wash our clothes. Have lived very well on fresh beef, mutton, pork, all the time besides apples and roasting ears."[46] John Hoge, in the 8th Virginia Cavalry, found time to stay with friends and family in Salem for a few days late in the month and took the opportunity to trade in his weary horse for a new one. Randolph McKim, the young man who resigned his post with the 2nd Virginia Cavalry to pursue training as a minister, made good on his original commitment to the Confederate army and rejoined his company on August 23. He immediately organized daily prayer services that lasted through the fall, recording in his diary that "attendance was 'very good.' "[47]

Life for civilians in the lower Valley turned harder and more dangerous by late August, as Sheridan and his force moved into the region and began burning mills and barns.[48] On August 17, Mathella Page Harrison in Millwood described her experiences:

> Night has closed at last on this day of horrors. Years almost seem to have rolled since I opened my eyes this morning. The first sound that greeted my ears was the rumbling of Yankee waggons. . . . At nine o'clock yankee pickets were stationed on every hill. Fires of barns, stockyards, etc. soon burst forth and by eleven, from a high elevation, fifty could be seen blazing forth. The whole country was enveloped with smoke and flame. The sky was lurid and but for the green trees one might have imagined the shades of Hades had descended suddenly. The shouts, ribald jokes, awful oaths, demoniacal laughter of the fiends added to the horrors of the day.

Harrison's observations confirmed the wisdom of William Gilmer's advice in his July newspaper article urging people to plant root crops that could survive attacks like these. Harrison immediately recognized that the loss of foodstuffs would hurt the most, especially for families in the area who already lived on spare resources:

> They demanded food when they had just applied the torch to the provisions of the year, and indeed, years, for now the seed which would have been sown, has been destroyed. In almost every instance every head of stock was driven off. Those young animals that refused to go were shot down. Near a farm where light fires were blazing, Caster [Custer?] and his staff sat exulting over the ruin they had wrought. Large families of children were left without one cow. In many of the barns were stowed in and around all kinds of farming implements, waggons, plows, etc. and in no instance did they allow anything to be saved. The loss is inestimable and unpardonable in these times, situated as we are, communications with our friends so difficult, and no trade with the enemy even if we asked for it.[49]

Sheridan's tactics stunned and angered Valley citizens but did not uniformly drive them to despair. Indeed, some civilians reacted by recommitting themselves to the defense of the Confederacy. Twenty-eight women of Harrisonburg sent a petition to Secretary of War Seddon asking for authority to create a regiment of female soldiers. Charles Minor Blackford, a staff officer stationed at Maj. Gen. George E. Pickett's headquarters near Petersburg in late August, wrote to his mother with instructions for how she should prepare for the coming winter:

> A letter I received a day or two since from Mr. Robt. Saunders informs me he has made some arrangement for purchasing you some flour or wheat with gold—and by so doing it will cost you only $120 a barrel in Confederate money which is comparatively cheap—I wrote him when to apply to Miller for the money & wrote to Miller he *must* provide it. . . . The flour being purchased coal & wood are the next things—and then you and Mary & Peggy—and Sue when she returns must keep a close watch & buy everything eatable you see that will keep during the winter, especially cabbage & potatoes.

This type of preparation revealed a commitment to continuing the war, even though it entailed sacrifice and deprivation. The soldiers also made a significant commitment. From August 7 to November 28, Union and Confederate forces met in 113 clashes in the middle and lower Valley.[50]

Confederate soldiers from Valley counties facing Grant in the eastern part of the state had to sustain themselves on letters from home and news reports about the progress of Federal troops in their home region. Early's successes may have partially satiated their desire to be present in the Valley and to protect their own families, but no doubt each man carefully considered the risks, and dishonor, of desertion against the dangers confronting his family. Confederate soldiers from the Valley who participated with Jones, Breckinridge, and Early in defending their own communities found themselves in the position of fighting for home and country simultaneously. The decision, by Lee and other Confederate military leaders, to deploy troops from the region to defend the Valley proved not only a wise choice in a tactical sense (these men often intimately knew the territory over which they fought) but also in terms of morale. In effect, by being assigned to defend their own region, Confederate commanders removed the most significant incentive to desert among Valley soldiers. In contrast to the common assumption that Confederate desertion increased steadily as the war progressed, statistics from three regiments composed of troops from Valley counties reveals that rates peaked in early 1862 and declined throughout 1864 (see figure 1).[51]

By early September, Confederate soldiers believed that military events were building toward a climactic battle. William Clark Corson wrote his future wife Jennie from near Winchester on September 9: "I have been unable to write regularly since we came to the valley for the command is rarely ever still twenty-four hours at a time. The campaign is a perfect mystery to me; Gen. Early is either advancing or retreating and the cavalry is never out of sight of the enemy skirmishing daily." Corson suspected that Early was trying to draw Sheridan into a trap, but Union troops refused to take the bait.[52]

Like the three preceding years, 1864 had been harder on civilians in the lower Valley than on those in many parts of Virginia. Corson noted the tension between civilians' desire for protection and their ability to support the army. "The people in the Valley are obliged to have us here and say they hope the army may remain here all winter," he wrote. "That will be impossible however as it is too far to haul supplies from Staunton. We have threshed out most of the wheat and secured nearly all the hay. The corn crop though late and small is very promising." Corson, like many other Confederate soldiers serving the region, felt well prepared for whatever conflict might come: "The boys are all well. My health is excellent. I can eat 14 ears of corn for supper and sleep in my saddle as soundly as a dead pig in a shuck-pen." John T. Cooley, of the 51st Virginia Infantry, needed a little more to sustain him than Corson required, but he also anticipated hard fighting to come. "We are energized in a war which we must *fight out*," he affirmed, "'And the harder the storm the sooner it will be

James E. Taylor titled this sketch "Sheridan falling back through Charlestown, fire from the Enemies field pieces sweeping the street on morning of the 22nd of Aug — and stampeding the Union cavalry." It portrays Union forces in the way residents in the Valley saw them for most of 1864 — in retreat — and helps reveal why Sheridan's victories in September and October surprised so many Confederates. Courtesy of the Western Reserve Historical Society, Cleveland, Ohio.

over.' I can stand the storm very well if I get plenty to eat, and can enjoy good health, and be permitted to peruse the thoughts of *my highly esteemed and affectioned Cousin Julia.*"[53]

Robert Thurston Hubbard Jr., serving with the 3rd Virginia Cavalry in the Valley, noted that Confederate civilians had continued to support their troops late into the year. As his unit entered Clarke, in the lower Valley, Hubbard noted "thanks for a kind Providence and a nobly generous self-sacrificing patriotic people we were met by the citizens of Clarke with every exhibition of joy and with the assurance that with all the meanness & vandalism of the infernal yankees they hadn't succeeded in destroying everything & of what was left if it pleased God we should have our full share." Elisha Hunt Rhodes, a Union officer with the 2nd Rhode Island Infantry, had been detailed with his unit near Charles Town and Clifton in early September. He noted in his diary that "the farms are well-cultivated." For Jedediah Hotchkiss, well south in Staunton, the situation remained quite bearable. In mid-September, he described "a fine cool day. The people are busy sowing grain. Grass is growing finely."[54]

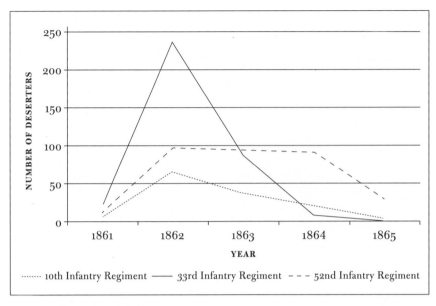

Figure 1. Desertion in Selected Valley Units

Both the busy people and the soldiers in the Valley drew satisfaction from Lee's stalemate with Grant on the eastern side of the state. They were proud of Lee's army and its blocking the larger Yankee force. The loss of Atlanta troubled many in the region who had closely followed Gen. Joseph E. Johnston's maneuvers against Sherman all summer, but for Richard Watkins that meant a longer rather than a shorter war:

> And Atlanta has fallen. Very well it is ordered by an all-wise Being and we have had too many reverses during this long war to retire at that. Would you to see the apparent unconcern manifested by our soldiers. "Well, Atlanta has gone up," and very little more is said about it. They go on whistling and singing & cooking. Tis in reality though a right serious matter and I fear will result in a prolongation of the war. It certainly affords encouragement to the North to persevere. And will no doubt add to our privation, both at home and in the army. But tis no good ground for despondency or discouragement as to the final result.[55]

On September 19, Sheridan's troops defeated Early's Confederates in the battle of Third Winchester. Early's little army fell back to Fisher's Hill, south of Strasburg, but were routed again on September 22. The soldiers in the Army of the Valley experienced their hardest fighting yet at Winchester, and many fled in fear during the fight at Fisher's Hill. Although the losses alarmed civilians in the area, they had lived through the cycle of defeats, occupations, and victories several times and knew their forces were still in the field and ably led. Chatting with civilians in Winchester after the battles, Rhodes noted that he had "met a lady a few days since who has had three brothers killed and one maimed for life since the war began. She is still very bitter and desires to have the war go on."[56]

That bitterness began to infiltrate the sensibilities of many of the diarists and letter writers living and fighting in the Valley in late 1864, but as with Rhodes's Winchester discussant, few showed an interest in abandoning the Confederacy. Soldiers who participated in the fighting conveyed news of their defeat to relatives and friends with shame but did not foresee more losses in the future. William Pettit, a lawyer from Fluvanna County, explained the unfortunate sequence of events at Winchester to his wife and concluded his account by reassuring her that they had retreated to a "line we fortified a month ago and shall give the Yanks a good drubbing if they attack us here. Outside the artillery, our loss was very slight." Many seemed too surprised at having lost to Union forces to think about anything else. Following the battle at Winchester, Rhodes "visited the Court House and talked with some of the Rebel officers. They were much depressed in spirits, for their defeat was a great surprise to them." The shock no doubt came from the sense of optimism and security that had built up over the spring and summer as Confederates defeated Union forces and enjoyed free rein in the Valley.[57]

Buckner Randolph, who had traveled home to Halifax for a brief furlough, returned to the Valley on September 25 and observed from his camp just below Port Republic that "the army [was] much broken & demoralized." Still, he noted that several days later his unit helped push the Yankees back across the Shenandoah River during a skirmish. Settled into camp in Waynesboro a few days following, Randolph reflected on the course of the fight at Fisher's Hill and its effect on the army in a lengthy letter to his mother:

When the enemy attacked, the cavalry gave way with so little resistance that we were scarcely aware of it, before the two divisions of the enemy had completely turned our left flank & come sweeping down the mountain at right angles with our breastworks & almost in our rear, at the same time a vigorous attack was made in front & our men became panic stricken & gave way in a disgraceful rout. I blush to say it, though I know some of the bravest of the brave were mixed up with it. . . . Our men are still considerably demoralized but they are recovered their confidence. They are not so much dispirited themselves, as that they have lost confidence in each other, I think.[58]

In this period of crisis and questioning, Confederate soldiers witnessing the destruction of the Valley's resources struggled to reorganize not just their army but also their conceptions of the changing nature of the war and of their role in it.[59] Richard Watkins, in a letter to his wife in early October from outside Staunton, spoke first of the damage he saw, the "night sky reddened with the glare from burning barns," and then of how he understood the shift in Union tactics. "The Yankees are seriously endeavoring to starve us into submission," he stated. "They are burning all the grain & all the mills within their reach." Recognizing that "the defeat of Early is the most serious disaster which Virginia has experienced during the war," Watkins agreed with his wife that they faced "the darkest hour of the war, but a just God still rules and controls the affairs of nations, and 'vengeance is mine I will repay saith the Lord.'" His final line of advice combined passive acceptance of events beyond their control with a deliberate choice to maintain his commitment to their new nation: "Let us not trouble ourselves too much about it, but go along like grown up folk and do our duty."[60]

Concern over loved ones in Sheridan's way and despair over the destruction often turned into anger against the North. William M. Willson, stationed at Fort Gilmer outside Richmond, corresponded in mid-October with his brother Francis, a member of the 14th Virginia Cavalry in the Valley. Anxious to know his brother's condition after the fighting around Winchester, Willson wrote, "I dislike very much to hear of our arms meeting with so many reverses there, where victory has always heretofore crowned them. It is almost enough to make the blood boil in ones veins to hear of the atrocities & vandalism Sheridan has committed. How much greater then must be the effect upon those who daily witness it with their own eyes? Surely the South can never be subdued by men who commit such outrages! The vengeance of a just God will most certainly overtake them sooner or later! God grant that we may be speedily ennobled to drive them from our borders."[61]

By the beginning of October, Confederate soldiers felt the pinch of scarcity their civilian friends and neighbors in the Valley already knew. George Peyton found it harder to obtain food and resorted to trading his tobacco for apples or grapes. On October 7, he recorded in his journal, "Got a letter from home written on the 3rd. . . . The Yankees had made around to Rapidan and burnt up everything there[.] Our house the mill the station and every vacant house in the place." Peyton's nonchalance over the destruction of his house came partly from the knowledge that his family had moved to another house on a neighbor's property. He maintained his focus on fighting the enemy and left managing the destruction at home to his family. Like many other soldiers and civilians in the Valley, Peyton could also take some comfort from the continual harassment which Confederate lieutenant colonel John S. Mosby and his partisan rangers inflicted on Union troops in the lower Valley.[62]

Confederate troops marched and fought continuously for the next several weeks. A weary John Hoge wrote this entry in his diary: "Oct 1: Marched to Staunton, staid there a while, and moved down the valley. It rained very hard all evening. We pitched camp about 3 P.M., built fires of rails, and were drying ourselves when the well known notes of the bugle said 'Boots & saddles.' With reluctance we obeyed, got ready & marched out into the road, stopping till all was ready & then marched on down the Valley." Even with this schedule, Virginia soldiers managed to keep some attention focused on the condition of their families and their homes. Andrew Jackson Dawson, a quartermaster from Albemarle, wrote to his wife in late October from Buckingham County: "I am in the hopes that Silver has been able to get the corn in from the fresh land on which I had the wheat seeded before I left, it was very important that it should bee got in soon as it was very much marked [?] down." He concluded the letter with instructions on how to feed the hogs and beef cattle for winter.[63] Albemarle fell under the control of Union forces in mid-October, but Dawson's focus, like that of many in central Virginia, was on maintaining an adequate supply of food and not on the perhaps temporary occupation by northern soldiers.

In addition to the physical and psychic strains of frequent combat, the Confederate losses at Winchester and Fisher's Hill generated recriminations between units and exacerbated latent tensions between the different branches of service. John Anthony Craig wrote to his mother in Lunenburg County from Maj. Gen. John B. Gordon's headquarters near Strasburg, in the lower Valley. "Since our late reverses in the valley we have had a hard time of it," he stated in language similar to that in numerous other letters from Early's infantrymen. "The greater portion of our Cavalry is utterly worthless, that is allows our infantry to be flanked on every occasion and has come near being the ruin of the army which is composed of troops that were considered the flower of the 'Army of Northern Virginia.' The troops have quite recovered their morale, and now occupy the same position at Fisher's Hill from which we were so disgracefully stampeded a few weeks ago." William Corson, of the 3rd Virginia

Cavalry, recognized the responsibility that his branch of the service held for the loss. He admitted to his wife that the rout at Fisher's Hill had been "the most complete and disastrous cavalry stampede of the war." Brimming with anger, Corson, who found time to write because he had been assigned to escort wounded men to Confederate hospitals, chafed to find another opportunity to smite the Yankees.[64]

Several weeks later, Confederates momentarily succeeded in exacting revenge upon Sheridan for his victories in September. The battle of Cedar Creek, fought near Middletown on October 19, opened with Confederate assaults that drove two-thirds of Sheridan's Army of the Shenandoah back in disorderly retreat. But the victory was lost when Sheridan rallied his fleeing troops, reversed the tide of the fighting, and soundly defeated Early's troops for the third time in a month. Daniel A. Wilson, secure in New Market after the battle, felt overwhelmed by the enormity of the disaster at Cedar Creek and by the confusing reversal that had occurred. He wrote a lengthy letter to his former colonel, now working in the War Department in Richmond, describing the battle: "Success is so blended with defeat—the shout of victory so mixed with the cry of 'all's lost' that I find myself totally unable to sift the details and place them upon paper in anything like form or method." Like many soldiers, Wilson reveled in the surprise that Early's troops had sprung on the Union forces, but after describing how Confederates had stopped to loot the Union camp, Wilson was unable to account for how quickly they broke when the Union forces returned. He did not blame Early; on the contrary Wilson closed with this assessment of his commander and their prospects for the future: "I believe he has done more than almost any other Lt. Genl. or officer other than Lee or Beauregard could have done with this army. The fact is—there is no army here. The very best *material* is indeed here, and in sufficient force or numbers, to drive Sheridan across the Potomac *if it was reorganized*. Until this is done it can not be depended on again."[65]

During the battle at Cedar Creek, Union forces wounded and captured Buckner Randolph, but he successfully escaped several days later. Writing in his diary from a hospital in Staunton, Randolph echoed both Wilson's comments about the need to reorganize the army and Corson's eagerness to resume the fight. "The army of the Valley has been inactive," he noted, "at least as far as campaigning & military moves are concerned I hear & hope . . . that they have been active in organizing & drilling, have also recruited considerably. I rather anticipate & hope for another fight, to retrieve the glory of our Valley army." While Wilson remained confident in Early, William Corson expressed

James E. Taylor's sketch titled "Custer Striking Early's Infantry on Hupp's Hill and
Making big Captures—QM Sergt David S. Scofield—5th NY Cavalry—Capturing a
Standard" conveys the ignominious end of the battle of Cedar Creek for Early's army.
Courtesy of the Western Reserve Historical Society, Cleveland, Ohio.

sarcastic doubts: "Early is now at New-Market, his army I suppose demoralized. I think he ought to sell out to another firm." Still, Corson assumed the war
would continue. Despite having his horse shot out from beneath him during
Cedar Creek, he had "been keeping up with the regiment on foot ever since I
got back. I shall come home after [a new] horse in a few weeks." Similarly, John
Cooley was embarrassed to admit to his "dear cousin" that Confederate troops
fled during the fighting at Cedar Creek, but in his letter written two weeks after
the battle, he closed by noting, "Everything indicates a winter campaign. Our
army is being recruited every day."[66]

Artillerist Henry Robinson Berkeley participated in the fight at Cedar Creek
and lost contact with his unit during the battle. Following the battle, he spoke
with members of a cavalry unit who said "if they were in my place that they
would take a furlough & go home for a week or two. I told them that I did not
think that this was a time for men to be going home, that General Early needed
every man, which he could possibly get—& many more than he had, & that if
we did not stand to our guns, the yanks might get to our homes before we did."
Berkeley had begun his diary entries for 1864 asking whether a soldier executed
for deserting to see his family died for his country. He scattered references to
the purpose of the war throughout his notes, mostly vague references to "our

future" or the fate of "our people." By the conclusion of the terrible year of fighting, he had refined his concern, focusing on the fate of his and his friends' "homes," and yet he remained convinced that the most effective way to defend those homes, and the loved ones inside them, was to stay in the army and continue fighting.[67]

Not all Valley Confederates found the energy or desire to rededicate themselves to the Confederate cause. Captain Rufus Woolwine, who had marshaled the men of the 51st Virginia Infantry to witness the execution of a deserter in April, recorded in December a challenge to Confederate authority that would have been unimaginable earlier in the year: "Dec. 6th 45th Va. Regt. Refused to Drill 51st went to arrest those that refused to drill. My Co. took possession of their arms. 7th I took command of the 45th." By the following day, Woolwine could report "all calm," but he remained in command of the rebellious regiment until December 18.[68]

Woolwine's experiences with Confederate military discipline revealed the substantial deterioration of the Army of the Valley. The April execution of a lone man elicited little sympathy from his comrades. By December, the soldiers of the 45th, who had experienced exceptionally high casualty rates during the summer fighting and suffered the humiliation of defeat three times in the fall, adopted a decidedly more independent-minded approach toward military order.[69] The breakdown in Confederate authority lasted less than two weeks, but it reveals that at least some of the soldiers in the Valley, who had begun the year expecting victory, had begun to harbor doubts about the likelihood of eventual success.

Most Valley Confederates, soldier and civilian alike, recognized that Union troops had finally accomplished their objective of eliminating the ability of regional farms to supply Confederate forces in the state. Both sides acknowledged that no more major battles would be fought in 1864. Still, many Confederate soldiers found themselves occupied in military actions against Federal units throughout November and into December, and the individual victories which Confederates scored over Union troops bolstered their sagging hopes.

Robert E. Lee wrote to Secretary of War Seddon ten days after Cedar Creek, describing a situation typical of military action that had been occurring all year in the Valley. "General Early reports that the enemy attacked General Lomax's forces at Milford on the 25th instant with one brigade and two pieces of artillery and were repulsed," stated Lee. "The next day they were attacked with two brigades and six pieces of artillery and were again driven back. General Lomax reports our loss very slight. Colonel Mosby reports that since the advance of the enemy up the Manassas Gap Railroad he has killed, wounded, and captured over 300, his own loss being 4 wounded and 1 captured." Jedediah Hotchkiss made notes of nearly daily fighting for the first half of November. His last entry for the month reveals the sustenance which men drew from the continued fighting in the Valley: "A fine, pleasant day. We heard of General Rosser's capture of New Creek; 800 prisoners, 8 pieces of artillery, &c. (This is my 36th birthday; how rapidly the years glide away! God grant that they may not have been spent in vain)."[70] Without the foresight to anticipate the defeat of Lee outside Petersburg the following spring, few of the Virginians living and serving in the Valley knew enough to despair.[71]

When it became apparent that fighting would continue, even Mathella Page Harrison, whose dramatic description of the burning and destruction of Millwood conveyed a sense of complete defeat, relished subsequent Union losses in the area. Her final journal entry, from two days after Christmas 1864, noted (accurately) that a large body of Yankees "have returned from their raid on Gordonsville, an unsuccessful one I am glad to say."[72]

William Wirt Gilmer of Albemarle closed his entries for 1864 on an even more committed note:

The last day of this eventful year. Gov. Vance of North Carolina in an address to his people says: — I command and adjure all good people, whither by law subject to mil. duty or not, who are able to stand behind breastworks & fire a musket of all ages & conditions to rally at Wilmington. The man who hangs back now & consoles himself with the much abused and mean-spirited plea that he can 'be of more useful service at home' will find it hard to make us believe that he is not pleading the cause of cowardice or disloyalty. The country needs their help, & if not rendered they must own that their souls are only fitted to enjoy the freedom purchased with other men's blood! — Good . . . if this will not bring them, let the slow finger of scorn, the hissing & mocking of all fall on them; And yet we see many here in Albemarle & all over the Confederacy who hang back & eat good things, drink good things, wear fine clothes & refuse to help the poor! — the soldier! or our beloved Country! — God forgive them . . . I never can. — This conduct will fall as a stigma on all who act thus, & on their children's children to remotest generations. — Rise my countrymen & fight for your birth-right, fight trusting in God & victory will at length come.

The winter is hard supplies scarce yet we can live on little, & give away much . . . Never surrender our beloved Country. . . . Fight even die for it if necessary! — "[73]

Gilmer's injunction probably echoed the feelings of many Valley residents and soldiers. Despite their reluctance to support the state's secession, Valley men supported the Confederate armies by volunteering in high numbers. Valley residents organized companies that enlisted 65 percent of the men between the ages of eighteen and fifty who lived in the region.[74] While men from the Tidewater region enlisted at an even higher rate, the two-thirds of Valley men who enlisted and stayed in the army illustrate the significant depth of support this region gave to the Confederacy.[75] Henry Robinson Berkeley, who served in a Virginia artillery battalion through the whole war, dreamed of this new world even in the midst of his unit's retreat up the Valley in late September. "We are ready to measure strength against with these vile yanks," he affirmed. "I don't see why they dont go home & leave us alone, that is all we ask. But here they are with a vile mercenary army, burning our towns, destroying our crops, desolating our country and killing our people. I wish all the yanks & all the negroes were in Affrica."[76]

Given Virginia soldiers' experiences in the first three years of the war, their continued support through 1864 should come as no surprise. Soldiers from the Valley, and especially those who fought there as well, derived enormous confidence from their victories over Yankees for most of the year.[77] They began the year not merely hoping for victory but expecting and assuming that independence lay just ahead. Many Confederate soldiers in the Valley fought to protect their homes as well as their new nation. In late October, after Sheridan's defeat of Early, most Confederates grew quite concerned about their prospects but did not abandon loyalty to their fledgling republic. Rather, hostility toward the Union accounted, in part, for the continued dedication that many people displayed through the defeats of the fall. Soldiers and civilians frequently revealed a genuine attachment to the Confederate nation; Union depredations in 1864 exacerbated already deep-seated antipathies toward the North. Soldiers remained members of their home communities throughout the war, reflecting the same fears and hatreds as civilians. Like Henry Robinson Berkeley, William Gilmer, and the fiery civilian Mathella Page Harrison, Charles Minor Blackford reacted with enthusiastic anger rather than despair when he heard that Union troops were approaching his home town of Lynchburg in June.

From camp near Richmond, he wrote to his wife, "To think that my whole family, wife, child, mother, sister, are probably this very morning subjected to the insults and indignities of a band of freebooters makes my blood boil."[78]

Confederate identity, like that in most fledgling nations, drew great strength from its opposition, and the people who built that identity drew effectively on their rivalry with the Union to mask internal dissent and conflict. Though not free from the tensions that marked most Confederate communities, Valley Confederates directed their energy against the North as the most dangerous and immediate enemy.[79] The losses of the fall severely shook the confidence of Valley Confederates, but by intensifying their dislike for the North, Sheridan's campaign of destruction had the unintentional effect of bolstering Valley citizens' endorsement of Confederate war aims.[80]

By late 1864, Valley citizens knew a hard winter lay ahead, and many began laying in supplies they had been cultivating through the year. Where Union or Confederate troops had seized grain or corn, Confederate civilians turned to root crops like cabbages, turnips, and onions that were easily preserved. Although by November most northern troops were again confined to the extreme northern end of the Valley, civilians treated the interlopers with more fear and suspicion than they had at the beginning of the year. Some Confederate soldiers criticized the decisions made by their commanders and expressed concern over the behavior of their comrades, but few had given up hope for the Confederacy altogether. Rather, the military losses in late fall and the barn- and mill-burning campaign led by Sheridan fired the hatred of Confederates for Federals to a harder temper, producing a sullen sheen of bitterness and mistrust that lasted well into the postwar years.

Appendix: Demographic Profiles

Name	Residence	Antebellum Regiment	Occupation	Family	Age	Service Record
Henry Robinson Berkeley	Amherst	Kirkpatrick's Battery	student	single		Enl. 5/17/61; POW 3/2/65
Benjamin Lewis Blackford	Lynchburg	11th Inf.	bookseller	single	29	Enl. Sgt. 4/23/61; in chg. Liberty Hosp.
Charles Minor Blackford	Lynchburg	2nd Cav.	lawyer	single	31	Enl. 1st Lt. 5/13/61; Cpt. 8/27/61; Jgd. Adv. 12/22/62
Henry Carpenter	S.W. Va.	45th Inf.				Enl. 4/6/62
John W. Carpenter	Washington	18th Cav.		wife	21	Enl. 12/3/62; Courier 10/20/64
Thomas Cleveland	Fluvanna	Fluvanna Arty.	wheelwright	wife+3	43	Enl. 8/6/61; Sgt. 2/10/62; sick 3/4/62, 6/29/62, 10/19/63, 3/2/65
John T. Cooley	Wythe	51st Inf.		single		Enl. 4/9/62; POW 3/2/65
William Clark Corson	Cumberland	3rd Cav.		wife	27	Enl. 5/14/61; sick 3–6/64
John A. Craig	Lunenburg	21st Inf.		single		
Andrew Jackson Dawson	Albemarle	_ master; 2nd Cav. [?]	farmer	wife+1	56	
William W. Gilmer	Albemarle	_ master	farmer			
Jasper Hawse	Hardy	11th Cav.	farmer/ teacher		29	Enl. 3/10/62
John Milton Hoge	Mercer	8th Cav.			20	Enl. Sgt. 8/12/62; Pres. 12/5/64
Jedediah Hotchkiss	Staunton	Topographical Engineer, 2nd Corps, A.N.Va.	cartographer	wife+2	36	
Robert Thurston Hubbard Jr.	Cumberland	3rd Cav.	student		25	Enl. 5/18/61; Lt. 4/62; wd. 4/1/65; prld. 4/65

Name	Residence	Regiment	Antebellum Occupation	Family	Age	Service Record
John H. Jones	Rockbridge	4th Inf.	student		21	Enl. 6/2/61; 2nd Lt. 8/30/62; wd. 5/5/64; surr. 4/9/65
Randolph Harrison McKim	Baltimore, Md.	2nd Cav.	student	single	22	Enl. 7/21/61; Chpl. 8/23/64; surr. 4/9/65
George Washington Miley	Woodstock	10th Inf.		single	24	Enl. 6/25/61; POW 5/12/64
William Pettit	Fluvanna	Fluvanna Arty.	attorney	wife+4	38	Enl. 3/22/62; Sgt. 5/16/62; Lt. 4/30/64; disch. 2/65
George Quintis Peyton	Orange	13th Inf.		single	21	Enl. 2/9/64; POW 10/19/64; rlsd. 6/16/65
Buckner Magill Randolph		49th Inf.				
Edward T. H. Warren	Harrisonburg	10th Inf.	lawyer	wife+3	35	Lt. Col. 7/1/61; Col. 5/8/62; WIA 5/3/63; KIA 5/5/64
Richard Henry Watkins	Prince Edward	3rd Cav.		wife	39	Enl. 6/24/61; Lt. 4/62; Capt. 10/62; wd. 10/31/62; wd. 10/9/64; ret. 3/31/64
Isaac White	Upshur	62nd Mt. Inf.	doctor	wife+2		POW 12/10/64
Daniel A. Wilson	Kanawha	22nd Inf.				Enl. 5/8/61; Corp. 6/6/61; dsrt. 9–10/62
Rufus James Woolwine	Patrick	51st Inf.			24	1st Lt. 5/5/62; Capt. ?; POW 3/4/65

Sources: Information drawn from manuscript collections cited in this essay; *The Roster of Confederate Soldiers, 1861–1865,* ed. Janet B. Hewett (Wilmington, N.C.: Broadfoot, 1995–); *Virginia Regimental History Series* (Lynchburg, Va.: H. E. Howard, 1967–) and 1860 Virginia Manuscript Census records.

Acknowledgments

I would like to thank Stephen Cushman, William G. Thomas, Edward L. Ayers, and Gary W. Gallagher for their support and their assistance on the many drafts of this essay.

Notes

1. Edward T. Warren to Virginia Warren, March 12, 1864, Warren Papers, Albert and Shirley Small Special Collections Library, University of Virginia, Charlottesville [repository hereafter cited as UVA].

2. Herman Hattaway and Archer Jones, *How the North Won: A Military History of the Civil War* (Urbana: University of Illinois Press, 1983), 572–76, 585–87, 600–603, 617–20; Brooks D. Simpson, *America's Civil War* (Wheeling, Ill.: Harlan Davidson, 1996), 172–73, 184–85. Mark Grimsley's book on "hard war" chronicles the evolution of northern policy over the course of the war and argues that Union general Philip Sheridan's tactics in the Valley explicitly "sought to detach Southern civilians from their allegiance to the Confederate government." Grimsley ultimately concludes that Union tactics were "discriminate and roughly proportional to legitimate needs," including operations in the Valley, which displayed a "directed severity" (Mark Grimsley, *The Hard Hand of War: Union Military Policy toward Southern Civilians, 1861–1865* [Cambridge: Cambridge University Press, 1995], 3, 219, 178). Popular histories of the campaign focus heavily on Sheridan's destruction of resources and often foreground the campaign's conclusion, emphasizing the inevitable nature of Union victory. See Edward J. Stackpole, *Sheridan in the Shenandoah: Jubal Early's Nemesis* (1961; reprint, Harrisburg, Pa.: Stackpole Books, 1992), and Thomas A. Lewis, *The Shenandoah in Flames: The Valley Campaign of 1864* (Alexandria, Va.: Time-Life Books, 1987).

3. U. S. Grant to Henry W. Halleck, July 14, 1864, in U.S. War Department, *The War of the Rebellion: A Compilation of the Official Records of the Union and Confederate Armies*, 127 vols., index, and atlas (Washington: Government Printing Office, 1880–1901), ser. 1, 37(2):301 [hereafter cited as *OR*; all references are to ser.1]. This is one of Grant's most famous lines and has come to epitomize the new style of warfare that he and Sheridan designed and executed in the Valley. The context for this dispatch and a reading of the whole text undercuts the traditional assumption that Grant's orders were implemented fully and without difficulty. Grant wrote the note just as Gen. Jubal Early was concluding a raid on Washington that embarrassed the Lincoln government. Grant desired that Gen. David Hunter (not Sheridan in this dispatch) follow Early back into the Valley "as rapidly as the jaded condition of his men will admit." Grant's use of the subjunctive in his famous command reveals his low expectation that Hunter would achieve in midsummer what he had failed to accomplish in June: "[Early] *should* have upon his heels veterans, militiamen, men on horseback, and everything that can be got to follow to eat out Virginia clear and clean as far as they go" (emphasis added).

4. Richard E. Beringer, Herman Hattaway, Archer Jones, and William N. Still Jr., *Why the South Lost the Civil War* (Athens: University of Georgia Press, 1986), 435, 320. Gary W. Gallagher has provided the most recent summary of the opposite view, that the Confederate defeat can best be explained on the battlefield. See Gallagher, *The Confederate War* (Cambridge, Mass.: Harvard University Press, 1997). James M. McPherson has also criticized "internalist" explanations for Confederate loss. See McPherson, "American Victory, American Defeat," in *Why the Confederacy Lost*, ed. Gabor S. Borritt (New York: Oxford University Press, 1992), 16–42.

5. The omnipresence of conflict in the Valley over the year made it difficult for both soldiers and civilians to visualize the long-term consequences of events they experienced firsthand and consequently made the meaning of the year's events much less certain for participants.

6. George Washington Miley to Tirzah Amelia Baker, January 10, 1864, George Washington Miley Papers, Virginia Historical Society, Richmond [repository hereafter cited as VHS].

7. Diary of Mathella Page Harrison, January 19, 1864, Mathella Page Harrison Papers, UVA.

8. For details on Staunton's strategic and logistical value, see Gary W. Gallagher, "The Shenandoah Valley in 1864," in *Struggle for the Shenandoah: Essays on the 1864 Valley Campaign*, ed. Gary W. Gallagher (Kent, Ohio: Kent State University Press, 1991), 2, 5.

9. Jedediah Hotchkiss, *Make Me a Map of the Valley: The Civil War Journal of Stonewall Jackson's Topographer*, ed. Archie P. McDonald (Dallas, Tex.: Southern Methodist University Press, 1973), 191. New Year's Day was a typical time for buying and hiring new servants; Hotchkiss mentions this practice in earlier years as well. The robust Augusta County economy drew strength from the hiring and leasing of slave labor throughout the prewar period. See J. Susanne Simmons and Nancy T. Sorrells, "Slave Hire and the Development of Slavery in Augusta County, Virginia," in *After the Backcountry: Rural Life in the Great Valley of Virginia, 1800–1900*, eds. Kenneth E. Koons and Warren R. Hofstra (Knoxville: University of Tennessee Press, 2000), 169–85.

10. Patrick Bowmaster, ed., "A Confederate Cavalryman at War: The Diary of Sergeant Jasper Hawse of the 14th Regiment Virginia Militia, the 7th Virginia Cavalry, the 17th Virginia Cavalry Battalion, and the 11th Virginia Cavalry," unpublished manuscript, VHS; Richard Henry Watkins to Mary Purnell (Dupuy) Watkins, January 1, 1864, Richard Henry Watkins Papers, VHS.

11. Details of the service records for these men can be found in the appropriate volumes of the Virginia Regimental History Series published by H. E. Howard of Lynchburg, Virginia. See William Marvel, *A Place Called Appomattox* (Chapel Hill: University of North Carolina Press, 2000), for evidence of men, especially those of the upper class, who avoided service.

12. Edward Warren to Virginia Warren, February 25, 1864, Warren Papers.

13. George Washington Miley to Tirzah Amelia Baker, undated [between March 20 and April 12, 1863], Miley Papers.

14. Randolph Harrison McKim, *A Soldier's Recollections: Leaves from the Diary of a Young Confederate, With an Oration on the Motives and Aims of the Soldiers of the South* (New York: Longmans, Green, 1910), 209. (The book is also available on-line at: ‹http://metalab.unc.edu/docsouth/mckim/mckim.html›.)

15. William Wirt Gilmer diary, late March 1864, Gilmer Family Papers, UVA; Edward Warren to Virginia Warren, March 9, 1864, Warren Papers. Gary W. Gallagher has argued persuasively that soldiers in the Army of Northern Virginia held high morale at the opening of the 1864 campaign in Virginia; see "'Our Hearts Are Full Of Hope': The Army of Northern Virginia in the Spring of 1864," in *The Wilderness Campaign*, ed. Gary W. Gallagher (Chapel Hill: University of North Carolina Press, 1997), 36–65. High morale among troops assigned to the Valley should not be surprising because many of them were drawn from the forces commanded by Lee in the Eastern Theater. However, the optimism expressed by Valley soldiers, and especially their perceptions of the war as it developed over the year, seem shaped specifically by their experiences in the Valley.

16. John William Carpenter to Mary Christina Burns, March 12, 1864, Burns Family Papers, VHS.

17. Cousin Marcey to John H. Jones, March 21, 1864, Marcey Family Papers, UVA.

18. Hotchkiss, *Make Me a Map*, 198–99.

19. Richard Henry Watkins to Mary Purnell (Dupuy) Watkins, April 12, 1864, Richard Henry Watkins Papers, VHS.

20. Edward Warren to Virginia Warren, April 5, 19, 1864, Warren Papers. Warren's service record is summarized in Terrence V. Murphy, *10th Virginia Infantry* (Lynchburg, Va.: H. E. Howard, 1989).

21. Diary of Henry Robinson Berkeley, January 8, 1864, Henry Robinson Berkeley Papers, VHS; Rufus James Woolwine diary, April 15, 1864, Rufus James Woolwine Papers, VHS; John T. Cooley to Julia Ann (Cooley) Price, April 21, 1864, Cooley Family Papers, VHS. In discussing the issue of desertion in Confederate armies, historians need to address more clearly the role that executions and other less severe punishments played in keeping men in the ranks. During the early phase of the war, most men enlisted with genuine enthusiasm; as the war ground on, military and civilian authorities worked hard to keep men in their units even if their enthusiasm waned.

22. H. M. Bell to J. C. Breckinridge, *OR*, 70(1):737. Lee was a strong advocate of impressment when necessary to feed the army at this stage of the war. See Gallagher, "'Our Hearts Are Full of Hope,'" 48–49.

23. Harrison diary, May 10, 1864; Levi Pitman journal, May 4, 1864, Levi Pitman Papers, UVA.

24. Benj. Lewis Blackford to Mrs. Wm. M. Blackford, June 7, 1864, Blackford Family Letters, UVA.

25. *OR*, 37(1):7, 151 (E. G. Lee to R. E. Lee, June 5, 1864), 155 (John D. Imboden to John C. Breckinridge, June 11, 1864).

26. Of the 555 Virginia companies that composed Early's Army of the Valley, 157 (or 28.3 percent) were organized in Valley counties. Scholars have defined the Valley in a variety of ways. I have adopted the regional boundaries identified by the Virginia

state auditor in response to a request from the 1861 Virginia Secession Convention. The report is Doc. No. 37, table A, in George H. Reese, ed., *Journals and Papers of the Virginia State Convention of 1861*, 3 vols. (Richmond: Virginia State Library, 1966), 3:[unpaginated; documents arranged in numerical order]. The following counties make up the Valley: Alleghany, Augusta, Bath, Berkeley, Botetourt, Clark, Craig, Frederick, Hampshire, Hardy, Highland, Jefferson, Morgan, Page, Pendleton, Roanoke, Rockingham, Shenandoah, and Warren.

27. Frederick Anspach to Robert Anspach, June 23, 1864, Anspach Family Letters, UVA. For a history of the battle of Lynchburg, see George S. Morris and Susan L. Foutz, *Lynchburg in the Civil War: The City — The People — The Battle* (Lynchburg, Va.: H. E. Howard, 1984).

28. Buckner Magill Randolph diary, June 19, 1864, Randolph Family Papers, VHS.

29. Frederick Anspach to Robert Anspach, June 23, 1864, Anspach Family Letters. References to the summer drought can be found in the Harrison and Gilmer collections previously cited. See also George Quintis Peyton diary, George Quintis Peyton Papers, UVA; Marcus Blakemore Buck diary, UVA; and Thomas Cleveland to Bettie Cleveland, July 18, 1864, in Ellen Miyagawa, ed., "The Boys Who Wore the Gray: A Collection of Letters and Articles Written By Members of the Fluvanna Artillery, 1861–1865," *Bulletin of the Fluvanna County Historical Society* 42 (October 1986):79.

30. Robert Young Conrad to Elizabeth Conrad, June 21, 1864, Robert Young Conrad Papers, VHS; E. G. Lee to Gen. S. Cooper, *OR*, 37(1):152–54.

31. Grant to Halleck, May 25, 1864, *OR*, 37(1):536 (see also the dispatches from Assistant Secretary of War Dana to Secretary of War Stanton and from Grant to Maj. Gen. George G. Meade, both June 5, 1864, in, *OR* 36[1]:89–90); Thomas Cleveland to Bettie Cleveland, June 28, 1864, in Miyagawa, ed., "Boys Who Wore the Gray," 75.

32. Randolph diary, June 21, 22, 1864; Peyton diary, June 22, 1864. Peyton's diary appears to have been written some time after the war, but he makes reference at the start to having used an original journal which he kept during his service. I have noted where he made specific references to using outside sources to reconstruct the sequence of battles.

33. Peyton diary, June 27, 1864. During this same period, Randolph noted, "We have fared elegantly on milk, butter, etc." See Randolph diary, June 27, 1864. For similar evidence of soldiers living rather well during this period, see J. Tracy Power, *Lee's Miserables: Life in the Army of Northern Virginia from the Wilderness to Appomattox* (Chapel Hill: University of North Carolina Press, 1998), 95.

34. Randolph diary, June 27, 1864. Other diarists noted their own or their comrades' visits with friends and family during this period. See journal of John Milton Hoge, late August and September 12, 1864, John Milton Hoge Papers, UVA; Berkeley diary, June 19, 1864; and Randolph diary, September 23, 1864.

35. Henry C. Carpenter to "My Dear Sister," June 22, 1864, Henry C. Carpenter Papers, Special Collections Department, University Libraries, Virginia Tech, Blacksburg. [repository hereafter cited as VT]. (The letters are also online at: ⟨http://spec. lib.vt.edu/mss/hccarptr.htm.⟩); Robert Young Conrad to Elizabeth Conrad, June 28, 1864, Conrad Papers; Isaac White to Mary Virginia (Day) White, June 27, 1864, Isaac

| AARON SHEEHAN-DEAN

White Letters, VT. (The letters can also be viewed online at: ⟨http://spec.lib.vt.edu/mss/white/white.htm⟩.)

36. J. E. Norris, ed., *History of the Lower Shenandoah Valley* (Chicago: A. Warner, 1890), 571–73. Using the Virginia Regimental History Series and the population schedules for the 1860 U.S. Census, I have compiled the absolute numbers and the proportions of eligible men who served in Virginia units from each county in the state. This material appears, in aggregate form, in figure 1 of Aaron Sheehan-Dean, "'Give the Yankees Hell': Enlistment and Service in the Virginia Infantry" (paper, annual meeting of the Southern Historical Association, Louisville, Kentucky, November 9, 2000). For a contrary interpretation of loyalty toward the Confederacy among Frederick County residents, see Michael J. Gorman, "'Our Politicians Have Enslaved Us': Power and Politics in Frederick County, Virginia," in *After the Backcountry*.

37. Gallagher, "Shenandoah Valley in 1864," 9.

38. Early to Breckinridge, July 3, 1864, *OR*, 71(2):591.

39. Berkeley diary, June 25, 1864. For additional observations of this practice, see Randolph diary, June 25, 1864, and Peyton diary, June 25, 1864. J. Tracy Power quotes several soldiers from other units who noted their passing by Jackson's grave (Power, *Lee's Miserables*, 93–94). I am drawing on the work of Drew Gilpin Faust, who argues that "nationalism is contingent; its creation is a process," in *The Creation of Confederate Nationalism: Ideology and Identity in the Civil War South* (Baton Rouge: Louisiana State University Press, 1988), 6. The practice of marching Confederate soldiers by Jackson's grave offers a dynamic counterpart to William DeHartburn Washington's painting "The Burial of Latane," which hung in the Virginia state Capitol at Richmond. Faust describes the effects of paintings from this heroic genre: "In their portrayal of virtue, personal sacrifice, and heroism as the essences of national greatness, these works invoke Christian iconography to extend a quasi-religious dimension to their subject matter; they are the visual counterparts to the transcendent language of the era's nationalist rhetoric" (*Creation of Confederate Nationalism*, 70). The process that Berkeley, Randolph, and Peyton observed accomplished the same thing on a wider scale by offering Confederate citizens heroic martyrs whom they could cherish. Daniel W. Stowall has recently explored the religious meaning of Jackson's death among Confederates. See Daniel W. Stowall, "Stonewall Jackson and the Providence of God," in *Religion and the American Civil War*, eds. Randall M. Miller, Harry S. Stout, and Charles Reagan Wilson (New York: Oxford University Press, 1998), 187–207. Although Stowall also sees Confederates creating a process of "corporate cultural ritual" in memories of Jackson's death, he reads these efforts as the prelude to how Confederates interpreted their eventual loss to the North. My sense is that during the war Confederate military leaders, and soldiers as well, used Jackson's image and memory to predict and model victory. Charles Royster makes a similar point in his analysis of the meaning of Jackson's death for his fellow soldiers, arguing that "even in death [Jackson's presence would] help to win Confederate independence." See Charles Royster, *The Destructive War: William Tecumseh Sherman, Stonewall Jackson and the Americans* (New York: Knopf, 1991), 204.

40. Dana to Grant, July 15, 1864, *OR*, 37(2):332.

41. Peyton diary, July 18, 1864; Gilmer diary, July 5, 28, 1864.

42. Gary Gallagher summarizes Early's accomplishments, highlighting his raid on Washington in July and the unsettling effect it had on northern politics, in "Shenandoah Valley in 1864," 11.

43. Robert E. Lee, July 19, 1864, *OR*, 37(1):346; Richard Henry Watkins letter, August 30, 1864, Watkins Papers.

44. Richard Henry Watkins letter, September 9, 1864, Watkins Papers; Henry C. Carpenter letter, July 19, 1864, Carpenter Papers. Watkins was correct that "a large majority have never owned slaves," and in comparison to Virginia's Piedmont region, Valley families held far fewer slaves. But according to the 1860 U.S. Census Population and Agricultural Schedules, 17 percent of Valley households owned slaves, a reasonably high proportion in comparison to other southern places. See Simmons and Sorrells, "Slave Hire and the Development of Slavery in Augusta County," for an example of the prominence of slavery in one Valley county.

45. Gilmer diary, August 9, 1864; Isaac White, August 9, 1864, White Letters.

46. Peyton diary, August 30, 1864. Evidence of the abundance of food at this time in the Valley abounds in most soldiers' accounts. Henry Robinson Berkeley noted in his diary on September 1 from Winchester, "We are getting an abundance of nice & ripe apples now. I weigh more now than I ever did before in my life." See also Power, *Lee's Miserables*, 105, which highlights the role that farmers in the Valley played in providing food and other crops to Confederate armies.

47. Hoge journal, late August 1864; McKim, *Soldier's Recollections*, 236.

48. See Gallagher, "Shenandoah Valley in 1864," 13–18, for more detail on Grant's decision to send Sheridan to the Valley and for a cogent summary of the fall campaign between Sheridan and Early.

49. Harrison diary, August 17, 1864.

50. Gallagher, *Confederate War*, 77; C. M. Blackford to Mrs. Wm. M. Blackford, August 28, 1864, Blackford Family Letters; *OR*, 43(1):8–11. In *Lee's Miserables*, 146, J. Tracy Power plays down the strategic consequences of these skirmishes and focuses on the declining morale among Early's notoriously ineffective cavalry units.

51. Explaining desertion requires considering a number of variables, including many specific to the company to which soldiers belonged, let alone individual predispositions toward service. See Kevin Conley Ruffner, "'A Dreadful Affect Upon Good Soldiers': A Study of Desertion in a Confederate Regiment" (M.A. thesis, University of Virginia, 1987) for an excellent study of desertion that examines a wide array of factors bearing on men's decision to remain in service. I drew the data on desertion figures from the unit histories of the 10th, 33rd, and 52nd Infantry regiments. See Murphy, *10th Virginia Infantry*, 121; Lowell Reidenbaugh, *33rd Virginia Infantry* (Lynchburg, Va.: H. E. Howard, 1987), 106; Robert J. Driver Jr., *52nd Virginia Infantry* (Lynchburg, Va.: H. E. Howard, 1986), 87. The following counties organized companies that served in these regiments: Page, Shenandoah, Augusta, Rockingham, Hampshire, Madison, and Frederick.

52. William Clark Corson to Jennie Hill Caldwell, September 10, 1864, William Clark Corson Papers, VHS. John Anthony Craig makes a nearly identical assump-

tion about Early's presumed course of action. See John Anthony Craig to Ann Parke (Jones), October 15, 1864, John Anthony Craig Papers, VHS.

53. William Clark Corson to Jennie Hill Caldwell, September 10, 1864, Corson Papers; John T. Cooley to Julia Ann (Cooley) Price, September 17, 1864, Cooley Family Papers (emphasis in the original).

54. Notebook of Robert Thurston Hubbard Jr., UVA (Hubbard composed his "Reminiscences of the Civil War" beginning in late July 1865); Elisha Hunt Rhodes, *All for the Union: The Civil War Diary and Letters of Elisha Hunt Rhodes*, ed. Robert Hunt Rhodes (New York: Vintage Books, 1985), 172; Hotchkiss, *Make Me a Map*, 228.

55. Richard Henry Watkins, September 8, 1864, Watkins Papers.

56. Power, *Lee's Miserables*, 149–61; Rhodes, *All for the Union*, 181.

57. William Pettit to Arabella Speirs, September 21, 1864, in Miyagawa, "Boys Who Wore the Gray," 83; Rhodes, *All for the Union*, 178.

58. Randolph diary, September 25, 1864; Buckner Magill Randolph to "Dear Mother," September 29, 1864, Randolph Family Papers.

59. William Thomas's essay in this collection explores the reactions of Valley civilians to the changing nature of the war and to the changing behavior of Confederate soldiers.

60. Richard Henry Watkins, October 3, 1864, Watkins Papers.

61. William M. Willson to J. Francis Willson, October 15, 1864, Elizabeth Ann Willson Papers, UVA.

62. See Rhodes, *All for the Union*, 186, 188, and Dennis E. Frye, "'I Resolved to Play a Bold Game': John S. Mosby as a Factor in the 1864 Valley Campaign," in *Struggle for the Shenandoah*, 107–26.

63. Hoge journal, October 1, 1864; Andrew Jackson Dawson to Milly B. Dawson, October 27, 1864, Dawson Papers, UVA.

64. John Anthony Craig to Ann Parke (Jones), October 15, 1864, Craig Papers; William Clark Corson, October 13, 1864, Corson Papers.

65. Daniel A. Wilson to Col., October 21, 1864, Daniel A. Wilson Papers, VHS.

66. Randolph diary, November 14, 1864; William Clark Corson, October 23, 1864, Corson Papers; John T. Cooley, October 30, 1864, Cooley Family Papers. J. Tracy Power also notes Early's efforts to reorganize and retrain units under his command following the loss at Cedar Creek (Power, *Lee's Miserables*, 175–76).

67. Berkeley diary, October 19, 1864. See Gallagher, *Confederate War*, 40, for a similar comment from another soldier in Early's army in late 1864.

68. Woolwine diary, December 6, 1864. There is no mention of the episode in the *OR*, but the regimental history of the 45th Infantry does briefly describe the event as Woolwine narrated it. See J. L. Scott, *45th Virginia Infantry* (Lynchburg, Va.: H. E. Howard, 1989), 51–52.

69. For evidence of the 45th's high casualty rates, see the report by Henry G. Cannon, the brigade inspector for Smith's brigade to which the 45th was assigned, in *OR*, 43(1):596. The regimental historian attributes the soldiers' behavior to frustration over their underequipped camp at New Market. The final straw was the lack of appropriate

winter clothing and a request from their commander to drill in the snow. See Scott, *45th Virginia Infantry*, 52.

70. Lee to Secretary of War James A. Seddon, October 29, 1864, *OR*, 43(1):553; Hotchkiss, *Make Me a Map*, 246.

71. Mark Grimsley makes the opposite case, arguing that "Sheridan's operations in the Valley produced not only an economic effect on Confederate supply, but also a psychological effect on Virginia civilians." He quotes a Vermont soldier who observed that Valley Confederates had begun "to feel that to hold out longer is to fight against inevitable destiny." As in this instance, Grimsley's evidence that Virginians were worn out and willing to quit comes from northern soldiers' observations, including Sheridan himself, who had good reason to exaggerate the effect of his triumphs. See Grimsley, *Hard Hand of War*, 167–68, 175–78, 183–85. Similarly, Hattaway and Jones quote Sheridan's October 7, 1864, dispatch to Grant in which he enumerated the destruction accomplished by his troops in order to evaluate Sheridan's "success" (Hattaway and Jones, *How the North Won*, 619). Without contextual information about the number of barns and livestock at the time, the economic effect of Sheridan's raids cannot be accurately assessed. William Thomas's essay in this volume offers quantitative evidence from the Confederate perspective on the effect of the 1864 campaigns that is at odds with Sheridan's assessment. Thomas's analysis of the damage done by Hunter and Sheridan to Rockingham County concludes by noting that county officials estimated their "losses represented less than a quarter of the county's production levels in 1860." In order to interpret the psychological reaction of Valley Confederates to the destruction (and the possibility of a concomitant decline in nationalist enthusiasm for the Confederacy), whatever its absolute scale, the reports of Union officers must be balanced by firsthand accounts from Virginians who experienced the raids.

72. Harrison diary, December 27, 1864.

73. Gilmer diary, December 31, 1864.

74. These figures are drawn from my own research. See tables 1.1 and 1.2 in Aaron Sheehan-Dean, " 'Give the Yankees Hell': Enlistment and Service in the Virginia Infantry." For a detailed examination of Virginia's secession, and especially of the debate between Unionists and secessionists in the Valley, see Daniel W. Crofts, *Reluctant Confederates: Upper South Unionists in the Secession Crisis* (Chapel Hill: University of North Carolina Press, 1995).

75. Men in Tidewater counties organized enough companies to enlist 75 percent of the eligible men from that region (tables 1-1 and 1-2 in Aaron Sheehan-Dean, " 'Give the Yankees Hell': Enlistment and Service in the Virginia Infantry").

76. Berkeley diary, September 23, 1864.

77. Kurt O. Berends has recently offered another explanation for why Confederate soldiers may have remained optimistic about the likelihood of victory until the very end of the war. The religious military press (RMP) of the Confederacy, which provided voluminous reading material to soldiers, adopted relentlessly positive interpretations of all battles, even those the Confederacy lost, and continued to predict imminent victory until the last weeks of the war. More substantively, Berends shows

that by articulating the religious dimensions of the conflict, RMP editors gave soldiers a way to understand military defeats as transient temporal setbacks that provided opportunities for atonement and repentance, which God would reward with ultimate victory (Kurt O. Berends, "'Wholesome Reading Purifies and Elevates the Man': The Religious Military Press in the Confederacy," in *Religion and the American Civil War*, 148).

78. Charles Minor Blackford to Susan Leigh Blackford, June 13, 1864, in Charles Minor Blackford III, ed., *Letters from Lee's Army* (1947; reprint, Lincoln: University of Nebraska Press, 1998), 255. The cliché of "boiling blood" and the theme of unbridled anger against the North surfaces frequently in soldiers' writings at the time. See materials in the collections of William Wilson, William Corson, Frederick Anspach, and Lewis M. Blackford.

79. Class, regional, and gender conflicts plagued most Confederate communities, as they did those in the North, throughout the war. The evidence I have seen, however, indicates that during crucial periods of the war, these tensions receded in the face of the threat posed by the Union military. Stephen Ash makes a similar argument for parts of the "Occupied South." See Stephen Ash, *When the Yankees Came: Conflict and Chaos in the Occupied South, 1861–1865* (Chapel Hill: University of North Carolina Press, 1995).

80. William Tecumseh Sherman's campaign through Georgia and South Carolina in late 1864 and early 1865 is the most famous example of a campaign of hard war against civilians. Much of the literature argues that Sherman's campaigns produced psychological devastation to match economic infrastructural damage, and ample evidence suggests that northern troops destroyed a great deal more property and equipment in the Deep South than they did in the Valley. Yet much analysis of Sherman's success at inflicting psychological damage upon Confederates reveals the same problem that weakens accounts of Sheridan in the Valley; namely, it relies overwhelmingly on northern soldiers' impressions of Confederate morale. See, for example, Royster, *Destructive War*, 4–33, 328–32, 339–42, and Grimsley, *Hard Hand of War*, 190–204. For a contrary view based on a close reading of Confederate sources, see Jacqueline Glass Campbell, *When Sherman Marched North from the Sea: Resistance on the Confederate Home Front* (Chapel Hill: University of North Carolina Press, 2003).

JOAN WAUGH

New England Cavalier

Charles Russell Lowell and the Shenandoah Valley Campaign of 1864

U nion cavalry officer Charles Russell Lowell epitomized New England's ideal soldier in the Civil War. "I do not think there was a quality," declared an admiring Maj. Gen. Philip H. Sheridan, "which I would have added to Lowell. He was the perfection of a man and a soldier." Brig. Gen. Wesley Merritt, Lowell's immediate superior during the 1864 Shenandoah Valley campaign, said that "a more gallant soldier never buckled on a saber. His coolness and judgment on the field was unequalled." Col. George B. Sanford, a fellow cavalryman, provided another warm commendation, describing Lowell as "an officer of singular merit and great gallantry," who was "quite young . . . of unusually fine appearance, and most courteous manners." Sanford ended his summation of Lowell by adding, "He commanded the respect of all who knew him, and in his own brigade was regarded with the warmest admiration and affection." By the time of the 1864 Valley operations, the ambitious and conscientious twenty-nine-year-old Lowell had compiled an admirable military record. His aggressive fighting against Lt. Gen. Jubal A. Early's forces near Rockville, Maryland, in July 1864 had impressed General Sheridan, who assigned Lowell to command the Reserve Brigade in Merritt's First Division of cavalry in the Army of the Shenandoah. Sheridan's decision soon bore fruit, as Colonel Lowell proved himself a first-rate combat leader in the battles of Third Winchester and Tom's Brook. Lowell's heroic actions at Cedar Creek on October 19, 1864, and death the next day from wounds received in the battle spurred northern papers to eulogize him as the "Beau Sabreur" of the United States. While Lowell fought at Cedar Creek, a commission was signed promoting him to brigadier general. Lowell's family, friends, comrades, and contemporaries mourned his death and memorialized his life. They believed his service demonstrated perfect sacrifice and courage, ennobling the terrible bloodletting that continued unabated. Charles Russell Lowell emerged, as did his brother-in-law, Col. Robert Gould Shaw of the 54th Massachusetts Infantry, as one of New England's greatest martyrs to Unionism.[1] Today, students, faculty, and visitors can contemplate a marble bust of Lowell by Daniel Chester French in Memorial Hall on the beautiful grounds of Harvard College.[2]

In reality, Lowell's career as a soldier from 1861 to 1864 was far from perfect. Like most mid-level officers of the Civil War, he had to learn from the ground up how to make men obey his orders and respect his leadership. His distinguished family lineage, Harvard education, and scholar's command of literature and philosophy meant little to soldiers on the battlefield. Rather, repeated demonstrations of courage in battle, an aggressive tactical approach, a willingness to bear the hardships of camp and campaign, and a concern for the welfare of his men shaped his reputation. Lowell's words reflected his deepest belief: "A man is meant to act and to undertake, to try and succeed in his undertakings, to take all means which he believes necessary to success."[3]

This essay will judge how well Lowell succeeded in "his undertakings." For him, those words meant more than success on the battlefield. Victories were meaningful only if they served the ideals of union and freedom for which the United States was fighting. These ideals, Lowell asserted, should be honored in thought *and* deed. He felt an obligation to take up arms and urged others of his background to do so. "If Southern gentlemen enlist," he insisted, "Northern gentlemen must also." Like the sons of the southern slaveholding class, the sons of New England Brahmins enrolled in the army at a higher rate than the rest of the population. Graduates of Harvard far exceeded the general rate of enlistment, and many were imbued with the righteousness of their actions. "This fight," Lowell wrote early in the war, "was going to be one in which decent men ought to engage for the sake of *humanity*." At times, he believed politicians and generals betrayed the people's trust on both the home front and the battle front. In addition, he often expressed concern about the northern people's level of support for the war effort. "I do not see that this war has done us as a nation any good," Lowell complained in late 1864, "except on the slave question, — in one sense that is enough; but how is it that it has not taught us a great many other things which we hoped it would?" Lowell honored the democratic principles of the United States, and he believed that the nation could only flourish with millions of what he called "useful citizens."[4]

Many of his views necessarily strike the modern reader as elitist and painfully idealistic, but Lowell viewed his military service as both a career and a sacred call to reinvigorate a nonslaveholding Union. Born in 1835 to a prominent Boston family, he was groomed early for leadership in business and public service. Lowell's region, his class, and his education shaped him in distinctive ways. His parents, Charles Sr. and particularly his mother, Anna Cabot Jackson, instilled in him a deep sense of social responsibility, not only toward ending slavery but also toward helping the less fortunate. Historian Reid Mitchell has placed the Lowell family, which also included a brother James and two sisters, Harriet and Anna, within a category he describes as "public families." Public families, both North and South, devoted time and resources to civic service in the arenas of government, politics, church, and philanthropy. Many in New England supported reform movements, such as abolitionism, that were relevant to the issues leading up to the Civil War; members of these families also articulated new principles for an expansive American nationalism in the postwar decades. Had Charles Russell Lowell survived the war, he undoubtedly would have been a leading figure in this effort.[5]

Children of public families were expected to carry on their parents' and grandparents' tradition of philanthropy and service. Lowell offers an excellent example of the process, demonstrating a clear consciousness of his "duty" as an officer, as a class exemplar, and as a devoted citizen of his country. This civic burden emanating from the private realm was especially heavy and momentous for the children who came of age during the Civil War. Lowell, at least, judged the sacrifice worthwhile. Upon hearing of the death of his fiancée's brother, Colonel Shaw, while leading his African American troops in battle at Fort Wagner, Lowell wrote, "I see now that the best Colonel of the best black regiment had to die, it was a sacrifice we owed, — and how could it have been paid more gloriously?" Here he linked Shaw's personal heroism with a far more important ideal of service in the cause of erasing slavery from the country.[6]

Lowell's inner life was animated by the ideas put forward by a close family friend, the transcendental philosopher and writer Ralph Waldo Emerson. Emerson's transcendentalism empowered the individual over institutions and celebrated the goodness inherent in all men. Emerson inspired many followers, including the young Charley Lowell, to liberate humans from all fetters, especially slavery; with freedom came the possibilities of improving all society through individual self-culture. Importantly, individuals had a role to play when government institutions floundered, as during the secession crisis. "When the public fails in its duty," Emerson wrote, "private men take its place.

Charles Russell Lowell and Josephine Shaw in a photograph taken after the announcement of their engagement, March 1863. Edward Waldo Emerson, *Life and Letters of Charles Russell Lowell* (Boston: Houghton, Mifflin, 1907), 228.

. . . This is the compensation of bad government, — the field it affords for illustrious men."[7] Throughout his short life, Lowell yearned to make explicit and real the link between thought and action, between the private basis of his intellectual beliefs and spiritual morality and the public display of moral courage. During the war, he strove to be one of Emerson's "illustrious men."

This essay deliberately offers more than an assessment of the military career of one officer during a particularly important campaign. It proceeds on the assumption that a more fully realized portrait of Lowell will be gained through an understanding of the cultural, social, political, and military forces that created the hero-soldier who died at Cedar Creek. That understanding, in turn, will be valuable in illuminating a perennial topic for those who study the Civil War soldier: "why men fought."[8]

In April 1861, Charles Russell Lowell quit his job as a manager for an iron mill in Mount Savage, Maryland. He carefully packed his belongings into a carpetbag and walked to Washington, D.C., to offer his services to the U.S. military forces. As he walked along the dusty, crowded roads, Lowell reflected on the experience and talents he possessed that might make him an outstanding soldier in the Union army. Outwardly modest, Lowell knew that he was considered by his peers and powerful patrons to be the best of his generation of Boston Brahmins.

A bright and energetic boy, Charley had excelled in both school and sports. He ranked as "first scholar" at Boston Latin School and, at age fifteen, the youngest of his class at Harvard, where he flourished. One classmate remembered that "of all the rest of us he won his way into my best graces by his vivacity, his thoroughly boyish open-heartedness, his eagerness for fun and frolic, and his indifference to high rank which at once he attained by easy strides and maintained." At college, Lowell became intimately familiar with the classics of literature and philosophy, counting himself a devoted follower not only of Emerson—the "sage of Concord"—but also of the British romantic poet Thomas Carlyle. He stood as a leader among his group of friends, with many of whom he would later serve in the war. Chosen at nineteen to give the valedictorian speech at the 1854 Harvard commencement, Lowell declared, "If young men bring nothing but their strength and their spirit, the world may well spare them, but they do bring it something better: they bring it their fresher and purer ideals."[9]

Lowell's contemplative bent was paired with the urgent necessity of righting the wrongs of society. He and his siblings had been exposed from earliest childhood to the literary and abolitionist reform circle of his uncle, James Russell Lowell, perhaps nineteenth-century America's most famous poet and critic. The elder Lowell doted on his three nephews—the brothers, Charley and James, and their cousin, William Lowell Putnam. All three died in the Civil War. A grieving uncle commemorated them in his poem "Memoriae Positum," which included the heartfelt line, "I speak of one while with sad eyes I think of three." Like his parents and his Uncle James, Charley was a staunch, although never a radical, abolitionist. In 1853, he stood among the angry crowd on the steps of the Boston Court House when federal marshals escorted the escaped slave Anthony Burns back to the South and slavery. Shocked and shaken by the experience, the teenage youth vowed to fight for emancipation. Later in the decade, Lowell seriously considered joining the free labor settlers in Kansas.[10]

Unlike his Uncle James, Charley proved unable to pursue his desired career as a writer or teacher who could influence the masses through the power of his mind. Part of a relatively impoverished branch of the powerful and wealthy Lowell-Jackson clan, Charley, as the oldest son, was expected to provide for the family. He did not want to be a businessman, but he accepted his fate with little complaint. "For our family, work is absolutely necessary," Lowell wrote his mother in 1855 from the Ames Company Iron Mill in Chicopee, Massachusetts, the first in a series of jobs where he worked as an ordinary laborer. Characteristically, Lowell strove to incorporate the idealism he treasured while studying at Harvard onto the mill factory floor. Toiling alongside workmen cleaning chains and filing iron brought forth the "hope of helping them to have richer and nobler lives."[11] To that end, he started a singing club, proposed a lending library, and often spoke of supporting a mild brand of socialism to mitigate capitalism's worst excesses. Lowell's good intentions were colored by an earnest paternalism, and one can only imagine the lukewarm enthusiasm his reforms engendered among the laborers. His great interest for improving the lives of the working poor was predicated, however, on the assumption that one day he would be a wealthy and influential man.

That goal seemed well within his reach as he advanced upward in business through his early twenties. John Milton Forbes, a millionaire Boston industrialist and philanthropist, had taken an interest in Lowell from the youth's Harvard days. Forbes was already grooming him to assume an important place in his thriving financial empire. "One of the strange things," Forbes wrote to a colleague after Lowell's death, "has been how he magnetized you and me at first sight. We are practical, unsentimental, and perhaps hard, at least externally . . . yet he captivated me just as he did you, and I came home and told my wife I had fallen in love; and from that day I never saw anything too good or too high for him."[12]

Slight and wiry, the adult Charles Russell Lowell possessed the fine features and sensitive mien of an upper-class Bostonian. He had blue eyes, wavy brown hair parted almost in the middle, and stood five feet ten in his stocking feet. A devastating bout with tuberculosis in his early twenties interrupted the upward trajectory of his business career. One of his doctors predicted he would not live past thirty, and the dire state of Lowell's health prompted his wealthy grandmother to fund a two-year sojourn in Europe. While abroad, months of horseback riding, walking and hiking trips, and rest and relaxation made him healthy and hardy. Lowell's stay encompassed trips to Spain, Switzerland, Austria, Germany, and Algeria and included attendance at the maneuvers of the French and Austrian armies.

Upon his return home in 1856, Charley's family and friends noticed a new steely quality to his gaze that contrasted with his gentle, mustached countenance and slender physique. He had acquired a reputation for expert horsemanship and seemed stronger in both body and mind. Lowell threw himself into his career, often working late into the night after colleagues had gone to sleep.

His reputation as a coming man in the world of business was burnished further after a stint working in Burlington, Iowa, an outpost in the Forbes' railroad domain. He next accepted the position that took him to the Maryland iron mill in 1860. Before leaving for Maryland, Lowell eagerly followed the Republican convention. An enthusiastic supporter of Abraham Lincoln, he wrote to a Boston acquaintance, "How does the Chicago platform and nomination please the Puritans, — it shows pluck, and that, in an American, generally argues strength. Deliberately I prefer Lincoln to Seward."[13] In the equally momentous wartime election four years later, Lowell again endorsed Lincoln.

From the vantage of a border state, Lowell watched the unfolding drama of the dissolution of the Union. Shocked at southern secession, he temporarily cast aside his commitment to emancipation: "Who cares now about the slavery question? Secession, and the new Oligarchy built upon it, have crowded it out." Then the Confederacy attacked Fort Sumter, and men from his own state of Massachusetts were killed in Baltimore on their way to protect the U.S. capital. As the stakes grew more serious, Lowell observed, "I fear our Government will be hard pushed for the next six months — it can raise 75,000 men easily enough, but can it use them after they are raised?" Lowell quit his job to join the regular army. In the first spring of the war, it seemed, as one of his friends later said, the "past was annihilated, the future was all."[14]

The Charles Russell Lowell who walked to Washington City in late April 1861 was anything but the typical inexperienced youth eager to enlist in the giant volunteer army being raised to suppress the rebellion. He was mature, intelligent, and a close and ardent student of the politics and character of America. Yet, like the vast majority of the early enlistees, he knew little of military life and nothing of war. Eager to learn, he approached the beleaguered capital determined to bring himself to the attention of those in charge of the U.S. Army. "I think . . . you will agree," he wrote his mother, "that I am right in trying to enter the regular army . . . that while the *volunteers* will furnish fully their share of military talent . . . it will fall mainly on the *Regular* organization to keep the armies in the field and to keep them moving."[15] He believed that the professional military desperately needed officers with experience in the management of men in business to defeat a dangerous, treasonous, but worthy foe.

A weary Lowell finally reached Washington and on April 23 wrote to Senator Charles Sumner of Massachusetts:

Dear Sir, — Have you at your disposal any appointment in the Army which you would be willing to give me? I speak and write English, French, and

Italian, and read German and Spanish: knew once enough of Mathematics to put me at the head of my class at Harvard — though now I may need a little rubbing up: am a tolerable proficient with the small sword and the single-stick: and can ride a horse as far and bring him in as fresh as any other man. I am twenty-six years of age, and believe I possess more or less of that moral courage about taking responsibility which seems at present to be found only in Southern officers.

Lowell waited impatiently for an appointment. While doing so, he helped the War Department by slipping into Virginia and Maryland and observing military preparations. He also acted as an agent for the state of Massachusetts. His decisive action and concise reports so impressed Secretary of War Simon Cameron that he recommended Lowell be sworn immediately into the newly expanded regular army. On July 1, 1861, Charles Lowell received his first orders as a newly commissioned captain in the Third U.S. Cavalry, a well-regarded unit under the command of Lt. Col. William H. Emory. The appointment to a regular unit marked an unusual distinction for a civilian."[16]

After joining the Third Cavalry, Captain Lowell journeyed to Pennsylvania and Ohio to recruit for the regiment, which was shortly renumbered as the Sixth U.S. Cavalry. Recruiting promised tedious duty in the best of times, and Lowell encountered many frustrations with the process. In Pennsylvania, he expressed dislike for the heavily antiwar sentiments of Democrats in the area, while in the Western Reserve of Ohio another unpleasant surprise awaited him. Lowell observed humorously that it must have been "a glorious place to recruit . . . two months ago." Now, he complained, "none but married men or elderly men are left." Although Lowell managed to scrape several companies together, he despaired of his lot as "a mounted officer without a horse, a Captain without a Lieutenant or a command." Anxious to get to the battlefield, he consoled himself by consulting books on the elements of military science and brought the same intense drive to his military career that previously characterized his business endeavors.[17]

Summer turned into fall, and finally the quota was filled. Lowell took charge of a squadron (two companies) of cavalry and looked forward to his first experience with the reality of war. "Like every young soldier," he said, "I am anxious for one battle as an experience." That experience remained in the future as the Sixth Cavalry trained near Washington, where the northern diarist George Templeton Strong viewed it on parade and drill. Strong commented about "one of the captains, Lowell of Boston, a notably promising officer, admired and commended by the regular brethren as the best appointment ever made from civil life." Frustrated with the inaction, except for drilling, Lowell entertained doubts about the way the war was being waged: "The Administration seems to me sadly in want of a policy — the war goes on well, but the country will soon want to know exactly what the war is *for*."[18]

In the spring of 1862, the Sixth Cavalry participated in Maj. Gen. George B. McClellan's ill-fated Peninsula campaign designed to capture Richmond. Lowell was pleased that his brother James, an officer with the 20th Massachusetts Infantry, was nearby. Captain Lowell's first taste of action occurred on May 5 at the battle of Williamsburg, where he commanded two companies in a cavalry attack. Outnumbered by southern forces, Lowell led his men in five charges, eventually succeeding in driving the enemy off. He made himself conspicuous by his aggressive fighting, which resulted in the capture of many Confederate prisoners. After Williamsburg, his command was ordered to go down the peninsula. In a parting of the ways for Charley and James, the 20th Massachusetts stayed to face the Confederates in the heavy fighting of the Seven Days' battles. Although disappointed to be out of the action, Lowell was recommended for brevet major — an honorary promotion that was not approved — and received an appointment to McClellan's staff.[19]

Pride in his early battle accomplishments paled alongside a tragedy that struck close to home. On July 4, 1862, James Jackson Lowell died of wounds received at the battle of Glendale. James was a lawyer in civilian life and, like his older brother, had finished first in his class at Harvard. Charley and their sister Anna, a nurse who worked on a hospital ship at Harrison's Landing (later she served in the same capacity in the Amory Square Military Hospital in Washington, D.C.), tried unsuccessfully to find James, who was unavoidably left behind by his comrades to die on the battlefield. Lowell consoled his grieving mother. "Your two last letters," he wrote her, "have told me more about Jimmy than I had learned from his friends here — they seem to bring me very near to him and also to you and Father."[20]

Captain Lowell had mixed feelings as he took up his duties on McClellan's staff. Throughout the war, he generally gave high praise to the controversial and charismatic Little Mac. Like many in the Army of the Potomac, Lowell admired McClellan's ability to inspire, to train, and to lead his soldiers. He also judged him to be a superb strategist. At the end of the Peninsula campaign, however, Lowell expressed less enthusiasm regarding McClellan's ability to win the smashing victory that would end the war. Lowell's unit met up with McClellan at Harrison's Landing, where the army gathered glumly to return to Washington, D.C. "He prepares very well," Lowell remarked about McClellan to a close friend who was visiting at the time, "and then doesn't do the best thing—strike hard."[21]

Despite reservations about McClellan, Lowell took pride in his service with the Army of the Potomac: "I have had my training in what I may now without boasting call a 'crack' regiment." His next opportunity for action came in the Maryland campaign. Lowell acted as a courier at the battle of Antietam on September 17, 1862. During that bloody day, he rode to the harried Union corps commanders delivering orders from McClellan. While so engaged that morning, he encountered part of Maj. Gen. John Sedgwick's Second Corps division retreating under severe fire just north of Sharpsburg. Lowell rallied the men and led them back into the fighting. After watching him in action, an officer remarked, "I shall never forget the effect of his appearance. He seemed a part of his horse, an instinct with a perfect animal life. At the same time his eyes glistened and his face literally shone with the spirit and intelligence of which he was the embodiment. He was the ideal of the *preux chevalier.*" Lowell managed to escape serious injury but did not emerge unscathed: "His horse was shot twice, his scabbard cut in two, and the overcoat on the saddle spoiled by a piercing bullet." Afterward, Lowell calmly resumed his staff duties. For his spectacular act of bravery during the battle, the young captain was selected by McClellan to carry thirty-nine captured Confederate battle flags from Maryland for presentation to President Lincoln. Once again, he was put up for promotion, and as with his failure to receive the brevet majority, once again he was denied.[22]

Lowell remained loyal to McClellan during what proved to be trying times for the "young Napoleon," but he was anxious to get another posting. He did not view Antietam as a triumph and anticipated the downward shift in McClellan's fortunes. "This is not a pleasant letter," he wrote to his mother. "We have gained a victory—a complete one, but not so decisive as could have been wished." He wrote another negative assessment for John M. Forbes, with whom he corresponded frequently. Forbes, an active and influential Union supporter, relied upon Lowell throughout the war for advice and insight on Union military policy and practice. Before and after McClellan's forced departure from command, Lowell often expressed concern to Forbes and others about the troubled state of the Army of the Potomac. According to Lowell, lax discipline, low morale, and "bickerings and jealousies" among officers of every rank plagued the army. "I see so many good officers kept back, because they are too good to be spared, and so many poor ones put forward merely as a means of getting rid of them, that I never worry," he wrote, reassuring his fiancée that he did not mind being ignored for promotion. Contemplating with disgust a vicious attack made by Maj. Gen. Joseph Hooker against McClellan, Lowell declared to Forbes in October, "Personally, I like Hooker very much, but I fear he will do us a mischief if he ever gets a large command. He has got his head in the clouds."[23]

In the midst of such worries, Lowell received an offer and an opportunity that he had been waiting for since the beginning of the war. Confederate victories in the all-important Eastern Theater brought a serious strain to Union military planning. High casualties and losses from short-term enlistments forced Lincoln to call for 300,000 volunteers in the summer of 1862. Worse was yet to come. It was commonly assumed that even this number would fall short of necessary manpower, and that the U.S. government, like its Confederate counterpart, would resort to an unpopular national draft. Other changes seemed necessary as well. The Peninsula campaign and Second Manassas had driven home the painful lesson that northern cavalry could not match its southern counterpart.[24] Reorganization followed, including plans to establish a Cavalry Bureau that could deploy Union resources more effectively and efficiently. A concerted effort to recruit more men into an expanded and revitalized cavalry corps was also undertaken. In New England, Amos A. Lawrence, a wealthy and patriotic Boston businessman, offered to help raise a three-year regiment of northern horsemen.[25] Hailed by other prominent Bostonians, including Lowell's mentor Forbes, this new unit, the 2nd Massachusetts Cavalry Regiment, was authorized by Governor John A. Andrew. Lowell was the unanimous choice to command. McClellan generously released him from his staff duties, and Lowell arrived in Boston as a colonel in November 1862. Exultant at this change in duty, Lowell had achieved his long-held wish to command a fighting regiment.

The 2nd Massachusetts Cavalry was immediately deluged with applications from men who wanted to serve as officers. They came mainly from Harvard students or graduates, who knew of and admired Colonel Lowell's military record and longed for the excitement of cavalry service. The lieutenant colonelcy went to Lowell's close friend Henry S. Russell, who later would command the 5th Massachusetts Cavalry, Colored. Capt. Caspar Crowninshield, originally from the 20th Massachusetts Infantry, was promoted to major and joined Russell as a trusted and battle-tested veteran officer. William H. Forbes, son of John Forbes, served as a captain. Officer recruitment was accomplished with lightning speed and to the satisfaction of the sponsors.

Filling the ranks was another matter altogether. During the winter of 1862–

63, Lawrence, Forbes, and Lowell directed the recruitment from Camp Quincy, located near the State House in the basement of Niles Block in Court Square. Lowell's experience in Pennsylvania and Ohio in June 1861 had prepared him for the difficulties of attracting truly patriotic volunteers. The situation had deteriorated a year later. Men neither enlisted in great numbers nor, when they did enlist, evinced great enthusiasm. More than ever, the business of recruiting proceeded on a cold, almost businesslike basis. Ever increasing bounties offered by states such as Massachusetts played an integral role in mobilizing northern men from early 1863 on, as did the specter of conscription. Many of the men who were "made to come or paid to come" would never be high quality soldiers, and some proved actively mutinous.[26]

Pickings were slim that fall and winter of 1862–63 as the 2nd Massachusetts Cavalry began recruiting in earnest. Generous cash bounties provided by wealthy backers of the regiment helped to fill two battalions (a battalion consisted of five companies) with local men, but more were needed. Members of the committee went to Canada and other states to hunt for extra volunteers. When the state of California offered two units to fight for the Union under the Bay State's quota, Governor Andrew gratefully accepted and paid $200 per soldier to cover traveling expenses for the arduous and expensive journey. The men of the "California Hundred" (Company A) and the "California Battalion" (Companies E, L, M, and F) accounted for half of the regiment and, unlike their eastern counterparts, had experience with horses. Shortly after the New Year, the California Hundred, under the command of Massachusetts-born Capt. J. Sewall Reed, arrived at Camp Meigs in Readville, a few miles from Boston.[27]

In camp, Lowell trained the new recruits in regimental, then squadron, and then individual drill. He also labored to teach the volunteers how to ride their horses as cavalry troopers. In a letter to John Forbes, Lowell commented, "My experience is that, for *cavalry*, raw recruits sent to a regiment in large numbers are worse than useless; they are of no account and they spoil the old men, — they should be *drilled* at least 4 months before they join their regiment." Lowell enjoyed training the horses, perhaps more so than the men who rode them. "I do not fancy horses who at the outset do not resist," he wrote in 1864, "but they must be intelligent enough to know when they are conquered, and to recognize it as an advance in their civilization." By February, Union headquarters pressed him to send a barely trained battalion to protect the Washington, D.C., area. "My first battalion leave on Thursday for Fort Monroe," a worried Lowell wrote a friend on February 15. As he feared, disaster marked the trip to Fort Monroe. "With the exception of the Californians, the men are a disgrace to the state which sent them," recorded Crowninshield. "They get beastly drunk and fight among themselves draw the sabres & pistols & cut & slash each other. . . . I hope to be able to make something like soldiers out of them — though like enough many will desert to the enemy."[28] It was not a particularly auspicious beginning for the regiment, which, as with other regiments formed at this time, would be afflicted with high rates of desertion until the summer of 1864.

Lowell faced a tough challenge in instilling discipline and professionalism in a sizeable number of the 2nd Massachusetts recruits, who had been attracted to the cash but not to the cause. Predictably, many of the local recruits were unruly and resistant to training from the outset. The new colonel was tested in a dramatic and potentially damaging incident that required fast thinking and decisive action. Early in the morning on April 9, Lowell arrived at Camp Quincy to find a group of sixty-eight freshly inducted soldiers in a state of mutiny against the sergeant in command. He firmly announced that the sergeant's order had to be obeyed even if the men found it objectionable. He also promised a fair hearing of the men's grievances after they carried out the order. Then, armed with his Colt revolver, he warned: "God knows my men, I don't want to kill any of you; but I shall shoot the first man who resists. Sergeant, iron your man." When the sergeant made a move toward the mutineers' leader, all the malcontents rushed him, many with knifes. Immediately, Lowell shot and killed twenty-three-year-old William Pendergast of Boston, whom he identified as one of the ringleaders. He then ordered the rest of the men off to drill and immediately walked to Governor John Andrew's office to report his action. After Lowell left, Andrew turned to an aide and said, "I need nothing more, Colonel Lowell is as humane as he is brave." Five of the men were held for trial at court martial proceedings. Later that same day, the remaining members of the company were sworn into service and taken to Camp Meigs.[29]

Confident that he acted within the bounds of military law, Lowell was vindicated by the verdict in a coroner's inquest held shortly afterwards.[30] He received strong support from his superiors for his action, and he had shown the men that he meant business. He had already gained a reputation among his troopers as a harsh disciplinarian. From Camp Meigs onwards, Lowell regularly issued orders enforcing strict discipline in camp regarding drinking, swearing, drilling, and the wearing of proper uniforms. He believed that hard training afforded the best education for good soldiers. The men of the 2nd Massachusetts who fought under Lowell for the remainder of the war did not always understand or appreciate the point of endless drilling. By 1864, however, Lowell was known for his fairness combined with firmness and earned the respect, if not the love, of his troopers. A fellow officer remembered that "Lowell was always kind to his men, duly considerate of all faults and failures on their part, he was, nevertheless, strict in his discipline."[31]

From February to April 1863, Lowell supervised the regiment's intensive training at Camp Meigs. Four hundred more Californians joined the camp on April 16. Filled with experienced riders and already acquainted with drill, the new men expressed open contempt for the inept Massachusetts recruits. Indeed, the men who brought the Bear Flag with them represented the strongest part of the regiment and embodied the best hope Lowell had for making the regiment a crack cavalry force. Yet Lowell had a serious leadership task with the Californians, most of whom had been born and raised in the Northeast. Put simply, many had grievances against what they perceived to be shabby treatment by both their Massachusetts officers and Massachusetts comrades. Perhaps the biggest protest concerned Lowell's decision to break up some of the California units to give the eastern men benefit of their superior background. His move earned him the enmity of many enlisted men and a few officers who understandably preferred to keep their cohesiveness and preserve their California identity.

In 1863 and early 1864, Lowell was regularly attacked in the pages of the *Daily Alta*, a major newspaper in San Francisco. The *Daily Alta*'s usual correspondent, Quartermaster Sgt. Thomas H. Merry of Company L, wrote, "We have just reason to complain of the colonel that the State chose to command this regiment, Col. Lowell, has done all in his power to spite us, both officers and men; he has divided and broken up our battalion . . . when it was specially agreed our battalion should remain intact, under the command of our own Major." In fact, there was no such agreement, but rather than engage in a debate, Lowell ignored the criticisms, preferring to let the glowing (and growing) reputation of the 2nd Massachusetts assuage such bitter feelings. When in July 1864 Lowell arranged for the California men to be equipped with new Spencer repeating rifles (paid for by the Bay State), he quipped that "it would convince the men that there were some advantages in belonging to a Massachusetts regiment—however revolting it might be to their pride."[32]

Another notable unit gathered at Camp Meigs. Col. Robert Gould Shaw was recruiting for and training the 54th Massachusetts Infantry, the first all-black northern regiment. Colonel Lowell heartily approved of the Emancipation Proclamation issued on January 1, 1863, and the passage a month later of the Negro Army Bill that led to creation of the 54th. He also approved wholeheartedly of its young commander: "I think it very good of Shaw . . . to undertake the thing." Lowell had earlier offered Shaw a command in the 2nd Massachusetts, which the latter declined, and the two colonels became close friends during the early months of 1863. They had much in common. Scions of New England ruling clans, they shared a strong commitment to Unionism that was heavily tempered with the realities of war, as well as great expectations and anxieties about what the future held for their respective regiments. Their mutual admiration increased when Lowell fell in love with Shaw's sister, Josephine. After the couple announced their engagement later that spring, Robert wrote to Charles that he hoped "this war will not finish one or both of us, and that we shall live to know each other well."[33]

Lowell received orders in May to move his command to the vicinity of Washington. Setting up camp east of the Capitol, Lowell prepared for duty under the command of Brig. Gen. Rufus King, who would oversee Union efforts to protect the line of the Orange and Alexandria Railroad. On May 19, Maj. Gen. Silas Casey reviewed the 2nd Massachusetts. The review went very favorably, and Lowell pronounced Casey "smiling and satisfied." Lowell and his troopers soon left for the area around Centreville, Virginia, where they guarded the supply and railroad lines of the Army of the Potomac. Lowell was a keen analyst of military strategy and, in a letter to Henry Russell dated May 23, predicted a new rebel movement. "You may rely upon it, Harry, that *Lee* will not remain idle if *we* do; he will send a column into Maryland again when the crops are ready: I look for a repetition of what occurred last summer."[34] Meanwhile, Union headquarters desperately needed cavalry to protect the supply lines to Meade's army at Warrenton, patrol the nearby mountain gaps, protect the Orange and Alexandria Railroad from Alexandria to Centreville, and safeguard engineers who were directing the repair of bridges and railroad lines. For excitement, the 2nd conducted the occasional foray against Confederates found in the countryside or the small towns nearby.

Despite the importance of his duty, Lowell agonized at being left out of the developing "Pennsylvania Movement." He had assumed that the 2nd Massachusetts would join the Army of the Potomac to contest Robert E. Lee's invasion that resulted in the battle of Gettysburg. It was not to be. His unit was deemed too valuable to leave the Washington area, despite many efforts made on his behalf and his own letters and pleas to superiors, including Secretary of War Edwin Stanton. In the ensuing months, Lowell's services were requested by prominent officers such as Brig. Gen. David McMurtrie Gregg, Maj. Gen. Samuel T. Heintzelman, and Maj. Gen. Nathaniel P. Banks. All of the requests were turned down promptly. "Stanton is so fond of us," Lowell wrote with a touch of sarcasm, "that he keeps us on the *safe* 'front' — the 'front' nearest Washington, whereby I am debarred from the rightful command of a brigade . . . in Gregg's division." Assigned to the Department of Washington, the 2nd Massachusetts remained on the sidelines, at least for the foreseeable future. "Don't you wish that your Colonel was one who belonged to the Army of the Potomac?" Lowell wistfully asked Josephine. "He does, I'm sure."[35]

Union military planners had another agenda for Colonel Lowell, who so far had performed assigned tasks with great competence and satisfactory results.[36] From August 1863 to August 1864, Lowell, first from Centreville and then Vienna, was directed to put an end to the activities of the colorful Maj. John Singleton Mosby and his 43rd Battalion of Virginia Cavalry, also known as Mosby's Raiders. The slight, blond Mosby was a former lawyer, equally smart and wily, who sported an ostrich plum in his hat, wore a gray cape with bright red lining, and in general cut a cavalier's arresting figure as he tore through the northern Virginia countryside. His operations were intended to divert men and supplies away from the major eastern Union army.[37]

Officially sanctioned by the Confederate Partisan Ranger Act of April 1862, as well as by orders Gen. Robert E. Lee and Maj. Gen. James E. B. Stuart issued in March 1863, Mosby's guerrilla operations were in full swing and creating havoc by the summer of 1863. Based in Loudoun and Fauquier Counties but often extending their activities into Fairfax and Prince William Counties, the raiders operated south of the Potomac and east of the Blue Ridge Mountains. Civilians loyal to the Confederacy dominated this area between Washington and the Army of the Potomac, which quickly became known as Mosby's Confederacy. Mosby and his men enjoyed rich opportunities for mischief, destruction, and plunder. Their favorite targets were the well-laden Union supply wagons.

To strengthen Lowell's hand against the elusive enemy, Washington placed him in command of an independent cavalry brigade. Included in this small brigade, which numbered about 1,200 troopers, were the 13th and 16th New York, a detachment from the 12th Illinois, and the 2nd Massachusetts. Lowell trained and disciplined disparate units, a difficult fact of life for him that would continue when he took part in the Shenandoah Valley campaign. Lowell received no advancement in rank to go along with the increased responsibility, although many expected that he would soon be promoted to brigadier general.

A harbinger of what Lowell could expect over the next year occurred in late July. On the thirtieth, Mosby struck a Union supply train near Fairfax Court House, capturing twenty-eight sutlers' wagons and a number of prisoners and horses. A magnificent haul, it was popularly dubbed the "Ice Cream Raid" because one of the wagons carried the desirable dessert. At Centreville, Lowell learned of the raid and immediately prepared his men for action. He led a detachment to some woods near Aldie, where he made camp on the evening of the thirtieth. Just after midnight, Lowell observed a line of Mosby's booty-laden raiders pushing down the road past the cavalry encampment. He organized an attack that quickly disbursed the unsuspecting rebels and recaptured all the Federal wagons, men, and horses. Lowell considered the victory incomplete, however, noting ruefully, "We retook them all [the wagons] but didn't take Mosby, who is an old rat and has a great many holes."[38]

Typically, Mosby and his men ambushed a supply train, stole horses, took prisoners and weapons, and then disappeared into the Virginia countryside. The partisan rangers, most of whom were native to the area, did not need great numbers to be successful. Their ability to disband instantly and then regroup at Mosby's bidding placed the drastically undermanned Lowell in an impossible situation. His strategy was by necessity reactive. One of his first orders increased the number of troopers protecting the vulnerable convoys traveling between Alexandria and Centreville. Although this improved security greatly, the lack of Union manpower for this type of activity guaranteed continued ambushes. Lowell answered reports of Mosby's depredations with swift operations that attempted to recapture the stolen materials, while inflicting heavy casualties on the raiders. To this end, Lowell launched counterraids, or sweeps, whose success often depended on a small, carefully nurtured, but often untrustworthy network of Union sympathizers. Federals captured eighteen raiders and thirty-five horses in November 1863 using vital information procured from one such informant, a southern deserter named Charlie Binns. Lowell combined raids with dismounted attacks to more aggressively fight the enemy.[39]

Advantages or knowledge gained from friendly southerners, however, were more than offset by bitter Virginians eager to hide, to provision, and to supply Mosby with detailed intelligence on the whereabouts of Lowell's men once they left the relative safety of their camp. Sweeps in response to large-scale plunder were just one part of contesting the raiders in Mosby's Confederacy. Other tasks were also dangerous. Picket duty, regularly scheduled reconnaissance missions, or specific scouting expeditions led by Lowell or another appointed officer sometimes resulted in disaster, as was reported to Lt. Gen. J. H. Taylor on December 13, 1863. "This morning at about 3 o'clock," wrote Lowell, "the picket at Germantown were surprised by a party of guerrillas, dismounted, some twenty strong. They crawled up and shot (without any warning), mortally wounding two men and capturing five horses and their equipment."[40]

Understandably, morale dropped and frustration rose among the Federal troopers. Another attack on a picket post on December 20 brought forth an outburst from a California soldier who complained that the colonel "had no regard for the lives and liberties of our men; sending five men to stand picket three and four miles from camp, where no assistance can reach them until it is too late."[41] Specific criticisms of Lowell's military acumen, however, failed to account for the larger picture. The give-and-take of guerrilla warfare created a vicious circle. Mosby's depredations invited Union attacks on southern property. The fresh hatred engendered by reprisals pushed even more civilians into active support for the guerrillas, leading to more destruction. "If there is any locality," wrote a soldier in the 2nd Massachusetts, "that has more than another suffered from the ravages of war, it is [Centreville]. . . . Nearly every house . . . has been either burned or torn down, and the whole country around it has been devastated."[42]

Lowell and his brigade moved in September from Centreville to Vienna, about fifteen miles from the capital. There, in comfortable quarters, he would spend the fall and winter of 1863–64 stalking Mosby. Charles A. Humphrey, who served as chaplain for the 2nd Massachusetts, kept a journal that recorded some of the life at Vienna. The Harvard-educated Humphrey and Lowell had much in common, including friends, relatives, and a love of discussing "metaphysics and mental philosophy." Both expressed frustration at the difficulties of fighting a war without clear guidelines. A highly principled man, Lowell had serious reservations about the kind of warfare he waged in Virginia. He was particularly distressed by having to roust and punish local civilians for hiding or otherwise aiding the partisan rangers. "I don't at all fancy the duty here, — serving against bushwhackers; it brings me in contact with too many citizens, — and sometimes with mothers and children." Lowell relished the times when he could let someone off easy, as he did with "a Quakerlike looking old lady" or with "a little fellow, only sixteen years old," who was drafted against his will. Conversely, he could be harsh against a well-defined enemy. "I had the satisfaction the other day," he wrote, "of arresting the Lieut.-Colonel who had charge of the draft in this and the neighbouring counties, and hoped I have stopped it for a time." Thus he commanded with a light hand, trying to distinguish between the enemy and those he deemed innocent victims. Whether many Virginians appreciated Lowell's calculated kindnesses is another question.[43]

Apart from his complex interaction with Confederates, Lowell provoked some carping within his own ranks. Maj. Caspar Crowninshield privately voiced concerns in letters to his mother. "I don't consider him much of a soldier," read one of Crowninshield's missives regarding Lowell, "although I do consider him the most talented young man I have ever met . . . but [he] is hasty inconsiderate and has not very good judgment. He has however a most unbounded confidence in his own ability." In another letter, Crowninshield remarked that Lowell "is so very ambitious, that he sacrifices everything for advancement." Crowninshield's reservations did not reflect the warm public support Lowell received from most of his officers.[44]

Some enlisted men also found reason to complain about elements of Lowell's leadership. One of the harshest and most persistent critics was the aforementioned Thomas Merry. Recounting a guerrilla ambush near Fairfax Court House on August 24, 1863, that resulted in a significant loss of 100 trained cavalry horses, Merry portrayed Lowell's tactical instructions (the colonel himself was not present) as woefully ineffective. Merry urged that instead of trying to fight by the rules Lowell should adopt purely guerrilla methods. "But Col. Lowell," he groused, "will never do it, for all the knowledge that he possesses of fighting Indians or guerillas has been acquired by reading Sylvanus Cobb's stories in the *New York Ledger*, while burning the 'midnight oil' at Harvard, but what he is deficient in this, he more than makes up in his knowledge of dress parades and policeing camps." Merry's comments must be placed in context. Even if Lowell wanted to engage in a "slash and burn" policy against the guerrillas and their supporters, which he did not, he was constrained by Union policy articulated in 1863. Draconian action entailed the mass removal of civilians from their homes and destruction of the surrounding countryside. This policy had proved counterproductive recently in Missouri, and Lincoln's top military advisor, Maj. Gen. Henry W. Halleck, issued an order forbidding such actions except in specific, and dire, circumstances.[45]

The war against Mosby's partisans proved immensely frustrating to Lowell and his command. The affair at Fairfax Court House that upset trooper Merry prompted Secretary of War Stanton to order a court of inquiry. Extremely upset at Stanton's action, Lowell believed strongly that even the minor rebuke issued was unjust and would adversely affect his chances of promotion. "I do not consider myself at all to blame," he wrote, "and really I shall not care for the finding." He added, "Heintzelman had told me he was more than satisfied, was gratified at what had been done." Lowell did not blame his men for their frustration, which he largely shared. He and most other Union officers who fought the Virginia guerrillas hated their jobs. The task of hunting guerrillas hidden among a supportive population was difficult and discouraging. At best, Lowell's and Mosby's clashes resulted in a tactical stalemate. The most desirable outcome for the Union would have been the capture of Mosby. That outcome eluded both Lowell and his successors. No clear-cut victory could be claimed; no triumph easily reduced to an exciting newspaper headline. Yet many of the men who composed Lowell's small brigade — led by the well-trained, drilled, and experienced 2nd Massachusetts — expressed visible pride in their service at this time. Samuel W. Backus of Company L of the 2nd wrote to his father on October 25, 1863: "We are always ready, if we see or hear any rebs, to give them a fight. Lately we have had a good many fights with them, in all of which we have whipped them badly. I think that we have crippled the gang of Moseby more than any other troops ever did before."[46]

In these months, Lowell staked out a position, born of growing experience, regarding the legitimate role destruction of enemy property could play in meeting Union goals. He believed officers should direct any such destruction to ensure it did not degenerate into wanton looting. Part of Lowell's thinking on this issue arose from his interest in the fate of the 54th Massachusetts commanded by his prospective brother-in-law, Robert Shaw. That regiment's participation in the plundering and burning of Darien, Georgia, on June 11, 1863, prompted Lowell to write a letter of protest to William Whiting, the solicitor of the War Department. On the other hand, Lowell increasingly became convinced that liberating Confederate slaves and enrolling them in Union regiments as free soldiers would deliver a major blow against the southern rebellion. "Negro Organization," he claimed, "is a more *aggressive* movement than the Army of the Potomac has ever ventured upon, and in a larger view, it is incomparably more important. Every black regiment is an additional guarantee for that settlement of these troubles which we regard as the only safe one, and will continue to be a guarantee for the permanency of that settlement when made." Later, Shaw's heroic death at the battle of Fort Wagner on July 18, 1863, struck Lowell hard. "The manliness and high courage of such a man never die with him," he wrote to Josephine, "they live in his comrades."[47]

Lowell's year of fighting Mosby's Raiders was interrupted twice. He obtained a generous leave to marry Josephine Shaw at her family's home in Staten Island in October. His new bride happily accompanied him back to Vienna, where she lived in camp with her husband for almost ten months. Another break came in February 1864 when Brig. Gen. James H. Wilson, the cavalry bureau chief for the Eastern Theater, asked Lowell to reorganize the Giesboro' Point Depot near Washington. Giesboro' Point was one of several huge depots run by the War Department in which thousands of worn-out horses were rehabilitated and thousands of new horses gathered for use by the cavalry forces. Lacking enthusiasm about Wilson's summons, Lowell explained to John Forbes, "I left Vienna, not from choice, but because I had to. I am sent over here to straighten out the Cavalry Depot. . . . There has been no head here, and there was a sad want of system."[48]

Lowell accomplished the reorganization by the end of March, returned to Vienna, and resumed active operations against Confederate guerrillas on April 4. One foray, taking place later that month, inspired Herman Melville's poem "The Scout Toward Aldie." The writer had a cousin, Lt. Col. Henry S. Gansevoort, who, along with Col. Henry M. Lazelle, commanded the New York regiments in Lowell's brigade. Gansevoort called Lowell "my model in arms" and acquainted Melville with the brigade's record. Melville visited the Vienna camp with his brother Alan in early April and was impressed by Lowell, who, he wrote, embodied "beauty and youth, with manners sweet, and friends." Melville also was fascinated with Lowell's opponent, declaring, "Of Mosby best beware." Knowing of Melville's desire to experience the war, Lowell invited him to accompany a large reconnaissance to check on reported sightings of Mosby and the partisan rangers somewhere between Aldie and Leesburg. The sortie netted eleven raiders but came up short, as Mosby again eluded capture. Melville's published Civil War writings experienced disappointing sales, but one stanza of his poem captured perfectly the exhaustion Lowell's soldiers felt after a days' long expedition:

The weary troop that wended now —
Hardly it seemed the same that pricked
Forth to the forest from the camp:
Foot-sore horses, jaded men;
Every backbone felt as nicked,
Each eye dim as a sick room lamp,
All faces stamped with Mosby's stamp.[49]

As he neared the end of a year's fighting against the raiders, Lowell's letters placed his war in perspective, demonstrating that he had reluctantly accepted his fate. "I dislike to have men killed in such an 'inglorious warfare,'" he wrote, "but it's not a warfare of my choosing, and it's all in the day's work." Lowell admitted that Mosby and his men operated within legally sanctioned boundaries. He also acknowledged that, in his judgment, the majority of Virginia guerrillas were not deliberately cruel and criminal, as were their unauthorized counterparts operating in Missouri and Kansas. "Mosby is more keen to plunder," Lowell stated. "He always runs when he can." Lowell concluded that "Mosby is an honorable foe and should be treated as such." This sentiment was in no way shared by many of Lowell's men, who suffered humiliation, defeat, injury, capture, and death at the hands of the guerrillas. "We must get over our nice points of etiquette and treat them as rebels," a soldier grumbled. The two top officers, however, admired each other's style. Mosby later wrote that "of all the Federal commanders opposed to me, I had the highest respect for Col. Lowell both as an officer and a gentleman."[50]

During and after the war, Mosby and his partisan rangers enjoyed a romantic and dashing reputation, while their Federal foes received scant if any recognition. Mosby unquestionably inflicted major embarrassments on the Union. There were good reasons for Confederate successes, including the fact that the huge area claimed by Mosby's Confederacy could not be covered adequately by the small number of Federals assigned to the task. A judicious assessment of Lowell's many cavalry operations would find much success, especially in the spring of 1864. Union supply trains, on mules and rails, rumbled through the countryside on a regular schedule to deliver their supplies relatively unhindered.[51] Lowell acquired a reputation as a superb cavalry officer who could spend long hours in the saddle without visible effect. Both of his commanding officers expressed confidence in his abilities. Brig. Gen. Robert O. Tyler, who led a division under Maj. Gen. Christopher C. Augur in the Department of Washington, provided this assessment: "With Colonel Lowell in command of the cavalry I have no fear of trouble." Augur himself praised Lowell for his successful engagements in April, stating, "I desire to commend in strong terms the zeal and ability displayed by Col. Lowell in these various expeditions.[52] In July, Lowell's "inglorious warfare" against the partisan raiders came to an end when events moved swiftly to bring him under the command of Maj. Gen. Philip Henry Sheridan in the Shenandoah Valley.

In early 1864, Abraham Lincoln reinvigorated the Army of the Potomac with new leadership and a grand strategy to win the war. The president brought east the hero of Shiloh, Vicksburg, and Chattanooga, Gen. Ulysses S. Grant, who planned to activate all Union armies simultaneously to strike Confederate forces in Virginia and Georgia, capture Richmond and Atlanta, and end the war swiftly. An important part of Grant's strategy was to clear the Shenandoah Valley of rebel soldiers while destroying its agricultural bounty.

Grant's proposed destruction of Valley farms and fields prompted Lee to order Lt. Gen. Jubal A. Early's Second Corps to the Valley with orders to remove the Federals in time for the harvest. Early defeated Maj. Gen. David Hunter at the battle of Lynchburg on June 18 and then turned north and invaded Maryland. He vanquished another hapless Union general, Maj. Gen. Lew Wallace, at the battle of the Monocacy on July 9, before setting his sights on Washington, D.C. Lee hoped Early's operations would lower northern morale by creating panic and chaos, as well as relieving Grant's pressure on the Army of Northern Virginia by drawing back to Washington thousands of Federal troops currently around Richmond and Petersburg.

On July 10–11, Early moved toward Washington and got as far as Fort Stevens, part of the defenses surrounding the city, after which he was forced to retreat. Lowell and the 2nd Massachusetts were ordered to harass Early's rear as he withdrew from Washington. While doing so successfully on July 14, Lowell and his men were surprised in the streets of Rockville, Maryland, by an attack from elements of Early's retreating army. Lowell and his troopers soon realized there would be no Federal victory gained on this day, only an escape from disaster, if possible. As panic infected some of his men, Lowell shouted, "Halt!" and "Dismount!" waving his sword above their heads. One of his soldiers later wrote about "the magical effects of his voice in asserting a calm authority." Their confidence restored, the troops formed a strong defensive line. Using their new Spencer repeating weapons to good effect, Lowell and the 2nd Massachusetts repulsed several charges by southern cavalry. The men performed superbly in a dangerous situation and, though suffering high casualties, retired in good order with their pride intact. Lowell explained his philosophy of command in this way: "You can usually make a man obey if you speak quickly enough and with authority."[53]

General Early's summer offensive was not finished. On July 30, cavalry attached to his small army attacked and burned Chambersburg, Pennsylvania, further alarming the northern population. This action, in conjunction with Old Jube's move on Washington, caused Grant to intensify his drive to shut down Confederate operations in the Shenandoah Valley. In early August, against the background of the siege of Petersburg and Sherman's battle for Atlanta, Grant placed Philip Sheridan in charge of defeating Early. Although Sheridan's background had been in the infantry, Grant appointed the son of Irish immigrants as chief of cavalry in the Army of the Potomac at the beginning of the Overland campaign. Sheridan quickly turned the cavalry into an impressive fighting force, infusing it with an exuberant aggressiveness that delighted Grant. When the Shenandoah operations bogged down, the general in chief turned to Sheridan. Grant ordered "that nothing should be left to invite the enemy to return, take all provisions, forage, and stock wanted for the use of your command. Such as cannot be consumed, destroy." Grant spelled out the means to achieve the end that had eluded so many other Union generals and armies. He combined four military districts to make up the Middle Military Division and created the Army of the Shenandoah, some forty thousand strong and including the Army of the Potomac's Sixth Corps, the Nineteenth Corps (recently arrived from Louisiana), and various units that had been operating in and near the Shenandoah Valley. Sheridan established headquarters at Harpers Ferry, where he presided over the assembling of his new army.[54]

On July 26, Lowell was released from service against Mosby and instructed to report with the 2nd Massachusetts for immediate duty in the Shenandoah Valley. Under the direction of the Army of the Shenandoah's chief of cavalry, Brig. Gen. Alfred T. A. Torbert, Lowell took charge of the Third Brigade in General Wesley Merritt's First Division. The Third Brigade, officially organized on August 9 and also known as the Provisional Brigade, included parts of the 2nd Massachusetts and the 14th and 22nd Pennsylvania and 1st Maryland regiments. Lowell had precious little time to prepare his men for action. On August 6, Sheridan reported to Grant that he had "ordered Col. Lowell with a portion of his command to make a reconnaissance on the south side of the river in the direction of Martinsburg." Sheridan soon began his move forty miles up the Valley to Strasburg, where Early's forces were entrenched. "Colonel Lowell led the advance, and next day met the enemy six miles north of Winchester, and after a sharp skirmish turned them about and drove them pell-mell through the town," related a report of the movement. On August 11–12, Lowell's brigade helped to secure the fords across Opequon Creek for the Union Army, which Sheridan declared indispensable to his plan of attack.[55]

With that engagement, Lowell began nine weeks of constant movement and fighting.[56] Due to alarm about Confederate reinforcements, Sheridan's army made an abrupt exit from Strasburg, and on August 16 Lowell received responsibility for guarding Sheridan's rear as he moved down the Valley toward Halltown, near Harpers Ferry. While protecting Sheridan's retreat, the cavalry was ordered to destroy anything of use to the enemy. "I had the right rear," Lowell explained to his wife, "with orders from Grant to drive in every horse, mule, ox, or cow, and burn all grain and forage — a miserable duty." Sheridan, who despised southerners, ruthlessly carried out Grant's instructions, expressing a grim satisfaction at a job well done. Afterwards Sheridan wrote, "Reduction to poverty brings prayers for peace more surely and more quickly than does destruction of human life." Lowell expressed more ambivalence. He executed his superiors' orders to destroy the countryside only after concluding that such destruction would end the conflict. Nevertheless, he worried that his actions might violate the rules of war, remarking that "the war in this part of the country is becoming very unpleasant to an officer's feelings."[57]

An incident during the third week of August reveals the character of fighting in the early phase of the Valley campaign. Leaving the area around Cedar Creek on the seventeenth, Lowell and his brigade had been lightly engaged all day when they were suddenly pressed by a more numerous enemy force. Ordered to fall back, Lowell constructed a defensive position on a small hill that offered some protection from Confederate artillery. He brought along a "quaker gun," a piece of wood on wagon wheels that from a distance resembled a cannon. Lowell instructed his men to "load" the wood, which immediately attracted rebel fire. He then swiftly moved his men away from the hill, temporarily out of cannon range. Lowell's orderly provided the rest of the story: "We fell back from there. We went down a hill and through the woods, and in a field we found our ammunition trains that had not been moved. Then the Rebs were on top of the hill behind us, and the Colonel had to turn and charge and drive them back from the ammunition trains; then he dismounted the men behind stone walls, and held them in check until they moved the ammunition. I saw the Colonel sitting behind the stone wall on his horse, and a shot from a cannon struck the wall by him, and for a good while I could not see him for the dust and stones that flew over and around him."[58]

As this incident demonstrates, Lowell displayed his by now polished skills to best advantage. His experience fighting against Mosby's raiders made him one of Sheridan's most valuable assets in the Valley campaign. "I never had to tell him what to do," Sheridan remarked. Lowell effectively combined mounted and dismounted attacks against Confederate cavalry or infantry, as the situation warranted. His skillful tactical maneuvers, which included a deadly use of repeating rifles, were complemented by his inspiring personal leadership. He led his men into battle in the full uniform of an officer. Robert Williams of the 2nd Massachusetts wrote his parents that Lowell "was always in the front when we were moving toward the enemy and in the rear when moving from them." That kind of display made Lowell a conspicuous target, and he knew the risk it entailed. But Lowell considered that risk a critical part of his duty as an officer. Once queried as to why he persisted in wearing an officer's crimson sash while pursing sharpshooters, he replied, "It is good for the men to have me wear it."[59]

Lowell also employed his saber to good effect, even though its usefulness was limited in the Civil War. On August 26, part of Lowell's command participated in an attack Sheridan ordered against Maj. Gen. Joseph B. Kershaw's division. Expressing a desire to view Lowell in action, Sheridan and his staff rode out to observe the action. The Confederates were entrenched behind a rail fence. Lowell observed that it was too high to leap over, and so he galloped along its length and struck enemy muskets with his sword while some of his troopers tore down sections of the barrier. Private Samuel Backus recalled that "Lowell led an attack against the advance of the enemy infantry and charged up a rail fence, behind which they were intrenched, and while he and a few of his men held them there—he himself actually whacking their leveled muskets with his saber—the rest tore down the barrier, and then they all charged again." Lowell's troopers captured seven officers and sixty-nine enlisted men, along with guns and other equipment. Sheridan turned to one of his aides and said, "Lowell is a brave man." One awed soldier praised Lowell's courage and described its effect on the men of his brigade: "Such a noble scorn of death and danger they never saw before and it inspired them with a courage that quailed at nothing."[60]

Lowell thoroughly approved of General Sheridan's sending out cavalry every day to meet the enemy. "It is exhilarating," he exclaimed, "to see so many cavalry about and to see things *right* again." The Valley's rolling terrain and good roads favored cavalry engagements, and Sheridan understood how to employ the mounted arm. He had forged the Army of the Potomac's horsemen into a deadly strike force that employed mobility, daring, and mastery of rapid-fire carbines. In the Valley, Federal cavalry contributed critically to Sheridan's success. The Union commander skillfully employed three cavalry divisions, which totaled more than 8,000 men, and twelve batteries of horse artillery to help achieve victories that sped the Confederates' final exit from the Valley. Lowell belonged to a group of talented officers who brought the Union cavalry to its greatest successes in battles such as Third Winchester, Fisher's Hill, Tom's Brook, and Cedar Creek. For his part, Lowell provided a favorable assessment of his commander: "I like Sheridan immensely, he is the first general I have seen who puts as much heart and time and thought into his work as if he were doing it for his own exclusive profit. He works like a mill-owner or an iron-master, not like a soldier—never sleeps, never worries, is never cross, but isn't afraid to come down on a man who deserves it."[61]

Sheridan also approved of his subordinate. On September 9, he appointed Lowell to lead the newly constituted Reserve Brigade in Merritt's division, which was composed of the First, Second, and Fifth U.S. Cavalry, Battery D of the Second U.S. Artillery, the 6th Pennsylvania, and Charley's own 2nd Massachusetts. Now in charge of three seasoned regular units, Lowell rightly concluded that Sheridan had paid him a high compliment. "I believe Sheridan is entirely satisfied with what we have done," he confided to John Forbes in relating news of his new command. Lowell and his troopers would be fighting alongside Col. James H. Kidd's First Brigade and Col. Gen. Thomas C. Devins's Second Brigade, and they would distinguish themselves in several notable engagements beginning with Third Winchester.[62]

In September, Lee recalled a portion of Early's army to Richmond, opening the way for Sheridan to attack the weakened Confederates at Winchester. Before dawn on September 19, General Merritt ordered Lowell to attack the enemy's infantry and establish a position across the Opequon Creek north of Winchester. Lowell's troopers moved toward the creek, where they scattered a Confederate picket line and captured several dozen prisoners. Throughout a long day's battle, Lowell's brigade joined other Union cavalry in pressuring Jubal Early's left flank. "In this campaign it had been Lowell's aim to educate his command up to attacking infantry and artillery," observed Edward W. Emerson in his edition of Lowell's letters, "and he showed the way himself, leaping the ditch or breastwork or rails, sword in hand." As part of the fight, Lowell attacked a battery with a small group of troopers who soon found themselves face to face with rebel cannons. One of the pieces fired, killing two horses, including Lowell's. Lowell swiftly found another horse and took the guns. General Merritt reported how the "noble Lowell, with his heroic little brigade, moved boldly forward," scattering rebels in confusion. "It was a noble work well done," concluded Merritt, "a theme for the poet; a scene for the painter." The next day, Lowell wrote to his wife about his horse troubles. "Poor Billy was shot in three places and is dead. . . . During the afternoon, I had one horse killed and two wounded, — all taken from orderlies." Lowell half-believed himself to be invincible, as if his death-defying actions were somehow miraculously protected. "Isn't it lucky that I keep always well and hearty?" he reassured his wife. "My friends never feel any anxiety on *that* account." And although Lowell had always ridden his mounts hard, during the Shenandoah campaign thirteen horses were shot from underneath him. "You see I am unlucky on horses," he ruefully quipped to a friend; ". . . it is the best form in which ill luck could come."[63]

The day-long battle at Winchester struck a bloody and devastating blow to the Confederates, yet the persistent and skilled Early showed no intention of withdrawing, much less admitting defeat. Lee sent reinforcements to Early, and the fighting continued. In late September and early October, Federal cavalry engaged in a systematic destruction of the Valley's countryside, known as The Burning. Lowell did not take part in the destruction but declared to Josephine that "if it will help end bushwhacking, I approve it, and I would cheerfully assist in making this whole Valley a desert from Staunton northward."[64]

In the wake of The Burning, Federal cavalry faced off on October 9 against their Confederate counterparts in the battle of Tom's Brook. Also known as "the Woodstock Races" because of the 26-mile Confederate retreat after the battle, this action marked the largest all-cavalry engagement of the Valley campaign. William J. Miller's essay in this volume details the tactical ebb and flow of the action, which need not be repeated here. Tom's Brook underscored the superiority of Sheridan's troopers in the Valley, and Lowell continued to collect praise for his battlefield performances. On horseback during the fighting, Lowell led his dismounted soldiers into action and inflicted heavy losses on the enemy. General Torbert reported that at Tom's Brook "the cavalry totally covered themselves with glory. . . . Brigadier-Generals Merritt and Custer and Colonels Lowell and Pennington, commanding brigades, particularly distinguished themselves." George Sanford was there and later described how "Lowell's Reserve Brigade, with the 1st cavalry leading, captured five pieces of artillery and then dashed on in pursuit. It was a great sight and the men were wild." A trooper in the 2nd Massachusetts recalled that in the battle Lowell exposed himself to Confederate bullets so fearlessly that he "dared not look at him for *I knew he would fall*, and yet he came back steadily and all right, his horse always wounded or killed, and himself never, until I began to feel that he was safe—but how, God alone knew." Overall, Lowell's conduct fully justified the words of one of Sheridan's aides, who, though not speaking about Tom's Brook, insisted that there was "no cooler head or better brain in all the army, no one to be more absolutely relied upon."[65]

The young colonel had for some time been performing the duties of a brigadier general, but as yet no promotion had materialized. His wife, his friends, and his supporters expressed anger and puzzlement that he still wore the "silver eagles on the yellow ground of a cavalry colonel." Lowell refused to lobby for the reward that he nonetheless thought was due him. Because he banned all reporters from his camp, his exploits were not featured prominently in the newspaper accounts of the battles. "I am very glad, my dear Mr. Forbes," Lowell explained to his old patron, "that we have not a hand writer among us. The reputation of regiments is made and is known in the Army,—the comparative

merits are *well* known there." He heaped scorn on those officers who culti-
vated the press and received supposedly undeserved notoriety. Lowell admitted, however, that he felt frustrated. In a letter to his wife on September 9, he
confessed weariness at always being in command of "patched up affairs" that
came with so many "prides and prejudices" with which to contend. "I . . . shall
try to do what I can," he concluded. "I don't think I now care at all about being
a Brigadier-General. I am *perfectly* satisfied to be a Colonel, if I can always have
a brigade to command; — that's modest, isn't it?"[66]

As his wry comment illustrated, Lowell was not a modest man. He strove for
excellence and expected, and even yearned, for approbation. He also planned
a postwar career that combined personal ambition with a patriotic agenda.
Despite the constant fighting, Lowell found time to write a series of letters
to family and close friends in the first two weeks of October. At first glance,
his reflections revealed a harder, more practical man than four years earlier.
He had given up the grand idealism that had captured his youthful imagination. Instead, Charley advised Henry Lee Higginson to "live like a plain republican," be forever "mindful of the beauty and the duty of simplicity," and
most of all, be an "unpretending hero," because if America did not produce
these "useful citizens" in great numbers, then "we are not going to have any
Country."[67]

Lowell warned others to throw their support to Lincoln and the Republican Party in the upcoming elections. To Charles E. Perkins, he sounded a
desperate note: "I hope and trust and believe that you are doing all you can
for Lincoln, — and I believe that McClellan's election would send this country to where Mexico and South America are. Do what you can to prevent it."
He depicted the war's results as "a great revolution [that] has been going on."
Lowell was convinced that the conflict would end in the near future. The time
had come for the men who successfully led the Union armies to be prepared to
guide the country through reconstruction. "What should we do with a peace,"
he asked, "until events have shaped out a policy which a majority of people at
the North will recognize as the necessary one for a successful reorganization
of the Southern territory and Southern institutions?" The sacrifices made by
the country must not be wasted, according to Lowell. He had always believed
in the importance of leadership, but his wartime experiences confirmed that
importance a thousand times over. Like so many, he grieved for the loss of relatives and friends to battle injuries, but he remained personally fearless. He always led his men in full officer's dress, and was thus a conspicuous target. One
horseman noted that "Lowell was known as one of the very bravest men in the

whole army." This observer explained, "He was a fatalist and believed that one must die when his time came and that no possible precaution could alter the fact." His valorous behavior might suggest recklessness but actually was very much in line with nineteenth-century ideas of courage and manhood. Lowell did not have a death wish; he eagerly planned his postwar future. In the fall of 1864, he expressed confidence that he would meet expectations in peacetime just as he had in wartime. Survival was the key. In one of his last letters to Josephine, Lowell wrote, "I don't want to be shot till I've had a chance to come home. I have no idea that I shall be hit, but I want so much not to now, that it sometimes frightens me."[68]

On October 12, Lowell's brigade arrived near Cedar Creek, a stream that lay in the shadows of Massanutten Mountain. The Valley seemed peaceful, with Early nowhere in sight. Lowell concluded that the Confederates' will to fight was utterly destroyed. He speculated that momentarily his unit might be sent on a raid to Charlottesville.[69] Lowell joined many others in thinking that operations were finished. Sheridan had carried out Grant's two-part plan to destroy the enemy forces and their breadbasket. The harvest that Lee hoped to save was lost; potential starvation loomed for his soldiers. The feisty Little Phil's success bred overconfidence. Sheridan believed his victory was secured, and he decided to leave the Shenandoah Valley to join Grant at Petersburg. Parts of the Sixth Corps were already moving east toward Ashby's Gap. Sheridan and Stanton planned to meet in Washington within days to discuss the further redeployment of the Army of the Shenandoah.

On October 15, the army lay near Middletown, arrayed behind the meandering Cedar Creek. Sheridan's left wing consisted of Brig. Gen. George Crook's two divisions from the Eighth Corps, and to his right, two divisions from Gen. William Emory's Nineteenth Corps. Lowell's and Col. James H. Kidd's brigades camped about four to five miles west of Emory. Their duty was to protect the army's right wing at Cedar Creek, which consisted of three divisions of Maj. Gen. Horatio Wright's Sixth Corps. Bivouacked on the relatively flat ground behind the creek, Wright's divisions were dangerously exposed to attack from the west. Lowell positioned his troopers nearly a mile west of the Sixth Corps encampment, behind Devin's and in front of Kidd's brigades. Although outwardly calm, the scene included disturbing signs that Early had not in fact withdrawn. Sheridan called back the departing troops from the Sixth Corps when, on October 16, intelligence reported rebel reinforcements being sent to Early's aid. Despite these precautions, Sheridan neither called off his trip (he expected to be back within twenty-four hours) nor expressed undue worry about the vulnerable position of his troops. On October 18, Sheridan left for the capital city, leaving General Wright in charge during his short absence.[70]

Many veterans later remembered that evening as particularly beautiful, with a full moon rising in the night sky. Lowell arose just after midnight, preparing to probe the right for an enemy presence. On October 19, reveille for the Reserve Brigade was at 3:30 A.M. Before troopers finished breakfast, they heard shots echo in the distance. Kidd's Michigan brigade had exchanged fire with some Confederates, and Lowell sent pickets groping through a foggy mist to investigate.[71] Meanwhile, thousands of northern soldiers slept, blissfully unaware that Confederate troops had spent the night moving en masse around the north slope of the Massanutten intent on destroying the entire Federal army with a single blow. Although much smaller than Sheridan's, Early's army throughout the campaign had exercised fully their advantage of experience and intimate knowledge of the countryside — an advantage never more evident than in the planning and execution of this imminent attack.[72]

At dawn, the rebels struck the camps of Crook's Eighth Corps. Within half an hour, the entire left of the Union army was in flight, panic was spreading to the Nineteenth Corps, and a major disaster appeared inevitable. Lowell and Kidd, hearing heavy fire on the army's far left, awaited instructions, but none came. Heavy fog still shrouded the battlefield, and the two officers discussed whether or not to move in the direction of the fire. Neither knew that orders had been given to move the cavalry from the army's right to its left, toward the Valley Pike. Lowell urged action, but Kidd hesitated, fearing to contravene his earlier orders. According to Kidd, he asked Lowell, "Colonel, what would you do if you were in my place?" Lowell answered, "I think you ought to go, too. . . . Yes, I will take the responsibility to give you the order."[73] Lowell led the brigades toward a rise just north of Middletown. From their position on a slight plateau, the pair watched as the rising sun revealed the extent of the Union calamity. Working hard to restore order, Wright ordered Lowell to move his brigade to support the frantic troops now falling back rapidly. The time was 9:00 A.M. The long cavalry column moved across the high ground and behind the rear of the Nineteenth Corps. Brig. Gen. William Dwight, a division commander with the corps, desperately sought to re-form his men. He stopped for a moment to watch the cavalry and described the scene: "They moved past me, that splendid cavalry. Lowell got by me before I could speak but I looked after him a long distance. Exquisitely mounted, the picture of a soldier, erect, confident, defiant, he moved at the head of the finest brigade of cavalry that at this day scorns the earth it treads."[74]

Despite the gravity of the situation, Lowell must have felt pride that severe fire from Confederate batteries did not cause any of his men to falter or the column to break, except for adjustments for the injured. His brigade had proven stalwart in recent battles, and now his horsemen again showed their courage. At 9:30 A.M., Lowell and Kidd arrived on high ground northeast of Middletown where Brig. Gen. George W. Getty's Second Division of the Sixth Corps was forming after putting up a strong fight on a hill near the Middletown cemetery. Lowell traversed the pike, deployed his men on the east side, and waited for direction that came within minutes. Merritt ordered him to attack a troublesome rebel battery — located behind some stone walls that formed a right angle to one of the roads bordering the northern edge of the village — that supported Brig. Gen. Gabriel C. Wharton's brigades.

Lowell immediately ordered most of his brigade to dismount and await the order to attack. He led the rest in a charge to force the Confederates back to a line of trees. While doing so, he had his thirteenth horse in thirteen weeks shot from under him. Quickly procuring another, Lowell returned to a desperate fight. General Merritt described Devin's and Lowell's brigades as confronting a "living wall of the enemy, which . . . emitted a leaden sheet of fire upon their devoted ranks." Lowell and his men came under considerable fire not only from rebel artillery but also from sharpshooters positioned on the roofs of houses in Middletown. Two charges later, a sniper's bullet hit Lowell in the chest, stunning him. The projectile did not penetrate his skin, but its force collapsed a lung, precipitating bleeding, faintness, and hoarseness. Despite the injury, Lowell continued fighting. Devin and Custer provided reinforcements, and the Confederates, facing a considerable number of Union cavalrymen, withdrew temporarily to a second set of stone walls. Lowell refused to leave the field, insisting that he be allowed to remain in command despite his weakened condition. "He was wounded painfully in the early part of the day soon after which I met him," wrote Wesley Merritt shortly after the battle. "He was suffering acutely from his wound but to ask him to leave the field was an insult to him." Lowell was carefully placed on the ground and covered with an overcoat provided by one of his staff.[75]

By late morning, the Confederates believed that they had won a major battle. They had routed decisively two of the three Union corps. This time, however, success made Jubal Early overconfident. A lull in the fighting allowed a goodly number of Union troops to reorganize for the expected second wave of battle. Sheridan, who was on his way back to Cedar Creek from Winchester, heard the sounds of guns. Moving purposefully southward, Sheridan reached his army by noon, and with his return demonstrated a brilliant generalship by regrouping his frightened soldiers and planning a counterattack. "When I arrived," Sheridan recalled, "this division [of Getty's Sixth Corps] and the cavalry were the only troops in the presence of and resisting the enemy." Sheridan's battle plan was simple and inspiring. He ordered his soldiers to attack the Confederates and regain their lost ground. Pride and victory were the goals. Sheridan asked Lowell whether or not he felt able to maintain his ground at the critical juncture. He wrote later that "Lowell replied that he could."[76]

At 4:00 P.M., Sheridan launched his assault on a weakened Confederate line. Faced with a renewed attack by a reinvigorated Army of the Shenandoah, Early's army wavered and then broke. Sheridan ordered Lowell's brigade to mount a third charge against the same guns that earlier had posed a formidable danger to Union soldiers. Unable to speak above a whisper, and despite protests from his subordinates, Lowell prepared to lead the attack. "I am well now," he murmured. Lifted back onto his horse, Lowell formed his brigade into battle line and led the charge on the battery. He immediately suffered another wound; the bullet severed his spinal cord, leaving him paralyzed below the waist. Caspar Crowninshield, who took command of the brigade when Lowell fell, recalled that "the charge in which Col. Lowell was killed was a very desparate one. We charged over an open field, the enemies infantry posted behind a stone wall and with 4 or 5 pieces of artillery. We charged all most up to the wall but we could not carry it. Their fire was perfectly fearful. Grape and Cannister and Musket balls came into us in perfect showers, we were driven back with considerable loss." Merritt's report described how "the fearless Lowell, at the head of as gallant a brigade as ever rode at a foe, fell in the thickest of the fray, meeting his death as he had always faced it — calmly, resolutely, heroically. His fall cast a gloom on the entire command." Sheridan wrote simply, "The accomplished Lowell received his death-wound in this courageous charge."[77]

Lowell's brigade won the fight for the battery, and the rest of the army salvaged victory from the wreck of the morning's debacle. The Union triumph at Cedar Creek ended Early's serious operations in the Valley and proved a harbinger of the end of the Confederacy. Sheridan would shortly rejoin Grant for the final months of the war. Meanwhile, Lowell was transported to a house in Middletown that served as a small hospital. His death was inevitable. Dr. Oscar De Wolf, the assistant surgeon attached to the 2nd Massachusetts, tended Lowell during his last hours. He recorded that Lowell accepted his fate calmly. The stricken colonel comforted the wounded around him and wrote a few words of farewell to his pregnant wife. Crowninshield, whose doubts about Lowell's

"Colonel Charles R. Lowell shot by sharpshooter from Brinker's House." In James E. Taylor's sketch, Lowell's horse rears as its rider is wounded. Taylor's memoir observed: "[T]hat accomplished officer received his death wound from a sharpshooter's bullet that sped on its mission of death from an upper window of . . . the Brinker house. . . ." Courtesy of the Western Reserve Historical Society, Cleveland, Ohio.

leadership had been put to rest in the preceding two months, visited Lowell briefly. He recounted that Lowell told him that "my only regret is that I cannot do something more for our war cause." Lowell lingered until dawn on October 20 and then died peacefully in his twenty-ninth year. "Colonel Lowell," wrote a sorrowful Crowninshield, "died like a hero and he certainly was one of the bravest of the brave." During the battle, Lowell's commission as a brigadier general was signed, too late to be delivered.[78]

Lowell's funeral was held on October 28, 1864, at the Harvard College chapel. That Friday morning dawned cold and rainy, matching the mood of the grief-stricken relatives and friends who gathered to pay their last respects. Charley's body, brought from his parents' house in a flag-wrapped coffin, was placed by soldiers on the chapel altar decorated with leaves, evergreens, and flowers. The attending minister read lines from a poem composed to honor the Union dead:

Wrap round his breast the flag that breast defended;
His Country's flag, in battle's front enrolled:
For it he died, — on earth forever ended
His brave young life lives in each sacred fold.

After the service, Lowell was buried at Mount Auburn Cemetery in Cambridge.[79]

Charles Russell Lowell—citizen and soldier—was mourned as one of the Union's best and brightest. His peers believed he embodied the virtues of the officer-gentleman: honorable, brave, and fair. Many soldiers aspired to these virtues, but few came as close as Lowell to manifesting them in the hard reality of war. His heroic actions in the battles of the Shenandoah Valley campaign, and especially at Cedar Creek, demonstrated a magnificent fulfillment of his military experience and his leadership potential. Those actions also reflected the maturation of the individual who had arrived at the battlefield in 1861 shaped by his social class, by his education, by his political preferences, and by his career aspirations. From beginning to end, his stated motivation for fighting the war never changed—it was for Union and for freedom.

It is now commonplace for historians to question the reputation of many Civil War heroes. This is especially true with those who survived the war and wrote about their experiences, often embellishing their accomplishments beyond recognition. Those who did not survive the war have often been ignored or their actions lost to the historical record. They had no one to speak for them. Lowell was not forgotten either in his own generation or to history. He was memorialized as a hero by his family, his admirers, and fellow soldiers. If they exaggerated his courage, if they elided his failures, they can be forgiven. They had an emotional stake in remembering Lowell and in honoring his place in the larger conflict.

Professional histories of the war have often included accounts of Lowell's wartime record, largely because of his contribution to the Shenandoah Valley campaign. And military scholars have usually portrayed Lowell's career in complimentary ways that would meet with the approval of his own generation. An added fascination for current scholars is his elite status. Here, some historians have cast a shadow on his reputation. They argue that his primary motivation for fighting the war, as with others of his class, was not idealistic or altruistic. Rather it was to reestablish control over an unwieldy working class and immigrant population that challenged the governing elite. The undemocratic Union that emerged from the conflict would be ruled by men like Lowell, who established their right to do so by their self-serving participation in the war.[80] Lowell did not fit neatly into this category, and because he died we can only speculate on how his life might have turned out.

We do know that despite his flaws, Lowell was tested in war as never during peace, and that he was not found wanting. "A man is meant to act and to under-

Fifteen days after Lowell's funeral, *Harper's Weekly* published this portrait and a short piece titled "Colonel Lowell" that included a quotation from General Custer: "'We all shed tears," said Custer, "'when we knew that we had lost him. It is the greatest loss the cavalry corps has suffered.'" *Harper's Weekly*, November 12, 1864.

take," he wrote, "and to try and succeed in his undertaking." Lowell excelled at the life of the soldier. He embraced the hardship and discipline required on the battlefield. He liked being an officer and believed that winning true laurels rested on his willingness to assert leadership through personal daring and courage. Lowell's achievements must not be judged solely in the service of his ambition. His stellar military record had meaning because it served, in the famous phrase of Frederick Douglass, for "something beyond the battlefield." On September 10, 1864, Lowell wrote to friend and fellow officer Francis C. Barlow: "There are better things to be done in the Country, Barlow, than fighting and you must save yourself for *them* too."[81] It is part of the vast tragedy of the American Civil War that Charles Russell Lowell died before he could fulfill the second half of his destiny.

Notes

1. *Harper's Weekly*, November 12, 1864; Gen. Wesley Merritt, "Written on the Death of General Charles R. Lowell," October 20, 1864, "Californians in the War" file, George Plummer Collection, Huntington Library, San Marino, Calif. [repository

hereafter cited as HL]; George B. Sanford, *Fighting Rebels and Redskins: Experiences in Army Life of Colonel George B. Sanford, 1861–1892,* ed. E. R. Hagemann (Norman: University of Oklahoma Press, 1969), 297–98. For a comprehensive account of Lowell's life, see Carol Bundy, *The Nature of Sacrifice: A Biography of Charles Russell Lowell* (New York: Farrar, Straus and Giroux, 2005). An indispensable earlier work is Edward Waldo Emerson, *The Life and Letters of Charles Russell Lowell* (Boston and New York: Houghton Mifflin, 1907). Emerson, the son of Ralph Waldo Emerson, worked closely with Lowell's widow in assembling the volume. Other useful sources on Lowell and his family include Mary Caroline Crawford, *Famous First Families of Massachusetts,* vol. 2 (Boston: Little Brown, 1930), 37–39, 44–45; Ferris Greenslet, *The Lowells and Their Seven Worlds* (Boston: Houghton Mifflin, 1946); Sarah Forbes Hughes, ed., *The Letters and Recollections of John Murray Forbes,* vol. 2 (Boston and New York: Houghton Mifflin, 1899); Bliss Perry, *The Life and Letters of Henry Lee Higginson* (Boston: Atlantic Monthly Press, 1921); James M. Peirce, "Charles Russell Lowell," in *Harvard Memorial Biographies,* ed. Thomas Wentworth Higginson (Cambridge, Mass.: Sever and Francis, 1867), 2:275–304; Joan Waugh, *Unsentimental Reformer: The Life of Josephine Shaw Lowell* (Cambridge, Mass.: Harvard University Press, 1997). Works on Lowell's military career will be cited below.

2. On the refurbishment of Memorial Hall, see "Harvard Is Preserving War Monument at Soldiers Field," *Civil War News* (October 2003), 52.

3. Emerson, *Life and Letters of Lowell,* 253.

4. Ibid., 204, 211, 314, 341. For a discussion of the rates of participation among northern elites, see Peter Dobkin Hall, *The Organization of American Culture, 1700–1900: Private Institutions, Elites, and the Origins of American Nationality* (New York: New York University Press, 1982), 223.

5. Reid Mitchell, "Generations, Gender and Public Families during the Civil War," unpublished paper in author's possession. See also Reid Mitchell, *The Vacant Chair: The Northern Soldier Leaves Home* (New York: Oxford University Press, 1993).

6. Emerson, *Life and Letters of Lowell,* 288–89.

7. Ralph Waldo Emerson, *Emerson's Antislavery Writings,* ed. Len Gougeon and Joel Myerson (New Haven, Conn.: Yale University Press, 1995), 102.

8. The phrase is taken from James M. McPherson, *For Cause and Comrades: Why Men Fought in the Civil War* (New York: Oxford University Press, 1997). See also McPherson, *What They Fought For, 1861–1865* (Baton Rouge: Louisiana State University Press, 1994).

9. Emerson, *Life and Letters of Lowell,* 6, 10.

10. Ibid., 16.

11. Ibid., 86, 371.

12. Ibid., 398–99. See also Hughes, *Letters and Recollections of Forbes,* 2:115.

13. Emerson, *Life and Letters of Lowell,* 187–88.

14. Ibid., 196–97; Higginson, *Harvard Memorial Biographies,* 1:iii.

15. Emerson, *Life and Letters of Lowell,* 206–7.

16. Ibid., 201–2, 211–13. Lowell stated on July 1 that he received his first orders that morning. Francis B. Heitman, *Historical Register and Dictionary of the United States*

Army, from Its Organization, September 29, 1789, to March 2, 1903, 2 vols. (Washington: Government Printing Office, 1903), 1:645, gives May 14, 1861, as the date of Lowell's commission as captain in the Third Cavalry.

17. Emerson, *Life and Letters of Lowell*, 214–16.

18. Ibid., 207, 212; George Templeton Strong, *The Diary of George Templeton Strong: The Civil War 1861–1865*, ed. Allan Nevins and Milton Halsey Thomas (New York: Macmillan, 1952), 195.

19. Emerson, *Life and Letters of Lowell*, 23–27. Lowell's wartime record is well covered in Thomas A. Lewis, *The Guns of Cedar Creek* (New York: Harper and Row, 1988), especially chapter 5; James McLean, *California Sabers: The 2nd Massachusetts Cavalry in the Civil War* (Bloomington: Indiana University Press, 2001); Jeffry D. Wert, *From Winchester to Cedar Creek: The Shenandoah Campaign of 1864* (Carlisle, Pa.: South Mountain Press, 1987).

20. Emerson, *Life and Letters of Lowell*, 221.

21. Ibid., 421.

22. Ibid., 222, 410, 29.

23. Ibid., 225, 243–44, 231.

24. On the challenges facing the Federal cavalry, see Edward G. Longacre, *Lincoln's Cavalrymen: A History of the Mounted Forces of the Army of the Potomac* (Mechanicsburg, Pa.: Stackpole, 2000), 1–52. The standard work on northern cavalry remains Stephen Z. Starr, *The Union Cavalry in the Civil War*, 3 vols. (Baton Rouge: Louisiana State University Press, 1979–84).

25. William Lawrence, *Life of Amos Lawrence* (Boston and New York: Houghton Mifflin, 1899), 186.

26. Bruce Catton, *A Stillness At Appomattox* (Garden City, N.Y.: Doubleday, 1953), 23. For Catton's discussion of the ill effects of the Union's draft and bounty system, see 22–36. See also James W. Geary, *We Need Men: The Union Draft in the Civil War* (DeKalb: Northern Illinois University Press, 1991).

27. Three very useful books on the California contingent of the 2nd Massachusetts are McLean, *California Sabers*; Thomas E. Parson, *Bear Flag and Bay State in the Civil War* (Jefferson, N.C.: McFarland, 2001); and Larry Rogers and Keith Rogers, *Their Horses Climbed Trees: A Chronicle of the California 100 and Battalion in the Civil War, from San Francisco to Appomattox* (Atglen, Pa.: Schiffer Military History, 2001).

28. Emerson, *Life and Letters of Lowell*, 290–91, 39, 236; Rogers and Rogers, *Their Horses Climbed Trees*, 87–88.

29. Emerson, *Life and Letters of Lowell*, 375; Rogers and Rogers, *Their Horses Climbed Trees*, 119–21.

30. In a face-to-face meeting a few weeks later, Secretary of War Edwin M. Stanton assured Lowell that he had acted properly. Stanton met Lowell when he presented the flags to Lincoln after Antietam. He told Lowell that he expected great things of the 2nd Massachusetts and promised Lowell a "post of honor" when the time came. The secretary admired Lowell and afterwards took a warm interest in his career (Emerson, *Life and Letters of Lowell*, 244–46). Another disciplinary case of interest occurred in Janu-

ary and February 1864. William Ormsby was a private from Company E of the 2nd Massachusetts who deserted and then joined Mosby's raiders. Upon capturing Ormsby, Lowell convened a drumhead court-martial that quickly came to a guilty decision and sentenced the deserter to death by shooting. Lowell knew he was contravening the 1862 law that said Lincoln had to pass on all sentences of death. Despite this, Lowell deliberately chose not to place the situation under review. He thought it critical to demonstrate that treason would be punished severely. He got away without a reprimand because his superiors (Maj. Gen. Christopher C. Augur and Secretary Stanton) approved of his action (Emerson, *Life and Letters of Lowell*, 450–51; Charles A. Humphreys, *Field, Camp, Hospital and Prison in the Civil War, 1863–1865* [Boston: George H. Ellis, 1918], 100–101, 105–111; Rogers and Rogers, *Their Horses Climbed Trees*, 232–35).

31. Emerson, *Life and Letters of Lowell*, 406.

32. "Our Letter from the Californians," *Daily Alta*, October 4, 1863, quoted in McLean, *California Sabers*, 51; Emerson, *Life and Letters of Lowell*, 317.

33. Emerson, *Life and Letters of Lowell*, 235; Robert Gould Shaw to Charles Russell Lowell, June 20, 1863, Shaw Family Papers, New York Public Library.

34. Emerson, *Life and Letters of Lowell*, 241, 244.

35. Ibid., 302–3, 273. General Gregg promised Lowell a brigade, while Banks claimed that Lowell's talents were vital to his department. See also Emerson, *Life and Letters of Lowell*, 229, 443–44.

36. From General Augur's headquarters for the Department of Washington came this praise for Lowell: "The Major General Commanding desires me to thank you for the very soldiery and effective manner in which have conducted the operations recently entrusted to you" (letter dated July 15, 1863, in Charles Russell Lowell, Military Service File, NATF 86, National Archives, Washington [hereafter cited as Lowell Service File]).

37. Much has been published on Mosby and his raiders. Among the more useful titles are John Singleton Mosby, *The Memoirs of Colonel John S. Mosby*, ed. Charles Wells Russell (1917; reprint, Bloomington: Indiana University Press, 1959); James A. Ramage, *Gray Ghost: The Life of Col. John Singleton Mosby* (Lexington: University Press of Kentucky, 1999); Jeffry D. Wert, *Mosby's Rangers* (New York: Simon and Schuster, 1990); Dennis E. Frye, "'I Resolved to Play a Bold Game': John S. Mosby as a Factor in the 1864 Valley Campaign," in *Struggle for the Shenandoah: Essays on the 1864 Valley Campaign*, ed. Gary W. Gallagher (Kent, Ohio: Kent State University Press, 1991), 106–27. Mosby was a major when Lowell first took the field against him but was promoted to lieutenant colonel in January 1864. His final promotion, to full colonel, came in December 1864.

38. Emerson, *Life and Letters of Lowell*, 294; U.S. War Department, *The War of the Rebellion: A Compilation of the Official Records of the Union and Confederate Armies*, 127 vols., index, and atlas (Washington: Government Printing Office, 1880–1901), ser. 1, 27(2):988–92 [hereafter cited as *OR*; all references are to ser. 1]; Ramage, *Gray Ghost*, 110–111; Wert, *Mosby's Rangers*, 91–92; McLean, *California Sabers*, 47–49.

39. Ramage, *Gray Ghost*, 111; *OR*, 29(1):652, 658; McLean, *California Sabers*, 61–62.

40. *OR*, 29(1):977; Emerson, *Life and Letters of Lowell*, 447.

41. *OR*, 29(1):987; McLean, *California Sabers*, 64. While Lowell was away from command, another tragic loss occurred. In February 1864, raiders ambushed a party from the 2nd Massachusetts returning from a two-day scouting trip. The casualty list was devastating. Capt. J. S. Reed of the California Hundred and nine of his men were killed, many others wounded, and fifty-five taken prisoner (*OR*, 33:587; Emerson, *Life and Letters of Lowell*, 451). On July 7, 1864, a clash between the raiders and Lowell's men resulted in the capture of William H. Forbes, the son of John Forbes (Emerson, *Life and Letters of Lowell*, 453–54; Rogers and Rogers, *Their Horses Climbed Trees*, 278–79).

42. Quoted in Rogers and Rogers, *Their Horses Climbed Trees*, 186.

43. Humphreys, *Field, Camp, Hospital and Prison*, 33; Emerson, *Life and Letters of Lowell*, 283–84.

44. Rogers and Rogers, *Their Horses Climbed Trees*, 205, 177.

45. Ibid., 189; *OR*, 29(2):98–99. For a discussion of Union policy toward guerrillas, see Mark Grimsley, *The Hard Hand of War: Union Military Policy toward Southern Civilians, 1861–1865* (New York: Cambridge University Press, 1995), 7–22, 111–19.

46. Emerson, *Life and Letters of Lowell*, 298–99, 311, 473; Rogers and Rogers, *Their Horses Climbed Trees*, 194–96, 202; *OR* 29, (1):658, 992.

47. Emerson, *Life and Letters of Lowell*, 265–66, 293, 286.

48. Ibid., 315–16. For official documents related to the two absences, see Lowell Service File.

49. "Beauty and youth" quote is from Herman Melville, "On the Grave of a Young Cavalry Officer Killed in the Valley of Virginia," in *Battle-Pieces and Aspects of the War* (1866; reprint, University of Massachusetts Press, 1972), 176. Other quotes from "The Scout Toward Aldie," 187, 222; Stanton Garner, *The Civil War World of Herman Melville* (Lawrence: University Press of Kansas, 1973), 307; *OR*, 33:306; Humphreys, *Field, Camp, Hospital and Prison*, 26; Ramage, *Gray Ghost*, 170–73.

50. Rogers and Rogers, *Their Horses Climbed Trees*, 151; Emerson, *Life and Letters of Lowell*, 295–96.

51. Ramage, *Gray Ghost*, 333–47. During the winter and spring of 1864, many of Mosby's men were captured. See *OR*, 33:306, 308. Assessments of Lowell's efforts against Mosby can be found in Ramage, *Gray Ghost*, 173, 224–25; McLean, *California Sabers*, 76–77.

52. Parson, *Bear Flag and Bay State*, 116. See also *OR*, 33:315–16, 985; Emerson, *Life and Letters of Lowell*, 76–77.

53. McLean, *California Sabers*, 96; Emerson, *Life and Letters of Lowell*, 373; *OR*, 37(1):250–52. Lowell's fight with Early is covered in Benjamin F. Cooling, *Jubal Early's Raid on Washington, 1864* (Baltimore: Nautical & Aviation, 1989), 182–83; Parson, *Bear Flag and Bay State*, 136–48.

54. U. S. Grant, *Papers of Ulysses S. Grant*, ed. John Y. Simon, 28 vols. to date (Carbondale: Southern Illinois University Press, 1967–), 11:378. A useful discussion of Federal leaders can be found in A. Wilson Greene, "Union Generalship in the 1864 Valley Campaign," in *Struggle for the Shenandoah*, 41–76.

55. Grant, *Papers*, 11:380; *OR*, 43(1):94, 486; Emerson, *Life and Letters of Lowell*, 457, 45; McLean, *California Sabers*, 118.

56. For enumerations of Lowell's engagements during the periods August 9–31 and September 8–October 4, see *OR*, 43(1):486, 490; Emerson, *Life and Letters of Lowell*, 445–48.

57. Emerson, *Life and Letters of Lowell*, 324, 353; McLean, *California Sabers*, 127; Philip H. Sheridan, *Personal Memoirs of P. H. Sheridan*, 2 vols. (1888; reprint, Wilmington, N.C.: Broadfoot, 1992), 228–29, 488.

58. Emerson, *Life and Letters of Lowell*, 48–49; McLean, *California Sabers*, 127–28.

59. Emerson, *Life and Letters of Lowell*, 64; Robert Henry Williams (acting adjutant of the 2nd Massachusetts under Lowell) to Richard and Ellen Williams, August 20, 1864, HM 22879 (1–6), HL; Greenslet, *Lowells*, 291.

60. Parson, *Bear Flag and Bay State*, 148; Emerson, *Life and Letters of Lowell*, 50; McLean, *California Sabers*, 132–33.

61. Emerson, *Life and Letters of Lowell*, 322, 46–47.

62. *OR*, 43(1):490, 111, 130; Emerson, *Life and Letters of Lowell*, 339. The 6th Pennsylvania was detached from the rest of Lowell's brigade and did not participate in the campaign's major battles.

63. Emerson, *Life and Letters of Lowell*, 56, 365, 327–28, 347–48; *OR*, 43(1):811, 490, 445; McLean, *California Sabers*, 136–41.

64. Emerson, *Life and Letters of Lowell*, 352–53. In this letter to Josephine, Lowell continued to express reservations about whether the wholesale burning fell within the rules of war. He spoke specifically about the destruction of the village of Dayton in response to the death by ambush of Lt. John R. Meigs of Sheridan's staff and of the execution of some of Mosby's raiders. See John H. Heatwole, *The Burning: Sheridan in the Shenandoah Valley* (Charlottesville, Va.: Howell Press, 1998) for a good overview of the topic.

65. *OR*, 43(1):431; Sanford, *Fighting Rebels and Redskins*, 284; Emerson, *Life and Letters of Lowell*, 61; Wert, *From Winchester to Cedar Creek*, 72.

66. Emerson, *Life and Letters of Lowell*, 473, 363–64, 337–38.

67. Ibid., 341.

68. Ibid., 362, 261, 357–58; Sanford, *Fighting Rebels and Redskins*, 273.

69. Emerson, *Life and Letters of Lowell*, 360.

70. See Wert, *From Winchester to Cedar Creek*, 170–73, for a detailed description of the Union positions on the eve of the battle of Cedar Creek.

71. For Kidd's viewpoint, see James H. Kidd, *One of Custer's Wolverines: The Civil War Letters of Brevet Brigadier General James H. Kidd, 6th Michigan Cavalry*, ed. Eric J. Wittenberg (Kent, Ohio: Kent State University Press, 2000), 110–16.

72. My account of the battle of Cedar Creek is based on the following: Lewis, *Guns of Cedar Creek*; Theodore C. Mahr, *Early's Valley Campaign: The Battle of Cedar Creek, Showdown in the Shenandoah* (Lynchburg, Va.: H. E. Howard, 1992); Wert, *From Winchester to Cedar Creek*.

73. J. H. Kidd, *Personal Recollections of a Cavalryman with Custer's Michigan Cavalry Brigade in the Civil War* (Ionia, Mich.: Sentinel Press, 1908), 412.

74. Elizabeth C. Putnam, *Memoirs of the War of '61: Colonel Charles Russell Lowell, Friends and Cousins* (Boston: George H. Ellis, 1920), 9–12.

75. *OR*, 43(1):450–51, 478–79; Wesley Merritt to Sgt. George Plummer, October 20, 1864, HM 16780, Plummer Collection. A member of the 2nd Massachusetts, Plummer wrote a regimental history, also at the Huntington Library, titled "Californians in the War: The Hundred and the Battalion," typescript, 21 pages, 1899, Washington, D.C. [date and place on the ms.].

76. Sheridan, *Personal Memoirs*, 2:84.

77. Rogers and Rogers, *Their Horses Climbed Trees*, 313; *OR*, 43(1):450–51; Sheridan, *Personal Memoirs*, 2:90. For an earlier, and almost identical, tribute to Lowell, see Wesley Merritt to Sgt. George Plummer, October 20, 1864, Plummer Collection.

78. Rogers and Rogers, *Their Horses Climbed Trees*, 314, 313. Ezra J. Warner, *Generals in Blue: Lives of the Union Commanders* (Baton Rouge: Louisiana State University Press, 1964), 285, states, "Upon the personal intercession of Sheridan, Lowell's commission as a brigadier general of volunteers was signed on the day of the battle." Heitman, *Historical Register and Dictionary*, 2:645, confirms that Lowell was promoted on the day of Cedar Creek.

79. For the poem, see Emerson, *Life and Letters of Lowell*, 365. The description of Lowell's death and funeral are taken from Waugh, *Unsentimental Reformer*, 82–84.

80. Analyses of the contributions of upper-class New Englanders to the war include Robert Gould Shaw, *Blue-Eyed Child of Fortune: The Civil War Letters of Colonel Robert Gould Shaw*, ed. Russell Duncan (Athens: University of Georgia Press, 1992); George M. Fredrickson, *The Inner Civil War: Northern Intellectuals and the Crisis of the Union* (New York: Harper & Row, 1965); Lawrence Lader, *The Bold Brahmins: New England's War against Slavery, 1821–1863* (Westport, Conn.: Greenwood, 1973); Gary Scharnhorst, "From Soldier to Saint: Robert Gould Shaw and the Rhetoric of Racial Justice," *Civil War History* 34 (December 1988):308–22; Lewis P. Simpson, *Mind and the American Civil War: A Meditation on Lost Causes* (Baton Rouge: Louisiana State University Press, 1989); Joan Waugh, "It Was A Sacrifice We Owed: The Shaw Family and the Fifty-Fourth Massachusetts Regiment," in *Hope and Glory: Essays on the Legacy of the 54th Massachusetts Regiment*, eds. Martin H. Blatt, Thomas J. Brown, and Donald Yacovone (Amherst: University of Massachusetts Press, 2001), 52–75.

81. Emerson, *Life and Letters of Lowell*, 344.

ROBERT K. KRICK

The Confederate Pattons

On September 26, 1918, Col. George S. Patton III, United States Army, engineered a rupture of the German lines near Cheppy, France. He forged the breakthrough by employing the military machine that he would make peculiarly his own in the next great war — the then still-novel armored and tracked tank. Patton recognized the need to push infantry through the gap to exploit the opportunity and desperately tried to rally some stragglers to that chore. Few were interested in moving forward into the hail of bullets screaming through the air. The colonel turned to the half-dozen men willing to advance, said, "It is time for another Patton to die," and began to run in the direction his tanks had taken. As he charged into the enemy muzzles, Patton later wrote, "I looked upon myself during the charge as if I were a small detached figure on the battlefield watched all the time from a cloud by my Confederate kinsmen and my Virginia grandfather." Amidst the rattle of machine guns and the grinding of armored vehicles powered by internal combustion, George Patton found inspiration from ancestral deeds in Virginia's Shenandoah Valley in the autumn of 1864. Somehow Patton managed to get within thirty yards of the German trenches before he was knocked down with a dangerous wound in his abdomen. The third George S. Patton survived his injury.[1] Not all of the spectral Confederate Pattons, from whom he had drawn inspiration, had fared so fortunately during the 1860s. The first George S. Patton, grandfather of the twentieth-century tanker, died at the head of his brigade at Winchester on September 19, 1864, in the first major battle of the 1864 Shenandoah Valley campaign.

The Patton forebears came from Scotland to America and settled in Virginia's Rappahannock River valley, bringing with them a redoubtable martial tradition. Apothecary and physician Hugh Mercer survived the deadly defeat of the Highlander army at Culloden in 1746 and emigrated to Philadelphia that same year. After serving with George Washington, a young soldier from

Fredericksburg, Virginia, in the ill-fated Braddock expedition of 1755, Mercer made his way to Washington's hometown and joined in the revolutionary talk fomenting there. Mercer operated an apothecary shop in town from which, according to Patton family lore, he helped Washington's mother Mary overcome her son's notions about temperance. "George thought his mother was hitting the bottle, and took all the liquor away from her," reported a daughter of George S. Patton III, "so she used to toddle down to Mercer's shop every afternoon . . . and he would give her 'by prescription' a nice whiskey toddy." Col. Hugh Mercer commanded a Virginia regiment in 1775. Brig. Gen. Hugh Mercer fell mortally wounded in Washington's successful crossing of the Delaware River and surprise attack at Princeton, New Jersey, on January 3, 1777. In 1793, Mercer's daughter Ann married tobacco merchant Robert Patton (another native of Scotland), a stern and demanding fellow: when a son muttered about committing suicide because of his father's demands, the old man sent him a nicely boxed set of imported straight razors, suggesting that he should use the best of utensils in all undertakings.[2]

Ann and Robert's eldest son, John Mercer Patton, married a regal Virginian named Peggy Williams in 1824. Peggy preferred her nickname, "French," because she thought that Peggy sounded undignified. Her parents came from the Slaughter family, who lived near Culpeper on Slaughter Mountain, and the Hite-Williams clan from the Shenandoah Valley near Strasburg. Both of "French" Williams Patton's ancestral home places became landmarks on bloody battlefields contested by Confederates in the next generation — Cedar Mountain and Cedar Creek. Her own offspring played a considerable role in forming the Confederate armies in Virginia. French bore a dozen children across a span of twenty-one years. Nine survived to become adults. Eight of those nine were boys. Seven of the eight bore arms for the Confederacy.[3]

John Mercer Patton attended Princeton, where his grandfather Mercer had died, then graduated from the medical department of the University of Pennsylvania in 1818. Despite his medical training and the Mercer medical tradition, John practiced law instead of the healing arts from his home in Fredericksburg. Law led to politics, in the American way. John served in the United States Congress beginning in November 1830, having been appointed to a vacant seat, then winning three elections that kept him in the national House of Representatives until April 1838. When Virginia's governor, Thomas W. Gilmer, resigned in 1841, Patton, the sitting lieutenant governor, acted as the state's chief executive for a time. The political base prompted Patton to relocate to Richmond, where he practiced law until his death in 1858.[4]

J. M. Patton's tenure in Fredericksburg unfolded in a town in which his father had long been a pillar. The senior Patton's name appeared in a local newspaper, the *Virginia Herald*, eighty times from 1790 to the 1820s. Several of the references detailed his role as manager of a lottery. Others reported on charitable and social activities. Young John and his wife bought property in several Fredericksburg locations, but they lived on the east side of Princess Anne Street near the corner of Amelia Street, on town lot 50, after buying the site from relatives in February 1833. John insured the house, "occupied by myself," together with an adjacent free-standing kitchen, for $2,800 in 1836. The Patton home stood two stories tall, built of wood, and measured 24 by 40 feet. French Patton had delivered John Mercer Patton Jr. at Spring Farm in Culpeper County on May 9, 1826, but her other two sons destined to wear three stars on their collars in the Army of Northern Virginia were born in Fredericksburg: George Smith Patton on June 26, 1833, and Waller Tazewell Patton on July 15, 1835. The original Patton home on Princess Anne Street survives today, entirely invisible, inside a house built around it almost a century ago.[5]

Soon after they bought their own home, John and French Patton joined with some relatives in a substantial philanthropic gesture. On June 30, 1834, the Pattons donated a tract facing Amelia Street, diagonally across the block from the Princess Anne house, to "the Directress and Managers of the Female Orphan Asylum," which soon thereafter built the gorgeous brick building that came to be known as Smithsonia to serve their charitable purpose. By 1840, the political and legal connections that had lured John M. Patton Sr. to Richmond prompted him to move his family to the state capital. The census enumerators found them there that summer. The Pattons did not sell their home place in Fredericksburg, however, until 1843, one day short of a decade after they had bought it.[6]

French continued to produce her large family in Richmond on an unrelentingly fecund schedule. One of the Patton brothers whom she bore fought through all four years of the Civil War and shed blood in the conflict without ever commanding troops. Hugh Mercer Patton was born in Richmond on April 6, 1841. He served as an enlisted man in Company B of the 12th Virginia Infantry and in the Charlottesville Artillery, then as adjutant of the 7th Virginia Infantry during which time he suffered a wound in the shoulder at Second Manassas. It looked for a time as though Patton would lose the arm, but he eventually recovered without an amputation. Mercer became a lieutenant and aide-de-camp on the staff of Brig. Gen. John Rogers Cooke on November 9, 1862, and served through to Appomattox. He married Fannie Dade Bull, a second cousin of General Cooke's wife, in 1870 and farmed in Culpeper. Hugh Patton died in Lynchburg three days after Christmas in 1917—not many months before his great-nephew would lead American tanks into action at Cheppy.[7]

A Patton brother too young for early war service was William Macfarland Patton, born in Richmond on August 22, 1845, and thus only fifteen years of age at secession. He nonetheless saw battle experience as a part of one of the most dramatic and famous episodes of the war in Virginia. William entered the family school, the Virginia Military Institute, on the first day of 1862; remained enrolled through all of the Institute's vicissitudes, including its relocation to Richmond after Yankees burned the Lexington campus; and graduated third in the rather large class of 1865. At New Market on May 15, 1864, Sergeant William Patton of the corps of cadets charged through the mud on the Bushong Farm with his fellow youthful student-soldiers and helped to capture the artillery that had been shooting at them all day. His big brother George commanded a regiment not many yards away on that rainy, bloody day. William's postwar career took him across the country and beyond. He held posts as a professor at his alma mater for three different tenures; worked as a mining engineer in the West Indies and Central America; built bridges across the Tombigbee, Mobile, Warrior, Susquehanna, Schuylkill, and Ohio rivers; served as engineer on the Mobile and Birmingham Railroad and the Louisville, St. Louis, and Texas Railroad; and, perhaps most challenging of all, taught at Virginia Tech, which named an engineering hall in his honor. William died in New York City on May 26, 1905, and was brought back to Virginia for burial in Lexington's Stonewall Jackson Cemetery.[8]

James French Patton, born in Richmond on September 19, 1843, attained modest rank during the war and survived it to leave a brief but impressive postwar mark on West Virginia. He went to war for the Confederacy in 1861 in the ranks of a company in the 22nd Virginia commanded by his brother, Capt. George S. Patton. In the spring of 1862, James accepted a commission as lieutenant in the 26th Virginia Battalion, which belonged to the same brigade as the 22nd. In 1863, under the nepotism that reigned as casual practice in that era, George—by then a colonel and acting brigade commander—made brother James an aide on his staff. Lieutenant Patton suffered "several wounds" during the war, "one of which narrowly escaped being fatal." The most serious came during the blood bath at Cold Harbor in June 1864, where a bullet hit James in the abdomen. After the war, the retired lieutenant became a judge in Pittsylvania County, Virginia, then a prosecutor in Monroe County, West Virginia. In 1881 Patton was appointed to the West Virginia Supreme Court, but he died the next spring and is buried, despite his exertions in favor of disunion, in Union, West Virginia.[9]

Isaac Williams Patton (his mother's father was Isaac Williams) achieved rank as high as George, John, and W. T., but in an arena farther from the center of the war's stage and far from his Virginian roots. Isaac was born in Fredericksburg on February 4, 1828. Somehow he missed out on the family's penchant for education at the Virginia Military Institute. He was attending a private school near Alexandria and reading law with his father when the Mexican War broke out. The youngster's family connections helped him secure a commission as second lieutenant in the Tenth United States Infantry early in 1847. He remained in the U.S. Army until 1855 (in 1853, he had not seen one of his brothers for six years), resigning as a first lieutenant in the Third U.S. Artillery. That background earned for Isaac the command of the "Screwmen's Guards," a Louisiana company that went to war in 1861. Patton and his wife, nee Frances E. Merritt, had moved from Virginia to Louisiana in 1857; he made his home there the rest of his life. The Screwmen's Guards became part of the 21st Louisiana Infantry, and Isaac rose to the rank of major in the regiment in March 1862, then to colonel in April 1863, with rank dating back to May 1862. On May 20, 1863, during the fighting around Vicksburg, Colonel Patton suffered a severe hip wound that hindered his mobility for the rest of his life. He convalesced as a paroled prisoner of war after Vicksburg at his father-in-law's plantation below New Orleans. Despite the disability, Patton later served actively at Mobile Bay and Spanish Fort and commanded a district headquartered at Pollard, Alabama. After the war, Colonel Patton became sheriff of New Orleans; played a leading role in the pitched street battles of Reconstruction there; was elected mayor of New Orleans; and served a term as city treasurer. The former colonel and mayor died at his home at 221 Washington Avenue, between St. Charles Avenue and Prytania Street, on February 9, 1890. An obituary boasted that his mayoral term resulted in steadily improved sanitary conditions in the city.[10]

John Mercer Patton Jr. graduated from V.M.I. before Maj. Thomas J. Jackson arrived on the Institute's faculty, but in 1861–62, Patton spent an exciting if strenuous tour in the field as a subordinate of the eccentric major — by then known as Stonewall. John performed quite well at V.M.I., with moderately good grades and a very strong military rating. At the end of his second year, young Patton stood seventh among twenty-four boys who finished. The next year he ranked sixth among seventeen, and at graduation in 1846 (the same month that Jackson was graduating from West Point), John finished eighth among sixteen seniors. His best standing was in French (third); his worst in conduct (tenth, with 85 demerits). Despite the modest ranking in conduct, Patton enjoyed the high honor of being cadet adjutant. His contentment with the V.M.I. experience shone through a speech he made to the institute's alumni association twenty-five years later. The "legitimate function of college education," Patton declared on July 4, 1871, was to combine rigor, discipline, and religion. He encouraged the school to continue its successful regimen, "relentlessly turn[ing] a deaf ear to all the modern sighing over the necessity of punishment." The graduate-orator also decried the decline of "Southern influence," which formerly had been "potent in the land and operated to check the growing license."[11]

John Jr. practiced law in Richmond, living at his parents' home for several years after graduation. In one law case, he represented the father of a V.M.I. cadet who believed that he had been overcharged in the institute's bill. John's military education doubtless served as the basis for his election as captain of the elite, highly social, Richmond Light Infantry Blues in 1852, and his reelection to two subsequent terms. Captain Patton of the Blues stares militantly out of a contemporary photograph, resplendent in a uniform bedizened with gilt and gewgaws. Patton married Sarah Lindsay "Sallie" Taylor on November 11, 1858, in Louisa County. Sallie died in 1872, and John married Lucy A. Crump in 1878. She survived the colonel by a decade, dying at their home at 215 South Third Street in Richmond in 1908. Two of John and Lucy's daughters survived, unmarried, in 1908, Susie French Patton and Agnes Park Patton. Five children of John and Sallie were alive in 1909, four of them sons.[12]

John Patton favored secession and said so prominently. On April 14, 1861, thousands of Richmonders gathered on the Capitol grounds to rejoice over the surrender of Fort Sumter. A local battery fired one hundred rounds in celebration, and Patton exhorted the crowd. Four days after the Virginia Secession Convention voted to leave the Union, John M. Patton became lieutenant colonel of the 21st Virginia Infantry by election. Precisely one year later, on April 21, 1862, Patton became colonel commanding the regiment. The 21st saw very little action through its first eleven months of existence but became intimately familiar with war at close range in the months thereafter. Robert E. Lee, who gave Patton a warm recommendation in May 1861, sent the young lieutenant colonel to Jamestown Island early in the war to organize volunteers there and arrange the area's defenses. That detail did not last long. The colonel of the 21st, Patton's immediate superior, was William Gilham, a long-time professor at V.M.I. Although neither of them remained with the 21st very long, Patton and Gilham clearly did a good job of organizing and training their regiment, as it became one of the sturdiest in the Army of Northern Virginia. In the wet, dreary, in-

Col. John Mercer Patton Jr.
A Souvenir of New Haven,
Connecticut, Fraternally
Dedicated to the Richmond
Light Infantry Blues of
Richmond, Virginia, by the
Second Company, Gover-
nor's Foot Guard, upon
the Occasion of their Visit
to New Haven, September
9, 10, 11, 1908 (n.p.: n.p.,
[1908]), 119.

conclusive campaign in western Virginia in 1861, no one accomplished much
on either side of the lines. Absence due to sickness kept Patton away from the
regiment through much of that frustrating period.[13]

Lieutenant Colonel Patton had returned to the 21st Virginia by the time it
marched out of Winchester on January 1, 1862, as part of Stonewall Jackson's
ill-fated Romney campaign. Balmy weather turned wintry, and operations deteriorated into a struggle for survival against nature's icy forces. Gilham displeased Jackson during these operations, and the army commander sent him
back to duty at V.M.I. That left Patton as the regiment's ranking officer and
commander—but he too left, on furlough (probably for health reasons again)
on January 11. Three weeks after he returned to duty on March 3, John Patton
led the 21st in the first major battle of what would become Jackson's storied
Shenandoah Valley campaign. At Kernstown on March 23, "Colonel Patton behaved very gallantly," wrote an admiring observer from a separate command,
"being always present in the thickest of the fight; his horse was wounded, and

he had a ball through his coat." The modern historian of Kernstown lauded Patton's "spirit and leadership" at the battle's critical point and credited him with having "saved the day." In his official report of his first combat, Patton reported losing 60 men out of 270 carried into action. He wrote with pride of the 21st's "gallant stand. . . . Though foot-sore and weary, their hearts were fired and they did great execution on the enemy."[14]

Through much of Jackson's rigorous campaign that spring, Patton commanded a brigade of Virginia regiments, his own 21st among them, as the senior colonel present. His admiration for the general whose exploits became legendary showed through in a letter he sent to Sallie in June 1862. Jackson "pounced like a lion," John told his wife, "first on one side, & then on another," using his "fangs" on the Yankees. Patton stood closest to center stage on June 8–9 around Cross Keys. For a time during the intervening night, he had tentative responsibility for the next morning's crucial rear-guard action, but Jackson reassigned that role to someone else by daybreak. Confusion over the mixed responsibility made its way into the history books, though not to Patton's discredit.[15]

The month after the end of the Valley campaign, Patton submitted his resignation. His family physician supplied a letter enumerating "disorders of the stomach, bowels, & liver, accompanied with great prostration of strength & emaciation." During the campaign, Patton had lost nearly 40 pounds off a frame that had not been particularly robust at the outset. The 21st's surgeon certified that the colonel had been absent sick through more than one-third of his tenure with the regiment. The resignation became effective on August 15, 1862. There is no surviving record of discontent with Patton from members of the 21st Virginia, but one artillery officer must have been delighted to see the colonel leave line command. Patton was "a pigeon headed fellow . . . with a mind as narrow as any King's that ever tormented mankind," the artillerist wrote pungently. The defects, he added thoughtfully, "as other things small and great . . . would not have been so well known or so soon but for the war."[16]

John Patton contemplated — apparently very briefly — running for elected office as soon as he left the 21st. The same Richmond newspaper that published a card from Patton's friends soliciting support for him for the Virginia House of Delegates also included a separate notice declaring that he was *not* a candidate. Patton instead spent the rest of the war back in the army, but in a sedentary staff role as a member of the military court of the Second Corps (Jackson's) of the Army of Northern Virginia; he surrendered with Lee at Appomattox in that post. A number of distinguished Virginians wrote in support of Patton's application for the courts post. Probably the most important letter came from his former law partner, John Randolph Tucker, one of the Old Dominion's most renowned barristers.[17]

The ex-Confederate colonel tried without much success to resuscitate the family estate in Culpeper County after the war, then threw himself into legal life with much energy, both practicing law and writing legal treatises. He operated much of the time from his wife's Albemarle County place, the Meadows. Patton became very active in V.M.I. matters for a time, both officially and as a regular but unofficial adviser to the institute's superintendent. In August 1865, he preferred, peculiarly, Dabney H. Maury over G. W. Custis Lee (both former Confederate generals) for an appointment on the faculty. During Reconstruction he resigned from the V.M.I. board because of his unwillingness to operate through the state's carpetbag government ("the bogus concern at Richmond," as he put it). Late in life the former colonel wrote an earnest religious book, *The Death of Death*. Colonel John Patton died in Ashland on November 24, 1898.[18]

The Confederate Patton who achieved the most fame other than George was Waller Tazewell Patton. Taz owed his contemporary prominence to diligence and bravery and skill, but his greatest lasting fame grew from his tragic end, when he was mortally wounded at the forefront of the dramatic attack at Gettysburg popularly known as Pickett's Charge.[19]

W. T. Patton joined the parade of Pattons who wended their way to Lexington for an education at V.M.I. Brother George had just graduated (though only two years older than Taz) and brother John had finished six years earlier. Taz fared very well academically. After two years, he stood first in a class of eighteen members, despite being twelfth in drawing. At graduation in 1855, he finished second, just behind Stapleton Crutchfield, who was destined to become Stonewall Jackson's chief of artillery and then die in battle during the war's closing scenes. Patton ranked second in natural philosophy (that is, physics), which Jackson taught. The bright youngster aspired to be an engineer, but admitted a few months after graduation that "it is not such a great thing to get out in the world as it is generally 'cracked up' to be, especially by the Cadets." Superintendent Francis Henney Smith of the institute gave Taz a strong recommendation with which to seek an engineering post; even better, he offered the new graduate a position on the faculty. Patton accepted with delight.[20]

Patton's return to V.M.I. to the other side of the lectern (he taught Latin) lasted only a few months. In January 1856, he fell into Smith's disfavor over a quarrel with a mess-hall steward. High-strung, still short of full maturity, Pat-

Col. Waller Tazewell Patton.
Courtesy of the Virginia Military Institute.

ton wrote an eight-page missive to Smith made up of declarations like "I could not consistently with my self-respect have returned to his table." Through the summer of 1856, Taz contemplated returning for another year on the V.M.I. faculty, but bad health drove him to White Sulphur Springs. He eventually determined upon a career in law instead of pedagogy and practiced in Culpeper until the war. As late as 1859, though, Patton still yearned enough for the academic life to apply for a professorship at the Louisiana State Seminary.[21]

When their state went to war, hundreds of young men with V.M.I. educations became the cadre upon which Virginia built an army to defend her frontiers. On May 7, 1861, two such men wrote a joint letter to the institute's superintendent. Lewis B. Williams and Waller T. Patton had much in common: they were cousins, through Taz's mother, and near neighbors (Orange and Culpeper); they graduated together in 1855; they served together on their alma mater's faculty in 1856, sometimes trading teaching roles; and in May 1861, both of them captains in the new 13th Virginia Infantry, they wrote jointly to the superintendent seeking recommendations.[22] Just more than two years later they would die together, each of them colonels, side by side at the forefront of Pickett's Charge.

Col. Lewis Burwell Williams. *Opening Celebration of the 1st Virginia Regiment Armory, Richmond, Virginia, Friday, May 29, 1914* (Richmond, Va.: State Printing Company, [1914]), unnumbered leaf [entire pamphlet lacks pagination].

Captain Williams and Captain Patton were each promoted to field-grade rank in the 7th Virginia Infantry. To Taz's disgust, Williams became lieutenant colonel of the 7th in mid-May. Six weeks later, Taz became the 7th's major, and Lewis Williams's immediate subordinate. James L. Kemper, a much distinguished Virginia politician, led the 7th as colonel. The following April, Williams transferred to the 1st Virginia Infantry with a promotion to colonel. Taz advanced to the 7th's lieutenant colonelcy, replacing Williams, then on June 3, 1862, to full colonel, when Kemper became a brigadier general and took command of a brigade that included both the 1st and the 7th regiments.[23]

Campaigning in the field did not always suit Taz Patton's constitution. On the last day of 1861, he wrote to Colonel Kemper to solicit advice and the extension of a sick furlough. The doctor diagnosed liver troubles. Patton hoped to secure command of the post at Culpeper, near home, because he hated cold weather and did not think he could stand up to winter in the field. Could Kemper help him land the Culpeper billet? Kemper's answer is not on record, but

Taz Patton returned to the 7th in time for the spring campaigns. His regiment's files include evidence that the young lieutenant colonel brooked no foolishness. He rigorously enforced his own notions of conscript laws and substitution (substitutes "are generally foreigners of doubtful character who desert . . . as soon as they have gotten their money") and defied the War Department over the way the 7th's quartermaster should function.[24]

War as a paperwork arena promptly gave way to sanguine combat in the spring of 1862. While major of the 7th, Patton had seen enough action at the battle of First Manassas to win honorable mention in the enormous official report filed by Gen. P. G. T. Beauregard. His first serious fighting came in the battle of Williamsburg on May 5, 1862. Brig. Gen. A. P. Hill, commanding the brigade that included the 7th, wearied of a stalemated firefight and ordered his men forward in a bayonet charge that carried the Federal position. Kemper led the 7th Virginia, Patton by his side. Hill's official report cited Taz as one of seven men who had been "brave, active, and energetic" in the charge. Again during the fighting around Richmond, Patton — now commanding the 7th — earned distinction, particularly during the savage contest on June 30 at Glendale, or Frayser's Farm. As he rode unscathed through sheets of lead and iron, men began to consider Colonel Patton lucky. Perhaps he agreed with them.[25]

Taz Patton's luck wavered on the plains of Manassas on August 30, 1862. As he led the 7th Virginia in that maelstrom, a bullet shattered his right hand. "There is a hole the size of a half dollar through his hand," wrote a friend, who estimated that Patton "will get off with the loss of a finger." Taz and his brother Mercer, adjutant of the 7th, who had suffered an even worse wound, convalesced for a time at the residence of Edward M. Spilman in Warrenton. The injured colonel eventually went to his mother's home (he never married) to complete his recovery. He was still absent wounded on the regimental rolls at the end of December. Taz's family noticed that the experience of war had changed him dramatically. The once "boisterous and flippant" youth, now twenty-seven years old, had become deeply religious and spoke of his wish "to lead a pure and holy life."[26]

Taz Patton's luck abandoned him for good at Gettysburg. En route through Culpeper toward Pennsylvania and a fatal destiny, he probably saw his ancestral home, "Spring Farm," where his brother had been born, for one last time. Federal occupation had devastated the house. A Pennsylvanian who visited that fall "found it a wreck, doors and window shutters all gone, floors ripped up, and nearly everything moveable taken away." In a dazzling display of Yankee rationalization, he blamed the destruction on the family for abandoning the house. "Had the family remained, no harm would have happened to it," he professed to know. "Where the family has abandoned the property it is taken for granted they do so because of their intense hatred of the Yanks, hence a retaliatory measure in the destruction of the building."[27]

Maj. Gen. George E. Pickett's division, which had brought only three of its five brigades to Gettysburg, played no role in the first two days of that titanic struggle. On the third day, July 3, 1863, Gen. Robert E. Lee in desperation sent Pickett's men, and a montage of other units, straight across nearly a mile of open country toward the heart of the Federal line on Cemetery Ridge. Kemper's brigade suffered dreadfully from artillery shells, then from canister as the range closed, and then from a deluge of musketry. Kemper went down horribly wounded. Somehow Colonels Taz Patton and Lewis Williams reached the stone fence that marked the enemy line. The two grasped hands and jumped atop the wall. "It's our turn next, Tazewell!" his cousin shouted, and the two young men crossed the wall and fell in a bloody heap. Colonel Williams died soon thereafter. Soldiers carried the mangled Kemper back across the field and eventually to Virginia. Patton fell into enemy hands.[28]

The bullet that laid Taz Patton low shattered his mouth and face. The three colonel-brothers of Virginia regiments resembled one another, especially George and Taz, but W. T. Patton looks calmly out of his surviving portrait with the most impressive mien of the kinsmen. Handsome features, an imposing but well-groomed beard, and a dignified composure convey a sense of worth and purpose. The steady eyes suggest a confident warrior. All of that external image vanished with the bullet's impact. Federal surgeons described the wound as in "Both Jaws." The victim himself told his mother that the wound "through the mouth" had fractured "the face bone badly on both sides." The damage made it impossible for him to speak most of the time, so he communicated with friends and nurses by writing on a slate. "Tell my mother that I am about to die in a foreign land," he wrote, "but I cherish the same intense affection for her as ever." Twelve days after his wounding, Taz reported a prognosis of "small" danger of a mortal result, although the wound was "serious, annoying, and will necessarily be a very long time in getting well." Nine days later he was dead, less than a week past his twenty-eighth birthday. A final note on the slate to his nurse said that, although he was "a young man and prized life, he would cheerfully lay down fifty lives in such a cause." Tazewell's mother received her son's optimistic letter of July 15 in the same envelope with another that reported his death. Her son's nurses said that they never would forget Patton's "beautiful chestnut hair on the pillow." They reported his dying words: "In Christ alone, perfectly content."[29]

By the time the 1864 Shenandoah Valley campaign began, only George S. Patton of the three colonel-brothers in the Virginia theater remained on stage. His war had been fought in Virginia, although not with Lee's army until 1864. That circumstance resulted directly from his prewar life and career, which had taken him away from the family's primary roots around Richmond, Culpeper, and Fredericksburg and into western Virginia.

George Patton forged a spectacular scholastic record at V.M.I. on the basis of a meteoric climb through the ranks in his senior year. After standing ninth in 1850, at the end of his second year, and dropping to fifteenth the next term, Patton somehow managed to rise to second among twenty-four graduates in the class of 1852. That standing included the highest marks in the classes for tactics, geology, French, English, and Latin and second in Professor T. J. Jackson's natural philosophy. Only inaptitude in drawing (eighteenth) kept Cadet Patton from climbing from the fortieth percentile all the way to first place in a single year. Classmates called George "Frenchy," in reaction to his facial hair, his meticulous habits of dress, and a relentless enthusiasm about the opposite sex.[30]

The superintendent of his alma mater promptly found young Patton a job teaching at a private school, but that fell through when the prospective employers offered an annual salary of $300 and Patton demanded $400. He apologized to Superintendent Smith for any embarrassment resulting from the "*contretemps*" and kept in touch with Smith steadily for the rest of his life. George remained around Richmond and Culpeper for several years, expecting to make a career in education. In 1853, he opened an exclusive preparatory school in the state capital in company with a German professor named Ernest Volger. "Volger & Patton" "succeeded very well," operating in a two-story brick academy, but at the end of the 1855 term Patton sold out his interest and moved to Kanawha County in western Virginia. For the few years of life remaining to him, George Patton became a member of that rather different society and culture than he had known in Virginia's flatlands. It certainly agreed with him. A few months after Patton settled in Kanawha, he called his location "a refined and intelligent neighborhood."[31]

Before he left eastern Virginia, George S. Patton had married a girl from Mobile, Alabama, on November 8, 1855 (a Thursday, atypical for wedding arrangements). Susan Thornton Glassell came from a Virginia family that had relocated to Alabama in her infancy. The ceremony's circumstances were fraught

Col. George S. Patton. Courtesy of the Virginia Military Institute.

with unknowable connections to a Confederate war still in the dim future. The couple exchanged their vows at St. Paul's Church in Richmond, where the Confederacy's leaders would worship, and where word would reach Jefferson Davis on a Sunday in 1865 of his capital city's collapse. The Reverend Philip Slaughter of Culpeper officiated at the 1855 wedding; seven years later his home and farm would be the scene of the battle of Slaughter's Mountain, or Cedar Mountain. George's bride was the only daughter of Andrew Glassell. Susan's brother William Thornton Glassell (1831–76), as a commander in the Confederate navy, would win renown by attacking the Federal gunboat *New Ironsides* in Charleston harbor in 1863 with a crude torpedo boat. Some of George's courtship correspondence with "My darling Sue" survives, revealing an ardent suitor of old-fashioned sentimental mien. He suggested to Susan ("my little scamp" and "Pet") that "the gentle eye and soft heart of woman should temper the afflictions, and pour balm on the sorrows of her loved partner." In early August, George bewailed the twenty-two-day absence from his fiancée, "the longest separation that we have yet had."[32]

George took his new bride to the Kanawha Valley, set up housekeeping, started a family, and became worshipful master of a local Masonic lodge. He read law, passed the bar, and went into practice with Thomas Lee Broun — who also became a Confederate colonel. In 1858, the Pattons bought an impressive home for $2,900. Looming war fever soon turned young Patton into the military man that V.M.I. had trained him to be. The invasion of Harpers Ferry, Virginia, by a band of raiders under John Brown galvanized much of the country in diametrically different ways. In Kanawha County, young men formed a volunteer military organization, named it the Kanawha Riflemen, and elected George Patton captain. As befitted his V.M.I. background, the captain proved to be "a martinet in discipline." He remained at the head of the riflemen, and the larger units into which they were subsumed, for the rest of his life. In 1859, Captain Patton wanted his regiment to look as crisp on parade as had his V.M.I. comrades, so he designed a snappy uniform. It featured bright brass buttons on dark green broadcloth, wide gold stripes on the trousers, gaudy headgear, white gloves, and crossed belts. Patton and his men would look back on that innocent uniform with amusement once real war had its way with them. The company's weapons, by contrast, were as businesslike as could be acquired. Patton somehow managed to outfit his men with Mississippi rifles, armament far better than the early-war Confederate norm.[33]

The Kanawha Riflemen responded predictably to Abraham Lincoln's demand for troops to invade the southern states by marching through Virginia. The mountain lads issued a declaration full of the same rodomontade that echoed across the whole country: "We . . . declare it to be our fixed purpose to never use arms against the state of Virginia, or any other southern state, in any attempt to coerce or subjugate them." Instead, inevitably, they pledged their loyalty to the Old Dominion and went to war under Virginia's standard. George mustered into state service on May 22, 1861, as captain commanding the riflemen, who soon became Company H, 22nd Virginia Infantry, and went into Confederate service. Early in June, the captain was commanding 350 men in a camp of instruction and soliciting support in getting a promotion. A few weeks later Patton held a commission as major so briefly that no full record survives, and on July 17, 1861, he became lieutenant colonel of the regiment.[34]

The company and regiment had not been Confederates many weeks before they went into action defending Virginia. The combat left George Patton badly wounded and entangled in a warren of military bureaucracy that extended across the lines between the armies. On July 17, 1861, the 22nd Virginia and a motley array of other Confederates fought a small army of Ohio troops on Scary Creek, near its confluence with the Kanawha River. The clash seemed a veritable Armageddon to the green soldiers, though it would barely rate as a skirmish by later-war standards. Brig. Gen. Henry A. Wise, a former governor and always a politician, filled his report of Scary Creek with such gasconade as "I ordered him to put the steel of his bayonet into their teeth." Patton galloped into the midst of his men to rally them. The colonel's "gallantry was most conspicuous," a superior wrote, but a bullet shattered his left shoulder. He was one of only ten Confederate casualties. The Federals lost fifteen killed, nine wounded, and seven missing.[35]

Patton would recover completely if slowly from his painful wound, but not nearly in time to retreat with Wise when he abandoned the Kanawha Valley not long after the Scary Creek encounter. That left Patton subject to capture. A Federal counterpart, Col. Jesse S. Norton of the 21st Ohio, proved to be Patton's salvation, but only after dealing with an intricate web of complications. Norton also had suffered a severe wound — through both hips — at Scary Creek and fell into Confederate hands. He and General Wise reached a gentleman's agreement that Norton and Patton would be exchanged at once. That way Norton could go home to convalesce while Patton accepted medical advice that he should not undergo "the fatigue & discomfort incident to a retreating army." The only strings affixed to the exchange stipulated that neither colonel could report anything he might have seen of his enemies' movements and strengths. That humane, pragmatic, and straightforward arrangement foundered on the bureaucratic notions of higher Federal command. Brig. Gen. Jacob D. Cox insisted that the arrangement had been a "parole" only for both men and arrested the still-enfeebled George Patton. Cox eventually gave Patton his freedom but only on parole, not as exchanged for return to duty. In March 1862, an exchange document came through and Patton gratefully rejoined the 22nd, only to learn of further complications when some Federal authority sought to revoke the exchange. Nine months after his wounding, the Confederate colonel remained in limbo, dreadfully frustrated with red tape but admitting that he had met with "courtesy & kindness" as a prisoner. In July 1862, fully a year after Scary Creek, Patton wrote to the Confederate secretary of war pleading for help in clarifying the mess. He even volunteered to go north under a flag of truce to attempt to achieve a resolution, being under "great anxiety to return to service" after resolving his "peculiarly perplexing predicament."[36]

During the brief interval in the spring of 1862 when George Patton thought he had a permanent exchange, he led the 22nd Virginia in action near Giles Court House on May 10. There he promptly suffered another wound while "carrying the last and probably most determined stand made by the enemy." Confederate

campaigns in western Virginia involved fewer men than those under Lee and
Jackson and garnered, then and now, far less attention. Participants found little
to gloat about in the relatively smaller absolute casualties because percentages
of loss were similar. George Patton surely got in the path of flying lead repeatedly. In another battle, Patton family tradition records, a bullet hit the colonel squarely in the abdomen for his third wound. Abdominal wounds usually
proved fatal. Patton told Brig. Gen. Henry Heth, "I am hit in the belly. It is all
over." Heth looked at the wound, probed a bit, pulled out a twenty-dollar gold
eagle, and said, "I think not, George." The Patton family held that dented coin
as an heirloom, in a safe deposit box, a century later.[37]

Through late 1862 and all of 1863, Colonel Patton ably led the 22nd in operations in western Virginia. On the third day of the new year, he was elected to
the rank of full colonel, to take rank from November 23, 1861, fourteen months
earlier. No doubt the promotion would have come much sooner had Patton actually been present with the unit instead of languishing in legally enforced neu-
trality. During much of this period, the regiment belonged to Brig. Gen. John
Echols's brigade. In the general's frequent absences because of chronic illness,
Colonel Patton commanded the brigade, winning encomiums from Echols in
the process. He fought as brigade commander against the Federal cavalry raid
into West Virginia in August 1863 and in the campaigns around Lewisburg in
November. His success in both regimental and brigade command led Colonel
Patton to hope for promotion to brigadier general. He elicited glowing recommendations from all of his superiors, who encouraged the War Department
to give George a general's wreath. Echols called Patton "energetic, ardent and
most effective . . . prompt, vigilant & highly intelligent, possessing the confidence & affection of his men . . . a gentleman of high order of accomplishment."
Brig. Gen. Samuel Jones, commanding the department, wrote of Patton's "zeal,
fidelity, and ability." Maj. Gen. John C. Breckinridge, former vice president
of the United States and soon to become Confederate secretary of war, commented "cordially" on Patton as an "officer of high merit." Brig. Gen. Gabriel
C. Wharton wrote just as warmly; Lt. Gen. Jubal A. Early docketed Wharton's
comments as "approved"; and Robert E. Lee forwarded the packet to the War
Department—two days after Patton had been mortally wounded in 1864.[38]

Colonel George Patton finally reached the Army of Northern Virginia in the
spring of 1864. The affiliation would cost him his life. Before he and his regiment crossed the mountains to help defend Richmond, Patton had an exciting
interlude in the capital city on his own. He was there on furlough when a Federal raiding party under Col. Ulric Dahlgren came toward the city, mayhem in

mind. Patton played a key role in organizing an "Officers' Battalion" among his fellow furloughed officers. The volunteer group hurriedly mustered on the evening of March 1 in front of Richmond's famous hotel, the Spotswood House, and formed into two companies. George Patton commanded one as its captain. His three lieutenants each were full colonels in their regular roles — one destined to die soon, another to become a general. Brother John M. Patton served as a lieutenant in the other company, which was led by Brig. Gens. Evander M. Law and Jerome B. Robertson. The "privates" in the ersatz battalion included majors and captains and lieutenants on furlough from the field armies, among them George's brother, Lt. Hugh Mercer Patton.[39] The quixotically comprised "Officers' Battalion" did not have a chance to fire a shot. Other troops disposed of Dahlgren north of the city.

A few weeks later, emergency-captain Patton was back in western Virginia and a full colonel again. General Echols extolled Patton's judgment to General Breckinridge on April 1 in contemplating how to resist the impending raid by Federal cavalry toward the Virginia and Tennessee Railroad. In early May, Breckinridge left southwestern Virginia and headed for the Shenandoah Valley to thwart an advance by Federals under Maj. Gen. Franz Sigel. George Patton went with him and would spend the rest of his life in the Valley, other than a brief venture to Richmond. Breckinridge and Sigel clashed at New Market on May 15, 1864. Patton led his 22nd Virginia near the right of the Confederate line "with distinguished gallantry." Not far to his left, little brother William charged with the V.M.I. cadets through the rain and mud into the muzzles of Sigel's artillery and helped to capture them at the climax of the Confederate victory.[40]

Just seventeen days after the victory at New Market, Breckinridge and Patton stood at center stage with Lee's Army of Northern Virginia at Cold Harbor in the outskirts of Richmond. They had been called over the mountains to help defend the capital, beginning the move on May 19. In Echols's absence, Patton commanded the brigade; he would retain that command for the few months of life left to him. On June 2, as the lines began to coalesce on ground that would be drenched with Federal blood the next morning, Patton jockeyed for a good position on the line in relief of Brig. Gen. Joseph Finegan's Florida brigade, driving off enemy skirmishers in the process. The next day, probably only by coincidence, Senator Allen T. Caperton wrote to General Lee urging that Patton be given permanent brigade command. Echols's delicate health kept him away from field duty so often that Patton had been de facto brigadier for some time, and under Patton the brigade (most of them Caperton's constituents) would be "ably managed." "According to the testimony of all," the senator wrote, "no one could have excelled him in gallantry or skill." Caperton already had floated his proposal successfully with Jefferson Davis. Breckinridge endorsed the plan ardently ("Patton is a very good officer"), and Lee forwarded it approved at once; but it disappeared into the maw of the Richmond bureaucracy.[41]

The massive Federal assault at Cold Harbor on June 3, 1864, has come to be remembered primarily for the dreadful slaughter of attackers thrown forward by Grant without a hope of success. On many parts of the line, that stereotypical view is precisely accurate, as Confederate defenders shot down their assailants in hecatombs without much risk to themselves. At one point, however, the Federals achieved a lodgment—precisely where Patton and his brigade defended an unhealthy salient projecting toward their enemy. Patton had tried to find Breckinridge during the night to recommend falling back to better ground but failed to locate the division commander, so remained where he was. The 26th Virginia Battalion of Patton's brigade lost about three-quarters of its men when Federals overran the salient. A member of the 22nd who survived Cold Harbor called it a "scene of confusion, and almost unparalleled slaughter" of "the mighty hosts of the Federals." Colonel Patton fought with his customary determination and contributed to the restoration of the position by hustling forward reserves from Finegan's Floridians and the 2nd Maryland Battalion.[42]

Patton's brigade hurried back to the Valley under Breckinridge as soon as Ulysses S. Grant's attacks at Cold Harbor had subsided. By June 8, Breckinridge had reached a position near the Blue Ridge Mountains intended to block Sigel's replacement, Gen. David Hunter. Gen. Jubal A. Early soon joined Breckinridge with the veteran Second Corps of the Army of Northern Virginia. Early repulsed Hunter in front of Lynchburg and chased him into the mountains, then turned north and thundered down the Valley toward the Potomac. Patton and his brigade marched with Early across the river to the outskirts of Washington. During the July 9 battle of Monocacy, en route to Washington, the brigade occupied a reserve position and suffered only a single casualty. Patton remained at the head of the brigade during Early's retirement through northern Virginia to the lower Valley and in the small battles of July 1864. Through all of August and the first half of September, Early maneuvered ceaselessly and to good effect, destroying Federal rail lines and logistical facilities and frustrating his opponent without serious fighting. Patton and his men marched wearily with Early's columns, grumbling incessantly—and with good cause—about short rations and no rest.[43]

The wearisome war of maneuver exploded into a violent war of musketry on

September 19, 1864. Early's opponent, Maj. Gen. Philip H. Sheridan, finally brought his elusive adversary to action in by far the largest engagement fought to that date in the Valley. The battle of Third Winchester caught Confederate columns strewn across a wide arc, too far apart to support one another effectively. East of town, on the Berryville Pike, infantry under Maj. Gens. S. Dodson Ramseur, John B. Gordon, and Robert E. Rodes stoutly resisted the onslaught and shot down their attackers in profusion, Rodes dying in the process. George Patton's brigade held a critical position in the northern edge of Winchester, at right angles to and northwest of Ramseur and his friends. Patton's men successfully resisted repeated Federal infantry assaults but then fell victim to an overwhelming attack by enemy cavalry that far outnumbered them. The cavalry's mobility enabled them to move around Patton's exposed left (western) flank and gallop into the rear. The Confederate line unraveled rapidly and completely, leaving Early no option but to retreat southward away from Winchester. As he attempted to rally his brigade to retard the Federal progress, George Patton went down badly hurt. A sizable piece of a rifled artillery shell tore through the colonel's shirttail and into his hip. Regretfully, but inevitably, Confederates scurrying out of town had to leave Patton behind in enemy hands. Ten days later a surviving Confederate referred to the fallen brigade commander as "an officer of highest gallantry and standing and a gentleman irreproachable in character."[44]

The desperately injured colonel struggled for life for six days at the home of his mother's cousin, Philip Williams, 25 West Piccadilly Street, but his shattered hip proved to be a mortal wound. Patton succumbed on September 25.[45]

Susan Glassell Patton awaited her husband, or word of him, at Woodville, the home of a friend near the James River Canal. Susan and her small children were lodging as refugees in "a wretched little house in the yard." When the dire news from Winchester reached Woodville, other refugee women in the neighborhood held "a long council . . . with streaming eyes to decide who should tell" the devastating news to the new widow. Eventually Patton's body servant Peter reached Susan, bringing with him the colonel's sword and saddle. Peter had made his furtive way home through enemy lines with the relics by hiding during daylight and traveling at night.[46]

Susan faced a bleak plight in the waning days of the Confederacy, when the barest necessities of life proved hard to secure for even those well situated. She received George's back pay of $539.50 in nearly worthless Confederate currency in January 1865. A friend attempted to secure food and supplies for Mrs. Patton and her orphans under the terms of legislation designed to help widows of Confederate officers but found farmers unwilling to accept paper drafts drawn on the tenuously surviving government. The county sheriff proved to be no help, and the Confederate secretary of war refused to intervene. Soon after the war Susan married George Hugh Smith, who earlier had succeeded George Patton as colonel of the 22nd Virginia. She died in California in 1883. George Smith helped keep George Patton's memory alive in stories he told his wife's grandson, George S. Patton III.[47]

The story of the dead Confederate Pattons extends beyond 1865. In the summer of 1866, Col. John M. Patton Jr. wrote to the superintendent of his (and most of his brothers') alma mater about the bodies of Cols. George S. and Waller Tazewell Patton. Both John's mother and George's widow (who was about to move to California) thought that the Stonewall Cemetery in Winchester would be a fitting final resting place for their loved ones. Taz's corpse had been embalmed and placed in a relative's vault in Baltimore. The V.M.I.'s good intentions about helping in the relocation of its distinguished graduates' remains came to naught in the Pattons' case and others, too. George's body went to Stonewall Cemetery, not many yards from where he had suffered his mortal wound, but Taz remained far from home. Finally in about 1876, George S. Patton Jr., son of Colonel George, traveled to Baltimore and brought back the body of his uncle Taz. Young George rode with the coffin in a freight train that only reached Winchester late at night. He worried about how to move the coffin to the cemetery through the darkness but need not have. A procession of Confederate veterans carrying torches escorted Tazewell Patton to his final resting place. As the second George Patton helped to enlarge the burial site, he uncovered the edge of his own father's grave; a lantern's light illuminated his father's face. Nearly fifty years later, George S. Patton Jr. brought his son, George S. Patton III, to the gravesite, and the two posed for a photo standing next to the single stone covering their two Confederate ancestors.[48]

For one Patton descendant, the 1864 Shenandoah Valley campaign lingered on in common memory as though in a parallel universe. George S. Patton III would have appreciated the 1870s graveside experience more than his father did. Years later he visited Gettysburg and at sundown sat on the rock fence where his uncles Taz Patton and Lewis Williams had been mortally hurt. "I could almost see them coming," he recalled. "I was quite happy. A strange pleasure yet a very real one." The George "quite happy" at the site of the breaking point of Pickett's Charge found ample cause to conjure up the Shenandoah Valley campaign in France in 1918, both at Cheppy and in another episode at St. Mihiel. He was after all by then a year older than his grandfather had been at Winchester on September 19, 1864, and that grandfather was keeping track of the new generation of Patton warriors from a convenient cloud.[49]

Acknowledgments

The author owes deepest thanks to Keith E. Gibson and Diane Jacob of the Virginia Military Institute — as does anyone working on history that touches that superb school — for their gracious and skilled professional assistance.

Notes

1. Martin Blumenson, *Patton* (New York: William Morrow, 1985), 112–14; Ladislas Farago, *Patton* (New York: Ivan Oblensky, 1964), 88–90. Within a few months of Colonel Patton's exploit in France, the journal of the Virginia Historical Society touted his deeds and compared them to those of his Confederate grandfather and great uncles (*Virginia Magazine of History and Biography* 27 [January 1919]:75).

2. John T. Goolrick, *The Life of General Hugh Mercer* (New York and Washington: Neale, 1906); Robert H. Patton, *The Pattons* (New York: Crown, 1994), 8–19; Joseph M. Waterman, *With Sword and Lancet* (Richmond, Va.: Garrett and Massie, 1941). R. H. Patton's book is very well constructed and written and is full of fine material from family manuscripts. The whiskey toddy tale is from Ruth Ellen Totten to "Dear Joe," June 1, 1984, Virginia Military Institute Archives, Lexington [repository cited hereafter as VMI Archives].

3. Patton, *Pattons*, 22–23, 25. An announcement of the wedding appeared in the *Virginia Herald* (Fredericksburg), January 10, 1824. The military careers of the seven boys are detailed in this essay. The eighth, Joseph, who appeared in the household in the 1850 Henrico County census (p. 344), age six, cannot be positively identified among the Confederate-records options.

4. *Biographical Directory of the American Congress, 1774–1949* (Washington: Government Printing Office, 1950), 1659; Lyon Gardiner Tyler, *Encyclopedia of Virginia Biography*, 5 vols. (New York: Lewis Historical, 1915), 2:53. A good obituary of John M. Patton Sr. appeared in the *Fredericksburg News*, November 2, 1858. For incidents in his political career, see the *Fredericksburg Political Arena*, March 8, 1831, and September 11, 1835.

5. Policy no. 9370, Mutual Assurance Society of Virginia, reel 14, vol. 97, filmed copy at Mary Washington College, Fredericksburg; Deed Book J, 218, Fredericksburg City Courthouse; Robert K. Krick, *Lee's Colonels: A Biographical Register of the Field Officers of the Army of Northern Virginia* (Dayton, Ohio: Morningside, 1991), 299–300. Patton's signature on the insurance document bears the date of November 15, 1836. French Patton probably had gone to her parents' home for the birth of John Jr. The physical description of the Patton house is from earlier Assurance Society policies (nos. 4286, 6185, and 7570) taken out by earlier Patton owners. The buildings that

now stand on that corner, including the one around the fabric of the old Patton house, date from ca. 1910 in the estimate of the estimable mayor of Fredericksburg, Bill Beck. Barbara Pratt Willis, the leading local historian, told me that when her mother-in-law, who lives in the house (1105 Princess Anne Street), had gutter work done a few years ago, opening up the northwest corner of the facade revealed an entirely undressed tree trunk as the primary supporting member.

6. Deed Book J, 416, and Deed Book M, 394, Fredericksburg City Courthouse. Other real estate documents involving John M. Patton Sr. are in Deed Books H, 357; H, 438; I, 79; and I, 111. The orphan asylum transaction actually was recorded as a sale, for a single token dollar. The Smithsonia name only came into use after the Civil War. The building is at 307 Amelia Street. Earlier Pattons had given the same site for use by the Presbyterian Church, a building gone by the 1830s.

7. Robert E. L. Krick, *Staff Officers in Gray: A Biographical Register of the Staff Officers in the Army of Northern Virginia* (Chapel Hill: University of North Carolina Press, 2003), 238; *Richmond Enquirer*, September 12, 1862.

8. William Couper, *The V.M.I. New Market Cadets* (Charlottesville: Michie, 1933), 150–51; W. F. Patton's file, VMI Archives. William married Annie Gertrude Jordan, a Rockbridge County woman, on January 7, 1875.

9. Terry Lowry, *26th Battalion Virginia Infantry* (Lynchburg, Va.: H. E. Howard, 1991), 143; Terry Lowry, *22nd Virginia Infantry* (Lynchburg, Va.: H. E. Howard, 1988), 183.

10. Francis B. Heitman, *Historical Register and Dictionary of the United States Army*, 2 vols. (Washington: Government Printing Office, 1903), 1:776; Isaac W. Patton's official Compiled Service Record [hereafter cited as CSR], M320, Roll 320, National Archives, Washington, D.C. [repository hereafter cited as NA]; "Unfiled Papers and Slips Belonging to Confederate Compiled Service Records," M347, NA [collection hereafter cited as "Unfiled Papers and Slips"]; Geo. S. Patton to F. H. Smith, May 14, 1853, VMI Archives; Works Projects Administration, Project 665-64-3-112, "Mayors of New Orleans, 1803–1926," unpublished typescript, March 1940; *New Orleans Daily Picayune*, February 10, 1890; *New Orleans Daily States*, February 10, 1890. Patton's precise dates of rank in the old army were as follows: 2nd Lt., March 8, 1847; assigned to 10th Infantry, April 9, 1847; assigned to 3rd Artillery, July 13, 1848; promoted to 1st Lt., October 2, 1853; resigned February 15, 1855. His Confederate ranks were as follows: elected captain of what became Co. A, 21st Louisiana, December 31, 1861; major on April 17, 1862, to take rank from March 9; colonel by election of April 4, 1863, to take rank from May 15, 1862. The 21st Louisiana consolidated at some point into the 22nd Louisiana.

11. John M. Patton Jr. file, VMI Archives; John M. Patton Jr., *Address Delivered Before the Society of Alumni of the Virginia Military Institute, July 4th, 1871* (Wytheville, Va.: D. A. St. Clair, 1871).

12. 1850 Henrico County census, 344; Patton to F. H. Smith, February 21, 1861, VMI Archives; *A Souvenir of New Haven, Connecticut, Fraternally Dedicated to the Richmond Light Infantry Blues . . . Upon the Occasion of Their Visit to New Haven, September 9, 10, 11, 1908* (New Haven, Conn.: n.p., 1908), 118–21; *Fredericksburg News,*

November 19, 1858; Patton's file, VMI Archives; *Virginia Magazine of History and Biography* 10 (October 1901): 203.

13. *Richmond Dispatch*, April 15, 1861; J. M. Patton's official CSR, M324, NA; Lee recommendation under Patton in "Unfiled Papers and Slips," M347, NA; Lee to Patton, May 7, 1861, in U.S. War Department, *The War of the Rebellion: A Compilation of the Official Records of the Union and Confederate Armies*, 127 vols., index, and atlas (Washington: Government Printing Office, 1880–1901), ser. 1, 51(2):70 [hereafter cited as *OR*; all references are to ser. 1]; Scott Shipp to Thomas T. Munford, June 26, 1903, Munford-Ellis Family Papers, William R. Perkins Library, Duke University, Durham, North Carolina.

14. J. M Patton's CSR, M324, NA; R. E. L. Strider, *The Life and Work of George William Peterkin* (Philadelphia: George W. Jacobs, 1929), 53; Gary L. Ecelbarger, *"We Are In For It!": The First Battle of Kernstown* (Shippensburg, Pa.: White Mane, 1997), 138, 166, 252; *OR*, 12(1):402–4.

15. Sarah C. Rives to Alfred Landon Rives, June 12, 1862, Rives Papers, Albert and Shirley Small Special Collections Library, University of Virginia, Charlottesville. (Sadie Rives was quoting to her husband from Sallie Patton's reading aloud of John M. Patton's letter.) For the Cross Keys episode, see Robert K. Krick, *Conquering the Valley: Stonewall Jackson at Port Republic* (New York: William Morrow, 1996), 285–86, 297–98, 541–42.

16. Letters of Dr. Wm. D. Meriwether, July 22, 1862, and Surgeon R. T. Coleman, in J. M. Patton's CSR, NA; John H. Worsham, *One of Jackson's Foot Cavalry*, ed. James I. Robertson Jr. (Jackson, Tenn.: McCowat-Mercer, 1964), 32n; J. H. Chamberlayne letter, December 31, 1861, in C. G. Chamberlayne, ed., *Ham Chamberlayne—Virginian* (Richmond, Va.: Dietz, 1932), 60. Patton's own account of the rigors of the Valley campaign is "Reminiscences of Jackson's Infantry ('Foot Cavalry')," in *Southern Historical Society Papers*, ed. J. William Jones and others, 52 vols. (Richmond, Va.: Southern Historical Society, 1876–1959), 8:139–42.

17. *Richmond Dispatch*, July 20, 1862; J. M. Patton's CSR, M331, NA.

18. Robert Garlick Hill Kean, *Inside the Confederate Government: The Diary of Robert Garlick Hill Kean*, ed. Edward Younger (New York: Oxford University Press, 1957), 209–10; J. M. Patton file, VMI Archives; J. M. Patton letters to the superintendent, August 30, September 13 (two of that date), and October 7, 1865, VMI Archives. Patton's papers at the Virginia Historical Society, Richmond, afford an extensive background on his life and nonmilitary career. The full title of Patton's religious book is *The Death of Death: or, A Study of God's Holiness in Connection with the Existence of Evil, In So Far as Intelligent and Responsible Beings Are Concerned, By an Orthodox Layman* (Richmond: J. W. Randolph & English, 1878). The book apparently met with success, because it was reissued in London in 1881 in an expanded (to 252 pages) edition. Patton's death has often been reported as occurring on October 9, but the *Richmond Dispatch* for November 25, 1898, provides full details, and Shockoe Cemetery burial records confirm the date. Another pietistic Patton piece is *Argument of Col. John M. Patton in Respect to the Validity of Ministerial Orders. . . .* (Richmond, Va.: Clemmitt & Jones, 1876).

19. The shortened familiar usage sometimes was rendered as "Taze," sometimes as "Taz."

20. W. T. Patton's file, VMI Archives; W. T. Patton to F. H. Smith, August 9, 15, November 29, 1855, VMI Archives.

21. Letters of W. T. Patton to F. H. Smith, January 16, July 15, 21, August 12, 1856, July 20, September 22, 1857, and July 13, 18, 1859, VMI Archives.

22. Krick, *Lee's Colonels*, 300, 400; W. T. Patton and Lewis B. Williams to F. H. Smith, May 7, 1861, and Patton alone to Smith, May 13, 29, 1861, VMI Archives. The last two letters include some unattractive grumbling by Patton about other officers given higher rank than his own despite his age and class ranking, especially W. S. H. Baylor. For a description of W. T. Patton parading his company in Richmond under a secession flag, see *Richmond Dispatch*, April 16, 1861.

23. Krick, *Lee's Colonels*, 300, 400; W. T. Patton's CSR, M324, NA. W. T. Patton's commission date as major was July 1, 1861. His appointment as colonel bore a date of June 24, 1862, but took rank from June 3 (it was not confirmed, typically, until months later—October 7, 1862).

24. W. T. Patton to J. L. Kemper, December 31, 1861, Kemper Papers, Alderman Library, University of Virginia, Charlottesville; W. T. Patton to Samuel Cooper, May 28, 1862, "Letters Received by the Confederate Secretary of War," document 295-P-1862, M437, NA; R. M. Graves to George W. Randolph, August 27, 1862, and W. T. Patton to Randolph, August 31, 1862, "Letters Received by the Confederate Secretary of War," document 565-G-1862, M437, NA.

25. *OR*, 2:445, 11(1):578; David F. Riggs, *7th Virginia Infantry* (Lynchburg, Va.: H. E. Howard, 1982), 6–14.

26. *Richmond Enquirer*, September 12, 1862; *Augusta (Georgia) Constitutionalist*, September 21, 1862; Patton, *Pattons*, 43; W. T. Patton's CSR, M324, NA.

27. Francis Adams Donaldson, *Inside the Army of the Potomac: The Civil War Experience of Captain Francis Adams Donaldson*, ed. J. Gregory Acken (Harrisburg, Pa.: Stackpole, 1998), 350–51, 476. The vengeful Captain Donaldson belonged to the 118th Pennsylvania.

28. George S. Patton III to Mrs. James C. Slaughter (his cousin), May 30, 1943, recounting both family lore and an account of his great-uncle's wounding told him by a Federal veteran, sold by Signature House Auction, Bridgeport, West Virginia, June 1998; Charles C. Coward to Edmund Berkeley, December 10, 1897, Prince William County WPA Reports, Library of Virginia, Richmond; Patton, *Pattons*, 49.

29. W. T. Patton's CSR, M324, NA; Patton, *Pattons*, 49–51; *OR*, 27(1):463–64; *Richmond Sentinel*, September 3, October 7, 1863; *Richmond Daily Whig*, September 1, 1863; *Southern Churchman*, November 11, 1863. W. T. Patton's dying words are inscribed on his tombstone in Winchester.

30. G. S. Patton's file, VMI Archives; Farago, *Patton*, 47.

31. John M. Patton to F. H. Smith, February 16, 1852, G. S. Patton to J. T. L. Preston, August 11, 1853, and G. S. Patton letters to Smith, July 26, October 1, 1852, May 14, July 17, 1853, July 9, 1854, January 3, 16, 1855, September 16, 1856, and June 9, 1857, VMI Archives. The letter of January 3, 1855 (misdated 1854 in the original), contains an

amusing plea from the former student to his former instructor for help in understanding "Osculatory Curves . . . [and] Integral Calculus" so that he can answer his own pupils' questions on those arcane subjects.

32. *Fredericksburg News*, November 12, 1855; *Virginia Magazine of History and Biography* 27 (January 1919):75; Tyler, *Encyclopedia of Virginia Biography*, 3:350–51; George S. Patton to "My darling Sue," July 18, August 1, 9, 1855, originals sold by, respectively, Signature House Auctions, Bridgeport, West Virginia, March 1999 and January 2000, and Remember When Auctions, Wells, Maine, May 2000. An equally devoted letter to "My dearest," written after eight years of marriage (December 29, 1863), was also in the Signature House auction in March 1999.

33. Krick, *Lee's Colonels*, 70–71; R. J. to Roy Bird Cook, October 8, 1946, VMI Archives; Blumenson, *Patton*, 21; Farago, *Patton*, 47; David Phillips, *Civil War Chronicles: A Soldier's Story* (New York: Metro Books, 1997), 18; Joseph Alleine Brown, *The Memoirs of a Confederate Soldier* (Abingdon, Va.: Forum Press, 1940), 3; Patton, *Pattons*, 31. The local volunteer company had existed since 1856, known first as the Kanawha Minutemen, but the Harpers Ferry crisis brought it into new focus with a new name. The house the Pattons bought in 1858 is preserved today as the Craik-Patton House in Charleston.

34. Lowry, *22nd Virginia*, 9–14, 183; Phillips, *Civil War Chronicles*, 20; Geo. S. Patton to F. H. Smith, June 4, 1861, VMI Archives; G. S. Patton's CSR, M324, NA. Colonel Patton's CSR is misfiled under Patten and therefore has eluded researchers over the years. Evidence of Patton's earnest efforts to prepare his charges for war survives at V.M.I. in the form of a signed and well-used copy of R. Milton Cary, *Skirmishers' Drill and Bayonet Exercise (As Now Used in the French Army), With Suggestions for the Soldier in Actual Conflict* (Richmond: West & Johnston, 1861).

35. *OR*, 2:292; Terry Lowry, *The Battle of Scary Creek* (Charleston, W.Va.: Pictorial Histories, 1982); John Echols to J. Randolph Tucker, July 1, 1863, in G. S. Patton's CSR, M324, NA. Patton wrote a detailed account of the battle to one of his brothers on the evening of July 17; it is in Miscellaneous File, Box 281, Huntington Library, San Marino, California (Patton's son, completely coincidentally, later became the first mayor of San Marino). An account by Patton of the battle also is in *West Virginia History* 33 (October 1971):55–60. *Battle of Scary Creek* is exhaustive and definitive and includes much valuable correspondence by, and other material about, George S. Patton. Terry Lowry, an oracle on Civil War events in the Kanawha Valley and curator of the Craik-Patton House in Charleston, is preparing a full biography of Colonel Patton (Terry Lowry to R. K. Krick, July 7, 2000).

36. Whitlaw Reid, *Ohio in the War: Her Statesmen, and Generals, and Soldiers*, 2 vols. (Cincinnati and New York: Moore, Wilstach, & Baldwin, 1868), 2:146, 148–49; Ohio Roster Commission, *Official Roster of the Soldiers of the State of Ohio in the War of the Rebellion*, 12 vols. (Akron, Ohio: Werner, 1893), 1:427; Geo. S. Patton to F. H. Smith, March 12, 19, 1862, VMI Archives; G. S. Patton to J. D. Cox, April (no day) 1862, in Patton's entry, "Unfiled Papers and Slips," M347, NA; G. S. Patton to George W. Randolph, July 4, 1862, document 392-P-1862, "Letters Received by the Confederate Secretary of War," M437, NA; Thomas J. Althauser, "Patton's Honor,"

Civil War Times 39 (August 2000):25–27. Norton resigned in December 1862. For a time during the late winter, Patton considered accepting a post on the V.M.I. faculty because he could do that while yet unexchanged, but then the temporary exchange came through.

37. *OR*, 12(1):493–95; Fred Ayers Jr., *Before the Colors Fade: Portrait of a Soldier, George S. Patton, Jr.* (Boston: Houghton Mifflin, 1964), 14.

38. G. S. Patton's CSR, M324, NA; Lowry, *22nd Virginia*, 183; *OR*, 29(1):53–56, 532–34. All of the letters of commendation and recommendation cited in the text are in Patton's CSR, M324, NA. Colonel Patton's role as commander of the 22nd Virginia Infantry makes him the key actor in the story told by Lowry's book. Anyone interested should see constant mentions of Patton throughout pages 2–111.

39. "The Officers' Battalion," *Mobile Advertiser & Register*, March 10, 1864, reprinted from the *Richmond Enquirer*, March 4, 1864.

40. *OR*, 33:1253–54; Lowry, *22nd Virginia*, 57–62; Jerry W. Holsworth, "The Patton Family at New Market," *Blue and Gray Magazine* 16 (April 1999):21.

41. *OR*, 36(3):864, 51(2):981–82.

42. Brown, *Memoirs of a Confederate Soldier*, 36–40; John K. Thompson to Col. George M. Edgar, July 22, 1902, Edgar Papers, Southern Historical Collection, University of North Carolina, Chapel Hill. Thompson was a captain in the 22nd and suffered a severe wound in the lung in the battle. The summary of the brigade's action in the text is based on information from Robert E. L. Krick, who is responsible for preservation and public use of Cold Harbor battlefield.

43. Lowry, *22nd Virginia*, 64–73.

44. A. S. Johnston, "Captain Beirne Chapman and Chapman's Battery," *Monroe Watchman*, May 21, 1903; *OR*, 43(1):597.

45. E. O. C. Ord to Isaac W. Smith, November 15, 1864, in G. S. Patton's CSR, M324, NA; *Richmond Daily Enquirer*, October 13, 1864; T. K. Cartmell, *Shenandoah Valley Pioneers and Their Descendants* (Winchester, Va.: Eddy Pr. Corp., 1909), 505; Garland R. Quarles, *The Story of One Hundred Old Homes in Winchester, Virginia* (Winchester, Va.: Winchester-Frederick County Historical Society, 1993), 192–93; Roger U. Delauter Jr., *Winchester in the Civil War* (Lynchburg, Va.: H. E. Howard, 1992), 80; Wayde Byard, "The Patton Brothers," *Winchester Star*, October 4, 1997. The Williams house was occupied by Colonial Art and Craft Shop in 1997.

46. "A Southern Lady Tells the News," *Tyler's Quarterly Historical and Genealogical Magazine* 10 (July 1928):66; Ayers, *Before the Colors Fade*, 14–15. John M. Patton Sr. had decreed upon his deathbed that the family slaves should be freed, but his wife ignored that directive. Apparently as a sort of compromise, George paid Peter a salary during the war (Patton, *Pattons*, 25).

47. Death claim filed January 25, 1865, by Isaac W. Smith on behalf of Mrs. Patton, in G. S. Patton's CSR, M324, NA; A. G. Grismore to James A. Seddon, November 29, 1864, document 264-P, 1864, "Letters Received by the Confederate Secretary of War," M437, NA; Patton, *Pattons*, 67, 79, 91–92. A highly useful summary of the postwar Glassell-Patton relocation to Southern California is in C. E. Parker to Jere M. H. Willis Jr., January 29, 1976, and attachments, in Patton folder, vertical file, Virginiana

Room, Central Rappahannock Regional Library, Fredericksburg. (It includes the interesting intelligence that Glassell connections to Orange County, Virginia—not the ubiquitous citrus fruit of the region—led to the choice of names for Orange County, California.)

48. J. M. Patton Jr. to Francis H. Smith, August 13, 1866, July 23, 1867, VMI Archives; Patton, *Pattons*, 51; Byard, "Patton Brothers"; "George S. Patton Visits Winchester," *Winchester Star*, November 22, 1997. The reburial probably took place in 1876. The brothers were there by the time of the 1877 Winchester Memorial Day on June 6 (a date chosen because of Turner Ashby's death), according to the *Winchester News*, June 9, 1877. The report of the 1875 Memorial Day did not mention them. The 1876 newspaper account of the annual event spoke of "the Brothers Patton," implying that both were buried there by that time (*Winchester Times*, June 14, 1876). I have not been able to ascertain the exact date of reburial nor find any purely contemporary accounts of it; more significant, neither has the nonpareil Winchester oracle, Ben Ritter. George Patton probably had been buried originally in a plot belonging to Philip Williams; Stonewall Cemetery did not open until after the war.

49. Patton, *Pattons*, 120, 184.

BIBLIOGRAPHIC ESSAY

The literature on the 1864 Shenandoah Valley campaign offers a rich array of campaign studies, biographies, and firsthand testimony from both civilians and soldiers. This brief overview points to some of the key titles, but readers should consult the notes accompanying the essays in this collection for other published items and manuscript collections.

As with every other Civil War military event, the most obvious source on the 1864 Valley campaign is U.S. War Department, *The War of the Rebellion: The Official Records of the Union and Confederate Armies*, 127 vols., index, and atlas (Washington: Government Printing Office, 1880–1901). The key volumes, both in series 1, are 37, parts 1–2, and 43, parts 1–2. Volume 37 contains approximately 1,550 pages of official reports, correspondence, and other documents relating to operations in the Shenandoah between mid-May and early August, which encompassed the battles of New Market, Lynchburg, the Monocacy, Stephenson's Depot, and Second Kernstown as well as the burning of the Virginia Military Institute and Chambersburg, Pennsylvania. Volume 43, totaling more than 2,200 pages, focuses on the confrontation between Sheridan and Early that stretched from early August through the late autumn and featured the battles of Third Winchester, Fisher's Hill, Tom's Brook, and Cedar Creek as well as "The Burning." Volumes 6–7 of part 1 of *Supplement to the Official Records of the Union and Confederate Armies*, ed. Janet B. Hewett and others, 100 vols. (Wilmington, N.C.: Broadfoot, 1994–2000), also contain some pertinent material. For particular military units, the "Record of Events" volumes in part 2 of the *Supplement*, which reprint information from the National Archives that includes details about personnel and movements, are very useful.

Published testimony from participants conveys a sense of the campaign's dramatic ebb and flow. A good starting point is Editors of Time-Life Books, *Voices of the Civil War: Shenandoah 1864* (Alexandria, Va.: Time-Life Books, 1998), a selection of Union and Confederate material enhanced by excellent illustrations by such contemporary artists as Alfred A. Waud and James E. Taylor. Volume 4 of the frequently cited *Battles and Leaders of the Civil War*, ed. Robert Underwood Johnson and Clarence Clough Buel, 4 vols. (New York: Century, 1887–88), offers about 60 pages on the 1864 Valley campaign, including articles by Jubal Early and Wesley Merritt. For Confederate accounts, see also *Southern Historical Society Papers*, ed. J. William Jones and others, 52 vols. (1876–1959; reprint, with 3-vol. index, Wilmington, N.C.: Broadfoot, 1990–92), and *Confederate Veteran*, 40 vols. (1893–1932; reprint, with 3-vol. index, Wilmington, N.C.: Broadfoot, 1984–86). *The Wartime Papers of R. E. Lee*, ed. Clifford Dowdey and Louis H. Manarin (Boston: Little, Brown, 1961), contains a good sampling of Lee's pertinent correspondence with Early, Jefferson Davis, and others.

On the Union side, volumes 7–8 of *The Collected Works of Abraham Lincoln*, ed.

Roy P. Basler, 9 vols. (New Brunswick, N.J.: Rutgers University Press, 1953–55), reveal how closely the president followed events in the Valley. Ulysses S. Grant's correspondence relating to the campaign, in volumes 11–12 of *The Papers of Ulysses S. Grant*, ed. John Y. Simon, 22 vols. to date (Carbondale: Southern Illinois University Press, 1967–), underscores the general in chief's concern about the Valley. Additional useful evidence from a Federal perspective can be found in the *Papers* of the Military Order of the Loyal Legion of the United States, 66 vols. and 3-vol. index (Wilmington, N.C.: Broadfoot, 1991–96), and in volume 6 of *Papers of the Military Historical Society of Massachusetts*, 14 vols. (1895–1918; reprint in 15 vols. with a general index, Wilmington, N.C.: Broadfoot, 1989–90).

Both army commanders wrote important accounts. Sheridan's two-volume *Personal Memoirs of P. H. Sheridan* (1888; reprint, Wilmington, N.C.: Broadfoot, 1992) and Early's *A Memoir of the Last Year of the War for Independence, in the Confederate States of America* (1866; reprint, Columbia: University of South Carolina Press, 2001) present their authors' actions in the best possible light, though Early's is the more honest of the pair (his 1866 narrative appeared virtually unchanged in a longer, posthumous memoir published in 1912). Among the best of other works by subordinate officers are Jedediah Hotchkiss's indispensable *Make Me a Map of the Valley: The Civil War Journal of Stonewall Jackson's Topographer*, ed. Archie P. McDonald (Dallas, Tex.: Southern Methodist University Press, 1973); George Crook's unvarnished *General George Crook: His Autobiography*, ed. Martin F. Schmitt (Norman: University of Oklahoma Press, 1960); Edward W. Emerson's engaging *Life and Letters of Charles Russell Lowell* (Boston: Houghton, Mifflin, 1907; reprinted with introduction by Joan Waugh, Columbia: University of South Carolina Press, 2005); John B. Gordon's often self-serving but widely quoted *Reminiscences of the Civil War* (New York: Scribner's, 1903); Clement A. Evans's revealing *Intrepid Warrior: Clement Anselm Evans—Life, Letters, and Diaries of the War Years*, ed. Robert Grier Stephens Jr. (Dayton, Ohio: Morningside, 1992); George B. Sanford's *Fighting Rebels and Redskins: Experiences in Army Life of Colonel George B. Sanford, 1861–1892*, ed. E. R. Hagemann (Norman: University of Oklahoma Press, 1969); James H. Kidd's *One of Custer's Wolverines: The Civil War Letters of Brevet Brigadier General James H. Kidd, 6th Michigan Cavalry*, ed. Eric J. Wittenberg (Kent, Ohio: Kent State University Press, 2000); George T. Stevens's *Three Years in the Sixth Corps* (Albany, N.Y.: S. R. Gray, 1866), a valuable early account by a Union surgeon; and Henry Kyd Douglas's immensely readable but sometimes unreliable *I Rode with Stonewall* (Chapel Hill: University of North Carolina Press, 1940).

Two books address the roles of major components of Sheridan's Army of the Shenandoah. Richard B. Irwin's *History of the Nineteenth Army Corps* (New York: G. P. Putnam's, 1892) tells in straightforward, somewhat dull fashion the story of the soldiers transferred from Louisiana to fight in Virginia, and Stephen Z. Starr does full justice to the potent northern mounted arm in *The Union Cavalry in the Civil War*, vol. 2, *The War in the East from Gettysburg to Appomattox* (Baton Rouge: Louisiana State University Press, 1981).

The James E. Taylor Sketchbook: With Sheridan Up the Shenandoah Valley in 1864,

Leaves from a Special Artist's Sketch Book and Diary, ed. Dennis E. Frye, Martin F. Graham, and George F. Skoch (Dayton, Ohio: Morningside, 1989) stands as a unique source. A sketch artist for *Frank Leslie's Illustrated Newspaper*, Taylor accompanied Sheridan's army for part of the campaign, sketching along the way. During the postwar years, he added many new drawings to his wartime sketches and written impressions to create a huge illustrated account of the campaign. Invaluable because of its depictions of many places and military scenes, it complements all other written accounts of the 1864 Valley campaign.

The leading biographies of Sheridan and Early, both of which are well written and emphasize narrative rather than analysis, are Roy Morris Jr., *Sheridan: The Life and Wars of General Phil Sheridan* (New York: Crown, 1992) and Charles C. Osborne, *Jubal: The Life and Times of General Jubal A. Early, CSA, Defender of the Lost Cause* (Chapel Hill, N.C.: Algonquin, 1992). Eric J. Wittenberg's *Little Phil: A Reassessment of the Civil War Leadership of Gen. Philip H. Sheridan* (Washington, D.C.: Brassey's, 2002) renders a harsh verdict about Sheridan in the Valley (and elsewhere). Two of Early's division commanders receive full-scale examination in Ralph Lowell Eckert, *John Brown Gordon: Soldier, Southerner, American* (Baton Rouge: Louisiana State University Press, 1989) and Gary W. Gallagher, *Stephen Dodson Ramseur: Lee's Gallant General* (Chapel Hill: University of North Carolina Press, 1985). Volume 3 of Douglas Southall Freeman's classic, *Lee's Lieutenants: A Study in Command*, 3 vols. (New York: Charles Scribner's Sons, 1942–44), deftly examines Early and all of his principal subordinates. A brace of Sheridan's lieutenants, one in the cavalry and the other in the infantry, are the subject of excellent coverage in T. Harry Williams's *Hayes of the Twenty-Third: The Civil War Volunteer Officer* (New York: Knopf, 1965) and Jeffry D. Wert's *Custer: The Controversial Life of George Armstrong Custer* (New York: Simon and Schuster, 1996).

Three analytical narratives provide a collective overview of the campaign. For the first phase, which ended with Early's return to the Valley after threatening Washington, see Frank E. Vandiver's sprightly *Jubal's Raid: General Early's Famous Attack on Washington in 1864* (New York: McGraw-Hill, 1960) and Benjamin F. Cooling's more detailed *Jubal Early's Raid on Washington, 1864* (Baltimore, Md.: Nautical and Aviation, 1989). The best study of the climactic phase between Sheridan and Early is Jeffry D. Wert's evenhanded *From Winchester to Cedar Creek: The Shenandoah Campaign of 1864* (Carlisle, Pa.: South Mountain Press, 1987). Gary W. Gallagher, ed., *Struggle for the Shenandoah: Essays on the 1864 Valley Campaign* (Kent, Ohio: Kent State University Press, 1991), supplements Wert's narrative with analysis of military leadership on both sides. For a well-illustrated popular treatment, see Thomas A. Lewis and the Editors of Time-Life Books, *The Shenandoah in Flames: The Valley Campaign of 1864* (Alexandria, Va.: Time-Life, 1987). Older works of continuing value include Henry A. Du Pont, *The Campaign of 1864 in the Valley of Virginia and the Expedition to Lynchburg* (New York: National Americana Society, 1925), which combines elements of personal reminiscence and historical analysis by an artillerist in Sheridan's army; George E. Pond, *The Shenandoah Valley in 1864* (New York: Scribner's, 1883), another history by a Union veteran; and Sanford C. Kellogg's *The Shenandoah Valley and Virginia*

1861 to 1865: A War Study (New York: Neale, 1903), a third of which covers the 1864 Valley campaign.

The campaign's principal engagements have received uneven attention. By far the most detailed and scholarly study of any of the 1864 Valley battles, Theodore C. Mahr's *The Battle of Cedar Creek: Showdown in the Shenandoah, October 1–30, 1864* (Lynchburg, Va.: H. E. Howard, 1992) explores every aspect of the complex and dramatic engagement. More smoothly written than Mahr's book, Thomas A. Lewis's *The Guns of Cedar Creek* (New York: Harper & Row, 1988) provides a good overview and focuses on leading commanders. Joseph W. A. Whitehorne's *The Battle of Cedar Creek: Self-Guided Tour* (Strasburg, Va.: Wayside Museum of American History and Arts, 1987) will help visitors make sense of the sprawling battlefield. Brandon H. Beck and Roger U. Delauter, *Early's Valley Campaign: The Third Battle of Winchester* (Lynchburg, Va.: H. E. Howard, 1997) offers a brief treatment of the bloody clash that opened Sheridan's final offensive drive. On the biggest battle during the first phase of the campaign, see B. Franklin Cooling's *Monocacy: The Battle That Saved Washington* (Shippensburg, Pa.: White Mane, 1997). Fisher's Hill, Tom's Brook, and other smaller engagements still await book-length attention, but John L. Heatwole's *The Burning: Sheridan in the Shenandoah Valley* (Charlottesville, Va.: Rockbridge, 1998) draws on folklore as well as more traditional printed materials to paint a graphic picture of civilian suffering in September and October.

Five broader treatments of the Valley during the Civil War illuminate elements of the 1864 campaigning. Laura Virginia Hale's *Four Valiant Years in the Lower Shenandoah Valley, 1861–1865* (Strasburg, Va.: Shenandoah Publishing House, 1968) reflects the hard labors of a local historian who collected an enormous amount of anecdotal material about Confederate soldiers and civilians who lived and campaigned in the lower Valley. Michael G. Mahon allocates one chapter to 1864 in *The Shenandoah Valley, 1861–1865: The Destruction of the Granary of the Confederacy* (Mechanicsburg, Pa.: Stackpole, 1999), maintaining that the Valley's importance as a Confederate granary has been exaggerated. Roger U. Delauter Jr., *Winchester in the Civil War* (Lynchburg, Va.: H. E. Howard, 1992); Edward H. Phillips, *The Lower Shenandoah Valley in the Civil War: The Impact of War Upon the Civilian Population and Upon Civil Institutions* (Lynchburg, Va.: H. E. Howard, 1993); and Richard B. Kleese, *Shenandoah County in the Civil War: The Turbulent Years* (Lynchburg, Va.: H. E. Howard, 1992) all devote considerable attention to 1864.

Finally, several titles help flesh out the experience of civilians and their soldier-relatives. Cornelia Peake McDonald, *A Woman's Civil War: A Diary, with Reminiscences of the War, from March 1862*, ed. Minrose C. Gwin (1935; Madison: University of Wisconsin Press, 1992) conveys the roller-coaster experience of civilians in Winchester. Unfortunately, the editor's introduction does nothing to enhance the value of McDonald's splendid diary. *Winchester Divided: The Civil War Diaries of Julia Chase and Laura Lee*, ed. Michael G. Mahon (Mechanicsburg, Pa.: Stackpole, 2002), juxtaposes testimony from one Confederate and one Unionist woman, while *Diaries, Letters, and Recollections of the War between the States*, ed. Garland Quarles and others (Winchester, Va.: Winchester-Frederick County Historical Society, 1955; published as vol. 3 of the Society's *Papers*), gives additional perspective on Winchester's citizens and soldiers. Lucy Rebecca Buck's *Sad Earth, Sweet Heaven: The Diary of Lucy Rebecca Buck during the War between the States*, ed. Dr. William P. Buck (Birmingham, Ala.: Cornerstone, 1973; reprinted as *Shadows on My Heart: The Civil War Diary of Lucy Rebecca Buck of Virginia*, ed. Elizabeth R. Baer [Athens: University of Georgia Press, 1997]) in some ways rivals McDonald as a valuable woman's account. Margaretta Barton Colt's *Defend the Valley: A Shenandoah Family in the Civil War* (New York: Orion, 1994) is a fine compilation of various kinds of testimony from several individuals that includes a long section on the 1864 campaign, and Thomas A. Ashby's *The Valley Campaigns: Being the Reminiscences of a Non-Combatant While between the Lines in the Shenandoah Valley during the War of the States* (New York: Neale, 1914) traces incidents of the campaign through the eyes of a teenage boy who lived in the path of the armies.

CONTRIBUTORS

WILLIAM W. BERGEN is an independent scholar who works as an administrator at the University of Virginia.

KEITH S. BOHANNON, a member of the Department of History at the State University of West Georgia, teaches courses on the Civil War and on the history of Georgia. He is the author of *The Giles, Alleghany, and Jackson Artillery* and a number of essays and articles, and coeditor of *Campaigning with 'Old Stonewall': Confederate Captain Ujanirtus Allen's Letters to His Wife.*

ANDRE M. FLECHE is a doctoral candidate in history at the University of Virginia whose articles and essays have appeared in *Civil War History* and other publications. He is completing a study of the influence of the European revolutions of the 1840s on Civil War–era Americans.

GARY W. GALLAGHER is the John L. Nau III Professor in the History of the American Civil War at the University of Virginia and editor of eight previous titles in the Military Campaigns of the Civil War series. His books include *The Confederate War* and *Lee and His Army in Confederate History.*

JOSEPH T. GLATTHAAR is the Alan Stephenson Distinguished Professor of History at the University of North Carolina at Chapel Hill. His books include *The March to the Sea and Beyond: Sherman's Troops in the Savannah and Carolinas Campaigns, Forged in Battle: The Civil War Alliance of Black Soldiers and White Officers,* and *Partners in Command: Relationships between Civil War Leaders.*

ROBERT E. L. KRICK, a Richmond-based historian, was reared on the Chancellorsville battlefield. He is the author of *The 40th Virginia Infantry,* a number of essays and articles, and *Staff Officers in Gray: A Biographical Register of the Staff Officers in the Army of Northern Virginia.*

ROBERT K. KRICK grew up in California but has lived and worked on the Virginia battlefields for more than twenty-five years. He has written dozens of articles and twelve books, including *Conquering the Valley: Stonewall Jackson at Port Republic* and *The Smoothbore Volley That Doomed the Confederacy: The Death of Stonewall Jackson and Other Chapters on the Army of Northern Virginia.*

WILLIAM J. MILLER, editor of *Civil War: The Magazine of the Civil War Society* for several years, is the author of *The Training of an Army: Camp Curtin and the North's Civil War* and *Mapping for Stonewall: The Civil War Service of Jed Hotchkiss,* editor and coauthor of the three-volume *The Peninsula Campaign: Yorktown to the Seven Days,* and editor of a forthcoming volume of Jedediah Hotchkiss's Civil War letters.

AARON SHEEHAN-DEAN is assistant professor of history at the University of North Florida. His articles and essays have appeared in *Civil War History* and elsewhere, and he is completing a book-length study of Virginia's soldiers and civilians during the Civil War.

WILLIAM G. THOMAS, the John and Catherine Angle Chair in the Humanities in the Department of History at the University of Nebraska-Lincoln, is coauthor of "The Valley of the Shadow: Two Communities in the American Civil War" website and of *The Civil War on the Web: A Guide to the Very Best Sites.*

JOAN WAUGH, a member of the Department of History at the University of California, Los Angeles, is the author of *Unsentimental Reformer: The Life of Josephine Shaw Lowell* and *Personal Memoirs of U. S. Grant: A History of the Union Cause*, editor of *Encyclopedia of American History: Civil War and Reconstruction, 1856–1869*, and co-editor and coauthor of *The Memory of the Civil War in American Culture.*

INDEX

Adams, Charles Francis, Jr., 92
African Americans: and slavery, 9, 249–
50, 255 (n. 53), 260, 291 (n. 9); emanci-
pation in Valley, 240, 243, 252 (n. 14);
service in Union army, 243–44, 300,
312, 318. *See also* Slavery
Alabama troops: 3rd Infantry, 178, 186;
61st Infantry, 165
Alexander, Peter W., 71–72
Allen, Eva Honey, 229, 231, 232, 234–35,
237, 249
Ambler, Lucy Johnson, 233
Anderson, Richard H., 114
Andrew, John A., 309, 310, 311
Ansley, Joseph, 165
Anspach, Frederick, 267, 268
Antietam, battle of, 7, 8, 308, 336 (n. 30)
Appomattox Court House, 86, 126 (n. 34)
Army of Northern Virginia, 7, 18–19, 56,
162, 164, 201, 211, 267, 321, 331, 346
Army of the Potomac, xi, 16, 38, 97, 116,
120, 201, 223, 313, 318, 321
Army of the Shenandoah, xvi, 9, 12, 14,
102, 103, 105, 108, 118, 322, 328
Army of Tennessee, 51
Army of the Valley, xii, 27, 50, 75, 105,
161, 189, 190, 246, 267, 278–79, 292
(n. 26); morale of, xvii, 165, 189–90,
284
Army of West Virginia, 14
Ashby, Turner, 142
Atkinson, Edmund N., 164, 181, 196
(n. 37)
Atlanta, Ga., xiii, 320, 321; fall of, 50,
200, 218, 237, 278
Augur, Christopher C., 46, 320, 337
(n. 30)
Averell, William Woods, 141, 171

Backus, Samuel W., 318, 324
Badeau, Adam, 113
Baird, Alexander S., 68
Baker, Norval, 173
Ball, Mottrom D., 150
Baltimore and Ohio Railroad, xii, xiii,
10, 15, 17, 31 (n. 22), 271
Banks, Nathaniel P., 46, 101, 313
Barlow, Francis C., 334
Baruch, Simon, 26
Bates, Edward, 39, 44, 48
Battle, Cullen A., 164, 165, 178, 184, 197
(n. 42)
Bean, Onslow, 165, 173, 198 (n. 43)
Beauregard, P. G. T., 352
Bedingfield, John Y., 27
Bell, H. M., 265
Benjamin, William H., 149, 150
Berkeley, Henry, 169, 190, 264, 271, 283–
84, 286, 288
Binns, Charlie, 315
Bissell, Lewis, 97, 126 (n. 34)
Blackford, Benjamin Lewis, 266, 288
Blackford, Charles Minor, 275, 286–87,
288
Blair, Montgomery: burning of home
of, 41, 43; and tension with Halleck,
43
Bomar, Thomas H., 59
Booth, George W., 174, 186
Boston Herald, 74
Boteler, Alexander A., 72
Bradford, Louisa Marcella, 89
Bradford, Slaughter S., 98
Bradwell, Isaac G., 67
Bragg, Braxton, 86, 95
Braxton, Carter M., 182, 183, 197 (n. 42)
Breckinridge, John C., 99, 162, 163, 187,